Polic...ng in ...

Edition 8

Policing in America

Edition 8

Larry K. Gaines
California State University-San Bernardino

Victor E. Kappeler
Eastern Kentucky University

Routledge
Taylor & Francis Group

LONDON AND NEW YORK

First published 2015 by Anderson Publishing

Published 2015 by Routledge
2 Park Square, Milton Park, Abingdon, Oxon OX14 4RN
and by Routledge
711 Third Avenue, New York, NY 10017, USA

Routledge is an imprint of the Taylor & Francis Group, an informa business

First Edition: 1994
Second Edition: 1997
Third Edition: 1999
Fourth Edition: 2003
Fifth Edition: 2005
Sixth Edition: 2010
Seventh Edition: 2011

Notices
No responsibility is assumed by the publisher for any injury and/or damage to
persons or property as a matter of products liability, negligence or otherwise,
or from any use of operation of any methods, products, instructions or ideas
contained in the material herein.

Practitioners and researchers must always rely on their own experience and
knowledge in evaluating and using any information, methods, compounds, or
experiments described herein. In using such information or methods they should
be mindful of their own safety and the safety of others, including parties for
whom they have a professional responsibility.

Product or corporate names may be trademarks or registered trademarks, and
are used only for identification and explanation without intent to infringe.

Library of Congress Cataloging-in-Publication Data
Gaines, Larry K.
   Policing in America / Larry K. Gaines, Victor E. Kappeler. -- Edition 8.
      pages cm
1. Police–United States. 2. Law enforcement--United States. I. Kappeler, Victor E. II. Title.
   HV8139.G35 2015
   363.20973--dc23
                        2014011995

British Library Cataloguing in Publication Data
A catalogue record for this book is available from the British Library

ISBN-13: 978-0-32-331148-9 (pbk)

Dedication

This book is dedicated to R. Steve Nobles, the former Chief of the Oldham County, Kentucky, Police Department. Steve joined the Oldham County Police Department on January 1, 1978, and was one of the Department's original three officers. He was appointed Chief in September 1979. During his tenure as Chief, he exemplified and modeled his department after what many believe to be the professional principles that should drive police management and operations. He was a community police officer before community policing was in vogue. He understood that police officers must not only serve their communities, they must also be a part of their communities. He believed that police officers and departments should be accountable for the human needs and problems that exist in their communities. As an example, he started a program whereby parents with small children who could not afford a child car seat could come to the police department to obtain one.

Steve was also a good friend. He constantly worked with other departments in an effort to improve policing in the Commonwealth of Kentucky. While as President of the Kentucky Association of Chiefs of Police, he started a state-level agency accreditation program. He worked with a variety of community groups on problems, such as domestic violence, driving under the influence enforcement, and crime prevention.

Steve's untimely death has had a tremendous effect on law enforcement. We miss him very much.

Larry K. Gaines

Contents

Acknowledgments

Writing an introductory text is a tremendous undertaking, and it usually involves the advice and counsel of a large number of colleagues. We depended upon the generosity of our colleagues to provide criticism, ideas, and information. At this point, we would like to acknowledge their contributions and express our gratitude.

First, we would like to thank Steven G. Brandl of University of Wisconsin–Milwaukee and Larry Miller of East Tennessee State University for their comments on earlier editions of this book. Their reviews resulted in a number of changes that substantially improved this text. Second, a number of our colleagues provided valuable information that we have included in this text. They include Tom Barker, Gary Potter, and Peter Kraska of Eastern Kentucky University; Rolando del Carmen and Victor G. Strecher of Sam Houston State University; and Mark Blumberg of Central Missouri State University. We thank Tom O'Connor of North Carolina Wesleyan College for assisting us in locating many of the Web sites included in this edition, as well as allowing us to reference his extensive Web sites on policing. Some of our current and former graduate students assisted with various aspects of developing this text. They include Brandon Marker, William Oakley, Greg Ferrell, Louis Cubellis, Tammy Garland, Natalie Powell, Lisa Conley, April Hatfield, Holli Sims, Daniel Wright, and Jordan Henson. Also, we would like to thank Aaron E. Kappeler, University of Toronto, for keeping us on the straight and narrow concerning the historical, anthropological, and archaeological records. He conducted a significant amount of research and critique for various editions. His future as a scholar is certain. We would like to express our gratitude to the many police departments and federal agencies that provided us with data and other information.

We would also like to acknowledge the efforts of the staff at Elsevier Science and Technology Books, and its affiliates. Mickey and Susan Braswell deserve special mention for their constant cajoling and encouragement. Marisa LaFleure, our editor, did a fantastic job of working with us on this edition, and during the final stages of manuscript development.

Larry K. Gaines
Victor E. Kappeler

Preface

Police work is becoming increasingly complex, specialized, and interwoven into the social fabric of American society. The activities and practices of American police officers are expanding into areas of social life that far exceed their traditional social role. As each year passes, police are becoming more involved in the day-to-day activities of citizens and their private lives. The 1970s and 1980s saw the federal government almost totally neglect our nation's cities and the many social problems that contribute to crime and other police problems. During those decades, governmental resources for policing became scarce. Government agencies, especially police departments, had to do much more with fewer resources. These factors created substantial strain and pressure on police departments and on police officers. These conditions seemed to change almost overnight as economic and political changes engulfed the United States in the 1990s.

The last decade of the twentieth century saw a general and broad-based improvement in American economic conditions; there was a resurgence of governmental and public interest in our cities and in policing. There was an increase in the number of television programs dealing with police work, and the news media gave more attention to police activities and crime. Decades of neglect changed to an urban focus with considerable money being spent to revitalize our nation's cities. Policing has been drawn into this focus. As our social gaze changed from neglect to almost an obsession with urban affairs, media and political leaders generated an unprecedented fear of crime among citizens, despite more than two decades of declining criminal victimization. There was a growing concern among citizens that they are not as safe as they once were. This situation, coupled with a renewed focus on the police, led to changes in the police institution as well as shifts in the philosophies that underpinned policing. Police became intimately involved in establishing order in what were characterized as "decaying urban centers" dubbed "pathological." The language of disorder, coupled with political leaders' preference for formal social control over the expansion of social programs placed policing once again in the political spotlight. These trends and the new language of policing, politics, and crime control contributed to the complexity and specialization of the American police institution. Such a situation led to no shortage of serious social issues confronting both the police and society. Most police agencies developed some form of community police program in response to these problems. Police became the major problem-solvers in the nation's cities, especially where political leaders failed in their responsibilities or developed poor social policy.

At the height of the police institution's focus on communities and local social problems, the nation experienced the tragedy of September 11, 2001. The terrorist attacks in New York City and Washington, DC altered the federal government's focus once again, away from local problems and the needs of citizens, to concerns with national security. Police agencies came under extreme pressure to alter their view and take a more national security focus. Federal funds and training dollars were shifted away from community policing and pumped into forging the police as first responders—intelligence gatherers for federal agencies—and much of the burden of federal law enforcement was pushed down to the local level. As this dynamic unfolds and as the economic recession continues, it remains to be seen whether the gains made by community policing, especially among minority communities, will be washed away in the changing role of the police. Concerns with controlling immigration, preventing domestic terrorism, and protecting critical infrastructure all promise to alter the police institution. Political leaders and the media have used the fear of terrorism to advance many misconceptions about police work, immigration, and terrorism itself, and these misconceptions inhibit policing from becoming fully responsive to the real needs of the people they are to serve. Today policing may face some of the worse circumstance is its history. Political leaders continue, and the public expects, the services provided by the police be expanded, even as they slash budgets and make derogatory comments about public servants. People are living under chronic economic stress, cities have smaller budgets, and the police are once again called on to do more with less. Often what the police are called upon to do is the result of political leaders inability to address or solve social problems like homelessness, high rates of unemployment and underemployment and issues associated with mental illness. This decade promises to by one of the most challenging for the police institution.

The purpose of this text is to provide an overview of contemporary police work, as well as an accurate assessment of where we are and where we need to go. This unique look at policing provides the reader with information to assist in gaining a better understanding of the complex relationship between police and society, to assist in making informed decisions about the many social issues facing the police institution, and to guide officials in their approaches to law enforcement operations and policies. We accomplish the goals of this text if readers come away with a better understanding of the complex issues facing the police and society.

Victor E. Kappeler
Larry K. Gaines

CHAPTER 1

The Police in American Society

Government, even in its best state, is but a necessary evil; in its worst state, an intolerable one.

—Thomas Paine

LEARNING OBJECTIVES

After reading the chapter, you should be able to:

- Describe the environment in which the police institution operates in America.
- Understand the government structure and how it relates to policing.
- Describe the place police hold in the criminal justice system.
- Articulate the role of police and the law in the criminal justice system.
- Understand and explain the roles and functions of police in modern society.
- Describe the research on police activities and police work.
- List and describe the various style of policing used by departments.
- Understand the roles and functions of federal, state, and local law enforcement agencies.

KEY TERMS

- Bill of Rights
- Case law
- Civil law
- Constitution
- Constitutional government
- Criminal justice system
- Decentralization
- Dual citizenship
- Executive branch
- Explanation
- Federal law enforcement
- Federalism
- Formal social control
- Government
- Governmental structure
- Harrison Act

INTRODUCTION

The American police fulfill their various responsibilities within the confines of a unique environment. This environment is constantly evolving and is composed of social, legal, economic, political, and intellectual forces that combine to create a unique climate. This environment substantially influences the behavior of American police officers and, to some degree, determines where and when they will enforce the law, how they will go about enforcing the law, and even which laws will be enforced and which ones will be ignored. Although the police can be distinguished from other social institutions and are a distinct

1

- Informal social control
- Judicial branch
- Judiciary Act of 1789
- Jurisdiction
- Law
- Law and order
- Law enforcement role
- Legalistic style
- Legislative branch
- Convenience norm enforcement
- Order maintenance role
- Police functions
- Police power
- Procedural law
- Role
- Separation of powers
- Service role
- Service style
- Social contract
- Social control
- Society
- State
- State police
- Substantive law

To learn more about the social contract and Rousseau, visit the Website **http://www.fordham.edu/halsall/mod/rousseau-soccon.asp**

governmental entity, their actions are largely controlled by forces within the environment that are external to police organizations. This is not to say that police are merely passive actors who respond to their environment. Police, in fact, are active in both responding to these forces and shaping their working and social environments. To really understand the policing and police behavior requires us to consider both the internal and external working environments of the police institution. In this chapter, however, we will focus on the external environment of American policing and how the police institution is structured.

The primary shapers of the American police institution are society and government. Because of their interdependence, the terms "state," "government," and "society" are often used interchangeably. They are, however, distinct. A *state* is an apparatus that has the recognized authority to use and maintain a monopoly on the use of force within a clearly defined geography or jurisdiction. *Government* is a political institution of the state that uses organization, bureaucracy, and formality to regulate social interactions and is most often recognized among societies that emerge as nation-states. *Society* is the totality of networks and patterns of social interaction occurring between members of a bounded social group, including those interactions within organizations and institutions. Societies can exist without the formation of a state or formal government, but states and government cannot exist without a social structure and citizens.

The relationship among the state, government, and society has occupied the attention of political scholars since the early days of philosophy. Many great political thinkers of the 1700 and 1800s spent considerable time examining the role of the state and government in society. Political philosophers such as John Locke, Thomas Hobbes, and Jean-Jacques Rousseau developed lengthy works on the ideal relationship between government and society. Collectively, these theories are referred to as the *social contract*. Under the social contract, members of society are assumed to have entered an agreement to create the state and a government to acquire security and order for the entire society. By entering into such a contract, citizens are said to surrender certain natural rights and vest government with the power to maintain social stability and protect the interests of its members. In exchange for relinquishing the right to use physical force—for defense and to secure the necessities of life—members of society expect the government to provide an effective system for regulating conduct and creating forums for resolving conflicts between citizens. While it is assumed that citizens and the governments they create will abide by the spirit of the social contract, inherent deviations on both sides of the contract exist. Conduct against the social good, whether by citizens or government, that violates the spirit of the social contract, requires political change, social control, and, in some cases, formal sanction.

While social contract theory provides us with a framework for considering the relationship between a state and members of society, it is not without problems. There are many variations of social contract theory. Some political philosophers describe the social contract as placing members of society in the dominant position, while others characterize the state as the controlling party. Still other philosophers dispute the notion that members of society would knowingly enter into an agreement that would require them to relinquish their rights to create a state—absent compulsion, coercion, or use of force .

Social contract theory does not apply to most historical forms of government but is usually associated with new democratic forms that are guided by the provisions of constitutions. In this sense, social contract theory is not an *explanation* for the formulation of states and forms of governance but, rather, an ethical or logical *theory* that is used to justify the creation of new states and governments (Figure 1.1).

Democratic systems of government are built on a delicate balance between individual rights and the collective needs of members of society. In this balance, the police perform the critical role of protecting individual rights and ensuring social order. In this context, Jerome Skolnick (1994) noted that *law and order* are constantly shifting terms balanced by the police. Indeed, the imposition of order creates disorder. As society changes and political

- Subsystem
- Theory
- USA PATRIOT Act
- Watchman-style

FIGURE 1.1
Jean-Jacques Rousseau (1712–1778). Engraved by R. Hart and published in The Gallery of Portraits with Memoirs encyclopedia, United Kingdom, 1833. *Copyright Shutterstock/Georgios Kollidas.*

leaders create new laws, emerging norms and values produce crime and deviance in a transformative process. Not only does too much order create disorder, but too much law also threatens the principles of democracy. When we seek order for its own sake, to the detriment of individual freedom, we move away from the democratic ideal toward the creation of a police state.

In all states, it is necessary for the police to restrict, or take away, the freedoms of some to protect the liberties and interests of others. It is the social and legal configuration of these interests among different classes, ethnic groups, and gendered communities that determines police orientation. Police officers arrest individuals who are "suspected of committing" criminal acts but, at the same time, they must ensure that their investigative procedures and behaviors do not violate a suspect's constitutional rights. If individual rights are neglected in favor of social order, government ultimately becomes totalitarian and repressive. Everyone's individual freedoms are slowly extinguished (Bayley, 2002; Chevigny, 2002). On the other hand, if individualism were allowed to completely overshadow collective societal needs, then there would be little order. These ideas "suggest that police are intricately intertwined in the social fabric of American democracy" (Kappeler, Sluder, & Alpert, 1998:2).

Democratic government embraces several unique principles that distinguish it from other forms of government. The concept of *democracy* includes belief in such fundamental principles as respect for the rule of law, individualism, civil rights, human dignity, constitutionalism, social justice, and majority rule. These principles are held in high regard and, historically, the desires for social control and order have been viewed as secondary concerns.

In terms of the social contract, democratic societies view the government as the minor party in the contractual arrangement and emphasize the process by which order and stability are achieved over the ends themselves. These principles make democracy a unique form of governance and policing a difficult challenge. Enforcement of social norms is less efficient in a political system that values civil rights, individualism, and respect for the rule of law over order and conformity. The balance between effective and efficient control of social behavior and the values of democracy is constantly in a state of flux.

THE GOVERNMENT STRUCTURE AND POLICING

The police institution operates within a *governmental structure*. This structure shapes the character of a nation's police. It is not uncommon for police systems to closely mirror the form of government under which they operate. For example, police systems operating in countries with dictatorships or totalitarian forms of government are much different from the police systems operating in democracies. These police systems have a tendency to be politically centralized and paramilitary in appearance and operation, and they are vested with authorities and powers that are not usually subject to formal review. Because government is a forum for making and carrying out public policy, the manner in which this is done shapes the character of a society and its social institutions. The police are no exception to this principle.

Government, in general, is another institution that addresses social problems; it provides a forum for debating solutions to problems, but, most importantly, government provides a system of formal social controls. *Social controls* are the collective practices by which a group attempts to ensure that individuals conform to the norms and values of the group. While government is but one institution that controls human behavior, it is by far the most formidable. Other social institutions such as religious groups, the family, and educational institutions also shape behavior in society and perform control functions, but these institutions are informal as compared to government. These institutions use *informal social controls* so that individuals are socialized into internalizing the norms and values of these institutions. *Formal social control* involves the use of sanctions for rule breaking. Through the political process, government determines what behaviors are acceptable and provides the means by which violations of acceptable behavior are sanctioned. Obviously, governmental agencies such as the police, who are charged with detection and control of crime, will closely resemble the structure of the society and government they serve and will tend to focus on rule-breaking behaviors and sanctions as they are formalized in the political process.

Constitutional Government

Because historical, political, social, and cultural differences exist in different countries, each country has a unique form of government with different methods of carrying out very different public policies. One way of distinguishing governments from one another is the presence of constitutions. *Constitutions* describe the social arrangements between a government and its citizens. These documents provide broad guidelines and limitations describing the relationship between people and their government. Constitutions detail the responsibilities of government and the rights of citizens by establishing a general framework within which the government should operate.

In the same broad fashion, constitutions distribute authority and limit the use of power. Not only are constitutions political instruments designed to curb abuses of power by the government, but they also have an administrative quality. Essentially, constitutions establish parameters that define a government's control over its citizens and indicate how such control can be established and maintained (Figure 1.2).

In terms of American law enforcement, the U.S. Constitution places restrictions on what police officers can do when enforcing the law or investigating crime. The first 10 amendments to the U.S. Constitution are known as the *Bill of Rights* and afford American citizens certain rights and protections. Citizens have the right to free speech, the right to peaceably assemble, and the right to protest governmental actions. The First Amendment protects these rights. The Fourth Amendment protects citizens from illegal searches and seizures and the improper use of police force. The manners in which police officers obtain confessions and conduct lineups are addressed by the Fifth Amendment, while the Sixth Amendment guarantees suspects the right to legal counsel. The Fourteenth Amendment, with its due process and equal protection clauses, helps ensure that police officers carry out their law enforcement role in a manner that protects citizens' rights. Finally, police officers sometimes are called upon to protect citizens as they exercise their constitutional rights. They must protect the privacy and domestic tranquility of complaining citizens while ensuring

FIGURE 1.2
"Scene at the Signing of the Constitution of the United States," by Howard Chandler Christy (oil on canvas, 1940). *Courtesy of Architect of the Capitol.*

that those who are causing the disturbance as a result of exercising their freedom of speech are equally protected. Box 1.1 presents the Bill of Rights to the U.S. Constitution.

Box 1.1 Bill of Rights to the U.S. Constitution

These amendments were ratified December 15, 1791

Amendment I

Congress shall make no law respecting an establishment of religion, or prohibiting the free exercise thereof; or abridging the freedom of speech, or of the press; or the right of the people peaceably to assemble, and to petition the Government for a redress of grievances.

Amendment II

A well regulated Militia, being necessary to the security of a free State, the right of the people to keep and bear Arms, shall not be infringed.

Amendment III

No Soldier shall, in time of peace, be quartered in any house, without the consent of the Owner, nor in time of war, but in a manner to be prescribed by law.

Amendment IV

The right of the people to be secure in their persons, houses, papers, and effects, against unreasonable searches and seizures, shall not be violated, and no Warrants shall issue, but upon probable cause, supported by Oath or affirmation, and particularly describing the place to be searched, and the persons or things to be seized.

Amendment V

No person shall be held to answer for a capital, or otherwise infamous crime, unless on a presentment or indictment of a Grand Jury, except in cases arising in the land or naval forces, or in the Militia, when in actual service in time of War or public danger; nor shall any person be subject for the same offense to be twice put in jeopardy of life or limb; nor shall be compelled in any criminal case to be a witness against himself, nor be deprived of life, liberty, or property, without due process of law; nor shall private property be taken for public use, without just compensation.

Amendment VI

In all criminal prosecutions, the accused shall enjoy the right to a speedy and public trial, by an impartial jury of the State and district wherein the crime shall have been committed, which district shall have been previously ascertained by law, and to be informed of the nature and cause of the accusation; to be confronted with the witnesses against him; to have compulsory process for obtaining witnesses in his favor, and to have the Assistance of Counsel for his defense.

Amendment VII

In suits at common law, where the value in controversy shall exceed 20 dollars, the right of trial by jury shall be preserved, and no fact tried by a jury, shall be otherwise reexamined in any Court of the United States, than according to the rules of the common law.

Amendment VIII

Excessive bail shall not be required, nor excessive fines imposed, nor cruel and unusual punishments inflicted.

Amendment IX

The enumeration in the Constitution, of certain rights, shall not be construed to deny or disparage others retained by the people.

Amendment X

The powers not delegated to the United States by the Constitution, nor prohibited by it to the States, are reserved to the States respectively, or to the people.

To learn more about the separation of powers watch a video at **http://www.youtube.com/watch?v=Nnqk-yGzYYg**

Separation of Powers

The U.S. Constitution created three branches of government: the *executive* branch, the *judicial* branch, and the *legislative* branch. The Constitution provides for the *separation of powers* between these branches of government. Ideally, each branch of government operates independently, acting as a source of checks and balances on governmental power and authority (Bowman & Kearney, 2009). The police come under the administrative control of the executive branch of government but fulfill the will of all branches of government. Police officers must enforce the laws that are passed by the legislature, and they must abide by the procedural guidelines promulgated by the courts.

This often causes conflict for the police because they must respond to different sources of authority. State legislators may, for example, enact a law for the police to enforce, but local government officials may be responsible for allocating funds for the police to carry out enforcement activities, and the courts may determine what practices are appropriate for enforcing the legislation. Police officers must respond to all of these political dictates when executing their responsibilities. While there is a tendency to think of police agencies as being separate from politics, or even apolitical, the police institution is inherently political. Not only are police agencies creations of government and the political system that control government, but also organizational activities are directed by the edicts of each branch of government.

Principles of Federalism

One unique feature of the American system of government is the principle of federalism. *Federalism* is a form of political organization that distributes authority and power among levels of government. This principle basically vests certain powers in the federal government, other powers in state governments, and the remaining powers and rights in individual citizens. One of the powers vested in state governments is the ability to allow the formation and regulation of units of local government. Although the Tenth Amendment to the U.S. Constitution reserves police powers for the states, law enforcement agencies have evolved at each of these three levels, and they have different operational responsibilities. Cole (1995) provided some background about how federalism has been applied and how federal agencies have come into existence:

> As a consequence of the bargain worked out at the Constitutional Convention, the general police power was not delegated to the federal government. No centralized national police force with broad

enforcement powers may be established in the United States. It is true that the national government has police agencies such as the Federal Bureau of Investigation (FBI) and the Secret Service, but they are authorized to enforce only those laws prescribed under the powers granted to Congress (1995:14–15).

To learn more about the Constitution and to view historical documents, visit the National Archives and Records Administration Website at: **http://www.archives. gov/exhibits/charters/constitution_ history.html**

This unique form of political subdivision has several implications for American police. First, *police power* is distributed among several levels of government, and administration of the police is divided among these levels. This helps ensure that no single police agency accumulates too much power and leads to various types of police organizations, each with unique laws to enforce and a unique set of responsibilities. For example, the FBI and the Drug Enforcement Administration (DEA) are federal agencies, while each state—except Hawaii— has a state police or highway patrol agency, and cities and counties often have police departments.

Second, because government in the United States is *decentralized*, the police institution is likewise decentralized. Although it has been debated that a centralized police system, such as the types found in Europe, may be a more efficient system of policing, decentralization helps ensure that police agencies do not amass too much power and are somewhat responsive and accountable to the unique populations they serve. Third, the principle of federalism provides members of American society with *dual citizenship*—citizenship of the United States and citizenship of the respective state in which each citizen resides. This means that the police must respond to the dual rights of citizens. Fourth, federalism results in the creation of a unique web of overlapping jurisdictions for law enforcement agencies. In some cases within a single city, more than a dozen agencies from all political subdivisions of government might have responsibility for law enforcement.

Finally, as a practical matter, decentralized policing can be a challenge to crime control. A single homicide, for example, might be dispersed across several jurisdictions. A suspect might live in one state, commit a crime in another state, dispose of the evidence of the crime in a third state, and even move or flee to still another state. In an increasingly global society, crime can even cross international borders. Multijurisdictional cases present a challenge to effective crime control and communications between police agencies.

POLICE AND THE LAW

Law is a binding rule that regulates conduct and provides sanctions for violations of its provisions. The law serves several functions:

- It legitimizes the existing social order and structure.

- It regulates social behavior.
- It curtails and defines freedom.
- It provides a system of dispute resolution.

In terms of legitimizing the existing social structure, the law embodies the basic agreements of a society, as they are decided through the political process. The extent to which one social group can guide or influence the political course of law, as compared to another social group, depends on the power that group can generate and their position in the social structure. The law regulates social conduct by establishing boundaries of acceptable behavior, providing some measure of order and predictability to our daily lives. To the extent that this is possible, the law attempts to hold constant existing social norms, values, and arrangements and thus lends legitimacy to the existing social structure. We expect other members of society to behave within legally prescribed boundaries, which foster a sense of well-being, order, and security. The law both curtails and defines our freedom. The amount of freedom that an individual has changes over time, as the result of the passage of new laws, court decisions, and the individual's position in society. In the end, it is the law and its enforcement (or lack of enforcement) that define what government and citizens can and cannot do. Finally, the law establishes the formal structures by which citizens and governments can resolve disputes. It formalizes the process of dispute resolution, which, in turn, further reinforces the existing social order (Figure 1.3).

Although there are many forms of law, essentially four types of law affect the police: substantive law, procedural law, civil law, and case law. *Substantive law*

FIGURE 1.3
Police personnel are called upon to give testimony in legal and legislative proceedings. *Photo courtesy of AP Photo/Andre J. Jackson, Pool.*

refers to criminal statutes that define which behaviors are acceptable and which behaviors are unacceptable in our society. The legislature passes laws that define crimes such as murder, robbery, rape, larceny, or burglary. These criminal statutes represent the bulk of a police department's "law enforcement" role. Police officers cannot arrest citizens unless they violate a substantive law. In this sense, the law directs the focus of the police on certain types of behaviors that have been criminalized.

Procedural law refers to laws that prescribe how police officers apply substantive laws. For example, many state legislators have passed laws dictating the circumstances in which police officers can use deadly force. The use of force by police officers must conform to the requirements of procedural law. These laws may also delineate conditions regulating the types and standards of evidence that may be admitted in a criminal trial. For example, legislators have described how police officers will apply breath tests and how their data will be admitted during a driving-under-the-influence case. Likewise, procedural law determines the practices in which police officers can engage while conducting a criminal investigation or making an arrest.

Civil law regulates social interactions arising from private, commercial, or contractual relations. Family law, the law of contracts, and business law are all considered forms of civil law. Certain codes for operating businesses, housing restrictions, and safety regulations are often embodied in the civil law. Historically, the police have had little to do with civil law enforcement. Today, however, because of changes in the orientation of many police departments, and newly enacted laws, police are more likely to become involved in civil law enforcement. In fact, some police departments, such as the New York City Police Department, use civil law to bolster criminal law enforcement. The owner of an apartment complex who has rented to drug traffickers may find the police enforcing city codes or safety regulations in an attempt to force the owner into cooperating with police enforcement objectives. Legislative bodies have enacted civil forfeiture laws that allow the police to confiscate personal property such as money, houses, and motor vehicles if citizens are suspected of being involved in certain crimes. Many of these laws do not require citizens to be convicted of a crime before their property is seized and becomes the property of the state. Civil enforcement and civil forfeiture of property are controversial legal trends in policing.

Case law refers to the written opinions of the courts. As disputes come before the courts, judges decide cases and formulate written opinions. These opinions have the force of law and often determine which police practices are acceptable and which practices are unacceptable. The courts provide guidelines relative to how police officers should apply the criminal code, as well as the procedures that officers should follow when enforcing the law. There are numerous U.S. Supreme Court decisions that dictate how police officers should collect evidence and how it is to be used in a criminal case. The case of *Mapp v. Ohio* (1961) provided guidelines relative to police searches, the case of *Miranda v. Arizona* (1966) dictated when officers would advise suspects of their constitutional rights against self-incrimination, and *Tennessee v. Garner* (1985) and *Graham v. Connor* (1989) provided additional requirements as to when police could use force in effecting arrests. Through the litigation and appeals process, the Supreme Court reviews state and federal laws and police procedures to determine whether they violate the U.S. Constitution. Because the U.S. Constitution is the highest law of the land, all other laws must be consistent with it.

POLICE IN THE CRIMINAL JUSTICE SYSTEM

In the United States, crime control and the administration of justice are handled by the criminal justice system. The *criminal justice system* is composed of three primary and discernible components: police, courts, and corrections. These components are sometimes referred to as *subsystems*. From this perspective, the components of the criminal justice system are seen as interrelated, interdependent, and striving to achieve a unified goal. This view of criminal justice often focuses on how cases flow through the system, causing ripple effects as cases move from one component to the next. The actions of police officers on the streets, for example, affect the workload of courts, and the decisions of judges in courtrooms affect the operation of jails and prisons.

Police hold a special place in the criminal justice system. Not only do the activities of law enforcement officers affect the operations of the entire criminal justice system, but also police are said to be the "gate keepers" of the system: "They are usually the first to make contact with accused offenders and are in a position to make some very important decisions about what will happen to those individuals. Perhaps the most frequent decision that a police officer makes is… to initiate an alleged offender's journey through the maze of American criminal justice" (Alpert & Dunham, 1997:11) (Box 1.2).

Although most citizens are never arrested or even experience a face-to-face encounter with the police in any given year, police are the most likely component of the criminal justice system to have an influence on their day-to-day lives. More often than not this influence is largely symbolic. People usually see the police while they are carrying out their day-to-day activities or when they are exposed to media depictions of the police. Police far outnumber members of other occupational groups in criminal justice. There are about 1.8 million public employees in the justice system; more than 1.1 million serve in a law enforcement capacity (Kyckelhahn, 2010). The police are not only the most numerous but also the most visible component of the criminal justice system. The vast majority of commissioned personnel in police agencies are uniformed, making them readily identifiable to the public. In addition, the majority of

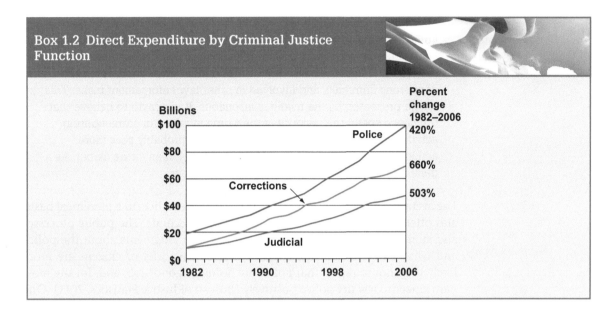

Box 1.2 Direct Expenditure by Criminal Justice Function

commissioned personnel in police agencies are assigned to patrol duties, and most work out of marked patrol vehicles (Kappeler et al., 1998). As we discuss in other chapters, visibility has been a major element in police crime control strategies and practices.

To learn more about the stages of the criminal justice system, refer to the chart at **http://www.bjs.gov/content/justsys.cfm**

THE ROLES AND FUNCTIONS OF POLICE IN MODERN SOCIETY

Citizens' perceptions and ideas about the police are based on global attitudes toward crime and social justice, past experiences with governmental agencies, and social status. Our knowledge about the police, what they do, and how they do it comes from a number of sources, and quite often represents distorted or incomplete pictures about the police. The public and media have had a long-running fascination with police work. From the *Keystone Cops* of the early cinema to the most current depiction of the police, many of us have grown up with media portrayals of policing. These images of policing usually carry with them certain recurrent themes that promote and shape views of the nature of police work in American society (Dowler, 2004). Prevalent in media images of police work is that policing is all about crime fighting, excitement, and danger. As Kappeler and Potter (2005) remarked:

> When citizens reflect upon the role of the police, invariably they think in terms of their law enforcement capacity. Whether they are being depicted in a police series on television or in a current movie, police

officers are portrayed almost solely as crime fighters. Citizens spend hours of leisure time watching cops engage in such activities as high speed pursuits involving wanted felons, questioning persons who are suspected of having committed serious crimes, shooting it out with dangerous criminals, and involved in other law enforcement tasks. This image presented by the media is erroneous. It is a myth to believe that the police spend the majority of their time involved in crime-fighting activity. In fact, the average cop on television probably sees more action in a half-hour than most officers witness in an entire career. As a general rule, most police work is quite mundane.

The average citizen collects information about the police on a piecemeal basis, and often this information is incomplete or inaccurate. The public processes and stores this information and uses it to make judgments about the police and what they do. Research suggests that the majority of citizens are more likely than not to report that police are doing a "good" job, and, for the most part, citizens view the police positively (Bureau of Justice Statistics, 2011). One should keep in mind, however, that the majority of American citizens are white and working and have never experienced a confrontation with the police. Even though a majority of citizens have a positive view of the police and support them, this support is not uniform across all segments of society and in all social settings.

Citizens with little or no contact with the police may draw on media depictions of policing or their global attitudes about crime and justice to form their views of the police. Research indicates, for example, that citizens who have no contact with the police have more favorable views of the police than citizens who have contact with the police. This finding seems to hold regardless of whether the police initiate the contact or the citizen calls the police. Likewise, while there is some indication that negative police actions—making an arrest, issuing a traffic citation, or aggressively questioning a citizen—lead to an unfavorable view of the police, citizen perceptions of being treated fairly determine their view of the police regardless of enforcement actions (Mazerolle, Antrobus, Bennett, and Tyler, 2013). In this fashion, experience with the police shapes citizens' global attitudes about crime and justice, and global attitudes about crime and justice shade specific experiences with the police. Public attitudes toward the police are addressed in more detail in Chapter 10.

Roles Performed by the Police

The police are called on to perform a wide range of tasks and activities. Although the obvious functions of the police are to "protect and serve" the public, police officers in some jurisdictions are expected to be responsible for nonlaw enforcement activities such as reading meters, serving as animal control officers, or inspecting homes for insect infestations during summer months. Some citizens expect the police to provide public services such as helping open locked doors, offering motorist assistance, or disseminating information about community problems and issues. Smaller jurisdictions sometimes require their officers to perform activities that are considered outside the traditional boundaries of police responsibility. Generally, police departments in smaller jurisdictions are more service orientated. The police are also called on to maintain public order by investigating disturbances, breaking up fights, and settling domestic disputes.

One important distinction that police scholars make when discussing the varied activities of the police is between roles and functions. A *role* refers to a basic or standardized social position that carries with it certain expectations. These expectations can be very specific or diffuse, and they are often associated with social institutions. Roles can carry with them specific functions. *Police functions* are the tasks and activities associated with a role of the police. The police are expected to carry out various social roles and engage in a variety of social functions or tasks.

For the most part, there are four primary roles over which the police have responsibility:

1. Law enforcement
2. Order maintenance
3. Provision of miscellaneous services
4. Convenience norm enforcement

Box 1.3 provides a partial listing of the various tasks or activities that police officers might perform in each of these roles. The listing in Box 1.3 represents a wide range of activities. Citizens and citizen groups have varying expectations about what the police should do—some are specific and some are diffuse. For example, merchants and business people typically envision and advocate that police officers' primary role should be to protect them and their businesses from burglars or perhaps remove panhandlers so that they do not obstruct their doorways. Residents in a housing project expect police officers to maintain order and provide them protection from the criminals and drug dealers who might reside in the area. Suburbanites, on the other hand, frequently expect the police to expedite the flow of traffic so they can travel to their jobs with the minimum amount of inconvenience.

What the police actually do, therefore, is the result of a complicated political and social process. The government, city council, mayor, and city manager will attempt to appease citizen constituents by pressuring various governmental agencies to provide expected services. Sometimes, citizens will band together in an effort to pressure government officials to change policies. The police also

---

Box 1.3 Police Roles and Activities

Law Enforcement
  Investigate criminal activities.
  Arrest perpetrators of crimes.
  Investigate crimes in progress.
  Serve warrants.
  Interrogate suspects.
Order Maintenance
  Force panhandlers or drunks to vacate an area.
  Investigate suspicious persons or vehicles.
  Investigate domestic disturbances.
  Break up bar fights.
  Quell riots or disorder.
  Intervene in noisy parties or gatherings.

Miscellaneous Services
  Assist stranded or lost motorists.
  Provide assistance during a medical emergency.
  Look for lost children.
  Assist people who have locked their keys in their automobiles.
  Provide information to citizens.
Convenience Norms
  Investigate traffic accidents.
  Issue traffic citations.
  Issue parking tickets.
  Direct traffic.
  Suggest engineering changes to facilitate traffic flow.

---

have an interest in the services they are called on to perform. Depending on the change that is being advocated, the police may support or resist the change.

Conflict often develops regarding what the police do and how they do it. Klockars (2006) discussed this issue in terms of the "Dirty Harry" problem, and Bittner (1974) deliberated the police role in an article titled "Florence Nightingale in search of Willie Sutton." Essentially, the police are confronted with role conflict when they are expected to effectively perform a sometimes dirty, undesirable job within the confines of a number of legal and constitutional limitations. In other words, the police are expected to apprehend criminals, but officers must follow legal and constitutional mandates when doing so. Officers sometimes use "dirty means" to accomplish "good ends," and when they do they essentially step outside legal, ethical, or moral boundaries.

In the end, the police are continually involved in providing a variety of services that have differential effects on citizens. Yet, police are at least expected to act within the legal and constitutional parameters that protect individual rights and accord citizens the due process of law. The relative importance and mix of these services and how they are performed change with the political winds. As society identifies new problems, police departments identify new priorities. Even though a number of attempts have been made to enumerate police activities or objectives, Goldstein (1977:52) identified those objectives that are most applicable:

1. To prevent and control conduct widely recognized as threatening to life and property;
2. To aid individuals who are in danger of physical harm, such as the victim of a criminal attack;

3. To protect constitutional guarantees, such as the right of free speech and assembly;
4. To facilitate the movement of people and vehicles;
5. To assist those who cannot care for themselves: the intoxicated, the addicted, the mentally ill, the physically disabled, the old and the young;
6. To resolve conflict, whether it is between individuals, groups of individuals, or individuals and their government;
7. To identify problems that have the potential for becoming more serious problems for the individual citizen, for the police, or for government; and
8. To create and maintain a feeling of security in the community.

Police Activities

Police officers typically view themselves as crime fighters or crook catchers (Manning, 2006), and many people seek careers in law enforcement because of the "exciting" connotation surrounding crime fighting (Kappeler et al., 1998). Some police officers view their sole role as that of law enforcement. They tend to relegate other duties and responsibilities to a lower level and, in some cases, argue that they are not obligated to perform them. This sometimes causes problems, when people go into the police occupation with unrealistic expectations about police work and because the public feels police should be involved in roles other than just law enforcement and crime fighting.

Perhaps the best way to understand the police role is to examine what they do. A number of studies have done this by researching police activities and police workloads. Although these findings present inconsistencies, they shed some light on defining the police role and sorting out the difference between perceptions of what the police do or profess to do and what is actually done.

One of the earliest studies, by Cumming, Cumming, and Edell (1965), found that about one-half of the calls received by one unidentified police department dealt with problem solving. Similarly, Wilson (1968) examined the calls received by the Syracuse, New York, Police Department and found that about 10% of the calls related to law enforcement, 30% to order maintenance, 22% to information gathering, and 38% to service calls. Bercal (1970) examined police calls in St. Louis and Detroit and found that only 16% were related to law enforcement, and Webster (1970), upon examining police department call cards (records of calls for service), again found that only 16% of the calls were law enforcement related. Meyer and Taylor (1975) found that the majority of police calls were of a service nature (64% service and 36% law enforcement), but, when proactive mobilizations were analyzed separately, the difference between law enforcement (41%) and service (59%) was not as great. Individual police officers tend to initiate law enforcement activities—the traditional police role as opposed to service.

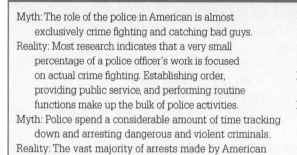

The Myth of Police as Solely Crime Fighters

Myth: The role of the police in American is almost exclusively crime fighting and catching bad guys.

Reality: Most research indicates that a very small percentage of a police officer's work is focused on actual crime fighting. Establishing order, providing public service, and performing routine functions make up the bulk of police activities.

Myth: Police spend a considerable amount of time tracking down and arresting dangerous and violent criminals.

Reality: The vast majority of arrests made by American officers are for relatively minor crimes like intoxication, traffic violations, and drug possession. In fact, on average, a police officer makes fewer than two felony arrests in any given year.

Myth: Television dramas about the police accurately reflect the reality of policing.

Reality: Although it depends on where officers work and their particular assignments, television cops probably see more crime-fighting action in single season than most cops see in their entire careers.

There are several problems associated with interpreting police workload studies (Greene & Klockars, 1991). First, the interpretation of police activities is based on the subjectivity of researchers' and citizens' own perceptions. The provision of "service" to one group in society may involve the targeted law enforcement of another group (Kappeler et al., 1998). Business people might want the police to move panhandlers from their storefronts and consider this a police service, but the homeless may perceive this as police harassment. Additionally, sometime police agencies provide services in hopes of developing better relations with citizens, making it easier to collect information that will be used for enforcement purposes. Second, researchers have not been consistent in categorizing specific activities or events. Third, data tend to include citizen descriptions of events or problems and police definitions rather than those of independent observers. Fourth, these studies generally include only patrol activities and do not count the activities of criminal investigation units or special response units, which have heavy workloads. Finally, numerous service or order-maintenance activities require officers to exercise law enforcement skills; police calls are not always clear cut in terms of being order maintenance, service, or law enforcement but instead may require all types of skills on the part of the responding officer.

A number of studies have attempted to identify how patrol officers spend their time through observation rather than just viewing records. Earlier studies examined dispatch records, while the more contemporary studies have been observational, where participant observers rode with officers and recorded what the officers did. Observational studies are more accurate because they are able to collect more detailed information about officer activities. When Frank, Brandl, and Watkins (1997) studied officers in Cincinnati, Ohio, they found that officers spent about one-third of their time on patrol (uncommitted), about 20% of their time responding to noncrime calls, and about 17% of their time responding to crime-related calls. About 13% of their time was devoted to administrative matters, such as court time or completing reports, and 9% of their time was considered to be personal time, such as eating or attending to personal matters. The remaining 7% of their time was devoted to dealing with the public in terms of providing assistance or information, problem solving, and attending community meetings. Famega (2005) reviewed a number of these studies and found that there is a measure of consistency across departments. She noted that about 75% of an officer's time is uncommitted, but officers conduct a substantial number of administrative and personal activities during this time. This finding was reinforced by Frank et al. (1997), who observed that only 30% of officers' time was devoted to dispatched calls. Obviously, officers complete administrative tasks such as writing reports and initiate contact with citizens during this time. But officers still have substantial amounts of free time that could be better utilized (Box 1.4).

It should be noted that there is considerable variation across police departments. For example, when Parks et al. (1999) examined workload in Indianapolis, they found that 26% of the officers' time was either spent patrolling or uncommitted and 6% of their time was devoted to administration. They also found that 14.58% of the officers' time was spent driving to calls, meetings, jail, or headquarters. It is difficult to compare the various workload studies, because they do not use the same categories to collect data; for example, travel time to calls was not included in the Frank et al. (1997) study.

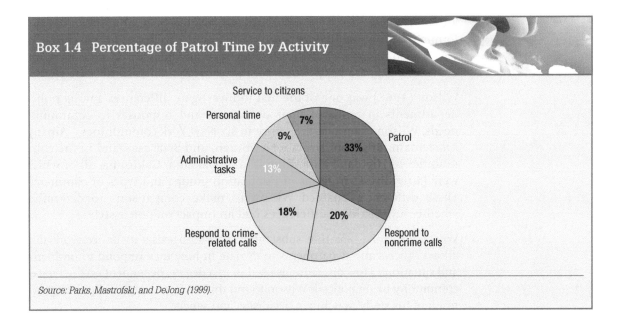

Box 1.4 Percentage of Patrol Time by Activity

Service to citizens — 7%
Personal time — 9%
Patrol — 33%
Administrative tasks — 13%
Respond to noncrime calls — 20%
Respond to crime-related calls — 18%

Source: Parks, Mastrofski, and DeJong (1999).

Most American police departments have adopted some form of community policing, which has resulted in greater emphasis on policing disorder and minor crime. Many police administrators have adopted Wilson and Kelling's (2006) "Broken Windows" approach with the belief that police action to reduce minor violations would ultimately have an impact on property and violent crime (McArdle & Erzen, 2001). This philosophy has spread throughout the United States, creating a greater emphasis on law enforcement, even in service and order maintenance situations, but there is little empirical support that it reduces crime.

Community policing has also resulted in changing how police officers interact with the community; for example, Kappeler and Gaines (2011) noted that community policing consists of problem solving and developing partnerships with community groups. Police workload studies show that police officers have ample time to engage in these activities. Police managers and supervisors must facilitate officers' engagement in these activities.

Styles of Police Departments

The above discussion points to the differences in how individuals, citizens, and police officers view the police occupation and the role of police in American society. It is important to realize that such differences exist in terms of how police departments operate. Each jurisdiction has its own unique set of problems, population groups, and socioeconomic structure, and the differences in these variables will cause each police organization to respond accordingly. Moreover, individual police officers within the same jurisdiction will view their jobs differently and respond accordingly when interacting with citizens and performing police duties (Broderick, 1987; Coates, 1972; Muir, 1977; White, 1972). This section explores what types of police departments exist in our society and the different approaches police departments use to fulfill their social roles.

Wilson (1968) was one of the first to investigate differences among police departments in terms of their operations and responses to community needs. Wilson examined the police in six New York communities—Albany, Amsterdam, Brighton, Nassau, Newburgh, and Syracuse—and in the communities of Highland Park, Illinois, and Oakland, California, all of which were fairly diverse in terms of population groups and types of commerce. These differences enabled Wilson to make comparisons to determine whether jurisdictional differences had an impact on police style.

Wilson's premise was that substantial discretion exists in police work that allows officers and departments to deviate in how they respond to problems and situations. How discretion is used is, to a degree, dependent on the type of community being policed. Wilson found three different styles of policing as a result of his study: watchman, legalistic, and service.

Watchman-style policing refers to policing that emphasizes order maintenance and crime control and generally can be found in larger industrialized cities. Watchman-style police officers are concerned with public order and "serious" crime. Police departments that adhere to the watchman style are not overly concerned with minor infractions of the law. Officers are less likely to invoke the criminal justice process when misdemeanors, traffic violations, or other minor infractions of the law occur. They are more likely to use extralegal methods such as verbal warnings, forcing people to leave an area, or onsite destruction of contraband as opposed to formally processing offenders. The watchman style of policing requires that officers consider any mitigating circumstances when deciding what actions to take; for example, juveniles are expected to "act up." Watchman-style police officers typically take a familial or in loco parentis view toward juveniles and use court referrals only as a last resort. Disputes between citizens are viewed as private matters unless they result in a disturbance of the peace. In the end, watchman-style police officers have two criteria in enforcing the law: (1) take action against serious crimes, and (2) ensure that domestic tranquility is maintained.

The *legalistic-style* police department is one in which authority is highly centralized or bureaucratic and requires officers to enforce one set of uniform standards on the public. Departments in the western United States, particularly California, have had a long-standing reputation as being legalistic. The exercise of police discretion is discouraged and, in some cases, it is not even recognized as a viable police option. All citizens, regardless of circumstances, should be treated the same. Uniformity of law enforcement is equated with fairness. Discretion is viewed as a possible first step to police corruption. The legalistic department generally implements the criminal justice process as frequently as possible, and offenders, regardless of their circumstances or the severity of their offense, seldom escape official sanctions. Legalistic departments write large numbers of traffic citations and arrest and detain persons for even the most minor criminal violations. Basically, there is no alternative to the criminal justice process.

Service-style agencies are usually found in homogeneous middle- and upper-class communities that generally surround metropolitan areas. These departments emphasize providing services to their residents. Officers in these departments consider all calls to be serious, regardless of their nature, but invoke the criminal justice process only when necessary. They see their primary function as protecting the community from unruly teenagers or criminals from outside the community. Service-style police departments are generally found in communities with substantial wealth and resemble security departments with an emphasis on public and community relations. In terms of security, officers closely monitor citizens' property, investigate strange vehicles seen in neighborhoods, and ensure that all strangers have legitimate purposes for being in areas of the jurisdiction. Citizens are treated with respect, and every effort is made to meet their needs and to conform to their idea of how the police should operate. Because these communities generally have ample tax bases and resources, officers who patrol these areas are usually paid well and are provided with state-of-the-art police equipment. These factors contribute to their willingness to work in service-style police agencies.

A great deal has changed in American policing since Wilson conducted his study in 1968. The distinctions he made between the three styles of policing have become blurred. Zhao and Hassel (2005) surveyed 482 large departments and found that departments had become more homogeneous in their styles of policing. They credited this change to police professionalization and departments' political environments having less of an impact on a department's operations. Today, however, examples of watchman-, legalistic-, and service-style departments can still be found. For example, a campus police department might adopt a watchman style of policing, a tourist community might use a service style, and an industrial city could adopt the legalistic style. Some departments may use all three styles of policing (Baillargeon & Smith, 1980). The styles of policing used are often associated with the community being served, its economic foundation, the composition of its citizenry and police officers, and the unique circumstances facing the community at a given point in time. A beachfront community may adopt a service style of policing during spring break and revert to a watchman style after that vacation season has ended. A police department in a single city may use one style of policing in an affluent neighborhood and still another style in a low-income part of the city. Police officers in large cities who are permanently assigned to a beat will adapt their policing style to meet the needs, or their own expectations, of the area. In these cases, police officers may decide, individually, which of the three styles they will use; therefore, it is possible that all three policing styles could be implemented within a single jurisdiction.

DIVERSITY OF THE POLICE ESTABLISHMENT

It is important to realize that there is a vast police institution in the United States. There are approximately 18,760 separate local, state, and federal law enforcement agencies in the United States, with more than 1.1 million employees and a combined operating cost of nearly $99 billion (Kyckelhahn, 2010). In addition to these agencies are various governmental agencies that normally are not thought of as police agencies but which have police powers; for example, most state social welfare departments have an inspector general's office or other type of investigative unit to investigate welfare or food stamp fraud.

The vast numbers of police agencies divided across levels of government have prompted critics to contend that American law enforcement is fragmented and that this fragmentation results in inefficiency and ineffectiveness. Indeed, a given jurisdiction may be policed by several agencies: a city police department, a sheriff's department, a state police organization, and several federal agencies. Each of these agencies would have jurisdiction for specific offenses, and, in some cases, several of them would have jurisdiction over the same offense. For example, a large organized drug operation involving firearms in a city could potentially involve the city police, the sheriff's department, the state police, the FBI, the DEA, and the Bureau of Alcohol, Tobacco, and Firearms (BATF). There seldom are situations in which this many different agencies would be involved in the same case, but on occasion conflicts between agencies do occur because of overlapping jurisdiction.

FEDERAL LAW ENFORCEMENT AGENCIES

As noted above, federal law enforcement agencies and police powers have evolved in response to specific political needs; consequently, federal police agencies have somewhat restricted responsibilities focusing on a limited number of criminal acts. Approximately 65 different federal law enforcement agencies employ about 105,000 men and women (Reaves, 2006). In November 2002, President George W. Bush signed legislation creating the Department of Homeland Security (DHS). Previously, most law enforcement agencies were housed in the Departments of Justice and Treasury. The legislation shifted a number of agencies from other federal departments into Homeland Security, giving Homeland Security a major law enforcement presence. Although Justice and Homeland Security contain most of the federal law enforcement responsibility today, other departments such as Treasury, Agriculture, Defense, Energy, and Human Services have some law enforcement responsibilities (see Box 1.5). The following sections address the major federal law enforcement agencies.

Justice Department Agencies

The Justice Department was created in 1870. It was charged with enforcing most of the criminal laws that were created by Congress. Box 1.6 provides a listing of the primary federal law enforcement agencies within the Justice Department. Each is discussed below.

Federal Bureau of Investigation

The Federal Bureau of Investigation (FBI) was created in 1908 as the Bureau of Investigation. Prior to 1908, the Justice Department staffed its law enforcement force with borrowed agents from the Treasury Department. In 1906, Charles Bonaparte, President Theodore Roosevelt's attorney general, requested funds for full-time Justice Department agents. Congress refused the request, largely because of a land fraud investigation that led to the indictment and conviction

Box 1.5 Department and Branch of Federal Agencies Employing Full-Time Officers with Authority to Carry Firearms and Make Arrests, by Primary Place of Employment, September 2008

| Department/ Branch | Federal Agency | Primary Place of Employment | | | Primary Duties of Law Enforcement Officers |
		Total	50 States and District of Columbia	U.S. Territories	
Agriculture	U.S. Forest Service, Law Enforcement and Investigations Organization	648	644	4	Uniformed law enforcement rangers enforce federal laws and regulations governing National Forest lands and resources. Special agents are criminal investigators who investigate crimes against property, visitors, and employees.
Commerce	Bureau of Industry and Security, Office of Export Enforcement	103	103	0	Special agents conduct investigations of alleged or suspected violations of dual-use export control laws.
Commerce	National Institute of Standards and Technology Police	28	28	0	Officers provide law enforcement and security services for NIST facilities.
Commerce	National Oceanic and Atmospheric Administration, Office of Law Enforcement	154	149	5	Special agents and enforcement officers enforce laws that conserve and protect living marine resources and their natural habitat in the U.S. Exclusive Economic Zone, which covers ocean waters between 3 and 200 miles off shore and adjacent to all U.S. states and territories.
Defense	Pentagon Force Protection Agency	725	725	0	Officers provide law enforcement and security services for the occupants, visitors, and infrastructure of the Pentagon, Navy Annex, and other assigned Pentagon facilities.
Energy	National Nuclear Security Administration, Office of Secure Transportation	363	363	0	Special agents, known as nuclear materials couriers, ensure the safe and secure transport of government-owned special nuclear materials during classified shipments in the contiguous United States.

Box 1.5 Department and Branch of Federal Agencies Employing Full-Time Officers with Authority to Carry Firearms and Make Arrests, by Primary Place of Employment, September 2008 *Continued*

Department/ Branch	Federal Agency	Primary Place of Employment			Primary Duties of Law Enforcement Officers
		Total	50 States and District of Columbia	U.S. Territories	
Health and Human Services	National Institutes of Health, Division of Police	94	94	0	Officers provide law enforcement and security services for NIH facilities.
Health and Human Services	U.S. Food and Drug Administration, Office of Criminal Investigations	187	183	4	Special agents investigate suspected criminal violations of the Federal Food, Drug, and Cosmetic Act and other related Acts; the Federal Anti-Tampering Act; and other statutes, including applicable Title 18 violations of the United States Code.
Homeland Security	Federal Emergency Management Agency, Security Branch	84	84	0	Officers are responsible for the protection of FEMA facilities, personnel, resources, and information.
Homeland Security	U.S. Customs and Border Protection	37,482	36,863	619	CBP officers protect U.S. borders at official ports of entry. Border patrol agents prevent illegal entry of people and contraband between the ports of entry. Air and marine officers patrol the nation's land and sea borders to stop terrorists and drug smugglers.
Homeland Security	U.S. Immigration and Customs Enforcement	12,679	12,446	233	Special agents conduct investigations involving national security threats, terrorism, drug smuggling, child exploitation, human trafficking, illegal arms export, financial crimes, and fraud. Uniformed immigration enforcement agents perform functions related to the investigation, identification, arrest, prosecution, detention, and deportation of aliens, as well as the apprehension of absconders.

Continued...

Box 1.5   Department and Branch of Federal Agencies Employing Full-Time Officers with Authority to Carry Firearms and Make Arrests, by Primary Place of Employment, September 2008 *Continued*

Department/ Branch	Federal Agency	Primary Place of Employment			Primary Duties of Law Enforcement Officers
		Total	50 States and District of Columbia	U.S. Territories	
Homeland Security	U.S. Secret Service	5226	5213	13	Special agents have investigation and enforcement duties primarily related to counterfeiting, financial crimes, computer fraud, and threats against dignitaries. Uniformed Division officers protect the White House complex and other presidential offices, the main Treasury building and annex, the President and Vice President and their families, and foreign diplomatic missions.
Independent	Amtrak Police	305	305	0	Officers provide law enforcement and security services for the passengers, employees, and patrons of the national railroad owned by the U.S. Government and operated by the National Railroad Passenger Corporation.
Independent	Federal Reserve Board Police	141	141	0	Officers provide law enforcement and security services for Federal Reserve facilities in Washington, D.C.
Independent	National Aeronautics and Space Administration, Protective Services	62	62	0	Officers provide law enforcement and security services for NASA's 14 centers located throughout the U.S.
Independent	Smithsonian National Zoological Park Police	26	26	0	Officers provide security and law enforcement services for the Smithsonian Institution's 163-acre National Zoological Park in Washington, D.C.
Independent	Tennessee Valley Authority Police	145	145	0	Officers provide law enforcement and security services for TVA employees and properties, and users of TVA recreational facilities.
Independent	U.S. Environmental Protection Agency, Criminal Enforcement	202	202	0	Special agents investigate suspected individual and corporate criminal violations of the nation's environmental laws.

Box 1.5 Department and Branch of Federal Agencies Employing Full-Time Officers with Authority to Carry Firearms and Make Arrests, by Primary Place of Employment, September 2008 *Continued*

Department/ Branch	Federal Agency	Primary Place of Employment			Primary Duties of Law Enforcement Officers
		Total	50 States and District of Columbia	U.S. Territories	
Independent	U.S. Postal Inspection Service	2324	2288	36	Postal inspectors conduct criminal investigations covering more than 200 federal statutes related to the postal system. Postal police officers provide security for postal facilities, employees, and assets, as well as escort high-value mail shipments.
Interior	Bureau of Indian Affairs, Division of Law Enforcement	277	277	0	Officers provide law enforcement services in some tribal areas. In addition to providing direct oversight for these bureau-operated programs, the division also provides technical assistance and some oversight to tribally operated law enforcement programs.
Interior	Bureau of Land Management, Law Enforcement	255	255	0	Law enforcement rangers conduct patrols, enforce federal laws and regulations, and provide for the safety of BLM employees and users of public lands. Special agents investigate illegal activity on public lands.
Interior	National Park Service, United States Park Police	547	547	0	Officers provide law enforcement services to designated National Park Service areas (primarily in the Washington, D.C., New York City, and San Francisco metropolitan areas). Officers are authorized to provide services for the entire National Park System.
Interior	National Park Service, Visitor and Resource Protection Division	1416	1404	12	Park rangers, commissioned as law enforcement officers, provide law enforcement services for the National Park System. Additional rangers serving seasonally are commissioned officers but are considered part-time and not included in the FLEO census.

Continued...

Box 1.5   Department and Branch of Federal Agencies Employing Full-Time Officers with Authority to Carry Firearms and Make Arrests, by Primary Place of Employment, September 2008 *Continued*

Department/ Branch	Federal Agency	Primary Place of Employment			Primary Duties of Law Enforcement Officers
		Total	50 States and District of Columbia	U.S. Territories	
Interior	U.S. Bureau of Recla-mation, Hoover Dam Police	21	21	0	Officers provide security and law enforcement services for the Hoover Dam and the surrounding 22-square-mile security zone.
Interior	U.S. Fish and Wildlife Service, Office of Law Enforcement	603	598	5	Special agents enforce fed-eral laws that protect wildlife resources, including endangered species, migratory birds, and marine mammals.
Judicial	Administrative Office of the U.S. Courts	4767	4696	71	Federal probation officers supervise offenders on probation and supervised release. In seven federal judicial districts, proba-tion officers are not authorized to carry a firearm while on duty and are excluded from FLEO officer counts.
Judicial	U.S. Supreme Court Police	139	139	0	Officers provide law enforcement and security services for Supreme Court facilities.
Justice	Bureau of Alcohol, Tobacco, Firearms and Explosives	2562	2541	21	Special agents enforce federal laws related to the illegal use and trafficking of firearms, the illegal use and storage of explosives, acts of arson and bombings, acts of terrorism, and the illegal diversion of alcohol and tobacco products.
Justice	Drug Enforcement Administration	4388	4308	80	Special agents investigate major narcotics violators, enforce reg-ulations governing the manufac-ture and dispensing of controlled substances, and perform other functions to prevent and control drug trafficking.

Box 1.5 Department and Branch of Federal Agencies Employing Full-Time Officers with Authority to Carry Firearms and Make Arrests, by Primary Place of Employment, September 2008 *Continued*

Department/ Branch	Federal Agency	Primary Place of Employment			Primary Duties of Law Enforcement Officers
		Total	50 States and District of Columbia	U.S. Territories	
Justice	Federal Bureau of Investigation	12,925	12,760	165	Special agents are responsible for criminal investigation and enforcement related to more than 200 categories of federal law. Criminal priorities include public corruption, civil rights violations, organized crime, white-collar crime, violent crime, and major theft. FBI police officers provide law enforcement and security for FBI facilities.
Justice	Federal Bureau of Prisons	16,993	16,835	158	Correctional officers enforce the regulations governing the operation of BOP correctional institutions, serving as both supervisors and counselors of inmates. They are normally not armed while on duty. Most other BOP employees have arrest and firearm authority to respond to emergencies.
Justice	U.S. Marshals Service	3359	3313	46	The agency receives all persons arrested by federal agencies and is responsible for their custody and transportation until sentencing. Deputy marshals provide security for federal judicial facilities and personnel.
Legislative	Library of Congress Police	85	85	0	Officers provided law enforcement and security services for Library of Congress facilities. On October 1, 2009, the agency ceased operations and its personnel, duties, responsibilities, and functions were transferred to the U.S. Capitol Police.

Continued...

Box 1.5   Department and Branch of Federal Agencies Employing Full-Time Officers with Authority to Carry Firearms and Make Arrests, by Primary Place of Employment, September 2008 *Continued*

Department/ Branch	Federal Agency	Primary Place of Employment			Primary Duties of Law Enforcement Officers
		Total	50 States and District of Columbia	U.S. Territories	
Legislative	U.S. Capitol Police	1637	1637	0	Officers provide law enforcement and security services for the U.S. Capitol grounds and buildings, and in the zone immediately surrounding the Capitol complex. The U.S. Capitol Police assumed the duties of the Library of Congress Police on October 1, 2009.
Legislative	U.S. Government Printing Office, Uniformed Police Branch	41	41	0	Officers provide law enforcement and security services for facilities where information, products, and services for the federal government are produced and distributed.
State	Bureau of Diplomatic Security	1049	1049	0	In the U.S., special agents protect the secretary of state, the U.S. ambassador to the United Nations, and visiting foreign dignitaries below the head-of-state level. They also investigate passport and visa fraud.
Treasury	Bureau of Engraving and Printing Police	207	207	0	Officers provide law enforcement and security services for facilities in Washington, D.C., and Fort Worth, Texas, where currency, securities, and other official U.S. documents are made.
Treasury	Internal Revenue Service, Criminal Investigation Division	2655	2636	19	Special agents have investigative jurisdiction over tax, money laundering, and Bank Secrecy Act laws.
Treasury	United States Mint Police	316	316	0	Officers provide law enforcement and security services for employees, visitors, government assets stored at U.S. Mint facilities in Philadelphia, PA; San Francisco, CA; West Point, NY; Denver, CO; Fort Knox, KY; and Washington, D.C.

Box 1.5   Department and Branch of Federal Agencies Employing Full-Time Officers with Authority to Carry Firearms and Make Arrests, by Primary Place of Employment, September 2008 *Continued*

Department/ Branch	Federal Agency	Primary Place of Employment			Primary Duties of Law Enforcement Officers
		Total	50 States and District of Columbia	U.S. Territories	
Veterans Affairs	Veterans Health Administration, Office of Security and Law Enforcement	3175	3128	47	Officers provide law enforcement and security services for VA medical centers.

Note: Table excludes offices of inspectors general (see Table 3), U.S. Armed Forces (Army, Navy, Air Force, Marines, and Coast Guard), Central Intelligence Agency, and Transportation Security Administration's Federal Air Marshals.
Source: Bureau of Justice Statistics, Census of Federal Law Enforcement Officers, 2008, Reaves (2012).

of several members of Congress. Bonaparte ignored the refusal and in 1908 created a small enforcement division of about 35 agents called the Bureau of Investigation (Unger, 1976). The Bureau began to grow rapidly following passage of the White Slave Act in 1910 and the Espionage Act in 1917.

In 1924, Attorney General Harlan F. Stone appointed J. Edgar Hoover as the Director of the Bureau of Investigation. At the time of his appointment the Bureau was characterized by a lack of leadership and internal corruption. The 29-year-old Hoover immediately set out to professionalize the agency. He focused on its image and its ability to investigate crimes and arrest lawbreakers. He also initiated a rule that the Bureau must hire only college graduates, especially those with degrees in law and accounting.

Also in 1924, the Bureau opened its Identification Division, which serves as a national clearinghouse for information on criminals. The Identification Division started with some 810,000 fingerprint cards, which were obtained from

Box 1.6   Law Enforcement Agencies in the U.S. Department of Justice

Federal Bureau of Investigation
Drug Enforcement Administration
U.S. Marshal Service
Bureau of Alcohol, Tobacco, and Firearms

the Federal Penitentiary at Leavenworth, Kansas, and from the International Association of Chiefs of Police. Today, the Identification Division has nearly 200 million fingerprints on file and processes several thousand inquiries each day. The Bureau's crime laboratory was opened in 1932, and within the first year 963 cases were processed. In 1935, the Bureau of Investigation formally changed its name to the FBI. Under Hoover's leadership, the FBI developed the image of a highly professional law enforcement agency. The Depression and Prohibition era of the 1920 and 1930s and the Bureau's many encounters with nationally known crime figures propelled the Bureau into a dominant position in American law enforcement (Figure 1.4).

In 1972, the FBI opened its new academy on the U.S. Marine Corps base located in Quantico, Virginia. The FBI Academy trains its agents, DEA agents, and more than 1000 local and state police officers every year. Other responsibilities of the FBI are the Uniform Crime Reporting (UCR) system, which collects national statistics on crime, criminals, and criminal justice agencies, and the National Crime Information Center (NCIC), which serves as a national database for wanted persons, wanted and stolen vehicles, and stolen property. In addition to its national academy, the FBI offers a number of training programs to local, state, and international enforcement officers. Since the latter part of the 1990s, the FBI has been establishing offices throughout the world that are known as legal attachés, or legats. These legats work with host-country agencies on cases that are of interest to the United States and the host country. Their purpose is to stop foreign crimes that may affect the United States and to help solve international crimes as quickly as possible. The Bureau operates 60 of these offices (FBI, 2014).

FIGURE 1.4
J. Edgar Hoover became the first FBI Director in 1924 and remained in office until his death in 1972.
Photo courtesy of the Federal Bureau of Investigation.

The FBI operates 56 field offices throughout the United States and has approximately 13,913 special agents and 22,161 other employees. The FBI enjoys an annual budget of more than $8.1 billion for salaries, operations, and expenses and has investigative responsibility for approximately 250 different criminal offenses (FBI, 2013). The FBI's top priorities include:

1. Protect the United States from terrorist attack.
2. Protect the United States against foreign intelligence operations and espionage.
3. Protect the United States against cyber-based attacks and high-technology crime.
4. Combat public corruption at all levels.
5. Protect civil rights.
6. Combat transnational and national criminal organizations and enterprises.
7. Combat major white-collar crime.
8. Combat significant violent crime.
9. Support federal, state, county, municipal, and international partners.
10. Upgrade technology to successfully perform the FBI's mission.

The FBI investigates a variety of crimes. As a result of having jurisdiction across the United States, it is involved in a number of complex investigations across numerous political jurisdictions. Box 1.7 provides a summary of the crimes investigated by the Bureau.

For more information about the FBI, visit their Website at: http://www.fbi.gov/

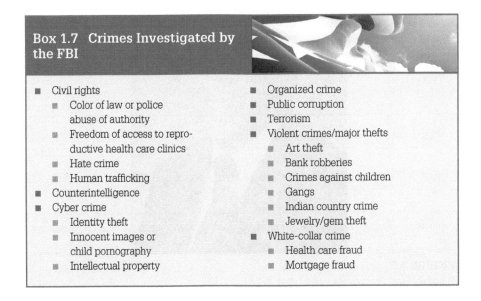

Box 1.7 Crimes Investigated by the FBI

- Civil rights
    - Color of law or police abuse of authority
    - Freedom of access to reproductive health care clinics
    - Hate crime
    - Human trafficking
- Counterintelligence
- Cyber crime
    - Identity theft
    - Innocent images or child pornography
    - Intellectual property
- Organized crime
- Public corruption
- Terrorism
- Violent crimes/major thefts
    - Art theft
    - Bank robberies
    - Crimes against children
    - Gangs
    - Indian country crime
    - Jewelry/gem theft
- White-collar crime
    - Health care fraud
    - Mortgage fraud

The contemporary FBI has not escaped criticism. In 1997, the FBI was the center of a national scandal involving false testimony of its experts and the practices at its crime laboratory. The capability and judgment of the FBI were further called into question because of its handling of the raid on the Branch Davidian compound in Waco, Texas. Following a botched raid by BATF agents, the FBI became involved in one of the longest standoffs in law enforcement history. In 1993, after a 51-day standoff, agents of the FBI stormed the Waco residence with tanks and tear gas. The compound was engulfed by fire and at least 70 residents, many of whom were children, were killed—some at their own hands, others because of the fire (Department of the Treasury, 1993; Stone, 1993).

In 2001, it was learned that a 25-year veteran of the FBI, Robert Hanssen, had been selling government secrets to the Soviet and Russian governments for decades. Hanssen faced 21 spying charges that stemmed from allegations that he took $1.4 million in cash and diamonds and sold secrets that could have resulted in the death of two federal agents. Over the years, a number of FBI agents have been disciplined or their behavior has discredited the FBI. Nonetheless, the FBI remains a highly professional organization with a number of congressionally mandated responsibilities (Figure 1.5).

The focus of the FBI was reshaped by the terrorist attacks of 9/11. Today, the primary emphasis for the bureau is countering domestic terrorist threats. Most of the FBI's counterterrorism efforts are housed in its National Security

FIGURE 1.5

Robert Hanssen. *Photo courtesy of AP Photo/FBI.*

Branch. It contains several divisions, including counterterrorism, counterintelligence, directorate of intelligence, weapons of mass destruction, counter proliferation, and the terrorist-screening center. The FBI investigates thousands of foreign nationals and U.S. citizens with suspected links to terrorist organizations such as al Qaeda. Al Qaeda and other terrorist groups have made numerous threats against the United States, and the FBI has been given the responsibility to collect intelligence, investigate suspicious persons and activities, and work with other agencies such as Homeland Security to counter terrorist threats. These activities are primarily conducted by the Bureau's Counterterrorism Division, which also coordinates many fusion centers (local-level antiterrorism groups consisting of local officials). The Bureau also participates in the Joint Terrorism Task Force, which includes all intelligence-collecting agencies that share terrorism intelligence to ensure all intelligence information is available on current terrorist activities. Fusion centers and the Joint Terrorism Task Force are discussed in more detail in Chapter 14.

The FBI is responsible for investigating a variety of criminal activities. The following provide a synopsis of a few of their cases. Notice the variety of investigations conducted by the Bureau:

- In Operation Ghost Click, an FBI investigation led to the arrest of six Estonians engaged in computer fraud. They infected approximately four million computers worldwide and manipulated Internet advertising, collecting $14 million in illicit fees.
- In Operation Delta Blues, a law enforcement task force assisted by the FBI arrested 70 people including five law enforcement officials in Arkansas for public corruption, drug trafficking, money laundering, and firearm offenses.
- In Operation Bad Medicine, an FBI-led task force investigation led to the indictment of 533 people for a $7 million health care fraud. The arrests included several doctors. The defendants were signing bogus accidental injury claims defrauding insurance companies.
- In a case investigated by the FBI and DEA, 35 members of the Barrio Azteca gang were charged with racketeering, murder, drug offenses, money laundering, and obstruction of justice.
- A Boston-area man was arrested for a plot to damage or destroy the Pentagon and U.S. Capitol using a remote controlled aircraft filled with C-4 plastic explosives (FBI, 2013).

Drug Enforcement Administration

Narcotics and drugs have long been considered a significant problem in the United States. In 1914, Congress passed the *Harrison Act*, which regulated opium, morphine, heroin, and cocaine. The Miscellaneous Division within the Internal Revenue Service was created in 1919 and assigned 162 agents to enforce the law (Bailey, 1995; Lyman, 2010). This unit was the first American law enforcement unit devoted to drug enforcement. The Narcotics Division was created during Prohibition. In each of these cases, drug enforcement was a minor endeavor.

In 1930, President Hoover appointed Harry Anslinger to head the newly created Federal Bureau of Narcotics (FBN). Once appointed, Anslinger quickly moved to increase his and the FBN's power and authority. He pushed for expanded enforcement powers and additional laws to use as weapons in the war against drugs. As the result of Anslinger's often questionable lobbying a number of federal laws were passed that were aimed at effecting better control over the narcotics problem. The FBN, for the most part, concentrated on the illegal importation of drugs into the United States.

In 1968, under President Lyndon B. Johnson, the FBN was removed from the Treasury Department and combined with the Bureau of Drug Abuse Control from the Department of Health, Education, and Welfare to create the Bureau of Narcotics and Dangerous Drugs (BNDD) in the Justice Department. This was the first time in history that the Justice Department was given authority to enforce drug laws. The creation of the BNDD was an effort to eliminate fragmentation in the federal government's drug enforcement efforts and to eliminate friction among agencies involved in drug enforcement.

For more information about the DEA, visit their Website at: **http://www.justice.gov/DEA**

In 1973, President Richard M. Nixon again reorganized our nation's drug enforcement system. He created the DEA by combining all the personnel and resources from the BNDD and the Office for Drug Abuse and Law Enforcement and the Office of National Narcotics Intelligence. The director of the DEA reported directly to the attorney general. Nixon envisioned that the DEA would mount a unified attack against drug suppliers and drug users. Agents were concerned not only with stopping the importation of drugs but also with drug networks at the state and local levels.

Today, the DEA has approximately 5000 agents allotted to 223 field offices in the United States and 86 foreign offices in 67 countries. The DEA's annual budget is approximately $2.87 billion. Agents are stationed in foreign countries in an attempt to collect drug exportation intelligence and assist and advise host-nation drug enforcement efforts. These foreign-based agents also work with INTERPOL and other international organizations on drug matters. The DEA's enforcement policy is to eliminate drugs as close as possible to the source and to disrupt drug trafficking systems by identifying, arresting, and prosecuting traffickers. More specifically, the DEA has nine major responsibilities in its mission statement:

1. Investigation and preparation for prosecution of major violators of controlled substances laws operating at interstate and international levels;
2. Investigation and preparation for prosecution of criminals and drug gangs who perpetuate violence in our communities and terrorize citizens through fear and intimidation;
3. Management of a national drug intelligence system in cooperation with federal, state, local, and foreign officials to collect, analyze, and disseminate strategic and operational drug intelligence information;
4. Seizure and forfeiture of assets derived from, traceable to, or intended to be used for illicit drug trafficking;
5. Enforcement of the provisions of the Controlled Substances Act as they pertain to the manufacture, distribution, and dispensing of legally produced controlled substances;
6. Coordination and cooperation with federal, state, and local law enforcement officials on mutual drug enforcement efforts and enhancement of such efforts through exploitation of potential interstate and international investigations beyond local or limited federal jurisdictions and resources;
7. Coordination and cooperation with other federal, state, and local agencies, and with foreign governments, in programs designed to reduce the availability of illicit abuse-type drugs on the U.S. market through nonenforcement methods such as crop eradication, crop substitution, and training of foreign officials;
8. Responsibility, under the policy guidance of the Secretary of State and U.S. Ambassadors, for all programs associated with drug law enforcement counterparts in foreign countries; and
9. Liaison with the United Nations, INTERPOL, and other organizations on matters relating to international drug control programs (DEA, 2013).

The DEA has a number of programs to facilitate achieving these responsibilities. First, the asset forfeiture program is where the DEA works with other law enforcement agencies to seize cash, real property, and other drug proceeds. Seizing assets is a tool to weaken drug trafficking organizations. Second, the domestic cannabis eradication program is designed to reduce the growing and distribution of marijuana. Third, the diversion control program works to prevent prescription drugs from being brought into the illicit market. Fourth, the DEA works with numerous local and state agencies through the High Intensity Drug Trafficking Areas program. These task forces facilitate cooperation among agencies in attempting interdict drugs and dismantle drug trafficking organizations. Fifth, through its financial investigations strategy, the DEA attempts to prevent money laundering. This directly affects drug cartels' businesses. Sixth, the Organized Crime and Drug Enforcement Task Force works with other agencies to investigate major drug trafficking organizations. Finally, the Southwest

Border Initiative is a comprehensive effort by federal law enforcement agencies in investigating and dismantling Mexican drug cartels (DEA, 2013). The DEA's programs represent a comprehensive law enforcement approach in dealing with America's drug problems.

Each year the DEA conducts a number of major operations designed to counter the drug problem. The following are examples of some of these programs.

- In 2010, for example, Project Deliverance resulted in the arrest of 2266 suspects on drug-related charges and the confiscation of more than 74 tons of illegal drugs when the DEA worked with numerous state and local agencies across the United States.
- The DEA conducted Operation Cuba Libre, an investigation of the Gramercy Medical Center in New York arresting 47 people including a doctor and his assistant for diverting over 500,000 prescription narcotic pills worth $10 million on the street.
- The DEA announced the results of Operation Knight Stalker where 30 members of the La Familia Michoacán and Knights Templar drug cartels were indicted in Southern California. The investigation resulted in the seizure of more than 1000 pounds of methamphetamine, 200 pounds of cocaine, 28 pounds of heroin, 320 pounds of marijuana, and $200,000.

U.S. Marshals Service

The office of U.S. Marshal was established by the *Judiciary Act of 1789* and is the oldest federal law enforcement agency in the United States. The Act provided that each judicial district would have one marshal who would in turn select deputy marshals to assist him as needed. "Originally, President George Washington nominated and the Senate confirmed 13 U.S. Marshals, one for each of the 11 states and one each for the districts of Kentucky and Maine" (Morris, 1995:796). Often U.S. Marshals were the only federal presence in new territories. The Marshals Service provided local representation for the newly established federal government. They were involved in taking the national census every 10 years, distributing Presidential Proclamations, collecting statistical information on commerce and manufacturing, and performing routine tasks needed for the central government (U.S. Marshals Service, 2008).

The Marshals Service expanded over the years as new states and territories were added to the nation. During the 1850s, U.S. Marshals were charged with apprehending fugitive slaves. Until 1861, the Marshals were under the direction of the Secretary of State, but after passage of legislation that year control of the Marshals switched to the attorney general. Since its inception, the Marshals have been called on by the executive and legislative branches of the federal government to engage in many controversial and unusual activities, including registering immigrants during wartime, capturing slaves, sealing borders, and trading spies with foreign countries (U.S. Marshals Service, 2014).

In 1969, the Marshals were given agency status when the U.S. Marshals Service (USMS) was created, and in 1974 it became a federal bureau. The President of the United States appoints each of the 94 U.S. Marshals. The USMS employs approximately 3925 deputies and has an annual budget of $1.186 billion (U.S. Marshals Service, 2014).

For more information about the U.S. Marshals Service, visit their Website at: **http://www.justice.gov/agencies/ index-list.html#USMarshal**

The USMS has five primary responsibilities. First, the USMS seizes property as the result of both criminal and civil actions to satisfy judgments issued by the federal courts. As a part of this responsibility, the USMS is responsible for maintaining, inventorying, and disposing of assets seized as the result of investigations by all federal law enforcement agencies. The USMS manages approximately $2.4 billion in property each year. Second, the USMS provides physical security for federal courtrooms and protects federal judges, attorneys, and jurors. The service provides security and protection for more than 13,000 members of the federal judiciary, and in 2013, the Marshals investigated over 1300 threats against the judiciary. Third, the USMS transports prisoners to and from federal penal institutions and courts. The USMS on average has about 60,000 in custody and receives about 233,000 prisoners each year. Fourth, the USMS protects government witnesses during court proceedings, especially when their testimony might jeopardize their lives. The Witness Security Division of the USMS provides for the security of witnesses in organized crime and other major felony cases when threats to their safety occur. Finally, U.S. Marshals execute federal, state, and local arrest warrants. In 2012, the USMS cleared 153,734 warrants and apprehended 123,006 fugitives.

The USMS remains out of public view and does not receive the notoriety that the FBI, DEA, Customs, or other federal agencies receive. They were the primary law enforcement in the western United States during the mid-1800s and were responsible for bringing countless numbers of criminals to justice. Marshals were used extensively during the civil rights movement. They protected James Meredith, the first African-American student at the University of Mississippi, when he first entered the university. They frequently were used to escort and protect Dr Martin Luther King, Jr, during his marches and speeches, and they were present at numerous other public gatherings during that period.

The USMS is involved in a variety of cases. The following are some examples,

- Marshals arrested Rashad Akeem Williams, who was wanted on two counts of attempting to commit the murder of two police officers.
- The USMS sold a home in Montclair, NJ that was once part of a Russian spy ring.

- Marshals arrested a Virginia fugitive in Vermont. The man was wanted for multiple sex crimes against a child.

Bureau of Alcohol, Tobacco, and Firearms

For more information about the BATF, visit their Website at: **http://www.justice.gov/agencies/index-list.html#ATF**

The BATF was created in 1972 by order of the Treasury Department. The order mandated that the BATF enforce all Treasury laws relating to alcohol, tobacco, firearms, and explosives. Prior to 1972, these law enforcement functions were housed with the Internal Revenue Service. Historically, the BATF has had two primary functions: (1) regulation and collection of taxes related to alcohol and tobacco, and (2) investigation of crimes related to firearms and explosives. The creation of the DHS resulted in BATF's enforcement operations being moved to the Justice Department; the tax collection division remained in Treasury. The BATF has an annual budget of more than $1.1 billion. Today, it employs more than 4800 people. Approximately 2450 of these employees are special agents who are assigned to 129 cities throughout the United States (BATF, 2013).

The BATF is engaged in a number of programs to accomplish its objectives. It has the Bomb Arson Tracking System to maintain a database on bomb and arson incidents, and to assist in such incidents, the BATF maintains certified explosives specialists and certified fire investigators. It also maintains experts in improvised explosive devices and has canines trained in explosives and accelerant detection. Its eTrace program assists in tracing and tracking firearms. The BATF conducts federal firearm compliance inspections and maintains information on some firearms sales. It also monitors tobacco sales to ensure that taxes are properly collected. The BATF has jurisdiction in crimes involving firearms, which results in the Bureau getting involved in the investigation of a host of crimes.

Department of Homeland Security

As noted above, much of federal law enforcement was reorganized as a result of the creation of the DHS. More than 100 units and bureaus from other departments were transferred to the new department. The mission of the DHS includes the following objectives (DHS, 2010):

1. Prevent terrorism and enhance security.
2. Secure and manage our borders.
3. Enforce and administer our immigration laws.
4. Safeguard and secure cyberspace.
5. Ensure resilience to disasters (Box 1.8).

The creation of the DHS resulted in one of the largest departments in the federal government. The DHS has approximately 200,000 employees across its many agencies. Agencies were organized into directorates and distinct departments. Box 1.9 shows the organizational chart for the DHS.

> **Box 1.8 Law Enforcement Agencies in the Department of Homeland Security**
>
> - U.S. Secret Service
> - Border and Transportation Directorate
> - Emergency Preparedness and Response Directorate
> - Science and Technology Directorate
> - Information Analysis and Infrastructure Protection Directorate

Transportation Security Agency

The Transportation Security Agency (TSA) has approximately 57,000 employees with an annual budget of over $7.6 billion (DHS, 2014). The primary responsibilities of the TSA are to protect our nation's transportation systems, including aviation, waterways, rail, highways, public transportation, and pipelines. The TSA attempts to ensure freedom of movement for people and commerce. The most visible members of the TSA can be found in our airports, where their responsibilities include using electronic screening devices on luggage and passengers to search for destructive devices. In 2012, the TSA screened more than 1.8 million passengers per day. In 2012, TSA found over 1500 guns. The agency screens all air cargo, including more than four billion checked bags, for explosives. These officers also use bomb-sniffing dogs in many of the nation's airports. The TSA conducted background checks for transportation-related employees, and checks passengers to determine if they are on the terrorist watch list.

The TSA has a number of other programs. On civilian aircraft, the Federal Air Marshal program deploys armed officers whose purpose is to intervene in possible hijackings or possible terrorist activities. The typical Federal Air Marshal spends about 900 h a year aboard aircraft (TSA, 2010). Under the *Vision 100—Century of Aviation Reauthorization Act* passed in 2003, the TSA is responsible for training airline crews in self-defense and pilots on how to use firearms, which are now stored in the cockpits of civilian aircraft. The TSA also monitors and regulates cargo that is being shipped by air, and the agency audits shippers to ensure that only approved cargo is transported. The Known Shippers Program ensures that only cargo from approved or known shippers can be transported in certain instances.

U.S. Customs and Border Protection

The Customs and Border Protection (CBP) has more than 21,370 border patrol officers and 21,186 officers stationed at our nation's ports. The CBP has an annual budget of over $11 billion (DHS, 2013). The agency has two primary

Box 1.9   Department of Homeland Security Organizational Chart

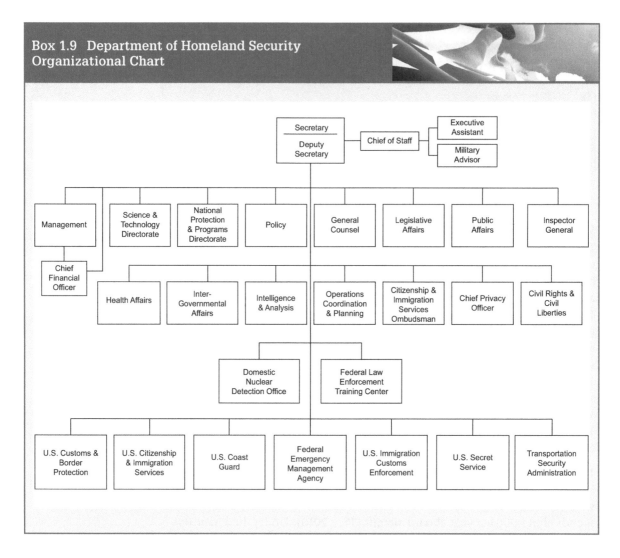

goals: (1) secure the nation's borders to protect the country from the entry of dangerous people and prevent unlawful trade and travel, and (2) ensure the efficient flow of legitimate trade and travel across U.S. borders (CBP, 2013).

The CBP is responsible for patrolling more than 6900 miles of Mexican and Canadian borders and 327 ports of entry (CBP, 2010). The most substantial obstacle is the terrain, especially along the Mexican border, which is where the greatest amount of smuggling and immigration activity occurs. The border is primarily desert and mountainous, which makes patrolling and observation extremely difficult. The CBP uses air and vehicular patrols, and in some cases all-terrain vehicles and horses are used. The patrols observe for undocumented immigrants or evidence that they are using a particular route. In some cases, fences have been constructed in areas that have a high traffic of immigrants. The fences alter immigrants' routes and reduce the amount of area that must be constantly patrolled. Additionally, the CBP has some 139 stations and 37 checkpoints where people crossing the border are checked to ensure that they have proper documentation. Automobiles, buses, freight trains, and marine craft are also inspected. It is anticipated that over the next several years the resources and activities of the CBP will increase substantially as the United States attempts to provide greater security for its borders.

CBP officers process approximately 339 million travelers per year at point of entry. It also processes 29.5 million trade entries (trucks and containers) per year. This is accomplished by border patrol officers as well as air and marine agents. These agents are primarily observing for illegal or undocumented immigrants, contraband such as controlled substances, counterfeit goods, diseased or prohibited plants and foodstuffs. CBP agents work with foreign governments to prevent smuggling.

As noted, CBP officers are responsible for investigating a host of crimes. The following are some examples of CBP cases:

- CBP officers arrested two women attempting to smuggle $61,340 into Mexico. Mexican drug cartels' ability to retrieve drug money from the United States is limited and they are now depending on smuggling cash back to Mexico.
- CBP officers intercepted a car in Baltimore. The care had been purchased with a stolen credit card and was being shipped to Lagos, Nigeria.
- In one weekend, CBP officers in Laredo, Texas intercepted cocaine and methamphetamine valued at more than $3 million.
- CBP agents in Nogales, Arizona arrested a man who was attempting to smuggle more than three tons of marijuana in boxes labeled vacuum pumps and lamp holders.

> For more information about the U.S. Immigration and Naturalization Service (INS) and the border patrol, visit the CBP Website at: **http://www.cbp.gov/xp/cgov/border_security/border_patrol/**

U.S. Secret Service

The Secret Service was established in 1865—two years after the United States adopted a national currency—with the mission of capturing counterfeiters. During the Civil War, approximately one-third of all the money in circulation was counterfeit. In 1901, President McKinley was assassinated, and Congress directed the Secret Service to provide protection for the President. Prior to that time, no federal agency was responsible for protecting the President. Today, this remains the primary responsibility of the Secret Service. The Uniform Division of the Secret Service was created in 1922 at the request of President Warren G. Harding to provide protection and security for the White House, the Treasury Building, presidential offices, the

Vice President's residence, and foreign diplomatic missions. In 2002, when President George W. Bush reorganized federal law enforcement in the wake of the 9/11 terrorist attacks, the Secret Service was moved from the Treasury Department to the DHS.

In addition to investigating the counterfeiting of currency, the Secret Service has authority to investigate credit card and computer fraud. In 1984, Congress enacted legislation making the fraudulent use of credit cards a federal violation. The Secret Service also investigates unauthorized access to automated teller machines and the possession and trafficking of counterfeit or stolen credit cards. "The mission of the United States Secret Service is to safeguard the nation's financial infrastructure and payment systems to preserve the integrity of the economy, and to protect national leaders, visiting heads of state and government, designated sites and National Special Security Events" (Secret Service, 2011). The *USA PATRIOT Act* increased the Secret Service's role in investigating fraud and related activity in connection with computers. The Act also authorized the Director of the Secret Service to establish nationwide electronic crimes task forces to assist law enforcement, the private sector, and academia in detecting and suppressing computer-based crime; increased the statutory penalties for the manufacturing, possession, dealing, and passing of counterfeit U.S. or foreign obligations: and allowed enforcement action to be taken to protect our financial payment systems while combating transnational financial crimes directed by terrorists or other criminals.

For more information about the secret service, visit their Website at: **www. secretservice.gov/**

Today, the Secret Service has a budget of approximately $1.8 billion. employs more than 4500 agents. In 2011, the agency arrested 5018 suspects for financial crimes, 2857 suspects for counterfeiting, and 863 for cybercrimes. Agents seized over $70 million in counterfeit currency, and prevented $5.6 billion in potential losses though financial crime investigations. In terms of executive protection, agents screened more than 1.4 million members of the public at events. The agency also screened 1.43 million mail items destined for the White House (DHS, 2013). Thus, the agency is immersed in a variety of activities.

Citizenship and Immigration Services

In 2003, service and benefit functions of the U.S. Immigration and Naturalization Service (INS) were transferred to the DHS as the U.S. Citizenship and Immigration Services (USCIS). The USCIS is responsible for the administration of immigration and naturalization adjudication functions and establishing immigration services policies and priorities. These functions include:

1. Adjudication of immigrant visa petitions
2. Adjudication of naturalization petitions
3. Adjudication of asylum and refugee applications

4. Adjudications performed at the service centers
5. All other adjudications performed by the INS

The USCIS has 18,000 employees and contractors working in approximately 250 headquarters and field offices around the world and has a budget of $3.0 billion (USCIS, 2013; DHS, 2013). As a result of the 9/11 terrorist attacks, governmental agencies have more closely examined the legality of numerous visitors' status in this country. Many visitors have overstayed their visas and otherwise entered the United States illegally. The service has several programs to accomplish this goal. The SAVE program is a web-based program that allows state and local governments to check the immigration status of people applying for benefits. E-Verify is a database that allows employers to check the immigration status of employees. In 2011, the service naturalized more than 692,000 new citizens and examined over 3000 cases involving national security (DHS, 2013).

Immigration and Customs Enforcement

Immigration and Customs Enforcement (ICE) was created by combining the law enforcement arm of the Naturalization Service and the former Customs Service. It is the largest investigative branch within the DHS. It has more than 20,000 employees operating in 400 offices around the world, and has a budget of $5.6 billion (ICE, 2011; DHS, 2013). Whereas the CBP is responsible for our borders, ICE is responsible for immigration enforcement within the interior of the United States. ICE has three primary objectives: (1) preventing terrorism and enhancing security, (2) securing and managing our borders, and (3) enforcing and administering immigration laws.

The agency has two primary operational units that carry out these objectives. First, Homeland Security Investigations has a number of responsibilities, including enforcing immigration-related laws; visa security activities; working with state, local, federal, and international agencies to dismantle human, narcotic, and weapons smuggling routes; protecting intellectual property from being illegally transferred; and preventing the trafficking of weapons and sensitive technology. Second, the agency's enforcement and removal operations have a number of duties, including detaining illegal aliens, of which it remove about 400,000 per year, and targeting criminal aliens for removal (DHS, 2013).

ICE has a number of responsibilities. The following examples demonstrate the diversity of the organization's activities.

> For more information about Immigration and Customs Enforcement, visit their Website at: **www.ice.gov**

- ICE returned a sixteenth century tapestry to Spain. ICE agents seized the tapestry in Houston.
- An ICE investigation led to the arrest of a Texas man on charges of transporting and possessing child pornography. He was distributing the materials via the Internet.

- ICE agents arrested two Mexican nationals in Albuquerque for selling fraudulent identity documents. Undercover agents bought a fraudulent social security card and a green card from the couple.
- Three business people in Orange County, California were charged with selling counterfeit goods after an ICE investigation.
- A result of an ICE investigation, two Maryland men were charged with conspiring to transport and entice females to travel interstate for prostitution, and sex trafficking by force (ICE, 2014).

U.S. Coast Guard

Historically, the primary responsibility of the U.S. Coast Guard was the enforcement of maritime laws pertaining not only to the Pacific and Atlantic Oceans, but also to intracoastal waterways such as the Mississippi and Ohio Rivers and the Great Lakes. Today, the U.S. Coast Guard's duties have been expanded to include watching for threats to our security. The agency is responsible for protecting more than 361 ports and 95,000 miles of coastline, America's longest border. It is the only military organization within the DHS. The 9/11 terrorist attacks altered the U.S. Coast Guard's mission, and today the agency is more involved in homeland protection. This is accomplished by:

1. Protecting ports, the flow of commerce, and the marine transportation system from terrorism;
2. Maintaining maritime border security against illegal drugs, illegal aliens, firearms, and weapons of mass destruction;
3. Ensuring that we can rapidly deploy and resupply our military assets by keeping Coast Guard units at a high state of readiness and by keeping marine transportation open for the transit of assets and personnel from other branches of the armed forces;
4. Protecting against illegal fishing and indiscriminate destruction of living marine resources and preventing and responding to oil and hazardous material spills, accidental or intentional; and
5. Coordinating efforts and intelligence with federal, state, and local agencies.

Some examples of the Coast Guard's activities include:

- In one year, recovered 75 metric tons of cocaine and 18 metric tons of marijuana destined for the United States. Officers interdicted 40 vessels and detained 191 suspected drug smugglers.
- Interdicted 2474 undocumented migrants attempting to illegally enter the United States.
- Responded to 20,510 search and rescue missions saving 3804 lives.
- Investigated 3000 pollution incidents.

The above sections have highlighted the primary agencies in the DHS. The Department is large, and there are dozens of other agencies directly involved in homeland security. The responsibilities of these agencies range from counter–agriculture terrorism to animal and plant health inspections. In essence, the DHS is responsible for initiating and coordinating the nation's response to any type of disaster or attack.

Miscellaneous Federal Law Enforcement Agencies
In addition to the investigative agencies in the Departments of Justice and Homeland Security, there are a number of other agencies with police or investigative powers. For example, the Department of Defense has several investigative and police agencies, including the Naval Criminal Investigative Service, Military Police in the Army, the Air Force has its Security Police, and within the Department of Defense there is the Defense Criminal Investigative Service. These and other units within the Department of Defense and armed services have extensive investigative and policing responsibilities.

There are numerous other agencies with police powers spread across other federal departments. The Department of Agriculture maintains an Office of the Inspector General, which is responsible for investigating fraud involving federal agriculture policies and programs. For example, they investigate the fraudulent use of food stamps and fraud associated with federal crop subsidy programs. The State Department maintains a force of investigators who provide protection for foreign dignitaries and investigate passport fraud. Finally, the Energy Department maintains a force of officers who are responsible for guarding and escorting nuclear materials that are associated with nuclear weapons or energy production.

The following sections examine state and local police agencies. It is informative to touch on the difference between federal police authority and state and local police authority. From the above discussion, it can be seen that federal law enforcement agencies were created to enforce specific laws, e.g. federal agencies do not enforce or investigate all federal laws, only those that have been assigned to them by Congress. State and local agencies, on the other hand, enforce all state laws. State and local police agencies have broader police powers. Many federal crimes are also state crimes. For example, the FBI investigates bank robberies, but bank robbery is also a state crime and is investigated by state and local authorities. Thus, state and local police officers have significant crime-related responsibilities.

STATE LAW ENFORCEMENT AGENCIES

The most common state law enforcement agency is the state police or highway patrol agency. Every state, with the exception of Hawaii, has a state police organization. In addition to these state police organizations, most states have several limited authority or limited-purpose law enforcement agencies. Limited-purpose agencies are those that have investigative or law enforcement responsibility for specific offenses or crimes involving certain classes of offenders (Table 1.1).

State Police and Highway Patrols

Historically, state police agencies were created for a number of reasons: (1) to assist local police, which frequently did not have adequate training or resources; (2) to investigate criminal activities that transcended jurisdictional boundaries; (3) to provide law enforcement in rural and other areas that did not have local or county police agencies; and (4) to break strikes and labor movements.

The first statewide police organization was the Texas Rangers, which was established in 1835. Initially, the Texas Rangers was created to patrol the border with Mexico and, therefore, was not a general-service state police agency. The Texas Rangers were first used to augment the American military. This group of men was often willing to engage in illegal activities and atrocities that the regular military would not, in order to advance the war. The Rangers later evolved into more of a general-purpose police agency. Massachusetts created the second state police organization in an attempt to control vice crime. Similarly, the Arizona Rangers police organization was created in 1901, and the New Mexico Mounted Police was established in 1905 (Smith, 1960). Perhaps the first general-purpose state police organization to be created in the United States was the Pennsylvania State Police (PSP) in 1905. The PSP was created in response to the Great Anthracite Coal Strike of 1902.

There are 26 highway patrols and 23 state police agencies in the United States, in addition to 35 state investigative agencies or segments of agencies that are not part of a state police or highway patrol agency. State police agencies in Kentucky, Michigan, Texas, New Mexico, Louisiana, Virginia, Pennsylvania, Rhode Island, Oregon, and New York are full-service police departments with statewide jurisdiction. That is, they are legally authorized to provide the same types and level of services that city or county police departments provide, only on a statewide basis. Highway patrols, on the other hand, have limited authority. They are limited either by their jurisdiction or by the types of specific offenses or duties that they have authority to control. Highway patrols are usually found in the south, but they can also be found in other parts of the country. Highway patrols are found in such states as Florida, Georgia, North Carolina, Ohio, and Nevada. Most of the highway patrols concentrate on traffic activities, such as the enforcement of traffic laws and the investigation of traffic accidents, and leave criminal investigation responsibilities to sheriff's departments or other statewide investigative agencies. They frequently limit their patrolling activities to state and federal highways. An agency title does not always properly describe the agency's activities; for example, the Washington State Highway Patrol actually has state police powers. As shown in Table 1.1, about 89,000 employees work for the 48 state police agencies.

Table 1.1 Full-Primary State Law Enforcement Agency Employees by State

Agency	Total	Percent Change from 2004	Per 100,000 Residents	Percent Change from 2004
US. Total	60,772	3.4	20	−0.5
Alabama Department of Public Safety	763	9.2	16	5.3
Alaska State Troopers	274	−5.2	40	−8.8
Arizona Department of Public Safety	1244	10.6	19	−2.0
Arkansas State Police	525	3.3	18	−1.0
California Highway Patrol	7202	1.7	20	−1.2
Colorado State Police	742	9.0	15	1.5
Connecticut State Police	1227	6.5	35	5.6
Delaware State Police	658	2.5	75	−3.3
Florida Highway Patrol	1606	−2.9	9	−8.4
Georgia Department of Public Safety	1048	−5.6	11	−13.2
Hawaii Department of Public Safety[1]	290	18.9	23	15.6
Idaho State Police	264	−8.3	17	−16.5
Illinois State Police	2105	4.8	16	3.2
Indiana State Police	1.315	13.6	21	10.5
Iowa Department of Public Safety	669	19.7	22	17.6
Kansas Highway Patrol	525	−3.0	19	−5.3
Kentucky State Police	882	−5.8	21	−8.8
Louisiana State Police	1215	14.3	27	15.3
Maine State Police	334	−1.2	25	−2.0
Maryland State Police	1440	−9.8	25	−11.6
Massachusetts State Police	2310	5.0	35	3.5
Michigan State police	1732	−7.0	17	−6.2
Minnesota State Patrol	530	−2.6	10	−5.4
Mississippi Highway Safety Patrol	594	11.0	20	9.0
Missouri State Highway Patrol	1028	−6.3	17	−9.4
Montana Highway Patrol	218	5.8	23	1.2
Nebraska State Patrol	491	−2.4	28	−4.6
Nevada Highway Patrol	417	−1.0	16	−11.8
New Hampshire State Police	350	21.1	26	18.4
New Jersey State Police	3053	10.3	35	9.6
New Mexico State Police	528	−6.7	27	−11.2
New York State Police	4847	3.9	25	3.0
North Carolina State Highway Patrol	1827	20.4	20	11.1
North Dakota Highway Patrol	139	3.0	22	2.1
Oho State Highway Patrol	1560	3.9	14	3.3

Continued...

Table 1.1   Full-Primary State Law Enforcement Agency Employees by State *Continued*

Agency	Total	Percent Change from 2004	Per 100,000 Residents	Percent Change from 2004
Oklahoma Department of Public Safety	825	2.1	23	−1.5
Oregon State Police	596	−4.0	16	−9.3
Pennsylvania State Police	4458	6.1	35	4.6
Rhode Island State Police	201	5.8	19	7.6
South Carolina Highway Patrol	967	23.2	21	14.9
South Dakota Highway Patrol	152	−1.3	19	−5.0
Tennessee Department of Safety	942	−3.1	15	−8.1
Texas Department of Public Safety	3529	2.7	15	−5.3
Utah Department of Public Safety	475	−11.7	17	−21.0
Vermont State Police	307	−5.5	49	−6.0
Virginia State Police	1873	0.2	24	−4.0
Washington State Police	1132	6.9	17	0.7
West Virginia State Police	667	4.1	37	3.4
Wisconsin State Patrol	492	−3.5	9	−5.5
Wyoming Highway Patrol	204	8.5	38	2.4

[1]*The Hawaii Department of Pubic Safety was previously classified in the CSLLEA as a special jurisdiction agency.*
Source: FBI (2010).

Investigative agencies that are independent of the state police or highway patrol can be found in 35 states. These agencies are commonly part of a Department of Public Safety or a Justice Department within state government. Such agencies are commonly found in states that have highway patrols and serve to investigate criminal activities; for example, Oklahoma has two state investigative agencies in addition to its highway patrol: (1) a State Bureau of Investigation, and (2) a State Bureau of Narcotics and Dangerous Drugs Control. Numerous configurations and arrangements exist for state police and the various investigative agencies.

Limited-Purpose State Law Enforcement Agencies

The states have developed specialized police or law enforcement agencies to meet particular law enforcement needs. To this end, there is a wide variety of these agencies within the 50 states. For example, most state attorneys general have investigative units whose responsibility includes the investigation of various forms of white-collar crime. The Office of the Attorney General commonly investigates food stamp and Medicare fraud, and it works closely with the state's human resources department to ensure that nursing homes are in compliance with state standards. Their investigators review unusually high Medicaid provider costs to make sure that charges are within government guidelines.

States generally have Alcoholic Beverage Control (ABC) commissions or similarly named organizations that are responsible for investigating the distribution and sale of alcoholic beverages. ABC commissions monitor alcohol distributors to be sure that they account for all alcoholic beverages that pass through their control so proper taxes are paid. These agencies, in addition to other state and local police officers, monitor bars and liquor stores to ensure that all relevant laws are followed. For example, they frequently analyze samples of liquor from bars to verify that lower-quality, inexpensive alcoholic beverages have not been placed in bottles and sold as more expensive alcoholic beverages. The ABC commissions in many states determine the number of licenses that are allotted to a particular jurisdiction and are responsible for revoking or suspending liquor licenses.

Another limited-purpose police organization is the Fish and Game Warden. Individuals in this group have law enforcement powers and are responsible for enforcing all laws relating to hunting and fishing. They patrol rural areas to make sure that individuals have hunting and fishing licenses, that they are hunting or catching the proper species, and that the species being hunted or fished are in season. In addition, they make certain that quotas are not exceeded.

Several states have motor vehicle compliance officers. These law enforcement officers work to ensure that interstate carriers or trucks are in compliance with state and federal laws. They verify that each vehicle has the proper permits, that it has special permits if oversized, and that each vehicle travels on designated or approved highways. These officers also operate the weigh stations that are commonly found on interstate highways (Table 1.2).

LOCAL LAW ENFORCEMENT AGENCIES

There are more local police agencies than any other type of law enforcement agency, and these local agencies employ the largest number of law enforcement officers. The most common local police agencies are city or municipal police agencies. There are 12,501 municipal agencies. The United States has approximately 3100 elected sheriffs. The largest sheriff's department, Los Angeles County, California, is a full-service police department with more than 9461 officers (Reaves, 2011). Sheriffs commonly have other duties in addition to law enforcement responsibilities; for example, they may be responsible for managing the jail or collecting certain types of taxes, and they typically are responsible for serving warrants, subpoenas, and civil papers. Different states have legislated different duties for sheriff's departments.

Table 1.2 Special Jurisdiction Law Enforcement Agencies and Full-Time Sworn Personnel, by Type of Jurisdiction, 2008		
Type of Special Jurisdiction	**Agencies**	**Full-Time Sworn Personnel**
Total	1,733	56,968
Public buildings/facilities	1,126	21,418
4-year university/college	508	10,916
Public school district	250	4764
2-year college	253	2648
State government buildings	29	1138
Medical school/campus	18	747
Public hospital/health facility	48	715
Public housing	13	250
Other state-owned facilities	7	240
Natural resources	246	14,571
Fish and wildlife conservation laws	56	5515
Parks and recreational areas	124	4989
Multifunction natural resources	16	2926
Boating laws	10	461
Environmental laws	7	368
Water resources	18	185
Forest resources	9	65
Levee district	6	62
Transportation systems/facilities	167	11,508
Airports	103	3555
Mass transit system/railroad	18	3214
Transportation—multiple types	5	2000
Commercial vehicles	12	1320
Harbor/port facilities	25	876
Bridges/tunnels	4	543
Criminal investigations	140	7310
State Bureau of Investigation	22	3527
County/city investigations	66	2006
Fraud investigations	13	636
Fire marshal/arson investigations	21	478
Tax/revenue enforcement	6	177
Other/multiple types	12	486
Special enforcement	54	2161
Alcohol/tobacco laws	22	1280
Agricultural laws	12	387
Narcotics laws	5	233
Gaming laws	10	231
Racing laws	5	30

Note: Excludes agencies employing less than one full-time or the equivalent in part-time officers.
Source: Reaves (2011).

County police departments are police organizations that report to a county commission or other form of county government and are generally independent of the sheriff. The largest county police department is located in Nassau County, New York. Many counties have both sheriff's departments and county police departments. Counties typically create county police departments when the population and workload in the county become too large for the sheriff to handle adequately or when county officials want to exercise more control over law enforcement operations. Because sheriffs are elected officials, they frequently have substantial independence from county governments in terms of priorities and policy formulation. Sheriffs have total control over their agencies' administration and operations, while county governments frequently have nothing more than budgetary control. County police departments generally are managed by a chief of police and operate similarly to municipal police departments (Figure 1.6).

The largest municipal police department in the United States is the New York City Police Department (NYPD). The NYPD has 36,023 police officers (Reaves, 2011). There are several fairly large police departments in the United States as shown in Table 1.3. The Chicago Police Department, the nation's second largest municipal department, has 13,129 sworn officers. In 2010, its officers made 181,669 arrests and answered 3,711,913 calls for service. This was accomplished on a budget of $1.23 billion (Chicago Police Department, 2011). Large police departments are quite active in terms of responding to community needs.

Tables 1.3 and 1.4 provide selected characteristics of the nation's largest municipal police and sheriff's departments, respectively. The number of

FIGURE 1.6
NYPD recruits listen during the swearing-in ceremony, Thursday, January 10, 2013 in New York. The 830 probationary police officers graduated in the summer after completion of their police academy training. *Courtesy of AP Photo/Mary Altaffer.*

Table 1.3 Fifty Largest Local Police Departments, by Number of Full-Time Sworn Personnel, September 2008

City/County	Full-Time Sworn Personnel, 2008			
	Total	Percent Change Since 2004	Per 100,000 Residents	Percent Change Since 2004
New York (NY)	36,023	−0.3%	432	−2.4
Chicago (IL)	13,354	1.7	472	2.4
Los Angeles (CA)	9727	6.9	256	6.7
Philadelphia (PA)	6624	−3.0	430	−4.7
Houston (TX)	5053	−0.8	226	−8.7
Washington (DC)	3742	−1.5	634	−3.2
Dallas (TX)	3389	15.5	265	11.4
Phoenix (AZ)	3388	18.5	216	7.5
Miami-Dade Co. (FL)	3093	−¹	268	12.0
Baltimore (MD)	2990	−5.4	469	−4.9
Las Vegas–Clark Co. (NV)	2942	10.0	216	0.5
Nassau Co. (NY)	2732	6.1	256	5.5
Suffolk Co. (NY)	2622	−2.6	194	−3.8
Detroit (MI)	2250	−35.9	247	−35.1
Boston (MA)	2181	11.2	343	6.1
San Antonio (TX)	2020	−1.7	150	−9.7
Milwaukee (WI)	1987	2.1	329	1.6
San Diego (CA)	1951	−7.2	149	−9.4
San Francisco (CA)	1940	−10.5	240	−14.3
Honolulu Co. (HI)	1934	7.7	214	6.7
Baltimore Co. (MD)	1910	6.2	242	5.0
Columbus (OH)	1886	6.1	248	2.9
Atlanta (GA)	1719	4.6	320	−8.7
Charlotte–Mecklenburg Co. (NC)	1672	12.7	220	1.9
Jacksonville-Duval Co. (FL)	1662	2.8	205	−1.5
Cleveland (OH)	1616	3.6	372	8.8
Indianapolis–Marion Co. (IN)	1582	−3.4	195	−5.1
Prince George's Co. (MD)	1578	17.4	248	31.1
Memphis (TN)	1549	−23.2	229	−22.6
Denver (CO)	1525	8.5	257	2.2
Austin (TX)	1515	11.2	197	1.0
Fort Worth (TX)	1489	14.0	211	−2.5
New Orleans (LA)	1425	−13.4	423	18.8
Kansas City (MO)	1421	9.5	296	4.6
Fairfax Co. (VA)	1419	4.5	144	2.2

Table 1.3 Fifty Largest Local Police Departments, by Number of Full-Time Sworn Personnel, September 2008 *Continued*				
	Full-Time Sworn Personnel, 2008			
City/County	**Total**	**Percent Change Since 2004**	**Per 100,000 Residents**	**Percent Change Since 2004**
San Jose (CA)	1382	3.0	146	−2.2
St. Louis (MO)	1351	−3.5	379	−5.1
Nashville–Davidson Co. (TN)	1315	8.5	216	2.4
Newark (NJ)	1310	0.8	472	0.5
Seattle (WA)	1283	2.8	213	−2.6
Montgomery Co. (MD)	1206	15.2	129	11.5
Louisville–Jefferson Co. (KY)	1197	1.6	188	−0.6
El Paso (TX)	1132	1.7	186	−2.7
Miami (FL)	1104	4.4	256	−8.2
Cincinnati (OH)	1082	3.2	325	2.8
DeKalb Co. (GA)	1074	13.1	168	10.0
Oklahoma City (OK)	1046	1.7	190	−2.9
Tucson (AZ)	1032	7.4	191	2.7
Albuquerque (NM)	1020	7.3	195	−0.3
Tampa (FL)	980	2.0	288	−3.8

[1]*Change was −0.03%.*
Source: Reaves (2011).

sworn officers ranges from a high of 36,023 in New York City to a low of 980 in Tampa, Florida. In terms of sheriff's departments, the largest is Los Angeles County with 9461 deputies. The fiftieth largest sheriff's department has only 454 deputies.

Discussions about municipal policing generally center on the nation's larger police departments; however, most of the police departments in the United States are small, as approximately 8800 departments have 10 or fewer officers; about 49% of all departments and about 2100 departments (12%) have only one officer (Reaves, 2011). Small police departments frequently have many of the same responsibilities and problems as the larger departments but on a smaller scale. All jurisdictions, regardless of their size, experience problems with drugs, serious crime, traffic congestion and accidents, demands by citizens for services, and the need for order maintenance. Large police agencies usually have specialized units to handle many of these activities, while patrol officers handle all police activities in most small departments.

Table 1.4 Fifty Largest Sheriffs' Offices, by Number of Full-Time Sworn Personnel, 2008

| Agency | Full-Time Sworn Personnel, 2008 | | Primary Duty Areas of by Sworn Personnel | | | |
	Total	Percent Assigned to Respond to Calls for Service	Law Enforcement	Jail Operations	Court Operations	Other
Los Angeles County (CA) Sheriff	9461	31	X	X	X	
Cook County (IL) Sheriff	5655	4	X	X	X	X
Harris County (TX) Sheriff	2558	25	X	X	X	X
Riverside County (CA) Sheriff	2147	72	X	X	X	X
San Bernardino County (CA) Sheriff	1797	56	X	X	X	
Orange County (CA) Sheriff—Coroner	1794	22	X	X	X	
Broward County (FL) Sheriff	1624	97	X		X	
Palm Beach County (FL) Sheriff	1447	38	X		X	
Sacramento County (CA) Sheriff	1409	23	X	X	X	X
Orange County (FL) Sheriff	1398	45	X		X	X
San Diego County (CA) Sheriff	1322	43	X	X	X	
Hillsborough County (FL) Sherif	1223	63	X			
Wayne County (Ml) Sheriff[1]	1062	23	X	X	X	
Alameda County (CA) Sheriff	928	19	X	X	X	X
Pinellas County (FL) Sheriff	863	42	X		X	
San Francisco (CA) Sheriff	838	0		X	X	X
Jefferson Parish (LA) Sheriff	825	68	X	X	X	X
Oakland County (Ml) Sheriff	796	37	X	X	X	X
Maricopa County (AZ) Sheriff[1]	766	84	X	X	X	
Ventura County (CA) Sheriff	755	55	X	X	X	X

Table 1.4 Fifty Largest Sheriffs' Offices, by Number of Full-Time Sworn Personnel, 2008 *Continued*

| Agency | Full-Time Sworn Personnel, 2008 | | Primary Duty Areas of by Sworn Personnel | | | |
	Total	Percent Assigned to Respond to Calls for Service	Law Enforcement	Jail Operations	Court Operations	Other
Marion County (IN) Sheriff	740	0	X	X	X	X
King County (WA) Sheriff[1]	721	66	X		X	X
Contra Costa County (CA) Sheriff	679	31	X	X	X	
Collier County (FL) Sheriff	628	39	X		X	
Lee County (FL) Sheriff	621	54	X		X	
Polk County (FL) Sheriff	600	71	X			
Calcasieu Parish (LA) Sheriff	592	31	X	X	X	X
Jefferson County (AL) Sheriff	556	81	X	X	X	X
Pima County (AZ) Sheriff	554	67	X		X	
Jefferson County (CO) Sheriff	537	30	X	X	X	X
Passaic County (NJ) Sheriff	530	21	X	X	X	
Bexar County (TX) Sheriff	526	38	X		X	
Milwaukee County (WI) Sheriff	524	19	X	X	X	
Fulton County (GA) Sheriff	516	0	X	X	X	X
Shelby County (TN) Sheriff	516	30	X		X	X
Tulare County (CA) Sheriff	513	25	X	X	X	
Kern County (CA) Sheriff	512	50	X	X	X	X
Richland County (SC) Sheriff	512	41	X	X	X	X
Orleans Parish (CA) Sheriff (Criminal)	505	9	X	X	X	X
Fairfax County (VA) Sheriff	499	0	X	X	X	X
Brevard County (FL) Sheriff	497	70	X		X	X
Johnson County (KS) Sheriff	496	16	X	X	X	X
Monmouth County (NJ) Sheriff	494	0	X	X	X	

Continued...

Table 1.4 Fifty Largest Sheriffs' Offices, by Number of Full-Time Sworn Personnel, 2008 *Continued*						
	Full-Time Sworn Personnel, 2008		Primary Duty Areas of by Sworn Personnel			
Agency	Total	Percent Assigned to Respond to Calls for Service	Law Enforcement	Jail Operations	Court Operations	Other
Pasco County (FL) Sheriff	485	46	X		X	
Manatee county (FL) Sheriff	476	62	X			
Fresno County (CA) Sheriff	461	43	X		X	X
Knox County (TN) Sheriff[1]	456	58	X	X	X	X
Franklin County (OH) Sheriff	455	23	X	X	X	
El Paso County (CO) Sheriff	454	26	X	X	X	
Dane County (WI) Sheriff	454	22	X	X	X	X

[1]*Percent responding to calls is based on the 2004 Census of State and Local Law Enforcement Agencies. Source: Reaves (2011).*

SUMMARY

One method by which society attempts to control and structure the interactions of its members is the creation of government. Government exists to serve the needs of its citizens and to create formal mechanisms for dispute resolution. Law is the most formal system of social control, and many of its provisions are enforced by police agencies. In democratic societies, law is enforced under the provisions of a constitution. In American society, the police institution closely resembles the structure of government. The principle of federalism results in three levels of policing in the United States: (1) federal, (2) state, and (3) local. A variety of agencies at each of these levels serve distinctive purposes. The police can be viewed as a unique component of the criminal justice system, as police agencies have their own distinct goals and objectives and develop specific programs to accomplish these goals.

The police are an important part of our government and are expected to provide a variety of services to the community. It is expected that the police will provide these services and engage in a variety of activities all within the bounds of law. In this respect, the police should be accountable to the community and the governments they serve and should attempt to provide services that are both required and expected. To this end, various types of police organizations have developed. The fact that there are different types of police departments reflects political and social circumstances as well as the desire that police be responsive to the attitudes and needs of communities.

REVIEW QUESTIONS

- Who are the primary shapers of the American police institution, and how is each entity distinctive?
- The U.S. Constitution places restrictions on what police officers can do when enforcing the law or investigating crime. What rights and protections are afforded to American citizens in the *Bill of Rights*?
- What is meant by the term *Law*, and what functions does the law serve in society? Essentially, what four types of laws affect the police and why?
- What primary components make up the criminal justice system?
- The police are expected to carry out various social roles and engage in a variety of social functions. What are the four primary roles over which the police have responsibility? Give an example of an activity for each role.

REFERENCES

Alpert, G. P., & Dunham, R. G. (1997). *Policing urban America* (3rd ed.). Prospect Heights, IL: Waveland Press.

Bailey, W. G. (1995). Drug enforcement administration. In W. G. Bailey (Ed.), *The encyclopedia of police science* (2nd ed.) (pp. 241–244). New York: Garland Press.

Baillargeon, D., & Smith, D. (1980). In pursuit of safety: alternative patterns of police production in three metropolitan areas. *Journal of Social Issues, 36*(4), 35–58.

Bayley, D. H. (2002). Law enforcement and the rule of law: is there a tradeoff? *Criminology & Public Policy, 2*(1), 133–154.

Bercal, T. (1970). Calls for police assistance. *American Behavioral Scientist, 13,* 681–691.

Bittner, E. (1974). Florence Nightingale in search of Willie Sutton: a theory of police. In H. Jacob (Ed.), *The potential for reform of criminal justice* (pp. 17–44). Beverly Hills, CA: Sage Publications.

Bowman, A., & Kearney, R. (2009). *State and local government.* Boston: Houghton Mifflin Harcourt.

Broderick, J. (1987). *Police in time of change.* Prospect Heights, IL: Waveland Press.

Bureau of Justice Statistics. (2011). *Sourcebook of criminal justice statistics.* Washington, D.C.: U.S. Department of Justice, Bureau of Justice Statistics. www.albany.edu/sourcebook/.

CBP. (2010). *Snapshot: A summary of CBP facts and figures.* Washington, D.C.: U.S. Customs and Border Protection.

CBP (n. d.). *Secure borders, safe travel, legal trade: U.S. customs and border protection fiscal year 2009–2014 strategic plan.* Washington, D.C.: (Author).

Chevigny, P. G. (2002). Conflict or rights and keeping order. *Criminology and Public Policy, 2*(1), 155–160.

Chicago Police Department. (2011). *Annual report 2010: A year in review.* Chicago: Author.

Coates, R. (1972). *The dimensions of police–citizen interaction: a social psychological analysis.* (Ph.D. dissertation). College Park: University of Maryland.

Cole, G. (1995). *The American system of criminal justice* (7th ed.). New York: Wadsworth Publishing.

Cumming, E., Cumming, I., & Edell, L. (1965). Police as philosopher, friend and guide. *Social Problems, 12,* 276–286.

Department of the Treasury. (1993). *Report of the Department of the Treasury on the Bureau of Alcohol, Tobacco, and Firearms investigation of Vernon Wayne Howell, also known as David Koresh.* Washington, D.C.: U.S. Government Printing Office.

DHS. (2010). *Quadrennial Homeland Security review report: A strategic framework for a secure homeland.* Washington, D.C.: Department of Homeland Security.

DHS. (2014). *FY 2013 budget in brief.* Washington, D.C.: Author.

Dowler, K. (2004). Media influence on citizen attitudes toward police effectiveness. *Policing and Society, 12*(3), 227–238.

Famega, C. (2005). Variation in officer downtime: a review of the research. *Policing: An International Journal of Police Strategies & Management, 28*(3), 388–414.

FBI. (2010). *Crime in the United States: Full-time state law enforcement employees.* Washington, D.C.: Federal Bureau of Investigation. www2.fbi.gov/ucr/cius2009/data/table_76.html.

FBI. (2013). *Quick facts.* Washington, D.C.: Federal Bureau of Investigation. www.fbi.gov/

Federal Bureau of Investigation (FBI), (2014). http://www.fbi.gov/

Frank, J., Brandl, S., & Watkins, C. (1997). The content of community policing: a comparison of the daily activities of community and "Beat" officers. *Policing, 20*(4), 716–728.

Goldstein, H. (1977). *Policing a free society.* Cambridge, MA: Ballinger Press.

Graham v. Connor. (1989). 490 U.S. 386.

Greene, J., & Klockars, C. (1991). What police do. In C. Klockars, & S. Mastrofski (Eds.), *Thinking about police: Contemporary readings* (pp. 273–284). New York: McGraw-Hill.

ICE. (2011). *ICE overview.* Washington, D.C.: U.S. Immigration and Customs Enforcement. www.ice.gov/about/index.htm.

ICE, (2014). http://www.ice.gov/

Kappeler, V., & Gaines, L. (2011). *Community policing: A contemporary perspective* (5th ed.). Newark, NJ: LexisNexis Matthew Bender.

Kappeler, V. E., & Potter, G. W. (2005). *The mythology of crime and criminal justice* (4th ed.). Prospect Heights, IL: Waveland Press.

Kappeler, V. E., Sluder, R., & Alpert, G. (1998). *Forces of deviance: Understanding the dark side of policing* (2nd ed.). Prospect Heights, IL: Waveland Press.

Klockars, C. (2006). The "Dirty Harry" problem. In V. Kappeler (Ed.), *Police and society: Touchstone readings* (3rd ed.) (pp. 413–423). Prospect Heights, IL: Waveland Press.

Kyckelhahn, T. (2010). *Justice expenditure and employment extracts, 2007.* Washington, D.C.: U.S. Department of Justice, Bureau of Justice Statistics.

Lyman, M. D. (2010). *Drugs in society: Causes, concepts and control* (6th ed.). Newark, NJ: LexisNexis Matthew Bender.

Manning, P. (2006). The police: mandate, strategies, and appearances. In V. Kappeler (Ed.), *Police and society: Touchstone readings* (3rd ed.) (pp. 94–122). Prospect Heights, IL: Waveland Press.

Mapp v. Ohio. (1961). 367 U.S. 643.

Mazerolle, L., Antrobus, E., Bennett, S., & Tyler, T. R. (2013). Shaping citizen perceptions of police legitimacy: a randomized field trial of procedural justice. *Criminology, 51*(4), 33–64.

McArdle, A., & Erzen, T. (2001). *Zero tolerance: Quality of life and the new police brutality in New York city.* New York: New York University Press.

Meyer, J., & Taylor, W. (1975). Analyzing the nature of police involvements: a research note concerning the effects of forms of police mobilizations. *Journal of Criminal Justice, 3,* 141–146.

Miranda v. Arizona, (1966). 384 U.S. 436.

Morris, S. E. (1995). United States marshals. In W. G. Bailey (Ed.), *The encyclopedia of police science* (2nd ed.) (pp. 796–798). New York: Garland Press.

Muir, W. (1977). *Police: Streetcorner politicians.* Chicago, IL: University of Chicago Press.

Parks, R. B., Mastrofski, S. D., & DeJong, C. (1999). How officers spend their time with the community. *Justice Quarterly, 16*(3), 483–518.

Reaves, B. A. (2006). *Federal law enforcement officers, 2004.* Washington, D.C.: U.S. Department of Justice, Bureau of Justice Statistics.

Reaves, B. A. (2011). *Census of state and local law enforcement agencies, 2008.* Washington, D.C.: U.S. Department of Justice, Bureau of Justice Statistics.

Reaves, B. (2012). *Federal law enforcement officers (2008).* U.S. Department of Justice, Office of Justice Programs, Bureau of Justice Statistics.

Secret Service. (2011). *Homepage U.S.* Washington, D.C.: Secret Service. www.secretservice.gov/.

Skolnick, J. (1994). *Justice without trial: Law enforcement in a democratic society* (3rd ed.). New York: John Wiley & Sons.

Smith, B. (1960). *Police systems in the United States.* New York: Harper & Row.

Stone, A. A. (1993) *Report and recommendations concerning the handling of incidents such as the branch Davidian standoff in Waco Texas.* Cambridge, MA: Harvard University, unpublished manuscript.

Tennessee v. Garner, (1985). 471 U.S. 1.

TSA. (2010). *Welcome to what we do.* Washington, D.C.: U.S. Department of Homeland Security, Transportation Security Administration. www.tsa.gov/what_we_do/index.shtm.

Unger, S. (1976). *FBI.* Boston, MA: Little, Brown & Co.

U.S. Marshals Service. (2008). *Historical perspective.* Washington, D.C.: U.S. Department of Justice.

U.S. Marshals Service, (2014). www.justice.gov/agencies/index-list.html#USMarshal.

Webster, J. (1970). Police task and time study. *Journal of Criminal Law, Criminology, and Police Science, 61,* 94–100.

White, S. (1972). A perspective on police professionalization. *Law and Society Review, 7*(1), 61–85.

Wilson, J. Q. (1968). *Varieties of police behavior: The management of law and order in eight communities.* Cambridge, MA: Harvard University Press.

Wilson, J. Q., & Kelling, G. (2006). "Broken Windows" and fractured history. In V. Kappeler (Ed.), *The police and society: Touchstone readings* (3rd ed.) (pp. 51–65). Prospect Heights, IL: Waveland Press.

Zhao, S., & Hassel, lK. (2005). Policing styles and organizational priorities: retesting Wilson's theory of local political culture. *Police Quarterly, 8,* 411–430.

CHAPTER 2

Historical Perspectives

Let us resolve to be masters, not the victims, of our history, controlling our own destiny without giving way to blind suspicions and emotions.
—John Fitzgerald Kennedy

LEARNING OBJECTIVES

After reading the chapter, you should be able to:

- Explain policing in ancient times and how it related to the development of policing in America
- Trace the development of police in England and explain how it relates to American policing
- Develop and understand American policing in retrospect
- Outline the modern era of American policing
- Describe and explain the social factors that gave rise to the policing institution
- Trace and describe some of the social turning points in the development of policing

KEY TERMS

- Bow Street Runners
- Community-oriented policing
- Community policing
- Community relations
- Constables
- County Police Act of 1839
- Day watches
- Draconian
- Frankpledge system
- Greek city-states
- Hammurabi
- Highwaymen Act
- Investigative commissions
- Kinship-based community

INTRODUCTION

Sometimes a history is nothing more than a story of places, people, and events. Ideally, however, history provides a background and understanding of the present; it should provide a backdrop or a context by which to better understand current affairs. As Victor G. Strecher (2006:66) noted, "…our understanding of the present … is little more than an elusive knife-edge between the past and future, or in a practical sense, a thin, recent slice of the past." By trying to understand the past, it is possible to better comprehend present, and possibly future, events. To some extent, the present and future are direct results of the past; hence, it is important for the student of policing to study and understand

- Labor riots
- Leges Henrici
- Legions
- Lipit-Ishtar Code
- London Metropolitan Police
- Magna Carta
- Metropolitan Police Act
- Mesopotamia
- Municipal Corporations Act
- Night watches
- Peelian reform
- Pendleton Act
- Police state
- *Polis*
- Political entrenchment
- Praetorian Guard
- Problem-oriented policing
- Professionalism
- Reform efforts
- Riots and strikes
- Roman Empire
- Science and technology
- Shire reeve
- Slave patrols
- Social differentiation
- Specialized police forces
- State as political organization

major events in the history of law enforcement and the social context in which they occurred.

In studying history, it is also important to examine the underlying culture and values that helped to shape the places, people, and events. It is inadequate to be satisfied by knowing only *what* happened; to maximize the significance of history, it is also important to attempt to understand *why* events happened. In so doing, it is more likely that learning from past mistakes can prevent certain undesirable events.

This chapter provides a chronological account of law enforcement. It attempts to explain why certain decisions were made and how historical events and decisions shaped law enforcement today. Insofar as it is impossible to examine the complete history of law enforcement in one chapter, a few incidents are presented that typify American policing, and a discussion of these events is provided to offer understanding about the historical evolution of American policing.

AN OVERVIEW OF POLICING IN ANCIENT TIMES

The police function has been a central part of government since people started creating governments. For the most part, however, the police function was vested with the military during earlier times. The army was responsible for protecting rulers from external threats, and in numerous instances select units or guards within the army were used to protect these same rulers from internal threats. Some of these threats included threats from the military leaders themselves. Thus, the actions of the protectors were guided not by law but by those who controlled them. Historically, policing has been linked to the development of civilizations, political organizations, and the control of people and economic resources. The origins of modern policing can be traced to the rise of the state and the movement away from kinship-based communities: "Specialized police agencies are generally characteristic only of societies politically organized as states" (Robinson, Scaglion, & Olivero, 1994:6).

Our information about ancient police is restricted to major events, and we have little detailed information about their operation. Although it is tempting to assume that police forces always existed, there is little evidence that any organized form of policing developed before civilization was well under way. We do know, however, that there are several prerequisites to the development of civilizations and the emergence of formal policing. Formal policing seems to require that societies develop to a point where they are distinguished by four interrelated and well-established themes:

1. The development of a formal legal system
2. The emergence of social differentiation

3. The production of a surplus of material resources
4. The emergence of the state as a form of political organization

These themes in the development of civilizations have been influential throughout ancient history and appear to be related to the emergence of the police institution. Generally, the level of complexity and the extent to which each of these themes is formalized within a given society also explain the complexity and formality of a civilization's policing function. Although these themes explain the development of the police institution in historical terms, they also influence the development, reform, and focus of modern police forces. Changes in any of these themes have resulted in modifications of the contemporary police institution.

- Taxation
- Texas Rangers
- Vigils
- Violent Crime and Law Enforcement Act of 1994
- Vizier
- Volstead Act
- Weed and seed

The Birth of Civilization in Mesopotamia

The first civilization is thought to have begun about 3500 BCE. in Mesopotamia, the land between the Tigris and Euphrates rivers. The first known city in this area was Uruk. Between about 3500 and 3000 BCE, the population of Uruk quadrupled from about 10,000 to 40,000 inhabitants. Before the rise of this city, nomadic peoples inhabited the steppes of Mesopotamia, and scattered villages were peppered throughout the region. Although nomadic peoples may have posed a threat to the villagers, it is more likely that villagers often raided other villages to secure resources and exploit other village dwellers. Eventually, after a succession of raids that included the capture of slaves from surrounding villages, and following the development of trading relations, villages became large enough to be somewhat self-sufficient. As villages such as Uruk grew in population and resources, social differentiation occurred, usually beginning with slavery, and a surplus of material resources developed owing to trade, production, warfare, and the exploitation of slave labor. The rise of other cities (e.g. Umma, Eridu, Lagash, Ur) followed a similar pattern of development and growth.

Between about 3000 and 2300 BCE, these cities were engaged in almost constant warfare for control of the southern region of Mesopotamia known as Sumer. Between 2334 and 2279 BCE, the reign of Sargon, King of Akkad, witnessed consolidation and expansion of the city into a state. A series of conflicts and military campaigns eventually led to the dominance of Sargon in the region between the rivers (Kishlansky, Geary, & O'Brien, 1991). A series of internal and external conflicts led to the downfall of Sargon's empire (Oliphant, 1992), which was later consolidated into a nation-state, and a system of coded laws was developed by Hammurabi, who was then King of Babylon around 1750 BCE.

To review a translation of the Hammurabi code, visit the Website **http://eawc.ev-ansville.edu/anthology/hammurabi.htm**

The laws of Hammurabi were carved in black stone basalt and uncovered by French archaeologists in the early 1900s. The code contains nearly 300 clauses of laws that address 13 areas of concern ranging from the administration of justice to the rights of free men, as well as penalties for criminal offenses differentiated by social position. One of the shortest sections of the code reads: "If a man has kidnapped the son of a free man, he shall be put to death." This section illustrates both the social differentiation of the time and concern with creating penalties for crimes based on social position. Although Hammurabi's Code is generally referred to as the oldest known code of law, it is actually predated by the *Code of Lipit-Ishtar*. Excavations in the 1940s unearthed this code of law, which predates Hammurabi's Code by at least 300 years. One striking difference between the two codes is that the Lipit-Ishtar Code does not contain the harsh sanctions associated with Hammurabi's Code, and it stresses compensation over corporal punishment (Saggs, 1989). However, the code exhibits social differentiation in the form of slavery and assesses penalties by social position (Figure 2.1).

FIGURE 2.1

Law Code of Hammurabi Stele inscribed on a basalt stele (c. 1790 BC) in the Akkadian language in the cuneiform script. These laws stand as one of the first written codes of law in recorded history. *Courtesy of Shutterstock.*

Civilization in Ancient Egypt

The earliest Egyptian people were nomadic hunter-gatherers who established their first villages in the oases surrounding the Nile in Northern Africa between 5500 and 4500 BCE. (Grimal, 1994). By 4000 BCE., villages such as Merimda in Northern Egypt had populations of more than 10,000, and people lived in fixed dwellings (Kishlansky et al., 1991). As villages developed and cities grew, Egypt formed two kingdoms—the Upper and Lower Kingdoms. The capitals of these two kingdoms were Memphis and Thebes. By 3200 BCE., the two kingdoms were united, with Memphis becoming the capital. During this time, Egypt began to have contact with the inhabitants of Mesopotamia, as evidenced by the presence of their culture and art.

Some classical authors, such as Cicero and Herodotus, indicated that Egypt had a complex system of written laws, but to date, no written legal codes have been discovered. However, archaeologists have uncovered an abundance of judicial records that indicate a well-developed judicial system and the practice of initiating and resolving lawsuits. Early Egyptian rulers established courts, which were administered by government officials, and set up marine patrols and customs houses to protect commerce. The extent to which these official functions were specialized, however, is not yet known. The chief official of Egyptian government was the *vizier*, who had responsibility over agriculture, labor, and the treasury, as well as justice.

The successful Egyptian dynasties established some form of police force to protect domestic tranquility (Reith, 1952/1975), but it seems that their primary functions were to regulate trade, ensure production of agriculture, and collect taxes. Like Mesopotamia, Egypt seemed to develop specialized police forces only when it became politically organized and once a clear social stratification and an economic surplus developed that required control and redistribution. Egypt must have had an extremely effective system of social control to compel its subjects and slaves to construct some of history's greatest monuments, including the Great Pyramid of Giza. Some scholars believe that after the decline of the "Old Kingdom" and the end of the first intermediate period Egypt became a police state, with the very nature of its social order being considered by its inhabitants to be divine (Stadelmann, cited in Roberts, 1995).

H.W.F. Saggs (1989:126) described the social organization of ancient Eastern cities in terms of the relationship between local and centralized authority and the problems that arose in Mesopotamia and Egypt:

> ...social organization of this kind would give rise to problems that could only be dealt with at the local level. Some form of policing was also essential, and necessarily locally based and administered, although at some points this could impinge upon the central government. The security of goods and of strangers was a case in point: everywhere

the responsibility for apprehending robbers or murderers of strangers, or, failing that, paying compensation, lay in the first instance with city authorities, but if the city authorities failed in these responsibilities the royal power could and would intervene. Other matters that were usually dealt with locally included family disputes or matters of inheritance or disputes between citizens.

The Rise of Greek City-States

Studying the ancient Greeks provides another means of understanding early policing and civilization. Unlike the rich river valley civilizations of Mesopotamia and Egypt, Greece was located on rugged and mountainous terrain surrounded by the Aegean and Ionian seas. Because of the volatile climate and isolating nature of the many islands that make up the area, Greece developed as groups of self-contained agricultural and artisan societies. The isolated nature of Greece seems to have insulated the area from the warring tendencies of other civilizations and allowed the Greeks to concentrate on intellectual and artistic endeavors. Before 2500 BCE, most Greeks lived in small villages until the development of the centralized Minoan civilization. Like other ancient societies, the Minoan civilization had an elaborate social stratification. This civilization, however, distinguished between a paid peasantry, artisans, and elites. Although there was exploitation in the early Greek civilizations, they did not construct the massive monuments that other civilizations built to honor their rulers. Around 1600 BCE, evidence suggests that a powerful warrior elite emerged at Mycenae. Shortly after the rise of the elites, fortified centers began to develop; however, by 1200 BCE, many of the fortified centers had been raided or destroyed and civilization disappeared, ushering in the Dark Age.

After the Dark Age, the Greek world reemerged between about 800 and 500 BCE, and Greece experienced a major population growth in its centers. During this time, the Greeks developed a well-defined division of labor and a clearly delineated political structure. Eventually, Greece had more than 150 *city-states*—each of which had its own laws and judicial system. The growing exploitation of farmers and artists at the hands of wealthy merchants and the elite created conflict; however, the city-states had no police forces to enforce the order, and they depended on *kin-police*, which functioned according to tribal custom and tradition. A person who was wronged served as the police and brought the transgressor before a magistrate. Ultimately, this system failed in many of the city-states. In response, in 621 BCE, the people of Athens granted Draco the power to revise the legal system, and he did so with a vengeance, giving rise to the term *draconian*.

Peisistratus, a soldier and politician, saw the need for police. After two failed attempts to seize control of Athens, he became the ruler in 545 BCE. by establishing a large contingent of bodyguards that served as his police force. Throughout Greek history, rulers used bodyguards to maintain their rule, and their opponents used opposing mobs of bodyguards to attack and sometimes defeat them. To a great extent, the absence of a formal, well-structured police force led to the downfall of the city-states because they had no competent forces to protect the rulers and their governments (Figure 2.2).

The Greeks contributed significantly to the development of laws. Plato, the Greek philosopher, contemplated the nature of people, the state, and law. He argued that laws were necessary to structuring the *polis*, or state. He postulated that laws and political order were the means by which to achieve virtue—laws were the rules that governed a state's rulers. Plato's concepts of law and government laid the foundation for most of our governmental structure today.

The Roman Empire's Contribution to Policing

The rise and fall of the *Roman Empire* is similar to the path taken by the Greek city-states. Rome essentially derived its power from its mighty army, or legions. The *legions* consisted of professional soldiers who were masterful in the field of battle. As new lands were conquered, the legions established order and were used to install Rome's appointed rulers. These rulers were obligated to maintain order and to collect a tribute, which was paid to Rome. Once the rulers were installed, the legions were recalled to Rome or sent to some other distant

FIGURE 2.2
Philosopher Plato (nineteenth-century neoclassical statue) outside Academy of Arts of Athens in Greece.
Copyright Shutterstock/Brigida Soriano.

land to do battle, and the newly appointed rulers were left to care for their territories. This meant that the new rulers had virtually no force with which to impose their will. Reith (1952/1975:212) commented on how ineffective the Romans were in maintaining order under this system:

> On the first appearance of friendly acquiescence and compliance, the legions are withdrawn from the area, revealing or suggesting Rome's manpower or other weakness. In the absence of means of enforcing Roman laws, there is temptation to refuse tribute and rebel. The legions suddenly return, crushing, slaughtering, enslaving, and are withdrawn again. Their fear-inspiring effect may be lasting, but they cannot be everywhere, and there is no other force that can be used, in their absence. A consistent feature of the story is the folly of Rome's sustained belief in the endurance of fear when troops were absent, in spite of repeated experience of its being short-lived.

Civil life in Rome paralleled its interventions and activities in its conquered lands. Again, there were no forces other than the military that could be used to maintain order. The Senate contained numerous individuals who constantly and fiercely competed for power and wealth. Rome was ruled by the wealthy, which created an inordinately large underclass that was prone to riot, rebellion, and crime. Senators, wealthy citizens, and soldiers were constantly securing small armies of bodyguards and mobs to forcibly seize power and control. The legions frequently had to be recalled from conquered lands to restore order. As disorder became a reality at home, Rome's ability to control its many conquered lands diminished, which created even more disharmony and pressure on the Empire.

In 44 BCE Julius Caesar, who was the dictator over Rome, was murdered. Caesar had been able to exert a reasonable amount of control over Rome by defeating his enemies. His death led to a renewed continuation of fighting and war among those who vied for power. In the end, Gaius Octavius, Caesar's grandnephew, fought Marcus Antonius, a distinguished general, for political control of the Empire. Octavius ultimately was able to defeat Antonius and consolidate his power. As the new ruler, he took the name Augustus Caesar and set about to reform the Empire and eliminate the problems that contributed to the constant disorder.

To this end, Augustus Caesar was the first Roman ruler to implement a police force. First, he created the *Praetorian Guard*, whose primary mission was to protect him from assassination. The Praetorian Guard consisted of nine cohorts, each with 1000 men. Three Praetorian cohorts were assigned to Rome and were housed in private lodging. They did not wear uniforms; instead, their swords were concealed under their togas. This low-profile lifestyle led to a higher acceptance of this military presence in Rome, which afforded Augustus Caesar greater control over the city and its citizens (Davies, 1977; Kelly, 1973).

Later, *vigils* were formed by Augustus Caesar to guard and fight fires. Before the vigils, firefighting (which proved to be inadequate) was performed by small groups of slaves. Reith (1952/1975:226) described how the vigils evolved into Rome's police force.

> Augustus [Caesar] created a city fire brigade of six hundred slaves, which functioned in fourteen separate regions, but it was a failure. He then formed the corps of vigils, and is believed to have been made of it a copy of a similar body in Alexandria. He had the wisdom to make it entirely non-military, and to ensure and to emphasize its civilian status by recruiting freedmen only. They wore the usual short sword, but their hand weapon was a baton or club. Their police duties were soon increased. The prefect of vigils was, at first, an obscure and almost powerless individual, but he was soon given summary powers including that of inflicting corporal punishment on thieves and robbers, and on individuals who neglected fire regulations. He was not allowed to judge serious cases; he was obligated to pass all these to the prefect of the urban cohorts. The vigils are believed to have taken on most of the night duties of the policing of Rome, and to have shared day duties with the urban cohorts.

This police system served Rome for a number of years. The jealousy arising from the special treatment enjoyed by members of the Praetorian Guard, as well as their participation in attempts to assassinate leaders, made them a constant target. Finally, the Praetorian Guard was incorporated into Rome's legions, where it became nothing more than another military unit. The removal of one of Rome's primary police forces significantly contributed to renewed violence and disorder and Rome's ability to control its subjects. This, along with many other factors, contributed to the final downfall of the Empire.

POLICE DEVELOPMENT IN ENGLAND

Most scholars recognize that the first modern police department was created in London in 1829. The creation of the London Metropolitan Police Force was the result of efforts extending over a period of several years. The English, like other people, were extremely resistant to police forces because they were used to suppress or take rights away from the citizenry. The *London Metropolitan Police Force* essentially came into existence as the result of an evolutionary process consisting of efforts by a number of leaders and government officials.

Because the origin of English policing is well documented and because it provides a rich history of the evolution of police, a brief history of the English experience is in order.

Medieval England

Until the beginning of the Industrial Revolution, law enforcement in Anglo-Saxon England was a local responsibility, with people having a collective social obligation for maintaining order. England was primarily a rural and agrarian society; however, systems were established and officials were appointed to maintain order and to deal with criminals. Policing was provided through a *frankpledge system*. Under the frankpledge system, each male above the age of 12 was required to form a group with nine neighbors known as a "tithing." 10 tithings were grouped into a "100." Hundreds were supervised by a hundredman. The frankpledge system handled all criminal and civil matters for the tithing and 100. The Anglo-Saxons also created geographical divisions known as *shires*, which were similar to counties, to assist in governing the country. An Ealdorman (a title later shortened to Earl) was appointed to govern each shire. Their duties largely included the collection of taxes. *Shire reeves* (sheriffs) were also appointed to reside over the King's courts (Roberts, Roberts, & Bisson, 2002).

In 1066, William, the Duke of Normandy, invaded and conquered England. Before the invasion, England consisted of numerous towns and villages with limited centralized government. The Normans brought with them a sense of collective security, as opposed to individual rights, and commenced to centralize governmental activities and operations establishing a feudal system of government. William established a system of castles that allowed dispatch of mounted horsemen into the countryside to squash political dissent, and he introduced curfews as a means of control. The intent behind the centralized government was to facilitate the collection of taxes and ensure control over the population and aristocracy. William believed a strong treasury would assist him in defeating any enemies who might attempt to wrestle the crown from him. In 1116, Henry I, son of King William, issued the *Leges Henrici* (Latin for "Laws of Henry"), which served as the foundation for our legal system today. The document established offenses against the crown; for example, crimes such as robbery, arson, murder, and false coinage became crimes against the crown and were punishable by the crown. Before the decree, criminal acts were considered acts against individuals, not the state, and individuals generally had the responsibility of bringing lawbreakers to justice. The *Leges Henrici* also established judicial districts and separated crimes into felonies and misdemeanors. Sheriffs were required to enforce prohibitions on entertaining strangers and harboring vagabonds (Robinson et al., 1994). The theme of controlling vagabonds, vagrants, and rogues, as well as compelling people to labor, was repeated in statutes well into the 1500s. Various law enforcement officials, sheriffs, constables, and town bailiffs were charged with enforcing labor laws (Figure 2.3).

Henry II formed juries consisting of 12 men to hear cases, a departure from trial by ordeal. This development allowed witnesses to be heard in court cases. English Common Law developed during this period, as well as the practice of keeping court records. Henry II also required every freeman to arm himself to protect the crown and keep the peace.

In the mid-1100s, the office of High Constable was created; the position was a high-level functionary in the king's government. The constables' duties

KING JOHN SIGNING THE GREAT CHARTER. (See p. 282.)

FIGURE 2.3
King John signed the Magna Carta in 1215, laying the foundation upon which the subsequent rights of the people would be established. *Illustration from Cassell's History of England (1902).*

included command of the army. Constables were also appointed at the local level, and their duties included keeping order. They also were responsible for finding and recording facts for the courts. The position of constable has remained a part of the English justice system.

In 1199, King John took the throne after the death of his brother, King Richard. John was a particularly brutal leader who quickly made enemies of both the common people and noblemen. John's repressive ways ultimately led to his being forced to sign the Magna Carta in 1215, a document that guaranteed basic civil and political rights. Initially these rights were only applied to nobility, but they were later extended to common people. Many of the liberties enjoyed by Americans because of the United States (U.S.) Constitution's Bill of Rights can be traced to the Magna Carta.

For more information on the *Magna Carta*, visit the Website **http://www.history.com/topics/magna-carta**.

In 1285, Edward I issued the Statute of Winchester, which required landowners to maintain a horse and armor for a knight. By forcing the landowners to maintain knights, it reduced the amount of money the king needed to maintain an army (Roberts et al., 2002). This decentralization allowed the king to maintain an army, which was crucial to maintaining control over the nobility and foreign monarchs. Moreover, the statute created the first remnants of the watch system discussed below.

Early English Law Enforcement

Around 1500, England was steadily becoming more involved in world trade. America had been discovered, and England had developed a great wool industry. At the time, wool was in short supply, and an increasing amount of farmland was converted into pastures for sheep; consequently, a large number of England's poor were forced to move to the cities. The poverty, joblessness, and overcrowding in the cities resulted in a tremendous increase in crime and disorder. Although numerous new laws were passed and an escalating number of people were punished, imprisoned, and executed, these factors had little effect on the rising crime and disorder. Historians note that by the 1500s, England was characterized by lawlessness and the proliferation of criminals (Pringle, 1955; Samaha, 1974). A visitor to the country in the sixteenth century remarked, for instance, "There is no country in the world where there are more robbers and thieves than in England" (as cited in Samaha, 1974:11). At the same time, however, Britain also had one of the harshest criminal codes in the world. Children as young as 7 years old could be sentenced to death for the theft of something as minor as a pocket handkerchief (Pringle, 1955). Between the years of 1509 and 1547, some 72,000 people were hanged for crimes (Clear & Cole, 2005:30).

Merchants began hiring their own private police, which led to the merchant police of England. Cities were divided into parishes. In some cases, parishioners alternated patrol, whereas in others they paid watchmen to patrol their parishes. In 1663, Charles II instituted a night watch for London, consisting of 1000 watchmen who patrolled from sunset to sunrise, but crime continued to rise. In 1692, passage of the *Highwaymen Act* provided rewards to citizens who were willing to offer assistance in apprehending criminals, which led to numerous cases of blackmail and false accusations. In 1737, George II allowed the city council to levy taxes for the purpose of a paid watchman system. This was the first instance of formal taxation for the purpose of providing law enforcement.

For the most part, crime control efforts were ineffective, and poverty and crime continued to plague England's cities. The corruption and ineffectiveness of justice officials became painfully apparent. Johnson (1981:12) summarized the situation:

> …whole districts had developed into criminal haunts where no law penetrated and no honest citizen ventured. Thieves became extremely bold, even knocking down their victims on the streets in broad daylight. In the early 1700s, under the direction of Jonathan Wild, London's most famous fence, many criminals joined an organization that systematically plundered the city's homes. The victims of these crimes arranged the return of their property by paying Wild to negotiate for them with the thieves. Although Wild was eventually hanged, his blatant behavior and tremendous success demonstrated how corrupt and unreliable law enforcement had become in London.

When England experienced a problem with gin houses and public drunkenness in the 1700s, laws were passed requiring gin sellers and makers to purchase prohibitively expensive licenses. In response to these toughened laws, constables were bribed not to enforce the law so the gin shops could remain open (Rubinstein, 1973). Developing economic relationships forged early links between the merchant class and corrupt constables. Magistrates accepted bribes, forced innocent persons to pay for release from custody, and provided protection for illegal businesses. Watchmen participated in burglary rings and would overlook offenses for a fee. Given the structure of the "justice system" and its corrupt nature, "One of…[its]…most striking features…was that no one concerned in the enforcement of the law had any incentive to prevent crime. On the contrary, the police force—if one could call it that—had a direct incentive to encourage it" (Pringle, 1955:48).

You can watch a video on the development of early English policing at: **http://www.youtube.com/watch?v=9P48YT-61zII**

In eighteenth-century England, not only was the law enforcement system corrupt, the political system and government were also rife with corruption. In the House of Commons, for example, it was common for votes to be sold and for members to buy their seats. Positions in the civil service system, the Army, the Navy, and the church were also commonly sold (Kappeler, Sluder, & Alpert, 1998). Thus, the corruption of the early law enforcement system was in many ways simply a reflection of the corruption occurring in many segments of British government.

The English Reformers

The English people and parliament were adamantly opposed to a powerful centralized government that could be used as a police force to deprive citizens of their rights. They were more tolerant of disorder and crime than they were of a powerful centralized government that had a tendency toward abuse of citizens. A second obstacle to a police force was England's repressive laws—by the early nineteenth century, a person could be hanged for any of 223 crimes. Reformers believed that more humane laws would be self-enforcing and would reduce crime and that reform efforts should focus on less strict laws (Johnson, 1981). Other reformers concentrated their efforts on the establishment of a police force, and five individuals can be identified who directly contributed to the creation of the first modern police department in London: Henry Fielding, Patrick Colquhoun, Robert Peel, Charles Rowan, and Richard Mayne (Reith, 1952/1975). Box 2.1 lists some of the major historical developments in early English policing.

Henry Fielding

Henry Fielding was a playwright and a novelist. In 1748, Fielding was experiencing financial problems and was unable to work in the theater as the result of problems with a competitor. One of Fielding's friends, George Lyttelton, was able to secure the appointed post of magistrate for Fielding. The position of magistrate is akin to our modern-day constable. At the time, magistrates were unpaid and generally derived their income from bribes and fees. They were held in low esteem, and in many cases were only marginally above the criminals they processed through their courts. Fielding's friends thought the job would provide Fielding with an income and a degree of security (Figure 2.4).

Fielding made two contributions to policing. First, as a consequence of his writing skills, he was able to advocate change and spread awareness about social and criminal problems facing London. He published a volume detailing the crime, poverty, and social condition of London at the time. *Enquiry into the Causes of the Late Increase of Robbers* was one of the first publications to examine crime and its related social problems. In Fielding's position as magistrate, he also condemned the senseless slaughter of dozens of citizens who were being executed at Tyburn prison for crimes such as theft.

For more information on early English policing, visit the Website http://www.met.police.uk/history/

Box 2.1 Historic Events in English Policing

1663	London begins to employ paid watchmen to guard the streets at night; however, the job attracts only old or infirm men, who are nicknamed "Charlies" after the king.
1753	Based on the recommendation of the magistrate and novelist Henry Fielding, more forces are created in London along the lines of the Bow Street Runners.
1796	At least 3000 old iron and rag shops in London are said to be receiving stolen property, and more than 5000 public houses and beer shops are reputed to be harboring highwaymen.
1800	The Bow Street Runners are about 70 officers strong, and London has approximately 120 full-time police officers.
1805	The Bow Street Runners are augmented by the Bow Street Horse Patrol, a group of 44 former cavalry troopers. They clear the roads of highwaymen and are the first English law officers to wear a uniform.
1829	The Metropolitan Police Act establishes the principles that will shape modern English policing. The Act defines the original Metropolitan Police district as an area about 7 miles in radius from Charing Cross.
1830	London has one police officer for every 450 to 500 citizens.
1831	The Special Constables Act is passed, empowering two or more county or borough justices to appoint constables where any tumult or riots have occurred.
1835	The Municipal Corporations Act assists boroughs to sort out their administrative structure and allows new towns to incorporate. Incorporated towns are obligated to set up police forces.
1836	The Bow Street Horse Patrol is incorporated into the force and operated in the outlying Metropolitan divisions.
1837	Of 171 boroughs, 93 have developed an organized police force.
1838	The Railway Act establishes a police force specifically for the railways, providing for the appointment of special constables, but only for brief, temporary periods of time. The force will grow to become the third largest force in the country.
1839	Royal Commission states that "criminals migrate from town to town, and from the towns where they harbor, and where there are distinct houses maintained for their accommodation, they issue forth and commit depredations upon the surrounding rural districts; the metropolis being the chief center from which they migrate."
1839	The Rural Constabulary Act causes some boroughs to reorganize their police forces to avoid the high-expense involvement with county forces. The Act falls short of creating a national police force under the authority of the Metropolitan police. The Act permits the hiring of one police officer for every 1000 citizens. The second Metropolitan Police Act converts the River Thames force into the Thames division, absorbs the Bow Street Foot Patrol, and extends the Metropolitan police district to a 15-mile radius. Rowan and Mayne became known as "commissioners of police of the Metropolis."
1840	Of 171 boroughs, only 108 have organized a police force.
1841	London has one police officer for every 900 citizens.
1842	A small group of men, two inspectors and six sergeants, is formed into a detective department within the Metropolitan police.
1844	The criminal investigation department is established in the Metropolitan police by Sir James Graham, Sir Robert Peel's successor. He allows 12 police sergeants to work in plainclothes. The innovation causes public resentment.
1848	Of 171 boroughs, 22 still have no police force.
1853	Of 52 counties, only 22 counties have police forces.
1855	There are only about 12,000 policemen in England and Wales.
1878	A director of criminal investigations is appointed to head the reorganized detective department, which would become known as the Criminal Investigation Department.

FIGURE 2.4

A stamp printed in USSR shows Henry Fielding (1707–1754), c. 1957. *Copyright Shutterstock/Olga Popova*

Second, Fielding organized a group of six householders who agreed to serve as paid, regular constables. This small plainclothed force, first known as "Mr Fielding's people" or the "thief takers," was successful in breaking up a number of criminal gangs. Later, in 1750, they were called the *Bow Street Runners*, and they were responsible for patrolling the streets to investigate and, when necessary, arrest criminals. Many criminals fled, but many were apprehended. Fielding's Bow Street Runners were the first group to emphasize crime prevention as opposed to depending on reactive responses to crime. At the turn of the century, the Bow Street Runners were about 70 officers strong, and London had about 120 full-time police officers. In 1805, the Bow Street Horse Patrol, a group of 44 former cavalry troopers, augmented the Bow Street Runners. The Bow Street Horse Patrol was known as the "Redbreasts" because they wore bright red waistcoats. They helped clear the roads into London of highwaymen and were the first English law officers to wear a distinctive uniform. The Bow Street police made a notable impact on crime in London as the forerunners of London's modern police department.

You can watch a short video on the bow street runners at: **http://www.youtube.com/watch?v=2rZfckouVKc**

FIGURE 2.5
Bow street Magistrate's court, London. *Courtesy of Wikipedia.*

The Bow Street police, however, were not without criticism, because "complaints of the rowdy goings-on of prostitutes and their customers became increasingly directed at the inefficiency or venality of the police, rather than the actual culprits. The Bow Street Police Office, in the heart of Covent Garden (the most vice-ridden area of town), came in for a good deal of abuse. Sir John Fielding's efforts at vice control were widely scorned, and his proposals for retraining prostitutes in more conventional trades were ridiculed. Beneath this ridicule, one usually finds oblique suggestions that he and his Runners had a financial interest in maintaining things as they were" (Simpson, 1996:51) (Figure 2.5).

Before 1750, London had no formal law enforcement system. When riots or disorder occurred, the government called upon the military to restore order. Once this was accomplished, the military forces retreated and criminals were essentially left unattended to possibly commit additional crimes. Wealthy people were able to afford armed servants and bodyguards for their protection, but those who could not afford such protection were left to defend themselves.

Patrick Colquhoun
While Henry Fielding, and later his brother John, were having some success on Bow Street, unfortunately nothing else was being done to combat crime in London. Some years later, Patrick Colquhoun, a successful businessman, was

appointed magistrate. He worked diligently to alleviate social problems and deal with crime. He worked toward relieving unemployment, establishing school districts, and providing food to the poor. Colquhoun understood Fielding's methods and began to apply them. In 1796, he wrote *A Treatise on the Police of the Metropolis*, which reviewed the various crime problems facing the city.

Particularly noteworthy was Colquhoun's description of prostitution, which seemed to be growing with little control. Although estimates varied, Colquhoun reported that London had 50,000 prostitutes in the 1790s (Colquhoun, 1806:340). The Bow Street Police did not escape the corruption of their forerunners. Citing *The Times* dated June 13, 1828, Simpson (1996:59) wrote that:

> Extortion of prostitutes was a time-honored practice within law enforcement agencies, and even the police of the pristine City of London did not have the heart to break with this tradition. The practice was well-known and the culprits rarely punished. A rare instance of a policeman being brought to book for attempting to exact more than financial tribute from streetwalkers occurred in 1828. Samuel Hall was charged at Bow Street with the indecent assault and it was claimed "that the watchmen, as a body, were a worthless and depraved set of fellows. Not only did they levy contributions on the pockets of the unfortunate women who walked the streets at night, but also it was a fact they reduced them to such a state of terror, that they durst not refuse them any favour they might demand."

Colquhoun also advocated a formal, structured police force, a suggestion that sustained substantial criticism. As a result of his book, Colquhoun was approached by the West India planters and merchants for suggestions to curb crime in the dock areas. He developed a plan that was financed by the merchants and approved by the government. The plan called for a new river police force consisting of 80 permanent and 1120 part-time officers who would watch the docks while the West India ships were unloaded. As a result of the new police force, crime and property losses at the docks were drastically reduced. It was so successful that the government assumed its operation in 1800, and it remained a distinct police force until 1829, when it was absorbed by the new police force (Reith, 1952/1975).

Sir Robert Peel

Sir Robert Peel assumed the office of Home Secretary in 1822. He took office amid widespread scandal and disorder. At the time, the country was experiencing one riot after another, and the government had been unable to effectively deal with them. In one case, 60,000 citizens had gathered at Manchester to listen to the famous orator William Hunt. The magistrates decided that the best course of action was to arrest Hunt to eliminate any problems before they could occur. As a result of the attempts to arrest Hunt and the subsequent attempts to rescue those who attempted to arrest him, 11 citizens were killed and 500 to 600 were injured. For the first time, there was a general call from all levels of society for the government to take action (Reith, 1952/1975).

Before 1829, the state of law and order in England was characterized by the following (Bloy, 1998:1):

1. Authorities had few resources to cope with riot, crime, and disorder.
2. Country parishes and smaller market towns had constables and the local watch and ward.
3. Troops were used to keep order.
4. Local militias were used for local problems.
5. Spies were used to track down those who were suspected of disaffection.

In 1829, Peel introduced a bill in Parliament, *An Act for Improving the Police in and Near the Metropolis*, known as the *Metropolitan Police Act*. The Act provided for a single authority that would be responsible for an area that covered approximately a 7-mile radius from the heart of the city (Walker & Richards, 1995). Peel deliberately made the bill vague in terms of the operation of the new police, which facilitated its passage. The Metropolitan Police Act was passed as a political compromise, and the Act applied only to London. The jurisdiction of the legislation was limited to the Metropolitan London area and excluded the City of London and provinces. The police force began operation on September 29, 1829, with 1000 officers in six divisions. The new police headquarters was located at four Whitehall Place, which opened onto a courtyard that had been the site of the residence used by the kings of Scotland. Subsequently, the police headquarters was named Scotland Yard. Following are the principles of the *Peelian reform* (Germann, Day, & Gallati, 1973):

1. The police must be stable, efficient, and organized along military lines.
2. The police must be under government control.
3. The absence of crime will best prove the efficiency of police.
4. The distribution of crime news is essential.
5. The deployment of police strength by both time and area is essential.
6. No quality is more indispensable to a policeman than a perfect command of temper; a quiet, determined manner has more effect than violent action.
7. Good appearance commands respect.
8. The securing and training of proper persons are at the root of efficiency.
9. Public security demands that every police officer be given a number.
10. Police headquarters should be centrally located and easily accessible to the people.

11. Policemen should be hired on a probationary basis.
12. Police records are necessary to the best distribution of police strength.

Many of these principles serve to guide modern police operations. Peel was able to build on the work of numerous other reformers in developing and implementing the Metropolitan Police Act.

The establishment of British police forces spread at a rapid rate. In 1835, the *Municipal Corporations Act* mandated that 178 English towns and boroughs establish police forces, and the *County Police Act of 1839* spread policing to the more rural areas of England and Wales. In less than 20 years, more than 180 police agencies had been established in Great Britain.

Charles Rowan and Richard Mayne

Peel selected Charles Rowan and Richard Mayne to be the police force's first commissioners. Mayne was a young lawyer, and Rowan was an older man with a military background. Rowan worked out most of the organizational matters, while Mayne developed the police force's legal mandate. In 1829, Mayne wrote:

> The primary object of an efficient police is the prevention of crime; the next that of detection and punishment of offenders if crime is committed. To these ends all the efforts of police must be directed. The protection of life and property, the preservation of public tranquility, and the absence of crime, will alone prove whether those efforts have been successful and whether the objects for which the police were appointed have been attained.

Peel successfully selected two men whose talents complemented each other. The force quickly developed high standards. Because of these high standards, during the first 3 years of operation there were 5000 dismissals and 6000 resignations. Officers were strictly supervised to ensure that Peel's principles were followed. Rowan and Mayne meticulously followed the professional dictates prescribed by Peel.

In an effort to avoid criticism, the newly appointed police force was not armed. The only weapon provided to each officer was a bludgeon, or nightstick. This police force provided additional services not normally thought of as law enforcement, including lighting lamplights, calling out the time, and watching for fires. "'Bobbies' or 'Peelers' were not immediately popular. Most citizens viewed constables as an infringement on English social and political life, and people often jeered the police. The preventive tactics of the early Metropolitan police were successful, and crime and disorder declined" (Bloy, 1998:1). The key to this success was that professional principles of policing were enumerated and followed. "Their pitched battles with (and ultimate street victory over) the Chartists in Birmingham and London proved the ability of the police to deal with major disorders and street riots. Despite the early successes of the Metropolitan police, the expansion of police forces to rural areas was gradual. The Municipal Corporations Act of 1835 ordered all incorporated boroughs to set up police forces under the control of a watch committee, but it was not until 1856 that Parliament mandated that provinces establish police forces" (Bloy, 1998:1).

AMERICAN POLICING IN RETROSPECT

The development of law enforcement in the U.S. closely paralleled the development of policing in England. English settlers coming to this country tended to bring English ideas about justice with them. Even though settlers from other countries came to America, the English dominated. Many of today's criminal justice offices and terms are rooted in the English tradition: circuit courts, sheriffs, bailiffs, and constables (which exist in several states). The American experience, however, was truly unique, and many of the circumstances in which early settlers found themselves forced changes in the English tradition.

Early American Policing

The history of American policing can be traced to its English origins (see Box 2.2), but the American system of policing evolved from an amalgamation of systems from England, France, and Spain. "Many policing problems plagued the new cities of America. They included controlling certain classes, including slaves and Indians; maintaining order; regulating specialized functions such as selling in the market, delivering goods, making bread, packing goods for export; maintaining health and sanitation; ensuring the orderly use of the streets by vehicles; controlling liquor; controlling gambling and vice; controlling weapons; managing pests and other animals" (Nalla & Newman, 1994:304). These early police services had little to do with crime control and were performed by volunteer citizens who served on slave patrols or night watches.

> To learn more about slavery and the American colonies, watch the video at: **http://www.history.com/topics/slavery/videos#origins-of-slavery**

Night watches, which later became police departments, had different primary objectives, depending on the part of the country in which they were located. For example, New England settlers appointed Indian Constables to police Native Americans (National Constable Association, 1995), and many southern police departments began as slave patrols. In 1704, the colony of Carolina developed the nation's first slave patrol. *Slave patrols* helped to maintain the economic order and assisted the wealthy landowners in recovering and punishing their slaves, who essentially were considered their property.

Box 2.2 The Justice System in Colonial Virginia

By the middle of the eighteenth century, colonial Virginians had developed a legal system that reflected both the authority of the British Crown and the development of local self-government. The courts enforced English common law, statutory law, and the criminal code, with modifications for local conditions. Punishments for crimes were swift and often physical. Although all Virginians accused of a crime had the opportunity to speak in court, only a small number of colonists ruled on their neighbors' innocence or guilt. Perhaps most foreign to Americans living in the late twentieth century, in the eighteenth century the courts were associated with more than justice. As central public meeting places for the exchange of information and goods, courthouses played had an essential social, economic, and political role in local communities...

Colonial Virginians were more likely to interact with their local courts than with the high courts at the Capitol. Two local courts met monthly at the Courthouse in Williamsburg, the Hustings Court (municipal court) for the city and the James City County Court for the county. The city's mayor, recorder, and six aldermen (members of the municipal council) formed the Hustings Court. The James City County Court consisted of 12 justices of the peace. Virginians used these courts to settle boundary disputes with their neighbors, obtain licenses to establish taverns or water mills, and to petition for the investigation of suspected wrongdoings, such as nonattendance at church, the use of profanity, and the mistreatment of orphans by their guardians or apprentices by their masters.

By the time of the American Revolution, 60 county courts, like the one for James City County, were in operation across Virginia. Within these courts, the justices of the peace held key positions. To serve as a justice, a Virginian had to be a white male who had reached age 21, practiced the Protestant faith, and owned property. Appointed by the governor with the advice of the Council, the justices of a county soon became a self-perpetuating body of elite residents. If one died, the other 11 recommended his replacement, and the governor rarely refused their selection. The office often passed from father to son in prominent families.

When a county court was in session, a chief justice, usually the most prominent or the most senior justice, presided. Another justice, the sheriff, enforced the laws and carried out the physical punishments handed out by the court. Because few defendants requested jury trials, the justices determined the outcome of most cases. In addition, the justices wielded significant power in their communities by levying taxes for local services, appointing road surveyors, nominating tobacco inspectors, and advising the legislature on where to locate new churches, warehouses, ferries—and courthouses...

White women did not participate in the colonial justice system as officeholders or as jurors. In the eighteenth century, voting and office holding were defined as privileges rather than rights. Although unmarried adult women (referred to as "femes soles" in legal terms) had the right to own property and enter into contracts independently, they did not have the privileges of full citizenship. Married women (referred to as "femes coverts" in legal terms) participated even less directly in the courts than unmarried women. A married woman could not give property away, make contracts, or sue others without her husband's consent. Most women who set foot in the courthouse came not as plaintiffs but as defendants, witnesses, or bystanders.

Slaves and free blacks of both sexes also had limited access to the courts. They could not hold office or serve on juries. As defendants in felony cases, slaves were tried by the county courts, rather than the General Court like whites. Slaves accused of crimes did not have the right to a jury trial. As witnesses, slaves, mulattos, and Native Americans could testify against each other, but not against whites. As onlookers when court was in session, slaves and free blacks stood outside the courthouse, listening through the windows. For African-Americans in some counties, courthouses also held the sorrowful distinction of being sites for slave sales.

Source: PBS. (1998). The Justice System in Colonial Virginia. Arlington, VA: Public Broadcasting Service, Teacher Resource Service.

In the American colonies, *constables* were among the first law enforcement officers. Their numbers varied depending on the size of the city they policed. Constables were charged with surveying land, checking weights and measures, serving warrants, and meting out punishment. The first constable on record in the colonies was Joshua Pratt. Pratt served as Constable for the Plymouth Colony in 1634 (National Constable Association, 1995). Constables were often assigned to oversee night watches, many of which later developed into police departments.

Many of the first police departments in the United States were in the Northeast. Boston created a night watch in 1636, and a rattle watch (a form of night watch that involved alerting people of problems) was created in New York in 1658. In 1700, Philadelphia formed a night watch, and St. Louis established a Constabulary in 1808 (Kappeler, 1995). Germann et al. (1973:66) described the effectiveness of these watches:

> These early watchmen, like their counterparts in England at the time, were very lazy and inept. Minor offenders were sometimes sentenced to serve the watch as punishment. Often called leather heads, these guards were so dull that the towns sometimes had to formalize even the [simplest] duties. New Haven, in 1722, had a regulation that "no watchman will have the liberty to sleep," and a 1750 Boston rule stipulated that "watchmen will walk their rounds slowly and now and then stand and listen."

The watchmen frequently slept and drank while on duty, and most cared little about the job or the people they were supposed to protect. Citizens often volunteered for service on the watches to avoid service in the military, or they were assigned the duty as punishment or conscripted by the town.

The first day watch was created in Philadelphia in 1833. In 1839, St. Louis, Missouri, augmented its constabulary, which served as a night watch, by creating a city guard composed of 16 men and a chief (Kappeler, 1995). In 1844, New York started a day police force composed of 16 officers; the night watch consisted of 12 captains, 24 assistant captains, and 1096 watchmen (Fosdick, 1915/1969). During this period, most American cities created day watches to supplement the activities of the night watches; however, the day watch generally was separate from the night watch, both in terms of activities and management.

Around 1835, a series of *riots* swept through the country. About 15,000 Irish citizens and firemen clashed in Boston in 1837. Riots in Philadelphia left scores of people dead, and, in 1844, Native American riots lasted for 3 months, leaving many persons dead or wounded and causing extensive property damage (Fosdick, 1915/1969). The riots and their devastating effects demonstrated the ineffectiveness of the day and night watch systems in cities. Subsequently, watch systems began to evolve into police organizations. For example, in 1844, the New York State legislature passed a law creating a day and night police with a strength of 800 under the direction of a chief of police appointed by the mayor with the consent of the council. In 1854, Boston followed New York's example and abolished a watch system that had been in existence for more than 200 years. Box 2.3 presents some of the major historical events that occurred in the early years of American policing.

Other law enforcement agencies developed for different reasons. The Pennsylvania State Police force was originally created to assist mine owners in breaking coal *strikes*. Labor unions had been formed in an effort to counter the dangerous working conditions in the mines and the extremely low salaries. The objectives of the police force were to protect the strike-breaking "scabs," to protect coal company property, and generally to assist in breaking the strikes through arrests and physical violence. The Massachusetts State Police was created in 1865, making it one of the oldest statewide law enforcement agencies in the nation. The initial force consisted of a constable and 33 men. The early agency was obscure until 1921, when the uniformed branch was organized with a group of 50 men whose duties were to police the rural communities. The creation of the Massachusetts State Police evolved out of the desire to control vice-related crime in rural Massachusetts.

The *Texas Rangers* are said to be the very first state police organization. Although the history of the Texas Rangers can be traced to 1823, the name did not appear in legislation until 1874. In 1823, Stephen F. Austin, often called the "Father of Texas," wrote about the need for a small group of men to protect his fledgling colony. In August of that same year, Austin sent a proclamation to Land Commissioner Baron de Bastrop, and on the back of that document he wrote that he would "employ 10 men…to act as rangers for the common defense…the wages I will give said 10 men is 15 dollars a month payable in property." These initial Rangers convened only when needed and worked on a voluntary basis. By 1835, a local council created a "Corps of Rangers" to provide frontier settlements protect from Native Americans (Figure 2.6).

However, the Texas Rangers became the stuff of legend in 1841 with the slaughter of the Comanche people under the direction of Captain Jack Hayes. The movement of the capital of Texas from Houston to Austin began a cycle of conflict between the Rangers and the Comanches when Rangers began surveying the Comanches' holy mountains. The Rangers became even more infamous when the war with Mexico was declared in 1846 and Zachary Taylor commissioned Texas Ranger Samuel Walker in the U.S. military. Samuel Walker and his Texas Rangers developed a reputation for engaging in activities that even the military could not condone. Among the Mexican people, the Texas Rangers became known as *Los Diablos Tejanos* ("the Texas Devils"). As one Texas

Box 2.3 Historic Events in American Policing

Year	Event
1634	Constable position established in Plymouth Colony
1636	Boston rattle watch established
1644	Some 10,000 slaves imported into the Americas
1649	Black slaves number about 300 in the Virginia Colony
1658	New York City rattle watch established
1700	Philadelphia night watch established
1704	South Carolina Slave Patrol Act
1734	Charleston slave patrol established
1738	Virginia Slave Patrol Act
1757	Georgia Slave Patrol Act
1794	North Carolina Slave Patrol Act
1803	Cincinnati night watch established
1804	New Orleans city patrol established
1806	Tennessee Slave Patrol Act
1807	Louisiana Slave Patrol Act
1808	St. Louis constabulary established
	St. Louis night watch established
	New Orleans day watch established
1825	Arkansas Slave Patrol Act
	Missouri Slave Patrol Act
1831	Mississippi Slave Patrol Act
1832	St. Louis slave ordinances
1833	Philadelphia day watch established
1834	New York race riots begin
	Boston riots begin
1835	Boston riots
1836	Boston riots
1837	Boston riots
1838	Philadelphia riots
	Boston day force established
	Native American riots
	Philadelphia race riots begin
1839	St. Louis city guard established
1842	Philadelphia race riots begin
1844	New York City police unified
1846	St. Louis police unified
1848	Kentucky Slave Patrol Act
1849	Philadelphia race riots
1854	Boston police unified

Source: Reichel (1992), Bailey (1995), Williams and Murphy (2006).

FIGURE 2.6
Texas Ranger Samuel Walker was killed on October 9, 1847, while leading a charge in Mexico. *Photo courtesy of Library of Congress.*

You can see a short video on the Texas rangers by going to: **http://www.youtube.com/watch?v=rhqM38XmjsU**

Ranger put it, their objective was to "demand blood for blood." Eventually, Taylor sent the Texas Rangers packing. One decade after the Mexican War, the Rangers reverted to their volunteer status.

Beginning in the 1840s, people in the urban areas began to use firearms at an increasing rate. Many Americans believed that they had not only a right but also an obligation to carry a firearm; consequently, the homicide rate increased drastically. As the rate of violence increased, so did the number of police fatalities as a result of the violence. Officers had no way of knowing when they would confront violence or become a victim of it. They began to carry firearms, even when prohibited by policy or public opinion, and American policing eventually drifted into the practice of carrying firearms. It is interesting that today, more than 170 years later, American state legislators are revisiting the issue of allowing people to carry concealed deadly weapons, and several states have passed statutes that allow citizens this privilege.

The use of force was a volatile issue in the mid-1800s. Numerous laws were passed prohibiting behavior that was commonplace. Many people believed that police officers were intruding into personal business by enforcing laws that prohibited gambling, drunkenness, or disorderly behavior. Johnson (1981:31) summarized:

> The social turmoil of the era between 1840 and 1870 also helped explain the use of force. Violence had become commonplace, and many people who supported police reform did so in the expectation that a more effective police [force] would reestablish order on the streets. These people did not always care overly much exactly how the police accomplished that goal. If a few heads got broken in the process, that was a cost they were willing to pay. This was especially true during the 1850s, though it has usually been the case since that time as long as excessive force was used against certain classes of people but not against others. Charges of police brutality appeared most often during the 1850 and 1860s when a patrolman made the mistake of clubbing a "respectable" citizen who blundered into an encounter with an "undesirable" drunken Irishman (or someone equivalent). In effect, then, excessive force was implicitly encouraged as a means of obtaining more peaceful cities.

POLICING AMERICA: THE MODERN ERA

American policing has gone through several phases (Fogelson, 1977; Kelling & Moore, 2006). Although there is general agreement regarding these phases, a number of differences remain (Kappeler, 1996; Strecher, 2006; Williams & Murphy, 2006). Here, the police are examined in terms of the following phases: political entrenchment, reform, professional, and public and community relations. The phases discussed here not only describe police evolution, they also depict societal values. The evolution of policing has somewhat reflected social evolution. In essence, these phases tell how policing advanced to where it is today in terms of what the police do, how they do it, and why they do it.

The Political Entrenchment Phase

Around the turn of the century, the big-city political machines ruled municipal government and policing. It was a time of political entrenchment in which American society was changing in terms of phenomenal growth and opportunity, which in turn created political entrepreneurship. Many politicians saw the police as a mechanism for solidifying their power by controlling political adversaries and assisting friends and allies. The police department not only was responsible for enforcing a city's laws but, in many respects, was also the primary social service agency of the time. Politicians long realized that they could garner more votes from their constituents by providing much-needed social services than by hampering them through arrests or citations. Many politicians therefore encouraged the police to provide as much social assistance as possible.

The police historically have provided a wide range of services. Whitehouse (1973) reported that, during the 1800s, the Boston police were held responsible for a variety of social services; for example, in 1834 they removed 1500 loads of dirt, emptied 3120 privies, and visited every house in Boston daily to check for cholera. In a 3-month period in 1853, the Boston police provided lodging for 1048 homeless persons. Similarly, the New York City Police Department provided lodging to 880,161 homeless persons over a 10-year period and arrested 898,489 persons during that same period. The police housed approximately equal numbers of arrestees and destitutes. The duties of early police in Boston and New York highlight the substantial differences in, and clashes over, the role of the police (service versus law enforcement) that not only affected the early police but are still present today.

The police provided basic health services, but they were also instrumental in performing many of the early social service functions in our society. For Christmas 1916, the New York City Police Department entertained 40,000 children in police stations. In 1917, the New York City Police Department assigned "welfare officers" to 10 precincts to look after wayward youths. The department also established a junior police program that involved 6000 boys between the ages of 11 and 16 in 32 different precincts. Police departments nationwide initiated programs to curb juvenile delinquency (Figure 2.7).

FIGURE 2.7
Tweed Courthouse on September 7, 2013 in New York. The Tweed Courthouse was built using funds provided by William M. Tweed, an influential and corrupt Tammany Hall politician.

In 1918, August Vollmer, "widely recognized as the patriarch of police professionalism" (Crank & Langworthy, 1992:353), presented a paper at the annual meeting of the International Association of Chiefs of Police entitled "The Policeman as a Social Worker," and he made a presentation on the topic of "predelinquency" at the 1921 annual meeting (Walker, 1977; Whitehouse, 1973). Vollmer's leadership, however, involved more than advocating a service orientation for the police. He was instrumental in creating an image of the police as professional and "scientific" crime fighters. Vollmer introduced the crime laboratory to American policing in 1916 and the lie detector in 1921. Crank and Langworthy (1992:353) noted that Vollmer

> ...has had a broad impact on police activities nationally and was instrumental in establishing many police practices that have subsequently achieved mythical stature. Vollmer's broad influence is revealed in the establishment of the Uniform Crime Reports (UCR). Vollmer initially proposed the UCR as a method to track crime in the United States. Today, the ritual of data collection for the UCR is accomplished by tens of thousands of reporting districts across the country, all of which use similar offense classifications for the labeling of reported and cleared crime. Thus, a particular technique for measuring crime has become institutionalized as a means of assessing whether a police department acts (i.e., making arrests) as a police organization is supposed to act. In spite of a great deal of contemporary evidence that the Uniform Crime Reports tell us very little about actual crime, attention to UCR data collection provides a police organization with ceremonial evidence that the organization is doing something about crime.

Although politicians and police leaders were interested in social services and pushed their police departments toward active social roles, some were also corruptive and inhibited justice. In many respects, the political stranglehold on the police was total and consuming. Politicians controlled how the departments were organized, who was appointed to the department and to managerial and supervisory positions, the activities they performed, and, in many instances, who was arrested and which laws were enforced (Kappeler et al., 1998). Appointments to the police department were often made by political ward or precinct bosses, who then would exercise absolute control over their officers once on the force. Candidates frequently had to pay these ward bosses to become police officers. The Lexow Committee investigated New York City police corruption in the 1890s and found that the going rate to become a sergeant was $1600, and $12,000 to $15,000 was the price for captains' positions (Fogelson, 1977).

The police represented a vast resource that the politicians could use to ensure the outcome of future elections, reward friends, and punish enemies. The police in many cities were responsible for enforcing election laws and monitoring the polls. The police frequently would be used to discourage supporters of political enemies from voting or to allow friends of the ruling party to vote numerous times. Bars, brothels, and businesses that were engaged in illegal activities could avoid police attention and intervention as long as they supported the winning political candidate, whereas those who supported the losing candidate or party could expect maximum police enforcement of laws and ordinances. Bribery and corruption were commonplace. The police, in essence, served as the collection agents for political bosses (Fogelson, 1977).

The Reform Efforts

The reform efforts actually were not distinctive—in terms of time—from the political entrenchment period, but they paralleled and extended beyond the most abusive, politically corrupt period. There were always pressures to reform the police and government in general. They came from a variety of sources ranging from reform-minded citizens and civic groups to political opponents who were suffering at the hands of the victors. Police reform was a long, slow evolutionary process punctuated with numerous gains and losses. For the most part, police reform activities can be discussed in terms of investigative commissions, reform initiated by police administrators, and political reform. In some cases, the various reforms and the sources for these reforms are distinctive, whereas in others it is difficult to distinguish who set the reform in motion.

Investigative Commissions

Commissions investigating police corruption and police practices have long been a part of the political arena. It seems that a commission is the answer any time government officials, citizen groups, or police administrators are faced with political or moral issues. The commission became a primary vehicle to investigate police and government corruption because it could be formed and financed by private donations or by community groups when government leaders were not interested in investigating themselves or any wrongdoing Box 2.4.

Although corruption and mismanagement were prevalent, specific offenses or atrocities generally inspired citizens or government officials to establish a commission. Fogelson (1977:72) compiled a sampling of incidents that, owing to their audacity, prompted public outrage and investigation:

> In 1909, Mayor Arthur Harper, Chief Edward Kern, and a prominent
> pimp formed a syndicate that attempted to monopolize prostitution in
> Los Angeles by instructing the police department to enforce the law
> and harass the prostitutes everywhere except in the vicinity of a few

Box 2.4 The Whiskey Rebellion: George Washington's Proclamation

Angered by an excise tax imposed on whiskey in 1791 by the federal government, farmers in the western counties of Pennsylvania engaged in a series of attacks on excise agents. The tariff effectively eliminated any profit by the farmers from the sale or barter of an important cash crop and became the lightning rod for a wide variety of grievances by the settlers of the region against the federal government.

Although citizens in the east did not find it difficult to abide by the concept that individual states were "subservient to the country," people west of the mountains were less accepting of decisions made by the central government.

The rebel farmers continued their attacks, rioting in river towns and roughing up tax collectors until the so-called insurrection flared into the open in July 1794, when a federal marshal was attacked in Allegheny County, Pennsylvania. Almost at the same time, several hundred men attacked the residence of the regional inspector, burning his home, barn, and several outbuildings. Pittsburgh was another scene of disorder by enraged mobs.

On August 7, 1794, President Washington issued a proclamation, calling out the militia and ordering the disaffected westerners to return to their homes. Washington's order mobilized an army of approximately 13,000—as large as the one that had defeated the British—under the command of General Harry Lee, the then-Governor of Virginia and father of Robert E. Lee. Washington himself, in a show of presidential authority, set out at the head of the troops to suppress the uprising.

This was the first use of the Militia Law of 1792, setting a precedent for the use of the militia to "execute the laws of the union, (and) suppress insurrections," asserting the right of the national government to enforce order in one state with troops raised in other states. Even more important, it was the first test of power of the new federal government, establishing its primacy in disputes with individual states. In the end, a dozen or so men were arrested, sent to Philadelphia to trial, and released after pardons by Washington.

Source: Based on a Presidential Proclamation published in Claypoole's Daily Advertiser, August 11, 1794.

houses recently purchased by the syndicate. Three years later several gunmen, who were allegedly acting for Lieutenant Charles Becker, head of one of New York City Police Department's vice squads, shot and killed Herman Rosenthal, a professional gambler who had just charged the force with protecting gambling and was scheduled to appear before the district attorney to substantiate his charges. A major scandal broke out in San Francisco in 1913 when the press reported that Frank Esola, Louis Droulette, and nearly a dozen other detectives had recruited a gang of swindlers and, in return for 15 percent of the estimated gross of $300,000 a year, protected its members from the rest of the police department. An even worse scandal erupted in Chicago a year or so later when several members of the underworld who operated out of the Twenty-Second Street Levee tried to cripple Major Metellus L.C. Funkhouser's moral squad by threatening his deputy's life, stabbing one officer, and shooting another.

Commissions were frequently called upon to investigate the police when incidents such as these came to public light.

The New York City Police Department (NYPD) likely has been the object of investigation by the largest number of commissions (see Box 2.5). As early as 1894, the Lexow Committee investigated police corruption in New York City, including Tammany Hall, which was one of the most successful and extensive political machines of all time. In 1973, the Knapp Commission investigated the NYPD and found widespread corruption. The Commission found that officers were engaged in activities ranging from stealing seized narcotics and selling them to receiving payoffs to protect gambling operations, in addition to a host of other, less serious activities. In 1993, the Mollen Commission once again addressed the issue of corruption in the NYPD. Although numerous commissions have investigated corruption in the NYPD, the issue of corruption is as alive today as it was in the 1800s.

You can view a video interview with an NYPD officer testifying before the Knapp Commission by going to: **http://www. youtube.com/watch?v=PoNkmAUKWEg**

Commissions have served as blunt-force instruments whereby people could not avoid seeing and comprehending the problems associated with their police. The commission became so popular that it was frequently used to govern police departments. Commissions appointed by the governor or the state legislature were commonly used to control the daily operations of many big-city police departments: Louisville, Los Angeles, San Francisco, Milwaukee, New Orleans, Indianapolis, and Atlanta (Fosdick, 1915/1969). Kansas City and St. Louis are still governed by such commissions today.

Box 2.5   Major Investigations of the New York City Police Department

Year	Name of Investigation	Focus of Investigation
1894	Lexow Committee	Corruption from gambling and prostitution operations; extortion of money from legitimate businesspersons; collusion with criminals; intimidation, harassment of citizens
1913	Curran Committee	Corruption from gambling and prostitution operations
1932	Seabury Committee	Corruption from the manufacture, distribution, sale, and consumption of illegal alcohol; extortion of money from prostitutes
1949	Brooklyn grand jury	Corruption from gambling payoffs
1972	Knapp Commission	Corruption from gambling and drugs; payoffs from citizens and the operators of legal and illegal businesses
1993	Mollen Commission	Drug corruption; robberies and thefts committed by officers; on-duty substance abuse; excessive use of force; effectiveness of internal affairs in detecting and investigating police wrongdoing

Source: Kappeler et al. (1998).

More recently, the Christopher Commission was appointed in Los Angeles in 1991 to investigate police brutality and excessive force. The Commission was appointed after at least 15 officers from the Los Angeles Police Department brutally beat Rodney King, an African-American motorist whom they had stopped for a traffic violation. A civilian bystander videotaped this incident, and the tape was televised nationwide. The turmoil surrounding this case prompted the city to appoint the Commission to investigate the incident and to make recommendations on reducing police use of excessive force in the Los Angeles Police Department. Although the Commission serves a vital political function, its potential as an instrument of reform is questionable (see Box 2.5). Despite numerous commission investigations in municipal police departments such as New York, patterns of corruption and abuse often continue.

Police Administrative Reform

Reform initiated by police administrators was an important source of change. Basically, a number of police administrators took their jobs seriously and wanted to provide quality law enforcement services to the public, and they resented the control and domination exerted by incompetent or uncaring politicians. As more and more diligent, conscientious police executives maneuvered into the top levels of police management, they began to explore ways to reduce the influence of the corrupt politicians.

To a great extent, this internal reform centered on personnel issues. The reform-minded police executives called for selection standards and testing, recruit training, civil service, and promotion testing. These measures were seen as vehicles to prevent incompetent officers from joining the force or from being promoted if they were not excluded. The reformers knew they could not totally isolate the police department from the politicians, but they could control or establish minimum standards that the politicians had to uphold.

Another kind of reform was police reorganization. During the height of political control in police departments, the police chief was little more than a figurehead, with most police operations being dictated and controlled by the precinct captains. The precinct captains, in turn, received their orders from the precinct or ward political leaders. The captains and every officer in the precinct owed their jobs to these politicians.

Reorganization reform took three forms: (1) the addition of midlevel management ranks, (2) redistricting or changing police precinct lines, and (3) the deployment of specialized police units. Police chiefs started adding ranks such as majors and assistant chiefs in an effort to gain better control over operations. These midlevel officials could assist the chief in developing and implementing operational plans and monitor the activities of officers in the various precincts. Police chiefs also attempted to combine or change precinct stations' boundaries so that they included territory from more than one voting ward or city precinct. This essentially diffused the power of the precinct or ward politicians, because more than one were involved with a given police precinct station. This diffusion allowed police commanders, the police chiefs, and their management staff to assume more control over the daily operations of the precinct stations. Finally, police chiefs strived to deploy centralized special units such as criminal investigation, traffic, or vice with jurisdiction-wide powers. Before these specialized units, all police powers were vested with the precincts where their operation was controlled by the captains and the precinct politicians. Centralization allowed police executives to exercise more control over a number of police responsibilities.

General Political Reform

Although they were highly visible, the police were not the only unit of local government plagued by politics. Many local and state governments were riddled with mismanagement or corruption. Abuses of power and ineffective government management caused citizens to push for commissions (as discussed above) and changes in laws with the intent to impede corrupt politicians. For example, the *Pendleton Act*, which provided the first civil service coverage to public employees, was passed in 1883. The Pendleton Act provided job security to certain federal employees, giving them some degree of independence in the execution of their responsibilities.

In summary, there were a number of forces that, in combination, helped policing become more autonomous. This is not to say that corruption and politics are no longer problems, and, indeed, they always pose problems, but the reform phase represented an era during which citizens and their government initiated laws and programs to minimize their obvious influences.

Professional Policing Comes to America

As reform efforts gained momentum and politics had a less obvious and less intrusive role in policing, law enforcement in this country began to be viewed as a profession. The so-called professional phase of law enforcement began in the 1920s. The professional phase of policing can be analyzed and best understood using three general perspectives: the law enforcement role, the bureaucratic model, and science and technology.

The Law Enforcement Role

The political spoils era emphasized the service role, for obvious reasons. The police did not adopt a law enforcement, or crook-catching, role until the 1920 and 1930s. Police departments continued to move toward a more professional model as a result of the various reform efforts. Then, during the decades of the 1920 and 1930s, two significant events occurred that helped orchestrate a move toward law enforcement: (1) passage of the Eighteenth Amendment to the U.S. Constitution, or the Volstead Act; and (2) the Depression and the resultant crime wave.

The Eighteenth Amendment, or the *Volstead Act* (more commonly called *Prohibition*), was this country's grand experiment in regulating public morals. The Act prohibited the manufacture, sale, and transportation of alcoholic beverages. Prohibition was an emotionally charged issue with numerous supporters and numerous opponents. Wilson (1969) noted that the Act placed police officers in an adversarial law enforcement role for the first time. Before the Act, officers allowed public opinion to dictate police enforcement policies regarding vice and victimless crimes. The police tended to enforce laws haphazardly, as they encountered criminal activity, rather than planning and concentrating on crime problems. Police officers were more concerned with order maintenance and maintaining relationships with people within their beats.

> You can watch a video on the Volstead Act by going to: **http://video.pbs.org/video/2111642308/**

Prohibition changed this relationship. As a result of Prohibition, police officers were expected to take a proactive approach to laws that many people opposed. These expectations sometimes forced police to choose between upholding the law and maintaining a good rapport with the community (Figure 2.8).

The Depression of the 1930s had a similar effect. During the Depression, the country experienced widespread unemployment, bank failures, foreclosures on homes and other property, poverty, and homelessness. This was a desperate time for most Americans. Many people had little choice but to commit crime to survive. The Depression also produced major criminals who repeatedly stole, robbed, and killed. Among them, John Dillinger, Baby Face Nelson, and Bonnie Parker and Clyde Barrow became public heroes because of their crime sprees. The criminals were viewed as the heroes, whereas the banks and other financial institutions that were profiting from people's misfortune were seen as the enemies.

Government officials at all levels quickly comprehended the magnitude of the problem. Subsequently, substantial pressure was placed on police forces at all levels to become more effective in enforcing the law. The provision of miscellaneous services and order maintenance became secondary police objectives as crime fighting took center stage.

Law enforcement as the primary police mission became public policy. In 1929, President Hoover appointed the National Commission on Law Observance and Law Enforcement, also known as the Wickersham Commission. The Commission was charged with studying the rising crime rate and the lack of an effective police response. In 1931, the Commission issued its report, noting numerous problems associated with the police ranging from inadequate

FIGURE 2.8
Bandits Bonnie Parker and Clyde Barrow are seen in an undated photo. *Photo courtesy of* www.fbi.gov.

training to politics. The Commission championed the idea that police officers should be crime fighters and that service activities did not constitute "real" police work. Police leaders such as O.W. Wilson and J. Edgar Hoover cultivated the public perception of police as crime fighters (Crank & Langworthy, 1992). Despite decades of declining criminal victimization rates, "Today, efforts by police administrators to acquire increased budgets are invariably justified on the basis of a perceived need to improve crime-fighting capabilities" (Crank & Langworthy, 1992:355). The crime-fighting role had become fixed in the minds of police officials, intertwined in the notion of police professionalism, and a mainstay in the public's perception of the police.

To read the findings of the Wickersham Commission, visit the website: **http://www2.potsdam.edu/hansondj/Controversies/Wickersham-Commission.html**

The Bureaucratic Model

By 1950, there had been meaningful and considerable changes in law enforcement to the point that policing was moving into the pinnacle of its "professional phase." O.W. Wilson published the first edition of his *Police Administration* text, which quickly became the Bible for police administrators. Wilson and other professional police chiefs of the time preached that police departments should be centralized so as to exert more control and thwart potential external political influences. Wilson and his contemporaries essentially adopted the military model for policing that was first advocated by Sir Robert Peel in 1829 when he was organizing the London Metropolitan Police Department. Professionalism was viewed as organizational efficiency and crime fighting. Classical organizational principles that produced the appearance of greater control and efficiency were adopted. Police departments operated under the military model, with officers being closely supervised and directed. Police departments abolished foot patrols in favor of motorized patrols, station houses were closed and functions consolidated, and command functions emanated from a central headquarters (Sherman, 1974; Uchida, 1993).

Science and Technology

Police officials became fascinated by science and technology. They believed that policing could not truly achieve professional status without technology. The human aspects of police work were abandoned for science. Police officials pursued technological innovations on all fronts: police record systems, fingerprints, chemistry, serology, toxicology, evidence collection, and radio communications. Police chiefs and their investigators increasingly depended on physical evidence to obtain criminal convictions. Interpersonal relations with the community were virtually eliminated from the police agenda. The professional phase of policing produced a more efficient police organization that was devoted to criminal apprehension. Officers were moved from foot patrol to vehicular patrol, and a variety of technologies were adopted. Police officers were discouraged from getting involved with people, for fear of breeding corruption. Also, efficiency of operation was considered more important than solving problems, and the application of human relations skills within the police organization or by its officers in their daily activities was viewed as being inefficient and therefore unprofessional. Police work became mechanical, with officers having less meaningful contact with members of the community. The adoption of technology by the police, however, is paradoxical. Technological change in "policing involved not just the patrol car, but the car in conjunction with the telephone and the two-way radio. These served to bring police officers into far more intimate contact with people than ever before. While the patrol car isolated police officers in some respects, the telephone simultaneously increased the degree of contact in other respects" (Walker, 2006:57). With the adoption of the motor vehicle, the telephone, and the two-way radio, police could be summoned to distant parts of cities and rural counties, and were thus invited into our homes. With these technological innovations also came different citizen expectations about the proper role of the police.

Public and Community Relations Return to Policing

The police professional model was rocked by civil disturbances in the 1960s. During the 1960s, the civil rights movement intensified. This, combined with feelings of impoverishment and helplessness in the ghettos, created civil unrest. Almost every major city in the U.S. had a major riot between 1964 and 1968. Rochester, Philadelphia, and New York experienced riots in 1964; the Watts section of Los Angeles, in 1965 (see Box 2.6); Chicago and Cleveland, in 1966; Newark and Detroit, in 1967; and Washington, Baltimore, Pittsburgh, and Chicago, in 1968.

View historic newsreel footage of the watts riots at the website: **www.youtube.com/watch?v=SRDvY_anJdc**

Most of these riots were prompted by police-related incidents. This is not to say that the police caused the riots, but their actions often sparked riots. Indeed, research after the riots pointed out that social and economic oppression were the underlying causes of the riots; for example, the President's Commission (1967:37) noted:

> The principal objects of attack were most often just those people or institutions, insofar as they were within reach, that the rioters thought of as being their principal oppressors: Policemen and white passers-by, or white-owned commercial establishments, especially those that charged high prices, dealt in inferior merchandise, or employed harsh credit policies. Loan offices were a favorite target. Homes, schools, churches, and libraries were, by and large, left alone.

Box 2.6   The 1965 Watts Riots

The 1960s seemed to mark a turning point in America; with the passage of the Civil Rights Act, a new age in race relations appeared to be dawning. However, the states acted quickly to circumvent the new federal law. California reacted with Proposition 14, which moved to block the fair housing components of the Civil Rights Act. This act and others created a feeling of injustice and despair in the inner cities.

On August 11, 1965, a routine traffic stop in South Central Los Angeles provided the spark that lit the fire of those seething feelings. The riots lasted for 6 days, leaving 34 dead, more than 1000 people injured, nearly 4000 people arrested, and hundreds of buildings destroyed.

After the riots, then Governor Pat Brown named John McCone to head a commission to study the riots. The report issued by the commission concluded that the riots were not the act of thugs, but rather symptomatic of much deeper problems: the high jobless rate in the inner city, poor housing, and bad schools. Although the problems were clearly pointed out in the report, no great effort was made to address them or to rebuild what had been destroyed in the riots.

Source: University of Southern California libraries Website (www.usc.edu/libraries/archives/la/ watts.html).

When asked why they rioted, a number of the demonstrators replied that they thought it would bring about change or force the government to do something about their situation (President's Commission, 1967).

Adding to the problem was the Vietnam War, which generated civil disobedience on college campuses nationwide. During the first half of the 1967–1968 school year, students held 71 demonstrations on 62 college campuses; during the second half of the year, 221 demonstrations were held on 101 campuses. Some students refused to honor the draft, some supported other students who fled the U.S. to avoid the draft, and some openly supported civil disobedience in support of the antiwar movement. It was also a time when some students and other young people were openly using drugs, which often created adversarial relationships between them and the more conservative police culture (Figure 2.9).

The nation experienced numerous assassinations of public leaders. In 1963, President John F. Kennedy was killed in Dallas, and 36 h later, his alleged assassin, Lee Harvey Oswald, was killed. American civil rights leader Martin Luther King, Jr, and Attorney General Robert F. Kennedy were killed in 1968.

FIGURE 2.9

Demonstrators push against a police car after rioting erupted in a crowd of 1500 in the Los Angeles area of Watts, August 12, 1965. The disturbances were triggered by the arrest of a black person on charges of drunken driving. More than 100 officers were called into the area. *Photo courtesy of AP Photo.*

Other public figures assassinated include Medgar Evers, Field Secretary for the NAACP; Malcolm X, a black Muslim leader; and George Lincoln Rockwell, leader of the American Nazi Party. Assassination became a means to voice political discontent that cut across all political lines.

It became evident that the police were not prepared for or capable of dealing with the civil strife that occurred in the 1960 and 1970s. In fact, police often contributed to riots and disorder. The National Advisory Commission on Civil Disorders (1968) went so far as to note that the relationship between the police and African-Americans—and other minority groups—was abrasive and contributed to the tension and disorder. Essentially, the police, in their pursuit of professionalism, had lost touch with the people they were sworn to protect. In many cases, when the civil disorders occurred, the police did not have advance intelligence information nor did they comprehend that the disorders were imminent.

You can watch a video of the 1968 riots in Chicago by going to: **http://www.history.com/videos/violence-batters-1968-democratic-convention#chicago-seven-conspiracy-trial**

The federal government took measures to bolster police and criminal justice resources. In 1968, the *Omnibus Crime Control and Safe Streets Act* was passed. The Act, and subsequent legislation, provided substantial resources for state and local police and criminal justice agencies. Large portions of the money were spent on equipment, training, and programs in policing. The power, size, and control capacity of the American police institution grew at breakneck speed.

One of the primary initiatives funded by the federal government, in addition to reducing crime, was the development of programs to improve relations between the police and the public. The federal government provided funding to state and local police departments to create a wide variety of police–community programs. Most of the larger departments created police–community relations units or divisions, and they implemented programs that ranged from officer-friendly to urban-referral operations and from classroom presentations in the schools to summer recreation activities for inner-city youth. Many of these programs had little impact on citizens' perceptions of the police and were viewed as little more than a whitewash of an increasingly unresponsive institution. However, the movement did affect the organization of policing.

You can learn more about the criminal justice system and period of American history by watching a video at: **http://www.youtube.com/watch?v=_Ja0vEaZAY0**

The police–community relations movement had a variety of effects on police organizational thought and operational practices. Many departments moved to decentralize decision making and operational planning. Precinct and district commanders in many departments were given more authority to develop programs to provide better services to citizens. Order maintenance and the provision of services were elevated and again were considered legitimate police objectives. Finally, police departments began to emphasize citizens' rights and the police duty to treat people accordingly.

The Community Policing Era

During the 1980s, the police–community relations model of policing began to evolve into community policing. Several factors set the stage for the birth of community policing, including (1) the isolation of officers in police cars, (2) narrowing of the police mission to crime fighting, (3) an overreliance on the scientific approach to management that stressed efficiency and effectiveness, (4) increased reliance on high-tech gadgetry instead of human interaction, (5) insulation of police administration from community input and accountability, (6) a longstanding concern about police violation of human rights, and (7) failed attempts by the police to reach the community, such as police–community relations and crime prevention (Kappeler & Gaines, 2008).

Community policing is rooted in two schools of thought: (1) problem-oriented policing developed by Goldstein (1979), which was first implemented through several projects developed by the Police Executive Research Forum; and (2) community-oriented policing, which focused on fear of crime and the development of community partnerships (Kappeler & Gaines, 2008). Goldstein noted that traditionally, the police focused on the symptoms of problems and failed to address the causes of problems. The police spent too much time answering calls rather than addressing their root causes. He advocated that the police spend more time addressing problems (problem solving), eventually reducing their workload by eliminating problems and repeat calls for service and contributing to a safer community.

Community-oriented policing evolved from work at Michigan State University (MSU). Researchers from MSU conducted several studies in Flint and found that fear of crime was more problematic than crime itself. The researchers advocated that police departments should form partnerships with community groups to address crime and fear issues. Essentially, the police cannot be successful without the cooperation of the population being policed. The work at MSU resulted in a number of programs in which the police attempted to form police–community partnerships not only to address crime problems but also to address a variety of quality-of-life issues (e.g., attending to broken windows). Here, police departments began to deal with such disorder problems as panhandling, vagrancy, public intoxication, and street drug trafficking. It was hypothesized that eliminating or containing disorder problems would reduce crime.

Ultimately, problem-oriented policing and community-oriented policing merged into an overarching philosophy, which came to be known as community policing. As such, community policing has two key elements: problem solving and community partnerships. Community policing became institutionalized in American policing when President William Clinton signed the *Violent Crime and Law Enforcement Act of 1994*, which provided more than $30 billion to fund community policing and was the largest anti-crime legislation in the nation's history. Elements of the legislation included hiring 100,000 additional police officers nationwide, the creation of the Office of Community Oriented Policing Services (COPS Office) to oversee the distribution of funding to local and state police agencies, and the funding of a number of innovative community policing projects and experiments. When Worrall and Zhao (2003) examined COPS funding, however, they found that many recipients were more interested in obtaining COPS funding as opposed to substantively changing their operational philosophy.

Police departments implemented a variety of programs under the rubric of community policing. There were efforts to forge better relations with the community. Typical programs included neighborhood meetings, citizen academies, neighborhood newsletters, and police athletic leagues. There was, however, also a law enforcement agenda in many community-policing departments. Many programs attempted to abate neighborhood disorder through curfew enforcement, code enforcement, enforcement of public intoxication and vagrancy laws, and eviction programs aimed at drug users and traffickers. There were also programs focusing on crime prevention: Drug Abuse Resistance Education, Gang Resistance Education and Training, school resource officers, and Crime Stoppers. Finally, the police used enhanced patrolling as the primary method of problem solving. Some types of patrols used included bike patrols, horse patrols, additional police substations, and aggressive patrolling.

One example of a community policing program is *weed and seed*. Weed and seed programs were funded by the Bureau of Justice Administration and consisted of focusing on an area that had high levels of crime and disorder, especially drug trafficking. The weed portion of the program consisted of aggressive law enforcement to rid the area of crime and disorder. Once law enforcement had taken back control of the area, the seeding portion of the program was said to begin. Here, the police worked with neighborhood residents to solve problems, contacted other social service agencies to obtain needed social programming, and generally worked to build the area into a viable neighborhood. The essence of the program was to use problem solving and community partnerships to enhance the quality of life in the neighborhood. More often than not, though, cities did not receive the necessary funds to seed the neighborhoods that they had attempted to clean up.

Major problems with community policing in many police departments included too much emphasis on aggressive policing strategies and a failure to involve the community in problems and problem solving. For example,

Greene (2004) examined the Youth Firearms Violence Initiative that was implemented in 10 cities, including Baltimore, Birmingham, San Antonio, and Seattle. The program used community policing strategies to combat youth gun violence. Greene noted that for the most part, these programs failed because of an overdependence on saturation patrols that failed to focus on the problem (guns and gang members), and the unit assigned responsibility for the program failed to coordinate with other units in the police department, resulting in lost efficiency and support from other units.

There are ample examples of situations in which the police have successfully implemented community policing (see Brito & Allan, 1999) but for the most part, the core functioning of police departments has changed little with the advent of community policing (Zhao, Lovrich, & Robinson, 2001). Police departments remained focused on professional crime fighting. Barlow and Barlow (1999) and Manning (1991) observed that many police departments have used community policing as a vehicle to manage their image. In essence, it is highly questionable whether most police departments have bought into the ideas of problem solving and community partnerships.

The Post-Community Policing Era and the Rise of the Surveillance State

The September 11, 2001, terrorist attacks against the World Trade Center and the Pentagon had not only a profound impact on the nation's psyche, but also a significant affect on politics and the operation of American policing. Although community policing constituted a significant effort to move law enforcement away from the professional, law-and-order model of policing, it appears, based on the earlier discussion, that much work remained. The events of 9/11 and concern regarding subsequent terrorist attacks resulted in law enforcement placing greater emphasis on aggressive and invasive policing tactics. Although the federal government, particularly the Department of Homeland Security, has primary responsibility for combating terrorist acts, local and state police departments began preparing strategies and action plans for potential terrorist events in their jurisdictions. Initially, these plans focused on how medical services, fire services, civil defense, and law enforcement services would be deployed in response to a terrorist event. However, these initial concerns quickly changed with the rise of intelligence-led policing and enhanced technological capabilities of the police. Local law enforcement has been called on to work with federal law enforcement agencies such as the Federal Bureau of Investigation and agencies from the Department of Homeland Security to investigate possible terrorist suspects. Although many of the data collection methods and investigative techniques involve telecommunications and surveillance of people, others reemphasize aggressive police tactics over community policing tactics.

Although there was a move to abandon community policing as a result of the 9/11 attacks, community policing remains an important and viable police strategy in an era of terrorism and homeland security. Murray (2005), Thacher (2005), and Brown (2007) each advised that police departments develop positive working relationships with the community to collect intelligence about possible terrorists and their activities. When such relations exist, people are more likely report suspicious persons and activities; thus, community policing is more important today than ever, and aggressive law enforcement likely is counterproductive (Figure 2.10).

The 9/11 attacks also resulted in police beginning to collect intelligence at the local level. A number of departments are now using intelligence-led policing (Carter, 2004; McGarrell & Freilich, 2007). Historically, a number of police departments have regularly collected intelligence about organized crime criminals, drug traffickers, and career criminals. Intelligence-led policing means that departments begin to incorporate terrorist information into their intelligence

FIGURE 2.10
Two New York City police officers speak to each other near the area known as Ground Zero after the collapse of the Twin Towers on September 11, 2001, in New York City. *Copyright Shutterstock/Anthony Correia.*

operations. The collection of this information requires that police departments have working relations with the community. Again, community policing complements a police department's efforts in counterterrorism.

Myths of Change in American Policing

Myth: The primary driving force behind change in American policing has been changes in the nature of crime.

Reality: Although crime prevention is a primary task of the police, change in policing has not been driven by changes in the nature of crime. Economic and political change has brought about most transformations in policing.

Myth: Crime itself is a fixed and unchanging feature of American society.

Reality: Both the nature of policing and the nature of crime change with broader social transformations.

Over the development of American history, the role of police has changed from morals enforcement to the regulation of slaves through crime control and intelligence collection.

Myth: The nature of policing never changes; just the technology and techniques police use change.

Reality: Changes in the political economy, the movement from an industrial society to a global information-based society will foster greater changes in policing well into the twenty-first century.

SUMMARY

The evolution of policing can be traced to the rise of the state as a form of political organization. With the demise of kin-based communities and the rise of the democratic nation-state, specialized police forces came into existence. As social stratification develops and the need to control the distribution of resources arises, police forces emerge or are augmented. The history of the American police institution can be traced to the development of civilian policing in England. American policing has undergone significant change over the past 200 years. There have been a number of changes in the police role. Around the turn of the century, the police were concerned primarily with maintaining order and providing service to the community. This later changed to a focus on crime fighting. This focus was accompanied by the adoption of science and technology to create professionalized police forces that were detached from the communities they policed. Today, American police attempt to balance crime fighting with order maintenance and service; yet, many of the historical concerns people have had with the idea of policing remain. As the police attempt to become more responsive to their communities by providing services and addressing community problems, they are also developing the capacity to use aggressive and invasive law enforcement practices and are showing less tolerance for minor violations and disorders.

The changes in policing have paralleled changes in society, with the police responding to political, economic, social, and cultural influences. Although we have identified several phases through which policing has evolved, these phases were not always progressive, but paralleled changes in society. Policing has always been political, it has always involved reforms, and it has, to some extent, always entailed a service component. The balance between these forces has shifted with politics, economics, and history. Finding the right balance of forces, however, determines whether we live in a free and democratic society or a police state.

REVIEW QUESTIONS

1. What is the earliest known code of laws? What roles or functions did early police have in ancient Egypt, Greece, and Rome?
2. Most scholars recognize that the first modern police department was created where and in what year?
3. What was one of the first law enforcement officers in the early American colonies? What early police service, usually performed by volunteer citizens, later developed into police departments?
4. American policing is generally agreed to have undergone several phases. What are the four phases discussed in this chapter, and how do they depict police evolution and societal values?
5. What is community policing, and what factors were instrumental in the creation of community policing? What impact did the terrorist attacks on September 11, 2001, have on the post-community policing era?

REFERENCES

Bailey, W. G. (1995). *The encyclopedia of police science* (2nd ed.). New York: Garland Press.

Barlow, D. E., & Barlow, M. H. (1999). A political economy of community policing. *Policing: An International Journal of Police Strategies & Management, 22*(4), 646–674.

Bloy, M. (1998). *The metropolitan police*. Rotherham, U.K: Rotherham College of Arts and Technology.

Brito, C. S., & Allan, T. (1999). *Problem-oriented policing: Crime-specific problems, critical issues, and making POP work*. Washington, D.C: Police Executive Research Forum.

Brown, B. (2007). Community policing in post-September 11 America: a comment on the concept of community-oriented counterterrorism. *Police Practice and Research, 8*, 239–251.

Carter, D. (2004). *Law enforcement intelligence: A guide for state, local, and tribal law enforcement agencies*. Washington, D.C: U.S. Department of Justice, Office of Community Oriented Policing Services.

Clear, T. R., & Cole, G. F. (2005). *American corrections* (10th ed.). New York: Thomson Wadsworth.

Colquhoun, P. (1806). *A treatise on the police of the metropolis* (7th ed.). London: J. Mawman.

Crank, J. P., & Langworthy, R. (1992). An institutional perspective of policing. *The Journal of Criminal Law & Criminology, 83*(2), 338–363.

Davies, R. W. (1977). Augustus caesar: a police system in the ancient world. In P. J. Stead (Ed.), *Pioneers in policing* (pp. 12–32). Montclair, NJ: Patterson-Smith.

Fogelson, R. (1977). *Big-city police*. Cambridge, MA: Harvard University Press.

Fosdick, R. B. (1915/1969). *American police systems*. Montclair, NJ: Patterson-Smith.

Germann, A., Day, F., & Gallati, R. (1973). *Introduction to law enforcement and criminal justice.* Springfield, IL: Charles C Thomas.

Goldstein, H. (1979). Improving policing: a problem-oriented approach. *Crime & Delinquency, 25*, 236–258.

Greene, J. (2004). Police youth violence interventions: lessons to improve effectiveness. In F. Esbensen, S. Tibbetts, & L. Gaines (Eds.), *American youth gangs at the millennium* (pp. 333–350). Prospect Heights, IL: Waveland Press.

Grimal, N. (1994). *A history of ancient Egypt*. Oxford: Blackwell.

Johnson, D. R. (1981). *American law enforcement: A history*. St. Louis, MO: Forum Press.

Kappeler, V. E. (1995). The St. Louis police department. In W. G. Bailey (Ed.), *The encyclopedia of police science* (2nd ed.) (pp. 701–704). New York: Garland Press.

Kappeler, V. E. (1996). Making police history in light of modernity: a sign of the times? *Police Forum, 6*(3), 1–6.

Kappeler, V. E., & Gaines, L. (2008). *Community policing: A contemporary perspective* (5th ed.). Newark, NJ: LexisNexis Matthew Bender.

Kappeler, V. E., Sluder, R., & Alpert, G. P. (1998). *Forces of deviance: Understanding the dark side of policing* (2nd ed.). Prospect Heights, IL: Waveland Press.

Kelling, G., & Moore, M. (2006). The evolving strategy of policing. In V. Kappeler (Ed.), *Police and society: Touchstone readings* (3rd ed.). Prospect Heights, IL: Waveland Press.

Kelly, M. A. (1973). The first urban policeman. *Journal of Police Science and Administration, 1*(1), 56–60.

Kishlansky, M., Geary, P., & O'Brien, P. (1991). *Civilization in the West*. New York: HarperCollins.

Manning, P. K. (1991). Community policing as a drama of control. In J. Greene, & S. Mastrofski (Eds.), *Community policing: Rhetoric or reality* (pp. 27–46). New York: Praeger.

McGarrell, E., & Freilich, J. (2007). Intelligence-led policing as a framework for responding to terrorism. *Journal of Contemporary Criminal Justice, 23*, 142–158.

Murray, J. (2005). Policing terrorism: a threat to community policing or just a shift in priorities? *Police Practice and Research, 6*, 347–361.

Nalla, M. K., & Newman, G. R. (1994). Is white-collar policing, policing? *Policing and Society, 3*, 303–318.

National Advisory Commission on Civil Disorders. (1968). *Report of the national advisory commission on civil disorders*. New York: Bantam Books.

National Constable Association. (1995). Constable. In W. G. Bailey (Ed.), *The encyclopedia of police science* (2nd ed.) (pp. 114–115). New York: Garland Press.

New York (N.Y.) Knapp Commission. 1973). *Knapp commission report on police corruption*. New York: G. Braziller.

Oliphant, M. (1992). *The Atlas of the ancient world*. New York: Simon & Schuster.

President's Commission on Law Enforcement and Administration of Justice. (1967). *The Challenge of crime in a free society*. Washington, D.C: U.S. Government Printing Office.

Pringle, P. (1955). *Hue and cry: The story of Henry and John fielding and their bow street runners*. London: William Morrow & Co.

Reichel, P. L. (1992). The misplaced emphasis on urbanization in police development. *Policing and Society, 3*, 1–12.

Reith, C. (1952/1975). *The blind eye of history*. Montclair, NJ: Patterson-Smith.

Roberts, D. (1995). Age of the Pyramids. *National Geographic, 187*(1), 1–42.

Roberts, C., Roberts, D., & Bisson, D. (2002). *A history of England: Prehistory to 1714*. Upper Saddle River, NJ: Prentice-Hall.

Robinson, C. D., Scaglion, R., & Olivero, J. M. (1994). *Police in contradiction*. Westport, CT: Greenwood Press.

Rubinstein, J. (1973). *City police*. New York: Farrar, Straus & Giroux.

Saggs, H. W. F. (1989). *Civilization before Greece and Rome*. New Haven, CT: Yale University Press.

Samaha, J. (1974). *Law and order in historical perspective*. New York: Academic Press.

Sherman, L. (1974). The sociology and the social reform of the American police: 1950–1973. *Journal of Police Science and Administration, 2*(3), 255–262.

Simpson, A. E. (1996). "The mouth of strange women is a deep pit": male guilt and legal attitudes toward prostitution in Georgian London. *Journal of Criminal Justice and Popular Culture, 4*(3), 50–79.

Strecher, V. G. (2006). Revising the histories and futures of policing. In V. E. Kappeler (Ed.), *Police and society: Touchstone readings* (3rd ed.) (pp. 66–79). Prospect Heights, IL: Waveland Press.

Thacher, D. (2005). The local role in Homeland security. *Law & Society Review, 39*, 635–676.

Uchida, C. (1993). The development of american police: an historical overview. In R. Dunham, & G. Alpert (Eds.), *Critical issues in policing: Contemporary readings* (2nd ed.). Prospect Heights, IL: Waveland Press.

Walker, S. (1977). *A critical history of police reform*. Lexington, MA: Lexington Press.

Walker, S. (2006). Broken windows and fractured history: the use and misuse of history in recent police patrol analysis. In V. E. Kappeler (Ed.), *The police and society: Touchstone readings* (3rd ed.) (pp. 51–66). Prospect Heights, IL: Waveland Press.

Walker, D. B., & Richards, M. (1995). British policing. In W. G. Bailey (Ed.), *The encyclopedia of police science* (2nd ed.) (pp. 41–48). New York: Garland Press.

Whitehouse, J. (1973). Historical perspectives on the police community service function. *Journal of Police Science and Administration, 1*(1), 87–92.

Williams, H., & Murphy, P. V. (2006). The evolving strategy of police: a minority view. In V. E. Kappeler (Ed.), *Police and society: Touchstone readings* (3rd ed.) (pp. 27–50). Prospect Heights, IL: Waveland Press.

Wilson, J. (March 1969). What makes a better policeman? *Atlantic Monthly*, 129–135.

Worrall, J. L., & Zhao, J. (2003). The role of the COPS office in community policing. *Policing: An International Journal of Police Strategies & Management, 26*(1), 64–87.

Zhao, J., Lovrich, N. P., & Robinson, T. H. (2001). Community Policing: is it changing the basic functions of policing? Findings from a longitudinal study of 200+ municipal police agencies. *Journal of Criminal Justice, 29*, 365–377.

CHAPTER 3

Police Human Resources

Never fear the want of business. A man who qualifies himself well for his calling, never fails of employment.

—Thomas Jefferson

LEARNING OBJECTIVES

After reading the chapter, you should be able to:

- Describe the involvement of minorities and women in policing.
- Describe the idea of affirmative action and the Civil Rights Act of 1964.
- Describe the steps of the police selection process.
- Discuss the difference between standards and selection tests.
- List and describe the different phases of police training and career development.
- Understand the impact of race and gender on police officer careers.

KEY TERMS

- ADA
- Affirmative action
- Background or character investigation
- Basic training
- Career development
- Civil Rights Act
- Disparate impact
- Disparate treatment
- Disparate rejection
- Drug use standards
- Educational standards
- Equal Employment Opportunity (EEO)

INTRODUCTION

The recruitment, selection, training, development, and retention of police officers are of critical importance to any police department. A police department is only as good as the aggregate of its membership, and, in some cases, it is only as strong as its weakest or least professional officers. Police administrators have long recognized this fact and subsequently have directed substantial effort and resources towards developing effective personnel systems. This chapter explores the organization and development of police personnel systems. It is intended to provide an overview of current policies, procedures, and techniques used in personnel processes. This chapter describes how individuals become police officers. In this sense, it is intended to provide an understanding of the processes that police departments use to fill entry-level positions. This chapter also provides agency personnel with information regarding the effectiveness of the

- Field Training Officer (FTO) Program
- Gender bias
- Gender ideology
- Human resource management
- In-service training
- Institutional barriers
- Lateral expansion
- Medical standards
- Minimum standards
- Minority officers
- Oral interview board
- Personal barriers
- Personal preferences
- Personnel planning
- Physical agility
- Policewomen
- Polygraph
- Population comparisons
- Psychological screening
- Recruitment
- Residency requirements
- Screening-in applicants
- Selection process

various procedures used in police personnel administration. In this sense, it provides guidance to the police policymaker.

Schultz (1984) postulated that organizations could save literally millions of dollars annually through more judicious selection procedures. He argued that selection procedures should be developed that best approximate the job and predict future job performance. Insofar as selection procedures are improved, so will there be improvements in an organization's productivity. Indeed, Schultz identified the crux of the selection task: Organizations must identify and employ those who are most capable of performing the job. Nearly 40 years ago, the ramifications of selecting unqualified police officers were succinctly summarized by Wilson and McLaren (1972:245):

> Incompetent, untrained, and undisciplined policemen invariably provide unsatisfactory service; they damage the reputation of their own department and promote unfavorable public opinion throughout the country. There is no place in a modern, progressive department for stupid, inept, uncouth, lazy, dishonest, or insolvent officers; and their presence on a force is evidence of the failure of their administrative head to give careful attention to his personnel-management duty.

Essentially, police administrators must clearly articulate the goals of the organization, understand the roles and tasks to be performed, and ensure that the department's procedures select those who are capable of performing the complicated tasks required of police officers. Even the best selection procedures will be inadequate if administrators do not understand the relationship between achieving organizational goals and selecting its employees. Furthermore, it should be emphasized that incorrect hiring decisions have long-lasting effects; it is extremely difficult to remove mediocre officers from service once they are employed and covered by civil service or merit systems. In this sense, a bad decision today may still haunt the department 20 years later. Moreover, once a department makes its selection decisions, it should make every effort possible to ensure that personnel are trained and managed properly.

This chapter addresses the management of human resources. Starling (2008:442) has defined *human resource management* as "attract an effective work force to the organization, develop the work force to its potential, and maintain it over the long term." Police departments must maximize their "human capital" to successfully meet citizens' expectations—the provision of efficient and effective services. Human resource managers must ensure that employees are capable of performing in accordance with today's expectations, and they must also develop programs that will prepare them for tomorrow's changes—changes that include promotions, reassignments, and an evolving work environment.

TOWARDS A THEORY OF POLICE SELECTION

Realizing that the department should select only those who are qualified and capable, administrators should embrace a philosophy that ensures that only qualified personnel are selected. Wilson and McLaren (1972) described the underpinnings for a theory on police selection. They noted that only the best qualified should be selected and promoted, and when there is a doubt, any decision should be made in favor of the department. In essence, they proposed that any selection decision should be made only when those responsible for selecting are absolutely certain that the candidate will be an effective police officer. Gaines and Kappeler (1992) stressed that personnel systems should be designed to *screen in* applicants as opposed to *screening out* applicants. Personnel systems that screen out applicants attempt to identify those who are unqualified and remove them from consideration. Once this is accomplished, employees are selected from the remaining applicant pool. Some have observed that in this process the survivors are not necessarily the cream of the crop. They merely represent "applicants whom the agency has found no reason to reject" (Doerner & Nowell, 1999:343). Screening in applicants, on the other hand, refers to a process whereby organizational goals, values, and tasks are clearly articulated, procedures are employed that identify the best qualified applicants, and selections are made from this more restricted pool. The difference between these two philosophies is that the former selects applicants from a pool of minimally qualified applicants and the latter selects applicants from a pool of highly qualified applicants.

AFFIRMATIVE ACTION AND POLICE SELECTION

Given the importance of the police selection process and, indeed, the total police human resource system, one must consider the implications of *equal employment opportunity* (EEO) laws and court decisions as they relate to police personnel policies. Also, federal and state laws and court decisions regulate how police agencies hire and promote employees. These factors provide parameters for administrative decisions about personnel policies. In essence, police administrators must develop and adopt policies that balance the need to select the best qualified applicants with a need to not discriminate against applicants.

At this point, it should be mentioned that some people believe that quality selection procedures and affirmative action cannot coexist; for example, Lott (2000) argued that many departments have lowered their selection standards to hire larger numbers of minorities. This has reduced the quality of both minority and majority officers and led to higher crime rates. On the other hand, Felkenes (1991) found that court-ordered hiring quotas for the Los Angeles Police Department did not negatively affect the quality of the personnel hired.

- Selection standards
- Sexual harassment
- Title VII
- Vertical expansion
- Vision standards
- Written tests

While the laws of employee selection may make it more difficult to readily select employees, there is no evidence that police departments cannot fill their ranks with well-qualified individuals, although conforming to legal requirements. It means that departments must make a more concerted effort to attract larger numbers of all types of applicants. EEO requirements may help American police departments in becoming more diverse and representative of the communities they serve.

Title VII of the 1964 Civil Rights Act

Title VII of the 1964 Civil Rights Act was the first federal legislative action taken in this country to prohibit discrimination in employment. The Act defined discrimination as the act of drawing distinctions from which to make selection and other personnel decisions based on considerations of race, color, sex, national origin, or religion. Section 703a of Title VII says it is unlawful to:

1. fail, refuse to hire, discharge any individual, or otherwise discriminate against any individual with respect to his compensation, terms, conditions, or privileges of employment because of the individual's race, color, religion, sex, or national origin; or
2. limit, segregate, or classify employees or applicants for employment in any way that would deprive, or tend to deprive, any individual of employment opportunities or otherwise adversely affect his stature as an employee because of such individual's race, color, religion, sex, or national origin.

The legislation contained two conditions that affected police personnel systems. First, it prohibited discrimination against individuals falling into certain classifications (*disparate treatment*). Employers cannot discriminate against individuals because of their race, color, sex, national origin, or religion. Second, the legislation was interpreted to mean that employers could not discriminate against classes or groups of people that fell under the protection of the Act (*disparate impact*) (Gaines & Kappeler, 1992; Kappeler & del Carmen, 1989). To illustrate the differences here, police administrators have been known to discriminate against individuals, such as a police chief refusing to hire a female applicant because he believes that females should not become police officers. Most discrimination cases, however, have resulted from departments discriminating against groups or classes of people; for example, the courts have found females or minorities underrepresented in a department and subsequently have ordered that department to hire or promote additional minorities or females. When the courts have found that departments discriminated against groups or classes, the courts have generally struck down some or all of the department's hiring practices. In numerous cases, height requirements have been eliminated because they had an adverse impact on the hiring of females, and culturally biased written tests have been found to be inappropriate because they discriminated against certain minority groups. Both of these avenues to discrimination litigation have been used extensively over the years to challenge entry-level written tests, polygraph examinations, background investigations, drug testing or screening, physical agility tests, and minimum educational requirements (Figure 3.1).

Historically, Title VII was not universally applied until 1971, when the U.S. Supreme Court rendered its decision in *Griggs v. Duke Power Co.* In this case, the Court established new standards by which to judge the existence of discrimination in agencies. First, the Court found that it did not matter if discrimination was intentional or unintentional; all discrimination had to be eliminated. Prior to Griggs, employers escaped liability by claiming that they did not intend to discriminate in their selection testing. Second, the Court found that once a plaintiff established the existence of discrimination, the burden of proof fell upon the defendant agency to prove that its selection procedures were a business necessity. That is, differences in hiring rates were allowed if it could be proven that the hiring practices were related to job performance. This finding forced police and many other organizations to research and validate their selection practices. The *Griggs* decision made it much easier for applicants who were discriminated against to file a Title VII action against a police department.

The primary methods for establishing discrimination in law enforcement were *disparate rejection* rates and *population comparisons*. With regard to disparate rejection rates, the courts have examined how well females and minority

FIGURE 3.1
President Lyndon Johnson signs the Civil Rights Act on July 2, 1964, in the East Room of the White House. *Photo courtesy of AP Photo.*

applicants succeeded in passing the various selection tests and requirements. Basically, their selection rates were compared to those for majority candidates, and if the rate was not at least 80% of the majority-passing rate, then the courts generally determined that discrimination existed. For example, the court in *Vanguard Justice Society v. Hughes* (1979) found that the Baltimore Police Department's 5 ft, 7 in height requirement excluded 95% of the female population, but only 32% of the male population was excluded as a result of the standard. This standard obviously rejected females at a rate exceeding the 80% rule. Population comparisons also were used frequently, especially in jurisdictions containing large minority populations. In these cases, for example, the courts would examine the percentage of minorities in the jurisdiction *vis-à-vis* the percentage of minorities on the police department. If there were extreme differences, the courts would determine that discrimination was taking place (Box 3.1).

The results of Title VII and the subsequent court decisions were profound for police administration. Essentially, police departments had to prove that their selection procedures were job related or were of a business necessity when discrimination occurred. Police departments began to examine their selection tests and criteria in relation to officer performance and productivity. The best example of this is police selection tests. Many of these tests use questions that are police related.

Historically, a number of discrimination suits have been filed against police departments. No nationwide data are available regarding the number and

Box 3.1   Methods for Establishing Discrimination

Disparate Treatment

Disparate treatment applies to groups and is commonly referred to as the 4/5 rule. In essence, the courts have held that the selection rate for minority applicants must be at least 80% of the acceptance rate for majority candidates. If not, a *prima facie* case of discrimination is established.

Restricted Policy

Restricted policy applies to groups where the employer adopts a policy that excludes members of a minority (e.g., not hiring females for fear that they are not physically capable of performing the job).

Population Comparisons

Population comparisons apply to groups. The courts compare the percentage of minority employees with the percentage of minorities in the community or job market (e.g., when minorities constitute 5% of the department and 45% of the community).

McDonnell–Douglas Test

The McDonnell–Douglas test applies when a qualified minority applicant applies for an advertised position and is rejected. Upon the rejection, the position remains open and the employer continues to advertise the position.

Source: Developed from Dessler (1984), Gaines and Kappeler (1992).

basis for these suits, but Slonaker, Wendt, and Kemper (2001) examined all police discrimination suits filed in Ohio with the Ohio Civil Rights Commission. The most frequently cited reason for males to file suits was race; females cited gender as the reason for the claim. Other causes for suits included not being promoted, being unfairly disciplined, being terminated, being harassed, and not receiving pay and benefits. In terms of disposition, the Commission found there was no probable cause in 81% of the cases, and 15% of the cases were settled by the department and the claimant prior to a hearing.

Minorities in Policing

The first African-American police officer in the United States was employed in Washington, D.C., in 1861 (Kuykendall & Burns, 1980). In the early 1900s, African-Americans constituted about 2.7% of the nation's police officers and firefighters, and the vast majority was hired in the larger cities. By 1940, however, African-Americans accounted for less than 1% of the nation's police officers. In 2007, however, racial and ethnic minorities comprised about 25.3% of full-time sworn personnel (Reaves, 2010b). The percentage of African-American police officers approximates their percentage of the population. The distribution of minority police officers is shown in Box 3.2.

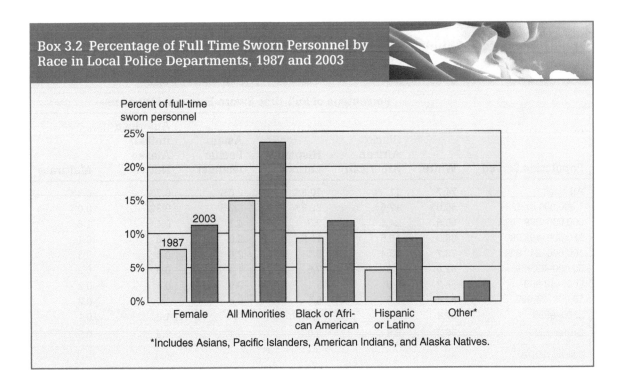

Box 3.2 Percentage of Full Time Sworn Personnel by Race in Local Police Departments, 1987 and 2003

*Includes Asians, Pacific Islanders, American Indians, and Alaska Natives.

The trends for Hispanics in the country are similar. In 1970, 4.5% of the American population was Hispanic, whereas only 2.7% of the police force was Hispanic. Today, Hispanics represent about 10.3% of the nation's police forces. It should be noted that most of these studies have surveyed large metropolitan departments that historically have had a much greater minority representation than smaller departments (Kappeler, Sluder, & Alpert, 1998). Minority representation declines drastically in cities with a population of less than 100,000 (see Table 3.1). Historically, there have been a number of reasons why minorities have not been adequately represented in the law enforcement workforce. These reasons fall into two broad categories: institutional barriers and personal preference. *Institutional barriers* refer to the formal and informal barriers police departments erect to dissuade minorities from seeking employment or continuing employment if they are hired. Such barriers include complicated applications, multiple-stage selection processes, the department's image regarding minorities, and perceived and real negative attitudes on the part of officers toward minorities. Such barriers are often very subtle, but in other cases they may be quite overt. Regardless, discrimination is discrimination.

Personal preferences refer to minorities' lack of interest in law enforcement as a career choice. Many African-American citizens consider police work an undesirable vocation. Buckley (2001) advised that a dominating antipolice attitude

Table 3.1 Race and Ethnicity of Full-time Sworn Personnel in Local Police Departments, by Size of Population Served, 2007

Population Served	White	Black/ African American	Hispanic/ Latino	Asian/ Pacific Islander	American Indian/ Alaska Native	Multirace
All sizes	74.7%	11.9%	10.3%	2.0%	0.7%	0.3%
1,000,000 or more	56.0%	17.6%	22.9%	3.2%	0.3%	0.0%
500,000–999,999	60.6	24.1	9.3	4.1	0.4	1.6
250,000–499,999	69.5	16.5	11.2	2.0	0.6	0.1
100,000–249,999	73.7	13.4	9.1	2.6	0.9	0.3
50,000–99,999	83.6	7.0	7.5	1.4	0.3	0.3
5000–49,999	88.2	5.0	5.1	0.9	0.6	0.2
10,000–24,999	87.5	5.6	5.1	0.6	1.0	0.2
2500–9999	87.9	5.1	4.4	0.6	1.8	0.1
Under 2500	88.3	5.8	3.0	0.1	2.3	0.5

Reaves (2010a)

in predominantly black neighborhoods likely impedes the recruitment of African-Americans for police service. Along these same lines, highly qualified minorities frequently are heavily recruited for better paying and more prestigious positions in government and private enterprise. Minorities often perceive that becoming a police officer will adversely affect their standing within the minority community. To address the variety of reasons why minorities are less inclined to seek careers in law enforcement, police departments must develop recruiting tools and modify working conditions to be more competitive (Figure 3.2).

Initially, African-Americans and other minorities were slowly assimilated into police work. Although some departments employed African-Americans in the late 1800s, it was not until the Civil Rights Era of the 1960s and 1970s that large numbers of minorities entered police departments across the

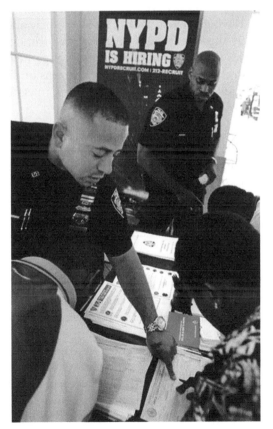

FIGURE 3.2
New York City Police Officers Ryan Jackson, top right, and Carlos Suarez, left, talk with some teenagers about becoming police officers (July 18, 2007). *Photo courtesy of AP Photo/Seth Wenig.*

nation. Even then, their entry into the workforce was not smooth. The courts forced many departments to hire minorities, and when they began their employment in the predominantly white or all-white police departments, they encountered resistance and resentment from all quarters. In some cases, their work assignments were restricted to minority neighborhoods, or they were only allowed to arrest minorities. It has taken decades for minorities to assimilate fully into police work, and even today vestiges of discrimination remain.

The integration of police departments has not been pursued only for the sake of eliminating discrimination. Indeed, other reasons for doing so include the following: (1) diversity makes a department more sensitive and effective in dealing with minority problems; (2) diversity tends to reflect a more positive image in many quarters of a community; and (3) integration ultimately results in more minority input in police policy formulation, which results in better police service to minority communities (Balzer, 1976; Walker, Spohn, & DeLone, 2004). Having a diverse police force also may affect the police culture. Weitzer (2000) suggested that a diverse police workforce may mitigate each group's attitudes and behavior toward other groups, help to socialize each group in terms of dealing and interacting with citizens of different races, and is symbolic of unity among officers of different races. Integration can lead to a more effective police department.

The primary motivation, historically, for integrating police departments was lawsuits and court orders (Sklansky, 2006). On its face, this strategy has been successful, as exemplified by the higher representation of minorities in policing; however, Sklansky questioned whether these changes have had a dramatic effect on policing and its culture. Have minorities changed law enforcement, or has law enforcement changed the minorities within the ranks? It is questionable if police departments today are any more sensitive to community cultural issues.

Women in Policing

The plight of women in American law enforcement is very similar to that of minorities. They, too, have faced extensive odds when attempting to assimilate into the ranks of police work. Although minorities have been discriminated against because of racial prejudice, barriers to women entering law enforcement have been gender ideology and gender bias. *Gender ideology* is a system of beliefs that attempts to justify differential treatment of women. In policing, for example, there has been a widespread belief that women cannot adequately perform what has always been a male-dominated vocation. In terms of *gender bias*, there have been and continue to be males in police work who have difficulty working with females. Historically, white males have been the power holders in our society, and they have been very reluctant to give up or share this power. Indeed, some police departments' culture tends to be male dominated or very machismo. Cordner and Cordner (2011) in a study of female officers in Pennsylvania found that 73% of respondents stated that the male-dominated culture in police departments was not woman friendly. This culture has a negative impact or recruiting females as well as retaining them once hired.

The first female police officer was appointed in Los Angeles in 1910. Her duties were described as "supervising and enforcing laws concerning dance halls, skating rinks, and theaters; monitoring billboard displays; locating missing persons; and maintaining a general information bureau for women seeking advice on matters within the scope of the police department" (Bell, 1982:112). Women were initially segregated within police departments and were not allowed to perform mainstream duties. Price (1996) noted that, "Women could only be promoted within their own bureaus because, as they were told by their police superiors, they had not had the full 'police experience' of being on general street patrol. It was, of course, the same male police administration that had refused over the years to assign women to general patrol and thus had blocked police women's access to the required experience." This essentially remained the practice in American policing until the 1970s, when Title VII litigation began to force departments to treat men and women more equally. Indeed, the National Center for Woman & Policing (2001) observed that court-imposed consent decrees were responsible for increases in female officers in American police departments. Zhao, Hi, and Lovrich (2006) investigated police hiring and found that departments with informal affirmative action programs hired larger numbers of female officers, especially white females.

Learn more about women in policing by visiting the Women Peace Officers Association of California website at **www.wpoaca.com**

There is no indication that females are inferior to or less effective than their male counterparts in policing (Bell, 1982; Hale & Wyland, 1993; Martin, 1990). For example, studies in Washington, D.C. (Block & Anderson, 1974), and New York (Sichel, Friedman, Quint, & Smith, 1978) found that male and female officers performed their duties similarly. David (1984) examined arrest rates for 2293 female officers in Texas and Oklahoma and found them to be almost identical to those of male officers. Grennan (1988) examined violent police confrontations and found that female officers used their firearms less frequently than male officers, had fewer instances of injuring citizens, and were no more likely to be injured. Price (1996) summarized the research by remarking that, "Almost all of the past research on women police has focused on the capabilities of women to perform police work; virtually all conclude that women, indeed, do have such ability. This capacity includes physical as well as mental and emotional fitness."

It seems the primary difference in performance for male and female officers is how they approach the job (Gilligan, 1993; Hale & Wyland, 1993; Rabe-Hemp, 2009; Worden, 1993). Gilligan suggested that male officers tend to subscribe to a "morality of justice," whereas women possess a "morality of care," and Rabe-Hemp observed that female officers do "gender" and "police work" collaboratively. Men tend to enact justice through the enforcement of rules and laws, whereas women tend to nurture, protect, and attempt to solve problems without necessarily depending on official sanctions. As such, women tend to be less physically aggressive, and males see this trait as a sign of weakness or inadequate performance. Paoline and Terrill (2004), however, examined male and female officers' use of force and found, contrary to conventional wisdom, little difference between them in terms of verbal and physical force. Given today's emphasis on community policing, the female officers' more diplomatic approach is gaining wider acceptance. Moreover, it should be noted that male officers become less aggressive as they mature on the job; thus, initial differences between males and females may be erased over time.

Women represent more than 50% of the nation's population, but in 2007, about 12% of American police officers were female (Reaves, 2010b). These figures show a substantial disparity in female representation in police departments. Like their minority counterparts, women have very little representation in smaller cities and towns (Langton, 2010). Nationally, however, women hold less than 7% of the top positions in law enforcement and less than 9% of all supervisory positions (NCWP, 1998). The plight of women of color in policing is even more alarming. Less than 4% of American police officers are women of color, and their representation in small cities and towns across the country is almost nonexistent.

Regardless of performance and modest increases in policing, female officers continue to face substantial resistance in the police workforce. Some of the resistance is in the form of sexual harassment (Hassell & Brandl, 2009), whereas other forms include avoidance, isolation, and total disregard of female officers by males. Martin (1990) and Morash and Haarr (1995) reported that some male officers harass females through displays of pornography, off-color jokes, and comments about women's sexuality. Morash and Haarr suggested that working conditions, not police work, create the greatest levels of stress. An International Association of Chiefs of Police (IACP) study of its members found that 12% of the departments they surveyed had been sued by one or more of its female officers for sexual harassment and that police departments only won 2% of these cases in court (IACP, 1998) (Box 3.3).

A number of departments have implemented programs specifically designed to attract and retain female officers; for example, in North Carolina, the Charlotte–Mecklenburg Police Department implemented a mentoring

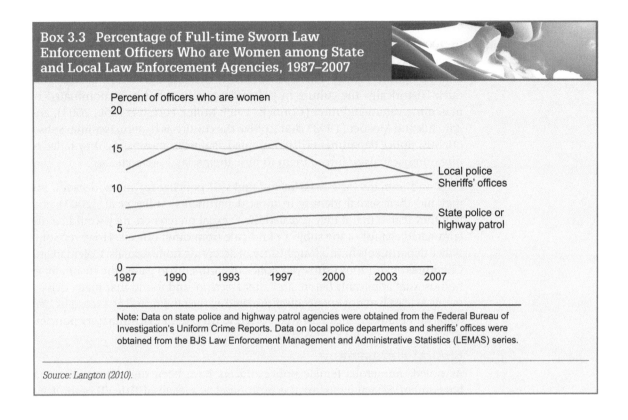

Box 3.3 Percentage of Full-time Sworn Law Enforcement Officers Who are Women among State and Local Law Enforcement Agencies, 1987–2007

Percent of officers who are women

Local police
Sheriffs' offices

State police or
highway patrol

Note: Data on state police and highway patrol agencies were obtained from the Federal Bureau of Investigation's Uniform Crime Reports. Data on local police departments and sheriffs' offices were obtained from the BJS Law Enforcement Management and Administrative Statistics (LEMAS) series.

Source: Langton (2010).

committee of women police officers that works with female recruits and officers (Maglione, 2002). Members of the committee meet with recruits to discuss problems and advise them on departmental expectations. They also discuss the important nuances of being a female officer. Essentially, the committee helps female officers understand their roles as police officers. The mentoring committee substantially cut female officer attrition rates and enabled the department to attract more female recruits.

Women have made modest strides in law enforcement employment over the past several decades. Large numbers of police departments have taken action to eliminate or reduce employment barriers and improve working conditions. This is not to say that undesirable conditions no longer exist or that female representation has reached an acceptable level (Kappeler et al., 1998). Indeed, Sklansky (2006) observed that, although minority representation in some departments approaches or exceeds the proportion of minorities in their community's population, female representation tops out at 25% for only a few departments, with most departments having less female representation.

Gay and Lesbian Police Officers

In 2003, the U.S. Supreme Court decided *Lawrence v. Texas*. The case struck down Texas' sodomy law on the grounds that such laws violate due process and the right to privacy. The case essentially decriminalized homosexual conduct. Historically, the culture in police departments has been dominated by masculine values and rules (Connell, 1995; Miller, Forest, & Jurik, 2003); and Zaitchik and Mosher (1993) characterize the culture as hypermasculine. Subsequently, police departments discriminated against homosexuals; they failed to hire homosexuals or forced them to hide their sexual preferences.

Gays and lesbians have been in the ranks of policing for many decades, but they hid their sexual identity in most departments. Miller et al. (2003) note that they feared that if they revealed their sexual preferences they would be discriminated against or the subject of ridicule from other officers. However, some police departments have a long history of accepting homosexuals. Coleman and Cheurprakobkit (2009) surveyed police departments to gauge the treatment of homosexual applicants before and after *Lawrence* and found that many departments at least had not openly discriminated against them, and as a result of *Lawrence*, and many departments were forced to drop their discriminatory policies.

Sexual Harassment

As noted, numerous female police officers have been the victims of sexual harassment. Sexual harassment is prohibited as a result of Title VII of the 1964 Civil Rights Act. *Sexual harassment* according to the Equal Employment Opportunity Commission is defined as follows:

> … unwelcome sexual advances, requests for sexual favors, and other physical or verbal conduct of a sexual nature constitutes sexual harassment when submission to or rejection of this conduct explicitly or implicitly affects an individual's employment, unreasonably interferes with an individual's work performance, or creates an intimidating, hostile or offensive work environment.

In 1986, the U.S. Supreme Court in *Meritor Savings Bank v. Vinson* clarified the issue of sexual harassment by specifying two distinct types of sexual harassment: (1) quid pro quo, and (2) hostile work environment.

Quid pro quo sexual harassment exists when there is a tangible economic detriment as a result of a refusal to succumb to sexual advances. Economic detriment can refer to any job condition or benefit, including work schedule, promotion, overtime, assignment, or other working condition. Thus, when an employer or superior insinuates that some working condition may be affected by the refusal to submit to sex or other affections, quid pro quo sexual harassment has occurred.

Hostile work environment, on the other hand, refers to situations in which unwelcome sexual conduct has the effect of "unreasonably interfering with an individual's work performance or creating an intimidating environment" (*Hall v. Gus Construction Co.*, 1988). The harassment must be "sufficiently severe or pervasive, so as to alter the conditions of the victim's employment and create an abusive working environment" (*Meritor Savings Bank v. Vinson*, 1986). Later, in *Harris v. Forklift Systems* (1993), the U.S. Supreme Court identified three factors that should be considered in determining whether a hostile work environment exists:

1. Was the conduct physically threatening or humiliating as opposed to being just offensive?
2. Did the conduct reasonably interfere with the employee's work performance?
3. Did the conduct affect the employee's psychological well-being?

Numerous court cases illustrate that behavior that some people may see as joking or playful may be offensive and hostile to another. Actions such as commenting on one's dress or appearance, allowing pornography or lewd pictures in the workplace, continued sexual or social requests, or telling sexually suggestive jokes can contribute to the creation of a hostile workplace. For example, Lonsway, Paynich, and Hall (2013) in a national sample of female officers found that 74% reported they had received unwanted sexual attention, 71.5% reported suggestive remarks made about them, and 34.5% reported officers attempting to have a romantic or sexual relationship even after the person was informed that such a relationship was unwanted. Anyone in a police organization can create a hostile work environment. Numerous departments have been sued as a result of sexual harassment, and these suits often result in substantial judgments. Departments can avoid sexual harassment by issuing policies, training officers, and ensuring that first-line supervisors properly control officers' behavior.

Recruiting Police Officers

As noted previously, the recruitment and selection of police officers are partially directed by Title VII law and court decisions. A number of other state and local statutes and requirements also impose restrictions on hiring police officers. These restrictions and qualifications determine the parameters for a department's recruitment pool and are incorporated in a department's minimum selection requirements.

Police recruitment is defined as the development of a pool of sufficiently qualified applicants from which to select officers. It should be remembered that recruitment and selection are separate and distinct processes, and the selection of officers cannot commence until an effective recruitment process has

You can learn more about policing as a career as well as see current job postings by going to: **http://discoverpolicing.org/**

been completed. If the department does not have an adequate number of qualified applicants, it will not be able to fill all its vacant positions or it must hire unqualified applicants. As an example, *The New York Times* recently reported that the Suffolk County Police Department hires only about 2% of those who take the written test (Kilgannon, 2007). Using the Suffolk County example, a department would need 5000 applicants to hire 100 officers. This hiring rate is not uncommon. Thus, recruitment is a key component in the hiring process, and police departments should expend the effort and resources necessary to ensure that adequate human resources are available for the selection process.

With the shortage of qualified police applicants, police departments are going to extraordinary lengths to find applicants. San Jose, for example, recently sent recruiters to Honolulu to recruit applicants. Honolulu, on the other hand, sent recruiters to San Diego and Portland. At the same time, Phoenix sent recruiters to Los Angeles (Waska, 2006). Recruiters from large city police departments are criss-crossing the country in an effort to attract applicants.

Police departments could learn a great deal about recruiting from industry and business. Industry and business frequently determine their personnel needs and then devise recruitment plans and programs to ensure that recruitment goals are met. *Personnel planning* entails constant monitoring of officer qualifications and a determination of what types of personnel are required by the department. For example, if the department plans to initiate a computerized crime analysis unit, then it must recruit and hire personnel with expertise in computer science or data processing. If the department is becoming more involved in white-collar crime investigations, it will need to recruit officers with expertise in business and accounting (Box 3.4).

To learn more about staffing agencies, watch the video at: **http://nij.ncjrs.gov/multimedia/video-nijconf2010-wilson.htm**

It becomes obvious that police departments must be more efficient in recruiting police applicants if they are to fully staff their agencies with qualified officers. Ridgeway et al. (2008) examined the San Diego Police Department's recruitment program to determine how it could be improved. They identified six factors affecting a department's ability to recruit officers:

1. Job seekers' propensity to join a particular department
2. Local labor market conditions
3. The opinions of community influencers toward the department
4. Recruiting resources, including the number of recruiters and the advertising budget
5. Efficiency of the department's recruiting process
6. Recruiter and resource management

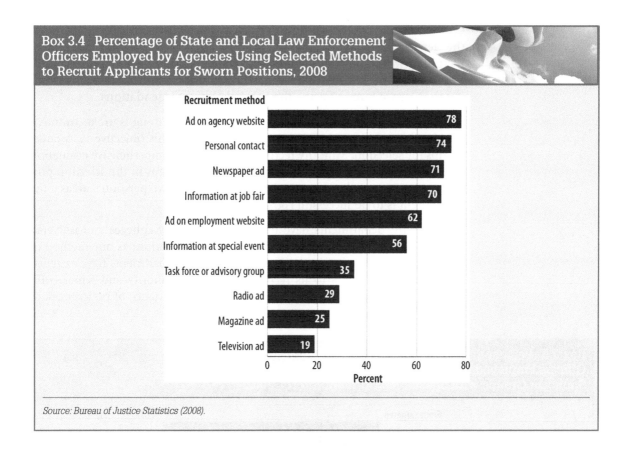

Box 3.4 Percentage of State and Local Law Enforcement Officers Employed by Agencies Using Selected Methods to Recruit Applicants for Sworn Positions, 2008

Source: Bureau of Justice Statistics (2008).

Consequently, Ridgeway and his associates recommended that recruiting materials should appeal to a broad range of potential applicants. Efforts here included brochures, a website, and using current police officers to recruit applicants. Taylor et al. (2005) found that large departments extensively used such techniques: 37% advertise statewide, 16% advertise nationally, 53% advertise at state college events, and 12% advertise nationally at college events. First, they recommended focusing on the local labor pool and selected areas as opposed to spreading the recruitment efforts over a large geographical area. Second, the department should examine its selection process. Many departments have selection processes spanning several months. If selection is expedited, fewer candidates would be lost. Along these lines, it was recommended that the selection criteria be examined, especially those tests that eliminated the largest number of candidates to determine how they contributed to selecting higher qualified candidates or

Visit the **Las Vegas Metro Police Department** to view a recruiting video: **http://www.youtube.com/watch?v=HgVxQB-2cO6E**

if other tests or criteria would serve better. Third, it was recommended that the department maintain a stable and adequate recruiting budget so that recruiting would be consistent over time. The majority of American police departments are having difficulty recruiting officers, and they should examine their procedures by using the San Diego recommendations.

One of the most important areas for recruitment planning is the recruitment of minorities and females. One way to accomplish this objective is to target groups for selection. Minority recruitment entails a comprehensive evaluation of how the department recruits applicants, and the steps in the selection process. Attention must be given to every aspect of these two personnel areas if the department is to be successful (Box 3.5).

Traditionally, departments have recruited at minority colleges and universities and other areas with high concentrations of minorities as one method of increasing minorities in the applicant pool. Many departments have assigned minorities and females to its recruitment teams. Minority and female officers can better explain the benefits, virtues, and importance of police work to

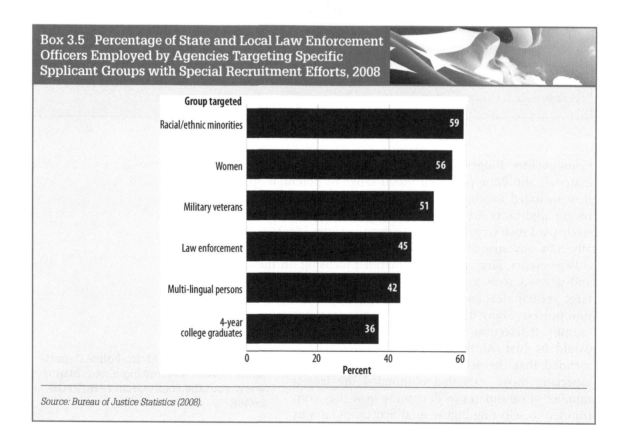

Box 3.5 Percentage of State and Local Law Enforcement Officers Employed by Agencies Targeting Specific Spplicant Groups with Special Recruitment Efforts, 2008

Group targeted

Racial/ethnic minorities — 59
Women — 56
Military veterans — 51
Law enforcement — 45
Multi-lingual persons — 42
4-year college graduates — 36

Percent

Source: Bureau of Justice Statistics (2008).

potential applicants. This is consistent with research by Whetstone, Reed, and Turner (2006), who surveyed 49 state police and highway patrol agencies and found that face-to-face recruiting efforts were more effective in securing larger numbers of applicants. In their survey of police departments, Jordon, Fridell, Faggaini, and Kubu (2009) reviewed police recruiting efforts and found that only 20% of the departments they surveyed had programs focusing on women and minorities, demonstrating that many departments need to examine their recruitment operations.

When asked for specific goals concerning the recruitment of minority candidates, most departments reported that their goal was to employ a police force that is approximately representative of the jurisdiction it serves. Today, many police departments maintain websites for recruiting police officers. These sites are designed to attract women and minorities to the police profession. Finally, most people are attracted to police work to help others (social service orientation) while obtaining good job benefits and job security (Raganella & White, 2004; White, Cooper, Saunders, & Raganella, 2010). These job attributes should be emphasized when recruiting applicants.

Establishing Minimum Selection Standards

Selection standards are rooted in court decisions and federal, state, and local laws, and reflect the department's concerns about what types of individuals can perform police work at an acceptable level. Regarding the vast majority of standards, there is very little uniformity across police departments. Some have established acceptance criteria higher or lower than the average, and these levels are, to a degree, dictated by the human resource market. If a police department's pay and benefits are substandard relative to the surrounding police agencies and industry, then in all likelihood it will have to adopt lower standards in order to fill its vacancies. The following paragraphs provide a discussion of some of the most common selection criteria used to screen applicants.

To find out about current employment opportunities in policing, visit the website **http://www.officer.com/careers**

Residency Requirements

Some departments recruit officers from around the country, but others have strict *residency requirements* limiting recruitment within the local jurisdiction or state. When a department limits its recruitment area, it effectively limits the potential pool of applicants. Residency requirements, for most jurisdictions, are a reflection of available personnel. A department that traditionally has a large number of qualified applicants can enforce residency requirements; conversely, if the number of qualified applicants is low, the department should expand its recruitment area. Politicians, especially those in small jurisdictions, frequently pressure police administrators to limit their search for officers to the local population because doing so is more likely to provide them with political allies at election time. Residency requirements are an outgrowth of the political spoils system, which gave jobs to loyal voters, but people who live outside the political jurisdiction are obviously not loyal voters. Proponents of residency requirements advocate them because they contribute to a jurisdiction's tax base although decreasing unemployment (Gonzalez, Mehay, & Duffy-Demo, 1991). Swanson, Territo, and Taylor (2007) advocated residency requirements as a method of having more police present in a jurisdiction and therefore reducing crime. Finally, residency requirements contribute to achieving racial and ethnic representation for departments. If a police department recruits strictly within the confines of its service community, the composition of the force is more likely to reflect that of the community.

Opponents of residency requirements argue that they restrict the applicant pool, thus reducing the overall quality of police selections (Dorschner, 1993). Residency requirements can affect the quality of life for police officers and their families, especially when they are required to reside in undesirable neighborhoods. Most police officers are opposed to residency requirements because of the quality-of-life issues.

Vision Standards

Most police departments have *vision standards*; however, there is a great deal of variability as to what levels of visual acuity are acceptable. Many administrators believe that 20/20 uncorrected visual acuity is the only acceptable standard (Holden, 1984). Cox, Crabtree, Joslin, and Millett (1987) observed that the adoption of strict standards is based on two rationales: (1) corrective lenses may become dislodged during the performance of critical police functions, and (2) optical blurring as a result of poor vision may hinder an officer's ability to recognize a suspect or a potential threat at greater distances. Research shows that dislodgment of corrective lenses occurs so infrequently that it should be nothing more than a minor concern. Optical blurring can occur in officers with good vision as well as in those with poorer vision, and the identification of suspects at great distances is improbable even with excellent vision.

The latitude found in police vision standards tends to illustrate that they are developed in a somewhat arbitrary fashion. Title VII does not cover vision standards; however, some state-level cases have held that the rejection of candidates because of vision requirements is discriminatory on the basis of a handicap (*Brown County v. LIRC*, 1985; Holden, 1991). Regardless, departments should be aware that adopting strict vision requirements may cause otherwise highly qualified applicants to be rejected. Departments should consider more liberal policies such as 20/80 correctable to 20/20. This policy would significantly increase the number of candidates in the applicant pool without jeopardizing officers' safety.

Educational Standards

Some police departments have adopted *educational standards* that go beyond the high school diploma, and this number continues to increase slowly. Only about 16% of local police departments have any college requirement at all, and only about 1% of departments require a 4-year college degree (see Table 3.2) (Reaves, 2010b). There is little uniformity with regard to these standards, and departments appear to have developed their standards based on the availability of qualified applicants. For example, the Tulsa Police Department requires every applicant to have a college degree; Multnomah County, Oregon, requires a 4-year degree; and the San Jose Police Department has required a minimum of 60 semester hours for employment since 1957. It is noteworthy that larger police departments are more likely to have education requirements as compared to smaller departments.

The legality of requiring college credit has now been sufficiently established in the courts. In *Davis v. Dallas* (1985), the court upheld the Dallas Police Department's entry requirement of 45 college hours. The court found that the job of police officer was complex enough to justify the educational requirement, even though the requirement adversely affected minority applicants. The court allowed the department to justify the requirement through expert testimony and opinions, as opposed to requiring the department to show a statistical relationship between performance and education.

Table 3.2   Education Requirements for New Officers in Local Police Departments by Size of Population Served, 2007

Population Served	Percentage (%) of Departments Requiring a Minimum of				
	Total with Requirement	High School Diploma	Some College[1]	2-Year College Degree	4-Year College Degree
All sizes	98	82	6	9	1
1,000,000 or more	100	62	38	0	0
500,000–999,999	100	68	16	16	0
250,000–499,999	98	65	9	17	7
100,000–249,999	99	72	16	7	4
50,000–99,999	99	68	14	14	3
25,000–49,999	99	68	15	14	1
10,000–24,999	99	83	7	9	[2]
2500–9999	98	80	5	13	1
Less than 2500	97	87	5	5	1

Note: Detail may not add to total because of rounding.
[1]*Nondegree requirements.*
[2]*Less than 0.5%.*
Reaves (2010c).

Police administrators are recognizing the importance of a college education. Johnston and Cheurprakobkit (2002) surveyed 100 police executives in Arkansas and Arizona and found that an overwhelming majority favored applicants with at least some college education. The police executives believed that a college education can improve officer attitudes, reduce citizen complaints, and result in better decision-making. About half of the departments had programs to assist or pay total educational expenses for officers. When Polk and Armstrong (2001) examined the effects of a college education on advancement in Texas police departments, they found that it reduced the amount of time before an officer is transferred to a specialized unit. College education also resulted in officers being promoted earlier in their careers. Education, it seems, assists officers in career development. Finally, Rydberg and Terrill (2010) found that college-educated officers were less likely to use force as compared to their less educated counterparts, and Mannis, Archbold, and Hassell (2008) found that college-educated officers were less likely to have allegations of police misconduct.

Physical Agility Standards

Physical fitness has long been recognized as a requirement to become a police officer. Even though the frequency of police officers' injuries in the line of duty has been declining (Brandl & Stroshine, 2012), police officers often suffer injuries. Moreover, Brandl and Stroshine examined about 5000 injuries in the Milwaukee Police Department and found that 41.7% were the result of dealing with a resisting or uncooperative subject. When officers are physically fit, they are less likely to be injured. Moreover, Lagestad (2012) points out that physical agility standards are not only important in situations that require a physical response, but they also are important from a health and psychological standpoint. *Physical agility* tests and standards are used to determine if police officers or applicants can perform the tasks associated with police work. The issue, however, is what level of physical fitness is required to be able to adequately perform police activities.

To learn more about police health go to the video: **http://nij.ncjrs.gov/multimedia/video-nijconf2012-closing-plenary.htm**

Historically, police departments gauged physical fitness through height and weight requirements. Departments required applicants to be of a minimum height (usually 5 ft, 6 in or taller) and to have a weight proportionate to their height. Such standards discriminated.

Against female and Hispanic applicants. Today, most departments have adopted some type of physical agility test as opposed to the standard height and weight requirements (Figure 3.3).

Over 80% of all police departments require a physical agility test during the selection process (Reaves, 2010b). The majority of large departments require the test, but smaller departments are less likely to use physical fitness standards at the entry level. The court in *Thomas v. City of Evanston (1985)* specified three basic requirements for a physical agility test to be acceptable. First, requirements must be based on a job analysis that determines the necessary physical

FIGURE 3.3
Today most police departments require that officers meet physical agility standards. (Photographed at the Border Patrol Academy, Artesia, New Mexico.) *Photo courtesy of AP Photo/Matt York.*

fitness for the job. Second, the test must represent the content of the job; that is, it must test what officers actually do. Third, the test must be scored to discern those who are capable of performing the job relative to those who cannot perform the job. In essence, physical agility testing must be job related.

Many departments' physical agility tests have an adverse impact on female applicants. Birzer and Craig (1996) conducted a study of a Midwestern police agency from the mid-1980s to the early 1990s to determine if female applicants would fail the physical ability test at greater rates than male applicants and whether the physical agility test actually measured critical police tasks. An examination of the validity of the test found that the test did not accurately reflect the actual physical tasks performed by police officers in the department. The inclusion of difficult agility items on the test that were not related to the actual duties of police officers more likely led to the drastic differences between male and female pass rates. The researchers found that, of a total of 841 applicants who took the test (743 males and 98 females), 93% of the males passed the test but only 28% of the female applicants did. Lonsway (2003) studied 62 police agencies and found that those with a physical agility test at the entry level had fewer female police officers as compared to departments that did not require the test.

COMPLETION RATES FOR RECRUITS IN STATE AND LOCAL ACADEMIES BY RACE AND GENDER

Perhaps the best method of physical fitness testing for entry is to adopt minimum standards that are easily met by healthy males and females (Box 3.6). Most basic academies have rigorous physical training, and generally recruits

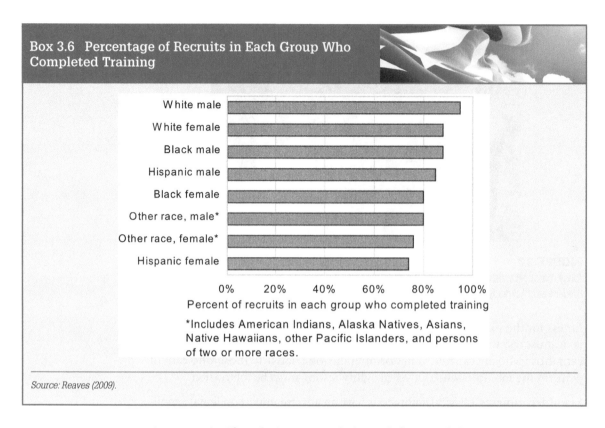

Box 3.6   Percentage of Recruits in Each Group Who Completed Training

Percent of recruits in each group who completed training

*Includes American Indians, Alaska Natives, Asians, Native Hawaiians, other Pacific Islanders, and persons of two or more races.

Source: Reaves (2009).

improve significantly in terms of physical fitness while in training (Gaines, Falkenberg, & Gambino, 1993). Stricter standards could be applied prior to graduation from the academy. Such an arrangement would give academy staff time to work with those who were not meeting the academy exit standard. This system could increase the number of female officers while maintaining high physical agility standards.

Background and Work History

Many police departments conduct extensive investigations into applicants' backgrounds. About 99% of the departments perform *background checks, criminal record checks,* and *driving record checks*. In addition, 61% of agencies perform a credit check on applicants (Reaves, 2010b). The objectives of these investigations are to uncover any criminal or undesirable behavior patterns and to determine whether applicants possess positive work attributes. Departments establish standards and then compare applicants with these standards. Standards are usually established in the following areas:

1. Driving and accident record
2. Criminal behavior

Table 3.3 Areas Tested during Polygraph Examination	
Honesty	97.3
Criminality	100.0
Sexual preference	25.0
Aggression	48.6
Racism	24.3
Loyalty	18.9
Sexism	21.6
Motivation	16.2
Phobias	10.8
Langworthy et al. (1995).	

3. Drug and alcohol usage
4. Honesty
5. Work record (attendance, productivity, etc.)
6. Interpersonal relationships with neighbors and coworkers
7. Financial management

A number of police departments use the polygraph in the selection process, but it is disallowed in some by state statute. Reaves (2010b) found that only 26% of departments use the polygraph with a higher percentage of larger departments using the screening device. The *polygraph* is frequently instrumental in uncovering information about an applicant's criminal history, drug and alcohol usage, and ethics. Because a great deal of this type of behavior occurs in a secretive manner and goes unreported to authorities, it is important that applicants are thoroughly investigated. It is quite possible, for example, that an applicant may have extensive experience in dealing drugs but has never been arrested. Police departments obviously cannot afford to hire individuals with extensive records of substance abuse, and the polygraph is the only effective tool to learn of such behaviors. Yet, less than half of local police departments use polygraph testing to screen their applicants. Furthermore, Horvath (1993) found that police administrators believed that using the polygraph resulted in: (1) more honest answers on applications, (2) higher-quality employees, and (3) fewer undesirable candidates being selected. Table 3.3 shows the areas typically tested during the polygraph examination and the percentage of departments examining each area.

The background or *character investigation*, on the other hand, consists of a process whereby officers contact the applicants' references and ascertain information about their work record, ability to get along with neighbors and others in the workplace, and lifestyle. Whereas the polygraph examination attempts to uncover negative attributes about the applicant, the background investigation attempts to determine whether the applicant possesses positive work and character attributes. The investigation of both aspects of an applicant's background is essential.

The Myth of Police Selection

Myth: Proper police selection techniques will ensure that departments do not experience police misconduct and poor performance.

Reality: Although proper selection techniques are necessary in establishing an agency free of misconduct and poor performance, they alone are insufficient to control misconduct and ensure proper performance.

Myth: The police Selection process ensure that "bad" cops are screened out of police agencies.

Reality: Because police misconduct is not only based on the fixed character of the individuals brought into policing, and because wrongful behaviors can be learned and encouraged by agencies, selection is only one step to used to reduce misconduct.

Myth: Proper police selection techniques can predict officer future behavior and predict who will and who will not be a "good" police officer.

Reality: The ability of most police selection techniques has very limited predictive validity in determining who will turn out to be a good officer.

Although all aspects of an applicant's background should be thoroughly investigated, one area requires particular attention—involvement with drugs. Drugs have become so pervasive in our society that they now pose a significant threat to the integrity of police services. Kraska and Kappeler (1988) found significant recreational drug use in a southern police agency that they studied, and, nationwide, the news media continuously report cases in which officers have either used or sold drugs. Research has shown that drug-involved officers are at a higher risk of corrupt behavior as compared to nondrug-involved officers (Lersch, 2002) Drug usage evaluation, either through drug tests or polygraph screening, is becoming more common among law enforcement agencies. Today, about 83% of local police departments use drug tests to screen their applicants (Reaves, 2010b).

This trend obviously affects police selection, and, indeed, departments must develop *drug usage standards*, especially when the polygraph is used. The polygraph generally leads to a significant number of admissions—a number that is typically so large that it sometimes becomes difficult for some agencies to hire enough drug-free officers to fill their vacant positions. Police departments that do not use the polygraph should ensure that their background investigations are extensive and that drug testing is an integral part of the probationary period. Most departments today have specified what drug-related behaviors are acceptable and which ones are not. When developing a policy, the department should consider the following areas:

1. Recency of usage
2. Patterns or frequency of usage
3. Types of drugs used
4. Involvement in sale and distribution of drugs (Box 3.7)

There is substantial variability in police drug standards for police applicants. In one study, Sharp (2003) found that 35% of the departments he surveyed outright rejected candidates who had previously smoked marijuana, although 60% of the departments reported that it was difficult to recruit enough applicants when marijuana was strictly forbidden. Many departments consider applicants who have experimented with soft drugs such as marijuana, but have strict prohibitions against long-term usage or the use of hard drugs such as cocaine, LSD, or opiates. Many departments have loosened their requirements as a result of shortages in officers and applicants.

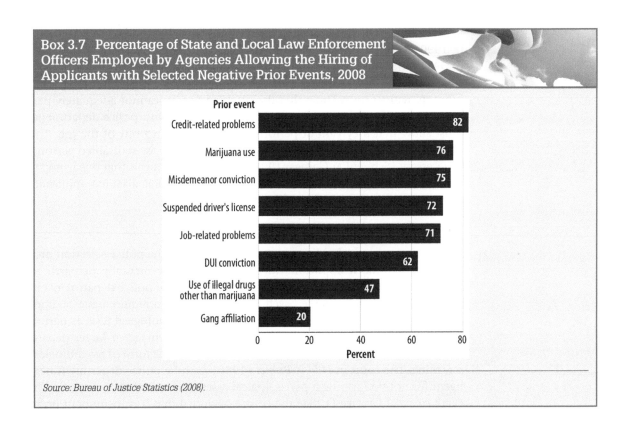

Box 3.7 Percentage of State and Local Law Enforcement Officers Employed by Agencies Allowing the Hiring of Applicants with Selected Negative Prior Events, 2008

Source: Bureau of Justice Statistics (2008).

A new avenue for police background investigations is social networks such as Facebook. Police departments increasingly are requiring applicants to give them access to personal accounts on social networks. Investigators can then review personal material and "friends" for problem behavior. Social networks can provide a wealth of information for background investigations. As an example, one investigator found a picture of an applicant smoking marijuana on his Facebook page. The applicant was disqualified.

Medical Standards

Applicants must be physically capable of performing the many tasks and responsibilities that are required of police officers; consequently, applicants are given a complete medical examination to ensure that they are healthy and can meet the demands of the job. A portion of the medical examination requires that applicants be free of diseases and other ailments that would interfere with job performance. The physical demands of law enforcement are often seen as the reason for administering medical examinations to police applicants, but these tests are most often used to help control the costs of workers' compensation and disability claims resulting from injuries on the job. About 89% of local police departments use some form of medical examination to screen their applicants (Reaves, 2010b).

In 1990, President George H.W. Bush signed the *Americans with Disabilities Act* (ADA), which protects persons with disabilities from discrimination in the workplace. The ADA requires that a police agency rejecting a disabled person for employment must show that the disabled person cannot adequately perform the job. In order to reject persons with a disability, police departments must show that they cannot perform the essential functions of the job. The department must make reasonable accommodations to assist disabled persons, if necessary (Schneid & Gaines, 1991). This does not mean that departments must hire all applicants with a disability; it means that disabled applicants must be able to proficiently perform police duties.

Psychological Screening

Psychological screening has become an integral part of the police selection process to determine if applicants to the profession are mentally prepared to assume the responsibilities of police work. Most major police departments in the United States have made psychological screening a requirement. Nationally, about 72% of local police departments use psychological tests as part of their selection process (Reaves, 2010b). A high percentage of larger departments, relative to smaller departments, tend to use some form of psychological screening. The court in *Hild v. Bruner* (1980) found a police department negligent for not performing a psychological assessment of its applicants, and in *Clark v City of Chicago* (1984) the court concluded that it is incumbent upon cities to determine the psychological fitness of potential police officers. If a department does not screen its officers, and an officer has psychological problems that later result in harm to a citizen, the department may be liable for the injuries because of negligent hiring practices (Box 3.8).

Although the ability of psychological tests to predict future behavior is very limited at best, a wide variety of psychological tests have been used to screen police applicants: the Minnesota Multiphasic Personality Inventory (MMPI), California Personality Inventory (CPI), Rorschach inkblot test, figure drawings, and sentence completion tests. Police departments use a variety of psychological screening tests. Most of these tests attempt to identify individuals who have personality problems, including emotional instability, excessive dependency, paranoid tendencies, sexual identity problems, schizophrenia, depression, and neurotic or psychotic tendencies. Other tests, such as the Inwald Personality Inventory (IPI), have been developed to identify those individuals

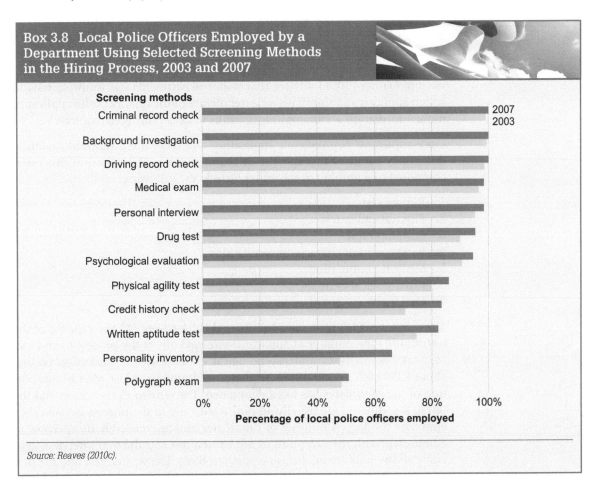

Box 3.8 Local Police Officers Employed by a Department Using Selected Screening Methods in the Hiring Process, 2003 and 2007

Screening methods

Criminal record check, Background investigation, Driving record check, Medical exam, Personal interview, Drug test, Psychological evaluation, Physical agility test, Credit history check, Written aptitude test, Personality inventory, Polygraph exam

Percentage of local police officers employed (0%, 20%, 40%, 60%, 80%, 100%)

2007
2003

Source: Reaves (2010c).

whose personalities are consistent with police work—a process of *screening in* applicants (Inwald & Shusman, 1984; Shusman, Inwald, & Kantz, 1987). When departments use the *screening out* process, they often are left with substandard candidates. Screening out does not distinguish between mediocre and outstanding candidates. Simmers, Bowers, and Ruiz (2003) examined psychological tests and found that the IPI was effective in predicting future job performance, academy success, commendations, attitude, absences, grievances, injuries, lateness, and termination demonstrating that the IPI is an effective tool when selecting police officers; the IPI was effective in screening in applicants. It is important for departments to ensure that their officers are psychologically prepared for police service so that future problems are avoided.

THE POLICE SELECTION PROCESS

Once an applicant pool has been established, police administrators attempt to select applicants who possess the qualities necessary to perform police duties at a high level. We use the word "attempt" here because selection is not a scientific proposition. The police selection process is a combined set of tests and standards that attempts to measure future behavior, which is a difficult proposition. Daniel (2001) advises that police departments use multiple tests to screen applicants so they have a clearer picture of the quality of the applicants; more information about applicants results in better hiring decisions.

Once applicants complete an application and meet the minimum qualifications, they progress through the selection process. The selection process is composed of a number of steps that include the following:

1. Written test
2. Physical agility test
3. Polygraph test
4. Background or character investigations
5. Medical examination
6. Psychological evaluation
7. Oral interview board

The order in which tests are administered is based on: (1) the expense of the test, and (2) the number of applicants screened out of the process by the test. Medical examinations and psychological evaluations are expensive, costing about $250 each per candidate, so they are administered last, after a large portion of the candidates has been eliminated. The written examination and the physical agility test are usually administered early in the process because they eliminate the largest number of candidates and are relatively inexpensive to administer. With the exception of the written test and the oral interview, generally all the tests are graded on a pass/fail basis. The written test and the oral interview are used to rank the applicants (Box 3.9).

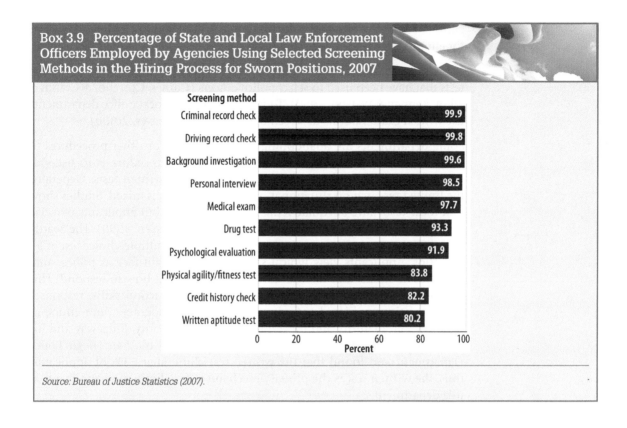

Box 3.9 Percentage of State and Local Law Enforcement Officers Employed by Agencies Using Selected Screening Methods in the Hiring Process for Sworn Positions, 2007

Source: Bureau of Justice Statistics (2007).

The Written Test

Nationally, police departments use a variety of written tests. Evidence suggests that written tests predict academy performance and future police performance (Henson, Reyns, Klahm, & Frank, 2010). Some of these tests are developed internally, specifically for the department, whereas others are purchased from a consultant or test maker and are used by numerous police agencies throughout the country. The written test is designed to measure an applicant's aptitude for police work; that is, the successful accomplishment of police work requires that each officer possess certain knowledge, skills, and abilities. For example, the Police Officer Examination marketed by Stanard & Associates evaluates candidates on arithmetic, reading comprehension, grammar, and report writing (Stanard & Associates, 2011). Job analysis shows that these dimensions are critical to the performance of police work.

Historically, police departments collectively have faced numerous Title VII lawsuits as a result of written examinations. *Written tests* generally have been used to identify qualified candidates and reduce the applicant pool to a manageable number of candidates For example, Ridgeway et al. (2008) examined selection procedures in the San Diego Police Department and found that the written test eliminated 62% of applicants; thus, the written test is the primary mechanism for eliminating applicants at this department.

Minorities tend to score lower than white candidates on a variety of written tests that have been used to select police officers (Gaines, Costello, & Crabtree, 1989; Kenney & Watson, 1990). Today, about 48% of local police departments use written examinations to screen their applicants (Reaves, 2010b).

Some departments are abandoning the written test for other procedures to avoid adverse impact and litigation. One popular procedure is to use video-based selection tests rather than multiple-choice written tests. Generally, the limited research on situational-based video testing is mixed. Studies show that these tests have adequate reliability and validity, but applicants perceive them as less fair than written tests (Truxillo & Hunthausen, 1999). The Seattle Police Department, for example, uses a video-based multiple-choice test of 54 scenarios. Applicants view typical situations they might face as police, analyze the situations, and make a quick judgment about how to respond. This testing method is designed to measure human interaction skills, responses to provocation, unbiased enforcement, situational judgment, and ethics, as well as social maturity and the ability to handle authority. Ridgeway and his associates (2008) examined selection procedures in the San Diego Police Department and found that the written test eliminated 62% of applicants; thus, the written test is the primary mechanism for eliminating applicants at this department.

The Oral Interview Board

The *oral interview board* generally occurs in one of two points in the selection process. Many departments use it as the last step in the selection process to determine the candidates' final ranking. At this point, a number of the candidates have been screened out of the process, and the remaining candidates should be of the highest quality. The level of quality is dependent on previously established standards and the rigor of any previous screening devices. The task of the oral interview board is to evaluate the remaining candidates and determine which ones the department should hire. Ideally, oral interview boards pose a series of standardized questions to applicants and rate their responses. The oral interview board usually ranks the remaining candidates, and selections are made consecutively from this list; in other cases, candidates are evaluated on a pass/fail basis. Some departments, however, administer the oral interview early in the selection procedure, after the written and physical agility tests. When it is administered early, it is used primarily to reduce the size of the applicant pool. The San Diego Police Department's oral interview eliminated 54% of the applicants who had passed the written test (Ridgeway et al., 2008).

Several oral interview board formats have emerged over the years. In some cases, the board asks each candidate a specific set of questions, and ratings are based strictly on the candidates' responses. In others, board members have complete access to each candidate's file and can inquire about that particular candidate's past or performance on other selection tests, in addition to asking any other questions that might assist in the ranking process. The latter type of board makes judgments based on the combined information from the selection process, whereas the former assumes that the remaining applicant pool consists only of the highest qualified and attempts to use questions to discern differences among the remaining applicants.

In the oral interview process, raters are provided with a set of dimensions or traits that they use to rate the candidates. Examples of such dimensions include appearance, confidence, motivation, dedication, oral communications, and judgment. Generally, the dimensions are weighted by their importance, and the scores are combined to create a composite score that determines the candidate's ranking. Selections are then made from the resulting list. Research has consistently called into question the utility, reliability, and validity of the process. Even the most carefully constructed interviews have been found to lack reliability (Doerner, 1997; Falkenberg, Gaines, & Cox, 1990). Still, about 98% of local police departments use some form of interview to assist them in making employment decisions (Reaves, 2010b).

TRAINING POLICE OFFICERS

Once qualified applicants have been selected, the department must ensure that they possess the knowledge and skills necessary to perform police work. Part of this process is accomplished in the selection process, in that testing ensures that newly appointed officers have the required personal characteristics and qualities. The remaining knowledge and skills must be learned during the training process. Training, in essence, is the imparting of specific and immediately usable skills and the provision of information that is useful for future long-term application. It is a process whereby officers are given the knowledge and skills necessary to accomplish police goals and objectives. Hennen (1996) suggested that training is the great equalizer, a force multiplier, a public relations device, and a way to avoid civil liability. Training results in the professional, efficient police force required to meet today's challenges.

States have established *minimum training standards* that are usually regulated by a state agency. The state agency ensures that all officers meet the minimum standards and that the training curriculum meets state requirements. In most states, a Peace Officer Standards and Training (POST) Commission performs this function. These standards have contributed to the highest level of police professionalism in our history.

Training is a complex endeavor; for example, on a statewide basis, the California Commission on Peace Officer Standards and Training trains more than 100,000 officers per year. Individual departments must also devote considerable resources and effort to training. Training needs and scheduling complexity confound the training process, but it must be successfully accomplished.

Police training consists of three phases: basic or academy training, field officer training, and in-service training. Basic training is designed to provide officers with a rudimentary level of competency before entering into police work; it provides officers with basic skills. Field officer training programs are designed to supplement basic training and have as their primary objectives: (1) to reinforce learning that occurred in basic training, (2) to ensure that officers are able to apply what was learned in basic training, and (3) to provide more detailed information about specific aspects of the job. Finally, in-service training attempts to keep veteran officers abreast of new or innovative procedures and techniques in law enforcement, and it is designed to provide specialized expertise to officers.

Basic or Academy Training

Basic training curricula are usually developed through some form of job analysis. The job analysis is used to specify the various tasks performed by incumbent officers and to identify the knowledge, skills, and abilities required to perform the various tasks. In some cases, training focuses on tasks; in others, the training emphasizes knowledge and skills. Generally, when instruction focuses on knowledge and skills, they are treated as building blocks for specific tasks, or they are required for developing skills for these tasks.

One particularly important part of the basic training program is the orientation. The orientation is used to incorporate employees into the department. Mathis and Jackson (2010) identified several functions of orientation: (1) to create an initial favorable impression, (2) to enhance interpersonal acceptance, and (3) to increase individual and departmental performance. In essence, this orientation process is actually a key to the socialization process, whereby rookie police officers learn not only official information but also unofficial boundaries and rules. Conti (2011) advises that this socialization process instills the department's norms and values on the trainees. He cautions, however, that this process can also imprint values that are counter to the department's values. For example, values imparted through war stories and police incidents may instill values that are counter to departmental needs and expectations. Training managers must ensure that the proper values are imparted (Figure 3.4).

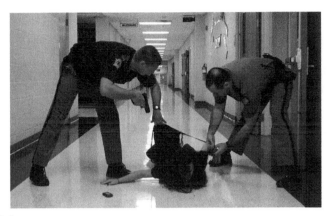

FIGURE 3.4
A Henderson County sheriff's deputy and a Kentucky state police trooper search a student or potential suspect in an "Active Shooter" training exercise held in conjunction with area police and emergency agencies. *Photo courtesy of AP Photo/The Gleaner, Mike Lawrence.*

Departments and states have adopted different training standards, all of which to some extent are based on POST standards. The national average for academy training is 613 h (Reaves, 2010b). Table 3.4 provides a breakdown of training requirements for police departments by size. Smaller states have centralized training where departments throughout the state use one centralized academy; in larger states, it is decentralized among numerous regional training centers. Larger departments generally operate their own academies rather than using a state facility.

A wide range of topics is generally addressed in the training academy. Specific topics are dictated by the job itself. The basic training curriculum shown in Table 3.5 satisfies the POST requirements for California police officers.

Essentially, basic training topics can be combined into the following areas:

1. **Introduction to the criminal justice system**—An in-depth examination of how the criminal justice system operates, covers trials, and what happens to citizens upon conviction so that officers can develop an understanding of the justice process.
2. **Law**—The study of substantive criminal law essentially ensures that officers understand the behavior that constitutes a criminal offense, and the study of procedural law develops an understanding of how police officers apply the law to citizens.
3. **Human values**—Various courses throughout a basic training curriculum attempt to "humanize" the officer so that he or she can more effectively deal with citizens and situations that call for police intervention.

Table 3.4 Training Requirements for New Officer Recruits in Local Police Departments by Size of Population Served, 2007 	Average Number of Hours Required		
Population Served	**Total**	**Academy**	**Field**
All sizes	922	613	309
1,000,000 or more	1700	1033	667
500,000–999,999	1783	1063	720
250,000–499,999	1542	906	636
100,000–249,999	1463	809	654
50,000–99,999	1341	731	610
25,000–49,999	1241	698	543
10,000–24,999	1101	666	434
2500–9999	979	634	345
Under 2500	691	538	153

Note: Average number of training hours excludes departments not requiring training.
Reaves (2010c).

4. **Patrol and investigation procedures**—The legal and technical aspects of patrol and investigation are covered. Content focuses on a number of applied topics, including how to patrol, collect evidence, interview suspects, and identify suspicious persons or situations.

5. **Police proficiency**—Trainees practice or apply police procedures in a training situation. Examples include moot court, firearms training, arrest techniques, and unarmed defense.

6. **Administration**—Trainees learn about how the department operates. Many police departments have extensive policy manuals that describe every aspect of the department's operation. Trainees must receive instruction on a department's operation if they are to be able to function effectively.

The various constituents of the process have diverse ideas about what is important in the training academy. Most of the trainees, for example, tend to value police proficiency or skills training. They usually find this training to be the most interesting, especially when they are practicing actual police procedures such as firing a pistol or shotgun, or practicing arrests on other trainees or academy staff. They see courses such as ethics, community relations, and diversity as being unimportant and not interesting. Buerger (1998) advised that an

Take a video and audio tour of the Colorado State Police Academy by visiting the website **www.state.co.us/gov_dir/cdps/academy/academy.htm**

Table 3.5 California Basic Academy Requirements 	
Subject Area	**Training Hours**
Ethics and Professionalism	8
Criminal Justice System	4
Community Relations	12
Victimology/Crisis Intervention	6
Introduction to Law	6
Crimes against Property	10
Crimes against Persons	10
General Criminal Statutes	4
Crimes against Children	6
Sex Crimes	6
Juvenile Laws	6
Controlled Substances	12
ABC Law	4
Laws of Arrest	12
Search and Seizure	12
Concepts of Evidence	8
Report Writing	40
Vehicle Operations	24
Use of Force	12
Patrol Techniques	12
Vehicle Pullovers	14
Crimes in Progress	16
Handling Disputes	12
Domestic Violence	8
Unusual Occurrences	8
Missing Persons	4
Traffic Enforcement	22
Traffic Investigation	12
Preliminary Investigations	42
Custody	4
Physical Fitness	40
Weaponless Defense	60
First Aid/CPR	21
Firearms/Chemical Agents	72
Information Systems	4
Persons with Disabilities	6
Gangs	8
Crimes against the Justice System	4
Weapon Violations	4

Continued...

Table 3.5 California Basic Academy Requirements *Continued*	
Subject Area	**Training Hours**
Hazardous Materials	4
Cultural Awareness	24
Total	603

underlying problem is that recruits come to the job with preconceived notions about police work that are usually based on news stories, novels, and movies. They view policing as crime fighting, not community service. Because trainees often consider instruction related to community service to be unimportant, they may not assimilate these ideas. In some cases, they might totally ignore the training (Conti & Nolan, 2005). This often results in conflicts with citizens and citizen complaints.

Administrators, on the other hand, view the study of administration, law, and human values as critical. Administrators typically are the individuals who are most aware of civil liability, citizen complaints, and negative media problems. They consider these areas of instruction to be the primary means of reducing problems. Finally, a number of segments within the community, especially minorities and women, see human values as being the most critical area of study. Human values training is viewed by this constituency as a means of ensuring that officers afford minorities and females greater respect and regard towards their problems when interacting with them. The key to basic police training is ensuring that officers receive adequate training across the full spectrum of topics so that they can function proficiently in all areas upon graduation.

A problem with basic academy training is instructional techniques. In a survey of police instructors, McCoy (2006) found them to be using traditional methods, such as lectures, which are not effective, especially when teaching community relations topics. Police training needs to develop trainees' skills in critical thinking, which is important to making decisions and applying police discretion. Training should be more interactive, particularly focusing on problem solving, so officers can more readily understand and accept new information, especially information that runs counter to their belief systems. One way to accomplish this objective is to use scenarios where trainees are given situations and asked to analyze and solve problems. The Idaho POST has implemented scenarios as a part of the training process and found it to contribute to learning (Werth, 2011).

Field Training Officer (FTO) Programs

The *field training officer* (FTO) program is a concept that originated in 1972 in the San Jose Police Department. Essentially, it is a program that attempts to bridge the gap between the academy and the practitioner. Within this context, police administrators implement FTO programs for a variety of reasons:

1. It serves as a vehicle for continued instruction. Some police concepts and procedures are not amenable to classroom instruction; therefore, teaching these concepts in the field is more effective.
2. The FTO program contributes to training standardization. The FTO program encourages officers in charge of basic academy programs to ensure that certain training objectives are met because their students later are evaluated on them. It also forces training officers to instruct and evaluate rookies on the same dimensions and criteria.
3. The FTO program allows managers to determine if rookie officers have assimilated information in the basic training academy. Trainers are able to observe rookies performing specific tasks and duties in the actual police setting.
4. As McCampbell (1987b) discovered in his study, 94.5% of the departments with FTO programs implemented them because of personnel problems and recognition of the need to improve training. The supervised performance of police tasks by rookies leads to a better understanding of the tasks and the police function in general. This understanding reduces problem behaviors and improves performance in a variety of situations.

Box 3.10 is a flow chart depicting the FTO program for the San Jose Police Department. Recruit training lasts 52 weeks. Phase I, the basic academy training, lasts 16 weeks. During this period, rookie officers are provided with the basic knowledge, skills, and abilities that are required to function as police officers. Phase II, which could be termed the "intensive evaluation phase," is the first part of the FTO program. This phase extends from week 17 to week 30.

Here, rookie officers are closely monitored. Training officers complete daily observation forms, and trainees are evaluated on a weekly basis. The rookies are assigned to a variety of training officers. They also work different shifts so that they can be evaluated under various police situations and on their ability to work with a variety of officers. Phase III, the final phase, is designed to evaluate how well rookies can work independently of their training officers. Here, the rookies are assigned solo beats, and they are evaluated less frequently relative to Phase II. During weeks 41–44, the rookies are reviewed by the Ten Month Review Board, which makes a determination as to whether the rookie is retained, dismissed, or required to complete remedial training. If rookies are required to complete remedial training, they are reevaluated during weeks 45–52.

Box 3.10   Flow Chart for the Field Training Officer
(FTO) Program for the San Jose Police Department

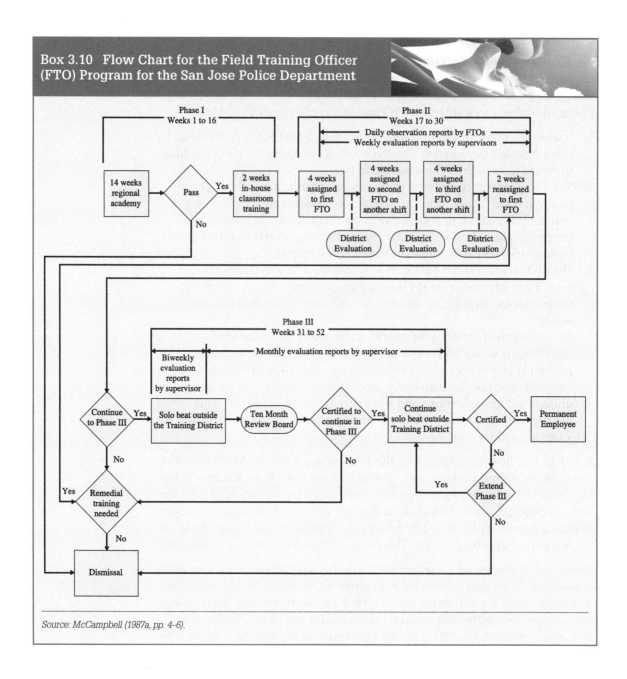

Source: McCampbell (1987a, pp. 4–6).

Although the San Jose FTO program has served as a model for other departments throughout the country, it should be noted that there is considerable variation in program structure and objectives across the country's police departments. The Largo Police Department in Florida assigns its rookie officers to units such as traffic, criminal investigation, and administration before they are assigned to patrol. The Flagstaff Police Department in Arizona similarly assigns its rookies to the criminal investigation unit during the last week of the FTO program. Both of these departments are attempting to provide rookies with a better understanding of the interworkings of the total department. Some jurisdictions vary the length of the program, whereas others vary substantially in the types and numbers of evaluations that are performed. Some departments (e.g., Newport News, Virginia) place a greater emphasis on training relative to evaluation. Regardless of program structure, FTO programs are now an integral part of police training.

FTO programs are not a panacea, and the programs themselves require extensive effort for development and evaluation if departments are to reach their program goals. Eisenberg (1981), upon studying FTO programs, identified several potential problems: (1) overemphasis on technical skills, (2) overemphasis on evaluation and not enough emphasis on training, (3) use of inexperienced or untrained field officers, (4) informally classifying rookies as being "good" or "bad" without depending on the formal evaluation system, (5) dealing with the recruits who are disliked versus those who are incompetent, and (6) developing a program with too short a time to do the job adequately.

Traditional FTO programs focus on accomplishing tasks such as pursuit driving, making felony traffic stops, writing reports, or interviewing witnesses or victims. This emphasis on skills does little to enhance the officers' cognitive abilities. The Reno Police Department has substantially modified its FTO program, and, rather than evaluating rookies' skills, they are rated on dimensions such as problem solving, conflict resolution, ethics, and cultural diversity. This system is more compatible with community policing and addresses more important dimensions (Hoover, Pitts, & Ponte, 2003) (Box 3.11).

In-service Training

In-service training refers to training that is designed to provide veteran officers with new skills or to update them on changes in the law, criminal procedures, departmental procedures, or general police procedures. Because police work is always evolving, officers, regardless of rank, must be provided with continuing education and training so that they will be better able to perform proficiently. In-service training should be given a high priority to ensure that officers maintain their knowledge and skill levels.

Police departments have experimented with a variety of methods for providing in-service training, including: (1) roll-call training, in which officers are provided short discussions on specialized topics during roll calls; (2) departmental in-service training sessions where officers are assigned to specific courses that last for one or more days; (3) courses where officers are sent to specialized

Box 3.11   A History of the San Jose Police Department Field Training and Evaluation Program

The concept of the police academy matured in the 1950s; however, the training did not adequately prepare new officers for the role of law enforcement. Many police departments throughout the United States began implementing field training programs that followed the academy. Typically, these programs consisted of "senior officers" who would guide new trainees through the initial experience of applying their academic training to the street. Although these field training programs proved to be helpful, they were popularity contests as often as they were not. If the new officer fit the image expected by the senior officer, the probability of success was high. If not, failure was certain. The senior officer was rarely instructed in the methodology of teaching and evaluation of performance, nor was any guide available to the trainer. Senior officers found themselves winging it based on their perception of what training was needed or, in some cases, what interested them.

If there was an evaluation system in place, it was standardized. Most of these systems included a numerical scale with no behavioral anchors. Officers simply relied on a slide-rule effect to decide what standards were to be met based on their personal likes and dislikes.

Finally, the phenomenon of the police culture prevented senior officers from taking action against a brother officer. It was highly unlikely that a recommendation for termination would be made. If such a recommendation were made, the likelihood that management would accept it was low.

In the late 1960s, a San Jose police officer was recommended for termination, but no system was in place to support the recommendation, and the officer was retained. He later became involved in a fatal accident and was dismissed. His lack of responsible attitude was a factor in the accident and had been noted during his training. This incident was the catalyst for the creation of a standardized and effective field training program in San Jose.

A twofold purpose exists in a program such as San Jose's. First, the program must fill a void in training that has existed for years in law enforcement. The academic knowledge and skills acquired in the academy must be applied to the street. The new officer needs to make a successful transition from classroom to real-life situations. Second, not all people who are hired into law enforcement are capable of doing the job. The field training program then becomes a vehicle that may be used to extend the selection process beyond entrance requirements. Officers have demanded that managers meet their responsibilities by hiring and placing competent police officers in their respective departments. Management now has the tools to do so.

The strength of the San Jose Field Training and Evaluation Program can be found in its standardized approach to training and evaluation. The San Jose model is based on at least two job task analyses that were conducted in San Jose and throughout California. These became the basis for the standards that were created and have become the central feature of the program. The definitions of behavioral anchors were derived from thousands of comments made by police officers in written narratives of trainee performance. Another unique characteristic of the program is that it is the first field training program that guides the trainer through the process in a foundation building manner.

The San Jose program was implemented in 1972. By 1974, it quickly caught on in the rest of the national law enforcement community. Although the evolution of the program is continuing, the basic model still exists and is effectively in place in hundreds of police departments.

Source: Keene, New Hampshire, Police Department (1998).

training academies or programs for one or more days; (4) extensive in-service training (lasting for several weeks or months) such as the Federal Bureau of Investigation's National Academy or the Southern Police Institute's Management Course; and (5) interactive learning systems featuring online courses and examinations.

There is no question that in-service training is an important component within any department's training scheme. Constant changes necessitate additional training for police officers. Police administrators should use a variety of techniques to determine specific training needs. These techniques include: (1) monitoring disciplinary reports to determine deficiencies, (2) examination of current court cases and newly enacted laws to discern changes, (3) review of police publications in an effort to identify better procedures, and (4) a discussion of current police issues and problems in staff meetings to identify problems that can be addressed through training. The police administrator must rely on a variety of techniques to ensure that all aspects of the department are reviewed and, when needs are identified, to ensure that adequate training is provided.

In some cases, training needs are specialized. As departments become larger, they tend to specialize; that is, they create specialized units such as traffic, criminal investigation, or narcotics to deal with specific problems. Officers assigned to these units should receive training when initially assigned, and they periodically should receive in-service training to update their skills. Officers assigned to selective traffic enforcement units should receive in-service training dealing with the use of radar and other speed-detection devices, traffic accident investigation, and possibly alcohol-detection and apprehension procedures for those driving under the influence. In-service training programs can address the areas of expertise required by traffic officers, and obviously the same holds true for all units within the police department.

As departments take on more of a community policing role, a significant need for in-service training develops, as departments cannot implement effective community policing without first training its officers. Florida and Illinois revamped their entire training curriculum to include more community policing, whereas many other training programs added community policing components (Chappell & Lanza-Kaduce, 2010). To enhance community policing, topics such as problem solving, ethics, communications techniques, community dynamics, and building alliances should be included in training. Finally, supervisory and management training should be mandatory parts of in-service training. Supervisors and managers frequently are not provided with training after promotion and later are not provided with appropriate in-service training. These individuals, upon each promotion, should be given training detailing their new duties and assignments, and training on how to supervise and manage employees and units within the department. Examples of supervisory and management in-service training topics include handling problem employees, allocation and distribution of personnel, counseling techniques, planning and decision-making, and criminal investigation case management.

Training is an important administrative function within any police department. Police officers not adequately trained will not be able to perform effectively. Regardless of lawsuits that are filed as a result of police departments that fail to properly train their officers, police administrators have moral and ethical obligations to the communities they serve to provide the best possible services, and this can only be accomplished when officers are properly trained.

Police Officer Career Development

Few successful efforts have been made in the area of *career development* in law enforcement. To a great extent, career development efforts have been limited by civil service, labor contracts, and other personnel restrictions that limit how employees are hired, transferred, and promoted within governmental agencies. Nonetheless, career development is an important human resource function. Police departments must prepare officers for promotion and to assume positions in specialized units such as criminal investigation and so on. Officers holding higher ranks in a police department are usually older, and consequently these positions turn over at a higher rate. A department must have younger officers who are prepared to assume these vacant positions (Box 3.12).

Lateral Expansion

One way to prepare officers for other positions in the department is *lateral expansion*. Lateral expansion occurs when officers are given a variety of job assignments in specialized units. Variety of assignment provides officers with a better understanding of the overall department. Specialized units in police departments include burglary investigation, sex crimes, selective traffic enforcement, juvenile or community relations, and so on. Patrol frequently is viewed as the basic assignment within the department. Decisions to transfer officers to a specialized unit are usually based on an examination of the officers' past work record and their education and training. For the most part, an officer's experience and specialized background determine which areas of specialization the officer is likely to pursue within the police department.

An interesting career development system has been implemented in the St. Louis County Police Department in Missouri. The department recognized that officers frequently wanted to be assigned to specialized units, especially investigative units, and implemented a length of assignment or tenure policy whereby all officers are routinely rotated through the various investigative units. Each assignment to an investigative unit has a maximum time limit; for example, an officer can be assigned to a burglary unit for a maximum of 5 years, to a drug enforcement unit for 2–1/2 years, or to a background investigation

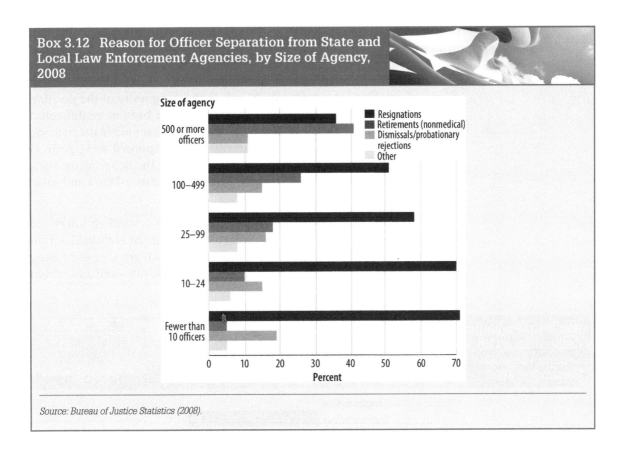

Box 3.12 Reason for Officer Separation from State and Local Law Enforcement Agencies, by Size of Agency, 2008

Source: Bureau of Justice Statistics (2008).

unit for 4 years. The majority of specialized positions are limited to a maximum tenure of 5 years. When investigators have completed their investigative assignment, they are rotated back to patrol. The department found that this policy led to an increase in morale and upgraded every officer's investigative capacity, and the department's clearance rates for serious and minor crimes exceeded the national averages (Kleinknecht & Dougherty, 1986). The program also provides an incentive to younger officers to excel as patrol officers so that they can be considered for an investigative assignment at an earlier stage in their careers.

Vertical Expansion

Vertical expansion refers to providing more opportunities for officers to advance within the department's rank structure. One example of vertical expansion is the Los Angeles Police Department's career police plan that was implemented in 1971. Essentially, the LAPD greatly expanded its rank structure by adding additional ranks at each level of rank within the department

(Lutz & Morgan, 1974). The rank of lieutenant, for example, was divided into lieutenants I and II, three grades of investigators were created, and, for the most part, all traditional ranks within the department were expanded in this manner. Once this occurred, the various positions or jobs within the department were assigned the new ranks based on the complexity of the position; for example, the job of a narcotics sergeant may have been more difficult or complex than that of a patrol sergeant, so the department made the narcotics sergeant a higher ranking sergeant (sergeant III as opposed to sergeant I). This plan allowed for more ranking positions within the department, and it allowed the department to distinguish positions in terms of rank and salary (Box 3.13).

In Missouri, the St. Louis County Police Department devised an interesting approach to vertical expansion. Basically, the department identified a number of technical and staff positions within the department that were designated as being "rank-and-assignment" positions. The rank-and-assignment

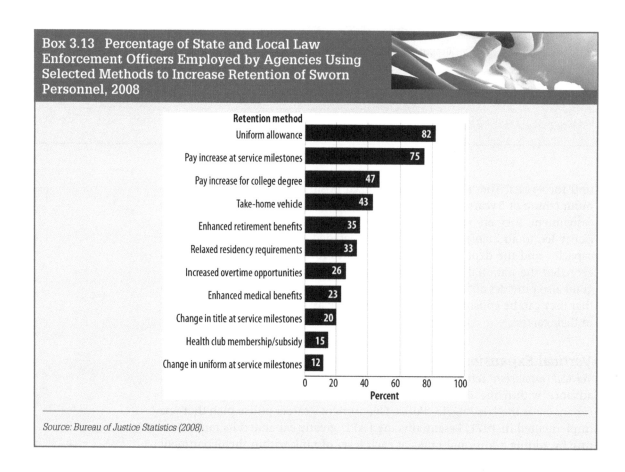

Box 3.13   Percentage of State and Local Law Enforcement Officers Employed by Agencies Using Selected Methods to Increase Retention of Sworn Personnel, 2008

Retention method

Retention method	Percent
Uniform allowance	82
Pay increase at service milestones	75
Pay increase for college degree	47
Take-home vehicle	43
Enhanced retirement benefits	35
Relaxed residency requirements	33
Increased overtime opportunities	26
Enhanced medical benefits	23
Change in title at service milestones	20
Health club membership/subsidy	15
Change in uniform at service milestones	12

Source: Bureau of Justice Statistics (2008).

positions allowed lower-level officers to be transferred to the positions based on their qualifications as opposed to their ranks; for example, a highly qualified officer of any rank might be able to occupy the position of director of training, and also draw the salary for the director's position. When an officer left the position, he or she would go back to the previous rank and salary. This scheme is similar to that used in business and industry, and it allows the organization a substantial degree of latitude in assigning personnel.

Most police departments have not adopted a system similar to St. Louis County's because of civil service rules and tradition; however, it should be noted that many departments throughout the nation have exempt rank positions where the chief is allowed to appoint staff personnel. These staff personnel can be reduced to their previous rank at any time, and be assigned to a position commensurate with the previous rank. The exempt rank positions are designed to give administrators latitude in appointing their staff. If chiefs of police are not allowed to appoint their own staff, in many cases they experience difficulty in implementing their programs.

IMPACT OF RACE AND GENDER ON POLICE OFFICER CAREERS

Although many departments have made strides in recruiting minorities and females, a problem facing many departments is minority and female representation in supervisory and management ranks in the department. Insufficient numbers of women and minorities in the upper levels of the department sends the wrong message to the community and to rank and file officers. Women and minorities have not been promoted in sufficient numbers. One problem may be that women and minorities do not have a desire to be promoted. Archbold, Hassell, and Stichman (2010) found that female officers were less interested in being promoted as compared to male officers. This is problematic, since it makes it more difficult to move female officers into management and supervisory positions. Implementing lateral and vertical job expansion can help remedy this situation. It may be advantageous for departments to establish career counseling and mentoring programs for officers to help advance their careers. It is critical for departments to have a pool of officers who are ready and capable of assuming new responsibilities in the department.

SUMMARY

This chapter examines the police human resource system in terms of how an individual enters and becomes a part of the police profession. Three critical components of this process are examined: selection, training, and career development. If a department is to successfully utilize its human resources, it must successfully develop and implement these three components of the personnel system.

During the selection process, the police department administrators attempt to identify and hire individuals who are capable of performing police duties and responsibilities. Traditionally, Title VII of the 1964 Civil Rights Act has played a key role in the design of selection systems, and the administrator should ensure that the department's composition represents all groups within the community.

During the training process, the police department provides its officers with the requisite knowledge, skills, and abilities that they need to execute the duties and responsibilities of police officers. The police administrator must develop and implement a training plan after evaluating the needs and resources of the department.

Finally, career development for police officers includes the department providing officers with career opportunities or alternatives when they have been with the department for a period of time. This aspect of human resource administration is important in maintaining morale and job satisfaction within the department. Moreover, a balance between the needs of the department and the needs of individual officers must be constantly maintained.

REVIEW QUESTIONS

1. *Title VII of the 1964 Civil Rights Act* was the first federal legislative action taken in the United States to prohibit discrimination in employment. Review the conditions that affected police personnel systems and the impact these conditions had on police hiring practices.
2. Women have faced similar tribulations in American law enforcement as minorities. What barriers have often stood in the way of women entering law enforcement?
3. Despite equal employment opportunity laws and ever changing policies, female officers continue to face substantial resistance in the police workforce. How does this resistance manifest itself?
4. What is meant by the term *police recruitment?* Review the three often-used standards for selecting potential recruits.
5. Review the police selection process. Once qualified applicants have been selected, police officer training begins. What are the three phases of police training and what does each phase entail?

REFERENCES

Archbold, C., Hassell, K., & Stichman, A. (2010). Comparing promotion aspirations among female and male police officers. *International Journal of Police Science and Management, 12*(2), 287–303.

Balzer, A. (1976). A view of the quota system in the San Francisco Police Department. *Journal of Police Science and Administration, 4*(2), 124–133.

Bell, D. J. (1982). Policewomen: myth and reality. *Journal of Police Science and Administration, 10*(1), 112–120.

Birzer, M. L., & Craig, D. E. (1996). Gender differences in police physical ability test performance. *American Journal of Police, 15*(2), 93–108.

Block, P., & Anderson, D. (1974). *Policewomen on patrol.* Washington, DC: The Police Foundation.

Brandl, S., & Stroshine, M. (2012). The physical hazards of police work revisited. *Police Quarterly, 15*, 262–282.

Brown County v. LIRC, 124 Wis. 2d 560 (1985).

Buckley, W. (2001). Wanted: policemen. *National Review, 53*, 54–57.

Buerger, M. (1998). Police training as a Pentecost: using tools singularly ill-suited to the purpose of reform. *Police Quarterly, 1*(1), 27–64.

Chappell, A., & Lanza-Kaduce, L. (2010). Understanding the lesson learned in the Paramilitary-Bureaucratic Organization. *Journal of Contemporary Ethnography, 39*, 187–214.

Chappell, A., Lanz-Kaduce, L., & Johnson, D. (2005). Police training changes and challenges. In (5th ed.) r. Dunham, & G. Alpert (Eds.), *Critical issues in policing* (pp. 71–88). Prospect Heights, IL: Waveland Press.

Clark v City of Chicago, 595 F. Supp. 482 (ND IL, 1984).

Coleman, E., & Cheurprakobkit, S. (2009). Police hiring and retention of sexual minorities in Georgia and Texas after Lawrence v. Texas. *Journal of Criminal Justice, 37*(3), 256–261.

Connell, R. (1995). *Masculinities.* Berkeley: University of California Press.

Conti, N. (2011). Weak links and warrior hearts: a framework for judging self and others in police training. *Police Practice and Research, 12*(5), 410–423.

Conti, N., & Nolan, J. (2005). Policing the platonic cave: ethics and Efficacy in police training. *Policing & Society, 15*(2), 166–186.

Cordner, G., & Cordner, A. (2011). Stuck on a Plateau? Obstacles to recruitment, selection, and retention of women police. *Police Quarterly, 14*, 207–226.

Cox, T. C., Crabtree, A., Joslin, D., & Millett, A. (1987). A theoretical examination of police entry-level uncorrected visual standards. *American Journal of Criminal Justice, 11*(2), 199–208.

Daniel, C. (2001). Is there "one best way" to select law enforcement personnel? *Review of Public Administration, 21*, 237–247.

David, J. (1984). Perspectives of policewomen in Texas and Oklahoma. *Journal of Police Science and Administration, 12*, 395–403.

Davis v. Dallas, 1986 777 F.2d 205, cert. denied, 106 S. Ct. 1972 (5th Cir. 1985).

Dessler, G. (1984). *Personnel management.* Reston, VA: Reston Publishing.

Doerner, W. G. (1997). The utility of the oral interview board in selecting police academy admissions. *Policing: An International Journal of Police Strategy & Management, 20*(4), 777–785.

Doerner, W. G., & Nowell, T. (1999). The reliability of the behavioral-personnel assessment device (B-PAD) in selecting police recruits. *Policing: An International Journal of Police Strategy & Management, 22*(3), 343–352.

Dorschner, J. (1993). The dark side of the force. In R. Dunham, & G. Alpert (Eds.), *Critical issues in policing*. Prospect Heights, IL: Waveland Press.

Eisenberg, T. (1981). July six potential hazards inherent in developing and implementing field training officer (FTO) programs. *The Police Chief*, 50–51.

Falkenberg, S., Gaines, L., & Cox, T. (1990). The oral interview board: what does it measure? *Journal of Police Science and Administration, 17*, 32–39.

Felkenes, G. (1991). Affirmative action in the Los Angeles Police Department. *Criminal Justice Research Bulletin, 6*(4), 1–9.

Gaines, L. K., & Kappeler, V. E. (1992). The police selection process: what works. In G. Cordner, & D. Hale (Eds.), *What works in policing? Operations and administration examined*. Cincinnati, OH: Anderson Publishing.

Gaines, L. K., Costello, P., & Crabtree, A. (1989). Police selection testing: balancing legal requirements and employer needs. *American Journal of Police, 8*(1), 137–152.

Gaines, L. K., Falkenberg, S., & Gambino, J. (1993). Police physical agility testing: an historical and legal analysis. *American Journal of Police, 7*(4), 47–66.

Gilligan, C. (1993). *In a different voice: Psychological theory and women's development* (6th ed.). Cambridge, MA: Harvard University Press.

Gonzalez, R. A., Mehay, S. L., & Duffy-Demo, K. (1991). Municipal residency laws: effects on police employment, compensation and productivity. *Journal of Labor Research, 12*(4), 440–452.

Grennan, S. (1988). Findings on the role of officer gender in violent encounters with citizens. *Journal of Police Science and Administration, 15*(1), 78–85.

Griggs v. Duke Power Co, 401 U.S. 424, 433 (1971).

Hale, D., & Wyland, S. M. (1993). Dragons and dinosaurs: the plight of patrol women. *Police Forum, 3*(2), 1–6.

Hall v. Gus Construction Co, 842 F.2d 1010 (8th Cir. 1988).

Harris v. Forklift Systems, 114 S.Ct. 367 (1993).

Hassell, K., & Brandl, S. (2009). An examination of the workplace experiences of police patrol officers: the role of race, sex, and sexual orientation. *Police Quarterly, 12*, 408–430.

Hennen, J. (1996). Staying prepared: nine fundamental principles for ongoing police training. *Law & Order, 44*(9), 85–87.

Henson, B., Reyns, B., Klahm, C., & Frank, J. (2010). Do good recruits make good cops? Problems predicting and measuring academy and street-level Success. *Police Quarterly, 13*, 5–26.

Hild v. Bruner, 496 F. Supp. 93 (D.N.J. 1980).

Holden, R. (1984). Vision standards for law enforcement: a descriptive study. *Journal of Police Science and Administration, 12*(2), 125–129.

Holden, R. (1991). Toonen v. Brown County: the legality of police vision standards. *American Journal of Police, 10*(1), 59–66.

Hoover, J., Pitts, S., & Ponte, D. (2003). *Reno police PTO manual*. Reno, NV: Reno Police Department.

Horvath, F. (1993). Polygraphic screening of candidates for police work in large police agencies in the United States: a survey of practices, policies, and Evaluative comments. *American Journal of Police, 12*(4), 67–87.

IACP.1998). *The future of women in policing: Mandates for action*. Fairfax, VA: International Association of Chiefs of Police.

Inwald, R., & Shusman, E. (1984). The IPI and MMPI as predictors of academy performance for police recruits. *Journal of Police Science and Administration, 12*(1), 1–11.

Johnston, C., & Cheurprakobkit, S. (2002). Educating our police: perceptions of police administrators regarding the utility of a college education, police academy training, and preferences in courses for officers. *International Journal of Police Science & Management, 4*(3), 182–197.

Jordon, W., Fridell, L., Faggaini, D., & Kubu, B. (2009). Attracting females and racial/ethnic minorities to law enforcement. *Journal of Criminal Justice, 37*(4), 333–341.

Kappeler, V. E., & del Carmen, R. V. (1989). The personnel staff exemption from the Civil Rights Act of 1964: may some criminal justice personnel be dismissed at will? *Criminal Law Bulletin, 25*(4), 340–361.

Kappeler, V. E., Sluder, R., & Alpert, G. P. (1998). *Forces of deviance: Understanding the dark side of policing* (2nd ed.). Prospect Heights, IL: Waveland Press.

Keene, New Hampshire, Police Department. (1998). *A history of the San Jose Police Department Field Training and Evaluation Program*. Keene, NH: City of Keene.

Kenney, D. J., & Watson, S. (1990). Intelligence and the selection of police recruits. *American Journal of Police, 9*(4), 39–64.

Kilgannon, C. (May 22, 2007). A race for jobs in Police Depts. on Long Island. *The New York Times* http://www.nytimes.com/2007/05/22/nyregion/22cops.html.

Kleinknecht, G. H., & Dougherty, M. (1986). A career development program that works. *The Police Chief, 8*, 66–67.

Kraska, P. B., & Kappeler, V. E. (1988). Police on-duty drug use: a theoretical and descriptive examination. *American Journal of Police, 7*(1), 1–28.

Kuykendall, J., & Burns, D. (1980). The Black police officer: an historical perspective. *Journal of Contemporary Criminal Justice, 1*(4), 103–113.

Lagestad, P. (2012). Physical skills and work performance in policing. *International Journal of Police Science and Management, 14*, 58–70.

Langton, L. (2010). *Women in law enforcement, 1987–2008*. Washington, DC: U.S. Department of Justice, Bureau of Justice Statistics.

Langworthy, R., et al. (1995). *Law enforcement recruitment, selection, and training: A survey of major police departments in the U.S.*. Highland Heights, KY: Academy of Criminal Justice Sciences, Police Section.

Lawrence v. Texas, 539 U.S. 558 (2003).

Lersch, K. (2002). All is fair in love and war. In K. Lersch (Ed.), *Policing and misconduct* (pp. 55–85). Upper Saddle River, NJ: Preentice-Hall.

Lonsway, K. A. (2003). Tearing down the wall: problems with consistency, validity, and adverse impact of physical agility testing in police selection. *Police Quarterly, 6*(3), 237–277.

Lonsway, K., Raynich, R., & Hall, J. (2013). Sexual harassment in law enforcement: incidence, impact, and Perception. *Police Quarterly, 16*, 177–210.

Lott, J. (2000). Does a helping hand put others at risk? Affirmative action, police departments, and crime. *Economic Inquiry, 38*(2), 239–277.

Lutz, C., & Morgan, J. (1974). Jobs and rank. In G. Stahl, & R. Staufenberger (Eds.), *Police personnel administration* (pp. 17–44). North Scituate, MA: Duxbury Press.

Maglione, R. (2002). Recruiting, retaining, and promoting women: the success of the Charlotte-Mecklenburg Police Department's women's network. *The Police Chief, 69*(3), 19–24.

Mannis, J., Archbold, C., & Hassell, K. (2008). Exploring the impact of police officer education level on allegations of police misconduct. *International Journal of Police Science and Management.* 10.

Martin, S. (1990). *Women on the move? A report on the status of women in policing.* Washington, DC: The Police Foundation.

Mathis, R. L., & Jackson, J. H. (2010). *Personnel: Human resource management* (13th ed.). St. Paul, MN: West Publishing.

McCampbell, M. S. (1987a). *Field training for police agencies: The state of the art.* Washington, DC: U.S. Department of Justice, Bureau of Justice Statistics.

McCampbell, M. S. (1987b). *Field training for police officers: The State of the Art.* Arlington, VA: U.S. Department of Justice, National Institute of Justice.

McCoy, M. (2006). Teaching style and the application of adult learning principles by police instructors. *Policing: An International Journal of Police Strategies & Management, 29*(1), 77–91.

Meritor Savings Bank v. Vinson, 474 U.S. 1047 (1986).

Miller, K. B., Forest, K. B., & Jurik, N. C. (2003). Diversity in blue: lesbian and gay police officers in a masculine occupation. *Men and Masculinities, 5,* 355–385.

Morash, M., & Haarr, R. (1995). Gender, workplace problems and stress in policewomen. *Justice Quarterly, 12*(1), 113–140.

NCWP.May 19, 1998). *Press release.* Beverly Hills, CA: National Center for Women & Policing.

NCWP.2001). *Equality denied: the status of women in policing.* Beverly Hills, CA: National Center for Women & Policing.

Paoline, E., & Terrill, W. (2004). Women police officers and the use of coercion. *Women & Criminal Justice, 15*(3/4), 97–119.

Polk, O., & Armstrong, D. (2001). Higher education and law enforcement career paths: is the road to success paved by degree? *Journal of Criminal Justice Education, 12*(1), 77–99.

Price, B. R. (1996). Female police officers in the United States. In M. Pagon (Ed.), *Policing in central and eastern Europe: Comparing firsthand knowledge with experience from the West.* Ljubljana, Slovenia: College of Police and Security Studies.

Rabe-Hemp, C. (2009). POLICEwomen or PoliceWOMEN: doing gender and police work. *Feminist Criminology, 4,* 114–129.

Raganella, A., & White, M. (2004). Race, gender, and motivation for becoming a police officer: implications for building a representative police department. *Journal of Criminal Justice, 32,* 501–513.

Reaves, B. A. (2009). *State and Local Law Enforcement Training Academies, 2006.* Washington, DC: Bureau of Justice Statistics.

Reaves, B. A. (2010a). *Census of State and Local Law Enforcement Agencies, 2007.* U.S. Department of Justice, Office of Justice Programs, Bureau of Justice Statistics.

Reaves, B. A. (2010b). *Local police departments, 2007.* Washington, DC: Bureau of Justice Statistics.

Reaves, B. A. (2010c). *Local police departments, 2007.* Washington, DC: U.S. Department of Justice, Bureau of Justice Statistics.

Ridgeway, G., Lim, N., Gifford, B., Koper, C., Matthies, C., Hajiamiri, S., et al. (2008). *Strategies for improving officer recruitment in the San Diego Police Department: Executive summary.* Santa Monica, CA: Rand.

Rydberg, J., & Terrill, W. (2010). The effect of higher education on police behavior. *Police Quarterly, 13,* 92–120.

Schneid, T., & Gaines, L. (1991). The Americans with Disabilities Act: implications for police administrators. *American Journal of Police, 10*(1), 47–58.

Schultz, C. (1984). Saving millions through judicious selection. *Public Personnel Management Journal, 13*(4), 409–415.

Sharp, A. (2003). Departmental divergences on marijuana use and new recruits. *Law & Order, 51*(9), 80–84.

Shusman, E., Inwald, R., & Kantz, H. (1987). A cross-validation study of police recruit performance as predicted by the IPI and MMPI. *Journal of Police Science and Administration, 15*(2), 162–169.

Sichel, J., Friedman, L. N., Quint, J. C., & Smith, M. E. (1978). *Women on patrol: A pilot study of police performance in New York City*. Washington, DC: National Institute of Law Enforcement.

Simmers, K. D., Bowers, T. G., & Ruiz, J. M. (2003). Pre-employment psychological testing of police officers: the MMPI and the IPI as predictors of performance. *International Journal of Police Science and Management, 5*(4), 277–294.

Sklansky, D. (2006). Not your father's police department: making sense of the new demographics of law enforcement. *Journal of Criminal Law & Criminology, 96*(3), 1209–1243.

Slonaker, W. M., Wendt, W. M., & Kemper, M. J. (2001). Discrimination in the ranks: an empirical study with recommendations. *Police Quarterly, 4*(3), 289–317.

Stanard & Associates. (2011). *The National Police Officer Selection Test*. Chicago, IL: Stanard & Associates. http://www.stanard.com/public-safety/police-test/the-national-police-officer-selection-test.

Starling, G. (2008). *Managing the public sector*. Belmont, CA: Wadsworth.

Swanson, C. R., Territo, L., & Taylor, R. W. (2007). *Police administration* (7th ed.). New York: Macmillan.

Taylor, B., Kubu, B., Fridell, L., Rees, C., Jordan, T., & Cheney, J. (2005). *The cop crunch: Identifying strategies for dealing with the recruiting and hiring crisis in law enforcement*. Washington, DC: Police Executive Research Forum.

Thomas v. City of Evanston, 610 F. Supp. 422 (N.D. Ill. 1985).

Truxillo, D. M., & Hunthausen, J. M. (1999). Reactions of African-American and White applicants to written and video-based police selection tests. *Journal of Social Behavior and Personality, 14*(1), 101–113.

Vanguard Justice Society v. Hughes, 471 F. Supp. 670 (D. Md. 1979).

Walker, S., Spohn, C., & DeLone, M. (2004). *The color of justice* (4th ed.). Belmont, CA: Wadsworth.

Waska, W. (2006). Police officer recruitment: a public-sector crisis. *The Police Chief, 73*(10), 45–48.

Weitzer, R. (2000). White, Black, or blue cops? Race and citizen assessments of police officers. *Journal of Criminal Justice, 28*, 313–324.

Werth, E. (2011). Scenario training in police academies: developing students' higher-level thinking skills. *Police Practice and Research, 12*(4), 325–340.

Whetstone, T., Reed, J., & Turner, P. (2006). Recruiting: a comparative study of the recruiting practices of state police agencies. *International Journal of Police Science & Management, 8*(1), 52–66.

White, D., Cooper, J., Saunders, J., & Raganella, A. (2010). Motivations for becoming a police officer: re-assessing officer attitudes and job satisfaction after six years on the street. *Journal of Criinal Justice, 38*, 520–530.

Wilson, O. W., & McLaren, R. C. (1972). *Police administration* (3rd ed.). New York: McGraw-Hill.

Worden, A. P. (1993). The attitudes of women and men in policing: testing conventional and contemporary wisdom. *Criminology, 31*(2), 203–237.

Zaitchik, D. L., & Mosher, D. L. (1993). Criminal justice implications of the macho personality constellation. *Criminal Justice and Behavior, 20*, 227–239.

Zhao, S., Hi, N., & Lovrich, N. (2006). Pursuing gender diversity in police organizations in the 1990s: a longitudinal analysis of the factors associated with the hiring of female officers. *Police*

CHAPTER 4

Organization and Management

The quality of an organization can never exceed the quality of the minds that make it up.

—Harold R. McAlindon

LEARNING OBJECTIVES

After reading the chapter, you should be able to:

- Elaborate on specific aspects of police administration.
- Describe the levels of administration and supervision.
- List and explain principles of organization and police administration.
- Understand basic organizational theory.
- Explain and describe crime analysis and COMPSTAT.
- Describe police collective bargaining.

KEY TERMS

- active supervisor
- administration
- appointment based on qualifications
- arbitration
- chain of command
- classical organizational theory
- collective bargaining
- communication
- COMPSTAT
- contingency management
- contract negotiations
- country club leaders
- crime analysis
- documentation

INTRODUCTION

Police administrators have specific duties when managing their departments. In essence, an organization is a collective that is brought together to accomplish a mission. Formal rules, division of labor, authority relationships, and limited or controlled membership distinguish organizations from other groups of people. Generally, the functions associated with administering police departments can be categorized as organization or management. Sometimes people use the terms "administration," "organization," and "management" synonymously. Each of these terms, however, has a distinctive meaning.

Organization refers to how a department is structured and shaped. By evaluating community needs, police administrators develop specialized units such as patrol, criminal investigation, traffic, or drug units. The establishment of these and other units dictates a department's structure. Determining the size and placement of these units within a police department is the act of organizing.

- employee benefits
- equity theory
- expectancy theory
- fact finding
- general orders
- hierarchy
- hierarchy of needs
- impasse resolution
- impoverished leaders
- innovative supervisor

The police administrator must organize the department in the way that most efficiently balances competing community needs and interests. For example, if a community is fairly small and is not experiencing a significant drug problem, it would be a waste of personnel to create a drug unit. As a department grows in size, organization becomes more important, because additional specialized units are added to the department. Organization is not critical in a small department consisting of five officers, but it is important to the New York City Police Department, which has almost 40,000 officers. Police executives in large departments must take great care in the manner in which they structure their departments.

Management is the processes that occur within the structure. Police administrators and supervisors must constantly make decisions, plan for activities, motivate subordinates, communicate information to various units and personnel within the department, and provide the department with leadership. All of these activities are managerial activities. How administrators and supervisors perform these activities establishes the managerial patterns for the department. Management style or technique should match the department's needs.

To learn more about management and watch a video, go to: **http://education-portal.com/academy/lesson/henri-fayols-management-principles-managing-departmental-task-organization.html**

The combination of organization and management embodies *administration*; that is, administrators are routinely involved in both organization and management decisions. They must decide whether the department's structure contributes to the effectiveness of the department, allowing it to meet the challenges put forth by the community, or, if not, how to restructure the department. Administrators must also decide the best ways to motivate, communicate with, and lead their subordinates. Organization and management are constant, interdependent considerations for the effective police administrator.

THE SPECIFICS OF POLICE ADMINISTRATION: POSDCORB

An early student of administration, Gulick (1937), postulated that administration consisted of seven activities. These activities form the acronym *POSDCORB* and are described below:

1. **Planning**—Development of a broad outline of what needs to be done and how the organization will accomplish the recognized purposes or objectives
2. **Organizing**—Establishment of a formal structure of units and people through which work is coordinated and accomplished

3. **Staffing**—The personnel function, including the recruitment, selection, training, and placement of people within the organization
4. **Directing**—The continuous process of making decisions; developing policies, procedures, and rules of conduct; and generally leading the organization toward the accomplishment of its designated mission
5. **Coordinating**—An organization creates an increasing number of specialized units as the organization becomes larger, and it is important that units work together toward common objectives
6. **Reporting**—The process of ensuring that everyone in the organization is aware of all other activities, generally accomplished through communications and record keeping
7. **Budgeting**—The task of fiscal planning for the organization to ensure that resources are available to implement programs necessary for the fulfillment of the organization's mission

These seven functions, broadly speaking, comprise police administration and outline how police administrators structure and manage their police departments. All seven functions must be constantly considered and effectively implemented; if any function is neglected, the organization will certainly suffer or become less efficient. Within this context, organizations consist of numerous parts and activities that must work together to achieve a predetermined mission, and this objective is accomplished through administration.

LEVELS OF ADMINISTRATION AND SUPERVISION

Administration occurs throughout the police department. Box 4.1 depicts the administrative structure that generally occurs in police agencies. At the top of the organizational structure are the administrators. These administrators have the broad-based responsibility of deciding upon the department's mission, devising programs by which to achieve goals, procuring fiscal and other resources from government, and generally ensuring that the department meets the needs of the community. Administration within a police department generally includes the chief, assistant chiefs, and majors.

Middle managers are the second tier of administrators within the police department. Middle managers generally have the rank of captain or lieutenant in larger departments and possibly sergeant in smaller agencies. They have the responsibility of commanding or administering specific units; for example, a captain in charge of a patrol shift or a lieutenant commanding a family violence unit would be considered a middle manager. The middle managers formulate strategies to accomplish objectives assigned to their units by the department's administrators, and they manage and control their units to ensure that the objectives are met (Figures 4.1–4.3).

- leadership
- management
- management prerogatives
- managerial grid
- mediation
- motivation
- operational planning
- organization
- organizational authority
- organizational documentation
- organizing
- participatory management
- policies
- policy planning
- POSDCORB
- procedural guidelines
- procedures
- quid pro quo
- specialization
- strategic planning
- supportive supervisor
- team leaders
- traditional police administration
- traditional supervisor
- vertical staff meetings

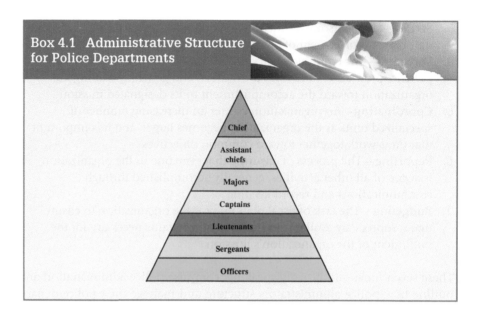

Box 4.1 Administrative Structure for Police Departments

Chief

Assistant chiefs

Majors

Captains

Lieutenants

Sergeants

Officers

Sergeants are the first-line supervisors in a police agency. They also are administrators from the perspective that they are responsible for managing officers and ensuring that work is completed correctly and timely. Sergeants generally are assigned to most units in a police department and have responsibilities such as supervising a squad of patrol officers or supervising subunits within larger specialized units (e.g., forgery unit within the criminal investigation unit).

FIGURE 4.1
Police officers in formation for parade march. *Copyright Shutterstock/Debbie Oetgen.*

FIGURE 4.2

Max Weber (1864–1920) was the first person to outline the principles of organization (c. 1894). *Photo courtesy of Wikipedia.*

FIGURE 4.3

Newly appointed Houston Police Chief Charles A. McClelland, Jr, smiles as Houston Mayor Annise Parker affixes the chief's badge to his uniform during a swearing-in ceremony in Houston in April 2010. *Photo courtesy of AP Photo/Houston Police Department.*

Another way to understand police administration is to examine the nature of its relative positions. Box 4.2 shows a typical police administrative structure in terms of the types of responsibilities assigned to officers at the various levels. Sergeants are more personnel and task oriented, whereas police administrators are more mission and goal oriented. Here, sergeants have the responsibility of directly supervising officers and specific tasks; for example, a sergeant might be given the responsibility to supervise five detectives assigned to a sex crimes unit. The sergeant would monitor the quality of investigations, assign cases, and ensure that all cases were adequately investigated.

In the past, sergeants and, to a large extent, middle managers were seen as conduits through which orders and communications flowed to officers. They were also seen as individuals who controlled subordinates and meted out discipline when officers failed to perform adequately. The contemporary police supervisor and middle manager, however, must possess significant human relations and organizational skills. Superiors at the lower levels of the police organization must not only supervise officers and tactics but also involve themselves with the community (Peak, Gaines, & Glensor, 2010). The strategic activities of top managers today are delegated to lower-level managers. These managers must in turn manage the police and citizen activities in their geographical area.

Interestingly, supervisors develop styles as they deal with subordinates and their responsibilities. Engel (2001) identified four distinct styles of supervision. *Traditional supervisors* encourage officers to produce large numbers of tickets and arrests. They see bean counting as good police work, although large numbers of tickets or arrests are not always good police work, unless the effort

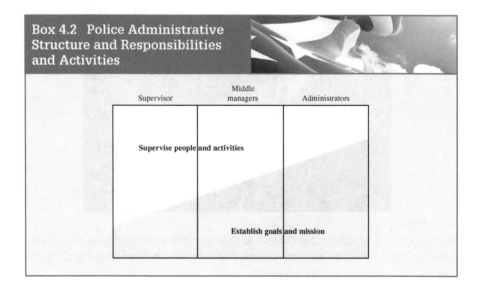

Box 4.2 Police Administrative Structure and Responsibilities and Activities

Supervisor   Middle managers   Administrators

Supervise people and activities

Establish goals and mission

is directed at solving a problem. *Innovative supervisors* mentor their officers, encouraging them to get to know citizens and focus on police and community problems. Innovative supervisors are best suited for community policing. *Supportive supervisors* attempt to develop positive relations with their subordinates and be "one of the boys." Supportive supervisors sometimes have difficulty disciplining officers or keeping them directed toward goals and objectives. Finally, *active supervisors* like to involve themselves in police work by answering calls, writing tickets, and making arrests. Their desire to do police work often overshadows their need to direct and supervise their subordinates. Middle managers must monitor their subordinates, sometimes rein them in, and ensure that they focus on priorities and that unit responsibilities are adequately addressed.

PRINCIPLES OF ORGANIZATION AND POLICE ADMINISTRATION

Modern police administration has its roots in the London Metropolitan Police Force. Robert Peel created a police force organized along military lines when he established the force in London in 1829. At the time, the military was the best example of how to administer large organizations. This quasi-military orientation was later adopted in the United States, and elements of this initial effort remain a central part of police administration for many police departments today.

To learn more about the issues that face today's police chiefs, visit the website of *The Police Chief* journal at **www.policechiefmagazine.org**

The tenets of the military organization are found in classical organization theory. Although numerous newer organizational variations such as community policing, decentralization, participative management, quality circles, and Total Quality Management have been discussed and attempted in policing, classical organization or bureaucracy remains the foundation from which these innovations are attempted (Gaines & Swanson, 1999).

Classical Organizational Principles

German sociologist Max Weber, the founder of modern sociology, was the first person to outline the principles of organization. Weber studied the church and army in an effort to understand why complex organizations were effective. As a result of his study, Weber identified six principles that have become the foundation of *classical organizational theory* and are used in police departments today:

1. The organization follows the principle of hierarchy; each lower office is under the control and supervision of a higher one.
2. Specialization or division of labor exists whereby individuals are assigned a limited number of job tasks and responsibilities.

3. Official policies and procedures guide the activities of the organization.
4. Administrative acts, decisions, and rules are recorded in writing.
5. Authority within the organization is associated with one's position.
6. Candidates are appointed on the basis of their qualifications, and training is a necessary part of the selection process.

Myths of Classical Organizational Theory and Policing

Myth: Classical organization and the paramilitary model are the best means for organizing the police because of the similarity between the police and the military.
Reality: The role and the functions of the police are very different than those of the military.
Myth: Classical organizational theory provides the best system for police accountability.
Reality: Classical organization principles may actually cause officers to become resentful of their agency because of the high level of control and because officers often see this form of organization as demeaning.

Myth: Classical organizational theory and the paramilitary model is the best was to organize the police because of the nature of police work.
Reality: Policing is a highly complex job that often requires high levels of discretion and good judgment. Classical organizational theory and the paramilitary model are designed to reduce discretion and are best suited for work that does not require a lot of judgment on the part of workers.

Hierarchy

The first of Weber's principles is hierarchy. Within the police organization this principle is the same as a *chain of command*, which means that officers of a higher rank have more authority than subordinates or officers working under them. Box 4.3 is the organizational chart for the Patrol Division for the Macon, Georgia Police Department. Notice that the city is divided into four precincts, and each precinct is commanded by a captain and staffed with a lieutenant, six sergeants, and about 30 privates or patrol officers. The captains report to a major. In Macon, like in other departments, sergeants have more authority than patrol officers but less authority than lieutenants or captains. Sergeants report to their lieutenant, who gives orders that lead to the accomplishment of the department's goals and objectives. Sergeants carry out these orders by providing subordinate officers direction. Lieutenants receive their direction from captains and majors. Hierarchy ensures that everyone in the department reports to a superior officer, and all officers know their responsibilities through the issuance of orders and directives. In essence, hierarchy is the lifeblood of an organization because hierarchy is the primary mechanism for controlling and coordinating everything in the organization. King (2004) observed that hierarchy distributes power among

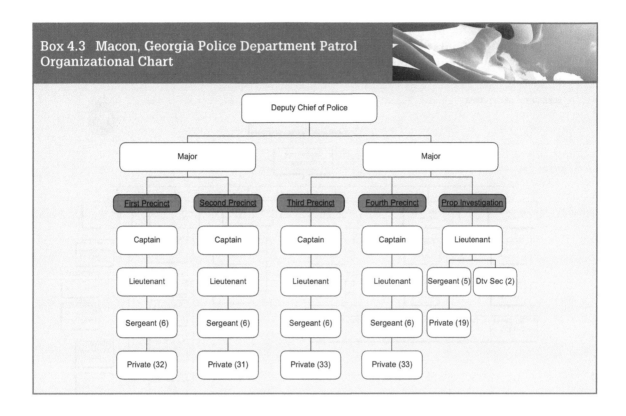

Box 4.3 Macon, Georgia Police Department Patrol Organizational Chart

the various levels and the people occupying those positions. This is necessary for work to be accomplished.

Hierarchy exists in all organizations, and, generally, hierarchy increases as the number of employees increases (Gaines & Worrall, 2011). Problems with hierarchy occur when a department creates too much or unnecessary rank. As the amount of rank increases within a department, fewer people are available to actually perform police tasks, and supervision is much closer. When supervision becomes too close or individualized, subordinates' creativity, initiative, and morale are stifled. The department becomes more bureaucratic. Police administrators should ensure that the chain of command adequately addresses the needs of the department but at the same time does not become burdensome.

Specialization

As police departments become larger, they must specialize. *Specialization,* sometimes referred to as the division of labor, is used to divide work among employees so that it can be performed more efficiently and effectively. Larger departments have larger numbers of specialists and specialized units. Box 4.4

Box 4.4   Organizational Chart for the Chicago Police Department's Bureau of Detectives

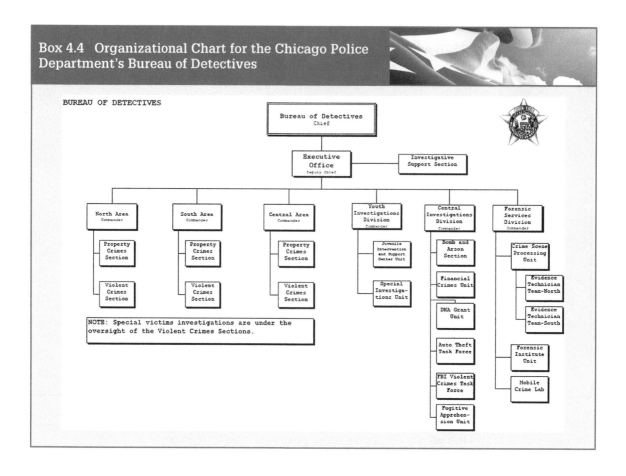

BUREAU OF DETECTIVES

Bureau of Detectives
Chief

Executive Office
Deputy Chief

Investigative Support Section

North Area
Commander

South Area
Commander

Central Area
Commander

Youth Investigations Division
Commander

Central Investigations Division
Commander

Forensic Services Division
Commander

Property Crimes Section

Property Crimes Section

Property Crimes Section

Juvenile Intervention and Support Center Unit

Bomb and Arson Section

Crime Scene Processing Unit

Violent Crimes Section

Violent Crimes Section

Violent Crimes Section

Special Investigations Unit

Financial Crimes Unit

Evidence Technician Team-North

DNA Grant Unit

Evidence Technician Team-South

NOTE: Special victims investigations are under the oversight of the Violent Crimes Sections.

Auto Theft Task Force

Forensic Institute Unit

FBI Violent Crimes Task Force

Mobile Crime Lab

Fugitive Apprehension Unit

shows how the criminal investigation Bureau of Detectives is organized in the Chicago Police Department. There are five major units. The North Area, South Area, and Central Area investigate property and violent crimes in a section of the city. The Youth Investigations Division investigates and intervenes in youth-related crimes and problems. The Forensic Services Division handles the collection and analysis of physical evidence. The Central Investigations Division investigates bombs and arson and financial crimes as well as having task forces that investigate auto theft and violent crime and apprehend fugitives. The Chicago Police Department's Bureau of Detectives is rather large, and as such, it has a number of specialized units. This specialization allows detectives to gain expertise while concentrating on a limited number of types of crimes. Specialization brings efficiency and effectiveness to investigations.

As noted, larger departments have more specialization than smaller departments. Table 4.1 provides a listing of some of the specialized units for larger police departments and compares 1990 and 2000. Notice that the percentages

Table 4.1 Special Units Operated by Police Departments Serving Cities with a Population of 250,000 or More				
	Percent (%) of Agencies with			
Full-time Special Unit			Full-time Special Unit or Part-time Personnel	
Type of Special Unit	1990	2000	1990	2000
Victim assistance	32	47	45	71
Crime prevention	95	76	100	87
Repeat offenders	68	34	77	57
Prosecutor relations	66	31	76	58
Domestic violence	50	81	61	97
Child abuse	87	77	95	92
Missing children	89	66	95	95
Juvenile crime	81	68	94	84
Gangs	69	84	89	98
Drug education	90	73	98	95
Drunk drivers	56	40	76	81
Bias-related crimes	34	26	58	71

Reaves and Hickman (2002).

have changed over time. In the 10-year period, a number of departments added domestic violence and gang units, but most other types of units declined in number. This demonstrates that police departments are constantly changing their priorities and organizational structure to meet changing demands and needs. As Crank (2003) suggested, police departments are a part of the environment; in their attempt to remain coupled with the environment, they must change to maintain a balance between departmental operations and community needs and desires.

There is no simple formula for determining the optimal number of specialized units or specialists within a particular department. Specialization decisions are generally based on two criteria. First, the police executive must determine the need by examining the amounts and types of work performed by the department; for example, an urban department with a high crime rate would definitely require proportionately more detectives than a suburban department that experiences a low crime rate but has a high rate of calls for services. With all other factors equal, the suburban department would be better served by having a larger contingency of patrol officers. Second, the quality of the department's personnel is a factor. Better trained, better educated officers are able to accept greater responsibilities, thereby reducing the need for specialization.

Oftentimes, departments must continually examine and adjust the levels of specialization to ensure that a proper balance is maintained.

Patrol units are also specialized, but specialization of patrol is based on time (shifts) and geography (beats and divisions or sectors). Police departments deploy officers across a 24-h period by assigning them to shifts. Each shift has a commander and supervisors who ensure that officers properly conduct police business. The commander is responsible for all personnel and activities that occur during his or her shift. Larger departments will divide the city into patrol divisions or sectors that operate as mini-police departments. Each division will have a commander, usually a captain. Each division will have shifts, with the shift commanders reporting to the division commander. Box 4.5 shows the North Central patrol division for the Dallas Police Department. The division has a number of patrol beats with officers assigned to each beat.

Procedural Guidelines
Basically, Weber believed that policies, rules, and procedures were an important part of administration. Without rules, there would be chaos in most

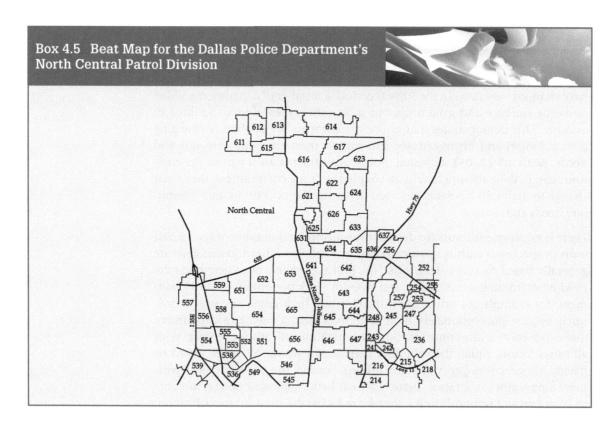

Box 4.5 Beat Map for the Dallas Police Department's North Central Patrol Division

organizations, because people would not clearly understand their duties, their relationships with other workers and units within the organization, or how they are supposed to perform when interacting with the public. To this end, most police departments have developed a system of written rules that include *policies*, which describe the department's position relative to some problem or area of concern; *procedures*, which describe how officers are to perform some function such as documenting the storage of physical evidence; and *rules* or *general orders*, which explicitly describe what an officer can or cannot do, such as the types of weapons the department will allow an officer to carry while on duty. Police departments often have extensive policy manuals covering almost every aspect of the job.

Police executives are pressured to limit discretion through procedural guidelines. Examples of such pressures include vicarious liability, public outcry, officer abuse of discretion, and political expectations for sound rules and regulations. Indeed, examples of improper behavior on the part of the police abound (Kappeler, 2006a, 2006b; Kappeler, Sluder, & Alpert, 1998; Kappeler & Van Hoose, 1995). As departments attempt to professionalize and adhere to national and state accreditation guidelines, they must do so through the implementation of policies, procedures, and rules. Rules are necessary to provide guidance on departmental goals, procedures, and officer productivity expectations. Alpert and Smith (1994) noted that, although rules can become bureaucratic, they are necessary. The police administrator, when deciding on the degree of discretion given to officers, may want to ensure that critical or high-liability areas have sufficient rules in place, whereas areas that are less crucial may require fewer rules. Further, as departments professionalize and the quality of their officers improves, the need to implement policies is reduced.

Organizational Documentation

The need to document decisions and activities is akin to the need for rules and regulations. *Documentation*, or ensuring that all or most communications are in writing, serves to inform others about what has previously occurred within the department and to hold people accountable. Police officers write reports and essentially document most everything they do, e.g., they write reports at the scenes of crimes, which often are used in court to document what occurred. In the past, everything was committed to paper. Today, many departments use e-mails and maintain a number of their reports electronically. Excessive dependence on the documentation of activities is generally indicative of extreme bureaucratization; that is, people within the department are overly dependent upon rules and regulations and are reluctant to exercise judgment and discretion. Furthermore, they are more interested in placing blame than resolving problems. Regardless, documentation is important. It allows incumbents to determine what has happened in the past, and it facilitates the collection of information that can be used in future planning and decision making; however, like policies and rules, documentation can quickly become counterproductive. Today, many police departments depend on e-mails to communicate and document activities. They are retained electronically in servers, and, in some cases, officers retain paper copies to submit with cases.

Organizational Authority

Weber observed that an individual's authority is derived from his or her position or assignment within the organization, rather than from his or her personality, standing in the community, or some other source. That is, a person's position within the chain of command dictates the amount of authority that person has. Weber believed this was critical in maintaining the organization's chain of command and controlling and directing the organization. When an individual possesses more authority than is signified by his or her position, conflict and organizational ineffectiveness generally result. An officer's authority to a large degree comes from policies, as policies often outline each unit's responsibilities.

Appointment Based on Qualifications

Here, Weber believed that only qualified persons should be selected and that the organization had an inherent obligation to train its employees. Positions within the police organization should be competitively filled, with selection being based on applicants' qualifications. To this end, police departments have developed comprehensive selection and promotion procedures, as discussed in Chapter 3. These procedures often involve a variety of requirements, tests, and practical applications.

All officers and civilian personnel should receive adequate training, regardless of rank or assignment. This requirement includes officers who are transferred from one type of job to another within the department.

Weber's organizational principles are the primary guidelines used by American law enforcement. They are appealing because they are prescriptive in nature and indicate exactly how the police administrator should organize and manage the police department and, to a large extent, they work (Gaines & Swanson, 1999). Even so, police administrators must be careful to not make the department overly bureaucratic, where administrators focus more on rules and formality than on facilitating work at the officer level. This has been a problem in the past (Moore & Stephens, 1991). Today, many police departments use community policing where officers are expected to solve neighborhood problems and work with people. Police officers need latitude or discretion to do this properly. Therefore Weber's principles when applied should build this into the organizational structure. Communication, coordination, and shared decision making should be ingrained in the department's structure.

Police Management

The previous sections examined police organization. The following sections examine police management. Proper management techniques are important since they allow the administrator to facilitate work—they are essential to properly serve the needs of the community.

Police Leadership

Leadership is the process of directing and influencing officers and units to achieve goals (Hitt, Miller, & Colella, 2006). Leadership serves as an interface between the organization and its officers. In order for leaders to influence subordinates, there must be a positive relationship between them. There must be mutual respect and understanding. Coinciding with this relationship is the leader's understanding of the department's goals—specifically, what must be accomplished. All ranking officers from the chief down to sergeants have a leadership role. However, there are some differences. Box 4.6 shows these differences for focal points.

Administrators, including chiefs, assistant chiefs, and majors, identify a vision or direction for the department. They must match departmental activities with community expectations. This necessitates that they sometimes shift the department's focus or direction. When they identify a problem or need, they establish new priorities and goals for units and their commanders. Commanders receive these goals and must translate them into programs and tactics. For example, if the chief advises the patrol commander of a robbery and felony assault problem in an area, the patrol commander examines his or her resources and devises a program or set of tactics to deal with the problem. Patrol sergeants are then given specific directions in terms of what they and their officers are to do, with the supervisors ensuring that officers comply with

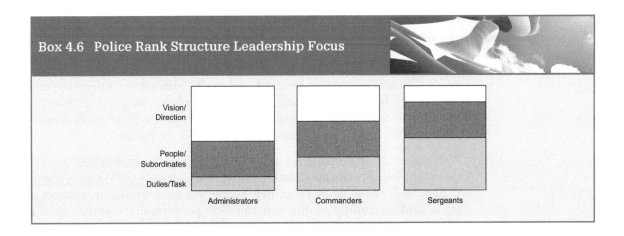

Box 4.6 Police Rank Structure Leadership Focus

the plan. If leadership breaks down at any point in this chain of events, the department may not successfully deal with the robbery and assault problems.

Previously in this chapter, Engel's (2001) types of supervisors were examined. Her research demonstrates that there is variability in how people approach leadership. The same is true for officers at the command and administrative levels. There have been numerous theories about what makes a good leader. The most accepted is the *Managerial Grid* developed by Blake and Mouton (1964). They stated that good leadership can be measured on two dimensions, concern for subordinates and concern for organizational objectives. Some leaders are low in both areas—they do not care about their subordinates or the department's goals. They are bureaucratic and only do the minimal amount of work necessary. Blake and Mouton characterized them as *impoverished leaders*. There are leaders who are high in concern or empathy for subordinates but low in goal achievement. These leaders try to be friends with their subordinates but not push them to do or excel on the job (*country club leaders*). Their officers often have low productivity. The third type, *authority-obedient*, concentrate on goals but show little regard for their subordinates. Although they sometimes are successful in accomplishing goals, over time they have little success because their subordinates are not motivated as a result of the negative relationship with their leader. Finally, *team leaders* are those who emphasize both goals and subordinates. They and their subordinates work as a team getting the job done. This is accomplished through being honest and transparent with subordinates, setting an example for subordinates in terms of performance and integrity, supporting subordinates, and being consensus builders (Fischer, 2009).

Motivation

Another important management process is motivation. *Motivation* can be defined as the qualities within the individual that account for the level, direction, and persistence of effort expanded at work (Schermerhorn, 2008). This definition implies that motivation is innate within officers and they have different levels of motivation. It also insinuates that their motivation should be directed toward work activities, which is accomplished through leadership. Leadership and motivation should be mutually reinforcing. Different people have variant levels of motivation, resulting in leaders attempting to forge different paths for their subordinates in order to maximize their productivity. A leader, to be effective, must attend to different officers' needs.

Although there are numerous theories describing the motivation process, two of the key theories are examined here. First, Adams' (1965) equity theory is discussed. *Equity theory* states that people examine rewards in relation to the rewards and efforts of others. If an officer perceives that another officer is receiving more benefits for doing the same job, the officer will perceive that there is inequity. This will often result in reduced motivation. Fairness plays an important role in workplace motivation.

A second motivation theory to consider is expectancy theory. Simply, *expectancy theory* states that officers will be motivated when they perceive that their work or effort will be appropriately rewarded (Porter & Lawler, 1968; Vroom, 1964). Appropriately rewarded means that rewards must be equal to or greater than the effort exerted by the officer. Not all work can be rewarded; officers must perform their regularly assigned duties. However, there should be rewards when officers' efforts exceed normal expectations.

Police departments are limited in the kinds of rewards they can bestow on officers. Civil service regulations and union contracts strictly dictate when officers are to receive salary increases and how promotions are made. However, superior officers can recognize work that goes beyond the expected by mentioning the work at roll call, thanking officers, recommending officers for commendations, and so on.

PLANNING

Planning occurs at all levels of the police department, as shown in Box 4.7. Police chiefs must ensure the department is responding to community needs, while sergeants often plan assignments for their officers. There is a hierarchy of planning. Chiefs and other top-level police administrators are involved in policy planning as they determine the department's direction or its goals and objectives by examining factors such as crime patterns, population shifts, economy, politics, and so on. Crime patterns may suggest that new anti-crime programs must be developed. Changes in the population may require the assignment of more officers in an area or unit. The economy affects the department's budget. Citizens and citizen groups often voice police-related concerns to politicians that must be addressed. Police policy planning establishes priorities for the department.

Policy planning outcomes are then interpreted in the strategic planning process. Strategic planning is where programs or strategies are developed to achieve goals and objectives emanating from policy planning. Unit commanders develop strategies for their units to accomplish the goals. Strategic planning may result in patrol commanders shifting officers from one area to another. It may result in selective traffic enforcement in newly identified area where there is a high volume of traffic crashes. It may result in the creation of a new unit to counter a growing problem. Strategic planning attempts to match resources and activities with community problems.

Finally, operational planning is where sergeants and lieutenants, through supervision, put the strategies into action. This may include shifting officers or giving them

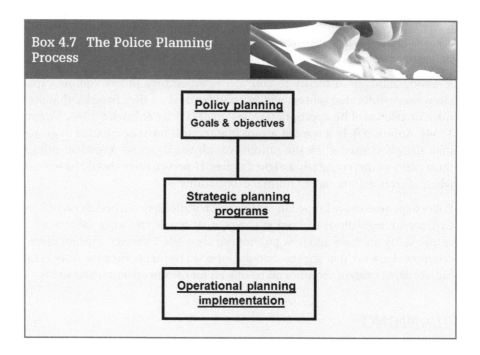

Box 4.7   The Police Planning Process

new duties. First-line supervisors ensure that strategies operate as planned. When this occurs, the department achieves its goals and is responsive to the community.

COMMUNICATIONS

Communication in a police department is critical. Simply stated, communication is the process of transmitting information and meaning between or among groups and individuals through a system of symbols, signs, and behavior (Lehman & DuFrene, 2008). Most everything a department does is information based. The unencumbered flow of information is directly tied to a department's effectiveness.

Police departments have expansive reporting systems where they collect information about crimes, traffic accidents, arrests, and calls for service. This information is distilled in a crime analysis unit (as discussed in more detail later in this chapter) and is used to direct police planning. This means that units and officers must have information. Patrol officers need information about dangerous locations on their patrol beat; detectives need information about victims, possible perpetrators, and similar cases when investigating a crime; traffic enforcement officers need information about the locations where large numbers of traffic crashes occur; and domestic violence investigators need information about their cases. All this information must be readily available through a communications network.

Police departments have elaborate communications networks. A great deal of information is sent to officers via the Internet and e-mail, with a number of departments having installed mobile communications terminals or notebook computers in police vehicles. There are two general types of information that departments should provide officers. First, officers need information that is operational in nature. This includes information about crimes and crime patterns, criminals and their modus operandi, dangerous locations such as gang or drug houses, and so on. This information is used by detectives and officers to better police the community.

The second general type of information is management related. Officers need to have access to and understand new orders and policies that are issued by police managers. Many police departments post their policies on the Internet, allowing officers to access them at any time. Box 4.8 provides the Minneapolis Police Department's policy on investigating bias crimes. The policy defines bias crimes and advises that all such crimes are to be investigated. It also provides a road map on how the crime should be investigated and the administrative actions of the responding officers. Policies provide officers guidance in doing their jobs. Policies are supplemented with supervisory direction and leadership.

In addition to management providing subordinates with formal communications, they also enhance leadership by effectively communicating with subordinates. This means that managers and supervisors must attempt to develop professional but friendly interpersonal relations with rank-and-file officers—a feeling of kinship should be engendered. When such relations exist, productivity is increased (Johnson, 2011; Nicholson-Crotty & O'Toole, 2004). Such relations can be encouraged in a police department. One way is through participatory management where officers from lower ranks are allowed to provide input into policies. This can be accomplished through meetings, surveys, and informal discussions. Vertical staff meetings are another vehicle for fostering subordinate input and better relations with managers and administrators. Here, officers from lower-level ranks are allowed to participate in the meetings where policies are formulated. Police administrators, managers, and supervisors must work to develop positive working relations with subordinates through communications and leadership. It results in a department that better responds to community needs.

Contingency Management

Contingency management represents a management philosophy rather than a distinct management theory. *Contingency management* assumes that there is no one best way to manage and that managerial decisions should be based on the particulars of the problem under consideration. Thus, contingency management is leadership based. Managers must constantly monitor organizational and environmental activities, and contingency management adds that these managers should monitor activities with a mind to reacting to problems and

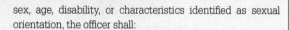

Box 4.8 7-304 Bias Crimes (9/26/07)

Proper investigation of bias crime incidents is the responsibility of all Minneapolis Police Officers. The actions taken by the MPD after a bias crime has occurred are visible signs of our concern and our commitment to the community.

Per Minnesota State Statute 626.5531, if a victim alleges that the offender was motivated to commit the act by the victim's race, religion, ethnic/national origin, sex, age, disability, or characteristics identified as sexual orientation, a police report shall be taken.

Sworn employees shall be aware of the following criteria, which may also be used to determine whether a criminal act falls within the mandatory bias/prejudice crime reporting requirements.

- The motivation of the perpetrator, as expressed in statements made to the victim (i.e., slurs, epithets).
- The nature of the symbols used to deface public or private property indicate bias or prejudice.
- The date and time of the occurrence corresponds to a holiday of significance.
- Observations made by the sworn employee(s) and common-sense review of the circumstances of the incident indicate bias or prejudice. Such observations may include the group or groups involved, the manner and means of the crime committed, and recurring patterns of similar incidents in the same area or against the same victim.

When an on-scene officer makes a determination that an incident is a criminal act and was committed because of the victim's perceived race, religion, ethnic/national origin,

sex, age, disability, or characteristics identified as sexual orientation, the officer shall:

- Provide necessary assistance to the victim(s).
- Conduct a preliminary investigation.
- Identify and arrest the suspect if possible.
- Protect and preserve the crime scene and evidence.
- Notify a supervisor.
- Ensure the victim(s) receive a Victim Assistance (blue) card.
- Complete a detailed police report.
- In CAPRS, check the box "Bias" on the M.O. screen.

Upon notification of a bias crime incident, the supervisor shall:

- Respond to the scene.
- Determine the seriousness of the incident and make appropriate notifications.
- For serious incidents (serious physical harm, significant event, felony level) the supervisor shall notify the on-duty Watch Commander.
- Request a Crime Lab response, to photograph the scene and/or victim(s) and recover any possible evidence.
- Complete a supplemental report.

The Intelligence Sharing and Analysis Center (ISAC) shall be responsible for the written reporting of bias-motivated crimes to the Bureau of Criminal Apprehension (BCA) as required by Minnesota Statute 626.5531.

Source: Minneapolis Police Department. http://www.minneapolismn.gov/police/policy/mpdpolicy_7-300_7-300.

potential problems. King (2009) and Giblin and Burruss (2009) observed that police departments alter their operations and structure in response to environmental demands. Leaders should consider internal and external conditions as they pursue organizational goals and objectives, and they must use a variety of leadership styles, the style exhibited by the leader being dependent on the situation and temperament of subordinates. A crisis situation such as a barricaded person or drug raid would require a different style of leadership as compared to organizing officers to direct traffic after a large event such as a football game.

Contingency management is a bottom-up philosophy in that organizational activities are dictated by changes and problems in the environment. Thus, management actions are dictated by activities at the lowest levels within the department. This also means that supervisors and middle managers assume more significant roles in managing departmental operations.

As noted above, management decisions are situationally based. Factors that influence decisions include the problem, the environment of the problem, and the available resources to solve the problem. With regard to the problem, the police manager must ensure that all aspects of the problem are understood. When this occurs, different approaches for dealing with the problem become available. The environment of the problem is important in terms of providing a better understanding of the problem. It is also important to examine the environment to ensure that the problem is not part of a larger problem or a complex set of other problems. Finally, the resources, personnel, equipment, and money that a manager has when dealing with a specific problem will limit the numbers and types of responses. Regardless, when all of these factors are considered, a number of alternative methods by which to approach a given problem become available, and the best approach should be selected.

Contingency management requires that police organizations be flexible. They must be able to quickly identify a problem and, with some immediacy, respond to it. In some cases, problems require that officers be shifted from one unit to another or reassigned to different geographical areas. For example, there may be an influx of gang activity in an area, resulting in an increase in robberies and assaults. The department may shift additional patrol officers to the area and make it a high priority for the gang unit to repress crime. Since some of these crimes may be committed by the same perpetrators, additional detectives could be assigned to these cases so that arrests can be made more quickly. In some cases, the department's organizational structure may be altered. Operation Ceasefire in Boston (Braga, Kennedy, Waring, & Piehl, 2013) and Operation Peacekeeper in Stockton, California are examples of contingency management where organizational change occurred. Both cities were experiencing high gang homicide rates. In both cities, officers were teamed with probation and parole officers, state and federal prosecutors, and community groups. When a homicide occurred, officers would flood the area and probation and parole agents would investigate gang probationers and parolees. These officers would not only investigate the violent crimes, they also sent a message to gang members that their behavior would not be tolerated. Community-based organizations such as churches were enlisted to send the same message. State and federal prosecutors fast-tracked prosecutions. These concerted efforts resulted in decreases in homicides in both cities. Contingency management often requires innovated alternatives.

MANAGING COMMUNITY POLICING

The previous sections outlined a variety of methods by which to facilitate communications and allow subordinates to provide input into decision making. A number of departments have adopted these methods when implementing community policing, but these efforts have been uneven and in some cases ineffective (Chappell, 2009; Morabito, 2010). To better understand community policing and its implementation, it is informative to examine community policing's objectives. Terpstra (2010) identified five primary goals: making policing more neighborhood oriented, a focus on problems in the neighborhood, prevention of crime and disorder, cooperation with other criminal justice agencies and community groups, and increased citizen involvement.

If community policing is to be implemented successfully, administrators must alter organizational arrangements to involve lower-ranking officers in the process. Traditional police management is a top-down process, whereas community policing necessitates more of a bottom-up process of decision making and goal setting. If police departments are to achieve the goals identified by Terpstra, policing must be decentralized where officers are able to work more closely with the community.

Community policing requires a redefinition of patrol operations. Rather than concentrating on a rapid response to calls for service, patrol officers must attempt to attend to the problems that are at the root of the calls. They must identify and solve problems and engage the community. This requires a shift in organizational control from top management to patrol commanders and supervisors (Kappeler & Gaines, 2009). Such a shift results in patrol commanders having more flexibility when deciding on tactics and dealing with crime and disorder problems—they must engage in contingency management. It also requires that unit commanders place a higher priority on problem solving.

To learn more about problem-oriented policing, visit the website **www.popcenter.org**

It is not easy to transform a police department from the traditional philosophy to a community policing department. Police departments and personnel are resistant to change. Although community policing has been around for over two decades, most police departments have not altered their organizational structure to facilitate its implementation (Zhao, He, & Lovrich, 2003; Zhao, Ren, & Lovrich, 2010). Police departments still cling to the organizational principles discussed earlier in this chapter. Cheurprakobkit (2001) studied community policing officers in one city and found that the officers had reservations about the chief's ability to adequately implement community policing, demonstrating a strain between the department's organizational structure and the need to change to a community policing format. Chiefs and their staffs must make community policing a priority and develop a plan for its implementation. This plan should include a discussion of the department's organization, unit responsibilities and duties, and training for officers to ensure they have the tools to effectively use community policing tools.

Most police departments have implemented community policing piecemeal. They tend to implement individual programs aimed at some narrow issue or problem. Some of the programs that they have implemented include neighborhood watches, Drug Awareness Resistance Education, bike patrols, curfew enforcement, and citizen academies. However, this is not community policing. These tactics do little to address problems in neighborhoods. If community policing is to be successful, it must be embedded throughout police responses to problems in the community. It should guide patrol and investigative operations.

The most logical method of implementing community policing holistically is to delegate operational control to field commanders. Field commanders, especially in patrol and criminal investigation, should be given the authority to make decisions about police tactics and operational priorities. Today, the most common method of accomplishing this is through COMPSTAT, which is discussed in the following section. Community policing is discussed in more detail in Chapter 11.

CRIME ANALYSIS AND COMPSTAT

One of the important technological innovations in law enforcement in recent years has been crime analysis and COMPSTAT. *Crime analysis* is the examination and mapping of crime and calls for service in order to discover patterns. When patterns have been discovered, the police have better information about activities and how to respond to them. *COMPSTAT* is a managerial process that uses crime analysis information. It gives administrators a measure of control as they direct police operations to specific crime and disorder problems such as gang or drug-dealing hot spots. It is a process where administrators, in conjunction with patrol, traffic, and investigative commanders and personnel, examine activities and cooperatively develop plans to address problems in specific geographical areas. It also adds accountability to the mix, as it provides a constant level of feedback relative to the success of operations. In other words, if a problem persists, it means that departmental actions have not sufficiently addressed the problem. Administrators can then discuss the lack of progress or successes with commanders. COMPSTAT provides a continuous examination of crime and disorder and serves to evaluate the department's efforts.

Crime Analysis

Police departments have been conducting crime analysis for many years; in fact, Harries (1999) noted that New York was mapping crime as early as 1900. It did not become an integral part of policing until the 1970s, though, when the costs of computers and software decreased to the point that they were widely affordable. Police departments began using computers to automate their records and dispatch information. This created a large paperless database that could provide considerable information about crimes, calls for service, and police activities. Over time, the costs of computers have continued to decline, and today there is ample software to allow departments to maintain robust databases. Such software allows officers to map activities by geography, time, and type of activity.

Essentially, crime analysis is the collating or sorting of data to allow officers to visualize or better understand activities. Gaines and Worrall (2011) categorized the several types of data collected:

1. Specific types of calls, across the jurisdiction or within a specific area for a given time period
2. Activities for a particular shift or watch
3. Activities for a particular beat or police district
4. Activities around a "hot spot" or concentration of crime and disorder
5. Concentrations of activities in an area over time
6. Police activities in relation to social and ecological characteristics

Usually this information is provided on a map along with a narrative report detailing the activities on the map. The information can then be used by patrol officers or detectives to direct or concentrate their activities toward a particular problem or problem area.

As an example, Box 4.9 provides a map of juvenile arrests in Redlands, California. Juvenile arrests appear to occur only in certain areas, and some of the areas have large concentrations of these arrests. The patrol, criminal investigation, and crime prevention units can all use this map. The areas where higher levels of juvenile crime occur require more patrol time relative to other areas. Detectives can use the information shown on the map to help them solve crimes committed by juveniles. Finally, crime prevention activities, especially those providing recreational or after–school activities for juveniles, could be implemented in the areas with the highest concentration of juvenile arrests. Crime analysis and mapping can substantially direct police activities.

COMPSTAT

COMPSTAT is an extension of crime analysis in that it incorporates management and crime activities. It is a strategic management tool. It gives decision makers immediate access to information relevant to problems and tactical decisions. Managers have more information about crime and disorder problems, and by closely examining this information they can make decisions about how to best

Box 4.9 Map of Juvenile Arrests in Redlands, California

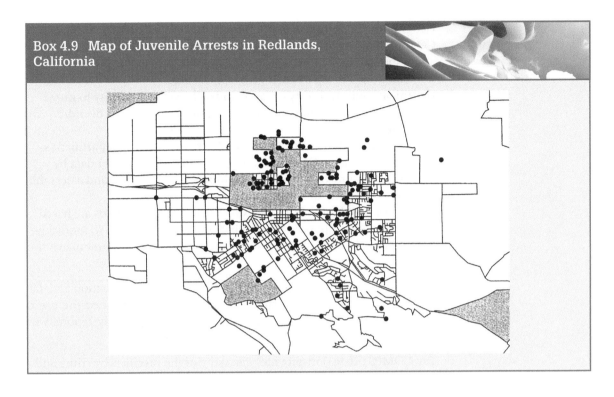

respond to them tactically. Some problems may require additional patrols, others may necessitate the creation of a special investigative task force, and still others may be solved through crime prevention efforts. The response to a problem can be fashioned after the data are thoroughly examined. When such information is readily available, managers can make more appropriate decisions. Administrators can monitor activities over time in certain geographical areas, such as patrol beats or patrol districts, and determine if police programs are effective in reducing problems. These administrators can also hold unit commanders accountable when conditions do not improve; for example, if the number of burglaries increases in a district, administrators may require the district commander to explain what actions were taken and why the situation did not improve. It also opens discussions about what other tactics may be more effective.

Willis, Mastrofski, and Weisburd (2003) examined several COMPSTAT programs and identified six core elements associated with them:

1. **Mission clarification**—Administrators are able to clarify core objectives for commanders and units and, through supervision, ensure that commanders and units actively pursue achieving these objectives.
2. **Internal accountability**—Operational commanders are held accountable for achieving core objectives and attending to crime and disorder problems (see Box 4.10).

3. **Geographical organization of operational command**—The focus of COMPSTAT is geographical areas where commanders are given authority and responsibility. This results in one individual being held accountable for what occurs in a particular geographical area.

4. **Organizational flexibility**—Commanders have the flexibility to move officers and change unit structures to respond to crime and disorder problems.

5. **Data-driven analysis of problems and assessment of a department's problem solving**—COMPSTAT generates crime and disorder data by geographical subdivision, allowing administrators to track and assess the department's ability to solve problems.

6. **Innovative problem-solving tactics**—Responses to problems are based on what works as opposed to what has been done in the past. Innovative solutions can be used, and solutions can be deployed that best match the problem.

For COMPSTAT to be effective it must provide units with information and data that they can use to fashion responses. Henry (2002) examined the use of COMPSTAT in New York and found that three distinct weekly reports were generated:

1. The COMPSTAT Report provides a ranking of the precincts by crime and arrests and allows management to make a determination about each precinct's problems and the efforts exerted to solve the problem. This

---

Box 4.10   Five Axed Over Bad Stats

A routine inspection last summer that uncovered an unusually high number of crimes that police in New Orleans' 1st District improperly downgraded to less serious offenses has snowballed into a scandal that led to the dismissal of five veteran officers in October for allegedly cooking their jurisdiction's books.

Police Superintendent Edwin Compass fired the 1st District's commander, Capt. Norvel Orazio, a 29-year veteran who won crime reduction awards in 2002 and 2003. According to an internal audit that scrutinized 690 reports from July 2002 until May 2010, 42 percent were wrongly downgraded from major crimes that should have been reported to the FBI for inclusion in the Uniform Crime Reports. Another 17 percent were questionable, said investigators from the department's Public Integrity Bureau.

A more cursory check of the city's seven other precincts, which looked at a fraction of the number of cases, found six that had error rates ranging from 10 percent to 25 percent. Only one district, the 3rd, had an error rate of zero.

A 225-page report issued after Compass announced the firings said that Orazio encouraged the systematic downgrading of incidents in an effort to win the crime reduction awards.

Source: Five Axed Over Bad Stats (2004).

report can also provide information on officer productivity to determine those officers who are making more and fewer arrests and issuing citations. This information would be helpful in identifying officers in need of additional supervision and training.

2. The Commander Profile Report serves as a report card on how managers are dealing with their crime problems and their units. The report contains information on population and demographics for each command area, number of assigned personnel, citizen complaints filed against officers in the command, vehicle crashes involving departmental vehicles, response time to calls for service, number of on-duty injuries to officers, and amount of overtime expenditures. This report allows administrators to examine commanders over time and with each of the other commanders. Such a comparison can identify problem commands.

3. The Crime Mapping Report provides commanders with visual accounts of crime and calls for service in their commands. Various maps can be generated examining individual or all major crimes for a short or extended period. This flexibility allows commanders to discover trends over time or in specific locations. The maps assist the commanders in developing better tactics for dealing with the problems in their areas.

In weekly COMPSTAT meetings administrators discuss these reports and the status of crime and police activity in each of the commands. Administrators query the commanders about their tactics and whether they are effective in dealing with identified problems. The discussions can also lead to commanders considering new tactics when current operational arrangements are not producing the desired outcomes.

> To learn more about COMPSTAT you can watch a video about the Los Angeles Police Department at: **http://www.youtube.com/watch?v=pltQi6aG4M8**

Silverman (1999) suggested that the discussion of high-profile cases and crime patterns with commanders reduces bureaucratic entanglements and facilitates communication. It allows for better identification of goals and objectives and a rapid change in tactics to meet evolving problems. It also holds commanders accountable when they fail to resolve high-profile cases or reduce crime in their areas. Although COMPSTAT has received widespread acceptance in policing, it remains questionable if it has reached its full potential. Problem analysis remains primitive or haphazard in many departments and is often superficial. Accountability is often absent, resulting in little or no pressure on commanders to exert more attention and effort to solving problems.

POLICE COLLECTIVE BARGAINING

The previous sections in this chapter examined police administration and management. A thorough examination of this topic cannot be accomplished without examining the impact of police collective bargaining on police management. *Collective bargaining* is where employees organize in a union or other organization to present their demands and grievances to management. Often, the employees negotiate salaries, working conditions, and benefits through unions. When police officers band together in a union, they have a stronger voice in many of the decisions that directly affect them.

To view a video of police testimony on first responder collective bargaining, visit the website **http://www.youtube.com/watch?v=yfsse4gcub8**

Most people associate collective bargaining with unions; however, police officers in the United States are represented by a variety of organizations. These organizations can be categorized as unions and fraternal organizations. Unions representing the police include the International Brotherhood of Police Officers; the American Federation of State, County, and Municipal Employees; and the International Brotherhood of Teamsters, among others. Fraternal organizations include the Fraternal Order of Police and police benevolent associations. There is no national union; rather, police collective bargaining tends to be locally based, with a patchwork of organizations throughout the United States.

Today, 40% of all police departments have some form of collective bargaining (Hickman & Reaves, 2006). As noted in Table 4.2, most large and medium-size police departments have collective bargaining, while most of the smaller departments do not. A state must pass legislation authorizing a police department to engage in collective bargaining. Many states have authorized it for larger cities but prohibited it in smaller jurisdictions. Other states have authorized it for all police agencies.

Organizations that represent employees are often concerned with: (1) better economic benefits; (2) better job conditions; and (3) a voice in management practices. In some cases, management and labor can cooperate on issues; for example, increases in salaries benefit not only line officers but also the department, as it is better able to attract highly qualified applicants. In other cases, the relationship can be adversarial; for example, the union may want promotions in the department to be based on longevity as opposed to performance on promotion tests. Unions certainly complicate the management process, but they are now present in many jurisdictions, and management must deal with them and their demands. Nonetheless, where deficient work conditions exist it is clear that unions can improve matters, especially in the areas of salary and supplementary compensation (Briggs, Zhao, & Wilson, 2008; Wilson, Zhao, & Ren, 2006).

Table 4.2 Collective Bargaining Authorized by Local Police Departments

Population Served	Percentage (%) of Agencies Authorizing Collective Bargaining for	
	Sworn Employees	Civilian Employees
All sizes	41	22
1,000,000 or more	81	63
500,000–999,999	84	67
250,000–499,999	66	54
100,000–249,999	69	60
50,000–99,999	71	59
25,000–49,999	75	59
10,000–24,999	70	48
2500–9999	50	21
Under 2500	13	2

Hickman & Reaves (2006).

Essentially, there are two basic types of issues: employee benefits and management prerogatives. *Employee benefits* refer to salary, vacation and holiday time, overtime compensation, fringe benefits such as health and life insurance coverage and retirement plans, and working conditions. *Management prerogatives* are management decisions that affect the operation of the department, such as hiring and promotion procedures, transfer policies, and the purchase of equipment. In most departments, employee benefits are negotiable, while management prerogatives are not; however, many unions attempt to bring the management prerogatives into the negotiation process. When this occurs, police administrators begin to lose control of their departments (Gaines & Worrall, 2011). When management prerogatives have been bargained away, they are difficult to recover.

The recession beginning in 2007 had a significant impact on police collective bargaining. The recession resulted in significant losses of income for governments at all levels, and this loss of income brought about cuts in government services, especially at the local level. Police departments across the country reduced their numbers of police officers, not replacing officers who left the department, furloughing officers, and laying off officers (COPS Office, 2011). In some cases, cities abolished their police departments. Officials in Camden, New Jersey eliminated its department and contracted with the county police to reduce costs (Laday, 2013). As cities began to look for ways to reduce expenditures, public safety contacts (police and fire) became a focal point, especially retirement and health benefits. In many cases, local governments unilaterally reduced retirement benefits and health benefits, resulting in numerous lawsuits from police and fire unions. Many such reductions were in violation of negotiated contracts.

The concern over police pay and benefits, to some extent, is misdirected or unfounded. First, research indicates that public employees, even with their benefits, are paid less than equally educated workers in the private sector. Lewin et al. (2011) found that public employees are paid from about 2–12% less than privately employed workers. Although public employee pensions and benefits often are better than private pensions and benefits, they do not totally make up the difference between the public and private sector in total wages and benefits. Also, Brandl and Smith (2013) studied the mortality of retired municipal employees from Detroit. They found that police officers on average died six years younger than other retirees and had retirements 74 months shorter than other city employees. Once police officers retire, their longevity is much shorter than other workers. This factor should be considered when examining police wages and benefits.

Contract Negotiation

The relations between labor and management are enumerated in the contract. Contracts generally are fairly substantial and address all points in the agreement. Contracts are negotiated for a specific period of time, usually for 1–3 years. Once the contract is agreed upon, it is binding for all parties. The contract serves as the authority for deciding issues that are addressed in it.

Contract negotiations usually begin 6–12 months before the expiration of the current contract. Both sides establish a set of demands to present to the other side. Once negotiations begin, it generally is a quid pro quo process whereby each side gives up or alters demands in order to come to an agreement; for example, the union may request a 10% salary increase over the course of the new contract but management can negotiate the increase to a lower percentage. Generally, both sides will reduce their demands in one area if the other side gives something in another area. The union may reduce its salary demand for an increase in health insurance coverage or other benefits.

In some cases, the two sides cannot come to an agreement. This is called an *impasse*. When this occurs, there are two options: some type of job action or the use of *impasse resolution* procedures. In terms of job actions, the union has a number of alternatives, ranging from media press releases and presentations to strikes. Other job actions include the "blue flu" (large numbers of officers calling in sick), demonstrations at police headquarters or at council meetings, letter writing campaigns to elected officials, ticket slowdowns to reduce the city's revenue, and ticket speedups to agitate citizens. The union will engage in job actions as a method of forcing the government to agree to its contract conditions.

There are several impasse resolution procedures, and their existence in a jurisdiction generally is a matter of state law. The first is *mediation*, which involves third-party intervention. The mediator works with both sides in an effort to facilitate the two sides' reaching an agreement. The mediator cannot force a settlement on the participants. Second is *fact finding*, which is similar to mediation except that a written report is produced. Fact finding places additional pressure on the parties as a result of the written report. Finally, *arbitration* allows both sides to present their demands, and evidence and documentation supporting those demands, to an arbitrator. The arbitrator, after considering the positions of both sides, has the authority to impose a final decision on the issues in dispute. Arbitration places additional pressures on the parties to come to an agreement, as the arbitrator's final decision may result in a greater loss compared to what had already been negotiated.

It sometimes appears that unions and police executives are on opposing sides, but for the most part, they generally agree and often work together. Police executives do disagree when unions attempt to become involved in management prerogatives such as hiring and promotion procedures, allocation of officers across units and other assignments, disciplinary actions, or police tactics. However, police executives have a vested interest when unions demand higher salaries and benefits. Gains in these areas reduce the attrition rate for the department and make it easier to recruit high-quality applicants. The relations between chiefs and unions for the most part can be characterized as a partnership.

SUMMARY

This chapter provides an overview of classical organizational theory as it relates to policing. It explores a number of definitions and terms that are critical to learning how police departments are administered. Today, the vast majority of police departments use classical organizational theory as their administrative foundation, which is referred to as *traditional police administration*. Classical organizational theory consists of a number of straightforward principles that are easily applied in law enforcement.

In addition to organization, this chapter provides an overview of police management. Management is the actions that occur within the organizational structure and facilitate productivity. Management includes behaviors such as leadership, planning, communication, and motivation. Police leaders use these processes to spur work. Moreover, these processes must be used effectively by police managers if they are to be successful.

The chapter provides an overview of crime analysis and COMPSTAT. Crime analysis gives police personnel a better understanding of crime and disorder in their community. It also provides information on how to best fashion responses to crime and disorder. COMPSTAT is a managerial process whereby authority is delegated to lower-level commanders. Commanders are expected to identify crime problems and devise individualized tactics to respond to the problems. Administrators review commanders' actions and successes, holding them accountable when problems are not resolved.

Finally, this chapter provides an overview of the police collective bargaining process. Most police officers in the United States are involved in the collective bargaining process. It is a mechanism that allows officers to have input in a variety of decisions that affect the job. Police administrators must be able to deal effectively with police unions if they are to successfully guide the department toward effective goal accomplishment.

REVIEW QUESTIONS

1. Who developed the acronym POSDCORB and what is it used to describe?
2. Describe the basics of organizational theory and its principles.
3. What is the administrative structure that generally occurs in police agencies? From what police force does modern police administration take its roots?
4. Who was Max Weber and what are the principles he identified as the foundation of *classical organizational theory?*
5. Describe the collective bargaining process.

REFERENCES

Adams, J.S. 1965. Inequity in social exchange. *Advances in Experimental Social Psychology.* 62:335–343.

Alpert, G., & Smith, W. (1994). Developing police policy: an evaluation of the control principle. In L. Gaines, & G. Cordner (Eds.), *Policing perspectives* (pp. 353–362). Los Angeles, CA: Roxbury.

Blake, R., & Mouton, J. (1964). *The managerial grid.* Houston: Gulf Publishing Co.

Braga, Anthony A., Hureau, David M., and Papachristos, Andrew V. (2013). Deterring Gang-Involved Gun Violence: Measuring the Impact of Boston's Operation Ceasefire on Street Gang Behavior, *The Journal of Quantitative Criminology,* 26: 1.

Brandl, S., & Smith, B. (2013). An empirical examination of retired police officers' length of retirement and age at death: a research note. *Police Quarterly, 16,* 113–123.

Briggs, S. J., Zhao, J., & Wilson, S. (2008). The effect of collective bargaining on large police agency supplemental compensation policies. *Police Practice and Research, 9,* 227–238.

Chappell, A. T. (2009). The philosophical versus actual adoption of community policing. *Criminal Justice Review, 34,* 5–28.

Cheurprakobkit, S. (2001). Organizational impacts on community policing: management issues and officers' perceptions. *Crime Prevention and Community Safety: An International Journal, 3*(1), 43–54.

COPS Office. (2011). *The impact of the economic downturn of American police agencies.* Washington, DC: Author.

Crank, J. (2003). Institutional theory of police: a review of the state of the art. *Policing: An International Journal of Police Strategies & Management, 28,* 186–207.

Engel, R. S. (2001). Supervisory styles of patrol sergeants and lieutenants. *Journal of Criminal Justice, 29,* 341–355.

Fischer, C. (2009). *Leadership matters: Police chiefs talk about their careers.* Washington, DC: Police Executive Research Forum.

Five Axed Over Bad Stats. (2004). *Law Enforcement News, 29*(613), 5.

Gaines, L., & Swanson, C. R. (1999). Empowering police officers: a tarnished silver bullet? In L. Gaines, & G. Cordner (Eds.), *Policing perspectives* (pp. 363–371). Los Angeles, CA: Roxbury.

Gaines, L., & Worrall, J. (2011). *Police administration.* Belmont, CA: Delmar.

Giblin, M., & Burruss, G. (2009). Developing a measurement model of institutional processes in policing. *Policing: An International Journal of Police Strategies & Management, 32,* 351–376.

Gulick, L. (1937). Notes on the theory of organization. In L. Gulick, & L. Urwick (Eds.), *Papers on the science of administration.* New York: New York Institute of Public Administration.

Harries, K. (1999). *Crime mapping: principle and practice.* Washington, DC: National Institute of Justice.

Henry, V. E. (2002). *The COMPSTAT Paradigm.* Flushing, NY: Looseleaf Law Publications.

Hickman, M. J., & Reaves, B. A. (2006). *Local police departments, 2003.* Washington, DC: U.S. Department of Justice, Bureau of Justice Statistics.

Hitt, M., Miller, C., & Colella, A. (2006). *Organizational behavior.* New York: Wiley.

Johnson, R. (2011). Officer attitudes and management influences on police work productivity. *American Journal of Criminal Justice, 36,* 293–306.

Kappeler, V. E. (2006a). *Critical issues in police civil liability* (4th ed.). Prospect Heights, IL: Waveland Press.

Kappeler, V. E. (2006b). *Police civil liability: Supreme court cases and materials* (2nd ed.). Prospect Heights, IL: Waveland Press.

Kappeler, V. E., & Gaines, L. (2009). *Community policing: A contemporary perspective* (5th ed.). Newark, NJ: LexisNexis Matthew Bender.

Kappeler, V. E., Sluder, R., & Alpert, G. (1998). *Forces of deviance: Understanding the dark side of policing* (2nd ed.). Prospect Heights, IL: Waveland Press.

Kappeler, V. E., & Van Hoose, D. (1995). Illegal drug use by narcotics agents: retiring the addicted centurion. *Criminal Law Bulletin, 31*(1), 61–70.

King, W. (2004). Toward a better understanding of the hierarchical nature of police organizations: conception and measurement. *Journal of Criminal Justice, 33,* 97–109.

King, W. (2009). Toward a life-course perspective of police organizations. *Journal of Research in Crime and Delinquency, 46,* 213–244.

Laday, J. (March 18, 2013). Camden police layoff plan approved by state, layoffs to begin April 390. *South Jersey Times.* http://www.nj.com/gloucester-county/index.ssf/2013/01/state_approves_camden_police_l.html.

Lehman, C. M., & DuFrene, D. D. (2008). *Business communication.* Belmont, CA: Thomson.

Lewin, D., Kochan, T., Cutcher-Gershenfeld, J., Ghiarducci, T., Katz, H., Keefe, J., et al. (2011). *Getting it right: Empirical evidence and policy implications from research on public-sector unionism and collective bargaining.* http://papers.ssrn.com/sol3/papers.cfm?abstract_id=1792942.

Moore, M., & Stephens, D. (1991). *Beyond command and control: The strategic management of police departments.* Washington, DC: Police Executive Research Forum.

Morabito, M. S. (2010). Understanding community policing as an innovation: patterns of adoption. *Crime & Delinquency, 56,* 564–587.

Nicholson-Crotty, L., & O'Toole, L. J. (2004). Public management and organizational performance: the case of law enforcement agencies. *Journal of Public Administration Research and Theory*.

Porter, L. W., & Lawler, E. E. (1968). *Management attitudes and performance*. Homewood, IL: Irwin.

Peak, K. J., Gaines, L. K., & Glensor, R. W. (2010). *Police supervision and management: In an era of community policing* (2nd ed.). Upper Saddle River, NJ: Prentice-Hall.

Reaves, B. A., & Hickman, M. J. (2002). *Police departments in large cities, 1990–2000*. Washington, DC: U.S. Department of Justice, Bureau of Labor Statistics.

Schermerhorn, J. (2008). *Management*. New York: Wiley.

Silverman, I. (1999). *NYPD battles crime: Innovative strategies in policing*. Boston: Northeastern University Press.

Terpstra, J. (2010). Community policing in practice: ambitions and realization. *Policing: A Journal of Policy and Practice, 4*, 64–72.

Vroom, V. (1964). *Work and motivation*. New York: Wiley.

Willis, J., Mastrofski, S., & Weisburd, D. (2003). *COMPSTAT in practice: An in-depth analysis of three cities*. Washington, DC: Police Foundation.

Wilson, S., Zhao, J., & Ren, L. (2006). The influence of collective bargaining on large police agency salaries: 1990–2000. *American Journal of Criminal Justice, 31*, 19–34.

Zhao, J., Ren, L., & Lovrich, N. (2010). Police organizational structures during the 1990s: an application of contingency theory. *Police Quarterly, 13*, 209–232.

Zhao, S., He, N., & Lovrich, N. P. (2003). Community policing: did it change the basic functions of policing in the 1990s? A national study. *Justice Quarterly, 20*(4), 697–724.

CHAPTER 5

Police Operations

It is common sense to take a method and try it. If it fails, admit it
frankly and try another. But above all, try something.

—Franklin D. Roosevelt

LEARNING OBJECTIVES

After reading the chapter, you should be able to:

- Describe the allocation of police personnel in law enforcement agencies.
- Understand the role of police patrol role in crime prevention.
- Explain and distinguish the different methods and techniques of patrol.
- Describe the various police patrol strategies.
- Describe and explain the various stages and purposes of criminal investigation.
- Understand the role of the police traffic function.
- Describe the purposes and changes in police paramilitary units.

KEY TERMS

- 311 call number
- Aircraft patrol
- Allocation of personnel
- Beats
- Beat boundaries
- Bicycle patrol
- Call priority system
- Committed time
- Control beats
- Crime suppression force
- Criminal investigation
- Differential police response
- Directed patrol
- D-runs
- Enhanced supervision partnership

INTRODUCTION

Police operations refer to the services provided to citizens and the methods used by police agencies when delivering these services. The police are called upon to do many things. They are the most accessible of all governmental agencies; they operate continuously, 24 h a day in most jurisdictions. Emergency 911 telephone numbers give the public immediate access to the police, and automobile patrols allow the police to respond rapidly to citizen complaints. For these reasons, the public has increasingly come to depend more on the police to solve their problems, regardless of the nature of the problem.

Police services are delivered by a variety of operational units within the police department. The number and nature of these units depend on the department's size, workload, and the community being policed—there is great variation in

- Follow-up investigation
- Foot patrol
- Fugitive apprehension units
- Hot spots
- Information-sharing partnership
- Interagency problem-solving partnership
- Investigative function
- Kansas City Patrol Study
- Latent investigation
- Modus operandi files
- Omnipresence
- Patrol function
- Police operations
- Police paramilitary units
- Postarrest enhancement
- Prearrest targeting
- Preliminary investigation
- Pretextual traffic stop
- Preventive patrol
- Proactive beats
- Pulling levers
- Racial profiling

the structure of police agencies. The majority of police services or operational activities emanate from three units: patrol, criminal investigation or detective, and traffic.

The *patrol function* is performed by patrol officers who are allocated across beats to respond to calls and to observe for crime and suspicious activities. Patrol is considered to be the most important operation in a police agency. Noted scholar and former Chicago Police Chief O.W. Wilson described it as "the backbone of policing" (Wilson & McLaren, 1977). Patrol is the primary unit responsible for answering calls, providing police services, and preventing crime. A majority of the officers in any given department will be assigned to patrol. In large agencies, it is given the organizational status of an independent bureau, division, or unit. In smaller departments, the patrol division may comprise the entire department.

The *investigative function* is directed at solving crimes reported to the police, apprehending criminals, and recovering stolen property. In large departments, this responsibility is vested with large detective units that specialize in the investigation of specific types of crimes. For example, a department might have an auto theft unit, homicide unit, and property crimes unit as well as other units in a detective division. Less specialization is found in medium-sized agencies, and detectives may adopt a generalist approach, investigating all crimes. Still, in small agencies, the responsibility for investigations may rest with patrol because many departments are too small to employ detectives.

The *traffic unit* is responsible for reducing the frequency and severity of traffic crashes and facilitating the orderly flow of traffic. Traffic units achieve these two objectives through: (1) *enforcement*, (2) *education*, and (3) *engineering*. Police officers develop enforcement plans that focus on accident-causing violations. Such selective enforcement is aimed at reducing the causes of accidents and deterring traffic violations through a police presence. Education refers to those programs whereby police departments attempt to educate the public on their driving responsibilities and the benefits of safe driving techniques. Examples of these programs include campaigns to raise awareness of the consequences of driving under the influence and the importance of wearing seat belts. Finally, engineering refers to when officers make suggestions about the need for stop signs, yield signs, and stop lights. The police frequently recommend changes in speed limits or suggest replacing yield signs with stop signs to reduce the frequency of accidents. The police traffic responsibility is substantial, and it is an important operational function.

ALLOCATING POLICE PERSONNEL

The allocation of police personnel refers to decisions about the number of officers assigned to the various units in the police department. Police chiefs are constantly bombarded by requests from unit commanders for additional personnel. Sometimes as a result of such requests, it seems that every unit in the department is understaffed; consequently, the chief must be judicious when deciding how new or additional personnel will be assigned within the department. They must be assigned on a basis of agency and community needs.

There is little consistency in how various managers assign officers within their departments. A study by Hickman and Reaves (2006) found the percentage of officers assigned to patrol ranged from a low of 54% to a high of 96%. Smaller departments generally have larger percentages of personnel assigned to patrol because they have fewer specialized units. When administrators assign officers to specialized or nonpatrol units, they automatically reduce the number of patrol officers, and the territory covered by the patrol beats is increased because of fewer patrol officers. It therefore becomes extremely important for administrators to ensure that personnel are allocated to specialized units only when necessary.

Allocation decisions are generally made after a workload analysis. For the most accurate decisions to be made, detailed reports of unit activities must be analyzed to determine the workload for each unit in the police department. This is accomplished by identifying the frequency of each activity performed by the unit and the average amount of time spent for each occurrence. For example, the workload of a sex crimes unit would be determined by identifying the various types of crimes investigated (e.g., rape, sexual assault, child molestation) and the average time spent investigating and processing each case (e.g., paperwork, court time). This process allows administrators to determine how much detective time is required by a unit and how the time is distributed. This process can be applied to each unit to make better personnel allocation decisions.

- Reactive beats
- Repeat offender projects
- Routine preventive patrol
- Saturation patrol
- Specialized enforcement partnership
- Split force policing
- Stop and frisk stops
- Suspect-oriented techniques
- Sweeps
- Symbolic assailants
- Traffic function
- Walk-throughs
- Water patrol
- Warrant services
- Where-are-theys
- Whodunits
- Zero tolerance

RECEIVING AND MANAGING CALLS FOR SERVICE

Most police work is the result of citizens calling the police, although a percentage of work is initiated by officers; for example, an officer may make a traffic stop after observing a violation or a crime. Thus, it is important to examine how police departments handle citizen calls or calls for service. This section focuses on how calls from citizens are handled by police departments.

This Website shows the location and nature of police calls for service in Tampa. **http://www.tampagov.net/appl_police_calls_for_service/frmCallsList.asp**

Police departments receive large volumes of calls. The Seattle Police Department answers between 800,000 and 870,000 calls per year (Seattle Police Department, 2013); the Fort Worth Police Department answers approximately 1.18 million calls per year (Fort Worth Police Department, 2014); and the St. Louis Police Department answers approximately 850,000 call per year

(St. Louis Police Department, 2013). It is interesting today in some departments that a majority of calls come from cell phones as opposed to land lines; in St. Louis, 78.9% of calls were from cell phones. This makes it more difficult for police departments to determine exact location of originating calls. Nonetheless, police departments across the country receive large volumes of calls from citizens.

Police departments receive a variety of calls. Box 5.1 shows the top five calls received by the Sacramento Police department. The most common call is incomplete because the caller hangs up before talking with a call taker. In many cases, patrol officers must be dispatched to the call location because the call could have been an interrupted emergency. Disturbance calls are second most common and can be altercations on the street, bar fights, and so on. All-units broadcasts are where all units are notified of a problem such as a drunk driver in a general location. The fourth most common call was misdemeanor assault often are the result of robberies and fights. Finally, domestic calls are the fifth most common. It is interesting that some form of conflict between citizens constitutes the most common legitimate calls to the police.

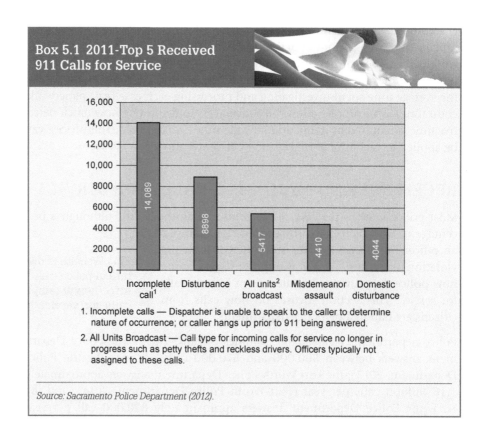

Box 5.1 2011-Top 5 Received 911 Calls for Service

Call Type	Number
Incomplete call[1]	14,089
Disturbance	8898
All units[2] broadcast	5417
Misdemeanor assault	4410
Domestic disturbance	4044

1. Incomplete calls — Dispatcher is unable to speak to the caller to determine nature of occurrence; or caller hangs up prior to 911 being answered.

2. All Units Broadcast — Call type for incoming calls for service no longer in progress such as petty thefts and reckless drivers. Officers typically not assigned to these calls.

Source: Sacramento Police Department (2012).

Table 5.1 Boston Police Department's Call Priority System		
Priority	**Type of Call/Response**	**Percent of Total Calls**
1	Immediate response	20.3
2	Medium-priority response	34.8
3	Low-priority response	32.5
9	Administrative	8.2
	Walk-ins to department	4.1

Source: Adapted from Nesbary (1998).

Generally, when a citizen calls the police, a call-taker records the pertinent information and forwards the call to a dispatcher, who then dispatches a police officer. In an effort to ensure that emergency calls are dispatched first, police departments use a priority system. There is no standard priority system, and the system often is dependent on the particular computerized dispatch system used by the department. Boston found that approximately 20% of all their calls were "immediate response" or emergency. These emergencies could range from a crime in progress to a traffic crash involving personal injury. Table 5.1 shows the distribution of calls in Boston based on their *call priority system*.

Police departments receive large volumes of calls. Today, in most urban areas, a caller will be put on hold when calling 911 because emergency dispatch centers are overwhelmed by the number of calls. The vast majority of calls to 911 are not emergencies, which hinders the ability of the police to respond adequately to emergency calls. Jurisdictions are now implementing a *311 call number*, which is a police nonemergency number that serves as a filter to allow emergency calls to be handled more quickly.

One of the first cities to implement 311 was Baltimore. During the first 2 years of implementation, 28.6% of 911 calls were migrated to the 311 number. Of course, the department still has to maintain a complement of dispatchers and officers to respond to the calls. Kennedy (2003) suggested that implementation of 311 service can result in an increase in the number of calls a police department receives. Whereas in the past someone may have been reluctant to call the police regarding a minor issue, having a 311 number available might encourage more such calls. When 911 emergency numbers were first implemented, the number of calls to police departments dramatically increased, and departments had to employ additional call-takers, dispatchers, and police officers to handle the increased workload.

POLICE PATROL

Historically, police administrators have envisioned a number of purposes for patrol. O.W. Wilson's view dominated the conventional wisdom that guided patrol operations for much of the twentieth century. For Wilson (1963:39–40), the purpose was to have an officer "patrol his beat [and] be alert for conditions that may jeopardize the comfort, safety and welfare of the people, and take actions to correct improper conditions." Today, this traditional view of patrol has been substantially expanded. Alpert and Dunham (1997:135) summarized the responsibilities of patrol:

- Deter crime through routine patrol.
- Enforce the laws.
- Investigate criminal behavior.
- Apprehend offenders.
- Write reports.
- Coordinate efforts with prosecutor.
- Assist individuals in danger or in need of assistance.
- Resolve conflicts.
- Keep the peace.
- Maintain order.
- Keep pedestrian and automobile traffic moving.

This list basically reflects patrol activities from a traditional standpoint. As community policing is included in departments' operational strategies, this list will be expanded to include community-based activities; for example, Kappeler and Gaines (2011) advised that community policing will require the police to work more closely with citizens and other governmental agencies when attempting to solve problems. This list may grow to include activities such as holding neighborhood meetings, working with other governmental and private agencies, and coordinating youth recreational activities. Community policing expands basic patrol activities well beyond traditional limits and involves officers in activities that previously were reserved for specialists from other units within the police department.

How well patrol officers perform traditional tasks and newly acquired tasks as a result of community policing has long been debated and studied. In simple terms, patrol officers are to provide a timely response to citizens' requests for service whether they relate to community policing or traditional needs. Their presence in a given area allows them to respond more quickly than if they were to be dispatched from a central location. When not responding to calls for service, officers' patrol activities are designed to create a high visibility for the department and allow them to become involved in officer-initiated activities. Historically, visibility was believed to repress crime. This *omnipresence* (an appearance that the police were everywhere) is thought to have a deterrent effect on potential criminals and at the same time increase the citizens' feelings of safety.

DEPLOYING PATROL PERSONNEL

It is no simple task to effectively deploy patrol personnel. Most departments establish beat boundaries by calculating patrol-committed time in a fashion similar to how workload studies are performed. *Committed time* refers to any time that an officer is committed to some call or police activity. Patrol officers are either on patrol (not assigned to an activity) or they are responding to some crime or citizen need. Today, computers allow administrators to plot police activities geographically and determine the amount of officer time required for each activity or type of activity. *Beat boundaries* are established by attempting to equalize committed time across all of the department's beats.

Large police departments divide the city into sectors, districts, or precincts that are commanded by a captain or major. These districts often are fairly independent from other districts in the police department and adopt distinct social norms and policing priorities. In some cases, there are significant differences in how the various districts are policed (Hassell, 2007; Klinger, 1997). Each district contains several beats. For example, Sacramento has six districts. Box 5.2 contains a map of the beats in district 3. Notice that the district contains five beats.

One common error in determining patrol assignments has been the use of aggregate data that compared the level of activity for given areas. Although some areas maintain a constant level of activity, it is far more common to find that demands for services vary according to time of day, day of week, or even season of year. An entertainment district may generate a relatively high amount of activity on the weekend followed by low levels of activity during the week. A university in an adjacent district may have higher demands for service during the week when students are on campus and relatively low levels of activity on the weekend when most of them return home. Using this same example, the entertainment district will have a higher level of activity during the evening hours, and the university will have a higher level of activity during the day. Aggregate data that merely summarize the total amount of activity over time might indicate that these two districts are comparable in the amount of work to be performed. If the aggregate data are used to assign officers, the entertainment district will be overstaffed during the week and understaffed on the weekends. The opposite would occur in the university district, where a majority of the activity occurs during the week, and relatively fewer demands for services occur on the weekend.

Box 5.2   Beat Structure for District 3 in Sacramento

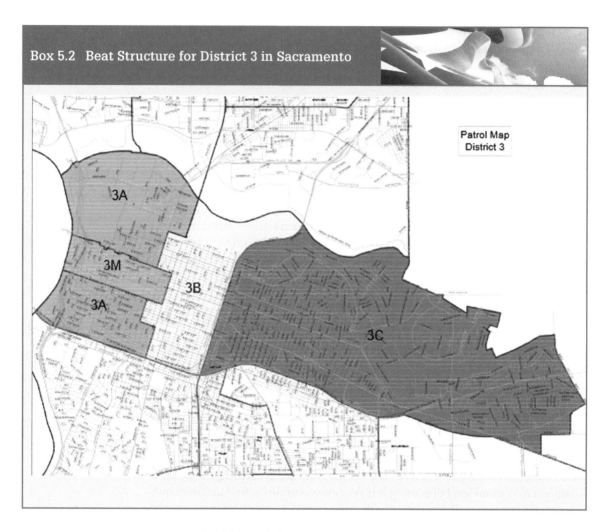

As a result of demand fluctuations, many departments have different beat con-figurations across shifts. The beats for the morning shift are different from the beat boundaries for the night shift. Box 5.3 provides an example of how police activities fluctuate over time. Also, in an effort to deploy police personnel more accurately, departments may change their beat structures periodically during the year. The pattern of activities for most cities during winter months is pro-foundly different from the pattern of activities during the summer months. Today, police administrators constantly monitor police activity to ensure that they have deployed their patrol personnel most effectively.

One-Officer and Two-Officer Patrol Units

One issue in patrol deployment has been whether to use one-officer patrol units or to staff patrol cars with two officers. Historically, patrol units were

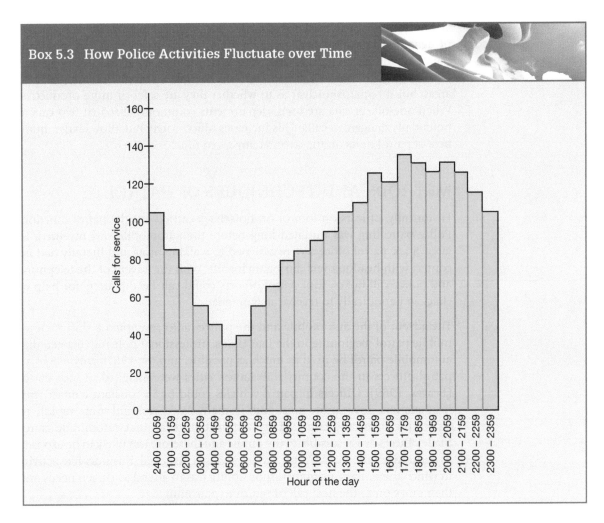

Box 5.3 How Police Activities Fluctuate over Time

staffed with two officers, assuming that two-officer units were safer; however, as personnel costs increased, police departments began to use one-officer patrol units. Boydstun, Sherry, and Moelter (1977) undertook the first study of patrol car staffing and found that one-officer units made more arrests, filed more crime reports, and had fewer citizen complaints. Kessler (1985) replicated the study and achieved similar results. Kessler also found that officers in one-officer units were less likely to be injured. In a more recent study, Wilson and Brewer (2001) found that officers in two-officer units encountered more resistance from citizens, indicating that officer demeanor or the dynamics of interactions with citizens changed as a result of the additional officer.

Officers tend to favor two-officer patrol units. In a Texas police department study, del Carmon and Guevara (2003) found that officers believed two-officer units were safer and that officers could observe more while on patrol. They also advocated their use in high-crime areas and at night. About a quarter of departments continue to use two-officer patrol units, with larger departments having a greater number of two-officer patrols. When a department uses two-officer patrol units, they generally are deployed at night or in high-crime areas, but it remains unclear as to whether they are safer or more productive. When one-officer cars are used, departments commonly dispatch two cars to potentially dangerous calls. This increases officer safety but allows larger numbers of patrol units on the street at any given time.

METHODS AND TECHNIQUES OF PATROL

Historically, officers on foot or on horseback carried out the patrol function. Police patrolling was initiated long before the automobile was invented. In large cities, patrol officers were assigned to walking beats and literally had no contact with headquarters during their shift. With the advent of the telephone and police call boxes, foot patrol officers could call headquarters for help or check in periodically to receive assignments.

The advent of the automobile and the police radio prompted a shift to automobile patrol. Beginning in the late 1950s, professional policing dictated that automobile patrol be used as much as possible, and, by 1987, only 6% of all patrol officers in the country's 59 largest cities were assigned to foot patrol (Reaves, 1989). Officers in patrol vehicles could be in constant contact with headquarters, cover more area, and, in many cases, respond more rapidly to citizen problems and crime. Many administrators felt that automobile patrol made officers less accessible to the public and therefore less likely to be exposed to corruptive influences. Patrol was viewed as a detached, business-like activity in which the officers' primary responsibility was to attend to citizen needs and then move on to the next call or return to patrolling.

Use of aircraft, boats, and bicycles and a return to officers on foot or horseback have allowed the police to address specific problems. Furthermore, police departments realized in the 1970s and 1980s that the police must work with citizens, and departments began to implement patrol methods that increased public contact and fostered better relations. Specialized patrol methods are recognized as a necessity today, and most large departments are using some form of specialized patrolling; for example, many of the nation's larger police departments are reinstituting foot patrols. In this section, we will examine the methods and techniques of patrol and their applicability to the patrol function.

Foot Patrol

Although significantly reduced or abandoned in favor of the automobile, the use of foot patrol has witnessed resurgence over the past 30 years. About 55%

of police departments use foot patrols (Reaves, 2010). One of the primary reasons for returning to this technique was to address the growing problem of decreased citizen–officer interaction. Before the automobile, officers were assigned relatively small patrol areas. Most departments would routinely assign officers to the same area for an extended period. The officer became familiar with the residents and their needs, whereas citizens became familiar with the officers and their limitations. In the past, the foot patrol officer was viewed as part of the neighborhood, a resource for citizens to turn to in time of trouble. In essence, the officer was more of a community advisor and helper than a law enforcement agent. This relationship was beneficial for the officers because residents who knew and trusted them were more likely to cooperate in crime prevention and suppression activities. Perhaps more importantly, foot patrol officers provided a link to other governmental services. The officers were expected to be familiar with a neighborhood and their problems, making referrals to government services as appropriate. Generally, foot patrol programs were designed to accomplish a number of objectives, which included the following (Trojanowicz, 1982:17–19):

1. Decrease the amount of actual or perceived criminal activity.
2. Increase citizen perception of personal safety.
3. Deliver residents a type of law enforcement service consistent with community needs.
4. Create community awareness of crime problems and methods for increasing the ability of law enforcement agencies to deal with actual or potential criminal activity effectively.
5. Develop citizen volunteer action in support of the police and aimed at various target crimes.
6. Eliminate citizen apathy about reporting crime to the police.
7. Increase protection for women, children, and the elderly.

Although it is not feasible to abandon the automobile, many agencies have incorporated foot patrols into their overall strategy. Realizing that not every area is geographically suitable for foot patrol, agencies have selected target locations to reinstitute the technique. Efforts in this regard generally focus on business and entertainment districts or residential areas with a high concentration of people or criminal activities.

Early programs in Michigan and New Jersey are generally cited as examples of successful efforts to reintroduce and evaluate the usefulness of foot patrol. The Flint Police Department started a neighborhood foot patrol program in 1978. By August 1983, nearly $3 million had been spent to support the foot patrol and its evaluation. Evaluations by researchers from Michigan State University indicated that the program was well received by officers and citizens alike, even though crime had actually increased. It was found that foot patrols increased citizen's perceptions of public safety. In 1983, with decreasing financial support, the department faced the prospect of reducing the program, but it was rescued by citizen support for it, and citizens voted for increased taxes on three separate occasions to support the program (Figure 5.1).

A similar study was conducted in Newark, New Jersey. An evaluation revealed that citizens were acutely aware of the foot patrol officers and a police presence. Citizens reported that they felt safer and that serious crimes were declining in their neighborhood, even though crime levels remained virtually constant. It seems the intimate contact between citizens and police officers as a result of the foot patrols engendered positive attitudes about the police and the community (Table 5.2).

More recently, the Philadelphia Police Department initiated foot patrols in high-crime areas in an effort to reduce violent crime. In 2008, the top 5% of street corners in the city accounted for 39% of robberies, 42% of aggravated assaults, and 33% of homicides. Street corners were divided into control and experimental areas, and pairs of foot patrol officers were assigned to the experimental corners. Violent crime decreased by 22%, vehicle-related crime decreased by 12%, and drug incidents were reduced by 28% in the experimental areas. The foot patrol officers' activities resulted in a 51% increase in pedestrian stops and a 33% increase in vehicle stops, and arrests increased by 13% (Radcliffe, 2010). Whereas the foot patrols in Flint and Newark did not have an

FIGURE 5.1
Louisiana State Troopers talk with a tourist during a foot patrol in Jackson Square in the French Quarter of New Orleans. *Photo courtesy of AP Photo/Alex Brandon.*

Table 5.2 Types of Regularly Scheduled Patrols Other Than Automobile Used by Local Police Departments by Size of Population Served

Population Served	Percent of Departments Using Each Type of Patrol Regularly						
	Foot	Bicycle	Motorcycle	Marine	Transporter	Horse	Air
All sizes	55	32	16	4	2	1	1
1,000,000 or more	92	100	100	69	31	77	100
500,000–9,999,999	81	100	94	52	29	61	71
250,000–499,999	78	89	91	26	24	50	57
100,000–249,999	59	71	90	12	15	17	14
50,000–99,999	56	69	74	12	6	5	5
25,000–49,999	52	58	55	6	4	2	1
10,000–24,999	50	44	25	5	2	1	1
2500–99,999	58	36	8	4	1	—[1]	0
Less than 2500	54	15	4	1	—[1]	0	—[1]

[1]Less than 0.5%.
Source: Reaves (2010).

appreciable impact on crime, the Philadelphia experience demonstrates that foot patrols can be highly productive in high-crime areas.

Given the results from Flint and Newark, it would seem that police departments should increase the levels of foot patrolling; however, police officials can use foot patrols only sparingly because of their substantial costs. Several officers are required to cover an area that one automobile patrol could cover. Foot patrol remains a strategy that can be used to police small, high-crime areas or that can be implemented temporarily and then removed when crime and order-maintenance problems have abated.

Horse Patrol

As with foot patrol, horse patrol has a long police history in the United States; for example, the San Francisco Police Department began using horse patrols in 1874. Many of the same reasons that prompted a return to foot patrol officers have been offered as justification for horse patrols. They are readily accessible to the public, they are a positive public relations tool that serves as a bridge to the community, and they can perform some duties more efficiently than officers in automobiles. They are well suited, for example, for rugged terrain such as parks and are especially useful in disorder situations. Horse patrol officers are able to cover a larger area than traditional foot patrol officers can. However, only about 1% of police departments deploy horse patrols with larger departments using them more as compared with smaller departments (Reaves, 2010) (Figure 5.2).

FIGURE 5.2
Police officers ride their horses downtown in New York on a main street in Manhattan on July 7, 2010.
Copyright Shutterstock/Jorg Hackemann.

In spite of their usefulness, horses have a number of limitations. The amount of equipment an officer can carry is limited, and horses are not suitable for patrol in many areas. With the exception of parking regulations, it is difficult to enforce traffic laws from atop a horse. They generally are restricted to daylight hours or patrol of well-lit areas. Finally, the acquisition, care, and maintenance of horses for horse patrols can be rather expensive compared with automobile patrols (Table 5.3).

Bicycle Patrol

The bicycle has a long history of use in Europe and in some cities in the eastern United States. Communities that are large in geographical area and low in population densities rarely use them for patrol because they are impractical. As urbanization continues and population density increases, many agencies are considering bicycles as an additional patrol technique. This factor, plus the current trend toward community policing that stresses enhanced police–citizen contact has led departments to create or reestablish bicycle patrol units with 32% of police departments using this type of patrol (Reaves, 2010).

Like the horse, bicycles have certain advantages over foot patrols. Officers are able to travel greater distances at a faster rate. Although readily visible while on routine patrol, the bicycle offers the option of concealment and stealth when approaching suspects. They can travel in places where automobiles cannot go, such as alleys, dirt paths, down stairwells, and on sidewalks. They are far more maneuverable in traffic than the automobile. Officers believe that bicycles are good public relations tools—so popular, in fact, that a normal part of their daily routine includes being photographed with tourists (Figure 5.3).

Table 5.3 Use of Animals by Local Police Departments by Size of Population Served	Percent of Departments Using:	
Population Served	Dogs	Horses
All sizes	29	1
1,000,000 or more	100	77
500,000–999,999	100	61
250,000–499,999	100	52
100,000–249,999	95	20
50,000–99,999	87	7
25,000–49,999	66	2
10,000–24,999	51	1
2500–9999	23	—[1]
Under 2500	10	—[1]

[1]Less than 0.5%.
Source: Reaves (2010).

Two studies have examined bicycle patrol productivity relative to automobile patrol productivity. First, Clark (2003) compared bicycle and automobile patrols in Cincinnati and found that bicycle patrols were more productive across a number of areas, including misdemeanor arrests, juvenile arrests, field interviews, property recovery incidents, warrants served, crimes discovered, vice incidents, and motorist assists. The only category in which automobile

FIGURE 5.3
Minneapolis Police patrolling in the Liberty Parade, in Minneapolis, August 31, 2008. *Copyright Shutterstock.*

patrols were more productive was felony arrests. In a similar study, Menton (2008) found that bike officers had more contacts with the public and were involved in more serious encounters. These studies demonstrate that bicycle patrols are highly productive and ideal in densely populated areas.

Aircraft Patrol

Patrol by airplane and helicopter is viewed as a necessity for many agencies. About 1% of police agencies have some form of air patrol with larger departments more often using airplanes or helicopters (Reaves, 2010). Aviation units serve a number of functions: search and rescue, medevac operations, transportation of prisoners and personnel, surveillance, tracking, and general support of ground operations. Aircraft are finding increased use in drug enforcement activities to track suspects and vehicles and to locate marijuana fields. Officer safety during car chases is improved because the aircraft allows patrol officers to slow down while the aircraft follows a suspect vehicle safely from the air. Helicopters are more prevalent than airplanes because of their versatility in surveillance and support activities. The Santa Barbara County Sheriff's Department's aviation program began in 1941 as a volunteer operation that used privately owned fixed-wing aircraft and civilian pilots. In 1995, however, the department acquired three Bell Jet Ranger helicopters. The department currently uses these aircraft for a variety of activities, including support for deputies on the ground, eradicating marijuana, surveillance of narcotics operations, and searching for lost hikers. The aircraft are also used to help coordinate firefighting efforts in brush land areas.

To learn more about the specialized patrols in this section of the chapter, visit the Website **http://www.officer.com/ topics/special-operations**

Aviation units are extremely expensive to institute and operate. In addition to personnel and training costs, aircraft require extensive maintenance and have high operational costs. The cost to purchase and equip a helicopter for police work exceeds $1 million and may range as high as $10 million or more for a command and control aircraft (McLean, 1990:33–35).

The forward looking infrared device is rapidly becoming an essential component of many aviation units' equipment. Although expensive to purchase (approximately $100,000), it dramatically increases the utility of already expensive air operations. The device clearly images objects that vary only slightly in temperature. Its heat and time elements make it possible to locate vehicles that have recently been driven and allow an observer to follow tracks at night, in the snow, and in dense underbrush. A trained operator can easily locate a human body (McLean, 1988). More recently, the device is being used to locate indoor marijuana-growing operations.

Several police departments are now using drone aircraft. These aircraft have been used successfully by the military to hunt down terrorists, but some police departments are now purchasing drone fixed-wing or drone helicopter aircraft. These aircraft can serve a number of functions similarly to traditional aircraft, but they are less expensive to purchase, less expensive to operate, and they do not place pilots in jeopardy. U.S. Customs and Border Protection are using the craft to patrol our border with Mexico. By 2011, the agency had used the aircraft to make 7500 arrests and seize thousands of pounds of drugs (Kaminsky, 2012). Police departments in Mesa County, Colorado; Seattle; Houston; and others have purchased drone aircraft. In some cities such as Seattle, the police department has experienced substantial resistance from the community and elected officials who had privacy concerns. For example, the Alameda County, California, Sheriff's Department wanted to apply for a homeland security grant to purchase drones to monitor unruly crowds and locate illegal marijuana crops, but the proposal drew opposition from the county board of supervisors.

Watercraft Patrol

The presence of a large body of water or navigable river creates the need for a water patrol unit. Policing on the water presents a unique set of challenges. Activities range from combating criminal activities such as drug smuggling to controlling tourists who fail to comply with safety regulations and precautions. Water patrol units vary in size and activities performed depending on their area of responsibility. According to a study by the Bureau of Justice Statistics (Hickman and Reaves, 2010) only about 4% of departments have some form of water patrol with larger departments using this form of patrol more frequently (Figure 5.4 and Table 5.4).

FIGURE 5.4
Los Angeles Port Police. *Copyright Shutterstock/Ron Kacmarcik.*

Table 5.4 Off–Land Vehicles Operated by Local Police Departments by Size of Population Served, 2007 			
	Percent of Departments Using:		
Population Served	**Boats**	**Helicopters**	**Airplanes**
All sizes	**6**	**1**	**_¹**
1,000,000 or more	77	100	38
500,000–999,999	61	74	19
250,000–499,999	41	50	15
100,000–249,999	22	9	2
50,000–99,999	19	2	_¹
25,000–49,999	14	_¹	0
10,000–24,999	8	_¹	0
2500–9999	5	0	0
Less than 2500	2	_¹	0

¹Less than 0.5%.
Source: Reaves (2010).

POLICE PATROL STRATEGIES

Patrol strategies are developed in an attempt to better respond to calls for service, deter crime, or apprehend criminals once crimes have occurred. Throughout much of the twentieth century, there was only one strategy: routine preventive patrol. Based on research that questioned the effectiveness of random patrol as a method to repress or prevent crime, administrators have developed different strategies for deployment and use of officers. In this section, we will review the use of random patrol and a number of directed patrol strategies.

Routine Preventive Patrol

With few exceptions, officers in marked police vehicles dispersed throughout an agency's jurisdiction provide *routine preventive* patrol or random patrol. Officers are assigned to patrol specific areas, often termed *beats*. The geographic boundaries of patrol areas are generally based on some form of workload analysis. Agencies attempt to balance the officer's workload by dividing the city into areas having equal amounts of activity. Under this traditional method of allocating resources, one officer may have a relatively large area to patrol while another may be restricted to an area comprising a few square blocks, depending on the workload of each officer.

Once beat boundaries are determined, officers are assigned to the beats and are expected to randomly patrol or observe when not assigned calls for service. By randomly patrolling, they hope to reduce the opportunities for criminal acts to be committed. When they are not able to prevent criminal acts, their patrol beat assignment facilitates a rapid response and possible apprehension of offenders when crime occurs. If patrol officers are not able to deter crime or intercept perpetrators, they are still available to investigate criminal activities and participate in other crime prevention activities.

Routine Preventive Patrol Reconsidered

Routine preventive patrol has increasingly been criticized for its ineffectiveness, and it requires large amounts of a department's resources. Critics charge that routine patrol is ineffective in deterring criminal activity, patrol units seldom apprehend criminals in the act of committing crimes, and uncommitted patrol time tends to provide little benefit to the department or the community. As Klockers (1983) noted, "it makes about as much sense to have police patrol routinely in cars to fight crime as it does to have firemen patrol in fire truck to fight fire" (p. 130).

The most frequently cited and perhaps most in-depth study of the effectiveness of routine preventive patrol was conducted by the Kansas City Police Department with assistance from the Police Foundation during 1972 and 1973 (Kelling, Pate, Dieckman, & Brown, 1974). The city's South Patrol Division was selected for the study. Fifteen patrol beats were divided into three groups. The first group, *reactive beats*, included five beats where patrol was withdrawn and police officers only entered the beats to respond to calls. When calls had been handled, officers were instructed to immediately leave the beat. Five other beats, *proactive beats*, contained two to three times the normal levels of patrolling. Finally, five *control beats* contained the normal patrol contingent. Box 5.4 shows the beat configuration used in the experiment.

If random patrol had an effect on crime or citizen satisfaction with the police, one would predict that where patrol was increased crime would decrease and citizen satisfaction would increase. Conversely, in the area where random patrol was eliminated, one would expect crime to increase and citizen satisfaction to be diminished. There should have been no changes in the area where patrol was maintained at its previous level. The results of the study shocked the police community. The researchers examined four different types of variables: victimization, citizen fear of crime, citizen attitudes toward the police, and police response time to calls for service. There were no significant differences in any of the three areas in the amount of crime or citizen satisfaction, and most citizens did not realize the patrol levels had been altered.

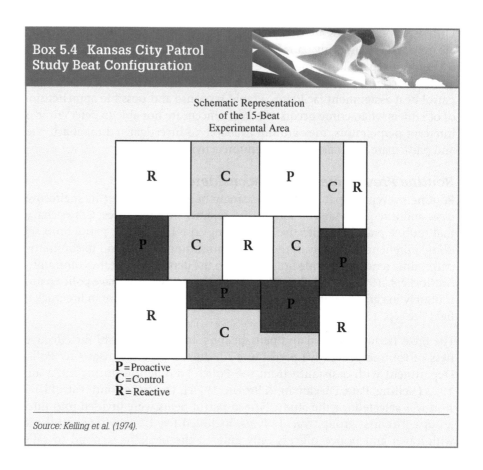

Box 5.4 Kansas City Patrol Study Beat Configuration

Schematic Representation
of the 15-Beat
Experimental Area

P = Proactive
C = Control
R = Reactive

Source: Kelling et al. (1974).

This study has been the focus of much debate and controversy. Some have mistakenly interpreted the study to mean that the police have no effect on crime; however, it merely points out that routine patrol has minimal effect on crime. The study also implies that specialized, aggressive patrol tactics should be considered as more appropriate tools to combat crime problems. Within this context, it is perhaps more important to focus on how the police spend their time. By restructuring activities, patrol can indeed become an effective way of combating crime (Koper, 1995; Worden, 1993). Sherman and Weisburd (1995) found that increasing patrols in high-crime areas could result in reductions in crime and disorder. In essence, targeted patrols, as opposed to random patrolling, can have an impact on crime (Figure 5.5).

Maximizing Resources for Directed Patrol

The implication from the Kansas City Patrol Study is that police departments should devote more resources to directed patrol. *Directed patrol* is where departments appropriate higher levels of officers and other resources to combat crime

FIGURE 5.5
A New York Police Department counterterrorism officer watches commuters entering the subway at Grand Central Station in New York. *Photo courtesy of AP Photo/Kathy Willens.*

or disorder problems in a specific location or geographical area. Directed patrol sometimes necessitates acquiring additional personnel, whereas some departments are able to implement directed patrol strategies by better using current resources. Better use of police resources to implement directed patrol can be accomplished by:

1. Patrol workload studies
2. Delayed police response
3. Differential police responses

Reducing Patrol Time

Administrators sometimes can obtain the personnel necessary to implement directed patrol by examining the department's workload. Famega (2005) examined a number of police workload studies and found that, on average, 75% of officers' time is not devoted to calls. This does not mean that officers do not do anything during this time. They often complete reports, serve warrants, attend to personal business such as meals, and become involved in self-initiated activities such as traffic or pedestrian stops. Even when these other activities are included in the workload, patrol officers generally are patrolling about one-third of their shift. Police managers could more effectively use this time by providing officers guidance in terms of patrolling high-crime areas and engaging in problem solving. Better managing patrol officer activities could significantly increase patrol effectiveness. Admittedly, some departments are understaffed and patrol officers are overwhelmed by the workload, but many departments can easily afford a reduction in patrols. The workload of every unit in the police department should be similarly examined to determine whether personnel could be reassigned to some form of directed patrol.

Delayed Police Response

A timely and rapid police response has long been an important strategy for patrol. Contemporary research shows that police response time does not necessarily increase apprehension rates (Pate, Ferrara, Bowers, & Lorence, 1976). First, it should be noted that the vast majority of calls to the police are not related to crimes. Most of the criminal or serious calls to the police are "cold," where the perpetrator has long since absconded, or the victim has waited an inordinately long period before calling the police. A national study of response times showed that approximately 75% of serious (Part I) crimes were cold when the citizen notified the police (Spelman & Brown, 1984). Citizen delays in calling the police are attributable to:

1. Apathy
2. Skepticism about the police's ability to do anything
3. Citizens notifying other persons before calling the police

It seems citizens wait at least 5 min before calling the police in about one-half of the serious crimes that are reported. These studies clearly indicate that rapid response does not contribute to increased apprehensions in the majority of crimes.

A second consideration with rapid response is citizen perceptions of police effectiveness. Untimely delays for a police response do cause citizen dissatisfaction with the police (Pate, Ferrera, et al., 1976; Percy, 1980); however, this dissatisfaction can be reduced and controlled through proper police communications procedures. In most cases, discontent is the result of the police response being slower than that which the police dispatcher indicated or led citizens to expect. Police dispatchers should calculate and advise citizens of delays for nonserious calls to reduce negative sentiment. Worden (1993) found that citizens were satisfied with the police response when they were appropriately advised of response time delays, but Frank, Smith, and Novak (2005) found that response time had little bearing on citizens' evaluations of police effectiveness. It appears that getting to the scene is less important than what the police do when they get there.

Many police departments control their responses through call prioritization. Call-takers categorize calls in terms of their severity, and the most serious calls are answered by officers, whereas nonserious calls are held until officers are available to answer them. Managers are able to schedule officers for the average workload during a shift as opposed to the maximum workload. This, in essence, frees up some officers for reassignment to directed patrol or other duties.

Differential Police Response

Historically, most departments adopted the policy that when a citizen called the police a patrol car was dispatched as soon as possible, regardless of the nature of the call. Emergency calls where life or property were in immediate danger received priority over other calls, which generally were handled in the order in which they were received. In reality, many calls did not require any patrol response at all.

A *differential police response* entails responding to citizen calls by means other than dispatching an officer. McEwen, Conners, and Cohen (1986) identified several alternatives to an immediate police response:

1. Telephone report unit for taking reports of minor crimes over the telephone
2. Procedures for a delayed police response (holding calls for 30–60 min)
3. Referring calls to other agencies
4. Using report-taking alternatives, such as scheduled appointments, walk-in reporting, or mail-in reports

They suggested that approximately 20% of the calls received by a police department can be handled without an on-scene response. Alternative police responses can substantially reduce patrol requirements and allow officers to be used for directed patrol.

Police workload studies, call prioritization, and differential police response represent procedures by which to better manage patrol resources. When Worden (1993) examined delayed police responses in Lansing, Michigan, he found that they could be properly managed so that the police responses were both efficient and equitable. Alarid and Novak (2008) surveyed citizens and found that they were receptive to telephone reporting but were not receptive to making reports by mail or the Internet.

Not Responding to Certain Calls

Most police departments dispatch a police officer to all calls that are received from citizens. Although many problems are best handled by another agency, citizens generally call the police, because they are readily available, especially after normal working hours. Rather than responding to these calls, the police should refer callers to agencies that can help them deal with the problems.

One area of particular interest is false burglar alarms. The number of alarms has increased drastically in many jurisdictions. In some places, all new houses are wired for burglar alarms, and with the increase in alarms comes an increase in burglary calls, with the vast majority being false. Sampson (2003) noted that, of the approximately 38 million alarm activations each year, somewhere between 94% and 98% of them are false. Each year, the Chicago police respond to more than 300,000 burglar alarms, with 98% of them being false. In essence, false burglar alarms in Chicago consume the equivalent of 195 full-time officers. Essentially, alarm companies market police services. They guarantee their clients an armed or police response to these alarms.

Several police departments have attempted to better manage alarm calls. Some of the tactics used include: (1) requiring alarm owners to register their alarms, (2) training for alarm owners, and (3) fines for false alarms. These tactics can reduce the number of alarms, but even after their implementation departments generally find that 8% of their calls for service are for alarms, which is a considerable portion of a department's workload.

Jurisdictions are now moving to a system of verified response. This requires that the alarm company send personnel or hire security firms to investigate alarms before calling the police. Because burglar alarms are of the lowest priority in many police departments, the response time likely would be reduced by having a third party initially investigate the alarm. Alarm companies object to the verified response approach because of the increased costs they incur. Police departments can substantially reduce their workload if a verified response is adopted.

Some police departments have stopped responding to other types of calls as a way of conserving resources. For example, as a result of the recession, in 2012, the San Jose Police Department stopped responding to some nonemergency calls including noise complaints, recycling thefts, noninjury traffic accidents, venders without permits, and illegal parking. The department also eliminated its horse patrols (Parlow, 2012). Police departments should examine their workloads to determine if additional resources can be obtained by not responding to certain calls or forwarding some calls to other agencies that are better prepared to handle the problem.

Directed Patrol

Directed patrol consists of a variety of strategies: saturation patrol, stakeouts, surveillance of suspects, and decoys, among others. Its implementation recognizes that crime and other police hazards are not equally distributed across space and time and that recognizable patterns can often be identified. Sherman (1996) described how calls for police services were concentrated in Minneapolis; 3% of the estimated 115,000 addresses and intersections in Minneapolis were the subject of 50% of the 321,174 calls to police between December 15, 1985, and December 15, 1986. Sixty percent of the addresses and intersections produced no calls to police at all. Of the 40% with any calls, the majority (52%) had only one call, whereas 84% had less than five. The top 5% of the locations with any calls produced 48.8% of the calls (p. 217).

Because chronic repeat call locations require an inordinate amount of police resources, it has been argued that the police should proactively attack these locations with tailored police responses. If these responses are successful, the police should have a disproportionate reduction in crime and problems. If the police concentrate on the "right problems" and the "right locations," they may substantially reduce their workload or enhance public order.

Many police departments today are focusing on "hot spots." *Hot spots* are concentrations of crime and disorder in a specific location or area and in some cases a particular time frame. A variety of activities can occur in a hot spot. A large number of disturbance and fight calls can come from a bar. There may be concentrations of drug dealing on a street corner. An area may have a high concentration of street assaults and robberies. A street or parking lot may have a high number of auto burglaries. It is important to identify the hot spots by examining crime reports. Next, a diagnosis of the hot spot should be conducted to determine the types of crime and activities that occur there. These two activities are generally performed by the crime analysis unit. Finally, the department should devise a strategy to alleviate the problem. This form of policing has been successful for attacking hot spots of crime and disorder (Sherman & Weisburd, 1995), drug-dealing locations (Weisburd & Green, 1995), drug markets (Hope, 1994), crack houses (Sherman & Rogan, 1995), armed robberies (McCampbell, 1983), and violent crime locations (Braga, Weisburd, Mazerolle, Spelman, & Gajewski, 1999).

D-runs

Directed patrol runs, or *D-runs* where officers are assigned travel to a specific location to have an impact on crime, disorder, or traffic problems, have been used in jurisdictions such as New Haven, Connecticut; Louisville, Kentucky; Arlington County, Virginia; and Montpelier, Vermont. D-runs are one strategy that police agencies can use to augment or replace routine patrol. The Arlington County Police Department used D-runs to target their seasonal problem of armed robberies. An analysis of the previous year's robberies revealed that they occurred primarily during the evening hours in four districts. To address the problem, officers were placed in small patrol areas and instructed not to leave their area except to answer a call. All uncommitted time was to be spent performing robbery prevention activities in the target areas. All available marked patrol cars were used, including unmanned vehicles parked in conspicuous locations. The vehicles were randomly moved to different locations during each shift. The emphasis was on high visibility to deter would-be robbers. At the conclusion of the project, robberies occurring during the evening hours in the target areas had been significantly reduced (McCampbell, 1983).

The Louisville Police Department, in a similar program, provided each patrol with D-run assignments. The assignment sheet contained a map of the beat and specific locations with descriptions of the various clusters of problems and the times at which the problems generally occurred. Problems ranged from rowdy or disruptive juveniles to traffic crashes. Patrol officers were encouraged to be in the areas at the designated times and to focus on the identified problems. D-runs can be useful when a problem occurs in a specific location during a specific time frame. Box 5.5 provides an example of a beat map with associated D-runs.

There is research supporting D-runs. Koper (1995) examined increased patrol time at crime hot spots. Patrol officers assigned to frequently go to hot spots on a random basis and spend time at the hot spot location. Koper found that when officers randomly and frequently spent about 15 min in each location crime was reduced. Telep, Mitchell, and Weisburd (2012) replicated Koper's work in Sacramento. They found the strategy reduced calls for service and Part I crimes. D-runs are a simple strategy that can be implemented without increases in police officers.

Split Force

The Wilmington, Delaware, Police Department is the best example of *split force policing*. In Wilmington, the patrol force was split into two separate patrol groups: the patrol call-answering group and the criminal interception group. The program was based on a belief that a patrol division is responsible for two essential functions: responding to calls for service and crime suppression and prevention.

The patrol force was responsible for calls for service and random patrol. When not handling complaints, they engaged in assigned activities that required short amounts of time to complete and that could be interrupted by service calls. These activities included monitoring schools at opening and closing times, traffic enforcement, security checks of property, and patrol of problem or nuisance areas. To provide adequate coverage for service calls, officers were scheduled according to an analysis of the workload demands. Research had shown that only 7% of their calls required an immediate response. The remainder of calls was nonemergencies that could be delayed until a patrol unit was available.

The *crime suppression force* devoted its time almost exclusively to crime prevention, deterrence, and apprehension activities. Additionally, officers were expected to respond to serious in-progress crimes. Various tactics were employed by the crime suppression force, including high-visibility saturation patrols, covert patrols, and decoy operations. Saturation patrols were directed at deterring crime, whereas covert and decoy operations addressed the need for detection and apprehension of offenders. Covert patrol was accomplished not only through the use of unmarked police vehicles, but also through the use of service vehicles such as taxicabs and delivery trucks. Activities were selected on

Box 5.5   District 1 Beat 8

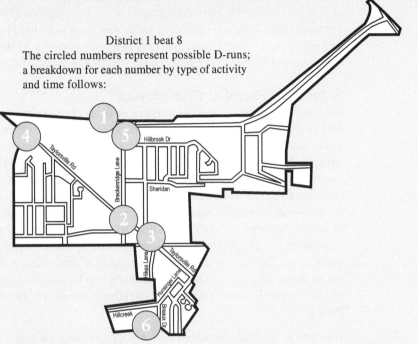

District 1 beat 8
The circled numbers represent possible D-runs;
a breakdown for each number by type of activity
and time follows:

No.	Time	Location	Activity
1.	0000–0359	2800 Breckinridge Lane (Apartments)	Burglary & Larceny
	0800–1159	2800 Breckinridge Lane (Apartments)	Burglary & Larceny
	2000–2359	2800 Breckinridge Lane (Apartments)	Burglary & Larceny
2.	0000–0359	Taylorsville Rd and Breckinridge Lane	Accidents
	0400–0759	Taylorsville Rd and Breckinridge Lane	Accidents
	0800–1159	Taylorsville Rd and Breckinridge Lane	Accidents
	1200–1559	Taylorsville Rd and Breckinridge Lane	Accidents
	1600–1959	Taylorsville Rd and Breckinridge Lane	Accidents
	2000–2359	Taylorsville Rd and Breckinridge Lane	Accidents
3.	0000–0359	3000 block Hunsinger Lane	Larceny
		Breckinridge Lane and Hikes Lane	Accidents
	0400–0759	Breckinridge Lane and Hikes Lane	Accidents
	0800–1159	Breckinridge Lane and Hikes Lane	Accidents
	1200–1559	Breckinridge Lane and Hikes Lane	Accidents
	1600–1959	Breckinridge Lane and Hikes Lane	Accidents
	2000–2359	Breckinridge Lane and Hikes Lane	Accidents
4.	2000–2359	3710 Taylorsville Road	Larceny
5.	No specific time available	Breckinridge Ln. from Hillbrook Dr. to Sheridan	High-crime area
6.	No specific time available	Hunsinger to Breaux Dr.; Hillcreek south to City Limits	High-crime area

Figure courtesy of the Louisville Police Department.

the basis of information generated by the crime analysis bureau, an essential element of the program. Unlike many agencies, the crime analysis bureau did not operate as a support function but assumed responsibility for identification of activities, direction of street operations, and coordination of efforts between the patrol and detective divisions. Daily meetings were held between the crime analysis bureau, patrol division, and detective division to devise strategies to address specific crime problems (Gay, Schell, & Schack, 1977:141–143).

Saturation Patrol or Crackdowns

Saturation patrol or *crackdowns* attempt to deter crime or problems in a specific area through sudden and dramatic increases in police officer presence, sanctions, and threats of apprehension either for specific crimes or for all types of crimes (Davis & Lurigio, 1996). In some cases, officers will use *zero-tolerance*, where all laws are enforced to bring order to an area. Zero-tolerance usually lasts for a period of weeks or months. On the other hand, *sweeps* are where the police deploy large numbers of officers in an area to make large numbers of arrests. Sweeps generally are short in duration, one or two days, but can be repeated as necessary. The strategy can be applied to virtually any type of street crime, including narcotics, prostitution, robberies, auto theft, burglaries, assaults, and gangs. These crackdowns can be used in a variety of settings, including public housing, specific neighborhoods, or an entire city (Scott, 2003).

The police in Indianapolis used a high volume of traffic stops, enforcement, and field interviews in drug market areas to reduce drug trafficking and crime. The enhanced enforcement resulted in decreases in auto thefts and burglaries (Weiss & McGarrell, 1999). The Houston Police Department added 655 additional officers to the seven highest crime beats. The officers used zero-tolerance policing, high-visibility patrol, and problem-solving to attack the crime problems (Caeti, 1999). The high-visibility patrol beats and the zero-tolerance beats experienced reductions in several Part I crimes. The Kansas City Police Department attempted to crack down on gun-related violence by intensive enforcement of gun laws, searches incident to an arrest, *Terry* stop or investigative pat-downs, and traffic enforcement. The strategy resulted in significant increases in gun seizures and reductions in gun violence (Sherman, Shaw, & Rogan, 1995). Dallas police, in an effort to reduce gang-related violence, enforced truancy and curfew laws and used high-visibility patrols with increased stops and frisks in gang areas. The strategy resulted in reductions in gang violence (Fritsch, Caeti, & Taylor, 1999).

Scott (2003) analyzed a number of saturation patrols and crackdowns and found that they had short-term positive effects. Sherman (1990) noted that crackdowns were an effective method of bringing order to an area that was plagued with disorder. In short, if we are willing to occupy a space with police, we can have a temporary effect on crime. Sherman advised that a crackdown's effectiveness could be increased if followed by additional intermittent crackdowns. Also, if crackdowns are followed with enhanced directed patrol, their effects can be enhanced.

Stop and Frisk

A tactic commonly employed to collect leads on crimes and to prevent crime is stop and frisk stops. *Stop and frisk stops* are where police officers observe a suspicious person, stop the person, and talk with him or her. Using the authority provided under *Terry v. Ohio* (1968), motorists and pedestrians who are suspicious (a reasonable suspicion that the person is involved in criminal activity) are stopped and questioned by officers. They may be frisked for weapons if the officer reasonably believes the person being stopped poses a danger. If an arrest is not made, the officer completes a report that details the subject's description and circumstances of the stop. The reports are used to provide intelligence information on known criminals and their associates, vehicles, and activities. Officers investigating criminal activity in the area also use these reports. Relatively few of these field interrogations lead to arrests, but they are thought to be a deterrent to would-be criminals.

Stop and frisk became a primary crime prevention strategy in New York City. In 2003, New York Police Department (NYPD) officers made 160,851 such stops, and as a result of the department's insistence that officers make such stops, the number climbed to about 600,000 in 2010. These stops resulted in thousands of arrests, mostly for minor crimes. There were many critics of the NYPD's stop and frisk policy, noting many of the stops were violations of people's Fourth Amendment rights and the right to privacy. Indeed, many of the stops were outside the bounds laid out in *Terry*. However, Mayor Bloomberg and Police Commissioner Kelly attributed a reduction in crime to the stop and frisk initiative. Weisburd, Telep, and Lawton (2013) examined crime in New York City and found that crime had declined even though the police department had fewer personnel. The researchers could not attribute the decline to the department's stop and frisk policy as its results could not be disentangled from other NYPD crime reduction efforts.

There is some evidence that the NYPD's stop and frisk policy may reduce crime. Groff, Johnson, Ratcliff, and Wood (2013) examined foot patrols in Philadelphia. Essentially, large numbers of police officers were assigned to foot patrol in high-crime areas to supplement random automobile patrols. The foot patrol officers were instructed to engage citizens and be involved in broken windows policing—attend to disorder and petty crime. Groff and her colleagues report that crime was substantially reduced as a result of the foot patrols. In New York, police officers as a result of being directed to conduct large numbers of stop and frisk stops essentially increased the number of "quality" citizen contacts in high-crime areas. Based on the Philadelphia research, it may be that the contacts, not necessarily the stop and frisks and subsequent arrests, resulted in a crime reduction. There is a need to examine this more closely.

The tactics or strategies discussed here represent police efforts to attack crime and disorder hot spots. There is consistent research that demonstrates that police concentration on hot spots can bring a reduction in crime and disorder or calls for service (Braga, 2005; Ratcliffe, 2010). Braga also found that, for the most part, little displacement of crime and disorder to other areas occurred. The key to policing hot spots is the identification of problem areas, usually through crime analysis, diagnosing the causes, and implementing the most effective strategy or combination of strategies.

Suspect-Oriented Techniques

Suspect-oriented techniques are ones in which agencies direct officers to concentrate on known suspects or classes of individuals. For example, when police officers and detectives believe they know who is committing certain crimes, they can concentrate on apprehending those people. In the 1970s, the Kansas City Police Department formalized what had been an informal process by implementing person-oriented patrols. The program consisted of officers conducting intensive surveillance on known robbers (Pate, Bowers, & Parks, 1976). The idea was for officers to concentrate on dangerous felons, observe them committing a criminal act, and arrest them when they committed crimes. Even though the program was labor-intensive, it was believed that a substantial reduction in the robbery rate, and possibly other criminal activity, could be achieved by concentrating on known, habitual robbers who committed a disproportionately high number of robberies. The program did increase the frequency of arrest for the robbers, but most of the arrests were for drug violations.

Person-oriented patrol was the forerunner of *repeat offender projects* (ROPs), which are designed to arrest large numbers of offenders who commit disproportionately large numbers of offenses. Spelman (1990) noted that about 10% of the offender population was responsible for approximately 50% of the crimes committed. Chaiken and Chaiken (1982) found that habitual offenders had crime commission rates 40 to 50 times higher than regular criminals. If a higher number of these habitual, multiple-offense offenders could be incarcerated, it would have a significant impact on the crime rates.

A survey of police departments found some variation in the way ROPs are implemented (Spelman, 1990). They generally fall into one of three categories:

1. Prearrest targeting, where officers use surveillance and stakeouts to apprehend suspects before or while committing a criminal act
2. Warrant services, where officers track down parole or probation violators or suspects wanted on warrants

3. Postarrest enhancement, where officers enter a case after a suspect has been arrested to assist the arresting officers in developing a stronger case against the suspect

The Washington, D.C., Police Department created an ROP unit to concentrate on habitual or professional offenders. The ROP unit used a variety of techniques and was able to arrest offenders who had long histories of criminal activities. Initially, ROP officers were to spend half their time on surveillance and the remaining time serving warrants. After 6 months, surveillance produced only 14% of the unit's arrests. The unit then implemented more proactive tactics such as stakeouts, buy-and-bust operations, stings, decoys, and other covert means. A Police Foundation evaluation of the program found that target offenders were eight times more likely to be arrested, and although ROP officers made fewer arrests relative to other officers their arrests were quality arrests for felony, drug, and weapons crimes (Martin & Sherman, 1986).

To summarize directed patrol, it first should be noted that it is used to supplement, not supplant, routine preventive patrol. Routine patrol remains the best vehicle for responding to calls for service. Second, there are numerous directed patrol strategies. The most appropriate strategy depends on the problem under consideration. Police managers must attempt to completely define the problem and devise a strategy that best meets the needs of the area. Third, a department may deploy multiple directed patrol strategies at any given time because departments are constantly facing a variety of problems.

Finally, patrol remains the backbone of American policing. Most contacts between the police and citizens are made by patrol officers, and it is responsible for the vast majority of tasks and assignments that a department provides its citizens. It is a function that must be properly managed so that the vast resources it consumes are effectively used. Research consistently supports supplementing random routine patrol with some form of directed patrols in high-crime or disorder hot spots.

Racial Profiling

The previous section described a number of aggressive patrol strategies that are being used to focus on crime problems. When the police become more aggressive and stop or investigate more people, it often leads to complaints of police harassment, especially when minorities are the targets of such investigations. In recent years, there have been complaints about the police racially profiling people they stop or investigate.

Racial profiling is one of the most controversial issues to face policing in recent years. Essentially, *racial profiling* is a charge leveled against police departments for stopping, citing, searching, or arresting a disproportionate number of minorities. Although most of the controversies around racial profiling involved police traffic stops, racial profiling can occur in other police activities. In 2013, the U.S. Justice Department ordered Los Angeles County and the cities of Palmdale and Lancaster to pay $12.5 million as a result of police officers in those cities and Los Angeles Sheriff's deputies targeting and harassing African-Americans and Hispanics in low-cost or Section 8 housing. Housing inspectors and officers routinely harassed residents (Faturechi, Winton and Shyong, 2013). These jurisdictions are not alone. In 2011, the Civil Rights Division of the U.S. Department of Justice issued a report detailing racial profiling in New Orleans (Civil Rights Division, 2011). Several cities have faced similar reviews.

The issue came to light when it was discovered that the New Jersey State Police and the Maryland State Police were disproportionately stopping minorities on portions of those states' freeways (Gaines, 2006). It was charged that officers stopped minorities as a result of race as opposed to an infraction of the law. It seems that officers believed that minorities were more likely to be transporting drugs, thus justifying the stops. As a result of the cases in New Jersey and Maryland, complaints were made and lawsuits were filed against departments throughout the United States.

Profiling has been used in law enforcement at a number of levels. Officers often attempt to profile drug couriers and traffickers, prostitutes, gang members, and terrorists. The problem is that too often race is used by officers as the primary or only indicator when deciding to investigate a citizen. Absent suspicious behavior or other indicators, it is improper to stop citizens solely on the basis of their race.

Today, police departments are using aggressive police tactics to tackle crime as discussed in this chapter. One tactic commonly used is the pretextual traffic stop. A *pretextual traffic stop* occurs where an officer uses the pretext of a traffic violation to stop a vehicle to investigate for other crimes. An officer might observe a vehicle whose driver appears to be a gang member and will wait for the driver to commit a traffic violation, such as speeding, driving on the center line, or failing to signal when turning. The officer then stops the vehicle for the traffic violation but investigates the driver for gang activities. In *Whren v. United States* (1996), the U.S. Supreme Court stated that such stops were reasonable as long as the officer had probable cause to believe that a violation had occurred. Citizens, especially minorities, see these practices as racial profiling and discriminatory.

The police have responded to the charges by noting that most aggressive police practices and traffic stops occur in high-crime areas and that high-crime areas frequently are inhabited primarily by minorities. They advise that they are not racial profiling but are engaged in "criminal profiling." Moreover, they note that residents in these high-crime areas deserve the same level of police protection as afforded in more affluent neighborhoods. In other words, the police should not allow problems to occur in lower class neighborhoods that would not be tolerated in middle or upper class neighborhoods.

Numerous studies validate police assertions that traffic stops are occurring in high-crime areas. Gaines (2006) examined traffic stops in Riverside, California, and found that the police predominantly made traffic stops in those areas with high levels of violent crime, property crime, drug trafficking, and citizens' calls for police service. Police officers are allocated based on the number of calls in an area. In many cities, poor and minority neighborhoods often experience the greatest amount of crime increasing the probability of stops in those areas. Other studies have discovered similar findings: Cincinnati (Ridgeway, Schell, Riley, Turner, & Dixon, 2006), San Jose (Lansdowne, 1999), Seattle (Engle, Smith, & Cullen, 2012), and Sacramento (Greenwald, 2001). Thus, even though minorities are overrepresented in traffic stops, it appears that at least for the most part, the police are making a high percentage of the stops in reaction to crime and disorder problems.

This is not to say that there are not problems. First, the overrepresentation of minorities in the numbers of traffic stops that occur on the nation's highways cannot be attributed to aggressive crime fighting because these areas do not constitute communities with high crime rates, calls for service, or large minority populations; for example:

- **Baltimore, Maryland**—Of 533 cars searched by Maryland state troopers on Interstate 95, more than half of the drivers were black and 10% were Hispanic. In all, 63% of drivers forced out of their cars were minorities.
- **New Jersey**—According to statistics presented in a lawsuit against the New Jersey State Police, troopers used widespread racial profiling along the New Jersey Turnpike. In 1994 and 1995, although African-Americans made up only 13.5% of the drivers along a stretch of the Turnpike, they constituted 46.2% of drivers stopped by police in that area.

Some police officers and some departments have racist orientations and stop minorities because of race. Skolnick and Caplovitz (2001) noted that some officers view minorities as *symbolic assailants* because their actions or dress may be nonconforming or they may fit officers' perceptions of what criminals look like. Police managers and supervisors must be ever-vigilant in monitoring individual officer's traffic stops and complaints from citizens to ensure that racial profiling is not occurring. Such monitoring and corrective action can reduce the number of complaints and improve police community relations. Additionally, Verniero and Zoubek (1999) suggested ways in which departments could reduce racial profiling problems:

1. Issue a policy prohibiting racial profiling.
2. Provide officers with in-service training about racial profiling.

3. Issue training bulletins discussing the issue.
4. Require officers to have a reasonable suspicion before asking permission to search, a requirement that exceeds the requirements of state and federal law.
5. Prohibit officers from spotlighting occupants of vehicles at night before deciding whether to stop a vehicle.

These actions establish a foundation and culture conducive to better police decision-making. They also send a message to individual police officers about the department's philosophy relative to racial profiling and traffic stops.

Criminal Investigations

Citizens frequently associate criminal investigations with detectives. These perceptions are probably based on the many popular television shows and novels that characterize the detective as the person responsible for investigating crimes and bringing criminals to justice. Investigations are not the exclusive domain of detectives. Other police personnel such as those assigned to patrol, traffic, or other units in the department perform investigations. Patrol officers investigate criminal cases in their capacity as the first officer on the scene, and they generally complete preliminary investigations in criminal cases. Traffic officers investigate traffic accidents and situations or conditions that cause accidents. Records clerks, dispatchers, crime analysts, and other support personnel are involved in investigations by sorting through records and providing information to detectives and other officers. Investigation is a function performed by all police officers.

The *investigative function* focuses on solving crimes reported to or discovered by the police. Osterburg and Ward (2010:5–6) identified a number of objectives for the investigator:

1. Determine whether or not a crime has been committed.
2. Decide if the crime was committed within the investigator's jurisdiction.
3. Discover all facts pertaining to the complaint:
    a. Gather and preserve physical evidence.
    b. Develop and follow up all clues.
4. Recover stolen property.
5. Identify the perpetrator.
6. Locate and apprehend the perpetrator.
7. Aid in the prosecution of the offender by providing evidence of guilt that is admissible in court.
8. Testify effectively as a witness in court.

It is not enough for officers to arrest a suspect as a result of an investigation, but they must attend to each of these objectives in every case.

INVESTIGATIONS: A HISTORICAL PERSPECTIVE

The term "detective" was first used in the 1840s (Kuykendall, 1986). The London police created a detective unit in 1842, and in the 1880s a Special Irish Branch was created to control for agitation for a separate Ireland. Henry Fielding's Bow Street Runners of the 1750s concentrated on investigative activities rather than patrolling. After examining the history of criminal investigation, Kuykendall (1986) identified three historical periods: the detective as secretive rogue, 1850s–1920s; the detective as inquisitor, 1890s–1960s; and the detective as bureaucrat, 1940s–1980s.

The Detective as Secretive Rogue

Up until the 1920s, police detectives themselves were unsavory characters and quite often were immersed in crime or corruption. Unlike today, these early detectives focused on criminals instead of crimes. They seldom investigated a crime unless there was public pressure or the possibility of personal gain; instead, they focused on individual criminals. These criminals were individuals who were committing large numbers of crimes, were easy targets of the investigators, or were enemies of the political administration. The apprehension of these criminals usually resulted in a monetary reward or recognition within the political regime.

Because detectives focused on criminals, rather than individual crimes, it was important for the detectives to fraternize with and infiltrate criminal organizations; consequently, detectives were always living on the edge. Sometimes it was difficult to distinguish the cops from the crooks. The detectives often became actively involved in criminal conspiracies. Sometimes they arrested the criminals, but on numerous occasions they continued the criminal activity and kept the profits. There was a fine line between corruption and duty, with the distinctions constantly changing.

The Detective as Inquisitor

The methods and techniques used by detectives evolved with changes in police administration. Around the turn of the century, sporadic efforts were made to eliminate police corruption and make the police accountable to the public. As the movement flourished, it brought changes in investigations. Police administrators elevated their expectations of detectives in terms of making arrests and clearing cases. The police "third degree" was born out of these new expectations. When faced with public, political, and departmental expectations for more arrests, detectives simply adopted methods that could produce these arrests. Police brutality and abuse of suspects became a way of life for detectives.

Hopkins (1931) studied one department and found that the police physically abused 289 of 1235 suspects. The Chicago Police Department had its "goldfish room," equipped with rubber hoses and blackjacks, which was used for interrogating suspects. The problem was well documented by the National Commission on Law Observance and Enforcement (Wickersham Commission) (1931). One complete volume of the Commission's report was devoted to police brutality. The Commission noted that suspects were beaten, starved, and forced to remain awake for long periods.

The police, during this period, depended too much on confessions and brutal third-degree techniques to solve cases. Detectives seldom collected evidence, interviewed witnesses, or used any of the other investigative techniques that are commonly used today. When the police identified a suspect, they proceeded to obtain a confession any way they could. Due process was nonexistent, so once a confession was obtained the case was solved.

The Detective as Bureaucrat

Two primary forces changed the nature of police investigations in the decades after World War II. First, efforts to professionalize the police escalated and put pressure on detectives to be even more accountable. Detectives began to focus on specific crimes and to respond to individual crime victims rather than only investigating criminals. Police managers began to control their detectives, making them complete reports and integrate their investigative efforts with other officers and units in the department.

Second, the due process revolution of the 1960s placed new legal constraints on police investigations. The U.S. Supreme Court handed down a number of cases that restricted how police officers performed investigations. For example, *Mapp v. Ohio* (1961) applied the "fruits of the poisonous tree doctrine" to the states. *Mapp* essentially prohibited any evidence that was obtained illegally or in violation of a suspect's rights from being admitted in court. In 1964, the Court handed down its decision on *Escobedo v. Illinois*, requiring that police officials allow suspects who are in custody to have access to an attorney when questioning becomes accusatory. *Miranda v. Arizona* (1966) required that police officers advise suspects of their rights to legal representation and against self-incrimination. These three cases not only made any evidence produced as a result of the "third degree" illegal, but also made it extremely difficult for police officers to elicit confessions at all. These, and other U.S. Supreme Court cases, placed many new constraints on police investigative procedures.

These court decisions, although deplored by much of the police community, had a positive, professionalizing effect on law enforcement. With confessions more difficult to obtain, investigators began to rely on developing better cases, carefully collecting physical evidence, and working more closely with victims and witnesses. The "third degree" and confessions had been an easy way out. Investigators essentially had to go about the actual task of investigating as a result of the U.S. Supreme Court due process decisions.

Investigators began to place more emphasis on investigative procedures and the associated paperwork as a result of the increased legal constraints and administrative supervision. Kuykendall (1986) maintained that this eventually resulted in the bureaucratization of criminal investigations. Detectives began emphasizing completing their reports, filing them on time, and investigating those cases that were most easily solved in order to produce better crime statistics. Detectives spent an inordinate amount of time behind their desks reading reports, completing paperwork, holding meetings, and in general discussing criminal investigative procedures (Ericson, 1981). The goal of bringing criminals to justice as a result of criminal investigations was supplanted with the goal of ensuring that the criminal investigation process was correct.

THE INVESTIGATION PROCESS

Nationally, 10–15% of a department's sworn personnel are assigned to a detective unit. In larger departments, investigations are the responsibility of detectives who are assigned full-time to this role. In smaller agencies, patrol officers are responsible for conducting investigations due to the limited number of employees and workload of the department. Some departments divide responsibility for investigations between patrol and detective units whereby patrols investigate minor offenses or, in some cases, the majority of all offenses. Generally, small municipal or county departments will have a state agency investigate crimes because they do not have the personnel or training to conduct sophisticated investigations. The percentage of departments investigating arson is lower because, in many jurisdictions, fire departments conduct arson investigations. The percentage of departments investigating environmental crimes is low because those crimes often are investigated by a state or federal agency.

The investigative workload in our nation's largest cities requires specialization within the detective unit. Greenwood, Chaiken, and Petersilia (1977) reported that the most common detective specializations are "crimes against property" units and "crimes against persons" units. Even more specialization frequently occurs within these two broadly defined units; for example, common units found in crimes against persons divisions include homicide, sex crimes, domestic violence, and crimes against children. Burglary, robbery, and auto theft are common crimes against property units.

Regardless of agency size or organizational structure, part of the criminal investigation responsibility will always be assumed by patrol. Their activities are particularly critical during the initial or preliminary investigation of a crime and provide a basis for the *follow-up investigation*.

Preliminary Investigations

The investigative process is conceptually divided into preliminary and follow-up or latent investigations. The *preliminary investigation* basically is an initial inquiry into a reported crime. The process remains the same regardless of whether the investigation is to be conducted by a patrol officer or a detective.

In most instances, the first officers responding to crimes will be patrol officers. These officers immediately establish control of the scene. They determine if additional assistance will be necessary and may request assistance from detectives, arson investigators, the coroner, or evidence technicians.

The scene is searched to determine whether the suspect is still present. If there are injuries, medical assistance is summoned and first aid is rendered to any injured parties. Access to the area is controlled to prevent the destruction of evidence. The order in which these activities are performed will vary and should be prioritized on the basis of danger to the officer or others present at the scene followed by taking the steps necessary to prevent the loss of evidence. Once the scene has been secured, the preliminary investigation begins.

An interview of the victim, witnesses, and suspects is conducted to determine what crime has been committed and to identify suspects. If an immediate arrest is not made, information can be broadcast to other officers to begin a search for suspects or observe for suspicious vehicles or persons. The crime scene is searched for physical evidence, and the physical evidence is secured for analysis by a crime lab.

To take a virtual tour of a crime lab, visit the Website **http://www.youtube.com/watch?v=1WnXFbcWBBQ**

When interviews have been completed and the physical evidence collected, the officer prepares a written report that documents the entire preliminary investigation. These reports will later be used by detectives for the follow-up investigation and by prosecutors in presenting the case in court. The preliminary investigation is crucial to the successful solution and prosecution of a crime. In fact, patrol officers make the majority of the felony arrests for any given police department. Mistakes made during the preliminary investigation can almost never be rectified, particularly those dealing with the collection of physical evidence (Box 5.6).

Finally, preliminary investigations generally are not extensive, even though they may encompass a number of tasks or responsibilities. Eck (1983) found that officers spend an average of about an hour on preliminary investigations. He found that officers spent an average of 53 min on burglaries and 66 min were devoted to robberies.

Follow-up or Latent Investigations

At the conclusion of the preliminary investigation, a decision must be made whether to assign the case for a follow-up investigation. When detectives are assigned cases they are one of three types: (1) *walk-throughs*,

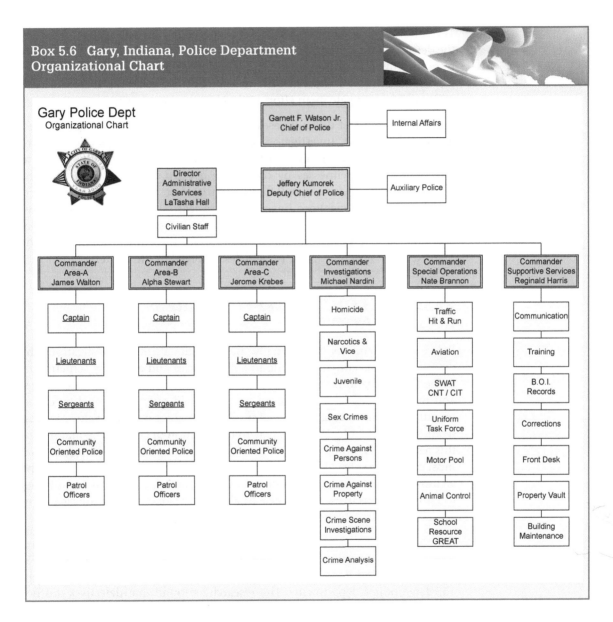

Box 5.6 Gary, Indiana, Police Department Organizational Chart

when the suspect has been identified and apprehended; (2) *where-are-theys*, when the suspect has been identified but officers have been unable to make an apprehension; and (3) *whodunits*, when the preliminary investigation did not result in identification of the perpetrator (Kuykendall, 1986; Sanders, 1977). The type of case will dictate the amount of effort exerted by the detective and the types of investigative actions taken. Walk-throughs and where-are-theys will receive considerably more attention than whodunits.

The follow-up investigation will be initiated when the case is turned over to the detective unit. If a suspect has already been arrested, the detective's primary responsibility is to process the materials and evidence gathered so the prosecutor can file charges and present the case in court. In some cases, the detective will further investigate in an effort to develop a stronger case.

Obviously, the most difficult cases are those in which the investigator must identify the suspect. Investigators sometimes retrace the steps already completed to ensure that no evidence was missed. An attempt will be made to locate additional witnesses by contacting everyone in the area where the crime occurred. *Modus operandi* files (files that describe how known suspects commit specific crimes) can be examined to learn if any similar crimes have been reported in the past. Informants can be interviewed in the hope that they will be able to provide information about the crime. Attempts will be made to trace stolen property or vehicles involved in the crime.

RESEARCH ON THE EFFECTIVENESS OF INVESTIGATIONS

Police administrators traditionally have assumed that investigations by detectives significantly contribute to solving cases and arresting perpetrators. Indeed, investigations were seen as the almost exclusive domain of detectives, and investigations were seen as an art that could only be applied by expert investigators; however, a number of studies have questioned the value of investigations and the role detectives play in the solution of crimes. The majority of this research, beginning with the President's Commission (1976), suggests that most crimes are solved because of arrests made by patrol officers or because the victim was able to supply the name of the suspect to investigators, as opposed to efforts by detectives. About 80% of all cases cleared by arrest are cleared in this fashion (Greenwood et al., 1977).

One of the first major studies to illuminate the interplay among detectives, evidence, and investigative activities was the Rand study published in 1975. In this study, the Rand Corporation examined the investigative practices in 153 large police departments. The researchers found that detectives did not generally solve cases by hard work, inspiration, or science but instead focused on and solved easy cases. Only about 3% of solved cases were solved by detectives exerting extraordinary investigative effort (Greenwood et al., 1977). Subsequent statistical examinations of how evidence affects case outcomes has substantiated these findings with only a few exceptions, such as when cases are solved as a result of specific suspect information provided by victims and witnesses. Other information has little impact on whether a case is solved (Eck, 1979; Gaines, Lewis, & Swanagin, 1983). Table 5.5 provides an example of how pieces of case information contribute to the solving of a robbery. In Table 5.5, if the additive value of the evidence does not equal or exceed 1000, it is very unlikely that the robbery will be solved as a result of routine investigation. The model substantiates that robberies are only solved when victims and witnesses provide fairly straightforward information.

To learn more about crime analysis, visit the Website **http://www.youtube.com/watch?v=NR5Z0s5noRg**

Eck (1983) attempted to refine our understanding of the investigative process and identified three categories of cases facing investigators: (1) weak cases that cannot be solved regardless of investigative effort (unsolvable cases); (2) cases with moderate levels of evidence that can be solved with considerable investigative effort (solvable cases); and (3) cases with strong evidence that can be solved with minimum effort (already solved cases). Eck found that cases within the "already solved" category did not require additional investigative effort or time, and the "unsolvable cases" should not be investigated because it would be a wasted effort. Eck concluded that detectives should be assigned the "solvable cases." Such cases have the potential to be solved with

Table 5.5 Solvability Factors Used to Investigate Robberies

Information Element	Weight
Suspect	
Suspect associate named	508
Suspect seen, suspect known, or suspect named	1000[1]
Clothing	
Clothing evidence only	335
Clothing match	670
Weapon	
Weapon evidence only	348
Weapon match	696
Property	473
License	431

Usage rules

1. Circle the weight for each information item present. In each group use only the largest weight possible.
2. Add up the circled weights.
3. If the resulting number is greater than 1000, classify the case as solvable; otherwise, classify the case as unsolvable.

[1]The weight for this information item actually exceeds the cutoff of 1000. This value shown is simpler to use and yields the same result.
Source: Gaines et al. (1983).

additional effort. Brandl and Frank (1994) examined a number of burglary and robbery cases relative to Eck's three types of cases and found that cases with moderate levels of evidence could be successfully investigated. Thus, contrary to the Rand study, criminal investigations can have positive results, but investigators must focus primarily on those cases that potentially can be solved.

Finally, several researchers have attempted to examine detectives' decision-making processes in terms of how they select cases and conduct investigations. Ericson (1981) and Waegel (1981) found that victims in higher socioeconomic strata received more investigative attention than those in lower strata. On the other hand, victim race, gender, and employment status did not affect the investigator's decision relative to the amount of effort given a case. Detectives will also exert greater efforts when more evidence exists for a given case (Bynum, Cordner, & Greene, 1982; Sanders, 1977). Corsianos (2003) found that high-profile cases tend to receive more attention from detectives. A case can become high profile as a result of media attention, the status of the victim or accused, and the desire to ensure that the police do not receive any negative publicity. Corsianos observed that detective managers and other administrators often took more interest in these cases, resulting in increased detective accountability. It appears, however, that the overriding factor determining an investigator's efforts is the amount of evidence (Brandl, 1993). Detectives tend to informally use evidence criteria to screen cases when deciding on the degree of effort.

Two developments that have significantly affected criminal investigations are the Automated Fingerprint Identification System (AFIS) and DNA testing. AFIS allows the police to check and compare large volumes of fingerprints. Before automation, fingerprint comparisons were performed manually, a feat that was extremely labor-intensive. The Federal Bureau of Investigation (FBI) operates the Integrated Automated Fingerprint Identification System, which includes mug shots, criminal history information and physical descriptions. The system includes more than 668,000 wanted persons and more than 600,000 sex offenders. There are more than 50 million queries per year for the system (FBI, 2013a). The system allows law enforcement officers to perform a nationwide fingerprint search in less than 30 s.

Deoxyribonucleic acid (DNA) testing was developed in the 1980s and allows the police to almost positively link suspects to crimes. DNA is the genetic code that determines the finite building blocks that contribute to our individualism. No two individuals, except for identical twins, have the same DNA. Every state and the federal government requires the collection of DNA from suspects under arrest and offenders convicted of certain crimes. DNA testing has also been used to free wrongfully convicted prisoners as well as identify and convict suspects.

The FBI manages a national database of DNA samples known as Combined DNA Index System (CODIS). The database contains more than 12 million DNA profiles. When DNA evidence is available, investigators can submit the DNA profile to CODIS to determine if the perpetrator has previously committed a crime and his or her DNA sample is on file. This has led to solving ongoing as well as cold cases. The FBI reports that as of 2013, CODIS has produced more than 213,000 hits assisting in more than 204,000 investigations (FBI, 2013b). This has led to many crime labs having a backlog of cases to analyze. In 2009, it was estimated that the backlog of DNA cases in the United States was more than 1 million (National Institute of Justice, 2011). DNA evidence has substantially increased law enforcement's ability to solve criminal cases, but crime labs have not expanded quickly enough to meet the demand. This is due in large part to law enforcement using DNA more frequently. Even though police departments are collecting more DNA evidence, these efforts can be increased. Telep and Weisburd (2012) advise that DNA collection in property crimes should increase, and the increase would lead to increased arrests. DNA frequently is left at the scene of property crimes, but they often have a low investigative priority.

Research on DNA testing shows that it is an effective investigative tool. DNA testing is five times more likely to identify a suspect as compared with fingerprints. Studies show that cases where DNA is used increases the arrests and convictions of suspects. For example, in a study in Denver, twice as many suspects were arrested and convicted when DNA was used as compared with traditional investigations without DNA. Research also shows that patrol officers can collect DNA evidence—the conviction rate for cases where patrol officers collected DNA was about the same as cases where DNA was collected by forensic specialists (Office of Justice Programs, 2013).

Regardless of technological advances, investigations are conducted by detectives collecting evidence and interviewing suspects and witnesses. Many departments have limited numbers of detectives, resulting in a reduction in the ability to investigate all cases that should be investigated. Recently, the Houston Police Department increased its investigative capacity by assigning some investigations to patrol officers (Kenney, White, & Ruffinengo, 2010). The police department assigned 45 patrol officers as Investigative First Responders (IFRs). The IFRs continue to answer calls for service but also perform criminal investigations. The results of the program so far have been impressive. First, the IFRs answered only one call less than regular patrol officers, so the assignment had minimum impact on their ability to perform patrol duties. Second, they investigated a large number of cases and made a significant number of arrests. Kenney et al. noted that many of the cases investigated by the IFRs would not have been investigated due to a shortage of detectives. Finally, as a result of the assignment, patrol officers' investigative report writing improved dramatically. Moreover, the program developed a pool of officers with proven investigative experience who could be transferred to criminal investigation when openings became available. It should be noted that the Houston program questions the traditional practice of having follow-up investigations exclusively assigned to detectives. Other departments should look at the Houston program as a way of expanding patrol officers' roles and career development.

In summary, contrary to how investigations are portrayed by the movies and television, it appears that detective work is fairly routine. Investigators adhere to an ordinary set of procedures. The distinguishing factor in determining how a case is investigated and the amount of time devoted to it is the amount of evidence available to the detective. Finally, even though investigations are fairly routine, technology in the form of AFIS and DNA testing has significantly improved the police's ability to identify and convict suspects.

THE TRAFFIC FUNCTION

No other police activity affects more people than the traffic function. Most people who have been driving for any length of time have been stopped by a police officer as a result of a traffic violation or have been involved in a traffic accident that required an officer to take a report. It is difficult to conceive of anyone who is not affected by the problems associated with the movement of pedestrians and vehicles. Because traffic is often a major problem, many departments have created special units that focus on the numerous traffic-related problems. Their activities include controlling the flow of traffic, enforcing traffic laws, investigating traffic crashes, making recommendations about traffic engineering, and developing education programs to induce voluntary compliance on the part of the public. The nature of the work creates special problems for the police. In recent years, public attention has become focused on enforcement of alcohol-related traffic laws and the dangers of police pursuits.

The Police and the Traffic Function

Critics argue that the traffic function is not properly categorized as a police function. Although it may be possible to assign responsibility for traffic enforcement to someone else, there may be tangible benefits to having it performed by the police. Police often fulfill their law enforcement role through traffic stops. It is commonly claimed that traffic enforcement leads to solving other crimes, more arrests, and the recovery of stolen property. Officers are given the opportunity to stop and interrogate suspects as a result of traffic violations. Wanted persons are routinely apprehended through computer checks of license and registration documents.

Nonetheless, controlled research calls to question the common wisdom that traffic enforcement leads to the suppression of other crimes and enhanced criminal enforcement. Weiss and Freels (1996) conducted a study of aggressive traffic enforcement and its effects on crime in Dayton, Ohio. The study sought to determine whether areas in the city subjected to aggressive traffic enforcement would experience lower rates of street crime and traffic accidents. The study collected data on whether aggressive traffic enforcement would result in increased arrests for certain types of crimes such as drunk driving. They found that increased traffic enforcement did not result in reductions in serious crimes, nor did it have any effect on traffic accidents. In fact, the researchers concluded that increased traffic enforcement activity resulted in significant reductions in arrests for drugs, weapons, and drunk driving. Although common wisdom may suggest that traffic enforcement results in crime reductions and increased arrests, research tends to indicate otherwise.

Enforcement of traffic laws is also said to contribute to the order-maintenance function. Unabated careless driving, congestion, and noise created by drivers have in the past contributed to an escalation of order-maintenance problems in neighborhoods. The service aspect of the traffic function should not be overlooked. Assistance rendered to stranded motorists enhances the public's perception of the police and may be repaid through future cooperation or information in criminal or other matters (Box 5.7).

The traffic control function is carried out through three activities: regulating flow of traffic, enforcing traffic laws, and investigating accidents. Traffic conditions may require the presence of a police officer to direct and control its flow. At some locations, this may occur on a regular basis, such as school crossings or busy intersections. Parades, demonstrations, athletic contests, or other special events may create the need for direction and control on an irregular basis. The goal of officers providing traffic direction and control is to promote public safety and maintain the orderly flow of traffic.

Proactive traffic enforcement is designed to reduce the number and severity of accidents. Selective enforcement is used to target those offenses that are believed to contribute most frequently to accidents or injuries. Particular locations may also be targeted because of the high number of accidents that occur. Officers exercise discretion in their enforcement activities. It is not always necessary to arrest a violator to achieve the desired result. In many cases, warning drivers of the potential consequences of their actions will accomplish the desired goal of accident reduction.

Accident investigations are conducted for two reasons: (1) to preserve human life by collecting information to prevent accidents from occurring in the future and (2) to assist insurance companies in determining fault or liability. Clusters of accidents at specific locations indicate the need for enforcement action. When

Box 5.7 Traffic Laws: Back to the Beginning

Man creates the automobile. In March 1896, Charles and Frank Duryea of Springfield, Mass., offer the first commercial automobile: the Duryea Motor Wagon.

Man hurts man with the automobile. Two months later, New York City motorist Henry Wells hits a bicyclist with his new Duryea. The rider suffers a broken leg. Wells spends a night in jail, and the nation's first traffic accident is recorded. On September 13, 1899, Henry H. Bliss steps off a New York streetcar and is hit by a passing automobile, resulting in the first traffic death.

Man creates the driver's license. In 1903, Massachusetts and Missouri, concerned about vehicular mayhem, enact the first driver's license laws. Five years later, Rhode Island becomes the first state to require a driver's test. Ohio and most other states follow suit within the next 10 years. "Since that time," says the U.S. Department of Transportation, "the testing and licensing of drivers have evolved into a comprehensive system based on the principle that driving is a privilege for those who can qualify."

Man creates traffic laws. On May 12, 1901, Connecticut is the first state to enact speed limits—15 mph on country roads, 12 mph in the city. Other states, including Ohio, adopt similar laws the next year. By 1908, cars are beginning to fill the streets of Columbus. Tickets, primarily for speeding,

are issued. At major intersections, officers direct traffic using large umbrellas painted with the words "Go" and "Stop." In 1911, Columbus police, adopting a "revolutionary measure," do away with their horse-drawn wagons in favor of Ford automobiles. The "mechanized era" of law enforcement—as dubbed by police—begins. By 1920, automobiles are so numerous—and tickets so plentiful—that Columbus' first traffic court session is held on May 19.

Man creates havoc behind the wheel. "I want the traffic slaughter in Columbus to stop," Mayor Myron B. Gessaman says in 1937. "The police have my instructions to go to the limit. Columbus must be made a safe city." Hundreds of traffic tickets are issued. The Dispatch publishes the names of violators and a daily tally of tickets as the death toll reaches 95 for the year. With streetcars and automobiles competing for road dominance, nearly 60% of the deaths involve pedestrians—many stepping off streetcars. In addition, the early cars lack power steering, proper headlights, and hydraulic brakes. "Authorities said 1937 will be marked as the greatest year of slaughter in the history of Columbus," a Dispatch article proclaims on New Year's Day 1938. Fifty-nine years later, the fatality record stands.

Source: Berens (1996).

To learn more about traffic safety, visit the Website **www.nhtsa.gov/**.

the police devise and implement enforcement plans based on accident-causing violations, they usually can reduce the number and severity of accidents occurring at a given location.

Enforcement plans should also consider citizen complaints about inappropriate driving; for example, when citizens complain of speeding in school zones or running traffic signs in specific locations, police officers should be dispatched to engage in selective enforcement. The enforcement of traffic laws at the request of citizens fosters goodwill and potentially reduces future accidents.

Driving-under-the-Influence Enforcement

Driving under the influence (DUI) of an intoxicating substance is a significant health problem in the United States. It was estimated that in 2011, almost 10,000 Americans were killed as a result of drunk drivers. It is also a significant law enforcement activity with about 1.2 million drunk drivers arrested each year. Drunk drivers constitute about 10% of all arrests (National Highway Transportation Safety Administration, 2012). A person is deemed to be driving under the influence when his or her blood-alcohol content is 0.08% or higher.

There have been three important legal policies that have resulted in the police making more DUI arrests (Rookey, 2012). First, primary enforcement of seat belt laws where officers can cite drivers who are not wearing seat belts. These laws increase the number of stops officers make and have resulted in officers identifying drivers who were under the influence. Second, open container laws prohibiting the consumption of alcoholic beverages in public have also resulted in officers making more stops and identifying drivers who are under the influence. Finally, the number of police officers has increased over time increasing the probability of a person who is DUI being observed by officers (Table 5.6).

Most, but not all, law enforcement and other criminal justice officials are committed to stricter DUI enforcement. Departments vary in their enforcement of DUI, as do officers within the same department. Mastrofski and Ritti (1996) reported substantial variation in the rate of DUI arrests for police officers in Pennsylvania. They found that officers in smaller departments (one to five officers) had an average arrest rate for DUI more than seven times that of officers from larger departments (more than 100 officers). They also found that 4.6% of the officers made 42% of all the DUI arrests (Figure 5.6).

Table 5.6 Traffic- and Vehicle-Related Functions of Local Police Departments by Size of Population Served

Population Served	Percent of Agencies Responsible for				
	Traffic Law Enforcement	Accident Investigation	Traffic Direction/ Control	Parking Enforcement	Commercial Vehicle Enforcement
All sizes	100	97	89	86	38
1,000,000 or more	100	100	88	88	81
500,000–999,999	100	100	97	71	57
250,000–499,999	100	100	95	73	61
100,000–249,999	100	99	94	81	56
50,000–99,999	100	99	90	88	51
25,000–49,999	100	99	91	93	52
10,000–24,999	100	99	95	92	45
2500–9999	100	98	90	89	39
Less than 2500	100	94	86	81	32

Source: Hickman and Reaves (2006).

FIGURE 5.6
Working out of a mobile DUI processing van, police officers from the Phoenix DUI squad process an alleged extreme DUI suspect. DUI, driving under the influence. *Photo courtesy of AP Photo/Ross D. Franklin.*

Mastrofski and Ritti (1992) identified several organizational factors that contribute to the level of commitment for DUI enforcement: (1) local demand for DUI enforcement, (2) the police leadership's priority for DUI enforcement, (3) the police leadership's capacity for command and control of the department, and (4) the disposition of the local police culture, organization structures, and other work issues. Additionally, Rookey (2012) found that DUI enforcement was lower in communities with pro-normative drinking climates, demonstrating that community attitudes play a role in DUI enforcement. Factors associated with each of these areas can result in a DUI enforcement program being reduced (Box 5.8).

Individual police officers frequently view DUI enforcement differently. Some officers on a department may make numerous arrests, whereas other officers seldom make DUI arrests. Mastrofski and Ritti (1996) suggested that officers may strictly enforce DUI laws because: (1) they are concerned about productivity, (2) they see DUI as a serious crime, or (3) DUI arrests come to be seen as bounty with official or peer group rewards. On the other hand, officers fail to enforce DUI laws because: (1) they are lazy or incompetent, (2) they do not view DUI as a serious offense or problem, or (3) they do not believe arresting DUI offenders will have any impact on the problem. Clearly, administrators create and have a variety of attitudes to contend with when developing DUI enforcement programs.

The two primary mechanisms by which the police approach the DUI problem are education and enforcement. The news media often display public service announcements describing the penalties associated with DUI. It is

Box 5.8 Drunk as a Skunk, and Quick as a Wink

Lawmakers nationwide focus on measures aimed at the most intoxicated drinkers—those with blood-alcohol levels twice the legal limit—as part of a plan to bring down the number of traffic deaths. Highway fatalities rose in 2002 to their highest level since 1990. There was a 3% increase in those caused by drunken driving during the same period in 2001. The initiatives include the creation of a new charge of aggravated drunken driving for hardcore offenders and the elimination of plea bargains when they could result in charges that do not include alcohol.

Drivers who receive a speeding ticket are 35% less likely to be killed in a crash within the following three to four months. The study, by researchers in Canada and the United States, found that drivers are more cautious after receiving a citation, regardless of their age, gender, or economic class. Getting a ticket even works as a deterrent to young male drivers, a high-risk group, the study said.

Traffic investigators from around the country are invited to attend a one-day course on blowouts offered by the tire manufacturer Michelin North America, Inc. At Tires 101, participants are taught that the proper response to a blowout is counterintuitive—to increase speed and steer straight ahead. When control is regained, pull over.

The Osceola County, Fla., Sheriff's Department came under fire for a sting operation that used deputies disguised as vagrants to catch speeders. Officials defended the initiative against homeless advocates, citing 107 deaths in 2001 from motorists who disregarded traffic signals.

Legislation signed by New Mexico Gov. Bill Richardson will give state and tribal criminal justice authorities the ability to share data on repeat drunk-driving offenders. Each of the state's 22 tribal governments may enter into an agreement with the government to file share. New Mexico, which ranks fifth in the nation in per capita drunk driving, is believed to be the only state to pass such legislation.

A 25-question Internet exam, plus $20 and a hefty fine for speeding, has drivers passing through Summersville, W.Va., hopping mad. Although the strategy does offer motorists a way to avoid notifying insurers, it also points to the town's militancy in collecting fees, they say. But police note that, in 2002, there was only one traffic-related death.

The Rhode Island State Police threw their support behind legislation that would allow tests to extract blood and urine samples from drunken-driving suspects. California is found to lead the nation in accidents involving hit-and-run drivers. … Critics challenge the findings of a Florida Department of Motor Vehicles study, which found cell phones responsible for only one in 170 accidents.

Source: Drunk as a skunk (2003).

believed that such announcements dissuade people from drinking and driving. In terms of enforcement, police departments often hold sobriety checkpoints where drivers are questioned, and if they appear under the influence, are given sobriety tests. A number of police departments use these checkpoints. However, one problem is that they often remain in one location for a long period. The advent of social media such as Twitter and Facebook allow such locations to be broadcast to large numbers of people enabling them to avoid the checkpoints. Police departments should frequently rotate the locations of these checkpoints.

POLICE PARAMILITARY UNITS

Most police departments in the United States now have police paramilitary units (PPUs). Initially PPUs constituted only a small portion of police work, and they were largely restricted to urban police departments. The initial activities of PPUs were rationalized on the rare need for police to address extreme criminal events such as hostage situations, terrorist acts, or sniper shootings. The growth and activity levels of PPUs since the early 1970s, however, have far exceeded the occurrence of these rare criminal incidents. These units have become so popular that they are now depicted on television shows and in movies. These units are not just popular with Hollywood but are also being developed even in the smallest of American police departments. Before discussing the research on the growth and activities of these units, it is necessary to briefly distinguish between PPUs and regular police.

Distinguishing PPUs from Regular Police

Kraska and Kappeler (1997:3) distinguished PPUs from regular police officers and other units within departments by noting that, "PPUs are equipped with an array of militaristic equipment and technology. They often refer to themselves in military jargon as the 'heavy weapons units,' implying that what distinguishes them from regular police is the power and number of their weapons." These weapons can range from submachine guns to military armored personnel carriers and specially equipped tactical cruisers. PPUs are structured after the military model; they operate and train under a military command structure and attempt to impose discipline on their members. They are "a squad of police officers trained to be use-force-specialists. These squads have an intensified operational focus on either the threatened or the actual use of collective force" (Kraska & Kappeler, 1997:4).

In essence, PPUs are highly organized and well-armed units that are rigidly focused on the possibility of applying force. Until very recently, their work

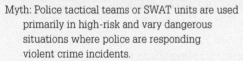

Myths about Special Weapons and Tactics (SWAT) Teams

Myth: Police tactical teams or SWAT units are used primarily in high-risk and vary dangerous situations where police are responding violent crime incidents.
Reality: The vast majority of police deployments of tactical teams are used for the service of routine search and arrest warrants.
Myth: SWAT teams are mainly used by big cities with high rates of violent crime.

Reality: SWAT teams have been created in all sizes of police departments across the country regardless of the rates of violent crime.
Myth: SWAT teams are composed of only the most highly trained use of force specialists.
Reality: The training and selections for SWAT teams varies widely across the country from those agencies that only use highly trained and well-screened officers to those who have no formal selection procedures and provide little to no training.

differed significantly from routine policing in that they reactively responded to a limited number of highly dangerous criminal events.

Generally speaking, for a police unit to be considered a PPU, it must (Kraska & Kappeler, 1997:4):

1. Be state sanctioned, operating under legitimate state authority
2. Be trained and operate as a military special teams unit with a strict command structure and discipline
3. Have at the core and forefront of their function to threaten or use force collectively, instantaneously, and not necessarily as an option of last resort

Kraska and Kappeler's survey of 690 of the nation's law enforcement agencies indicated that, in the early 1970s, fewer than 10% of police departments had PPUs, but that by 1995 more than 89% of police departments had established a unit. Of the departments without PPUs, about 20% were planning on developing one in the near future. Box 5.9 shows the number of units

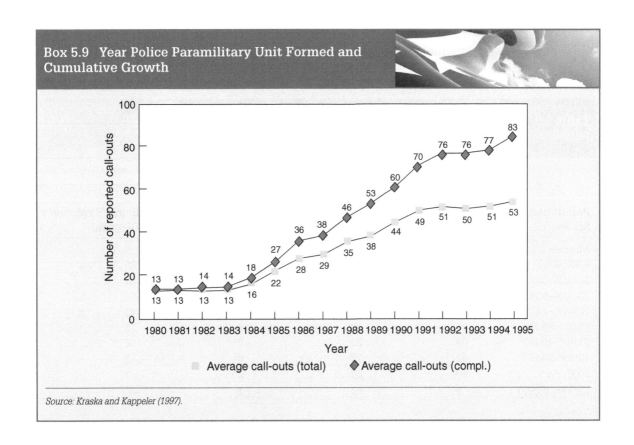

Box 5.9 Year Police Paramilitary Unit Formed and Cumulative Growth

Source: Kraska and Kappeler (1997).

established in each year since the 1960s and the cumulative growth of these units by year. As the figure illustrates, there has been tremendous growth in these units (Table 5.7).

To learn more about PPUs, visit the Website of the National Tactical Officers Association at **http://www.ntoa.org**.

In addition to the tremendous growth of these units, Kraska and Kappeler found that the activities performed by PPUs had increased drastically and that the nature of the activities performed by PPUs changed substantially since they were first created. In 1980, PPUs were called out to respond to a dangerous situation on the average of about 13 times a year. By 1995, however, these units were being used an average of 83 times a year despite a dramatic decline in the nation's crime rate. This represented a 538% increase in the use of PPUs since just 1980. Box 5.10 shows the average number of times these units were deployed since 1980.

Perhaps more important, Kraska and Kappeler found that the nature of the activities performed by these units had changed since their inception. Although citizens normally think of PPUs as responding to dangerous situations such as terrorist acts, snipers, or hostage situations, the researchers found that these activities constituted a very small percentage of what

Table 5.7 Special Operations Functions of Local Police Departments by Size of Population Served

Population Served	Percent of Agencies Responsible for			
	Tactical Operations (SWAT)	Search and Rescue	Underwater Recovery	Bomb/Explosives Disposal
All sizes	25	21	4	3
1,000,000 or more	100	63	56	88
500,000–999,999	97	49	44	87
250,000–499,999	100	29	27	76
100,000–249,999	93	26	17	42
50,000–99,999	86	19	16	18
25,000–49,999	68	20	8	6
10,000–24,999	43	19	6	3
2500–9999	20	20	2	1
Less than 2500	8	22	2	—[1]

[1]*Less than 0.5%.*
Source: Hickman and Reaves (2010).

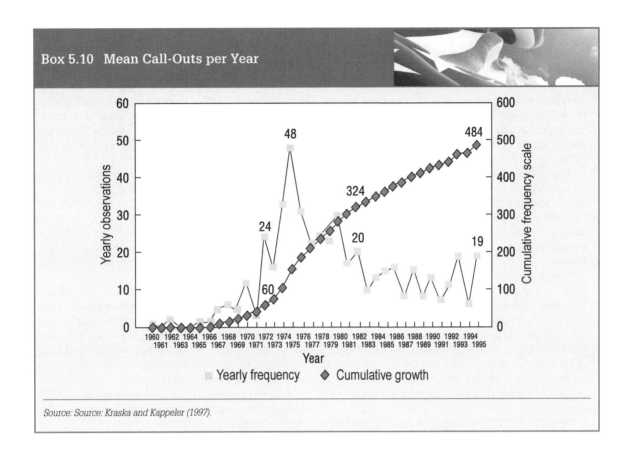

Box 5.10 Mean Call-Outs per Year

Yearly frequency   ◆ Cumulative growth

Source: Source: Kraska and Kappeler (1997).

these units actually do. In fact, the bulk of these units' activities involved the execution of proactive warrants where police officers were not called out to respond to a crisis situation, but rather to initiate an investigative raid on a residence, usually to either serve a warrant or conduct a drug investigation. In 1995, "Of the total number of call-outs, civil disturbances accounted for 1.3 percent, terrorist incidents .09 percent, hostage situations 3.6 percent, and barricaded persons 13.4 percent. ... Warrant work accounted for 75.9 percent of all paramilitary activity" (Kraska & Kappeler, 1997:7). Additionally, the researchers found that more than 20% of the police departments they surveyed used PPUs for patrolling urban areas on a somewhat regular basis (Box 5.11).

POLICE PARTNERSHIPS

Previous sections described a number of police operational strategies and programs. A fairly new innovation in policing is the development of

Box 5.11   Jet Gets Its Wings Clipped So Florida Sheriff's Tactical Training Can Take Off

In addition to the rappelling tower, the structures used for mock disasters and the bomb disposal depot, you can now add one Boeing 727 to the facilities at the Hillsborough County, Fla., Sheriff's Department training center in Lithia.

The 135-ft-long jet was donated to the agency last year by an Orlando air freight company. It arrived in December, all 12 ft wide and 30,000 pounds of it, minus its wings and tail. Officials said the plane will be available to any local, state, or federal law enforcement agency that wants to practice its antiterrorism tactics and homeland security response.

"This is a huge honor for us, and the training that this facility will provide is invaluable in this post-9/11 world," said Sheriff Cal Henderson.

Capital Cargo International, based in Orlando, was going to use the plane for parts when Hillsborough Deputy William Hill received a call from his brother, Ed Hill, the company's director of maintenance. Hill said the firm decided to donate the craft to law enforcement and then learned that Henderson wanted to increase his agency's antiterrorism training.

More than $500,000 was raised from private business and in-kind donations to cover the cost of moving, reassembling, and refurbishing the aircraft. The sheriff's department added approximately $150,000 of its own money. Hill spent months working on the logistics of getting the plane to the Lithia training site. A transport company towed the plane over country roads from the Orlando International Airport to the center in roughly 10 h.

The only other fuselage available for such exercises belongs to the FBI at its training center in Quantico, Va. That facility, however, is available only to federal law enforcement.

"Law enforcement from all over will come to Tampa Bay to ensure all Americans will continue to live free, safe, and secure," said Florida Attorney General Charlie Crist.

The sheriff's department's SWAT team has already conducted an exercise at the Anti-Terrorism Training Facility. More than a dozen members of the unit jumped from tanks and helicopters, storming the plane with rifles and handguns. About 50 "passengers," who included Crist, Henderson, and local disc jockey Skip Mahaffey, were told to put their hands on their heads.

Another exercise was scheduled in January by the FBI's hostage rescue team to train local agents, Tampa police, and sheriff's deputies in anti-terrorism tactics.

Source: Jet gets its wings (2004).

partnerships with other criminal justice and social service agencies. Partnerships allow for more comprehensive responses to problems; for example, it may be beneficial for police officers to work with social service agencies in areas with gang problems. The police could address crime-related problems, and the social service personnel could focus on those social and economic conditions that foster gangs. This approach couples enforcement and crime prevention. In many cases, problem-solving can best be accomplished through partnerships.

Police departments across the country have teamed up with a variety of agencies to form partnerships that focus on an assortment of problems. Perhaps the most common partnership is between the police and probation officers. Parent and Snyder (1999) identified five types of partnerships. *Enhanced supervision partnerships* are made between police and probation or parole officers

(Worrall & Gaines, 2006); probation and police officers visit probationers to ensure that they are complying with stipulations or rules imposed by the court. *Fugitive apprehension units* partner with other police departments or probation or parole officers to arrest suspects that are committing large numbers of crime. *Information-sharing partnerships* involve several agencies to develop comprehensive approaches to problems. *Specialized enforcement partnerships* are best represented by drug task forces. Finally, *interagency problem-solving partnerships* involve various agencies affected by a specific problem that band together to solve it.

One partnership that received a significant amount of attention was Boston's Night Light Program, an arrangement between the police and probation. From 1990 to 1995, probationers committed a high percentage of the city's homicides, and a large percentage of victims were or had been on probation (Jordan, 1998). Police–probation teams were created such that the probation officers could enforce terms and conditions of probation, whereas the police had the authority to investigate and arrest for new offenses. Because probation was a part of the team, the teams could conduct searches of probationers' homes, which sometimes resulted in arrests for new crimes. This technique allowed police to conduct searches without securing warrants from the courts. The teams used a *pulling levers* approach. That is, when they discovered probationers who were not conforming to the terms of probation, they had the authority to institute a number of sanctions that police officers or probation officers each have individually. The teams essentially were able to tailor enforcement and supervision based on the actions of the probationer. The police–probation teams were able to share information and better control a population of offenders who were responsible for a large volume of crime.

Police partnerships have a great deal of potential. When entering a partnership, there must be a clear understanding about the problem. Each agency involved in the partnership should have a full understanding of its role and what is to be accomplished. In other words, partnerships have great potential, but they are only effective when preceded by strategic and tactical planning (Murphy & Worrall, 2007). Also, these practices raise questions about civil liberties and can erode into the police conducting "fishing expeditions" that are not supported by probable cause and sanctioned by judiciary review.

SUMMARY

This chapter examines how police operations are carried out through the patrol, investigative, traffic, and PPUs. Historically, patrol has undergone a number of changes. Patrol traditionally was viewed as an activity that would prevent crime. As researchers began to question the effectiveness of random patrols in combating crime, new strategies were developed. Today, patrol is not viewed as a singular strategy, but is considered as a flexible set of tactics that can be implemented to target specific problems.

The investigative function is directed toward solving crimes, arresting perpetrators, and recovering stolen property. While some agencies may use detectives who specialize in this task, others assign the responsibility to patrol officers. The investigative process is divided conceptually into preliminary and follow-up investigations. A preliminary investigation is an initial inquiry into a reported crime, and a follow-up investigation is initiated in those cases where identification of the suspect appears likely. The efficiency of the investigative function has been questioned. Some researchers question the value of detectives in solving crimes, but others point to the practical problems created by assigning responsibility for this task to patrol officers.

The traffic function affects more people than any other activity performed by a police agency. By regulating the flow of traffic, enforcing traffic laws, and investigating accidents, police agencies seek to reduce the amount of property damage and severity of injuries attributable to accidents. Enforcement of DUI and seat belt laws results in reduced loss of life and injuries.

One of the most recent developments in American police operations is the rise and normalization of PPUs. Since the early 1960s, these units have increased dramatically and the nature of their activities has changed. These units are now engaged in proactive warrant and drug raids, and in a substantial number of cases they are used on routine patrol. Because the bulk of these units were created in the 1980s and 1990s, their effect on police departments as organizations and the police as an occupational culture is still not fully known. Their dramatic rise and proactive nature, however, warrant close scrutiny.

REVIEW QUESTIONS

1. What is meant by the term police operations? What is considered the most important operation of a law enforcement agency?
2. What are the responsibilities of police patrol in the traditional sense, before the implementation of community policing?
3. Name the various methods and techniques of police patrol. What are the common patrol strategies?

4. What is the investigative function of law enforcement and what are the objectives for an investigator?
5. How do Kraska and Kappeler distinguish PPUs from regular police officers and other units within departments? What constitutes the bulk of PPU activities?

REFERENCES

Alarid, L., & Novak, K. (2008). Citizens' views on using alternative reporting methods in policing. *Criminal Justice Policy Review*, *19*, 25–39.

Alpert, G., & Dunham, R. (1997). *Policing urban America* (3rd ed.). Prospect Heights, IL: Waveland Press.

Berens, M. J. (November 17, 1996). Traffic laws: back to the beginning. *Dispatch Staff Reporter*.

Boydstun, J., Sherry, M., & Moelter, N. (1977). *Patrol staffing in San Diego: One- or two-officer units*. Washington, DC: Police Foundation.

Braga, A. (2005). Hot spot policing and crime prevention: a systematic review of randomized controlled trials. *Journal of Experimental Criminology*, *1*, 317–342.

Braga, A. A., Weisburd, D. L., Mazerolle, L. G., Spelman, W., & Gajewski, F. (1999). Problem-oriented policing in violent crime places: a randomized controlled experiment. *Criminology*, *37*, 541–580.

Brandl, S. (1993). The impact of case characteristics on detectives' decision making. *Justice Quarterly*, *10*(3), 395–416.

Brandl, S., & Frank, J. (1994). The relationship between evidence, detective effort, and the dispositions of burglary and robbery investigations. *American Journal of Police*, *13*(3), 149–168.

Bynum, T., Cordner, G., & Greene, J. (1982). Victim and offense characteristics: impact on police investigative decision making. *Criminology*, *20*, 301–318.

Caeti, T. (1999). *Houston's targeted beat program: A quasi-experimental test of police patrol strategies*. Ann Arbor, MI: University Microfilms International.

del Carmon, A., & Guevara, L. (2003). Police officers on two-officer units: a study of attitudinal responses toward a patrol Experiment. *Policing: An International Journal of Police Strategies and Management*, *26*, 144–161.

Chaiken, J., & Chaiken, M. (1982). *Varieties of criminal behavior*. Santa Monica, CA: Rand Corporation.

Civil Rights Division, U.S. Department of Justice. (2011). *Investigation of the New Orleans Police Department*. http://www.justice.gov/crt/about/spl/nopd_report.pdf. Accessed 29.07.13.

Clark, W. (2003). Electric bicycles: high-tech tools for law enforcement. *Law Enforcement Technology*, *30*(11), 78–82.

Corsianos, M. (2003). Discretion in detectives' decision making and "high-profile" cases. *Police Practice and Research*, *4*(3), 301–314.

Davis, R., & Lurigio, A. (1996). *Fighting back: Neighborhood anti-drug strategies*. Thousand Oaks, CA: Sage.

Drunk as a skunk, and quick as a wink. *Law Enforcement News*. (December 15/31, 2003). XXIX(611, 612) www.lib.jjay.cuny.edu/len/2003/12.31/page6.html.

Eck, J. (1979). *Managing case assignments: The burglary investigative decision model replication*. Washington, DC: Police Executive Research Forum.

Eck, J. (1983). *Solving crimes: The investigation of burglary and robbery.* Washington, DC: Police Executive Research Forum.

Engel, R. S., Smith, M. R., & Cullen, F. T. (2012). Race, place, and drug enforcement: reconsidering the impact of citizen complaints and crime rates on drug arrests. *Criminology and Public Policy, 11,* 603–636.

Ericson, R. (1981). *Making crime.* Toronto, Canada: Butterworth.

Escobedo v. Illinois (1964). 364 U.S. 478.

Famega, C. (2005). Variation in officer downtime: a review of the research. *Policing: An International Journal of Police Strategies and Management, 28*(3), 388–414.

Faturechi, R., Winton, R., & Shyong, F. (2013). U.S says sheriff's deputies harassed Antelope Valley resident. *Los Angeles Times. http://www.latimes.com/news/local/la-me-sheriff-civil-rights-20130629,0, 715202.story.* Accessed 16.07.13.

Federal Bureau of Investigation. (2013a). *Integrated automated fingerprint identification system: Fact sheet.* http://www.fbi.gov/about-us/cjis/fingerprints_biometrics/iafis/iafis_facts. Accessed 29.07.13.

Federal Bureau of Investigation. (2013b). *CODIS-NDIS statistics.* http://www.fbi.gov/about-us/lab/biometric-analysis/codis/ndis-statistics. Accessed 29.07.13.

Fort Worth Police Department. (2013). *Annual report.* Fort Worth, TX: Author.

Frank, J., Smith, B., & Novak, K. (2005). Exploring the basis of citizens' attitudes toward the police. *Police Quarterly, 8,* 206–228.

Fritsch, E., Caeti, T., & Taylor, R. (1999). Gang suppression through saturation patrol, aggressive curfew, and truancy enforcement: a quasi-experimental test of the Dallas anti-gang initiative. *Crime & Delinquency, 45*(1), 122–139.

Gaines, L. (2006). An analysis of traffic stop data in Riverside, California. *Police Quarterly, 9*(2), 210–233.

Gaines, L., Lewis, B., & Swanagin, R. (1983). Case screening in criminal investigations: a case study of robbery. *Police Studies, 6,* 22–29.

Gay, W., Schell, T., & Schack, S. (1977). Improving patrol productivity. *Routine patrol .* (Vol. I) Washington, DC: Law Enforcement Assistance Administration.

Greenwald, H. (2001). *Final report: Police vehicle stops in Sacramento, California.* Sacramento, CA: City of Sacramento.

Greenwood, P., Chaiken, J., & Petersilia, J. (1977). *The investigative process.* Lexington, MA: Lexington Books.

Groff, E. R., Johnson, L., Ratcliff, J. H. ,, & Wood, J. (2013). Exploring the relationship between foot and car patrol in violent crime areas. *Policing: An International Journal of Police Strategies and Management, 36,* 119–139.

Hassell, K. D. (2007). Variation in police patrol practices: the precinct as a sub-organizational level of analysis. *Policing: An International Journal of Police Strategies and Management, 3,* 257–276.

Hickman, M. J., & Reaves, B. A. (2006). *Local police departments, 2003.* Washington, DC: U.S. Department of Justice, Bureau of Justice Statistics.

Hickman, M. J., & Reaves, B. A. (2010). *Local police departments, 2003.* Washington, D.C.: U.S. Department of Justice, Bureau of Justice Statistics.

Hope, T. (1994). Problem-oriented policing and drug market locations: three case studies. In R. V. Clarke (Ed.), *Crime prevention studies* (Vol. 2). Monsey, NY: Criminal Justice Press.

Hopkins, E. (1931). *Our lawless police.* New York: Viking.

Jet gets its wings clipped so Fla. Sheriff's tactical training can take off. *Law Enforcement News* 2004). XXX(616).

Jordan, J. (1998). Boston's "Operation Night Light". *FBI Law Enforcement Bulletin, 67*(8), 1–6.

Kaminsky, J. (November 27, 2012). Seattle police plan for helicopter drones hits severe turbulence. *The Chicago Tribune.* *http://www.chicagotribune.com/news/sns-rt-us-usa-drones-seattle-bre8aq10r-20121127,0, 6950306.story.* Accessed 29.11.12.

Kappeler, V. E., and Gaines, L. K. (2011). *Community Policing: A Contemporary Perspective* (6th Ed.). Waltham, MA: Anderson Publishing.

Kelling, G., Pate, T., Dieckman, D., & Brown, C. (1974). *The Kansas City preventive patrol experiment: A summary report.* Washington, DC: The Police Foundation.

Kennedy, L. (2003). Issues in managing citizens' calls to the police. *Criminology and Public Policy, 2*(1), 125–128.

Kenney, D., White, M., & Ruffinengo, M. (2010). Expanding the role of patrol in criminal investigations: Houston's investigative first responder project. *Police Quarterly, 13*, 136–160.

Kessler, D. (1985). One- or two-officer cars? A perspective from Kansas City. *Journal of Criminal Justice, 13*, 49–64.

Klinger, D. (1997). Negotiating order in patrol work: an ecological theory of police response to deviance. *Criminology, 35*, 277–306.

Klockers, C. (1983). *Thinking about the police.* New York: McGraw-Hill.

Koper, C. S. (1995). Just enough police: reducing crime and disorderly behavior by optimizing patrol time in crime hot spots. *Justice Quarterly, 12*, 649–672.

Kraska, P. B., & Kappeler, V. E. (1997). Militarizing American police: the rise and normalization of paramilitary units. *Social Problems, 44*(1), 1–18.

Kuykendall, J. (1986). The municipal police detective: an historical analysis. *Criminology, 24*(1), 175–201.

Lansdowne, W. (1999). *Vehicle stop demographic study: Covering July 1 to September 30, 1999.* San Jose, CA: San Jose Police Department.

Mapp v. Ohio, (1961). 367 U.S. 643.

Martin, S., & Sherman, L. (1986). Selective apprehension: a police strategy for repeat offenders. *Criminology, 24*(1), 155–173.

Mastrofski, S. D., & Ritti, R. (1992). You can Lead a horse to water...: a case study of a police department's response to stricter drunk-driving laws. *Justice Quarterly, 9*(3), 465–491.

Mastrofski, S. D., & Ritti, R. R. (1996). Police training and the effects of organization on drunk driving enforcement. *Justice Quarterly, 13*(2), 291–320.

McCampbell, M. S. (1983). Robbery reduction through directed patrol. *The Police Chief, 50*(2), 39–41.

McEwen, J., Conners, E., & Cohen, M. (1986). *Evaluation of the differential police response field test.* Washington, DC: National Institute of Justice.

McLean, H. (1988). A zap in the dead of night. *Law and Order, 36*(10), 26–31.

McLean, H. (1990). Getting high on crime. *Law and Order, 38*(7), 30–36.

Menton, C. (2008). Bicycle patrols: an underutilized resource. *Policing: An International Journal of Police Strategies and Management, 31*, 93–108.

Miranda v. Arizona. (1966). 384 U.S. 436.

Murphy, D., & Worrall, J. (2007). The threat of mission distortion in police–probation partnerships. *Policing: An International Journal of Police Strategies and Management, 30*, 132–149.

National Commission on Law Observance and Enforcement. (1931). *Police*. Washington, DC: U.S. Government Printing Office.

National Highway Traffic Safety Administration. (2011). *Alcohol-impaired driving*. http://www-nrd. nhtsa.dot.gov/Pubs/811700.pdf. Accessed 29.07.13.

National Institute of Justice. (2011). *Making sense of DNA backlogs, 2010 – myths vs. reality*. Washington, DC: Author.

Nesbary, D. (1998). Handling emergency calls for service: organizational production of crime statistics. *Policing: An International Journal of Police Management & Strategies, 21*(4), 576–599.

Office of Justice Programs. (2013). *Program profile: DNA field experiment*. . https://www.crimesolu-tions.gov/ProgramDetails.aspx?ID=155. Accessed 29.07.13.

Osterburg, J., & Ward, R. (2010). *Criminal investigation: A method for reconstructing the past* (6th ed.). Newark, NJ: LexisNexis Matthew Bender.

Parent, D., & Snyder, B. (1999). *Police–corrections partnerships*. Washington, DC: National Institute of Justice.

Parlow, M. (2012). *The great recession and its implications for community policing*. Marquette Law Scholarly Commons. Retrieved 10.01.13 from http://scholarship.law.marquette.edu/cgi/view-content.cgi?article=1607&context=facpub.

Pate, T., Bowers, R., & Parks, R. (1976). *Three approaches to criminal apprehension in Kansas City: An evaluation report*. Washington, DC: Police Foundation.

Pate, T., Ferrara, A., Bowers, R., & Lorence, J. (1976). *Police response time: Its determinants and effects*. Washington, DC: The Police Foundation.

Percy, S. (1980). Response time and citizen evaluation of police. *Journal of Police Science and Administration, 8*(1), 75–86.

President's Commission on Law Enforcement and Administration of Justice. (1976). *Task force report: The police*. Washington, DC: U.S. Government Printing Office.

Ratcliffe, J. (2010). *The Philadelphia foot patrol experiment*. Philadelphia, PA: Research Brief Temple University.

Reaves, B. A. (1989). *Police departments in large cities, 1987*. Washington, DC: U.S. Department of Justice, Bureau of Justice Statistics.

Reaves, B. A. (2010). *Local police departments, 2007*. Washington, D.C.: U.S. Department of Justice, Bureau of Justice Statistics.

Ridgeway, G., Schell, T., Riley, K., Turner, S., & Dixon, T. (2006). *Police–community relations in Cincinnati, year two evaluation report*. Santa Monica, CA: Rand Corp.

Rookey, B. D. (2012). Drunk driving in the United States: an examination of informal and formal factors to explain variation in DUI enforcement across U.S. counties. *Western Criminology Review, 13*, 37–52.

Sampson, R. (2003). *False burglar alarms*. Washington, DC: Office of Community Oriented Police Services.

Sacramento Police Department. (2012). *Sacramento police department 2011. Annual report*. http://www.sacpd.org/pdf/publications/ar/ar11.pdf.

Sanders, W. (1977). *Detective work*. New York: Free Press.

Scott, M. (2003). *The benefits and consequences of police crackdowns*. Washington, DC: Office of Community Oriented Policing Services.

Seattle Police Department, (2013). https://www.fortworthpd.com/

Sherman, L. (1990). Crackdowns: initial and residential deterrence. In M. Tonry, & N. Morris (Eds.), *Crime and justice: A review of research* (Vol. 12). Chicago, IL: University of Chicago Press.

Sherman, L. (1996). Repeat calls for service: policing the "hot spots". In G. Cordner, L. Gaines, & V. Kappeler (Eds.), *Police operations: Analysis and evaluation*. Cincinnati, OH: Anderson Publishing.

Sherman, L., & Rogan, D. (1995). Deterrent effects of police raids on crack houses: a randomized controlled experiment. *Justice Quarterly, 12*, 755–782.

Sherman, L., Shaw, J., & Rogan, D. (1995). *The Kansas City gun experiment*. Washington, DC: National Institute of Justice.

Sherman, L., & Weisburd, D. (1995). General deterrent effects of police patrol in crime "hot spots": a randomized controlled trial. *Justice Quarterly, 12*, 625–648.

Skolnick, J., & Caplovitz, A. (2001). Guns, drugs, and profiling: ways to target guns and minimize racial profiling. *Arizona Law Review, 8*, 135–152.

Spelman, W. (1990). *Repeat offender programs for law enforcement*. Washington, DC: Police Executive Research Forum.

Spelman, W., & Brown, D. (1984). *Calling the police: Citizen reporting of serious crime*. Washington, DC: U.S. Government Printing Office.

St. Louis Police Department. (2013). *Annual report*. http://www.kcmo.org/idc/groups/police/documents/police/2annual2011final.pdf.pdf.

Telep, C. W., Mitchell, R. J., & Weisburd, D. W. (2012). How much time should the police spend at crime hot spots? Answers from a police agency directed randomized field trial in Sacramento, California. *Justice Quarterly, 29*, 1–29.

Telep, C. W., & Weisburd, D. (2012). What is known about the effectiveness of police practices in reducing crime and disorder? *Police Quarterly, 15*, 331–357.

Terry v. Ohio. (1968). 392 U.S. 1.

Trojanowicz, R. C. (1982). *An evaluation of the neighborhood foot patrol program in Flint, Michigan*. East Lansing, MI: Michigan State University.

Verniero, P., & Zoubek, P. (1999). *Interim report of the state police review team regarding allegations of racial profiling*. Trenton, NJ: Office of the Attorney General.

Waegel, W. (1981). Case routinization in investigative police work. *Social Problems, 28*(3), 263–275.

Weisburd, D. L., & Green, L. (1995). Policing drug hot spots: the Jersey City drug market analysis experiment. *Justice Quarterly, 12*, 711–736.

Weisburd, D. L., Telep, C. W., & Lawton, B. A. (2013). Could innovations in policing have contributed to the New York City's crime drop even in a period of declining police strength?: the case of stop, question and frisk as a hot spots policing strategy. *Justice Quarterly, 30*, 1–25.

Weiss, A., & Freels, S. (1996). Effects of aggressive policing: the Dayton traffic enforcement experiment. *American Journal of Police, 15*(3), 45–64.

Weiss, A., & McGarrell, E. (1999). Traffic enforcement and crime: another look. *Police Chief, 66*(7), 25–28.

Whren v. U.S. (1996). 116 U.S. S. Ct. 1769.

Wilson, C., & Brewer, N. (2001). Working in teams: negative effects on organizational performance in policing. *Policing: An International Journal of Police Strategies and Management, 24*, 115–127.

Wilson, O. W. (1963). *Police administration* (2nd ed.). New York: McGraw-Hill.

Wilson, O. W., & McLaren, B. (1977). *Police administration* (4th ed.). New York: McGraw-Hill.

Worden, R. E. (1993). Toward equity and efficiency in law enforcement: differential response. *American Journal of Police, 12*(4), 1–32.

Worrall, J., & Gaines, L. (2006). The effect of police–probation partnerships on juvenile arrests. *Journal of Criminal Justice, 34*, 579–589.

CHAPTER 6

Police Discretion

One can pass on responsibility, but not the discretion that goes with it.
—Benvenuto Cellini

LEARNING OBJECTIVES

After reading the chapter, you should be able to:

- Distinguish between the various types of discretion used in policing.
- Discuss various situations in which police officers use discretion.
- Discuss and describe how police discretion differentially effects certain groups in society.
- List and describe the variables that influence police use of discretion.
- Discuss the various factors that influence police decisions to arrest.
- Discuss how police discretion is effected during vice, domestic violence, prostitution, and hate crimes investigations.
- Describe the various forms of control used to guide and limit police discretion.

KEY TERMS

- Administrative discretion
- Bar girls
- Child pornography
- Civilian review boards
- Court control
- Crime control model
- Deinstitution-alization policies
- Demeanor
- Discretion
- Discrimination
- Disenfranchised populations
- Domestic violence
- Due process model
- Enforcement discretion

Discretion is at the heart and soul of policing. In fact, it is the very foundation of our criminal justice system. It is an inescapable part of our justice process. Discretion is when the effective limits on a public official's power leave him or her free to make a choice among a number of possible courses of action (Davis, 1980). It is virtually impossible to provide employees with rules and regulations governing how every aspect of a job is to be performed except in the most mechanistic, repetitive jobs. Workers on an assembly line have few choices about how to do their jobs, but police officers, prosecutors, and judges deal with human behavior and constantly are encountering new, unique situations. It is impossible to provide criminal justice practitioners guidance in every situation because there are so many potential situations, and to even attempt to do so would result in a set of rules that would be too voluminous to

- Entrapment
- Escort services
- External controls
- Gambling
- Gender and discretion
- Hate crimes
- Homeless
- Human trafficking
- Internal controls
- Judgmental context
- Legislative control
- Mental illness
- Offender variables in discretion
- Pornography
- Prejudice
- Prostitution
- Race and discretion
- Situational variables in discretion
- Socioeconomic status
- Streetwalkers
- System variables in discretion
- Vice crimes

comprehend. Therefore, we must depend on the police and other practitioners to use "good judgment" and exercise discretion.

Indeed, everyone in the criminal justice system makes discretionary decisions. The police make these decisions every day. They must decide if a case is to be investigated, whether a suspect should be arrested, or if a traffic violation is severe enough to warrant a citation. Even though a police department can provide some guidance through training, rules, and supervision, there are situations in which the police officer does not have ample official guidance, and the officer must make decisions or use discretion when proceeding.

The police are not the only participants within the criminal justice system who exercise discretion. Prosecutors exercise immense discretion when they decide how to proceed on individual criminal cases. They examine the evidence collected by police officers; analyze the circumstances surrounding the offense, victim, and suspect; and then decide whether to dismiss, plea bargain, or prosecute the case. Historically, prosecutors have been severely criticized when they refuse to prosecute or plea bargain a case, but prosecutors generally dismiss or plea bargain cases only when they feel that the evidence is not strong enough to obtain a conviction. A plea-bargained guilty plea to a lesser offense is much better than a not-guilty verdict. Here, prosecutors use discretion in the best interest of justice.

Judges also exert discretion. They decide on the applicability of various motions as to the admissibility of evidence. Judges exert substantial discretion as a trial progresses. Beyond the technical aspects of the trial, judges exercise discretion when they consider probation or incarceration. Even when a judge decides to incarcerate an offender, the judge must exercise discretion when deciding on the length of the sentence. Thus, criminal justice can be viewed as a series of discretionary decisions commencing when an officer ponders whether to make an arrest until a suspect is ultimately released from the criminal justice system.

Given the setting in which discretion is used, it appears that there are two aspects that should be considered: judgmental and contextual. Judgment refers to whether discretionary decisions should be made. Prior to the 1950s, it was assumed by almost everyone that discretion was nonexistent within the criminal justice system (Walker, 1993). Supposedly, when police officers observed violations of the law, they wrote a citation or made an arrest. Prosecutors would then prosecute the case to the letter of the law, and judges would hand down inflexible sentences that were the same for every offender regardless of station in life or circumstances.

Even though no one would admit to the existence of discretion, most, if not all, police officers exercised discretion; however, the practice of discretion was viewed as being improper and, in some cases, illegal. Police corruption, which was rampant at the time, was considered to be the result of officers straying away from strict legal standards. Indeed, any deviation from accepted standards for any reason whatsoever was viewed as inappropriate. Discretion was also viewed as being extralegal, insinuating that it had no constitutional or legal foundation and therefore was improper. By the 1960s, discretion came to be viewed as a necessary evil. Discretion is a way criminal justice practitioners can counteract some of the imprudent or unworkable laws passed by legislative bodies. Laws frequently are passed in a vacuum to address a narrow range of behaviors, but police officers encounter a wide range of behaviors in a variety of situations. They must use discretion when applying laws to different behaviors; in some instances, they may apply a law strictly, whereas, in other cases, the same law may be applied very loosely. Because there is not always an exact fit, police officers must consider the context in which laws are applied.

The context in which discretion is applied is also important. Context refers to the facts of the situation, which is important because all situations are different. Guyot (1991) examined how officers use discretion and found that officers, in order to apply discretion contextually, should possess certain qualities. First, officers should be curious. They must have the will to inquire into situations, especially those that are unusual or suspicious. Second, officers must be able to perceive danger. The ability to evaluate a situation in terms of dangerousness is critical to the safety of police officers, but officers tend to view many situations as dangerous when they might not be, which often results in an overreaction on their part (Kappeler & Potter, 2005; Skolnick, 1994). Third, Guyot maintains that officers must have what Muir (1977) characterized as a tragic perspective. In essence, officers must be empathetic and have a compassionate understanding of the people and situations they police. Bureaucratic responses do not always lead to just outcomes. Fourth, officers must be decisive; when confronted with a situation, officers must be able to identify a workable solution. Fifth, officers must exercise self-control. Officers must always be aware of their roles, responsibilities, and duties; vigilantism has no place in law enforcement. Finally, officers must learn to use varied approaches to unique problems. Here, problem-solving rules the day. Officers must be able to analyze situations and solve them, rather than treating their symptoms. If officers possess these six qualities, they should be able to exercise discretion in a just, fair way.

THE NATURE OF POLICE DISCRETION

Discretion can have both positive and negative connotations. In the previous chapter on police operations, we discussed the difficulties faced by police departments that do not have sufficient resources to respond to every request for service. In effect, the department exercises discretion when it prioritizes calls for service or selects a patrol technique. It would be virtually impossible to arrest everyone who has committed a crime. Seldom are the police criticized by people who benefit from a discretionary decision not to arrest them; however, under the same circumstances, officers may be criticized by the victim, bystanders, or by the public for their lack of action.

Discretion also holds the potential for abuse. Decisions to perform a duty or refrain from taking action can be based on inappropriate criteria, such as gender, age, race, religion, physical appearance, political preference, or other prejudices held by the officer (Kappeler, Sluder, & Alpert, 1998). It is not discretion that is harmful to a department and community; rather, it is the inappropriate use of discretion. Because police officers often deal with circumstances in which the legal solution is not clear, their decisions must be guided by ethical considerations, which are discussed in Chapter 8.

ADMINISTRATIVE DISCRETION

It is possible to establish a conceptual distinction between discretion exercised by administrators and operational personnel. The existence of administrative discretion is implicit in the structure of police agencies. Police departments typically reflect a bureaucratic structure with a well-defined hierarchy. The administrative function is designed to establish policies and procedures that guide the actions of operational personnel; that is, administrators are responsible for such activities as planning, organizing, staffing, directing, coordinating, and budgeting. These activities are how administrators ensure that operational personnel perform their expected duties. As such, administrators have substantial discretion in their final operational decisions and dictates. Administrative discretion is the vehicle through which uniform policies and procedures develop. Although administrators exercise a choice among options, street-level officers theoretically translate their decisions into uniform activities (Chappell, MacDonald, & Manz, 2006; Riksheim & Chermak, 1993).

Administrative discretion is exercised in determining the role orientation of the agency. This should reflect the administrator's perception of the needs and expectations of the community as a whole and the various neighborhoods that exist within the larger community. Every agency operates under fiscal constraints, and it is not possible to meet all the demands for services that are requested. Through the process of budgeting and controlling expenditures, administrators are able to prioritize the types of services offered, thereby establishing the primary role and focus of the agency. Funding levels for programs reflect the degree of importance afforded different activities. For example, the number of officers assigned to different units, such as domestic violence, foot patrols, criminal investigation, and so on, are a product of discretion. Activities and problems that receive the greatest resources are those deemed most important by the administrator.

Administrators attempt to control not only what officers do but also how they do it. Alpert and Dunham (1990) found that nearly one-third of police pursuits resulted in traffic crashes, with a majority of the pursuits being for minor traffic violations. Many crashes of this type involve innocent third parties or police officers. Given the relative dangerousness and possibility of civil litigation, police administrators have established rules dictating when pursuits can occur and how they are to proceed. In some cases, departments have completely discouraged pursuits except for felony situations in which there is a threat to life. These rules have reduced the number of crashes associated with police pursuits—they have also reduced officer discretion.

Along these same lines, Fyfe (1979) studied the incidence of police shootings in New York City. He found that the city's restrictive policy governing police use of deadly force resulted in an almost 30% reduction in the number of instances in which officers shot people, and there were no negative consequences of the policy. Crime did not increase, nor was there an increase in assaults on police officers. A critical component of administrative discretion is controlling officer discretion. Administrators' decisions place parameters around what operational personnel can or cannot do. From this perspective, administrative discretion is exercised through policies and direction and by establishing goals and objectives for operational units.

Administrators attempt to control discretion using a number of tools. Stroshine, Alpert, and Dunham (2008) observed that departments attempt to control discretion through rules; Mastrofski, Reisig, and McCluskey (2002) advised that control often is exerted through the disciplinary process; Mastrofski (2004) identified recruitment, training, and the structuring of work as ways of controlling officer discretion; and LaFrance and Allen (2010) added mentorship to the list of methods for controlling police discretion. Mastrofski (2004) noted that control is often layered in a department. Different modes of control are enacted in a piecemeal fashion, but it is not known which form of control has the greatest or any effect. Even when control is implemented, officers tend to maintain their autonomy to the point that some disregard departmental control mechanisms. Mastrofski (2004) suggested that when discretion is not controlled it can lead to "organized anarchy." The presence of weak control mechanisms often leads to problems of abuse of force, under or over-enforcement of the law, police deviancy, and police legitimacy problems.

ENFORCEMENT DISCRETION

Administrators attempt to control officers' discretion by establishing policies and providing direction through orders and supervision. Even so, officers still have substantial enforcement discretion in terms of how they enforce the law, provide services, and otherwise maintain order. Officers use discretion in making a variety of decisions, such as whether to enforce specific laws, to investigate crimes, to stop and search people, to arrest or detain an individual, or whether to refer cases to the prosecuting attorney for the filing of formal charges. The racial profiling controversies that have emerged in many jurisdictions are examples of where enforcement discretion has gone awry. Discretion is routinely exercised in deciding whether to stop and interrogate or search individuals. Suspicious circumstances can be ignored by officers who are essentially reactive or may be investigated by those who are proactive.

Although discretion can be abused, when properly structured, it can be very positive. Community policing requires officers to be given discretion if they are to be responsive to the needs of the community. Community policing requires that officers consider and utilize a number of different responses to problems. The focus of their behavior is outcomes, not codified police procedures. Today's police environment requires officers who can exercise good judgment while making decisions.

THE POLICE DECISION-MAKING PROCESS

The nature of police work requires officers to make decisions about whether the criminal justice process will be initiated. In effect, this power of discretion makes them the gatekeepers of the criminal justice system (Alpert, Dunham, & Stroshine, 2005; Terrill & Paoline, 2007). Officers have wide latitude to decide whether to act when they observe someone who appears to be violating the law. They may ignore the situation altogether or decide to investigate further. Their investigation may lead them to believe no crime has been committed, or that someone else has committed it. If they determine that a person has committed a crime, they may decide to make an arrest or may believe some other type of disposition is warranted. Even after the arrest, their power to influence the criminal justice process is considerable. Officers may decide not to seek formal charges or may request the filing of a less serious charge. In making these decisions, officers effectively determine who is subject to the criminal justice process; hence, this is their role as gatekeeper.

THE DECISION TO INVOKE THE CRIMINAL JUSTICE PROCESS

Police work is a complex mix of different roles and functions, but the arrest is perhaps the quintessence of police work. It is most frequently the objective sought by officers and detectives as they perform their duties, and it is the activity that many people associate with the successful completion of a police endeavor. It is most certainly an important police function to the citizen subjected to it. As such, it is prudent to examine how police officers exercise discretion when making arrests.

Numerous studies have examined the decision to arrest. Although, almost all research concludes that the most significant factor affecting an officer's discretion is the seriousness of the offense. Crimes of violence receive more credence as opposed to property crimes. Nonetheless, there are other legal factors considered by officers. In addition to crime seriousness, Kochel, Wilson, and Mastrofski (2011) have identified four other legal factors that affect officers' discretion. First, does probable cause exist? Officers will only make an arrest when they have probable cause to believe a crime has been committed and the suspect committed the crime. Second, is there a credible victim or witness who is willing to testify in court? Third, the suspect's criminal record often plays a key role. Officers perceive those who have previously committed crimes as being guilty. Finally, mandatory arrest laws for crimes such as domestic violence or driving under the influence (DUI) increase the likelihood of arrest.

Other extra-legal factors also influence the decision-making process. The various decision elements can be grouped into three broad categories: (1) offender variables, (2) situational variables, and (3) system variables. Offender variables include considerations of gender, age, race, socioeconomic status, and demeanor. Situational variables affecting the decision may revolve around the seriousness of the offense, whether officers were summoned by someone else, or the visibility of their actions. System variables would include such factors as the officer's perception of the law, peer-group relationships, community attitudes, department philosophy, and the system's capacity to process legal violations.

Offender Variables

Offender variables are attributes of the offender that influence officers to take action. Research has identified several factors that affect officers' decision-making regarding, for example, making an arrest, issuing a traffic citation, or allowing the offender to go free with only a warning.

Myths of Police Discretion in Arrest Situations

Myth: Police fully enforce the law in all situations and with impartiality.

Reality: There are many situations in which police do not practice full enforcement of the laws.

Myth: Police enforce the law without regard to factors external to a legal consideration.

Reality: Although the seriousness of an offense is the best predictor of police decisions to arrest, the demeanor of a suspect greatly impacts the police decision to arrest.

Myth: Police enforce the law equally regardless of a suspect's race, age or gender.

Reality: Research consistently shows that police tend to stop, search, and arrest people of color, youths, and males at higher rates even when other factors are held constant.

Age

Research conducted on the relationship between age and the decision to arrest indicates that officers take adults' complaints more seriously than those made by juveniles. An arrest is more likely if the victim is older and the offender young (Dunham & Alpert, 2009). Other research suggests that younger suspects are more likely to be arrested (Sherman, 1980), whereas elderly offenders are more likely to be treated with leniency (Forsyth, 1993). Research also indicates that juveniles with previous police contacts are more likely to be arrested (Black & Reiss, 1970; Carter, 2006; Cicourel, 1976). One can only speculate as to why age would affect an officer's decision. It seems that adults are perceived to be more credible. It may also be possible that age is related to the demeanor of those involved; adults may appear to be more cooperative with the police and therefore receive better service or more lenient treatment (Alpert & Dunham, 2004). It is also important to note that young people commit crimes at a higher rate as compared to older persons, increasing the number of contacts with the police and possibly causing police officers to label younger people as being more criminal.

Race

Many studies have examined the effect of race on officers' behavior. Most studies have found that people of color are likely to be treated more harshly by police than whites (Brooks, 2001; Kochel et al., 2011). Here, we address three related issues: arrests, traffic stops, and drug enforcement.

There have been a number of studies examining race and arrests. Kochel et al. (2011) reviewed and reanalyzed 23 previous studies to investigate the effects of race on arrests. The studies in their dataset came from police agencies throughout the United States. They controlled for factors such as suspect demeanor, offense severity, presence of witnesses, quantity of evidence, whether the suspect was under the influence, whether the victim requested an arrest, and the suspect's past criminal record. After controlling for these factors, they concluded that race mattered. Minority suspects were more likely to be arrested by police than their majority counterparts. D'Alessio and Stolzberg (2003) found that white suspects were more likely to be arrested for robbery, aggravated assault, and simple assault as compared to black offenders. Alpert et al. (2005) found that officers are more likely to become suspicious of minority group members than whites, but they are no more likely to take action against them than against white people. Although minorities are often more often overrepresented in arrests, this is often because of more police officers being assigned to high crime and disorder areas, resulting in officers coming into contact with larger numbers of people of color.

In terms of race and traffic stops, there are numerous studies showing that minorities are stopped, questioned, and searched more frequently than their white counterparts. For example, one study of police traffic enforcement decisions based on a review of over 10,000 traffic stops found that "drivers' race and gender" had a significant effect on an officer's decision to search a driver/vehicle and invoke a legal sanction. African American male drivers were more likely than white drivers to be searched, but were less likely to receive a legal sanction" (Moon & Corley, 2007). This finding could indicate that police are more likely to stop African-American motorists to fish for evidence of criminality and, not finding any evidence, more likely to allow them to leave without taking enforcement action. Minorities are more likely to be stopped by the police based on less evidence of a violation than their white counterparts. Rosenfeld, Rojek, and Decker (2011) examined this issue further and found that younger African American males were more likely to be searched, but those over 30 years of age were no more likely to be searched as compared to white drivers. Race continues to play a key role in officers' decisions to investigate motorists in many jurisdictions.

Drug enforcement is another area that has received attention. Research by Beckett, Nyrop, and Pfingst (2006) on drug enforcement in Seattle found that it is very difficult to explain the overrepresentation of minority arrests in race-neutral terms. They explained that: the majority of those who deliver methamphetamine, ecstasy, powder cocaine, and heroin in Seattle are white; African Americans are the majority of those who deliver only one drug: crack. Yet, 64% of those arrested for delivering one of these five drugs is African American. This disparity appears to be the result of three main organizational factors. First, the focus on crack offenders is an important cause of racial disparity in drug arrests. Second, the police often focus on outdoor drug activity, but this does exacerbate racial disparity—African Americans are also overrepresented among indoor arrestees. Third, outdoor drug markets are not treated alike: predominantly white outdoor drug markets receive far less attention than racially diverse markets located downtown. It, thus, appears that the geographic concentration of law enforcement resources is a significant cause of racial disparity. In a similar study, Mitchell and Caudy (2013) examined national drug arrest data and, after controlling for a number of socioeconomic variables, concluded that racial biases play a role in minority overrepresentation in drug arrests.

Socioeconomic Status

Socioeconomic status is a person's or group's class position in a society based on income, occupation, and social position as compared to other people in the society. Socioeconomic status has been shown to affect the manner in which police respond to requests for service (Black, 1980; Smith & Klein, 1984) and the probability of being arrested (Black, 1971; Reiss, 1971). Those in the middle- or upper-income brackets generally receive more attention from the police when they file a complaint and are less likely to be arrested. Those in the lower socioeconomic strata are more likely to receive harsher treatment when encountering officers (Riksheim & Chermak, 1993). Belvedere, Worrall, and Tibbetts (2005) found that police encounters in areas deemed dangerous by the police resulted in higher rates of suspect resistance. This may be attributable to lower-class neighborhoods having a greater amount of crime and disorder. Lee, Zhang, and Hoover (2013) examined domestic violence arrests in Houston and found that socioeconomic class played a key role in the decision to arrest.

Demeanor

A substantial body of research suggests that people who show deference to the police by cooperating are more likely to be treated fairly. This research finds that suspects who are uncooperative are more likely to be arrested than those who are respectful (Black & Reiss, 1970; Carter, 2006; Lundman, 1996; Piliavin & Briar, 1964; Worden & Shepard, 1996). Klinger (1994) advised, however, that previous research was flawed because of definitional problems in that demeanor was not properly defined and, as such, resulted in measurement problems. In other words, what behaviors constitute demeanor? Research that attempted to better define and operationalize demeanor after Klinger's criticism still showed that demeanor affected police officers' decision to arrest (Brown & Frank, 2005; Engel, Sobol, & Worden, 2000; Novak & Engel, 2005). Some research has shown that officers were more likely to use force when confronted by disrespectful offenders (Garner, Maxwell, & Heraux, 2002; Sun & Payne, 2004). People's demeanor has an effect on how they are treated by police officers.

Gender

Intuitively, one would believe that gender would make a difference in how officers react to complainants and suspects. The research on this issue has achieved mixed results. Some early research indicates that gender has little or no effect on police discretion (Klinger, 1994; Smith & Visher, 1981), but other studies have found that females are less likely to be arrested than their male counterparts, especially when they commit crimes typically considered to be "male" offenses (Sealock & Simpson, 1998). One study of police officers' decisions to issue traffic tickets found that females are more likely to receive more lenient treatment by the police than are males (Liu & Cook, 2005). Gabbidon, Higgins, and Potter (2011) surveyed a national sample of African Americans to measure their perceptions about how they were treated by the police. Females tended to believe that they were treated more fairly than males. The preponderance of research tends to indicate that there are gender differences with females receiving different treatment as compared to males.

Situation Variables

Situation variables are the nuances of the interaction between officers and citizens. They are the context in which officers perform police activities. Research has examined situation variables that affect the officer's decision-making.

Seriousness of Offense

Almost every study ultimately reaches the conclusion that the single most important factor in officers' decision-making is the seriousness of the offense. "Arrest is more likely for serious offenses than for relatively minor ones. This is an established finding from four decades of research explaining the effect of situational variables on police officers' decisions to arrest" (Carter, 2006:596; Riksheim & Chermak, 1993; Sherman, 1980). Officers can more readily justify ignoring a relatively minor situation, whereas they feel compelled to take some type of action when a serious crime has been committed (LaFave, 1965; Smith & Visher, 1981; Wilson, 1968). Officers tend to associate importance and success on the job with arrests in serious crimes. Also, there is a general expectation by the public, government, and police officials that officers make arrests in serious crimes. Such expectations do not always exist for less serious crimes.

The decision may be further influenced by factors such as the presence of a weapon or the offender's prior criminal record. The presence of a weapon generally results in officers' taking official action. Research indicates that police officers are more likely to initiate formal actions for property crimes than minor crimes against persons. This may result from their belief that property crimes will generate requests from insurance companies for a copy of the report (Ericson, 1982) or that interpersonal crimes are best handled through mediation (Bayley & Mendelsohn, 1969).

Visibility of the event and the presence of others are other considerations. The nature of police work affords officers the opportunity to make decisions that are often concealed from the general public's view. These decisions are often not known or reviewed by their superiors. Decisions that are not likely to become known give officers more discretion. The decision to arrest may be guided by the probability of a complaint being filed, the ability to control others at the scene, and the availability of assistance. Officers may be subjected to criticism for either arresting or not arresting someone. Their decision to arrest or release may be influenced by their belief that a particular course of action is the least likely to result in a complaint. In the presence of larger crowds, the officer may feel it necessary to arrest the offender to prevent any further problems. Officers tend to take more official bureaucratic responses when witnesses are present.

Officer-Initiated Actions and Citizen Calls for Assistance

How officers become involved in an event affects their discretion. One would assume that officers have less discretion when summoned by a citizen because they must report the disposition of such complaints to the communications center, but research indicates the contrary. Activities initiated by the police are more likely to result in a formal report or arrest than those initiated by a citizen's complaint (Black, 1971; Reiss, 1971; Wilson, 1968). It seems that officers do not initiate actions unless they have already decided to take some action. Another explanation is that a large number of citizen calls are made for which no law has actually been violated.

System Variables

System variables are the idiosyncrasies of the criminal justice system that may influence officers to exercise their discretion for reasons other than those already discussed. Often mentioned as a justification for discretion is the lack of system capacity to arrest, prosecute, and incarcerate every individual who commits a crime. Even beyond the system's capacity is the officers' perceptions of inequities in the law and the justice system that stem from statutes that are overreaching, ambiguous, obsolete, or contrary to community's needs and expectations. This results in some officers over-enforcing the law, while other under-enforce the law. For example, Florida increased the penalty for the failure to wear a seat belt and the volume of traffic citations immediately declined. It seems that officers believed that the penalty was too severe and subsequently refused to invoke the criminal justice process.

Community Expectations

The community's expectations and standards will influence an officer's interpretation and application of the law. Some laws are seldom or never enforced. Police officers typically make decisions to enforce the law based on their perceptions of community expectations. Police officers are more tolerant of minor offenses if they believe residents are tolerant. Expectations vary across communities and within communities. People living in a rural or suburban community likely have different ideas about crime and how the police should behave as compared to people residing in urban areas. Neighborhoods also adopt different expectations. People living in lower socioeconomic neighborhoods are likely to be more tolerant of some behaviors as compared to people in middle and upper-class neighborhoods. Police officers often recognize these differences and act accordingly. This can have negative consequences. Klinger (1997) advised that police officers often become cynical when dealing with citizens who are uncooperative and policing high crime and disorder neighborhoods and react by providing more lenient services. Regardless, police officers often respond differently in affluent neighborhoods as compared to poorer neighborhoods.

Departmental Culture

Police departments have unique cultures that create norms, values, and attitudes that guide officers' decision-making. This culture has remained somewhat consistent over time (Loftus, 2010). Both the formal and informal norms of the department affect an officer's actions. Formal norms are taught in the police academy and reinforced through supervision and policies. The officer's peers convey informal norms. The peer group can influence subtly or bring direct pressure on an officer to behave in a certain way (Ericson, 1982; Lundman, 1979; Westley, 1970). Mastrofski (2004:104) suggested that the police culture is "a defense mechanism of street-level officers coping with pressures from management and environmental threats." By granting or withholding their approval, peers indicate what actions are acceptable (Kappeler et al., 1998). A department's culture, through the creation of norms, places limits on police discretion by identifying activities that are important and those that are not important. Officers often consider these norms when deciding to make an arrest or intervene in a situation. Indeed, officers see efforts to control discretion as an affront to their job autonomy. Officers often push back or attempt to protect their autonomy. Sometimes, officers become confrontational when trying to protect their autonomy or discretion. For example, Boivin and Cordeau (2011) documented how Montreal police increased crime reports when there was no apparent increase in crime. Their increased reporting was intended to overload management as a result of collective bargaining issues. Culture has a profound impact on police discretion. Culture can have a significant impact on police officer decision-making.

Community Policing

The philosophy of a police organization or a unit within a police department can affect officers' arrest decisions. An interesting study conducted by Novak, Frank, Smith, and Engel (2002) looked at the differences between traditional beat officers and community-oriented policing (COP) officers and their use of discretion. These researchers found that "Beat officers are more likely to use indicators such as minority status, gender, intoxication, and hostile demeanor when making their decision to arrest." On the other hand, "COP officers are less likely to use discriminatory factors (such as race or gender) and signs of nonconformity (including intoxication and hostile demeanor) when making their decisions to arrest. … Furthermore, COP officers are more likely to act on the preferences of the victim or a witness, indicating they are more responsive to the community that they serve." Similarly, Terrill and Paoline (2007) found that the officers in the St. Petersburg, Florida, Police Department were less likely to make arrests as a result of the department's community policing philosophy. This is demonstrated in Box 6.1. It appears that the adoption of community policing can have an effect on decision-making.

Box 6.1 Different Arrest Rates Across Departments

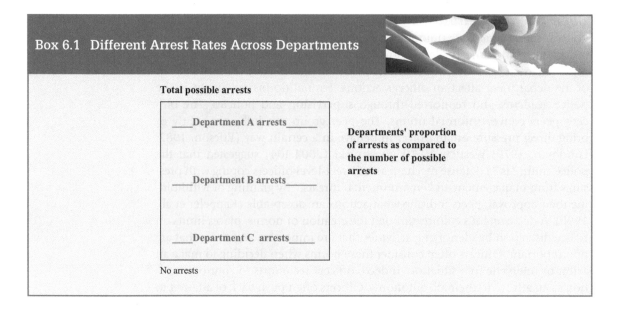

Total possible arrests

_____Department A arrests_____

_____Department B arrests_____

_____Department C arrests_____

No arrests

Departments' proportion of arrests as compared to the number of possible arrests

DISCRETIONARY SITUATIONS IN LAW ENFORCEMENT

Although decision-making is required in almost every facet of law enforcement, certain situations are thought to involve more discretion than others. These include domestic violence, vice crimes, hate crimes, and problems encountered with disenfranchised populations. In this section, we will explore these areas and the types of discretionary decisions officers must make.

Domestic Violence

Domestic violence is crime that results in physical harm or threats of harm by one intimate partner against another. "An intimate partner is a current or former spouse, boyfriend, girlfriend, or same-sex partner. Violence between intimates includes homicides, rapes, robberies, and assaults committed by partners" (Bureau of Justice Statistics, 2006:1). The primary focus, however, has been on spouses because of the high levels of violence in these relationships. On average, 30% of all women murdered in the United States are murdered by intimates (Bureau of Justice Statistics, 2006; Catalano, 2006). Husbands or boyfriends commit these murders. Every year, about 475,900 women in the United States fall victim to violence by intimates (Bureau of Justice Statistics, 2006) (Box 6.2).

Historically, arrest was the least used alternative in domestic violence situations. Police officers viewed domestic quarrels as private affairs that would, in all likelihood, only be made worse by official intervention and by processing the

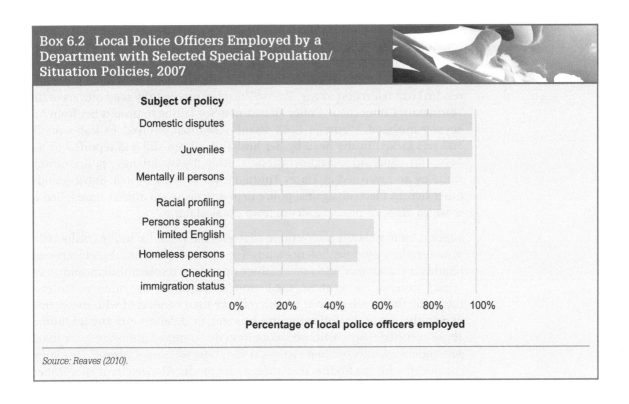

Box 6.2 Local Police Officers Employed by a Department with Selected Special Population/Situation Policies, 2007

Source: Reaves (2010).

parties through the criminal justice system. Victims were viewed as uncooperative because they were often reluctant to sign complaints and unwilling to follow through with prosecution if an arrest was made. Many states followed the common law rule that prohibited officers from making a misdemeanor arrest unless they had actually witnessed the crime taking place. This substantially reduced the probability that police officers would take any action whatsoever.

A number of factors influence police officers' decisions to arrest in domestic violence cases. Buzawa and Buzawa (2003) identified situational and incident characteristics, victim traits, and suspect traits that intervene in the officer's decision-making. Situational and incident characteristics include whether the suspect was present when officers arrived, who called the police (victim or third party), and the presence of weapons, injuries, or children. Victim traits include the victim–offender relationship, victim preference for arrest, drug or alcohol involvement by the victim, and the victim's demeanor. Suspects are evaluated in terms of criminal history, relationship with victim, drug or alcohol usage, and demeanor. Police officers often weigh a number of factors when determining the intervention for a domestic disturbance.

To learn more about domestic violence, visit the Website of the Violence against Women Office of the Department of Justice at **http://www.ovw.usdoj.gov/**

In the late 1970s, citizen groups began a campaign to change the police response to domestic violence. Pointing to the dangers of the recurring cycle of violence that occurs in domestic situations, they sought to limit police discretion and force officers to make arrests. In a nationally publicized incident that resulted in a television movie, Tracey Thurman successfully sued officers of the Torrington, Connecticut, Police Department for failing to protect her from her abusive husband. During a 1983 assault, Thurman received 13 stab wounds and was kicked in the head by her husband, whom she had reported to the police for abuse on several occasions. During the disturbance, police officers stood by and watched as Tracey Thurman was brutally beaten. Subsequently, other victims filed suit against police departments when officers have failed to make an arrest or protect a victim from physical harm.

Support for mandatory intervention strategies was provided by the results of the Minneapolis Domestic Violence Study. For a period of 18 months, officers were required to randomly select one of three options to resolve misdemeanor-level family violence cases: arrest, mediation, or requiring the offender to leave the home for an 8-h period. Interviews were then conducted with the victims during the 6 months following the incident to determine if any additional abuse occurred. Those who were not arrested committed almost twice as many subsequent assaults on their victims as did those who were arrested. The study concluded with the finding that arrest alone produced a deterrent effect (Sherman & Berk, 1984).

Under political pressure from citizens concerned with domestic violence and facing the ever-increasing threat of lawsuits, legislators were quick to enact presumptive or mandatory arrest laws. Relying on the proof of the well-publicized Minneapolis experiment, they legislatively limited officers' discretion in an attempt to reduce domestic violence. States required officers to make arrests when there was evidence of physical violence or abuse. Subsequent studies that replicated the Minneapolis experiment were conducted in Omaha, Charlotte, Dade County, Colorado Springs, and Milwaukee. Using similar research designs, dramatically different results were reached: making an arrest did not result in fewer subsequent incidents of assault, and the danger to the victim was not increased or decreased by an officer's choice to use mediation, to separate the parties, or to arrest the offender (Dunford, Huizinga, & Elliott, 1986). Other studies have reached different conclusions.

However, Dugan (2003) examined the effects of mandatory arrests and found that the laws reduced the incidence of domestic violence and reporting of such incidents to the police. When Maxwell, Garner, and Fagan (2002) reexamined the data from Omaha, Charlotte, Colorado Springs, Dade County, and Milwaukee, they pooled the data and found that arrest reduced the recurrence of domestic violence by 30%. They also found that older batterers were less likely to do so again, but batterers who had been previously arrested were more likely to batter again. They also found that low-cost legal sanctions were not an effective method of reducing the problem. Even though the research is somewhat mixed, it appears that arrest does reduce domestic violence.

Only a small percentage of the domestic violence cases are reported to the police. Dugan (2003) found that about half of cases are reported, whereas Felson and Pare (2005) found the reporting percentage to be 16%. Felson, Messner, and Hoskin (2002) identified factors that encourage and discourage reporting. The factors discouraging reporting include fear of reprisal and a desire to protect the offender. If the police arrest a batterer, there certainly will be court costs, fines, and possibly jail time. Victims have a vested interest in protecting their batterer, especially when loss of time at work is involved. On the other hand, the factors motivating victims to report violence are the desire for protection, belief that the violence is not a private matter, and belief that the incident is not trivial. Victims weigh these factors when deciding to call the police, and victims' experience with the batterer and the police will affect their ultimate decision.

Eigenberg, Scarborough, and Kappeler (1996) conducted a study of domestic violence enforcement in a medium-sized, midwestern police department to determine whether police handled domestic assaults differently from other assaults and to determine what factors affect police decision-making in different kinds of assaults. The researchers examined a random sample of police reports. Results revealed, even when controlling for situational variables, that police officers are less likely to arrest in domestic violence cases than in non-domestic cases. In addition, injuries were about equally likely to be present in cases of arrest for domestic and nondomestic assault, although victims were more likely to experience minor injuries in domestic assaults. Thus, although victims of domestic violence cases are more frequently victims of minor violence, the level of injuries by itself has relatively little to do with arrest in either domestic or nondomestic assaults. It appeared that police officers were more willing to consider domestic assaults as real assaults only when weapons were used. Similar results have been obtained by other researchers who have examined the police handling of domestic violence cases (Fyfe et al., 1997).

Finally, there has been criticism of mandatory arrest policies as a result of a the significant increase in the number of women being arrested for domestic violence. Gerstenberger and Williams (2013) examined over 3000 domestic violence arrests in Connecticut. They found that about 74% of the arrests were for males; whereas 26% of the arrests were for females. This finding is consistent with Chesney-Lind's (2002) findings. Chesney-Lind (2002) examined the domestic violence arrests in a number of cities and found that sometimes females accounted for about one-quarter of the arrests. Mandatory arrest laws require officers to make an arrest when there is evidence of physical harm, regardless of gender. Officers who had more discretion often did not arrest the female. More recent research into this issue examined the effect of expanding police power to make arrests for domestic violence. Simpson, Bouffard, Garner, and Hickman (2006:312) found that a "legislative initiative to expand police arrest powers positively affected the percent of reported cases that resulted in arrest … arrest rates increased similarly and significantly for both male and female offenders as a result of the legislative change." Contrary to the researchers' expectations, it did "not appear that expanding police powers to arrest necessarily impacts women more than men. Nor are black women at a greater risk for arrest as a consequence of the legislation than are white women."

VICE CRIMES

Crimes of vice, prostitution, pornography, gambling, and narcotics have received varying attention by society, policymakers, and the police throughout history. Vice refers to criminal activity that is against the public order or public morality, but they are also enacted to curtail the economic benefits of these activities. Vice includes activities such as prostitution, gambling, pornography, illegal sales of alcoholic beverages, and trafficking in drugs. Such crimes are considered to be victimless, as parties involved in such activities participate willingly. Also, because the activities are consensual, there are no complaints, which substantially complicate their investigation. Vice activities consist of three types of activities: (1) illegal selling of goods or services, (2) illegal consumption of goods or services, and (3) illegal performance (McCaghy & Cernkovich, 1987).

Vice statutes generally are enacted to regulate or control morality. They are seen as instruments by which persons are protected from their own behavior. Sheley (1985) suggested that some believe that such activities result in spiritual and even bodily harm to those engaging in them. The legislation of vice laws is the result of group conflict in our society. Some groups are more tolerant or condone vice behavior, while others believe that it should be strictly regulated. Generally, the more conservative, religiously fundamental groups are less tolerant of vice activities; however, individuals opposed to vice laws are quick to point out that sin should not necessarily equate with crime. The enforcement of vice crimes often depends on which group comes to political power.

The enforcement of vice laws is controversial and problematic for the police. Because there is no clear consensus in our society on such laws, the police frequently are placed in the untenable situation of enforcing unpopular or unenforceable laws. McCaghy and Cernkovich (1987) identified a number of problems associated with the enforcement of vice laws:

1. The laws are almost unenforceable. The police, when enforcing vice laws, must depend on peripheral individuals or persons who might have been witnesses to such an act and offended as a result of the act. This leads to a very small number of vice activities being reported to the police.

2. There is no uniformity in the manner in which vice laws are enforced. Police officers enforce them as opportunities avail themselves. Enforcement tends to be discriminatory, sporadic, and ineffective.
3. Vice laws encourage illegal activities by police officers. Illegal searches, planted evidence, and entrapment are some of the techniques that officers sometimes use to enforce vice statutes.
4. Enforcement of vice laws is extremely time-consuming and expensive. Because there seldom are any witnesses or victims, enforcement tactics include undercover operations, payments to informants, and stakeouts. These tactics are labor intensive relative to investigations of street crimes.
5. Vice laws encourage police corruption. The secrecy and large amounts of money associated with organized crime activities continuously lead to police corruption.
6. Vice laws encourage organized crime. Organized crime groups ranging from the Mafia to rural criminal groups are involved extensively in vice activities because they are lucrative and difficult for the police to investigate.

Vice laws constitute only a small portion of police enforcement activity. In Tables 6.1 and 6.2, vice violations accounted for only a small percentage of all arrests, and most of those arrests were for drug violations.

Prostitution and Human Trafficking

Prostitution is engaging in sexual behavior in exchange for money. It often is referred to as the world's oldest profession. For example, the term "hooker," which is used to refer to prostitutes, dates back to the Civil War when Union General Joe Hooker employed prostitutes for himself and his army (Winick & Kinsie, 1971). Prostitution traditionally has been an enforcement and order-maintenance problem in most of America's major cities. For the most part, the police have two objectives when dealing with prostitution. First, the police enforce prostitution laws in an effort to control it. The police will never be able to eliminate prostitution, but through enforcement they can attempt to confine it to specific areas or make it less visible and intrusive to the public. Second, the police are responsible for investigating and preventing crime associated with prostitution.

Traditionally, there are several different types of prostitution. Streetwalkers are commonly found in a city's vice or drug district. They work out of alleys, stairwells, cars, and cheap "hot sheet" hotels. They are vulnerable to problems such as diseases, arrests by the police, and physical abuse by customers and pimps. They receive little economic reward for their efforts and generally are poverty-stricken women who are attempting to exist or support a drug habit. Bar or club girls (b-girls) work in bars, restaurants, and taverns, most often with the consent of management. B-girls attempt to sell patrons

Table 6.1 Estimated Number of Arrests in the United States, 2012

Total[1]	12,196,959
Murder and non-negligent manslaughter	11,075
Forcible rape	18,098
Robbery	103,661
Aggravated assault	388,362
Burglary	283,582
Larceny-theft	1,282,352
Motor vehicle theft	68,845
Arson	11,433
Violent crime[2]	521,196
Property crime[2]	1,646,212
Other assaults	1,199,476
Forgery and counterfeiting	67,046
Fraud	153,535
Embezzlement	16,023
Stolen property; buying, receiving, possessing	97,670
Vandalism	228,463
Weapons; carrying, possessing, etc.	149,286
Prostitution and commercialized vice	56,575
Sex offenses (except forcible rape and prostitution)	68,355
Drug abuse violations	1,552,432
Gambling	7868
Offenses against the family and children	107,018
Driving under the influence	1,282,957
Liquor laws	441,532
Drunkenness	511,271
Disorderly conduct	543,995
Vagrancy	27,003
All other offenses	3,448,856
Suspicion	1532
Curfew and loitering law violations	70,190

[1]Does not include suspicion.
[2]Violent crimes are offenses of murder and non-negligent manslaughter, forcible rape, robbery, and aggravated assault. Property crimes are offenses of burglary, larceny-theft, motor vehicle theft, and arson.

Table 6.2 Drug and Vice Enforcement Functions of Local Police Departments, by Size of Population Served

Population Served	Percent (%) of Agencies with Responsibility for the Enforcement of	
	Drug Laws	Vice Laws
All sizes	88	51
1,000,000 or more	100	100
500,000–999,999	100	100
250,000–499,999	100	100
100,000–249,999	99	99
50,000–99,999	99	94
25,000–49,999	95	91
10,000–24,999	93	75
2500–9999	90	56
Under 2500	82	33

Source: Reaves and Goldberg (2010).

expensive, diluted drinks before offering or selling their sexual services. B-girl operations are often found adjacent to military bases and factories. In a similar fashion, a number of hotels maintain a list of call girls for exclusive clientele. Brothels, or houses of prostitution, are where clients can choose a specific type of sexual service and partner. Many brothels have been replaced by escort services, massage parlors, photographic studios, or tanning operations. Using the cover of a legitimate business makes it more difficult for the police to make arrests and for citizens to recognize that prostitution exists. Finally, there are private prostitutes who restrict their services to an exclusive list of wealthy clients. They add new clients only through referral (Box 6.3, Figure 6.1)

Prostitution is a compelling social problem because of the number of underage people engaged in prostitution. Some authors estimate the number of juvenile prostitutes in the United States to be between 100,000 and 300,000 (Flowers, 2001). Hagan (2010) estimated that in New York City alone there are 10,000 underage male prostitutes ("chicken hawks"). Many female prostitutes are underage, and a significant clientele prefers underage prostitutes. Prostitutes can have long histories of sexual and physical abuse by family members. This abuse often is a precursor to prostitution. Nadon and Koverola (1999), in a study of prostitutes, found that 60–70% had been abused as children.

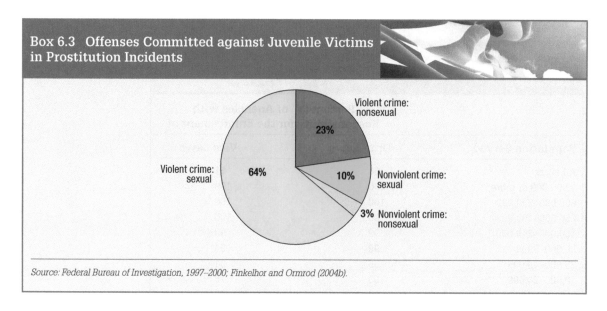

Box 6.3   Offenses Committed against Juvenile Victims in Prostitution Incidents

Violent crime: nonsexual 23%

Violent crime: sexual 64%

Nonviolent crime: sexual 10%

Nonviolent crime: nonsexual 3%

Source: Federal Bureau of Investigation, 1997–2000; Finkelhor and Ormrod (2004b).

The police have used a variety of tactics to deal with the prostitution problem. They sometimes use reverse stings to arrest clients ("johns"): "Reverse prostitution stings, sometimes referred to as operations, crackdowns, John stings, and roundups, have been conducted in many urban areas. In Savannah, Georgia, a task force headed by Prostitution Czar Juliette Tolbert began using female decoys and within one week 22 men had been arrested. … The city touted a conviction rate of 95% for men apprehended in these stings"

FIGURE 6.1

Homeland Security investigations dismantles an international sex trafficking ring in February 2014, rescuing 12 victims and convicting 23 defendants. *Photograph courtesy of the U.S. Immigration and Customs Enforcement* https://www.ice.gov/news/releases/1402/140220savannah.htm.

(Dodge, Starr-Gimeno, & Williams, 2005:3). Another way to control prostitutes is to eliminate their customers. In Aurora, Colorado, the city council passed an ordinance allowing police to purchase advertising space in a local newspaper and publish the pictures of arrested johns. In a more controversial program, the St. Paul Police Department created a web page that shows pictures of people arrested for prostitution. Many of these people have yet to be convicted of a crime, and the practice raises serious legal issues.

Most activities of law enforcement agencies aimed toward sexually oriented businesses are not initially based on a complaint from citizens or other governmental agencies. Although it is commonly asserted that these types of businesses and activities generate additional crime, some research indicates the contrary. Ruiz (1996) reported findings from a survey of 18 Texas police agencies that regulate sexually oriented businesses. This research found that sexually oriented businesses in these jurisdictions ranged from nude dancing to prostitution and the sale of obscenity. None of police agencies, however, reported that these businesses generated serious crime in the area or in the neighboring community. Likewise, although common sense suggests that police responded to these businesses because of citizens' complaints, the researcher found that the vast majority of law enforcement action was based on officer initiatives.

> To view the St. Paul web page, go to
> **www.stpaul.gov/index.aspx?nid=2167**

More recently, public and police attention has turned toward the international trafficking of human beings to service the sex industry. Human trafficking as a social and legal problem in the United States can be traced as far back as passage of the Mann Act in 1911, which made it illegal to transport women across state lines for purposes of prostitution. Historically, though, local police knew little about human trafficking and paid little attention to it as a local police problem. "In the United States, until the passage of the Trafficking Victims Protection Act (TVPA) in 2000, human trafficking was approached as an immigration problem, which meant that police viewed trafficking as a federal rather than a local responsibility" (Newman, 2006:1). The TVPA defines human trafficking as:

1. Sex trafficking in which a commercial sex act is induced by force, fraud, or coercion, or in which the person induced to perform such an act has not attained 18 years of age.
2. The recruitment, harboring, transportation, provision, or obtaining of a person for labor or services, through the use of force, fraud, or coercion for the purpose of subjection to involuntary servitude, peonage, debt bondage, or slavery.

Wilson et al. (2006:149–150) wrote that "Trafficking in human beings is a modern form of slavery that is one of the fastest growing forms of crime throughout the world." They reported that it has been estimated that 700,000 to 1 million women and children are trafficked each year across the globe, and 50,000 of them are imported into the United States, which has become a major importer of sex slaves. These numbers are only estimates, though, as human trafficking is a hidden transnational commerce that occurs in private homes or under the facade of legitimate businesses. Local police are more likely to confront both the victims of human trafficking and the perpetrators of these crimes than are federal law enforcement officials (De Baca & Tisi, 2002), but they "are ill prepared to recognize human trafficking victims or investigate this emerging crime problem. … Local police agencies view trafficking as a problem 'elsewhere' and for 'other' law enforcement agencies. Consistent with the attitudes that this was not really a local law enforcement problem, the majority of agencies believed that trafficking in human beings is 'best addressed by federal law enforcement.'" (Wilson et al., 2006:158). A number of departments are becoming more active in investigating human trafficking; for example, the Boston Police Department created a human trafficking unit. Human trafficking, unlike prostitution, cannot be seen as a victimless crime, because most of the workers involved in this trade are forced into the sex industry and many are children (Box 6.4).

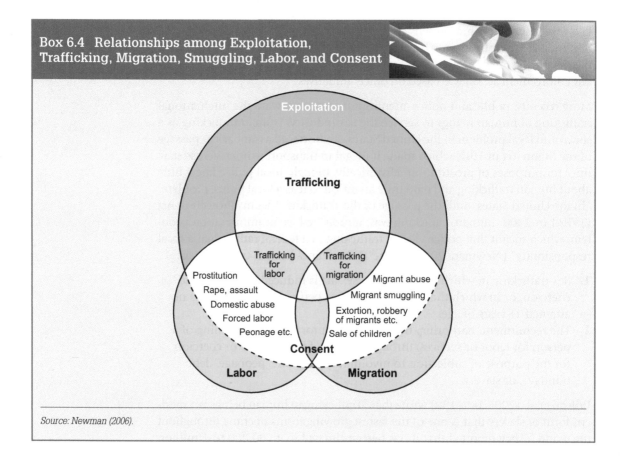

Box 6.4 Relationships among Exploitation, Trafficking, Migration, Smuggling, Labor, and Consent

Source: Newman (2006).

Pornography

Pornography is the depiction of lewd, obscene, or erotic sexual behavior without any artistic merit or value. Pornography is a complex law enforcement issue primarily because there are varying levels of public acceptance. Residents of cities, such as Los Angeles, Las Vegas, or New York City, are very likely to be more accepting than residents of the Bible Belt or cities that have large concentrations of fundamentalist religious groups. There is little agreement about pornography in most jurisdictions. Conservative, fundamentalist groups oppose pornography, whereas merchants and businesspeople frequently do not oppose it because it attracts business to the community.

To learn more about the issues of free speech, visit the Website for the Thomas Jefferson Center for the Protection of Free Expression at **www.tjcenter.org/**

The U.S. Supreme Court attempted to provide legal guidelines for the regulation of pornography in the case of Miller v. California (1973). The Court opted to leave definitional problems to each local community, declining to even attempt to establish a national standard as to what is obscene. The standard used to enforce obscenity laws is "that which violates the prevailing norms of the community," which results in substantial discretion and little consistency of enforcement. Specifically, the court established three standards:

1. The average person, applying contemporary community standards, would find the work, taken as a whole, appeals to prurient interests.
2. The work depicts or describes, in a patently offensive way, sexual conduct specifically defined by the applicable state law.
3. The work, taken as a whole, lacks serious literary, artistic, political, or scientific value.

Although there is general social acceptance of pornography, there is little acceptance of child pornography. Child pornography is the exploitation and abuse of minors by depiction of them in sexual situations. Affording children legal protection from sexual exploitation is a relatively modern development. "As late as the 1880s in the United States, the age of consent for girls was just 10 years. In 1977, only two states had legislation specifically outlawing the use of children in obscene material. The first federal law concerning child pornography was passed in 1978, and the first laws that specifically referred to computers and child pornography were passed in 1988. Since that time, there has been a steady tightening of child pornography laws." (Wortley, 2006:4). But there has also been growth in the industry. The kiddy porn industry is estimated at more than $1 billion U.S. annually. It is linked to pedophile rings that are involved in making children available for sexual relations with adults. These rings have extensive networks for recruiting young children and delivering a variety of sexual services (Box 6.5).

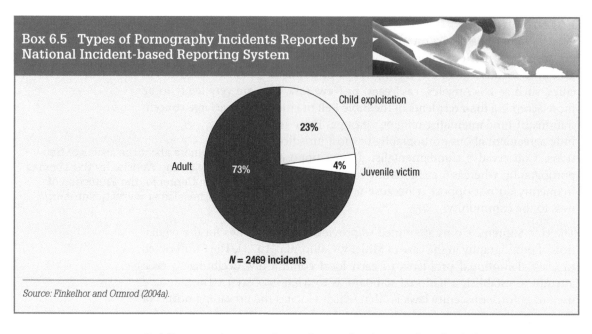

Box 6.5   Types of Pornography Incidents Reported by National Incident-based Reporting System

Child exploitation

23%

Adult 73%   4%   Juvenile victim

N = 2469 incidents

Source: Finkelhor and Ormrod (2004a).

Public attention was brought to the issue of pedophiles recently when veteran San Francisco police officer Donald Rene Ramirez was arrested in Phnom Penh for allegedly having sex with a 14-year-old girl. While in jail, the officer reportedly shot himself. According to Gary Delagnes, President of the Police Officers Association "Everyone knew—absolutely—what he was going over there for. … Nothing was ever written up, but they called him on the carpet and told him to knock it off," Delagnes said. "His response was basically, 'It's my time and I can do whatever the hell I want'." (Matier & Ross, 2006).

More attention is being paid to the issue of child exploitation, especially because of the Internet. Police have also begun using reverse stings to catch would-be pedophiles over the Internet. In Detroit, three men were arrested for soliciting sex from people they thought were teens over the Internet. In one case, the operation involved an undercover agent posing as a 13-year-old boy. The officer corresponded with suspects on the Internet, and a suspect who propositioned the agent to meet him for sex was arrested. In another case, a man was arrested for soliciting sex while chatting online with a sheriff's deputy who he thought was a 14-year-old girl. In still another case, a U.S. Secret Service agent assigned to the state's Internet Crimes against Children Task Force posed as a 13-year-old girl. He arrested a man who solicited sex online and e-mailed adult pornography to the investigators (Angel, 2006).

In perhaps one of the most widely publicized cases, Polk County (Tampa Bay) undercover detectives created fictitious online profiles to catch would-be child pornographers and pedophiles. In the course of their investigations, U.S. Department of Homeland Security Deputy Press Secretary Brian J. Doyle was arrested on about two dozen felony charges for having sexually explicit conversations with a person he thought was a 14-year-old girl. Detectives said Doyle had sexually explicit online and telephone conversations with the undercover detective, whom he contacted after reading the "girl's" profile on the Internet. Doyle sent the undercover detective sexually explicit digital movies and encouraged her to buy a web camera so she could send graphic images of herself to him, officials said. The Federal Bureau of Investigation's (FBI) Innocent Images National Initiative, meanwhile, made more than 11,000 arrests nationwide between 2001 and 2012 (FBI, 2013a).

The problem of pornography has traditionally been a local issue, but federal and state officials aggressively investigate and prosecute those involved in making and distributing child pornography and attempting to sexually exploit children. The U.S. Customs Service, for example, has several offices that attempt to intercept child pornography as it enters the United States, and the U.S. Postal Service attempts to monitor and prosecute individuals who use the mails to distribute pornography.

Gambling

Gambling includes a wide variety of activities, all of which involve the element of chance. Bets or wagers are risked by a player who hopes to win by beating the odds. It is an ambiguous law enforcement issue because many forms of gambling have been legalized in recent years. There are numerous forms of legal gambling including horse or dog racing, bingo, lotteries, and casinos on Native American reservations. Nevada and Atlantic City have legal casinos, and a number of states have legalized riverboat casinos. Consequently, the police do not see gambling as a major issue, and indeed, in 2011, there were only 8600 gambling arrests made in the United States (FBI, 2013b). Today, even though there has been a renewed interest in gambling because of the Internet, it receives a low priority in most police departments, and no priority whatsoever in many departments. Even with "thousands of Websites taking billions of dollars in wagers each year, fewer than 25 people have ever been prosecuted in the United States for online gambling. Most were bookies who were also taking sports bets by telephone." (Rose, 2006:1). With some form of state-supported gambling existing in most states, few police officers or citizens view it as being harmful, especially in light of the many other problems facing society. Because most gambling offenses are misdemeanors and substantial effort is required to investigate gambling, police departments are not willing to devote the resources necessary to control it.

THE INVESTIGATION OF VICE

The basic investigative techniques required to enforce laws against prostitution, gambling, and narcotics are similar. Each of these crimes requires the use of undercover officers, informants, and wiretapping or surveillance. The use of wiretaps and physical surveillance may produce some of the most convincing evidence of a crime, but they are expensive to conduct and, in the case of wiretapping, are subject to strict legal requirements and controls. They cannot obtain a wiretap order from the court without sufficient evidence to convince the judge that a crime is being committed, but, without the wiretap, it is impossible to develop the evidence necessary to show that the crime is being committed. Moreover, a number of states do not allow state and local officers to conduct wiretaps, which further complicates the investigation of vice activities. Regardless, police departments frequently spend thousands of dollars to investigate crimes that result in fines of less than $500.

Undercover operations present many problems for the department. Officers are forced to assume a different lifestyle that thrusts them into the criminal subculture where they must do things that would otherwise be illegal. This extracts a heavy toll on individual officers who must be separated from family, friends, and other department members for extended periods. Officers who remain in undercover positions for too long a period may begin to become corrupt. There are examples where undercover officers became drug dependent and, in some cases, engaged in the illegal sale of drugs. Furthermore, Langworthy (1989) suggested that some undercover operations actually cause additional criminal activities. As a result of his analysis of a Birmingham undercover antifencing operation, he concluded that the operation caused a substantial amount of crime by creating a market for stolen goods. If the police operation had not existed, no market would have existed and criminals would have stolen less.

Any undercover operation is subject to claims of entrapment. Although officers can do things that facilitate the commission of a crime, they may not induce someone to commit a crime. Because undercover operations generally may be initiated without prior judicial authorization, the results are subject to strict scrutiny by the court. Allowing police to make discretionary decisions to initiate undercover investigations based on a mere suspicion has been the subject of much criticism (Schoeman, 1986). Recognizing the magnitude of the problem, the FBI now requires that large-scale undercover operations first be reviewed by their Criminal Undercover Operations Review Committee.

Informants are particularly helpful and often necessary in the investigation of vice crimes, but they are problematic because police must sometimes overlook illegal acts committed by the informants. Narcotics users or lower level dealers may be allowed to continue violating the law so investigators can make cases against their suppliers. In order to move up the distribution network, officers may find it necessary to cooperate with dealers who are selling a significant amount of drugs. Moreover, information provided by informants may not be correct resulting in police operations that do not result in the arrest of any suspects.

Vice enforcement requires making a number of discretionary decisions. Administrative discretion is exercised in determining what activities will be pursued. Operational discretion is exercised in determining who will be targeted for investigation. Because police do not have the resources to investigate every crime, they engage in selective enforcement; they enforce only particular types of violations or target specific types of offenders. Police managers must ensure that vice enforcement focuses on those offenses that contribute to substantial levels of crime. With the exceptions of drugs and child pornography, officers may come to view enforcement of vice crimes as a waste of time. There is no evidence that their enforcement efforts will have any effect on limiting these activities, and the penalties received for conviction are relatively minor. Officers not specifically assigned to vice control units may be more likely to exercise discretion and not initiate any formal actions, preferring to resolve immediate problems through other means.

POLICING HATE CRIMES

In 1990, Congress passed the Hate Crime Statistics Act, which forced the police to collect statistics on crimes motivated because of a victim's race, religion, sexual orientation, ethnicity, or national origin. Crimes against persons with disabilities became an element of hate crime statistics with passage of the Violent Crime and Law Enforcement Act of 1994. In 1996, the Church Arson Prevention Act was signed into law, extending data collection to the destruction of churches. Today, about 12,417 law enforcement agencies in 49 states provide information regarding hate crimes to the Hate Crime Data Collection Program. Hate crimes are crimes that manifest evidence of prejudice based on certain group characteristics. As such, "hate crimes are not separate, distinct crimes; instead, they are traditional offenses motivated by the offender's bias. An offender, for example, may damage or vandalize property because of his/her bias against the owner's (victim's) race, religion, sexual orientation, ethnicity/national origin, or disability. … Because motivation is subjective, it is difficult to know with certainty whether a crime was the result of the offender's bias. Law enforcement investigation is imperative in that it must reveal sufficient evidence as to whether the offender's actions were motivated, in whole or in part, by bias." (FBI, 2006:1) (Box 6.6).

In some instances, the enforcement of hate crimes is problematic. The legal definition of a hate crime is often ambiguous and motive is often difficult to determine (Bell, 2002); enforcement is sometimes wrought with political

Box 6.6 Percentage of Hate Crime Incidents

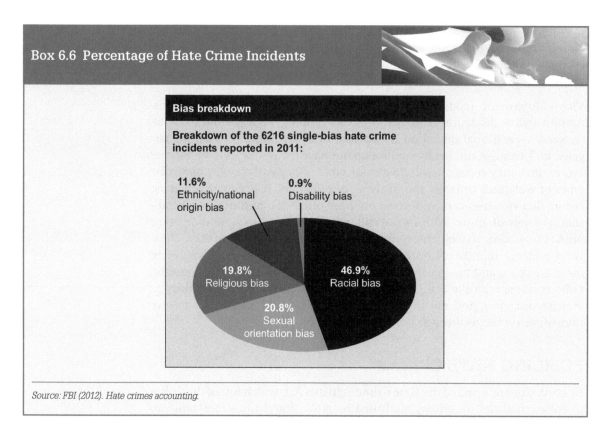

Bias breakdown

Breakdown of the 6216 single-bias hate crime
incidents reported in 2011:

11.6%
Ethnicity/national
origin bias

0.9%
Disability bias

19.8%
Religious bias

46.9%
Racial bias

20.8%
Sexual
orientation bias

Source: FBI (2012). Hate crimes accounting.

circumstances that drives police decision-making rather than the rule of law
(Bell, 2002; Cogan, 2002); and people in some communities expect to assign
officers or to establish specialized units to investigate hate crimes when the
department does not have adequate resources for enforcement (Balboni &
McDevitt, 2001). These problems add to the complexity of investigating hate
crimes (Table 6.3).

Clearly, African Americans, Jewish people, and homosexuals are the groups
targeted for hate crimes most frequently. Many right-wing groups identify these
people as enemies. After the 911 attacks in 2001, there was an increase in the
number of bias crimes directed toward Muslims and Arabs as a result of the
war on terrorism and the wars in Iraq and Afghan-
istan. Recently, there has been an increased interest
in policing hate crimes against the homeless. They
are victimized with great frequency, and numerous
homeless persons are murdered each year.

To view a video on hate crime, visit the Website **www.youtube.com/
watch?v=NXxY681UgoA**

There are more than 1000 active hate groups in the United States (Southern
Poverty Law Center, 2013). They include the American Nazi Party, Arizona

Table 6.3 Incidents, Offenses, Victims, and Known Offenders by Bias Motivation, 2011

Bias Motivation	Incidents	Offenses	Victims[1]	Known Offenders[2]
Total	6222	7254	7713	5731
Single-bias incidents	6216	7240	7697	5724
Race	2917	3465	3645	2787
Anti-white	504	577	593	594
Anti-black	2076	2494	2619	1935
Anti-American Indian/Alaskan native	61	67	70	60
Anti-Asian/Pacific Islander	138	165	175	120
Anti-multiple races, group	138	162	188	78
Religion	1233	1318	1480	590
Anti-Jewish	771	820	936	287
Anti-Catholic	67	68	84	21
Anti-Protestant	44	49	51	32
Anti-Islamic	157	175	185	138
Anti-other religion	130	139	155	74
Anti-multiple religions, group	60	63	65	37
Anti-Atheism/Agnosticism/etc.	4	4	4	1
Sexual orientation	1293	1508	1572	1511
Anti-male homosexual	760	871	891	978
Anti-female homosexual	137	168	174	123
Anti-homosexual	359	429	465	362
Anti-heterosexual	16	17	19	19
Anti-bisexual	21	23	23	29
Ethnicity/national origin	720	891	939	749
Anti-hispanic	405	506	534	452
Anti-other ethnicity/national origin	315	385	405	297
Disability	53	58	61	87
Anti-physical	19	23	26	29
Anti-mental	34	35	35	58
Multiple-bias Incidents[3]	6	14	16	7

[1]The term victim may refer to a person, business, institution, or society as a whole.
[2]The term known offender does not imply that the identity of the suspect is known, but only that an attribute of the suspect has been identified, which distinguishes him/her from an unknown offender.
[3]In a multiple-bias incident, two conditions must be met: (a) more than one offense type must occur in the incident and (b) at least two offense types must be motivated by different biases.

Patriots, Aryan Brotherhood, Aryan Nations, Christian Defense League, Christian Patriots Defense League, Identity Church Movement, Ku Klux Klan, Posse Comitatus, and skinheads, to name a few. In addition, more than 200 militias are operating in 39 states and over 1360 antigovernment "Patriot" groups were active in 2012. Many of these militias have racist or neo-Nazi ties (Southern Poverty Law Center, 2013). Almost all of the militias are based on an antigovernment platform. Computer bulletin boards and other forms of sophisticated communications link various groups together. Their goals range from the dissemination of hate materials to the coordination and commission of criminal acts against target groups and individuals. Some openly espouse the overthrow of the government (Figure 6.2).

The rationale for police involvement in hate crimes is that one of their primary roles is the enforcement or reinforcement of community values. Even though a particular hate crime may appear to be relatively minor and unorganized (e.g., graffiti, simple assault, or disorderly conduct), it may attack the very fiber of a community because of its effects on the victim or the community as a whole (Martin, 1996). Hate crimes have a compounding effect that touches a group of people, a neighborhood, or a whole community. They undercut our idea of

FIGURE 6.2
Ku Klux Klan ceremonial cross burning. *Photograph courtesy of AP Photo/Jeff Kowalsky.*

justice, fairness, and constitutionalism that is the very foundation of our social order. As such, the police must react decisively to hate crimes to ensure that public confidence is maintained and that deterioration of the community does not occur.

The primary law enforcement activity relative to hate crimes is the reporting and documentation of such crimes. If these crimes are not properly reported and documented, authorities cannot successfully mount enforcement actions. The police must exhibit a commitment to eradicate such crimes by thoroughly investigating them. For example, Garofalo (1991) found that 90% of the bias crimes in New York City resulted in three or more investigative reports, 76% of the nonbias crimes resulted in no reports, and only 7% of the nonbias crimes resulted in three or more investigative reports. Indeed, the New York City Police Department (NYPD) was exerting extra effort in bias cases (Martin, 1996) and hoped that its commitment to such cases was communicated to the perpetrators, victims, and community. Many jurisdictions, however, fail to adequately report and investigate hate crimes (Nolan & Akiyama, 2002), resulting in significant underreporting of the problem. Martin (1995, 1996) investigated determinants of police responses to hate crimes, including the types of bias and subjective judgments made by officers. Officers are more likely to make an arrest for crimes against persons than for property crimes, and they are more likely to make an arrest for hate crimes involving sexual orientation and race as compared to other types of bias. The police tend to exert greater efforts when the crimes are more severe (Wilson & Ruback, 2003) (Table 6.4).

DISENFRANCHISED POPULATIONS

A large segment of the American population has been disenfranchised from the rest of society because of our political economy and the stigma we attach to these people. This presents a special challenge for the police. Disenfranchised people include the mentally ill, public inebriates, drug abusers, and the homeless. Although many of the people in these categories experience homelessness, society tends to deal with them as the "homeless."

The Homeless

The best estimate of the number of homeless people was done by the National Alliance to End Homeless (2013) there are approximately 633,782 homeless people in the United States (Estimates also indicated that about 1% of the U.S. population experiences homelessness each year). The homeless are a diverse group of people and do not constitute a single group or a single social problem; treating them as such is an oversimplification. About 39% of the homeless are children, 17% are single women, and 33% are families with children. Although almost all homeless people are poor, many are employed. Poverty

Table 6.4 Incidents, Offenses, Victims, and Known Offenders by Offense Type, 2011

Offense Type	Incidents[1]	Offenses	Victims[2]	Known Offenders[3]
Total	6222	7254	7713	5731
Crimes against persons	3754	4623	4623	4631
Murder and non-negligent manslaughter	4	4	4	7
Forcible rape	7	7	7	10
Aggravated assault	677	895	895	1095
Simple assault	1336	1595	1595	1790
Intimidation	1720	2106	2106	1711
Other	10	16	16	18
Crimes against property	2611	2611	3070	1256
Robbery	131	131	157	288
Burglary	124	124	147	72
Larceny-theft	152	152	165	88
Motor vehicle theft	6	6	6	1
Arson	42	42	52	20
Destruction/damage/vandalism	2125	2125	2510	759
Other	31	31	33	28
Crimes against society	20	20	20	34

[1]The actual number of incidents is 6222. However, the column figures will not add to the total because incidents may include more than one offense type, and these are counted in each appropriate offense type category.
[2]The term "victim" may refer to a person, business, institution, or society as a whole.
[3]The term "known offender" does not imply that the identity of the suspect is known, but only that an attribute of the suspect has been identified, which distinguishes him/her from an unknown offender. The actual number of known offenders is 5731. However, the column figures will not add to the total because some offenders are responsible for more than one offense type; and are, therefore, counted more than once in this table.

and a lack of adequate shelter seem to be the only binding threads that unite the people we call homeless (Box 6.7).

Lumping all disenfranchised people into a single group is ineffective and deceptive and results in the police having to deal with these problems rather than social service agencies and public programs. For the most part, homelessness, drug abuse, alcoholism, and mental illness are intermingled. The U.S. Conference of Mayors (2010) found that about 30% of the adult homeless had an alcohol disorder or drug problem, and 22% had severe mental disorders. This becomes a significant problem for the police. A major problem is that there are not enough shelter beds in most communities to house or care for the homeless.

A number of departments have developed strategies or programs to deal with the homeless. The Los Angeles Police Department implemented the

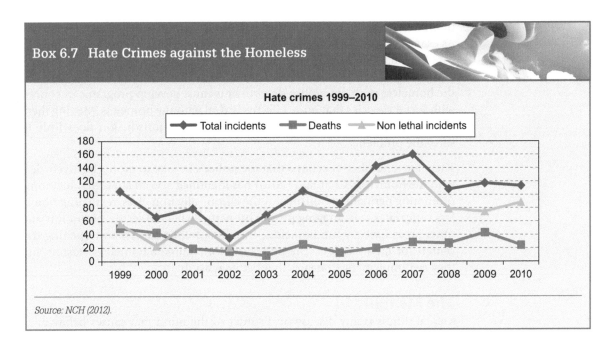

Box 6.7   Hate Crimes against the Homeless

Hate crimes 1999–2010

Total incidents — Deaths — Non lethal incidents

Source: NCH (2012).

Safer Cities Initiative (Berk & MacDonald, 2010; Braga, 2010). Los Angeles had a significant homeless population, primarily located in concentrated encampments. These encampments attracted prostitution, drug dealing and consumption, property crimes, and some violence. The department, under the guise of disorder policing, assigned large numbers of officers to these areas. They made arrests, issued citations, and forced residents out of the encampments. When the resident homeless population had been removed, the encampments were cleared. The result was a nominal decrease in crime in the affected areas (Berk & MacDonald, 2010), but it did not solve the homeless problem; it only dispersed it.

The City of San Bernardino passed an ordinance making it an offense to given panhandlers money. The police department tried to encourage the homeless to use the city's shelters, but very few did so. The program did not have an impact. It is not known if the police cited anyone as a result of the ordinance— doing so would add to the courts' workload and it is questionable if anyone would be convicted.

To learn more about the issues associated with the homeless, visit: **http://www. nationalhomeless.org/**

Another method by which police departments have dealt with the homeless has been the dumping of troubled persons in other jurisdictions (King & Dunn, 2004). Officers pick up homeless people, mentally ill people, prostitutes, and other problem persons and dump them in another political jurisdiction. King and Dunn identified four American cities where police engaged in dumping: Cleveland, Miami, Washington, D.C., and Schenectady, New York. As examples, the Washington, D.C., police transported 24 prostitutes to Arlington, Virginia, and Miami was the recipient of dumping by other cities in the area. This practice has resulted in several lawsuits and obviously does not solve the homeless problem. Police departments must develop programs in concert with social agencies that more effectively deal with the homeless. Moving them about a jurisdiction or dumping them in another jurisdiction does little to solve the problem.

There are a number of actions that the police can take to more effectively deal with the homeless. Chamard (2010) has identified several strategies, including promoting permanent housing for the chronically homeless, regulating homeless camp sites, encouraging private property owners to secure vacant lots and other areas used by the homeless, installing public toilets, and opening day centers for the homeless. The police cannot eliminate homeless persons, but they can implement strategies that better assist them.

The Mentally Ill

Mental illness is any disease or disorder of the mind that causes behavior or emotional problems that impairs a person's ability to function in society. Persons who are mentally ill account for a significant number of the calls for police service, although it has been pointed out that "mental illness is not, in and of itself, a police problem. Obviously, it is a medical and social services problem. However, a number of the problems caused by or associated with people with mental illness often do become police problems." (Cordner, 2006:1). Nonetheless, the police, in many instances, have become the agency responsible for handling the mentally ill. This is especially true for the lower socioeconomic segments of our society. Although all socioeconomic groups experience mental illness, the poor do not have access to private care, so they tend to call the police in hopes of obtaining necessary care for family members or others suffering mental illness.

The problem is significant for the police. LaGrange (2000) surveyed one large police department and found that 89% of the officers in the department had contact with mentally disoriented persons in the previous year. Cordner (2006:1) reported that "seven percent of police contacts in jurisdictions with 100,000 or more people involve the mentally ill. A three-city study found that 92 percent of patrol officers had at least one encounter with a mentally ill person in crisis in the previous month, and officers averaged six such encounters per month. Police in Lincoln, Nebraska, 'handled over 1500 mental health investigation cases in 2002, and spent more time on these cases than on injury traffic accidents, burglaries, or felony assaults.' The NYPD responds to about 150,000 'emotionally disturbed persons' calls per year."

The most effective way for the police to deal with people with mental illness is the crisis intervention team (CIT) model. Here, police officers are specifically trained to deal with persons with mental illness with a goal to divert them to mental health services rather than subjecting them to the criminal justice system. Researchers examining the CIT model in Chicago found that CIT officers directed more persons to mental health services as compared to non-CIT officers, CIT officers also were better able to handle or deal with mentally ill subjects.

Similar difficulties exist with people who are chronic public inebriates. Decriminalization of public intoxication coupled with jail overcrowding has limited the ability of police to do anything with these individuals. In areas where public intoxication is still a crime, the jails do not always have room to house them. They either discourage police from arresting such people or refuse to admit them to the facility. There is a general lack of adequate detoxification centers in this country, leaving police with few alternatives. In areas where public intoxication is no longer a crime, these centers are often the only alternative. If facilities are not available, the police generally must allow these people to remain on the streets.

Handling disenfranchised persons, particularly those with mental illness, is problematic. For the most part, officers do not receive adequate training on recognizing and handling mentally disturbed citizens. One recent study (Ruiz & Miller, 2004) found that only about half (53.2%) of the officers participating in the study believed they were qualified to handle mentally ill persons. Teplin (1986) found that the police tended to use informal dispositions, such as calming the person down or taking them to their homes in 72% of the cases; they made an arrest in 17% of the cases and used a civil commitment in 12% of the cases. King and Dunn (2004) identified instances in which officers essentially transported disenfranchised persons to another jurisdiction and dumped them, which raises a number of legal and ethical issues (see previous discussion on the homeless). The use of informal dispositions often is the result of a lack of adequate training, inadequate departmental policies, or the absence of community programs and facilities to deal with these individuals.

CONTROLLING POLICE DISCRETION

There has been considerable discussion since the 1960s about the use of police discretion and the extent to which it should be controlled. Even today, many departments do not provide formal guidelines to officers in such important areas as the decision to arrest, patrol and investigative procedures, or the use of force. It is impossible to eliminate discretion. Instead, administrators must examine the manner in which discretion can be regulated or controlled.

The police traditionally have been viewed as a ministerial agency responsible for implementing policies established by elected officials or the courts. Use of discretion effectively allows them to form policy or establish the boundaries of legal versus illegal conduct through their decisions. Discretion allows for arbitrary enforcement of the law, which, in turn, leads to discriminatory practices. The police have a tremendous amount of power that includes the authority to use deadly force. Critics are quick to show that the police have a history of exceeding their authority and abusing citizens (Kappeler et al., 1998).

Equally vocal are those who oppose attempts to restrict the use of discretion. Decision-making is an important and necessary function of the police. Attempts to reform the system should focus not on limiting discretion but on improving officers' capacity for judgment and teaching them how to make decisions properly. Focusing on the control of police discretion ignores the relationships among the law enforcement, order maintenance, and service roles. These roles cannot be compartmentalized into separate activities. Of necessity, they are often performed simultaneously. Each requires some degree of discretion. The decision to approach a particular situation from the law-enforcement, order-maintenance, or service perspective is itself a discretionary decision that cannot be controlled without a great deal of regulation.

Leaving the philosophical arguments aside, it is not possible in a practical sense to eliminate discretion. The question becomes one of how to structure and control the police decision-making process. Although both internal and external control mechanisms can be imposed, it is generally conceded that measures designed and implemented by the police are the most effective. Ultimately, the success of any attempt to control police discretion rests on the willingness of officers to comply.

UNDERSTANDING THE NEED FOR CONTROL MECHANISMS

Police officers become involved in undesirable situations because of, for example, using bad judgment or being indiscrete about where they commit illegal acts. In some cases, the behavior is deliberate, whereas in other cases it is accidental or unintentional. Internally, supervisors may observe or otherwise become aware of such activities and take immediate action to address them. If the transgression is severe enough, a supervisor may initiate formal charges against the officer in question. In other cases, a citizen may observe the behavior, or a citizen may believe that officers treated him or her improperly. In some cases, they may lodge formal complaints against the officer with the department. Once such complaints are made, some form of investigation or inquiry usually ensues. Police departments have an obligation to ensure that officer behavior, agency procedures, and actions are reasonable and effective. One aspect of meeting this obligation is allowing citizens a readily accessible process of lodging complaints against the department and its officers. This process must be conducted in a prompt and fair manner to create citizen confidence (U.S. Department of Justice, 2001).

Citizen complaints are a significant problem. Hickman (2006) determined that large police departments receive about 9.5 citizen complaints each year per 100 officers. Fyfe and Kane (unpublished:67) reported that, in a single year, the Internal Affairs Bureau of the NYPD processed 25,091 complaints against officers, 1203 of which involved allegations that could have led to criminal charges or terminations.

People file a variety of complaints against police officers. Table 6.5 shows the percentage of complaints filed by type for the San Francisco Police Department in 2011.

Internal Control Mechanisms

Police departments must actively establish policies and other guidelines to control officers' behavior. Civil liability and the national move toward departmental accreditation have resulted in many departments comprehensively examining their policies and operating procedures and taking action to ensure that they are consistent with real-world necessity. Policies and procedures not only control what officers do but also provide guidance when officers are confronted with situations where they need assistance. In the absence of such

Table 6.5 Type of complaints Filed Against San Francisco Police Officers	
Type of Complaint	Percentage of Total Complaints
Unnecessary force	3
Unwarranted action	36
Conduct reflecting discredit on the department	28
Neglect of duty	23
Racial slur	<1
Sexual slur	<1
Discourtesy	3

Source: The Office of Citizen Complaints 2011 Annual Report. http://www.sfgov3.org/modules/showdocument.aspx?documentid=1938.

policies, officers conceivably could do anything they wished to resolve a situation. Such a laissez-faire attitude has resulted in substantial civil liability in the past, especially in areas such as domestic violence, pursuit driving, false arrests, and use of force (Kappeler, 2006). Policies have been used to give officers direction and reduce the department's liability.

Policies that directly affect a department's ability to detect and correct abuses of discretion or authority include requirements that officers and interested parties who witness such abuses must report them. To encourage the reporting of police abuses, the U.S. Department of Justice (2001:7–8) recommended that:

1. Law enforcement officers should be required to report misconduct by other officers that they witness or of which they become aware. The failure to report misconduct should be subject to appropriate discipline.
2. Agencies should have in place appropriate protection against retaliation for officers who report misconduct.
3. Law enforcement officers should be required to report to their agency any instance in which they are: arrested or criminally charged for any conduct, named as a party in a civil suit regarding on-duty conduct, or named as a party in a civil suit regarding off-duty conduct where the allegations are related to the officer's ability to perform law enforcement duties (e.g., improper force, fraud, or discrimination).
4. Law enforcement agencies should seek to be notified whenever a court or a prosecutor concludes that an officer engaged in misconduct in the course of criminal investigations or proceedings (e.g., engaged in false testimony or dishonest conduct, or improperly charged an individual with resisting arrest, assault on an officer, or disorderly conduct in an attempt to justify inappropriate use of force).

Simply issuing policy directives is not enough. Departments must also train officers and provide supervisory mechanisms to ensure that the policies are properly communicated and implemented. The training should begin with recruits in the academy, but it is also necessary to continually retrain officers in the field. Agencies must be willing to supervise employees consistently. Many agencies are adopting the early warning system (EWS) approach to monitor officers' behavior (Alpert et al., 2005; Kappeler et al., 1998). The department keeps track of all complaints, justified or not, to identify officer behavior patterns. When officers begin to accumulate a number of complaints, their entire record is reviewed in an attempt to identify problem areas and provide early assistance. In some cases, the complaints may be an unjustified attempt to have an officer removed from the department. Others may reflect early signs of substance abuse, marital problems, or emotional difficulties that can be addressed if identified early enough. The EWS collects the following types of information about officers, supervisors, and managers (U.S. Department of Justice, 2001):

1. Information on shootings and use of force.
2. Arrests, traffic stops, searches and seizures.
3. Citizen complaints and commendations.
4. Criminal charges and traffic violations.
5. Lawsuits against officers.
6. Misconduct allegations.
7. Disciplinary actions and remedial actions.
8. Training and job performance history.
9. On-duty traffic accidents.
10. Use and abuse of sick leave.

Brandl, Stroshine, and Frank (2001) investigated the characteristics of officers who most frequently receive complaints and found that numbers of arrests, officer age, and officer gender differentiated officers with high numbers of complaints. Females received fewer complaints, probably because they tend to use reason and dialogue in confrontational situations, and they often are perceived as being less threatening to citizens. Younger officers received more complaints; one explanation is that they generally are more active, making larger numbers of stops and arrests. They also are more likely to use force relative to older officers.

Perhaps the most effective internal control a police department can use to ensure that officers are not abusing their discretion or authority is the development of an adequate process for the investigation of citizens' complaints. McCluskey and Terrill's (2005) research into citizens' complaints and actual police behavior on the streets shed light on the importance of using complaints to predict behavior. Their research suggests that "knowing that officers with a greater number of discourtesy complaints are also more inclined to use higher levels of force may change the dynamic of how these types of complaints are perceived by administrators. In other words, such complaints may offer a warning sign that simple verbal disrespect leads to coercion, and more severe forms of it."

The investigation of citizens' complaints against the police is usually handled by the Internal Affairs Unit of the police department. In this process, citizens should be provided the opportunity to have a full and fair investigation into their grievance against the officer or department. The U.S. Department of Justice (2001:7) recommended that:

1. Civilians should be allowed to file complaints in person, by mail, by telephone, by facsimile transmission, or, where possible, by e-mail. A complaint form should be offered, but completion of the form should not be required to initiate a complaint. Individuals should be able to obtain and file complaint forms at places other than law enforcement agencies.

2. Officers and other employees should be prohibited from refusing to accept complaints, or attempting to dissuade a civilian from filing a complaint. Civilians should not be required to meet with or speak with a supervisory officer as a requirement for filing a complaint.
3. Complaints should be accepted from all individuals, including those who request anonymity. Complaints should be accepted from third parties to ensure that witnesses of abuse or misconduct, as well as victims of such misconduct, can file complaints.

Box 6.8 shows the complaint investigation procedures used by the Boston Police department.

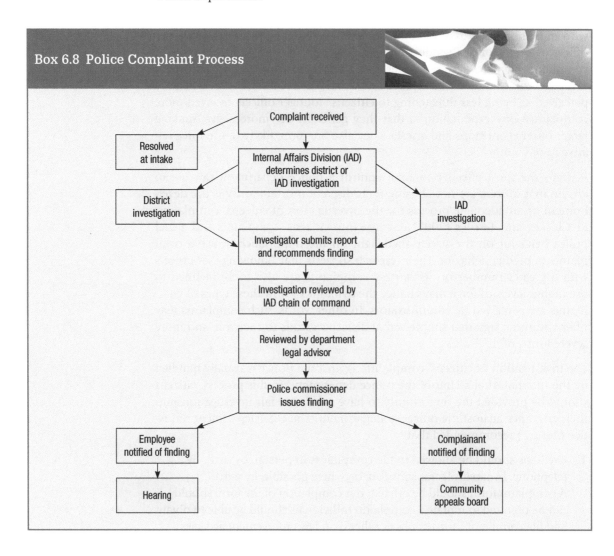

Box 6.8 Police Complaint Process

Through a process of policy formation, training, and adequate supervision, departments can begin to restrict and control discretionary decision-making. Although it is generally conceded that the most effective methods of controlling police behavior are those imposed by the police themselves, internal control alone is insufficient. It is necessary to utilize external methods of control as a way to ensure proper police conduct.

Finally, how the department operates has influence on police misconduct. Wolf and Piquero (2013) advocate that organizational justice can play an important role in curbing misconduct. They surveyed officers in the Philadelphia Police Department and found that those officers who believed their department was fair and just were less likely to adhere to a code of silence or believe that police corruption in pursuit of a noble cause is justified as compared to officers who perceived the department as being unfair. It seems that how a department's management structure is viewed by officers has influence on their behavior.

External Control Mechanisms

Unlike internal control mechanisms that reflect an attempt by the police to address inappropriate behavior, external control mechanisms are imposed on the department by other agencies or individuals who may or may not have an understanding of the police role and functions. This control can be achieved through civilian review boards, legislative oversight, or the court system.

Control by the Citizens

External control of policing is usually associated with civilian review boards (CRBs). Many were created as a result of community outrage over police misconduct in the 1960s. CRBs were created to "(1) maintain effective discipline of the police, (2) provide satisfactory resolution of citizen complaints against officers, (3) maintain citizen confidence in the police, and (4) influence police administrators by providing feedback from citizens." (Maguire, 1991:186). In terms of functioning, they can assume several roles: oversight, rulemaking, investigative, and judicial. Walker and Bumphus (1992) identified three distinct types of CRBs in their survey of the nation's 50 largest cities: (1) fact finding is performed by civilians, (2) fact finding is performed by sworn officers but dispositional recommendations are made by civilians, and (3) fact finding is performed by civilians and dispositional recommendations are made by civilians to civilians who have ultimate authority over the final disposition. The most controversial CRBs are the ones that have a measure of judicial or dispositional power over police officer wrongdoing. Almost from their inception, review boards were resented by the police, who viewed them as an unwarranted intrusion. Many officers believed that they reflected a lack of trust on the part of the public and did little to improve police–community relations. Police officers saw the majority of complaints as coming from citizens who were the recipients of police actions and feared that CRBs would be used as a method of retaliation against them (Goldstein, 1977). Research, however, indicates that CRBs are no more punitive than internal police boards when determining guilt or meting out sentences (Walker & Bumphus, 1992).

The number of cities utilizing CRBs is increasing with many of the larger cities using some form of CRB. In some cities, they have had a long tenure and have been, to some extent, accepted by rank and file officers. It remains to be seen if they are any more effective than internal controls.

Legislative Control

The legislative branch of government can affect the exercise of discretion in three ways: (1) enactment of laws, (2) allocation of funds, and (3) legislative oversight. Legislators can decrease an officer's discretion by writing laws clearly. When statutes are written in broad terms, they are subject to diverse interpretation, which creates more room for discretion. In recent years, legislators have enacted laws that restrict or eliminate an officer's discretion to arrest under certain circumstances. A number of states now require officers to make an arrest in domestic violence situations. Missouri's law governing protective orders issued by the court to prevent domestic violence (Missouri Revised Statute § 455.085, 1989) is illustrative of legislative attempts to control discretion. A court order may be issued to prevent an abuser from returning to the residence or engaging in further acts of abuse or harassment. When called to a disturbance, the law gives officers the authority to make arrests, even if they did not witness the offense. If they do not arrest the offending person, they must submit a written report detailing their reasons. When a second call is received at the residence within 12 h, the officers must make an arrest if there is probable cause and they can determine who is the "primary aggressor."

The law seeks to limit officers' discretion and to impose reporting requirements so that their actions can be reviewed. One of the difficulties with legislative attempts to limit discretion is the manner in which the law is written. In our example above, a paragraph in the law stipulates that officers must make arrests whenever an act of abuse occurs. Some argue that this completely removes an officer's discretion, whereas others maintain that they have limited discretion under the "12-h rule." Determining who the "primary aggressor" is and whether there is probable cause are, in themselves, discretionary decisions.

Through the budgetary process, the legislature can control expenditure of funds, thereby establishing priorities for law enforcement. Specific instructions in the law as to which programs are to be initiated can effectively limit administrative discretion that would otherwise be permissible. For example, legislatures often allocate monies to police departments for DUI enforcement, drug programing, gang enforcement, etc. Legislative oversight as a method to control discretion has not been the subject of much research. Although it is common for the federal government to hold oversight hearings, some states also use this process. Legislative committees are given the authority to review the activities of government agencies. This review process is designed to ensure operational efficiency and integrity. The relative power of the committee to affect the overall operation of an agency will determine whether this method of oversight is effective.

Control by the Courts

The courts are perhaps the most visible bodies of external control over discretion exercised by the police. Although appellate courts are responsible for determining the constitutionality of a law, they also have the authority to govern procedural aspects of the law and to limit the manner in which it is enforced by the police. One difficulty that arises in the court's attempt to control discretion is the manner in which cases are reviewed and in which the decisions are reported. Courts will normally take the narrowest approach possible when deciding an issue. The written decisions are often lengthy and difficult to understand, leaving room for various interpretations. Seldom does the court tell police specifically what they may or may not do. One notable exception is the now famous Miranda v. Arizona (1966) decision. In this case, the U.S. Supreme Court specifically set forth the steps that must be taken and the language that must be used to advise a suspect of his or her constitutional privilege against self-incrimination.

The criminal courts are generally restricted to dismissing cases or refusing to admit evidence as remedies for inappropriate exercise of discretion. Civil courts have the option of issuing a writ of mandamus to require agencies to do particular things or issuing injunctions that prohibit them from committing certain acts. Officers and departments that make inappropriate decisions are subject to lawsuits that can require the payment of enormous damage claims (Kappeler, 2006). With the proliferation of lawsuits against police, agencies are likely to take additional steps to define the boundaries of discretionary decisions in an attempt to limit their civil liability.

SUMMARY

Discretion allows officers to make decisions as to what course of action will produce the most desirable outcome in a given situation. Properly used, discretion can be a positive aspect of the criminal justice system. When used improperly, it results in actions that are discriminatory, unethical, or illegal.

Use of discretion by administrators is implicit in the bureaucratic structure of police agencies. Through their discretionary function, administrators are expected to develop policies and procedures that are translated into uniform activities by street-level officers. Operational personnel typically exercise more discretion. This is felt to be problematic because these are generally the officers with the least amount of training and experience. Many factors influence an officer's decision-making process. Research consistently shows the primary factor in the decision to formally process a case is the seriousness of the offense.

Although decision-making is required in almost every area of law enforcement, certain situations more readily lend themselves to discretionary decisions, particularly domestic violence and vice crimes. In recent years, attempts have been made to structure and control the use of discretion by police. While no one seriously proposes eliminating discretion, most feel it should be structured so as to limit its harmful effects. Discretion can be controlled internally by the department through development of policies, procedures, training, and supervision. External controls may be imposed by CRBs, the legislature, or the courts. Of these methods, internal controls are thought to be the most effective. In the final analysis, any attempt to control an officer's discretion rests on the willingness of the officer to comply. For most activities in law enforcement, there are no effective limits on officers' behavior other than those imposed by the officers themselves.

REVIEW QUESTIONS

1. What is meant by the term discretion? Is discretion a significant part of our criminal justice system?
2. What are administrative and enforcement discretion?
3. What are some on the most important areas in which police use discretion?
4. What problems did the deinstitutionalization policies of the 1960s and 1970s concerning the mentally ill create for police?
5. There has been considerable discussion since the 1960s about the use of police discretion and the extent to which it should be controlled. What are some of the numerous objections to the unstructured use of discretion?
6. What are some of the control mechanisms that have been utilized in an attempt to control discretion?

REFERENCES

Alpert, G., & Dunham, R. (1990). *Police pursuit driving: Controlling responses to emergency situations.* Westport, CT: Greenwood Press.

Alpert, G., & Dunham, R. (2004). *Understanding police use of force.* New York: Cambridge University Press.

Alpert, G., Dunham, R., & Stroshine, M. S. (2005). *Policing continuity and change.* Prospect Heights, IL: Waveland Press.

Angel, C. (November 16, 2006). *3 men arrested in web stings.* Detroit Free Press.

Balboni, J., & McDevitt, J. (2001). Hate crime reporting: understanding police officer perceptions: departmental protocol, and the role of the victim: is there such a thing as a hate crime? *Justice Research and Policy, 3*, 1–27.

Bayley, D. H., & Mendelsohn, H. (1969). *Minorities and the police*. New York: The Free Press.

Beckett, K., Nyrop, K., & Pfingst, L. (2006). Race, drugs, and policing: understanding disparities in drug delivery arrests. *Criminology, 44*(1), 105.

Bell, J. (2002). *Policing hatred: Law enforcement, civil rights, and hate crime*. New York: New York University.

Belvedere, K., Worrall, J., & Tibbetts, S. (2005). Explaining suspect resistance in police–citizen encounters. *Criminal Justice Review, 30*, 30–44.

Berk, R., & MacDonald, J. (2010). Policing the homeless: an evaluation of efforts to reduce homeless-related crime. *Criminology and Public Policy, 9*, 813–840.

Black, D. (1971). The social organization of arrest. *Stanford Law Review, 23*, 1087–1111.

Black, D. (1980). *The manners and customs of the police*. New York: Academic Press.

Black, D., & Reiss, A. (1970). Police control of juveniles. *American Sociological Review, 35*, 63–77.

Boivin, R., & Cordeau, G. (2011). Measuring the impact of police discretion on official crime statistics: a research note. *Police Quarterly, 14*, 186–203.

Braga, A. (2010). The police, disorder, and the homeless. *Criminology and Public Policy, 9*, 807–812.

Brandl, S., Stroshine, M., & Frank, J. (2001). Who are the complainant-prone officers? An examination of the relationship between police officers' attributes, arrest activity, and assignment. *Journal of Criminal Justice, 29*(6), 521–529.

Brooks, L. (2001). Police discretionary behavior: a study of style. In R. Dunham, & G. Alpert (Eds.), *Critical issues in policing* (pp. 117–131). Prospect Heights, IL: Waveland Press.

Brown, R., & Frank, J. (2005). Race and officer decision making: examining the differences in arrest outcomes between black and White officers. *Justice Quarterly, 23*, 96–126.

Bureau of Justice Statistics. (2006). *Intimate partner violence declined between 1993 and 2004*. [press release] Washington, D.C.: U.S. Department of Justice, Bureau of Justice Statistics. www.ojp.usdoj.gov/newsroom/pressreleases/2006/BJS07007.htm.

Buzawa, E., & Buzawa, C. (2003). *Domestic violence*. Thousand Oaks, CA: Sage.

Carter, T. J. (2006). Police use of discretion: a participant observation study of game wardens. *Deviant Behavior, 27*, 591–627.

Catalano, S. (2006). *Intimate partner violence in the United States*. Washington, D.C.: U.S. Department of Justice, Bureau of Justice Statistics.

Chamard, S. (2010). *Homeless encampments*. Washington, D.C.: Center for Problem-Oriented Policing.

Chappell, A., MacDonald, J., & Manz, P. (2006). The organizational determinants of police arrest decisions. *Crime & Delinquency, 52*, 287–306.

Chesney-Lind, M. (2002). Criminalizing victimization: the unintended consequences of pro-arrest policies for girls and women. *Criminology and Public Policy, 2*(1), 81–90.

Cicourel, A. (1976). *The social organization of juvenile Justice*. New York: John Wiley & Sons.

Cogan, J. C. (2002). Hat crime as crime category worthy of policy attention. *American Behavioral Scientist, 46*, 173–185.

Cordner, G. (2006). *People with mental illness*. Problem-Oriented Guides for Police, Problem-Specific Guides Series No. 40. Washington, D.C.: U.S. Department of Justice, Office of Community Oriented Policing Services.

D'Alessio, S., & Stolzberg, L. (2003). Race and the probability of arrest. *Social Forces, 81*, 1381–1397.

Davis, K. C. (1980). *Discretionary justice: A preliminary inquiry.* Westport, CT: Greenwood Press.

De Baca, L., & Tisi, A. (August 2002). Working together to stop modern-day slavery. *The Police Chief*, 78–80.

Dodge, M., Starr-Gimeno, D., & Williams, T. (2005). Puttin' on the sting: women police officers' perspectives on reverse prostitution assignments. *International Journal of Police Science and Management*, 7(2), 71–85.

Dugan, L. (2003). Domestic violence legislation: exploring its impact on the likelihood of domestic violence, police involvement and arrest. *Criminology and Public Policy*, 2(2), 283–312.

Dunford, F. W., Huizinga, D., & Elliott, D. S. (1986). The role of arrest in domestic assault: the Omaha police experiment. *Criminology*, 28(2), 183–206.

Dunham, R. G., & Alpert, G. P. (2009). *Critical issues in policing: Contemporary readings* (6th ed.). Prospect Heights, IL: Waveland Press.

Eigenberg, H. M., Scarborough, K. E., & Kappeler, V. E. (1996). Contributory factors affecting arrest in domestic and non-domestic assaults. *American Journal of Police*, 15(4), 27–54.

Engel, R., Sobol, J., & Worden, R. (2000). Further exploration of the demeanor hypothesis: the interaction effects of suspects' characteristics and demeanor on police behavior. *Justice Quarterly*, 17, 235–258.

Ericson, R. (1982). *Reproducing order: A study of police patrol work.* Toronto: University of Toronto Press.

FBI. (2013a). *Overview and history: Online child pornography/child sexual exploitation investigations.* http://www.fbi.gov/about-us/investigate/vc_majorthefts/cac/overview-and-history.

FBI. (2013b). *Uniform Crime Reports.* . http://www.fbi.gov/about-us/cjis/ucr/crime-in-the-u.s/2011/crime-in-the-u.s.-2011/tables/table-29.

FBI. (2006). *2006 Hate Crime Statistics.* Washington, D.C.: Federal Bureau of Investigation. www2.fbi.gov/ucr/hc2006/index.html.

Felson, R., Messner, S., & Hoskin, A. (2002). Reasons for reporting and not reporting domestic violence to the police. *Criminology*, 40(3), 617–648.

Felson, R., & Pare, P. (2005). *The reporting of domestic violence and sexual assault by nonstrangers to the police.* Washington, D.C.: National Institute of Justice.

Finkelhor, D., & Ormrod, R. (2004a). *Child pornography: Patterns from NIBRS.* Washington, D.C.: Office of Justice Programs.

Finkelhor, D., & Ormrod, R. (2004b). *Prostitution of juveniles: Patterns from NIBRS.* Washington, D.C.: Office of Justice Programs.

Flowers, R. B. (2001). *Runaway kids and teenage prostitution: America's lost, abandoned and sexually exploited children.* Westport, CT: Praeger/Greenwood.

Forsyth, C. J. (1993). Factors influencing game wardens in their interaction with poachers: the use of discretion. *Free Inquiry in Creative Sociology*, 211, 51.

Fyfe, J. J. (1979). Administrative interventions on police shooting discretion: an empirical examination. *Journal of Criminal Justice*, 7, 309–324.

Fyfe, JJ., Kane, R. (undated) *Bad cops: a study of career-ending misconduct among New York city police officers.* Washington, D.C.: U.S. Department of Justice, unpublished.

Fyfe, J. J., Klinger, D. A., & Flavin, J. M. (1997). Differential police treatment of male-on-female spousal violence. *Criminology*, 35(3), 455–473.

Gabbidon, S., Higgins, G. E., & Potter, H. (2011). Race, gender, and the perception of recently experiencing unfair treatment by the poilce: exploratory results from an all-black sample. *Criminal Justice Review*, 30, 5–21.

Garner, J., Maxwell, C., & Heraux, C. (2002). Characteristics associated with the prevalence and severity of force used by the police. *Justice Quarterly, 19*, 705–746.

Garofalo, J. (1991). Racially motivated crimes in New York City. In M. Lynch, & E. Patterson (Eds.), *Race and criminal justice*. New York: Harrow and Heston.

Gerstenberger, C. B., & Williams, K. R. (2013). Gender and intimate partner violence: does dual arrest reveal gender symmetry or asymmetry? *Journal of Interpersonal Violence, 28*, 1561–1578.

Goldstein, H. (1977). *Policing a free society*. Cambridge, MA: Ballinger Publishing.

Guyot, D. (1991). *Policing as though people matter*. Philadelphia, PA: Temple University Press.

Hagan, J. (2010). *Introduction to criminology: Theories, methods, and criminal behavior* (7th ed.). Chicago, IL: Nelson-Hall.

Hickman, M. (2006). *Citizen complaints about police use of force*. Special Report. U.S. Department of Justice. Washington, D.C.: Bureau of Justice Statistics.

Lee, J., Zhang, Y., & Hoover, L. T. (2013). Police response to domestic violence: multilevel factors of arrest decision. *Policing: An International Journal of Police Strategies & Management, 36*, 157–174.

Kappeler, V. E. (2006). *Critical issues in police civil liability* (4th ed.). Prospect Heights, IL: Waveland Press.

Kappeler, V. E., & Potter, G. W. (2005). *The mythology of crime and criminal justice* (4th ed.). Prospect Heights, IL: Waveland Press.

Kappeler, V. E., Sluder, R., & Alpert, G. P. (1998). *Forces of deviance: Understanding the dark side of policing* (2nd ed.). Prospect Heights, IL: Waveland Press.

King, W., & Dunn, T. (2004). Police-initiated transjurisdictional transport of troublesome people. *Police Quarterly, 7*(3), 339–358.

Klinger, D. (1997). Negotiating order in patrol work: an ecological theory of police response to deviance. *Criminology, 35*, 277–306.

Klinger, D. (1994). Demeanor or crime? Why "hostile" citizens are more likely to be arrested. *Criminology, 32*, 475–493.

Kochel, T. R., Wilson, D. B., & Mastrofski, S. D. (2011). Effects of suspect race on officers' arrest decisions. *Criminology, 49*, 473–512.

LaFave, W. (1965). *The decision to take a suspect into custody*. Boston, MA: Little, Brown and Company.

LaFrance, T. C., & Allen, J. (2010). An exploration of the juxtaposition of professional and political accountability in local law enforcement management. *International Journal of Police Science and Management, 12*(1), 90–118.

LaGrange, T. (November 15–18, 2000). *Distinguishing between the criminal and the "crazy": decisions to arrest in police encounters with mentally disordered*. Paper presented at the american society of Criminology, San Francisco, CA.

Langworthy, R. (1989). Do stings control crime? An evaluation of a police fencing operation. *Justice Quarterly, 6*, 28–45.

Liu, P. W., & Cook, T. A. (2005). Speeding violation dispositions in relation to police officers' perception of the offenders. *Policing & Society, 15*(1), 83–88.

Loftus, B. (2010). Police occupational culture: classic themes, altered times. *Policing & Society, 20*, 1–20.

Lundman, R. (1979). Organizational norms and police discretion: an observational study of police work with traffic violators. *Criminology, 17*, 159–171.

Lundman, R. J. (1996). Demeanor and arrest: additional evidence from previously unpublished data. *Journal of Research in Crime and Delinquency, 33*(3), 306–323.

Maguire, M. (1991). Complaints against the police: the British experience. In A. Goldsmith (Ed.), *Complaints against the police: The trend to external review*. Oxford, UK: Clarendon Press.

Martin, S. E. (1995). A cross-burning is not just an arson: police social construction of hate crimes in Baltimore County. *Criminology, 33*(3), 303–326.

Martin, S. E. (1996). Investigating hate crimes: case characteristics and law enforcement responses. *Justice Quarterly, 13*(3), 27–49.

Mastrofski, S. (2004). Controlling street-level police discretion. *Annals of the American Academy of Political and Social Science, 593*, 100–118.

Mastrofski, S., Reisig, M., & McCluskey, J. (2002). Police disrespect toward the public: an encounter-based analysis. *Criminology, 40*, 101–133.

Matier, P., & Ross, A. (November 5, 2006). *Within SFPD, little surprise over allegations that officer visited Asia for sex with children.* San Francisco Chronicle B.1.

Maxwell, C., Garner, J., & Fagan, J. (2002). The preventive effects of arrest on intimate partner violence: research, policy and theory. *Criminology and Public Policy, 2*, 51–80.

McCaghy, M. C., & Cernkovich, S. A. (1987). *Crime in American society.* New York: Macmillan.

McCluskey, J. D., & Terrill, W. (2005). Departmental and citizen complaints as predictors of police coercion. *Policing: An International Journal of Police Strategies & Management, 28*(3), 513–529.

Miller v. California, (1973). 413 U.S. 15.

Miranda v. Arizona, (1966). 384 U.S. 436.

Missouri Revised Statute § 455.085 (1989).

Mitchell, O. D., & Caudy, M. (2013). Explaining racial disparities in drug arrests. *Justice Quarterly,* http://www.tandfonline.com/doi/pdf/10.1080/07418825.2012.761721 Accessed 01.08.13.

Moon, B., & Corley, C. J. (2007). Driving across campus: assessing the impact of drivers' race, and gender on police traffic enforcement actions. *Journal of Criminal Justice, 35*(1), 29–37.

Muir, W. (1977). *Police: Streetcorner politicians.* Chicago, IL: University of Chicago Press.

Nadon, S. M., & Koverola, E. H. (1999). Antecedents to prostitution: childhood victimization. *Journal of Interpersonal Violence, 13*, 206–221.

National Alliance to End Homelessness. (2013). *Snapshot of homelessness.* http://www.endhomelessness.org/pages/snapshot_of_homelessness. Accessed 22.05.13.

NCH. (2012). *Hate crimes against the homeless: Violence hidden in plain view.* Washington, D.C.: National Coalition for the Homeless. www.nationalhomeless.org/publications/hatecrimes/hatecrimes2010.pdf.

Newman, G. R. (2006). *The exploitation of trafficked women.* Problem-Specific Guides Series Guide No. 38. Washington, D.C.: U.S. Department of Justice: Office of Community Oriented Policing Services.

Nolan, J., & Akiyama, Y. (2002). Assessing the climate for hate-crime reporting in law enforcement organizations: a force-field analysis. *Justice Professional, 15*(2), 87–103.

Novak, K., & Engel, R. (2005). Disentangling the influence of suspects' demeanor and mental disorder on arrest. *Policing: An International Journal of Police Strategies & Management, 28*, 493–512.

Novak, K. J., Frank, J. F., Smith, B. W., & Engel, R. S. (2002). Revisiting the decision to arrest: comparing beat and community officers. *Crime & Delinquency, 48*, 70.

Piliavin, I., & Briar, S. (1964). Police encounters with juveniles. *American Journal of Sociology, 70*, 206–214.

Reaves, B. A. (2010). *Local police departments, 2007.* Washington, D.C.: U.S. Department of Justice, Bureau of Justice Statistics.

Reaves, B. A., & Goldberg, A. L. (2010). *Local police departments, 1997.* U.S. Department of Justice, Bureau of Justice Statistics.

Reiss, A. (1971). *The police and the public.* New Haven, CT: Yale University Press.

Riksheim, E., & Chermak, S. (1993). Causes of police behavior revisited. *Journal of Criminal Justice, 21*, 353–382.

Rose, N. (2006). Gambling and the law: an introduction to the law of internet gambling. *UNLV Gaming Research & Review Journal, 10*(1), 1–14.

Rosenfeld, R., Rojek, J., & Decker, S. (2011). Age matters: race differences in police searches of young and older male drivers. *Crime & Delinquency, 49*, 31–55.

Ruiz, J. (1996). Regulation of sexually oriented businesses. *TELEMASP Bulletin, 3*(4), 1–11.

Ruiz, J., & Miller, C. (2004). An exploratory study of Pennsylvania police officers' perceptions of dangerousness and their ability to manage persons with mental illness. *Police Quarterly, 7*(3), 359–371.

Schoeman, F. (1986). Undercover operations: some moral questions. *Criminal Justice Ethics, 5*(2), 16–22.

Sealock, M. D., & Simpson, S. S. (1998). Unraveling bias in arrest decisions: the role of juvenile offender type-scripts. *Justice Quarterly, 15*, 427.

Sheley, J. F. (1985). *America's crime problem*. Belmont, CA: Wadsworth.

Sherman, L. (1980). Causes of police behavior: the current state of quantitative research. *Journal of Research in Crime and Delinquency, 17*, 69–100.

Sherman, L. W., & Berk, R. A. (1984). The specific deterrent effect of arrest for domestic assault. *American Sociological Review, 49*(2), 261–272.

Simpson, S. S., Bouffard, L. A., Garner, J., & Hickman, L. (2006). The influence of legal Reform on the probability of arrest in domestic violence cases. *Justice Quarterly, 23*(3), 297–316.

Skolnick, J. H. (1994). *Justice without trial: Law enforcement in a democratic society* (3rd ed.). New York: Macmillan.

Smith, D. A., & Klein, J. (1984). Police control of interpersonal disputes. *Social Problems, 31*(4), 468–481.

Smith, D. A., & Visher, C. (1981). Street level Justice: situational determinants of police arrest decisions. *Social Problems, 29*, 167–178.

Southern Poverty Law Center. (2013). *Active U.S. hate groups*. Montgomery, AL: Southern Poverty Law Center.

Stroshine, M., Alpert, G., & Dunham, R. (2008). The influence of "Working rules" on police suspicion and discretionary decision making. *Police Quarterly, 11*, 315–337.

Sun, L., & Payne, B. (2004). Racial differences in resolving conflicts: a comparison between black and white police officers. *Crime & Delinquency, 50*, 516–541.

Teplin, L. A. (1986). *Keeping the peace: The parameters of police discretion in relation to the mentally disordered*. Washington, D.C.: National Institute of Justice.

Terrill, W., & Paoline, E. (2007). Nonarrest decision making in police-citizen encounters. *Police Quarterly, 10*, 308–331.

U.S. Conference of Mayors. (2010). *Status report on hunger & homelessness city policy associates*. Washington, D.C.

U.S. Department of Justice. (2001). *Principles for promoting police integrity: Examples of promising practices and policies*. Washington, D.C.: U.S. Department of Justice.

Walker, S. (1993). *Taming the system*, Oxford, New York.

Walker, S., & Bumphus, V. (1992). The effectiveness of civilian review: observations on recent trends and new issues regarding the civilian review of the police. *American Journal of Police, 11*, 1–26.

Westley, W. (1970). *Violence and the police: A sociological study of law, custom, and morality*. Cambridge, MA: The MIT Press.

Wilson, D. G., Walsh, W. F., & Kleuber, S. (2006). Trafficking in human beings: training and services among U.S. Law enforcement agencies. *Police Practice and Research, 7*(2), 149–160.

Wilson, J. Q. (1968). *Varieties of police behavior*. Cambridge, MA: Harvard University Press.

Wilson, M. S., & Ruback, R. B. (2003). Hate activity in Pennsylvania, 1984–1999: case characteristics and police responses. *Justice Quarterly, 20*(2), 373–398.

Winick, C., & Kinsie, P. M. (1971). *The lively commerce: Prostitution in the United States*. Chicago, IL: Quadrangle Books.

Wolf, S. E., & Piquero, A. R. (2013). Organizational Justice and police misconduct. *Criminal Justice and Behavior, 38*, 332–353.

Worden, R. E., & Shepard, R. L. (1996). Demeanor, crime, and police behavior: a reexamination of the police services study data. *Criminology, 34*(1), 83–105.

Wortley, R. (2006). *Child pornography on the internet*. Washington, D.C.: U.S. Department of Justice, Office of Community Oriented Policing Services. Problem-Oriented Guides for Police, Problem-Specific Guides Series No. 41.

CHAPTER 7

Police Use of Force

Force without wisdom falls of its own weight.

—Horace

LEARNING OBJECTIVES

After reading the chapter, you should be able to:

- Define the meaning of the police use of force.
- Describe the legal requirements for use of force by the police.
- Discuss the patterns of police use of force.
- Explain how use of force is controlled in police agencies.
- Explain the difference between lethal and less-than-lethal force.
- Estimate the real dangers of police work.
- Define and explain the concept of net widening and it applicability to police work.
- Discuss suicide by cop.

KEY TERMS

- Brutality
- CALEA
- Conducted energy devices
- Deadly force
- Early Warning System
- Excessive force
- Excessive use of force
- Extralegal violence
- Fleeing felon doctrine
- *Graham v. Connor*
- Hidden suicide
- Less-than-lethal force
- Necessary force
- Net widening
- Oleoresin capsicum spray

INTRODUCTION

On the surface, from the public's perspective, police use of deadly force seems commonplace. Indeed, a review of the nation's major newspapers and television news shows would likely reveal discussions of a police shooting at least weekly. Although not as frequent, this same review would show that some police officers are assaulted or shot at by assailants. Examination of these cases would show that deadly force confrontations occur in numerous police situations, ranging from responding to felonies in progress to officers being shot while sitting in their patrol cars. In some of the cases, it is apparent that officers had no choice but to use deadly force. In other cases, it is clear that officers

- Physical force
- Reasonable force
- Suicide by cop
- Taser®
- *Tennessee v. Garner*
- Unnecessary force
- Use-of-force continuum

abused their power in their use of force. Citizens, politicians, and the media tend to second-guess officers' judgment and play a "what if" or "what should have been done" game. Sometimes this criticism is justifiable, as it is readily apparent in many cases that police officers could have avoided using deadly force or abused their authority.

There is evidence that the police use excessive force and abuse citizens. Large numbers of people report they have been abused by the police (Weisburd, Greenspan, Hamilton, Williams, & Bryant, 2000). In 2002, for example, more than 26,000 people filed complaints of police abuse of force (Hickman, 2006). A random survey of emergency physicians found that 99.8% believed that excessive force actually occurs and 97.8% stated that they have managed patients with suspected excessive use of force (Hutson, Anglin, Rice, Kyriacou, & Strote, 2009). Although many instances of police use of force are minor and do not include police violence, many do. For example, in 2013, six Kern County, California deputies, a sergeant, and two California Highway Patrol officers were involved in an altercation that resulted in the death of a suspect. The suspect was beaten repeatedly while on the ground and the suspect died shortly after the altercation. The FBI investigated the case. What makes this case more interesting is the fact that in 2010 the sheriff's department paid a $4.5 million judgment in the death of a suspect; his attorney alleged the man was struck 33 times with batons and Tasered 29 times. In 2005, the department had a $6 million judgment after a jail inmate was killed (Pringle & Winton, 2013). There is a need for police administrators to monitor and control officers' use of force.

You can watch a video of a brutal police–citizen encounter by going to: **http://www.youtube.com/watch?v=McFbZ7vB8io**

THE MEANING OF EXCESSIVE FORCE

Many police officers use force or coercion on nearly a daily basis. It may range from a verbal command to the use of a weapon against a suspect. It is part of their job. The police have a duty to the citizenry to provide them services and to protect them. To do so, police officers are empowered to use force when necessary to enforce the law or to apprehend offenders. A problem arises, however, when the police use unnecessary, abusive force or excessive force. There is substantial disagreement among experts as to when an incident involving the use of force represents the use of excessive force.

Klockars (1995) suggested three criteria that could be used to determine whether or not force is excessive: (1) criminal law, which states that an officer's use of force shall not constitute a crime; (2) civil liability, which relates to the idea that an officer's use of force shall not cause injury to an individual to the point that the courts would award payment to the person or his or her heirs; and (3) fear of scandal, where the nature of the officer's behavior would result in embarrassment to the department. Although these are important issues, they are of little use in actually determining excessive force. Unfortunately, they depend on the incident being reported and to some extent on the department's willingness to investigate the officer's actions. Also, the courts are often unwilling to rule against the police in such cases, especially when the plaintiff is of questionable repute, has a criminal history, or comes from a lower socioeconomic background. A wide range of abusive behaviors would go unrecognized using these criteria. Klockars' criteria, however, are noteworthy in that many police departments have come to view excessive force in these terms and often fail to investigate or take action unless one of these three criteria is triggered.

McEwen (1996) distinguished between *excessive force* and *excessive use of force*. He notes that excessive force is present when an officer applies too much force in a specific situation. On the other hand, excessive use of force is where officers legally apply force in too many incidents. The first case includes situations where officers use so much force that it constitutes an illegal act, whereas in the second case, officers resort to legal force too frequently to accomplish legal objectives.

Fyfe (1995) defined two types of excessive force. *Extralegal violence* or *brutality* occurs when officers willfully and wrongfully use force that exceeds the boundaries of their authority. The public often labels any questionable use of force by the police as brutality. On the other hand, *unnecessary force* is force used by well-intentioned officers who are unable to handle a situation and resort to force too quickly or needlessly. These distinctions often become blurred in the eyes of the public. Officers who use unnecessary force may be prone to using extralegal violence.

Within this framework, Klockars (1995) defined *excessive force* as "the use of any more force than a highly skilled police officer should find necessary to use in that particular situation." This definition raises questions about an officer's training, physical fitness, and experience. In a given department, what percentage of officers could realistically be considered "highly skilled"? Given these definitions, determining excessive and unreasonable force is often very subjective. There are, however, legal standards developed by the courts to control police use of force.

LEGAL STANDARDS AND POLICE USE OF FORCE

In 1985, the U.S. Supreme Court handed down its decision in *Tennessee v. Garner* (1985). The case dictated the circumstances in which police officers could use deadly force to make an arrest. The case involved the shooting death of an unarmed 15-year-old juvenile, Edward Garner, who had broken into an unoccupied home and stolen a ring and $10. When police officers arrived on the scene, Garner ran. A Memphis police officer shot and killed Garner, which was consistent with the Tennessee statute that allowed officers to use deadly force against a fleeing felon.

The Court ruled that police officers could not use deadly force to prevent the escape of a felon unless the suspect posed a significant threat of death or serious physical injury to the officer or others. In making its decision, the Court attempted to balance the government's interests in providing effective law enforcement and the intrusion into a suspect's rights. The Court noted that Garner's death was an unreasonable violation of the Fourth Amendment. In effect, the Court struck down the *fleeing felon doctrine*, which allowed police officers to use deadly force against any fleeing felon and required that police weigh the dangerousness of shooting a suspect and his or her crime with the probability of immediate or future harm caused by the suspect if he or she escaped.

A number of studies have attempted to determine the impact of *Garner* on police use of deadly force. Culliver and Sigler (1995) conducted a mail survey of large and medium-sized police departments in Tennessee. They compared the number of shootings before and after the *Garner* decision and found that the number of shootings was lower in the post-*Garner* period. Sparger and Giacopassi (1992) examined the Memphis Police Department's shooting policies before and after *Garner* and concluded that "both the overall shooting rate and the apparently discriminatory application of lethal force were reduced greatly as a result of the post–*Garner* deadly force policy." Finally, Tennenbaum (1994) used national police justifiable shooting data collected by the FBI to see if the case had a national impact. He found that police shootings were reduced by more than 16% as a result of *Garner*.

You can learn more about the issues surrounding police use of force by reading an International Association of Chiefs of Police report at: **http://www.theiacp.org/portals/0/pdfs/emerginguseofforceissues041612.pdf**

When *Garner* was decided, many states had already adopted statutes regulating the police use of deadly force. (See Box 7.1 for Kentucky's statute; notice that the statute is very restrictive in outlining when an officer can use deadly force.) Walker and Fridell (1992) noted, however, that the decision struck down statutes in 22 states that were too permissive. Blumberg (1997) observed that many of these departments likely revised and tightened their policies in the wake of *Garner*. About one-third of the major departments in the United States altered their policies as a result of *Garner* (Walker & Fridell, 1992). The *Garner* decision established a uniform national standard regulating when officers could use deadly force, and it led to a reduction in the number of police shootings.

Box 7.1 Kentucky Police Use of Deadly Force Statute

KRS503.090(2): Use of Physical Force by Law Enforcement

The use of deadly physical force by a defendant upon another person is justified … when:

1. The defendant is effecting the arrest; is authorized to act as a peace officer; and

2. The arrest is for a felony involving the use or threatened use of physical force likely to cause death or serious physical injury; and

3. The defendant believes that the person to be arrested is likely to endanger human life unless apprehended without delay.

The *Garner* decision clarified many important issues concerning police use of deadly force. Questions remained, however, as to its applicability to all circumstances in which police use force. In other words, was *Garner* applicable to cases of non-deadly force? In *Graham v. Connor* (1989), the U.S. Supreme Court answered this question.

Graham, a diabetic, had asked a friend to drive him to a nearby convenience store to purchase some orange juice to stave off an oncoming insulin reaction. At the store, Graham decided that the lines to the cashier were too long and opted to go to a friend's house for the orange juice. A Charlotte, North Carolina, police officer observed Graham's furtive movements in the store and his hasty departure. The officer became suspicious and stopped Graham and his companion when they left the store. The officer then called for backup assistance. During this time, Graham exited the vehicle and passed out on the curbside. In the confusion of the backup arriving, Graham was handcuffed. Officers then placed him on the hood of his friend's vehicle. Graham regained consciousness and requested the officers to verify his condition with the diabetic decal he carried in his wallet. He was told to "shut up" and was then thrown head-first into a squad car. As a result of these actions, Graham suffered a broken foot, cuts on his wrists, a bruised forehead, and an injury to his shoulder, and he continued to suffer from incessant ringing in his right ear. He later filed a lawsuit, alleging that the officers used excessive force during the investigatory step.

The Supreme Court ruled that police use of force must be objectively reasonable—that an officer's actions were reasonable in light of the facts and circumstances confronting him, without regard to his underlying intent or motivation. The Court stated that while "reasonableness … is not capable of precise definition or mechanical application" (*Graham v. Connor*, 1989:1871), a number of factors require careful consideration before an officer can use force against a citizen. These factors include the following (Kappeler, 2006):

1. Whether the suspect poses an *immediate* threat to the officer or others
2. The *severity* of the crime
3. Whether the suspect is *actively resisting* arrest
4. Whether the suspect is a *flight risk* or *attempting to escape* custody

PATTERNS OF POLICE USE OF FORCE

A national survey in 2008 estimated that 16.9% of the population age 16 or older had some contact with the police. Of the persons coming into contact with the police, one in four had more than one contact (Eith & Durose, 2011). Table 7.1 provides a breakdown of the reasons for police contacts.

The overwhelming majority of contacts between police and citizens did not involve any force whatsoever; however, about 1.4% of the people having face-to-face contact with the police reported officers using some level of force, and about 74.3% of those citizens felt the force was excessive. The most common force used by officers was handcuffing suspects, which is consistent with many departments' policies Generally, more than one-half of those citizens who had force used on them were minorities, and male. Males and minorities are increasingly represented as the level of force increases. These data indicate an inequality in the treatment of minorities (Eith & Durose, 2011). What is not known is whether this inequality is the result of biases or situational circumstances. Do police interact with those groups more frequently and in a more violent manner?

Since 1976, the police have killed an average of 373 citizens nationwide each year. In 1978, half of those killed by the police were white and 49% were African-American; however, in 1998, 62% of those killed by the police were

Table 7.1　Reasons for Police–Citizen Contacts	
Reason	**Percent of All Contacts**
Traffic-related	59.2
Resident reported crime/problem to police	20.9
Police provided assistance or service to citizen	6.3
Police investigating crime	5.6
Police suspected resident of wrongdoing	2.5
Other reason	5.5
Source: Eith and Durose (2011).	

white, and 35% were African-American (Brown & Langan, 2001). These data suggested that the police were shooting an increasing percentage of whites and a decreasing percentage of African-American citizens; however, based on population statistics, the rate of African-American deaths as a result of police actions was actually about four times that of whites.

Brown and Langan (2001) found that the average age of those killed by the police is 32 years. The highest rate of police homicide of citizens is for young African-American males; in 1998, the police killed 48 African-American males, and young African-American males were being killed at a rate six times greater than young white males.

Although American police officers kill larger numbers of whites than minorities, they kill minorities at a much greater rate, especially younger African-American citizens.

Many shootings are questionable; that is, it appears that the police could have avoided the use of deadly force or may have used it too quickly. Shootings from across the country highlight this problem. A number of communities have forced police departments to take action to better control officers when they use force. Moreover, there are ramifications for police shootings. In 2013, the Anaheim Police killed Manuel Diaz, a documented gang member. This was the sixth police shooting in six months, with all of them fatal except one, in a city of 340,000. The Diaz shooting resulted in protests involving over 1000 people. Protesters roamed the streets, setting fire to Dumpsters, breaking windows, and damaging more than 20 businesses. The police had to use pepper-spray balls and bean bags to control the crowd. Additionally, after the Diaz shooting, the Justice Department and FBI conducted an independent review (Cruz, 2013). Police shootings, justified or questionable, can have expensive consequences on cities.

Determinants of Police Use of Force

There have been several studies that examined officer and situational characteristics in police use-of-force cases. Garner, Schade, Hepburn, and Buchanan (1995) and Garner, Buchanan, Schade, and Hepburn (1996) examined officer use of force in Phoenix and found that arrestees who were involved in a violent offense, antagonistic, male, involved in a gang, intoxicated, or known to have a weapon or who had a reputation of being resistant toward officers were more likely to be handled by the police more forcefully. Terrill and Mastrofski (2002) obtained similar findings in their study of St Petersburg and Indianapolis. They found that male, nonwhite, poor, and younger suspects received more force, but they did not find that disrespectful citizens were recipients of greater levels of force. Police officers seem to see certain types of people as being more threatening or dangerous, and they tend to escalate the level of force when encountering them.

Several officer characteristics have been examined to determine their relationship with use of force. Hickman, Piquero, and Greene (2000) found that officer race did not affect the amount of force officers used when dealing with suspects. Studies regarding length of service as a determinant of levels of force used by police officers have had mixed results (Garner et al., 1996; Paoline & Terrill, 2007; Worden, 1995). A least one study suggested that more experienced officers are less likely to rely on verbal and physical force than inexperienced officers and that officers with a college education are also less prone to using force (Paoline & Terrill, 2007). Terrill and Mastrofski (2002) also found that less educated officers tended to be more forceful. Again, mixed results were obtained by research into the effect of officer gender. Garner et al. (1995) found that male officers were more likely to use force, but Worden (1995) found no differences between male and female officers in the application of force. Finally, Terrill, Paoline, and Manning (2003) found that officers who were more aligned with the traditional police culture were more likely to use force. This research demonstrates that several officer traits, situational variables, and cultural differences affect the level of force used by officers.

CONTROLLING POLICE DISCRETION IN SITUATIONS INVOLVING THE USE OF FORCE

The preceding sections have focused on the police use of deadly force; however, it should be noted that less-than-lethal force is of equal concern. More citizen complaints are generated as the result of police use of less-than-lethal force. Many citizens believe that the police often use excessive or abusive force. Here, we examine four important use-of-force issues: the use-of-force continuum, use-of-force policies, controlling off-duty use of force, and establishing early warning systems to identify problem officers.

Use-of-Force Continuum

Most police departments have adopted a *use-of-force continuum*. For example, in a sample of departments studied by Terrill and Paoline (2013) 80% of responding departments had a use-of-force continuum policy. The continuum outlines the level of force that officers can use when subduing a suspect. It is based on the principle that officers should use only the *reasonable force* necessary to effect the arrest or subdue a suspect. The use-of-force continuum is used to guide officers so they are less likely to use excessive force. Officers are expected to use more force than a resisting suspect, but excessive force should not be used. An officer is expected to use that force which minimizes the likelihood of injury to the officer and the suspect. An officer would not be expected to use his or her baton on a drunken suspect who was merely resisting verbally; on the other hand, an officer may be justified in using the baton if the suspect was physically fighting or resisting arrest. Police departments have incorporated the use-of-force continuum in their training and policies.

Terrill and Paoline found that departments use a variety of use-of-force formats. They typically contain the same elements, but in some cases they are arranged in different order. The use-of-force continuum for many departments is as follows:

1. **Physical presence of the officer based on the officer's police authority**—Most suspects become subdued or cooperative in the presence of an officer. Many people recognize a police officer's authority to intervene in situations.

2. **Soft hands**—This refers to a situation in which an officer physically grabs a suspect to control him or her. Soft-handed force is commonly used when a suspect verbally resists or becomes abusive. Soft-handed force is often used to prevent a situation from escalating. It brings the officer into direct contact with the suspect and increases the probability that the resisting suspect can harm the officer.

3. **Pepper spray and conduct energy devices**—When the soft-handed approach fails to adequately subdue a suspect, the officer may resort to pepper spray. Terrill and Paoline (2013) observed that pepper spray and conduct energy devices are often placed between the passive or cooperative stage and the assaultive stage of resistance, but in their study they found them to occur at different points in the use-of-force continuum.

4. **Hard hands**—This refers to when an officer literally fights with the suspect. Such fighting may include pushing, hitting, or other physical action to subdue the suspect. Officers should be leery of hard-hands combat with a suspect. It places the officer in greater danger, and essentially it places the officer and offender at the same level on the use-of-force continuum.

5. **Police baton**—The use of the baton increases the likelihood that there will be physical injury to the suspect, and a baton should be used only when the suspect cannot be overcome by using any of the previous stages in the continuum. Officers are trained on how to use the baton and where to strike a suspect (e.g., shin, shoulder, chest). Officers are trained to not hit a suspect in the head, as it could result in substantial injury.

6. **Threat of deadly force**—If the officer is not able to overcome the suspect with the baton and other physical means, the officer can threaten to use deadly force by unholstering his or her firearm. It is hoped that this action will cause the suspect to conform to the officer's orders and allow the officer to take him or her into custody.

7. **Deadly force used**—Deadly force occurs when an officer discharges his or her firearm at a suspect. The vast majority of police departments

You can learn more about police use of force and watch videos on the topic by going to: **http://www.policeone.com/use-of-force/page-4/**

have policies prohibiting warning shots; thus, when a weapon is discharged it is to shoot the suspect. Deadly force can be used only in instances where the officer believes there is a threat of "great bodily harm" to the officer or to another person.

Officers do not necessarily start at the beginning of the use-of-force continuum. An officer who encounters a suspect with a gun would immediately go to stage six in the use-of-force continuum—threat of deadly force. Officers must evaluate particular situations and determine the appropriate level of force, with the guideline being use force that is greater than that being displayed by the suspect. Police officers are not expected to fight fairly or evenly (Table 7.2).

The use-of-force continuum, however, begins with the proposition that police officers are merely responding to the acts of provocative citizens. That is to say, police only apply force in response to a citizen's actions. We know, however, that in many cases police are active participants in violent encounters and that they have the ability to either escalate or de-escalate confrontations. A police officer with a poor attitude can provoke a violent confrontation on almost any tour of duty. Additionally, the continuum presupposes a one-to-one relationship in the use of force—a single officer using a single level of force that is raised or lowered based on the suspect's actions. As we discuss later in the chapter, these are very simplistic and misleading assumptions about how force is used in policing.

Table 7.2 Use-of-Force Policies

Policy Area	Percentage (%) of Agencies Addressing Area
Purpose of the policy	90.6
Definition of less-than-lethal force	47.9
List of authorized duty weapons	96.9
List of unauthorized weapons for duty officers	45.8
Training requirements	62.5
Avoiding excessive force	51.0
Medical aid when force used	33.3
Reporting requirements when force used	72.9

Garner et al. (1996) examined 1777 arrests by the Phoenix Police Department to determine how often officers used various types of force. The researchers found that officers did the following:

1. Used threats or shouts less than 4% of the time
2. Pursued a fleeing suspect 7% of the time
3. Placed cuffs or restraints on 77% of the suspects
4. Used a weaponless tactic (holding, hitting, etc.) in 17% of the arrests
5. Threatened to use a weapon, but did not do so, in 3.7% of the arrests
6. Used a weapon in 2% of the arrests, with the most common weapon being a flashlight

These findings indicate that officers use physical force on an infrequent basis, and, when they do use it, it tends to be at the lower levels of the use-of-force continuum. In fact, in more than one-half of the arrests examined, the highest level of force used was some type of restraint, and in approximately 22% of the arrests, no restraint was used. Chemical weapons were used in only two arrests. Officers did threaten to use their firearms in 54 arrests (3.4%). These findings are consistent with Eith and Durose (2011), who, in a national study, found that officers used force in only about 1.4% of their encounters with citizens.

Even though officers use physical force sparingly, they frequently use non-physical force or verbal force (voice commands or threats). Terrill (2003) examined police confrontations in St Petersburg and Indianapolis and found that force, verbal or physical, was used in more than one-half of the police encounters with citizens. Citizens displayed substantially lower levels of force in the encounters (12% of the cases) and lower levels of resistance (passive resistance or noncompliance). Terrill found that their level of resistance seldom increased. His findings call into question the police tactic of immediately "taking charge" of the situation. It may be more productive for officers to initially use reasoning and dialogue rather than immediately taking charge. If reasoning and dialogue are not successful, then officers can begin progressing up the use-of-force continuum. Regardless, officers must understand that citizens use resistance in only a small percentage of encounters with the police.

Use-of-Force Policy Considerations

The use-of-force continuum is just one component of police agencies' policies regarding the use of force. A number of departments have attempted to develop a comprehensive policy that gives officers substantial guidance and reduces their discretion when using force. Police accrediting bodies have established that departments should have use-of-force standards (Box 7.2).

McEwen (1997) surveyed 96 police departments in an effort to determine the areas their use-of-force policies addressed. Almost all of the policies reviewed

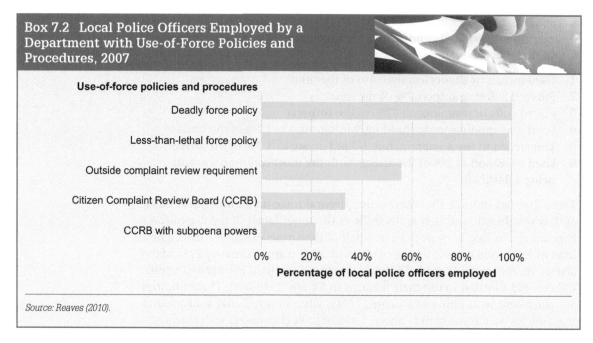

Box 7.2 Local Police Officers Employed by a Department with Use-of-Force Policies and Procedures, 2007

Source: Reaves (2010).

by McEwen contained a purpose statement. The purpose statement serves to convey the department's values relative to the use of force. The thrust of the value statement was that although force cannot be separated from the job, it must be used with restraint. These policies contained wording such as "reasonable force" or "reasonable and necessary force." The policies attempted to convey that officers should not use excessive force. Alpert and Smith (1994) have been critical of such verbiage because it does not concretely describe when force can be used. Most departments now provide a use-of-force continuum or matrix that provides additional guidelines about when and how much force can be used. About 51% of the departments had policies defining excessive force that supplemented the purpose statement. In many cases, the excessive force policy prohibited some behaviors, such as striking someone in the head with a baton (McEwen, 1997).

The policies of almost 50% of the departments contained information about less-than-lethal force (McEwen, 1997). Generally, any force other than the discharge of a firearm at a suspect is considered less-than-lethal force; however, it should be remembered that less-than-lethal force could cause grave bodily harm or death, so departments attempt to control less-than-lethal force through policy formulation. Again, this is linked to a use-of-force continuum in an effort to reduce the possibility of excessive force.

Many police departments include a listing of authorized or unauthorized weapons in their use-of-force policy. In McEwen's (1997) study almost all of the departments had a list of authorized weapons (e.g., type of firearm, nightstick, flashlight, chemical spray), and 45.8% of the departments listed unauthorized weapons. Some agencies, through policy, give officers flexibility in the types of weapons they can use; for example, the department may prohibit only some types of handguns, nightsticks, or other weapons. A department can reduce the incidence of excessive force by controlling the types of weapons officers carry and ensuring that officers are properly trained to use them.

A little more than 62% of the departments had policies regulating training requirements. Today, police departments provide training on the weapons they issue or authorize officers to carry. Such training is required because officers must know how to best use the weapons to avoid excessive force, and police liability dictates that officers be trained (Kappeler, 2006). A department is in a precarious situation when an officer injures someone while using a weapon that he or she has not been properly trained to use.

One-third of the departments had statements relative to medical aid. Liability dictates that the police provide medical attention to an injured arrestee as soon as possible (Kappeler, 2006). When medical aid is withheld or not provided in a timely fashion, there is the likelihood that an injury can result in more severe medical problems. In terms of reporting requirements, 72.9% of the departments had a policy requiring officers to report their use-of-force incidents. These policies outline the kinds of incidents that must be reported and how they are reported within the department. Most departments now have a use-of-force form that must be completed.

As noted, many police departments are now requiring officers to submit use-of-force reporting forms whenever an officer uses force. Usually, the policy requires officers to report any incidence of physical force but not verbal force, such as issuing a command to a suspect. Alpert and MacDonald (2001) found that these policies significantly lowered the amount of force used by officers, although it may be that some officers are failing to complete reports. Doing so, however, could result in possible disciplinary action at a later time. Another explanation is that officers move from verbal to physical force only when absolutely necessary in order to avoid completing the report. In these instances, the report causes officers to seriously consider the amount of force they use and results in less use of force overall.

Use of Force by Off-duty Police Officers

Police departments have long had policies regulating police officers' use of force while on duty, but it has been only in the past 20 years that departments began to regulate police officers' use of force off duty. This is an important policy area because arrests and instances where officers use force can occur while they are off duty. White (1999) found that 20% of police shootings in

Philadelphia occurred while the officers were off duty; similarly, it has been found that 24% of New York City police shootings have occurred while officers were off duty.

Off-duty police officers' use of force seems to be different from on-duty involvements. White (2000) listed four differences. First, off-duty use of force generally occurs when the officer is out of uniform and does not have radio contact. Second, off-duty officers tend to become involved in incidents that on-duty officers would not (e.g., personal disputes, victims of crime). Third, when an off-duty shooting occurs, it is more likely to violate departmental policies for on-duty use of force and state statutes. Finally, off-duty officers are more likely to use deadly force when they are under the influence of alcohol. Many off-duty use-of-force incidents occur when off-duty officers are socializing. These differences result in a strict need to control officers' off-duty use of firearms and deadly force.

There are considerable arguments for arming police officers while they are off duty. Geller and Scott (1992) observed that police officers, even when off duty, are expected to take action when in the presence of a crime being committed. Fyfe (1980) suggested that officers should be afforded some level of protection from suspects who might seek revenge on officers who investigated or arrested them. Fyfe also noted that off-duty officers being armed perhaps provide a deterrent effect, preventing some individuals from engaging in criminal behavior. While the first rationalization is a strong argument to arm off-duty police, the last two are questionable. There is little, if any, empirical research to suggest that individuals they have arrested confront police officers or that these people pose any significant threat to officers. Additionally, the deterrence theory assumes that citizens know that the person sitting next to them in a pub or standing in line with them at the bank is a police officer. The real question becomes: do the benefits of arming off-duty police officers outweigh the problems?

When White (2000) examined off-duty shootings in Philadelphia, he found that in one sample of off-duty shootings about 25% occurred in bars. The number of officers firing their weapons in an unauthorized fashion was substantially higher for off-duty discharges. He also found that officers were more likely to be injured in off-duty incidents than in on-duty incidents. He found that when the department instituted a shooting policy, it reduced the number of on-duty and off-duty discharges.

Historically, police departments required officers to be armed at all times so they could intervene in criminal activity. Today, many police departments have developed a more reasonable policy. Some departments prohibit the carrying of weapons off duty, while others make it optional. Such a policy is designed to ensure that officers do not have weapons when they visit bars or other establishments where problems might occur. A number of years ago, the New York City Police Department instituted such a policy, which substantially reduced the number of off-duty shootings (Fyfe, 1988).

Early Warning Systems to Identify Problem Officers

Many police departments have problem officers. They come to light when their actions result in lawsuits, the questionable death of a suspect, or multiple citizen complaints about the officer's demeanor or use of force. The problem began to receive national attention as a result of a report by the *Independent Commission on the Los Angeles Police Department* (Christopher Commission, 1991). The Commission found that some officers were over-represented in use-of-force statistics. The Los Angeles Police Department (LAPD) database contained 44 officers who had an inordinate number of complaints. The Commission found that of approximately 1800 officers against whom an allegation of excessive force or improper tactics was made from 1986 to 1990, more than 1400 had only one or two allegations. But 183 officers had four or more allegations, 44 had six or more, 16 had eight or more, and one had 16 such allegations. Of nearly 6000 officers identified as involved in use-of-force reports from January 1987 to March 1991, more than 4000 had fewer than five reports each. But 63 officers had 20 or more reports each. The top 5% of the officers (ranked by number of reports) accounted for more than 20% of all reports.

The Commission took note that the discrepancies possibly could be accounted for by the fact that these officers *may* have been assigned to high-crime or high-activity areas. However, the Commission also noted that, if this was the case (assignment was not examined by the Commission), then there was an ample number of other officers working such areas who did not generate the kind of complaint activity as those officers identified as receiving the most complaints or using the most force.

Toch (1995) argued that chronic deviants are a significant part of the use-of-force problem for police departments. *Chronic deviants* are those officers who repeatedly use excessive force and are abusive and disrespectful. Toch suggested that police agencies should identify and target these chronic deviants before their behavior gets out of hand. One method of accomplishing this task is to implement the *Early Warning System* (EWS) for problem police officers. The EWS is designed to identify officers who, as a result of their performance, may exhibit behavioral problems in using force and dealing with citizens. The benefits of such a system are that it potentially could reduce the number of civil suits against the department, reduce the incidence of excessive force and abuse, and ultimately foster better police community relations.

The first EWS was developed by the Miami Police Department (Walker, Alpert, & Kenney, 2000). The Miami EWS contained four performance criteria:

1. **Complaints**—An officer receiving five or more sustained or inconclusive complaints in a 2-year period
2. **Use of force**—An officer involved as a principal in five or more use-of-force incidents in a 2-year period
3. **Reprimands**—An officer receiving five or more reprimands in a 2-year period
4. **Discharge of firearms**—An officer who has three or more discharges in a 5-year period

When a Miami officer hit one of the above thresholds, supervisors would review his or her file, which contained all complaints, reports, and investigative materials. The supervisor would then meet with the officer with the goal of reducing the number of incidents that were occurring. The supervisor had a number of corrective options, including additional training, transfer, counseling, and disciplinary action. Once the supervisor made a recommendation, the commander of the internal affairs unit reviewed it. Eventually, the Miami EWS contributed to a reduction in the rate of complaints lodged against the department. It most likely improved officers' performance, reduced the number of civil suits against the department, and saved some officers' careers.

LESS-THAN-LETHAL FORCE

Each year there are cases where the police use deadly force and cases where they use less-than-lethal force that ends in death. In recent years, police officers and criminal justice planners have been searching for ways to reduce the incidence of police use of deadly force. Officials have been searching for effective, nondeadly alternatives to the use of conventional firearms. If the police could find or develop an effective alternative to deadly force or the use of firearms, lives would be saved and police departments would avoid a substantial amount of negative criticism by the media and citizens. This search has been a complex and very elusive quest (Figure 7.1).

Today, police departments around the world use various forms of less-than-lethal force. The phrase "less-than-lethal" is somewhat misleading because almost any use of force can result in fatal consequences. A better way of understanding the concept is to note that *less-than-lethal force* is any use of force that is not intended or likely to lead to death or serious physical injury. The most common less-than-lethal force weapons include the baton, pepper spray, and

FIGURE 7.1
Police in riot gear holding the line in downtown Portland, Oregon during an Occupy Portland protest on the first anniversary of Occupy Wall Street, November 17, 2011. *Copyright Shutterstock/JPL Designs.*

conducted energy devices. Pepper spray and conducted energy devices have been adopted by police departments because they are seen as being safer as compared to the baton, which when used can result in significant injuries (Table 7.3).

Table 7.3 Less-than-Lethal Weapons Authorized for Use by a Majority of Local Police Departments by Size of Population Served

Population Served	Percent (%) of Departments Authorizing the Use of		
	Pepper Spray	Baton	Conducted Energy Device[1]
All sizes	97	93	60
1,000,000 or more	92	100	100
500,000–999,999	100	100	77
250,000–499,999	100	100	93
100,000–249,999	100	99	76
50,000–99,999	99	99	78
25,000–49,999	99	98	70
10,000–24,999	99	96	67
2500–9999	98	93	58
Under 2500	94	91	55

[1]*Includes Tasers and stun guns.*
Source: Reaves (2010).

Police across the country use pepper spray and conducted energy devices to reduce the frequency of deadly force. Bailey (1996) examined the effects of less-than-lethal technology on police use of deadly force. He found that although the idea of less-than-lethal technology theoretically had promise, it did not have a significant impact on the number of deaths. Essentially, we have not identified a less-than-lethal technology that effectively meets law enforcement's needs. For such a technology to be effective, it must be issued and available to officers when they encounter deadly force situations, and, second, it must work better (be safer for officers and citizens when deployed).

Oleoresin Capsicum Spray

Oleoresin capsicum (OC) spray, or pepper spray, has become one of the primary weapons used by the police to subdue suspects. It is on the low end of the use-of-force continuum. Pepper spray contains derivatives of cayenne pepper; when a suspect's face is exposed to it, the eyes burn and swell shut, nasal passages drain, bronchial passages constrict, and breathing becomes more difficult. A suspect normally becomes subdued and less resistive, making arrest much easier; consequently, police departments across the country are adopting pepper spray in an effort to reduce the number of injuries sustained by officers and resisting suspects (McEwen & Leahy, 1993).

Lumb and Friday (1997) examined the use of pepper spray in the Concord Police Department in North Carolina. At the time of the study, the department had 75 officers, and the study covered a period of 1-1/2 years. They examined the use-of-force reports that officers were required to file when force was used. They found that pepper spray was used in a variety of incidents, calls, or crimes that escalated to the point where officers determined that it was appropriate to use pepper spray. As noted in the discussion on the use-of-force continuum above, it is noteworthy that pepper spray is seen as the stage of force where the suspect is using assaultive resistance. Pepper spray is not supposed to be used when the suspect is using passive resistance. The types of incidents where pepper spray was used were violent persons (39.3%), drunk and disorderly (29.5%), property offenses (19.7%), drug offenses (8.2%), weapons (1.6%), and unknown (1.6%). The variety of incidents where pepper spray has been used indicates that about any police encounter may escalate to where officers use force, and pepper spray may be effective in dealing with the situation.

In Concord, the use of pepper spray was not the most common type of force used. Pepper spray was used in only 16.4% of the cases where force was used. The most common form of force was physical, which was used in 47.5% of the cases. In 31 of the use-of-force encounters (34.4%), officers used the threat of deadly force. Finally, officers used the baton once out of a total of 61 use-of-force cases.

A unique aspect of Lumb and Friday's study is that they were able to study the use of force prior to the introduction of pepper spray (6 months), in a period when pepper spray was available to officers (6 months), and in a period when it was prohibited as the result of a civil suit involving its use (6 months). Essentially, they found that the introduction of pepper spray increased the frequency of officers using force. Perhaps this was the result of its novelty or net widening (using it in more situations that are less serious). However, they also found that as a result of pepper spray there was a reduction in the number of incidents where officers used serious physical force and threat of deadly force. Although officers tended to use force more frequently, they tended to use less physical alternatives.

There is some concern that pepper spray is not as effective as the manufacturers tend to indicate. There is some evidence that pepper spray is not effective in dealing with all suspects, particularly those who are intoxicated, violent, goal oriented, or mentally ill. Some have projected its effectiveness rate at about 85% (ACLU of Southern California, 1995; Norwicki, 1995), but when Morabito and Doerner (1997) examined the use of pepper spray in the Tallahassee Police Department they found its effective rate to be well below the level suggested by manufacturers. A recent study of Dutch officers conducted by Adang, Kaminski, Howell, and Mensink (2006) confirmed these findings. Their research found police officers need to be prepared for those situations where pepper spray "has no effect or may be less effective, but also those in which exposure to OC may actually cause suspects to become more aggressive." These researchers found that one-fifth of the subjects in their study "became a little more or very much more aggressive after being sprayed with OC." In fact, "there is a 132 percent increase in the odds that initially non-aggressive suspects will become aggressive after being sprayed with OC" (Adang et al., 2006). Although pepper spray is an effective police tool in that it reduces the number of injuries to officers and suspects alike, it does not subdue all suspects and is subject to abuse by officers.

Impact Munitions

Another less-than-lethal-force weapon increasingly being used by police departments is impact munitions. Impact munitions include rubber or wooden bullets and small beanbags that are fired from 12 gauge shotguns or 37 mm gas launchers. Such weapons are often used in riots and confrontations with unruly crowds. They are also increasingly being used when dealing with mentally and emotionally disturbed citizens (Hubbs & Klinger, 2004). These weapons can de-escalate violent encounters, allowing officers to avoid the use of deadly force. Police officers often cannot reason with these people, and in many cases pepper spray is not effective; consequently, confrontations with armed mentally disturbed subjects have often ended when police officers resorted to the use of deadly force. Impact munitions provide an alternative means of dealing with them.

When Hubbs and Klinger (2004) performed a national study on the use of impact munitions, they found that almost half the cases requiring the use of impact munitions involved a mentally disturbed person with suicidal tendencies. Another 20% of the cases involved suspects who refused to comply with officers' orders to surrender. In about 15% of the cases, officers fired projectiles at suspects who had barricaded themselves in buildings or vehicles. Additionally, there were a small number of instances in which they were used in hostage situations and civil disturbances. Hubbs and Klinger's study demonstrated that impact munitions have a role in law enforcement and can result in less violent confrontations between police officers and citizens. One must keep in mind, however, that these are police accounts and their characterizations of their use of force, not the version given by citizens.

The lethality of these weapons is of concern. In other words, does their potential for physical injury and death as well as police abuses outweigh their benefits? Hubbs and Klinger found that in almost 90% of the cases where impact munitions were used, the suspect had a weapon. In about half of the cases the suspect had an edged weapon, and in about 25% of the cases the suspect had a gun. The most common injury sustained by the suspect was a bruise, abrasion, or laceration (87%). Suspects received bone fractures in 3.5% of the cases, the projectile penetrated the skin in 1.8% of the cases, and the suspect was killed in 1.3% of the cases. The data indicate clearly the potential for death and serious injury when impact munitions are used, and there is evidence that police officers have used these weapons against peaceful individuals who posed no serious threat to anyone.

Conduct Energy Devices

To view a video on police Taser training, go to: **www.youtube.com/watch?v=AUquJQ_OgeE**

One of most popular "less-than-lethal" weapons used by police is the *conducted energy device* (CED), more often referred to as a Taser® or stun gun. The CED is a handheld weapon, shaped like a handgun, that delivers an instantly incapacitating 50,000 V shock to its target. The device is designed to interfere with the body's neuromuscular system and drops its target to the ground. The device can be operated in two modes—as a projectile device or as a contact stun device. As a projectile device, the weapon fires two barbed darts that are attached to two copper coils. The projectiles are designed to travel a distance of up to 21 feet. The barbs attach to the clothing or skin of the target, and the coils deliver a high-voltage, low-amperage 5 s electric shock. The deploying officer can lengthen the duration of the shock, and repeated bursts of electricity can be delivered. These devices are becoming more popular with police departments. In one national study, it was found that about 80% of departments use them. Moreover, as their use has increased, the use of other less-than-lethal weapons has decreased (Taylor, Alpert, Kubu, & Woods, 2011).

These devices are becoming very popular with law enforcement, correctional, and military agencies. Worldwide, they are used by law enforcement in over 50 countries and have been used in the Iraqi war (Amnesty International, 2006). Although estimates vary, it is thought that about 11,000 law enforcement agencies are currently using the weapon (Amnesty International, 2008). Moreover, officers in some jurisdictions are using them fairly frequently. Officers in Cleveland used the CEDs 969 times in a 5-month period (Shaffer, 2013). The device, however, is not without controversy. Although the available research and reports on these weapons are relatively limited, their use does raise a number of real concerns.

It has been determined that, since 2001, at least 500 people in the United States have died after being shocked by these devices (Amnesty International, 2012). Amnesty International reviewed a number of cases where the Taser had been used. Most of the deaths were attributable to causes other than the Taser, but medical examiners have listed the Taser as the cause or contributing cause in 60 deaths. In 90% of the cases, the suspect had been unarmed, and many victims were subjected to multiple shocks. As an example, in 2011 Roger Anthony fell off his bicycle and died after an officer shot him with a stun gun. The officer stunned Anthony because he did not respond to orders to pull over. Anthony most likely did not respond to the officer's orders because he was disabled and had hearing problems. It is obvious that the police cannot have a cavalier

FIGURE 7.2 A common police Taser.
Photo courtesy of Shutterstock.

attitude about the use of CEDs. It also appears, based on the number of deaths and reports of inappropriate police use of Tasers, that departments must evaluate their policies (Figure 7.2).

Although the Taser is touted as an effective alternative to the use of deadly force by police and in some cases is described as a "last resort" weapon, there is growing evidence that in the majority of police applications these weapons are not being used as an alternative to deadly force or as a weapon of last resort. In fact, an examination of 74 Taser-involved deaths found that "most of those who died were unarmed men who, while displaying disturbed or combative behavior, did not appear to present a serious threat to the lives or safety of others" (Amnesty International, 2006). There is also growing concern about police use of these weapons on vulnerable populations. CEDs have been used against schoolchildren, "unarmed mentally disturbed or intoxicated individuals, suspects fleeing minor crime scenes, and people who argue with police or fail to comply immediately with a command. Cases ... include the stunning of a 15-year-old schoolgirl in Florida, following a dispute on a bus, and a 13-year-old girl in Arizona, who threw a book in a public library" (Amnesty International, 2006) (Box 7.3).

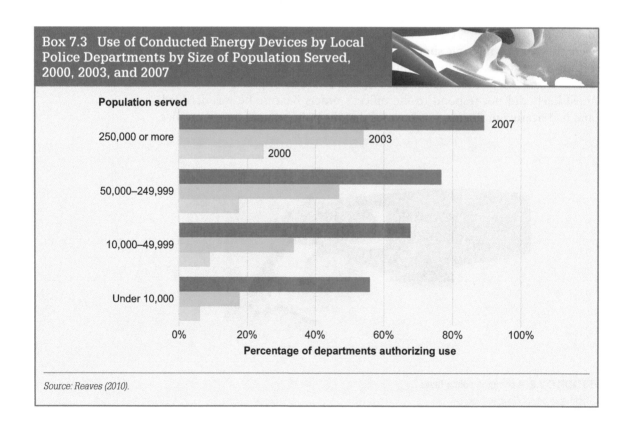

Box 7.3 Use of Conducted Energy Devices by Local Police Departments by Size of Population Served, 2000, 2003, and 2007

Source: Reaves (2010).

Finally, there is serious question as to whether these devices have actually reduced the police need to use force or merely allow police to use force on a greater number of citizens in far less serious situations. Sousa, Ready, and Ault (2010), in a study of police use of force, found that officers equipped with CEDs were less likely to deploy pepper spray or their batons when confronted with suspect resistance or aggression, and they were less likely to discharge their firearms. In a similar study, Lin and Jones (2010) examined over 1000 police use-of-force reports and found that CEDs decreased officer injury rates and tended to supplant other forms of force. There is a considerable need to evaluate these weapons relative to other weapons and to examine policies on their use.

Net Widening and Use of Force

Some research may indicate that police use of less-than-lethal weapons, such as pepper spray and CEDs, can decrease police use-of-force incidents and the number of serious citizen injuries associated with more traditional weapons, but this is not always the case. In fact, the introduction of new force or control technologies can result in an increased use of force against citizens. While the overall level or severity of the force used by police officers may decrease, the actual number of use-of-force incidents may increase. Police officers possessing less-than-lethal weapons may be more inclined to use these weapons in cases where they would not have been legally justified in using traditional weapons, or for that matter any force at all. This phenomenon is known as *net widening*. As use-of-force technologies improve, police may be more likely to apply force to a greater number of people, apply force in less serious confrontations, use force against women and children, or resort to force in cases where citizens simply defy police authority.

A commission report written by the LAPD 5 years after the beating of motorist Rodney King provides ample evidence of the net-widening phenomenon. The commission remarked that the LAPD had made substantial progress toward improving many of the critical problem areas identified by the original Christopher Commission. According to the new commission (Bobb, Epstein, Miller, & Abascall, 1996):

> The use of force declined in absolute numbers, although not as a percentage of arrests; the severity of force used decreased with the deployment of chemical spray, which has all but eliminated the use of the baton. … Ugly incidents have diminished and, although arrests are down, the reductions in serious injury to suspects have not been accompanied by feared increases in the crime rate or by significant increases in the number of officers injured.

The commission reported that between 1990 and 1995 use-of-force incidents dropped dramatically in the LAPD. According to the commission, there was a 36%

reduction in use-of-force incidents during this time period. The commission found that the number of use-of-force incidents dropped from 3403 in 1990 to 2187 in 1995. On its face, this would represent a remarkable turnaround in the LAPD.

Kappeler, Sluder, and Alpert (1998), however, observed that the commission never acknowledged that the most dramatic decline in reported use-of-force incidents came in the very year that Rodney King was beaten and before the Christopher Commission released its findings and recommendations for reform. In fact, 81% of the 36% reduction in use of force occurred in 1991. According to the commission, since 1991, the number of reported use-of-force incidents remained relatively stable. This, however, is only part of the story about change in the LAPD. When the number of arrests made by LAPD officers is taken into account, the rate of arrests involving force actually increased between 1990 and 1995. Perhaps the most dramatic decline in the use of force by the LAPD was found in officers' use of batons. From 1990 to 1995, the use of batons declined from 500 reported incidents in 1990 to only 43 in 1995. Once again the commission failed to note that the most drastic reduction in use of the police baton occurred in 1991. In fact, reported use of the baton that year alone dropped from 500 incidents to 167 incidents.

This trend, however, was also met with an increase in the use of chemical agents such as pepper spray. Between 1990 and 1994, the number of reported uses of chemical agents by LAPD officers rose from 21 to 835. If the commission had compared the number of incidents in which LAPD officers reported the use of either a baton or a chemical agent in 1990 (521) to the use of either of those two instruments of force in 1994 (878), they would have found a 68% increase in officer use of force. Because the number of arrests made by the LAPD decreased 61%, officers were more likely than ever to use force in arrest situations. In essence, the use of force by the LAPD increased as much as their arrests decreased. In the 5 years following the Rodney King beating, the LAPD had widened the net on the numbers of citizens who were subjected to police use of force while officer injuries, the arrest rate, and the overall crime rate declined. In the aftermath of one of the most publicized police beatings in American history, the LAPD increased its use of force against citizens.

A similar pattern of net widening seems to be developing with the use of CEDs (Amnesty International, 2004):

> Data from the Orange County Sheriff's Office in Florida showed that, by May 2002—just over a year after they were first deployed—CEDs had become the most prevalent force option for the department, constituting 68% of all use-of-force incidents. ... CEDs use reportedly rose to 77.6% of all force incidents in 2003. However, the data also reveals that, while police use of chemical sprays, police dogs, physical force and firearms dropped by about 21% in the year after CEDs were

introduced, the overall number of times force was used by Orange County deputies actually increased by 37%. A brochure on Taser International's website reports a staggering 72% increase in use of force by Orange County deputies from 1999 to 2002, in line with increased Taser use. Similarly, in May 2004, a local news agency reported that the use of force against suspects in the city of Orlando, Florida, had "nearly doubled in the last 14 months since Tasers were issued to police," although they arrested fewer suspects.

HOMICIDES AND ASSAULTS OF POLICE OFFICERS

The FBI Uniform Crime Reports show that between 2001 and 2010, 541 police officers were feloniously killed in the line of duty, with the highest number of officers (70) being killed in 2001 and the lowest number of officers (41) in 2008. In 2010, 56 law enforcement officers were feloniously killed (FBI, 2010). However, each decade since the 1970s has shown a substantial decline in officers feloniously killed.

Police officers encounter a variety of dangerous situations. It is commonly believed that more officers are killed when intervening in domestic disturbances, but actually, in 2010, more officers were killed in ambushes. Box 7.4 provides a breakdown of the situations where officers were killed.

The number of assaults on police officers has also fluctuated over the decades. In 1980, there were 57,847 assaults by citizens on police officers. Assaults of

Box 7.4 Situations Where Officers were Killed

- 15 officers were killed in ambush situations.
- 14 officers died as a result of felonious attacks during arrest situations.
- 8 officers were slain while investigating suspicious persons/circumstances.
- 7 officers were killed during traffic pursuits/stops.
- 6 officers were murdered answering disturbance calls.
- 3 officers were slain during tactical situations (barricaded offender, hostage taking, high-risk entry, etc.).
- 2 officers were killed while conducting investigative activity (surveillance, search, interview, etc.).
- 1 officer was killed while transporting or maintaining custody of a prisoner.

Source: FBI (2013).

police officers reached their height in 1992 (81,150) and declined to 54,774 by 2011 (FBI, 2010, 2012). Today, about 10% of police officers are assaulted in the line of duty in a given year. The three most common types of calls where police are assaulted are disturbance calls that include family quarrels, bar fights, etc.; officers attempting to make an arrest; and officers assaulted while transporting prisoners. There are several explanations for the decline in deaths and injuries. First, citizens are less likely to use deadly force against the police today than in the past. Second, part of the decline in deaths relative to the number of assaults is that an increasing number of officers are provided body armor. Third, it is possible that police officers receive better emergency medical care today than they had in the past (Box 7.5).

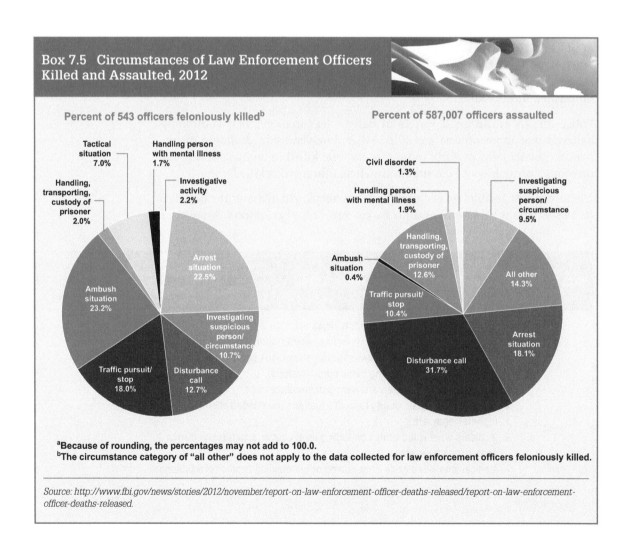

Box 7.5   Circumstances of Law Enforcement Officers Killed and Assaulted, 2012

Percent of 543 officers feloniously killed[b]

- Tactical situation 7.0%
- Handling person with mental illness 1.7%
- Handling, transporting, custody of prisoner 2.0%
- Investigative activity 2.2%
- Arrest situation 22.5%
- Ambush situation 23.2%
- Investigating suspicious person/circumstance 10.7%
- Traffic pursuit/stop 18.0%
- Disturbance call 12.7%

Percent of 587,007 officers assaulted

- Civil disorder 1.3%
- Handling person with mental illness 1.9%
- Investigating suspicious person/circumstance 9.5%
- Ambush situation 0.4%
- Handling, transporting, custody of prisoner 12.6%
- All other 14.3%
- Traffic pursuit/stop 10.4%
- Arrest situation 18.1%
- Disturbance call 31.7%

[a]Because of rounding, the percentages may not add to 100.0.
[b]The circumstance category of "all other" does not apply to the data collected for law enforcement officers feloniously killed.

Source: http://www.fbi.gov/news/stories/2012/november/report-on-law-enforcement-officer-deaths-released/report-on-law-enforcement-officer-deaths-released.

One way for police departments to reduce police officer deaths and injuries is protective body armor. Not all police departments issue officers body armor; and many that do, do not require officers to wear it at all times while on duty. Research shows that body armor can save police officers' lives. LaTourette (2010) calculated the effects of body armor on police fatalities. He found that outfitting police officers with body armor would save about 8.5 police officers a year. Body armor more than triples the likelihood that an officer will survive a gunshot to the torso (Box 7.6).

Several studies have examined offenders who kill police officers to gain insight into why officers are killed. In 1992, the FBI issued a paper, *Killed in the Line of Duty*, which analyzed 51 incidents between 1975 and 1985. The FBI concluded that there are predominantly two types of offenders who kill police officers: those who are antisocial and those who are psychologically dependent. Most of the offenders in their sample

You can listen to a podcast taped by the FBI on the issue of law enforcement officers killed by going to: http://www.fbigov/news/podcasts/thisweek/law-enforcement-officers-killed-and-assaulted-report-2011.mp3/view

were of the antisocial type. Other research, however, suggests that personality disorder is of little importance in predicting shootings, as the primary motivation for such shootings is to escape apprehension (Margarita, 1980). The FBI

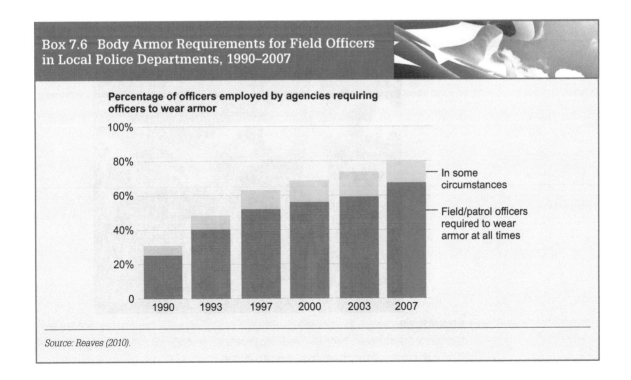

Box 7.6 Body Armor Requirements for Field Officers in Local Police Departments, 1990–2007

Percentage of officers employed by agencies requiring officers to wear armor

In some circumstances

Field/patrol officers required to wear armor at all times

Source: Reaves (2010).

reported that offenders often had criminal records, which supports the idea that most shootings occur as the shooters attempt to escape.

A considerable body of literature has developed examining social and demographic variables and police homicides. These studies seem to indicate that police homicides tend to occur more frequently in the south and are correlated with factors such as the number of civilians killed by the police, the general homicide rate, gun density, volume of crime, and poverty rate (King & Sanders, 1997). These factors tend to indicate those areas where shootings are more likely to occur, but they are general in nature and do not help predict specifically where shootings will occur. What can be said, however, is that poverty and subcultures of violence contribute to police homicides (Figure 7.3).

There is some research examining the characteristics of officer victims. The FBI study found that officer victims generally were easygoing, friendly, liked by the community, and reluctant to follow the rules (FBI, 1992). The FBI also found that the victims in their study generally made one of two mistakes during their fatal encounter: 41% of the victim officers made improper approaches to suspects or suspect vehicles, and 54% of the victim officers failed to control persons or situations that eventually got out of hand. These findings indicate that officers should maintain control of situations at all times and follow training guidelines when approaching suspects. A number of departments now emphasize these policies on a regular basis to reduce

FIGURE 7.3
Members of the Wilmington, North Carolina Police Department celebrate police memorial day on May 14, 2009 in Wilmington. *Copyright Shutterstock/Kevin Chesson.*

officer homicides. These assertions, however, are more likely the product of police culture and lore than an empirical reality. Police desire to blame procedure when an officer is killed in the line of duty, as such an explanation brings order and predictability to a senseless act of violence. The downside of this "professional" emphasis is to make it appear that officers are uncaring.

As noted above, a substantial number of assaults on police officers do not lead to death or injury to the officer. Garner and Maxwell (1999) examined assaults on police officers in six cities. They found that in 7512 arrest situations the arrestee attempted to use a weapon in only 52 cases (less than 1%). Thus, the police encounter suspects with weapons in only a few cases, and the average police officer seldom or never encounters a suspect brandishing a weapon. They found that the most common weapon used by suspects was a firearm (handgun, rifle, or shotgun). The next most common weapon was a knife, followed by a stick or club.

The Dangers of Policing in Context

Scenes of officers being attacked and killed by ruthless criminals are staples of film and television, reinforced by the occasional real-life incident in which a police officer is gunned down. When such a tragic event occurs, the evening news includes footage of the deceased officer's funeral and scenes of the hundreds of officers from other departments paying their last respects to the slain officer. Invariably, the story includes a commentary to the effect that police officers are on the front line in the war against crime, facing the possibility of death from a crazed assailant at any given moment. Law enforcement agencies promote this image of the occupation. Consider the FBI's explanation for several police killings: "Ten officers were victims of violent attacks that were as unexpected as they were unprovoked. In three of these instances, the unsuspecting officer walked into an ambush situation; in seven others, the officer was gunned down for no apparent reason, perhaps just for being a law officer. Law enforcement is a high-risk occupation" (FBI, 2002). These images, however, do not match the reality of the actual dangers of police work. The risk associated with police work has declined substantially over the years, and many of the deaths and assaults on police officers occur during routine police activities.

The data indicate that police deaths are relatively rare events that have declined dramatically in recent years. From a high of 134 in 1973, police killings declined to 41 by 2008. In fact, when the period from 1972 to 1980 is compared to the period from 2000 to 2009, the average annual number of killings drops from 102 to about 54. It is noteworthy that this risk associated with police work has declined, despite the restrictions that have been placed on police use of firearms, the alleged increases in the rate of violent crime, the

The Myths of Police Danger and Violence

Myth: Policing is one of the most dangerous occupations in American society.

Reality: As measured by both fatalities and injuries on the job, police work is not one of the top 10 dangerous occupations.

Myth: Police routinely use force, including deadly force, as a normal part of their everyday work.

Reality: Most police officers will never use deadly force in their entire careers. Likewise, the vast majority of police–citizen encounters never result in any use of force whatsoever.

Myth: The use of police force is evenly distributed across all segments of society and is strictly controlled.

Reality: Police use of force is disproportionately used against people of color, the poor, and young males.

claimed proliferation of semiautomatic weapons on the streets of U.S. cities, the war on drugs, and reported increases in the level of gang-related violence.

To some extent, these statistics on police killings mask the reduction in risk that has occurred because the number of law enforcement personnel has increased substantially during this period. Because the number of police officers has actually *increased* significantly in the past three decades, the *rate* at which officers are killed has declined significantly. There were about 594,209 persons employed full-time in law enforcement at all levels of government in 1973. Today, it is estimated that more than 969,070 people are employed full-time in law enforcement. Because there were 134 killings of police officers in 1973, the aggregate risk per officer was approximately one chance in 4434 that year. With 41 deaths in 2009, each officer stood about a one in 23,635 chance of being slain. This represented a significant reduction in the chance of being killed in the line of duty. This is the aggregate rate of risk for all law enforcement personnel. Some officers patrol neighborhoods or perform assignments that place them in somewhat greater danger. Overall, the number of law enforcement personnel feloniously killed annually on the job declined by more than 60% in 36 years.

Another way to examine the question of danger and put it into context is to compare the fatality rate of police officers with that of persons working in other occupations and professions. In 2012, the Bureau of Labor Statistics published the rates of fatal injuries by occupational sector. People working in the fishing industry sustained a fatal injury rate of 32.3 per 100,000; transportation, 13.3; mining workers, 15.6; agriculture and fishing, 21.2; and construction workers, 9.5. Police officers, on the other hand, do not even show up in the top 10 occupations (Bureau of Labor Statistics, 2012). What this means is that fishermen and loggers, as well as other workers, are far more likely to be fatally injured performing their jobs than are police officers. It should be noted that this rate included fatal injuries that were the result of accidents as well as homicides. Less than one-third of the total number of police who sustained fatal injuries on the job were the victims of homicide. In fact, when accidents are removed from the equation, the rate of fatal injuries among police officers drops to just slightly above the rate for all U.S. workers (Box 7.7).

Overemphasis on the dangers of police work has a number of consequences for law enforcement. First, this misperception results in an increased level of public support. A belief that law enforcement personnel routinely confront danger generally leads citizens to give the police the benefit of the doubt when it comes to various controversies involving the propriety of certain actions. Second, the public perception that the police are armed and ready to deal with danger 24 h a day can be beneficial when it is time to engage in contract negotiations. Third, the belief that being a law enforcement officer is akin to the work of a soldier

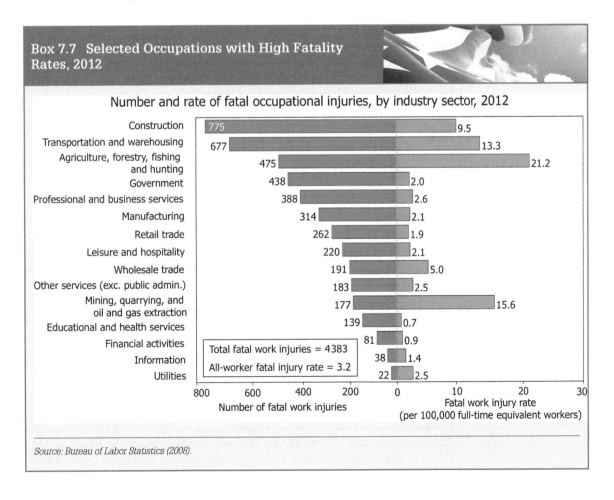

Box 7.7 Selected Occupations with High Fatality Rates, 2012

Number and rate of fatal occupational injuries, by industry sector, 2012

Total fatal work injuries = 4383
All-worker fatal injury rate = 3.2

Number of fatal work injuries

Fatal work injury rate
(per 100,000 full-time equivalent workers)

Industry sector	Number of fatal work injuries	Fatal work injury rate
Construction	775	9.5
Transportation and warehousing	677	13.3
Agriculture, forestry, fishing and hunting	475	21.2
Government	438	2.0
Professional and business services	388	2.6
Manufacturing	314	2.1
Retail trade	262	1.9
Leisure and hospitality	220	2.1
Wholesale trade	191	5.0
Other services (exc. public admin.)	183	2.5
Mining, quarrying, and oil and gas extraction	177	15.6
Educational and health services	139	0.7
Financial activities	81	0.9
Information	38	1.4
Utilities	22	2.5

Source: Bureau of Labor Statistics (2008).

on the front lines can have a deleterious effect on the officer's spouse. Fourth, the pervasive sense that their mission is dangerous affects the way that police officers deal with the public. One can only speculate about how many times officers use excessive force or are abrupt in their dealings with citizens because they perceive a world that is more dangerous than is actually the case. Finally, the fixation with danger likely results in a number of highly qualified people deciding to forego a career in law enforcement. Police departments across the country have difficulty in attracting enough qualified applicants.

SUICIDE BY COP

The shooting of civilians by police officers leads to a number of problems for officers, departments, and communities. As noted in this chapter, there have been a number of efforts to control police shooting behavior; however, there are some instances where police use of force seems unavoidable. One such area may be *suicide by cop*, which is a victim-precipitated homicide in which the victim takes action that causes the police to use deadly force. Kennedy, Homant, and Hupp (1998) provided several examples. In one case, a man drove his car onto the lawn of the Detroit Police Department headquarters and began shooting at the building. Detroit officers shot and killed him. In another case, officers were dispatched to a domestic violence call. Upon arrival, they encountered the victim's boyfriend with a rifle. The boyfriend, upon seeing the officers, slowly began raising the weapon to point it at the officers. The officers shot and killed him. The rifle was found to be unloaded. These, of course, do not represent the typical police shooting but are a very select group of sensational cases culled from literally hundreds of police shootings that occur each year.

Suicide by cop is a form of *hidden suicide*, which has long been suspected in numerous accidents such as automobile crashes, airplane crashes, and work-related accidents. By using hidden suicide, victims are able to accomplish their goals without losing their self-esteem. In some instances, it is easier to have another commit the fatal act, rather than having the victim do it himself or herself. There are few data examining such suicides, and we are not sure how frequently they occur. In numerous police shootings the victim's behavior has been considered bizarre or uncharacteristic, but in the past such circumstances were given little consideration. Today, we recognize that individuals can use the police to commit suicide.

Parent and Verdun-Jones (1998) observed that some individuals seek out the police to assist in their suicide because the police are equipped with the necessary weapons and they are available 24 h a day. Foote (1995) suggested that many victims of suicide by cop see themselves as victims and set a chain of events into motion to ensure their deaths and their victimization.

Geberth (1993) offered the opinion that some of the victims intend to make the police look bad and possibly cause unrest in the community, but many of the victims do not have the fortitude to commit the act of suicide themselves. Van Zandt (1993) noted that such suicides allow the victim to obtain substantial media coverage and attention, which compensate for feelings of inadequacy. Geberth also observed that some see suicide by cop as a better alternative than being arrested. It is apparent that a number of factors contribute to suicide by cop.

Suicide by cop is a dangerous event for the police as well as possibly innocent bystanders. Homant, Kennedy, and Hupp (2000) examined some of these suicides and found that, in 56% of the cases, there was a real threat to police officers. Moreover, some cases involved a family member being held hostage, or at least family members in close approximation, resulting in the police having to give them protection and exposing the officers to additional danger.

There is no certainty in quantifying how many police shootings are suicide-by-cop events. Research shows that many suicides by cop have many of the same characteristics as other suicides, including a history of mental illness, drug or alcohol abuse, past suicide attempts, suicide ideation, interpersonal crisis, and a criminal history (Lord, 2014). These personal characteristics can be found in a large number of people with whom the police come into contact. One major problem with determining the number of "suicide-by-cop" case is that most of the research done is based on either newspaper reports or the perceptions and reports of police officers involved in the shootings. It is to the police officers' advantage to characterize a shooting victim as crazed, on drugs, or suicidal (Kappeler et al., 1998), given the potential criminal and civil sanctions. Hutson et al. (1998) examined newspaper descriptions of shootings from a variety of cities. In most of the shootings, the researchers were unable to determine if suicide was a possible motivating factor due to insufficient detail describing the events.

Obviously, suicide by cop raises a number of issues for the police. When such an event occurs, there is little information other than the police account to indicate that it was a suicide. The event often is considered another instance where officers used deadly force. This, in turn, results in considerable scrutiny and criticism of the police.

SUMMARY

This chapter examines police use of force, which is one of the most significant problems facing police departments and society today. Each year, police officers kill a large number of citizens and use excessive force against many others. Citizens, politicians, and the media question whether the police use too much force too quickly. Ample anecdotal information suggests that officers use excessive force. On the other hand, while performing their duties police officers are sometimes confronted with hostile citizens who assault officers and attempt to take their lives.

Police departments must take actions to control officer discretion and reduce the levels of excessive force. These actions have centered around the development of a use-of-force continuum, implementing restrictive use-of-force policies, development of early warning systems to identify officers with behavioral problems, and a new focus on less-than-lethal weapons. None of these actions can be considered a panacea, because the problem continues. Policing has made a number of strides, but we must continue to address the problem.

Furthermore, police use of force is a complex problem. On the one hand, the media, citizens, and minority groups impeach police departments for not controlling their officers. On the other hand, police and unions advocate less restrictive policies because they feel they unfairly place officers in danger. Moreover, the police generally have the support of the public. Fear of crime remains a major social problem, and many citizens support the police, even when they take extralegal measures. These citizens favor community safety over citizen rights. Regardless, we must continue to improve how we enforce the law, use authority, and apply force.

REVIEW QUESTIONS

1. What did the U.S. Supreme Court rule in the 1985 decision in *Tennessee v. Garner*?
2. What happened in the case of *Graham v. Connor* and what ruling did the Supreme Court make in this case? What four factors did the Court identify as requiring careful consideration before an officer can use force against a citizen?
3. Describe the *use-of-force continuum* and how it is used to guide police officers in most police departments today.
4. What is meant by the term *less-than-lethal force*? Name some examples of less-than-lethal technologies that officers can deploy.
5. According to the Bureau of Labor Statistics, what is the job-related fatality rate of police officers compared to people working in other fields?
6. What is *suicide by cop?*

REFERENCES

ACLU of Southern California. (1995). *Pepper spray update: More fatalities, more questions.* Los Angeles, CA: Author.

Adang, O., Kaminski, R. J., Howell, M. Q., & Mensink, J. (2006). Assessing the performance of pepper spray in use-of-force encounters: the Dutch experience. *Policing: An International Journal of Police Strategies & Management, 29*(2), 282–305.

Alpert, G., & MacDonald, J. (2001). Police use of force: an analysis of organizational characteristics. *Justice Quarterly, 18*(2), 393–409.

Alpert, G., & Smith, W. (1994). How reasonable is the reasonable man? Police and excessive force. *The Journal of Criminal Law and Criminology, 85*(2), 481–501.

Amnesty International. (2004). *Excessive and lethal force? Amnesty International's concerns about deaths and ill-treatment involving police use of tasers.* London: Amnesty International.

Amnesty International. (2006). *Amnesty International's continued concerns about taser use.* London: Amnesty International.

Amnesty International. (2008). *USA – Stun weapons in law enforcement.* London: Amnesty International.

Amnesty International. (2012). *USA: Stricter limits urged as deaths following police taser use reach 500.* http://www.amnesty.org/en/news/usa-stricter-limits-urged-deaths-following-police-taser-use-reach-500-2012-02-15. Accessed 26.08.13.

Bailey, W. C. (1996). Less-than-lethal weapons and police–citizen killings in U.S. Urban areas. *Crime & Delinquency, 42*(4), 535–553.

Blumberg, M. (1997). Controlling police use of deadly force: assessing two decades of progress. In R. Dunham & G. Alpert (Eds.), *Critical issues in policing* (3rd ed.) (pp. 507–530). Prospect Heights, IL: Waveland Press.

Bobb, M. J., Epstein, M. H., Miller, N. H., & Abascall, M. A. (1996). *Five years later: A report to the Los Angeles police commission on the Los Angeles police department's implementation of independent commission recommendations.* Los Angeles, CA: City of Los Angeles.

Brown, J. M., & Langan, P. A. (2001). *Policing and homicide, 1976–98: Justifiable homicide by police, police officers murdered by felons.* Washington, DC: U.S. Department of Justice, Bureau of Justice Statistics.

Bureau of Labor Statistics. (2008). *National census of fatal occupational injuries in 2007.* Washington, DC: U.S. Department of Labor, Bureau of Labor Statistics. www.146.142.4.22/news.release/archives/cfoi_08202008.pdf.

Bureau of Labor Statistics. (2012). *National census of fatal occupational injuries. U.S. Department of Labor.* Washington, DC: Bureau of Labor Statistics.

Cruz, N. S. (2013). *Third Anaheim police shooting comes as more protests planned.* The Los Angeles Times. http://articles.latimes.com/2012/jul/27/local/la-mew-third-anaheim-police-shooting-mobile. Accessed 10.09.13.

Culliver, C., & Sigler, R. (1995). Police use of deadly force in Tennessee following Tennessee v. Garner. *Journal of Contemporary Criminal Justice, 11*(3), 187–195.

Eith, C., & Durose, M. R. (2011). *Contacts between police and public, 2008.* Washington, DC: Bureau of Justice Statistics.

FBI. (1992). *Killed in the line of duty: A study of selected felonious killings of law enforcement officers.* Washington, DC: Federal Bureau of Investigation.

FBI. (2002). *Law enforcement officers killed and assaulted, 2005.* Washington, DC: Federal Bureau of Investigation. www2.fbi.gov/ucr/killed/2005/.

FBI. (2010). *Law enforcement officers killed and assaulted, 2009.* Washington, DC: Federal Bureau of Investigation. www2.fbi.gov/ucr/killed/2009/.

FBI. (2012). *Law enforcement officers killed & assaulted 2011.* http://www.fbi.gov/about-us/cjis/ucr/leoka/2011/tables/table-65.

FBI. (2013). *Officer feloniously killed.* http://www.fbi.gov/about-us/cjis/ucr/leoka/leoka-2010/officers-feloniously-killed.

Foote, W. (1995). Victim-precipitated homicide. In H. V. Hall (Ed.), *Lethal violence 2000: A sourcebook on domestic, acquaintance, and stranger aggression* (pp. 174–202). Kamuela, HI: Pacific Institute of Conflict.

Fyfe, J. J. (1980). Always prepared: police off-duty guns. *Annals of the American Academy of Political and Social Science, 452,* 72–81.

Fyfe, J. J. (1988). Police use of deadly force: research and reform. *Justice Quarterly, 5*(2), 165–205.

Fyfe, J. J. (1995). Training to reduce police–civilian violence. In W. A. Geller & H. Toch (Eds.), *And justice for all: Understanding and controlling police abuse of force* (pp. 163–176). Washington, DC: Police Executive Research Forum.

Garner, J. H., Buchanan, J., Schade, T., & Hepburn, J. (1996). *Understanding the use of force by and against the police.* Washington, DC: National Institute of Justice.

Garner, J. H., & Maxwell, C. D. (1999). *Measuring the amount of force used by and against the police in six jurisdictions. Use of force by police: Overview of national and local data* (pp. 25–44). Washington, DC: National Institute of Justice and Bureau of Justice Statistics.

Garner, J. H., Schade, T., Hepburn, J., & Buchanan, J. (1995). Measuring the continuum of force used by and against the police. *Criminal Justice Review, 20,* 146–168.

Geberth, V. J. (1993). Suicide by cop: inviting death from the hands of a police officer. *Law & Order, 41*(7), 105–108.

Geller, W. A., & Scott, M. S. (1992). *Deadly force: What we know.* Washington, DC: Police Executive Research Forum.

Graham v. Connor, 1989 490 U.S. 386, 109 S. Ct. 1865.

Hickman, M. (2006). *Citizen complaints about police use of force.* Washington, DC: U.S. Department of Justice, Bureau of Justice Statistics.

Hickman, M., Piquero, A., & Greene, J. (2000). Does community policing generate greater numbers and different types of citizen complaints than traditional policing? *Police Quarterly, 3,* 70–84.

Homant, R. J., Kennedy, D. B., & Hupp, R. T. (2000). Real and perceived danger in police officer assisted suicide. *Journal of Criminal Justice, 28*(1), 43–52.

Hubbs, K., & Klinger, D. (2004). *Impact munitions database of use and effects.* Washington, DC: U.S. Department of Justice.

Hutson, H. R., Anglin, D., Rice, P., Kyriacou, D. N., & Strote, J. (2009). Excessive use of force by police: a survey of academic emergency physicians. *Emergency Medicine Journal, 26,* 20–22.

Hutson, H. R., Anglin, D., Yarbrough, J., Hardaway, K., Russell, M., Strote, J., et al. (1998). Suicide by cop. *Annals of Emergency Medicine, 32,* 665–669.

Independent Commission on the Los Angeles Police Department. (1991). *Report of the independent commission.* Los Angeles, CA: Author.

Kappeler, V. E. (2006). *Critical issues in police civil liability* (4th ed.). Prospect Heights, IL: Waveland Press.

Kappeler, V. E., Sluder, R., & Alpert, G. (1998). *Forces of deviance: Understanding the dark side of policing* (2nd ed.). Prospect Heights, IL: Waveland Press.

Kennedy, D. B., Homant, R. J., & Hupp, R. T. (1998). Suicide by cop. *FBI Law Enforcement Bulletin, 67*(8), 21–28.

King, W. R., & Sanders, B. A. (1997). Nice guys finish last: a critical review of killed in the line of duty. *Policing, 20*(2), 392–407.

Klockars, C. B. (1995). A theory of excessive force and its control. In W. Geller & H. Toch (Eds.), *And justice for all: Understanding and controlling police abuse of force* (pp. 11–30). Washington, DC: Police Executive Research Forum.

LaTourette, T. (2010). The life-saving effectiveness of body armor for police officers. *Journal of Occupational and Environmental Hygiene, 7,* 557–562.

Lin, Y., & Jones, T. R. (2010). Electronic control devices and use of force outcomes. *Policing: An International Journal of Police Strategies & Management, 33,* 152–178.

Lord, V. (2014). Factors influencing subjects' observed level of suicide by cop intent. *Criminal Justice and Behavior, 17,* 79–100.

Lumb, R. C., & Friday, P. C. (1997). Impact of pepper spray availability on police officer use-of-force decisions. *Policing: An International Journal of Police Strategies & Management, 20*(1), 136–148.

Margarita, M. (1980). Police as victims of violence. *Justice Systems Journal, 5,* 218–233.

McEwen, T. (1996). *National data collection on police use of force.* Washington, DC: U.S. Department of Justice, Bureau of Justice Statistics.

McEwen, T. (1997). Policies on less-than-lethal force in law enforcement agencies. *Policing: An International Journal of Police Strategy & Management, 20*(1), 39–59.

McEwen, T., & Leahy, F. (1993). *Less-than-lethal force technologies in law enforcement and correctional agencies.* Washington, DC: Institute for Law and Justice.

Morabito, E. V., & Doerner, W. G. (1997). Police use of less-than-lethal force: oleoresin capsicum (OC) spray. *Policing: An International Journal of Police Strategy & Management, 20*(4), 680–697.

Norwicki, E. (1995). Spray day. *Police, 19*(1), 36–39.

Paoline, E. A., & Terrill, W. (2007). Police education, experience, and the use of force. *Criminal Justice and Behavior, 34*(2), 179–196.

Parent, R. B., & Verdun-Jones, S. (1998). Victim-precipitated homicide: police use of deadly force in British Columbia. *Policing: An International Journal of Police Strategies & Management, 21*(3), 432–448.

Pringle, P., & Winton, R. (May 14, 2013). *They just beat him up: Kern county deputies are investigated in man's death.* Los Angeles Times, A1, A8.

Reaves, B. A. (2010). *Local police departments, 2007.* Washington, DC: U.S. Department of Justice, Bureau of Justice Statistics.

Shaffer, C. (2013). *New police order would bar Cleveland officers from shooting at or from moving vehicle.* Cleveland.com. http://www.cleveland.com/metro/index.ssf/2013/08/new_police_order_would_bar_cle.html. Accessed 05.09.13.

Sousa, W., Ready, J., & Ault, M. (2010). The impact of TASERs on police use-of-force decisions: findings from a randomized field-training experiment. *Journal of Experimental Criminology, 6,* 35–55.

Sparger, J., & Giacopassi, D. J. (1992). Memphis revisited: a reexamination of police shootings after the Garner decision. *Justice Quarterly, 9*(2), 211–225.

Taylor, B., Alpert, G., Kubu, B., & Woods, D. (2011). Changes in officer use of force over time: a descriptive analysis of a national survey. *Policing: An International Journal of Police Strategies & Management, 34,* 211–232.

Tennenbaum, A. N. (1994). The influence of the Garner decision on police use of deadly force. *Journal of Criminal Law and Criminology, 85*(1), 241–260.

Tennessee v. Garner, 1985 771 U.S. 1.

Terrill, W. (2003). Police use of force and suspect resistance: the micro process of the police-suspect encounter. *Police Quarterly, 6*(1), 51–83.

Terrill, W., & Mastrofski, S. (2002). Situational and officer-based determinants of police coercion. *Justice Quarterly, 19*(2), 215–248.

Terrill, W., & Paoline, A. (2013). Examining less lethal force policy and the force continuum: results from a national use-of-force study. *Police Quarterly, 16,* 38–65.

Terrill, W., Paoline, E., & Manning, P. (2003). Police culture and coercion. *Criminology, 41*(4), 1003–1034.

Toch, H. (1995). The "violence prone" police officer. In W. Geller & H. Toch (Eds.), *And justice for all: Understanding and controlling police abuse of force* (pp. 99–112). Washington, DC: Police Executive Research Forum.

Van Zandt, C. R. (1993). Suicide by cop. *Police Chief Magazine, 60*, 24–30.

Walker, S., & Fridell, L. (1992). Forces of change in police policy: the impact of Tennessee v. Garner. *American Journal of Police, 11*(3), 97–112.

Walker, S., Alpert, G., & Kenney, D. J. (2000). Early warning systems for police: concept, history, and issues. *Police Quarterly, 3*(2), 132–152.

Weisburd, D., Greenspan, R., Hamilton, E., Williams, H., & Bryant, K. (2000). *Police attitudes toward abuse of authority: Findings from a national study*. Washington, DC: U.S. Department of Justice.

White, M. D. (1999). *Police shootings in Philadelphia: An analysis of two decades of deadly force* (Ph.D. dissertation). Philadelphia, PA: Temple University.

White, M. D. (2000). Assessing the impact of administrative policy on the use of deadly force by on- and off-duty police. *Evaluation Review, 24*(3), 295–318.

Worden, R. (1995). The "causes" of police brutality: theory and evidence on police use of force. In W. Geller, & H. Toch (Eds.), *And justice for all: Understanding and controlling police abuse of force* (pp. 31–60). Washington, DC: Police Executive Research Forum.

CHAPTER 8

Police Culture and Behavior

I have always thought the actions of men the best interpreters of their thoughts.

—John Locke

INTRODUCTION

What we know and think about police culture and personality are largely dependent on how one views behavior. Police behavior can be seen from several different perspectives. Social scientists use different "cognitive lenses" from which to view behavior. Not unlike researchers studying cells under a microscope, adjusting magnification of the instrument for clarity, social scientists study behavior from different points of view. Although no single perspective gives a clear and complete understanding of the many varieties of police behavior, using several different points of view allows us to gain greater perspective of

- Predispositional model
- Problem-solver
- Professionalization
- Professionals
- Psychological perspective
- Realists
- Reciprocators
- Rule applier
- Secrecy
- Socialization model
- Sociological perspective
- Solidarity
- Stress
- Stress effects
- Stressors
- Subculture
- Subculture of violence
- Symbolic assailant
- Task officers
- Themes
- Tough cop
- Worldview

the police. These perspectives allow us to examine the behaviors of individual officers, police as a social group, and policing as a unique occupational culture. Depending on the point of view used, researchers draw different conclusions about police behavior.

Some people contend that police officers do not have personalities or cultures different from people in other occupations. Others maintain that police officers are very different in both personality and culture. Despite the debate, it can be said that the police roles and functions set officers apart from other members of society; therefore, the police as an occupational group can be distinguished from other members in society. This distinction has led to many studies on police personality and culture, including a wealth of theory about police behavior.

In this chapter, we will explore the police personality and culture from several different perspectives. Several models of police behavior will be advanced to gain a better understanding of the men and women who become police officers. A better understanding of the factors that shape police personality and culture allows us to understand many of the problems associated with police deviance, misconduct, and civil liability. These topics will be given greater attention in subsequent chapters. For now, we will consider the police from three different views—psychological, sociological, and anthropological. Each perspective gives us insight and helps to explain why police officers behave and perhaps think the way they do.

THE PSYCHOLOGICAL PERSPECTIVE

Traditional psychology involves the systematic study of mental and emotional factors. Psychologists often focus on the perceptions, emotions, and intelligence of people. Psychology as a field of study often emphasizes individual characteristics and personalities. Many researchers adopting the *psychological perspective* feel that personality is fixed and does not change significantly by occupational choice or personal experience. This perspective of personality holds that each person has a core personality that remains static throughout life (Adlam, 1982). Although events, experiences, and social situations change, a person's basic personality is thought to stay the same. When this individualist, fixed perspective of personality is applied to the police, researchers tend to focus on the personality characteristics exhibited by people who become police officers as compared to people entering other professions. Researchers then compare the "police personality" with personality characteristics of people in other occupations (Balch, 1972; Rubinstein, 2006).

This type of research allows the development of a *predispositional model* of police behavior. Under this model, researchers assume that behavior is predetermined by a static, preexisting personality shared by people entering the law enforcement profession. Persons with certain types of personalities enter policing and behave in certain ways (Balch, 1972; Genz & Lester, 1976; Sherman, 1980; Symonds, 1970). This predispositional model of police behavior and the fixed personality perspective have led some people to conclude that police recruits are more authoritarian than people who enter other professions.

The *authoritarian personality* is said to be conservative, aggressive, cynical, and rigid. People having these characteristics are said to have a limited view of the world and see issues strictly in terms of black and white. People are good or bad, likable or unlikable, friends or enemies. People with this psychological makeup are said to be more conservative and have a dislike of liberal ideals. This personality type is also characterized by tendencies to make simplistic judgments about people and events, assess individual guilt and responsibility, and seek harsh retribution for social transgressions. The authoritarian personality is also characterized by a rigid view of the world. Some have argued that police see the world simply in terms of good and bad people who deserve what happens to them. From this point of view, even crime victims deserve what happens to them or they can be blamed for their victimization (Lambert, Burroughs, & Nguyen, 1999). People with an authoritarian personality are often submissive to their superiors and tend to follow the status quo, but they do not tolerate persons who do not submit to their authority (Adorno, 1950).

Research from this perspective has focused on personality characteristics of the police. Carpenter and Raza (1987) found that police applicants differ from other occupational groups in several significant ways. First, these researchers found that police applicants, as a group, are more psychologically healthy, less depressed and anxious, and more assertive in making and maintaining social contacts. Second, their findings indicated that police officers are a more homogeneous group of people and that this "greater homogeneity is probably due to the sharing of personality characteristics which lead one to desire becoming a police officer." Finally, they found that police officers were more like military personnel in their conformance to authority.

In another study of police personality, researchers administered a battery of psychological tests to two samples of 275 police applicants (Lorr & Strack, 1994). They found that applicants seeking admission into police training programs fell into one of three personality profiles. The largest subgroup was considered normal, or what some would refer to as good or typical cops. One in four of the applicants (27%), however, fell into a group with relatively high levels of paranoia, schizophrenia, and psychasthenia. The third group fell in the middle range on emotional adjustment, integrity, and intellect, but scored the lowest on interpersonal relations.

A study of Israeli police officers found that, as compared to airport security guards, soldiers, and a control group, the police work situation and their "authoritarianism led them to seek a career in which they could be aggressive with the approval of established authorities" (Rubinstein, 2006:759). It would seem that these officers sought out opportunities for aggression but did so under circumstances where their aggression would be tolerated. Conclusions of this nature regarding the police personality have been called into question by researchers who adopt different perspectives of behavior (Bayley & Mendelsohn, 1969; Niederhoffer, 1967).

In contrast to the psychological fixed-personality perspective, other researchers have taken a more social perspective and view personality as developmental and therefore subject to change, given differential socialization and experience (Adlam, 1982). Instead of assuming that personality is fixed, these researchers see personality as dynamic and changing with an individual's experiences. These researchers have a tendency to focus on the role police perform in society and how training, socialization, and professionalization influence individual personality and behavior. From this perspective, researchers study how police training, the work environment, and peers all influence and shape a police officer's personality and behavior over time. In a recent study of inexperienced and experienced police officers, Laguna, Linn, Ward, and Rupslaukyte (2010) found that both groups tended to be psychologically healthy. Moreover, they found that more experienced police officers were no more authoritarian than less experienced officers. They did, however, find that experienced officers had higher scores on reactions to stressful events. The authors asserted that this may be because of experienced officers having dealt with more dangerous situations, and younger officers possessing more bravado. Experienced officers likely had learned to better respond to more dangerous situations. They also found that the less experienced officers scored higher on the antisocial practices scale. This finding is attributable to new officers being less mature and unfamiliar with proper comportment for officers. Evans, Coman, and Stanley (1992) studied 271 police officers and found that police personality differed with the length of service. Generally, they found that the most profound difference was between younger officers and officers with 12 or more years of experience. As compared to younger officers, the more experienced officers were more competitive, conscientious, and cynical. They often displayed traits of aloofness, tough-mindedness, aggression, hostility, and authoritarianism.

Many of these researchers, however, still view behavior from an individualistic level—focusing on an individual officer's unique experiences and the development of individual personalities. In all, most research suggests that police personality—"who an officer is"—has little to do with how an officer behaves (Crank, 1993:118; Worden, 1989). Researchers adopting a sociological perspective of police behavior have questioned the psychological approach.

THE SOCIOLOGICAL PERSPECTIVE

Several studies have rejected the concept of an individualistic socialization process for a group socialization model (Sherman, 1974a, 1974b, 1982; Stoddard, 2006; Westley, 1953, 1970). Van Maanen (2006) rejected the notion that police officers have certain personality characteristics, such as authoritarianism, that might predetermine their behavioral patterns. Instead, these researchers and others adopt the perspective that behavior is based on group socialization and professionalization. *Professionalization* is the process by which norms and values are internalized as workers begin to learn their new occupation. It is maintained that, just as attorneys and physicians learn their ethics and values through training and practice, so too do police officers. Exposure to a police academy training, regular in-service training, and field experience all shape the social characteristics of police officers as a group. Officers learn how to behave and what to think from their shared experiences as they become police officers.

From this *socialization model,* many researchers find that police officers beginning their careers are psychologically healthy, like members of other professions who come from similar backgrounds. This model of behavior assumes that police officers learn their social personality from training and through exposure to the unique demands of police work (Skolnick, 1966). Kappeler, Sluder, and Alpert (1998) suggest that police socialization results in "an ideology and shared culture that breeds unprecedented conformity to the traditional police norms and values" (p. 84). If officers become cynical, hard, and conservative, it is not because of their preexisting personality or their unique, individual experiences, but because of the demands of the occupation and shared socialization experience.

Some research is supportive of the position that recruit and probationary officers values are affected by their training. Conti (2009) described how academy staff through interaction with recruit officers would degrade recruits' civilian inclinations, although rewarding characteristics that strictly adhered to the police culture. The process effectively socialized the recruits to be "good" police officers. Chappell and Lanza-Kaduce (2010) compare police training to military boot camp where recruit officers are subjected to stressful situations and an emphasis on physical training, defensive tactics, weapons, and use of force. This contributes to group think and a police esprit de corps. Rookies leaving the academy often have a uniform mindset (Figure 8.1).

Police officers undergo extreme socialization as they are trained for their work. The group adopts a set of norms and values that are constantly reinforced within the group setting through shared experiences. These norms and values

FIGURE 8.1
Police academy recruits from Prince George's County, Maryland, search for evidence on the property where four bodies were found in a garage in Riverdale on August 6, 2010. *Photo courtesy of AP Photo/ Jacquelyn Martin.*

are also reinforced through department policies and the chain of command. Socialization is a continuous process. As a result of this process, officers begin to socialize more with other members within the police social setting and begin to withdraw from nonwork friends Obst and Davey (2003).

TYPES OF POLICE OFFICERS

Based on the idea that police officer behavior is driven by either individual personality or work socialization, researchers have attempted to classify police behavior (Broderick, 1987; Coates, 1972; Muir, 1977; White, 1972). Studies have developed typologies of police behavior that could be used to explain how police officers perform their jobs and to explain differences between individual police officers when such differences exist. Essentially, these typologies assist in understanding how the police interact with the community.

Coates' (1972) typology consists of three types: (1) legalistic-abusive officers, (2) task officers, and (3) community service officers. Coates modeled his police officer types after Wilson's (1968) styles of police departments. The *legalistic-abusive officer* category refers to officers who typically come from legalistically oriented departments. These officers see themselves as protectors of the right moral standards. They tend to be rigid in their adherence to the criminal justice process and have little sympathy for anyone, regardless of circumstances, who violates the law. They make large numbers of arrests and write numerous tickets. *Task officers* are street-level bureaucrats who follow the department's rules and regulations without exception. They are very similar to the legalistic-abusive officers except that their motivation is adherence to the rules and the legalistic-abusive officers' motivation is the advancement of public morality. Finally, the *community service officer* uses discretion liberally and has a primary objective of helping people as opposed to enforcing law. They are the type of officers needed in community policing programs.

White (1972) examined police behavior and developed a typology consisting of four types: (1) tough cop, (2) problem solver, (3) crime fighter, and (4) rule applier. White developed her typology by examining police officer values and techniques used when performing police tasks. *Tough cops* see their jobs as keeping criminals under control. They typically use very repressive methods and are more concerned with the outcomes of their actions than the actions themselves. *Problem solvers* are police officers who tend to be more sympathetic to people's needs, viewing people as clients, not adversaries. They are commu- vocab nity oriented and view the law as one of many instruments that can be used to solve a specific problem. *Crime fighters* are zealots who see their role as enforc- vocab ing the law and view other police activities as being outside real police work. They typically are associated with legalistically styled police departments. Finally, the *rule appliers* are bureaucrats who operate by the book. They remain detached from their jobs and the citizens they serve.

Muir (1977) also classified four types of police officers: (1) professionals, (2) enforcers, (3) reciprocators, and (4) avoiders. Muir developed his classification system by examining the perspective from which police officers viewed their jobs, as well as the "morality of coercion" (whether the use of force is acceptable to the officer). *Professional* police officers are those who have an integrated sense of coercion and have sympathy for peoples' problems. Professional officers consider a complete range of solutions and mediate the rule of law and citizen needs when they select solutions. They understand that their job requires them to assume a variety of roles including law enforcer, social worker, counselor, and psychologist. The enforcer tends to be cynical and is coercion oriented. *Enforcers* tend to adhere to a "tough guy" model whereby they overindulge in law enforcement activities and see themselves as protecting law-abiding citizens from the numerous criminals who roam the streets. They seldom are empathetic and see the law as being "black and white." *Reciprocators* are officers who are sympathetic toward citizens and have difficulty applying coercive force. These officers want to help people, but they are hesitant to use force. They tend to give people the benefit of the doubt, and when things do not work out they become frustrated because of their proclivity to avoid force. They shun law enforcement activities and focus almost entirely on providing services to citizens. Finally, the *avoiders* are officers who avoid the use of coercion and have little sympathy for people. Basically, they are not suited for police work because they have difficulty with its two primary elements—they shirk their duties and withdraw from responsibility.

Broderick (1987) examined police behavior in terms of emphasizing the need for social order and due process of law. He identified four types of officers: (1) idealists, (2) enforcers, (3) optimists, and (4) realists. *Idealists* are high in their regard for both the need for social order and individual rights. Idealists frequently are frustrated because the protection of a suspect's rights interferes with the idealist's ability to maximize social order; subsequently, they become cynical and withdraw from their responsibilities. *Enforcers* emphasize law enforcement at the expense of due process and individual rights. Enforcers believe that the "ends always justify the means." They typically are very cynical and approach the job as crime fighters. They tend to view even the most minor infraction as being serious. *Optimists* have a high regard for due process but have little regard for social order. To them, people are more important than crime. Optimists are committed to their jobs and tend to emphasize community service. Finally, the *realists* have little concern for social order or due process. They take a "to hell with it" attitude and typically withdraw from as many of their responsibilities as possible.

The research by Coates (1972), White (1972), Muir (1977), and Broderick (1987) identified a number of differences between police officers within

Box 8.1   Comparison of Police Types

Researcher	Types
Coates (1972)	Legalistic-abusive officer
	Task officer
	Community service officer
White (1972)	Tough cop
	Problem solver
	Crime fighter
	Rule applier
Muir (1977)	Professional
	Enforcer
	Reciprocator
	Avoider
Broderick (1987)	Idealists
	Enforcers
	Optimists
	Realists

Box 8.2 Dimensions Used to Classify Police Behavior

Researcher	Dimensions
Coates (1972)	Used self-perceptions of police officers to develop typology. Did not attempt to use predetermined dimensions.
White (1972)	Used police officer values and the application of techniques. Either dimension could be anchored as particularistic (recognition that differences exist among people) or universalistic (belief that no differences exist).
Muir (1977)	Used morality or willingness to use coercion or force and perspective about citizens (either cynical or empathetic) as the classification dimensions.
Broderick (1987)	Used emphasis on the need for social order and emphasis on due process and individual rights as the dimensions in the classification system.

any given police department. Box 8.1 lists the various types of officers these researchers used to categorize police behavior. Box 8.2 identifies the characteristics the researchers used when developing their typologies. As suggested by Wilson (1968), the type of police department may affect the types of officers in a given jurisdiction.

These typologies demonstrate that police officers are not all the same, and every police department will have a variety of types of police officers on the street at any given time. A variety of influences, both formal and informal, may affect police behavior. Some types of officers may exist in one police department and not in another, and the proportion of each type likely is dependent on the socialization process.

THE ANTHROPOLOGICAL PERSPECTIVE

The *anthropological perspective* of police behavior holds that officers are influenced and shaped by their culture. Beliefs and values are transmitted from one generation of officers to the next in a learning process by which a cultural group teaches what behaviors are acceptable and unacceptable. This approach to understanding police behavior can be termed a *culturalization model*. This model assumes that culture determines both personality and behavior. One can, therefore, study the culture of a group to understand the behavior of its members. Although this model focuses on cultural characteristics instead of personality, neither is necessarily distinct, and many anthropologists study personality by systematically examining the cultural setting in which personality is developed and where behaviors are carried out.

FIGURE 8.2

Brockton police officers Matthew Graham, bottom left, and William Carpenter, bottom right, wait to be honored during the 26th annual Trooper George L. Hanna Jr. Memorial Awards ceremony for bravery at the House of Representatives Chambers at the Statehouse in Boston. *Photo courtesy of AP Photo/Lisa Poole.*

Of the three models of police behavior, the culturalization model is the broadest and will be explored in greater detail in the sections that follow. Figure 8.2 shows the relationships among three perspectives of police behavior, three basic models of behavior, and their ability to account for individual and group behavior (Box 8.3).

THE POLICE SUBCULTURE

The term _culture_ is often used to describe differences between large social groups. Culture is the entire array of human symbols and artifacts. To study culture is to study not only symbols and artifacts, but also how they are created and given meaning and value. Social groups differ in many aspects, and people from different cultures have varying beliefs, laws, morals, customs, and other characteristics that set them apart from people of other cultures. These values and artifacts are unique to a given people and are transmitted from one generation to the next in a learning process. Cultural distinctions are easy to see when one compares, for example, the American and Japanese cultures. Clearly, Americans have different laws, language, customs, religions, and art forms than do the Japanese. These characteristics make each of these cultures unique compared to other cultures around the world.

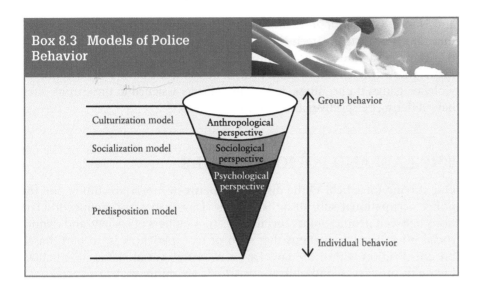

Box 8.3 Models of Police Behavior

There can also be cultural differences between people who form a single culture or social group. People who form a unique group within a given culture are members of a *subculture*. The difference between a culture and a subculture is that members of a subculture, although sharing many of the values and beliefs of the larger, more dominant culture, also have separate and distinct values. A subculture serves as a means by which individual and group identity are created through the expression of values, beliefs, and rituals that deviate from those of the larger culture. These differences make subculture members unique when compared to the larger, more dominant culture. Clearly, police officers in America share the same cultural heritage, speak the same language, operate under the same laws, and share many of the values of other Americans. But, there are certain aspects of the police subculture that make officers different from other members of society. The unique role and social status of the police in American society help to set police officers apart from other members of society; therefore, some scholars have maintained that the police are a unique occupational subculture.

From this point, it is possible to begin a discussion of the various elements of the police subculture that tend to shape the police social character and contribute to the unique behaviors of our nation's law enforcement officers. Although each police organization develops a unique and distinct subculture, many police organizations contain the same elements of culture described below. These elements, including world views, cultural themes like bravery, solidary and isolation, vary depending on the environment, organization, and social composition of the particular police department, and have both positive and negative results on the police and society.

The police subculture is complex in that some cultural values pervade the police department, whereas others may only exist within certain units. Klinger (1997) and Hassell (2007), upon examining police operations in large cities, found that police districts or precincts often are policed differently, demonstrating that there is variation in goals and culture across groups in a police department. These differences are more evident across some units such as domestic violence, gangs, traffic, drugs, and so on. Officers assigned to these units often have differing perspectives and cultural attributes.

THE LAW AND POLICE CULTURE

One driving force behind the distinction between American culture and the police occupational subculture is the law. Law shapes and defines interactions between people, grants social status to members of society, and defines social roles. The social status that each of us experiences is, in part, based on our position within the law. Law can bestow social status by articulating rights, privileges, and obligations. The law's ability to define social position can be as simple as the designation between who can and who cannot consume alcoholic beverages or as complex as who has the right to use the material resources of a society. The law defines who can do what, where, and when, and these distinctions are distributed differentially across members of society.

The police, by virtue of their social role, are granted a unique position in the law. Police officers have a legal monopoly on the sanctioned use of violence (Reiss, 1971; Reiss & Bordua, 1967; Westley, 1956) and coercion (Bittner, 1970; Westley, 1953) against other members of society. The legal sanctions that prevent citizens from resorting to violence are relaxed for police officers (Kappeler et al., 1998). Police officers often resort to violence or coercion to accomplish their goals of controlling crime and maintaining order. The police, therefore, are set apart from other members of society because of their unique position in the law and their ability to legally use violence. This distinction between citizens and the police sets officers apart from the larger American culture.

The effect of the law on the police as an occupational group, however, is more complex than just setting officers apart from citizens. The law shapes police perceptions of events, situations, and even their own self-image. Herbert (1998:353) remarked that officers routinely attempt to define situations in terms of existing law: "The law thus works … as a prism through which officers view an event for evidence of wrongdoing, and base their response accordingly." The law serves as a fundamental value of police culture, as well as a window that frames their view of the world. One must remember, however, that the cultural window on the world works two ways. Although police officers use the law to help define situations, other aspects of police culture determine what situations police feel are in need of their attention. The law itself is interpreted from a police value system that in part determines when and how the law is to be applied to the situations they encounter. In essence, police culture and the law represent a complex dance between reading the law as a fundamental value and interpreting the law based on police occupational values.

THE POLICE WORLDVIEW

The concept of a cultural _worldview_ can be defined as the manner in which a culture sees the world and its own role and relationship to the world (Redfield, 1952). This means that various social groups, including the police, perceive the world, people, and situations differently from other social groups. Attorneys may view the world, and events that happen in the world, as sources of conflict and potential litigation. Physicians may view the world as a place of disease and illness. These views of the world set the stage for determining what events or circumstances constitute problems, what solutions might be appropriate to solve these problems, and what courses of action are to be taken. The police worldview develops because of the "combined features of their social situation" and causes officers to "develop ways of looking at the world distinctive to themselves; cognitive lenses through which to see situations and events" (Skolnick, 1966). The way the police see the world has been described as a "we–they" or "us–them" orientation. Police officers tend to see the world as being composed of cops and others. If a person is not a police officer, he or she tends to be considered an outsider who is viewed with some level of suspicion (Figure 8.3).

Various factors contribute to the development of a "we–they" worldview. Police officers undergo a formal socialization experience when they enter the police academy. Bahn (1984:392) noted that in the police academy: The rookie soon learns that the way to "survive" in the academy (not to be singled out for attention or ridicule) is to maintain a "low profile," by being one of the group, acting like the others. Group cohesiveness and mutuality are encouraged by the instructors as well. The early roots of a separation between "the police" and "the public" are evident in many lectures and classroom discussions. In "war stories" and corridor anecdotes, it emerges as a full blown "us–them" mentality.

Officers learn about and experience the potential for danger through these "war stories" and field training after graduation from the police academy. Both the authority and danger inherent in police work indisputably form a great part of the American police officer's picture of the world. Police officers often see the world as a place of danger and potential injury; thus, officers tend to view citizens as potential sources of violence or even as enemies. These elements of

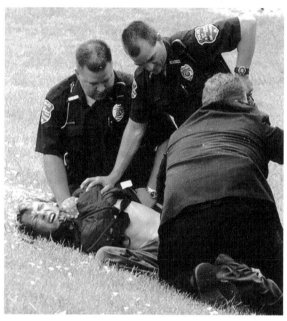

FIGURE 8.3

In Wisconsin, West Bend Police Department officers arrest a suspect in the robbery of a bank. *Photo courtesy of AP Photo/West Bend Daily News, Nathan Pier.*

To view a video of a Kentucky state trooper funeral procession, go to **http:// youtube.com/watch?v=1mXX3H1U7e4**

the police subculture do much to foster the "we–they" police worldview. Because the primary tools used by the police are violence and coercion, it was easy for the police to develop a paramilitary model of organization (Bittner, 1970). In this military model, likeness of dress, action, and thought is promoted. This military model has done much to foster the "we–they" perspective of police. Such a model allows police officers to see themselves as a close-knit, distinct group, and can even promote a view of citizens as "outsiders and enemies" (Sherman, 1982; Westley, 1956). Woody (2006) quoted a police officer in the following statement that captures the power of the police worldview: "The world is a jungle; there are a lot of bad people who will harm you and then go home and sleep like a baby; all that stands between good and evil is law enforcement; our survival depends on taking care of each other; there is no other dependable source."

The real and exaggerated sense of danger inherent in police work indisputably influences a police officer's picture of the world, such that citizens are viewed as potential sources of violence or enemies. Citizens become symbolic assailants to the police officer on the street (Skolnick, 1966). The *symbolic assailant* is further refined in appearance by taking on the characteristics of the marginal segments of society that police frequently come into contact with. The image of the symbolic assailant takes on the characteristics of the populations police are directed to control. To the cop in southern Texas, the young Latino man becomes the potential assailant; in Atlanta, it is the poor, inner-city African-American man; in Chinatown, it is the Asian who may resort to violence against the police (Kappeler et al., 1998). The element of danger emphasized by the police culture does much to foster the "we–they" worldview; it also focuses police attention on selective behaviors of certain members of society.

Research on the actual dangers of police work calls into question the stereotypic conception of the hazards associated with police work (Kappeler & Potter, 2005). Brandl and Stroshine's (2003) examined the injuries sustained by police officers and concluded that assaults on officers are relatively rare events, as are serious injuries and deaths. Rather, most injury incidents are a result of accidents. Yet, police officers consider the potential for assault as one of the most stressful aspects of police work. The aspect of danger in police work is so powerful that one study (Garcia, Nesbary, & Gu, 2004) concluded that "concern for a fellow officer being injured or killed … reinforces the frequent perceived potential for crisis situations, even during a period of low crime. This aspect continues to differentiate police work from most other occupations."

POLICE BRAVERY, AUTONOMY, AND SECRECY

Bravery is a central component of the social character and culture of policing. As such, it is related to the perceived and actual dangers of law enforcement. The potential to become the victim of a violent encounter, the need for support by fellow officers during such encounters, and the legitimate use of violence to accomplish the police mandate all contribute to a subculture that stresses the virtue of bravery. Also, the military trappings of policing, organizational policy (such as "never back down"), the increasing use of military tactics in the war on drugs, and informal peer pressure all contribute to instilling a sense of bravery in the police subculture. Herbert (1998) observed that "Officers thus encourage each other to summon the necessary bravery to handle potentially perilous calls. They also encourage each other to ensure the preservation of their own life and the lives of others. … Roll calls regularly end with the admonishment "stay safe out there." Officers express satisfaction when a tour of duty ends without mishap."

The real and exaggerated sense of danger inherent in police work and obsession with safety manifest themselves in forms of police behavior that are grounded in the *ethos* of bravery. Police behaviors can range from the violation of law because of the perceived need for safety, to the evaluation of probationary officers based on their ability to demonstrate bravery. It is not unusual for training officers to wait until a new recruit has faced a dangerous situation before recommending that the recruit be given full status on the department. Peer acceptance usually does not come until new officers have proven themselves in a dangerous situation. Officers in the department are often very concerned with how new officers will deal with dangerous situations. Will they show bravery?

An excessive concern with professional *autonomy* is also evident in the police subculture's use of and focus on discretionary law enforcement. The nature of police work results in officers demanding, and normally receiving, much autonomy in law enforcement and legal sanctioning. As the frontline of the criminal justice process, police officers must make authoritative decisions about who to arrest and when to use force. This desire for autonomy in decision-making often exists despite departmental, judicial, or community standards designed to limit the discretion of street enforcement officers. The need for autonomy can contribute to a sense of personally defined justice by members of the police subculture, and a widespread belief that one who has not done police work should have little or no input in restricting police authority. Personal interpretations of justice and personal preferences could lead to abuses of discretion and authority.

In many police subcultures, *secrecy* is a central organizing concept of police values. The police code of secrecy is often the result of a fear of loss of autonomy and authority as external groups try to limit police discretion and decision-making ability. A second factor supporting the development of a code of secrecy is the fact that policing is fraught with the potential for error. Officers feel that they are called upon to make split-second decisions that can be reviewed by others not directly involved in policing. The desire to protect one's coworkers from disciplinary actions and from being accused of making an improper decision can promote the development of a code of secrecy (Manning, 2006) and the use of cover stories or lies (Hunt & Manning, 1994) when police are confronted with wrongdoing (see Box 8.4).

The police code of secrecy is also a product of the police perception of the media and their investigative function. Some researchers suggest that police officers are very concerned with the manner in which the media reports their actions (Berg, Gertz, & True, 1984). This, coupled with a police perception of the media as hostile, biased, and unsupportive, contributes to friction in police–media relations and increased police secrecy. However, it is also often necessary for officers to refrain from making media releases, participating in public discussion, or commenting on current criminal investigations. The media, citizens, and others often interpret this practice as a self-imposed

Box 8.4 Sounds of Silence

One of policing's dirty little secrets is out: The so-called "blue wall of silence," in which cops close ranks to minimize, cover up, or lie about wrongdoing to protect accused colleagues, is now a matter of federal record, following the recent conviction on civil-rights charges of a fired New York City police officer who choked a man to death....

Francis X. Livoti, who was acquitted in state court two years ago of charges of criminally negligent homicide stemming from the death of Anthony Baez, 29, of the Bronx, was convicted June 26 by a jury in Federal District Court that took just five hours to reach a verdict. Livoti, 38, faces up to 10 years in prison when he is sentenced by Judge Shira A. Scheindlin on Sept. 24.

The death of Baez, who was confronted by Livoti after a football he was throwing landed on the officer's cruiser, prompted a fiery debate on police brutality and the role that the blue wall of silence plays in ensuring that officers are not held accountable for in-custody deaths or other actions.

The blue wall of silence was a central element of the prosecution's claim that officers who arrived at the scene of the confrontation and those who subsequently investigated Baez's death had lied and covered up to protect Livoti.

A juror said after the verdict that the panel agreed with federal prosecutors that three officers connected to the case lied on the stand. "All three lied," said a 25-year-old city resident who was not identified by the local media. "It wasn't just that they were trying to cover up for Livoti, but for themselves, because if they were witnesses to a crime, they were conspirators in the act."

The verdict, said Mary Jo White, the U.S. Attorney for the Southern District of New York, "shows that police officers who commit acts of brutality can be prosecuted and convicted, even, as the Government stated in its summation, when other officers fabricate testimony or cover up the truth."

Livoti was booted from the Police Department last year after an in-house trial found him guilty of using a banned choke-hold restraint on Baez.

Livoti, who had an extensive record of brutality complaints, was kept on patrol despite recommendations by his commander that he be transferred to a desk job or to a less stressful precinct. Prosecutors suggested Livoti's status and connections as a delegate for the Patrolmen's Benevolent Association, the powerful city police union, prevented the commander's recommendation from being carried out.

White hinted that investigations of three officers suspected of lying in the case are being pursued, perhaps with an eye toward federal perjury charges. White would say only that the investigation "of the entire matter, including a review of all trial testimony, is continuing."

The officers from the 45th Precinct—Sgt. William Monahan, who was Livoti's supervisor on the night of Baez's death, and officers Anthony Farnan and Mario Erotokritou—were stripped of their guns and badges and placed on modified duty, prompting speculation that they'll soon have perjury charges filed against them, The New York Daily News reported. Their claims that Baez was still alive after Livoti released him from the choke-hold were contradicted by another officer at the scene....

Prosecutors detailed meetings held between Livoti and officers on the scene in the hours and days following the incident, including meetings in the precinct house parking lot, and with their lawyers at PBA headquarters.

The jury was not allowed to hear testimony from Officer Daisy Boria, the only officer on the scene who said Baez did not rise and walk a few steps after Livoti released him from the hold, in which she claimed that officers concocted a cover story blaming a fictitious black man for choking Baez to death before running off into the night. Boria did provide testimony about post-incident meetings of officers who discussed the case outside the precinct house.

Most of the meetings were held during the period under the department's "48-hour rule," which gives officers involved in shootings or in-custody deaths a two-day grace period from having to face internal investigators. Prosecutors charged that the rule, which the city is attempting to have removed from future police labor contracts, provided the delay needed to get their stories straight.

Monahan did not give a full account of the incident to his own superiors or the Bronx District Attorney's Office. He made no statement for months, and then, only after meeting with Livoti. "He's got to make up a story," said assistant U.S. Attorney Andrew S. Dember during his summation to the jury. "But before he tells anybody the story, he meets with the defendant in the PBA offices and they discuss the case."

Boria is seeking to quit the NYPD and has filed for a tax-free disability pension. She reportedly became the target of threats following her testimony in Livoti's 1996 state homicide trial. The judge presiding over the bench trial acquitted Livoti, although he complained of a "nest of perjury" in conflicting testimony given by Boria and the three other officers.

Source: "Sounds of Silence," Law Enforcement News, September 15, 1998, p. 7.

censorship of information. Perceptions of this nature can promote the separation of the public and the police and create the impression of a secret police society.

POLICE ISOLATION AND SOLIDARITY

Isolation is an emotional and physical condition that makes it difficult for members of one social group to have relationships and interact with members of another group. This feeling of separateness from the surrounding society is a frequently noted attribute of the American police subculture (Harris, 1973; Kirkham, 1974; Manning, 2006; Reiss & Bordua, 1967; Sherman, 1982; Skolnick, 1966; Westley, 1953, 1956, 1970). Social isolation, as a theme of police subculture, is a logical result of the interaction of the American police worldview and code of secrecy. The self-imposed social isolation of the police from the surrounding community is well documented (Baldwin, 1962; Banton, 1964; Cain, 1973; Clark, 1965; Skolnick, 1966; Swanton, 1981).

Police isolation reinforces the police worldview. Persons outside the police subculture are viewed somewhat warily as potential threats to the members' physical or emotional well-being, as well as to the officers' authority and autonomy. Police officers isolate themselves from other social groups and begin to restrict their interactions to other members of their own profession. This limited interaction results in officers sharing and reinforcing an occupationally generated but very limited view of the world—a view constructed by the police. According to Baldwin (1962) and Skolnick (1966), police officers impose social isolation upon themselves as a means of protection against real and perceived dangers, loss of personal and professional autonomy, and social rejection. Rejection by the community stems, in part, from the potentially undesirable consequences that arise from police actions when laws are enforced (Clark, 1965). Clark (1965) and Westley (1953, 1956, 1970) noted that self-imposed restrictions on personal interactions with the community are not the only factors of police isolation. This theme is supported by the police occupational structure, one that looks inward to its own members for validity and support (Box 8.5).

Swanton (1981) examined the theme of police isolation and identified two primary groups of determinants that promote social isolation and are specific to the police subculture. Swanton maintained that these determinants were either (1) self-imposed by the police or (2) externally imposed upon the police by the community. Self-imposed police determinants identified by the author generally concerned work-related requirements of the policing profession: administrative structures, work structures, and personality structures. Swanton found that the nature of police work—enforcing the law, detecting and apprehending criminals—creates a sense of suspicion in police officers, resulting in

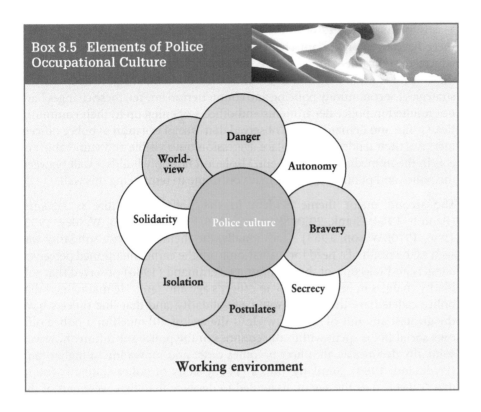

Box 8.5 Elements of Police Occupational Culture

Danger
World-view
Autonomy
Solidarity
Police culture
Bravery
Isolation
Secrecy
Postulates

Working environment

their frequently equating attempts at community interaction or kindness with subterfuges designed to compromise the officer's official position.

An additional deterrent to the maintenance of cordial relations with members of the general community outside the police subculture is the ambiguity evident in the police officer's on-duty and off-duty status. Swanton noted that the long and often irregular working hours—a result of shift schedules and possible cancellation of days off or vacations—coupled with the community's perception of police work as socially unattractive, contribute to the police officer's sense of isolation. Swanton's publicly initiated determinants of isolation include the following:

1. Suspicion that police compromise their friendships with higher loyalty to their employer.
2. Resentment at police-initiated sanction or the potential thereof.
3. Attempts at integrations by those wishing to curry favor, which are resented by others.
4. Personality of police being perceived as socially unattractive, thereby reducing the motivation of nonpolice to form close relationships with them.

Mastrofski and Willis (2010) note that this isolation has endured even though there have been significant changes in law enforcement. Officers are better educated, police departments have adopted an array of technology to better understand community conditions, and police departments have adopted new strategies for community policing and counterterrorism. Yet, these changes have not resulted in police departments and officers opening up to their communities. Griffin and Bernard (2003) observed that "social isolation of police officers increases their tendency to displace aggression onto visible and vulnerable targets in the immediate environment." Isolation not only builds a wall between the police and public, but it also may contribute to reinforcing this wall.

The second major theme evident in the police subculture is *solidarity* (Banton, 1964; Crank, 2010; Skolnick, 1966; Stoddard, 2006; Westley, 1953, 1956, 1970; Wilson, 1963). Traditionally, the theme of police solidarity was seen as the result of a need for insulation from the earlier mentioned perceived dangers and rejection of the community. Ferdinand (1980) observed that solidarity changes in proportion to an officer's age and rank. He maintained that police cadets have the least amount of solidarity, and that line officers have the greatest amount of solidarity. Until the age of 40, much of a police officer's social life is spent within the confines of the police subculture; however, solidarity declines as an officer becomes older and moves into a higher rank (Ferdinand, 1980). Similarly, Britz's (1997) study of police solidarity found that "officers over the age of 40 tended to disagree that 'they were part of the gang.' … Young officers may display a need for organizational belongingness, whereas the primacy of organizational fit may diminish for older officers who tend to be more comfortable in their social networks." Older officers and members of the police administrative hierarchy are frequently seen by line officers in much the same perspective as members of the community and other nonpolice characters—namely, as threatening to the welfare of the subculture.

Police solidarity, therefore, may be said to be an effect of the socialization process inherent to the subculture. New members are heavily socialized to increase their solidarity with the group, and those who move away from the subculture, through either age or promotion, are gradually denied the ties of solidarity. This socialization, or cohesion, is based, in part, upon the sameness of roles, perceptions, and self-imagery of the members of the police subculture, rather than any inherent personality characteristics of police recruits.

POLICE POSTULATES AND THE CODE

Postulates are statements of belief held by a culture that reflect its basic orientations. Postulates are expressions of general truth or principle that are accepted by a subculture. Such statements enable one to understand the nuances of a subculture. Postulates act as oral vehicles for the transmission of culture from one generation to the next, and they tend to serve as a reinforcer of the subcultural worldview. Postulates basic to an understanding of the police subculture have been collected and arranged into a semiformal code of police conduct. Reuss-Ianni (1983), drawing from the research of many others (Manning, 2006; Savitz, 1971; Skolnick, 1966; Stoddard, 2006; Westley, 1953, 1956), identified 21 police postulates that may be divided into three separate categories: postulates that support the earlier discussed concepts of the police subculture's worldviews, ethos, and themes:

Postulates indicative of the "we–they" worldview and supportive of police isolationism:

1. Don't tell anybody else more than they have to know; it could be bad for you and it could be bad for them.
2. Don't trust a new guy until you have checked him out.
3. Don't give them (the bosses) too much activity.
4. Keep out of the way of any boss from outside your precinct.
5. Know your bosses.
6. Don't do the bosses' work for them.
7. Don't trust bosses to look out for your interests.
8. Don't talk too much or too little.
9. Protect your ass.

Postulates indicative of bravery:

1. Show balls.
2. Be aggressive when you have to, but don't be too eager.

Postulates indicative of secrecy and solidarity:

1. Watch out for your partner first and then the rest of the guys working.
2. Don't give up another cop.
3. Don't get involved in anything in another cop's sector.
4. Hold up your end of the work.
5. If you get caught off base, don't implicate anybody else.
6. Make sure the other guys know if another cop is dangerous or "crazy."
7. Don't leave work for the next tour.
8. Don't make waves.
9. Don't look for favors just for yourself.
10. Don't take on the patrol sergeant yourself.

Through exposure to postulates, new generations of police officers combine their experiences and perceptions of the world viewed through a police officer's eyes with these "truths" and develop a belief system that dictates acceptable and unacceptable behavior. These postulates serve as unconscious reinforcers of the police worldview and act as part of the socialization process for members of a subculture. Violations of these canons may lead to immediate sanctions from fellow subculture members, frequently resulting in some form of expulsion from the security of the group. Ironically, therefore, police officers who violate the precepts of the subculture are doubly isolated—first from the community they service, by nature of the profession, and later by the subcultural community, for violating its norms of conduct.

POLICE SUBCULTURES OF VIOLENCE AND SOCIAL CONTEXT

The emergence of strong occupational cultures with policing can have negative consequences for both those who work within the profession and those exposed to the police. Citizens and police officers alike are affected by the police culture. In some incidents, police organizations overemphasize certain elements of their subculture. This can manifest itself in a decadent subculture. One area of growing research in the study of police culture is the emergence of *subcultures of violence*. Some police organizations have emphasized the bravery and danger elements of policing to such an extent that they have created an environment conducive to citizen victimization. Although seemingly countless acts of police violence have been captured by the media, several historic cases of police brutality illustrate the sometimes systemic and negative consequences of police subcultures. Each of these tragic cases brought police violence to the attention of the public and has generated reforms to the police institution. Perhaps no other case in American police history has attracted more public attention and resulted in more reform than did the Los Angeles Police beating of motorist Rodney King.

On Sunday, March 3, 1991, from the balcony of his apartment, amateur video camera enthusiast George Holliday captured footage of Los Angeles Police Department (LAPD) officers beating a 25-year-old, unemployed African-American man after a traffic stop. Rodney King's vehicle was speeding on the Foothill freeway. King's vehicle apparently approached a California Highway Patrol (CHP) car from the rear and ultimately passed it. The CHP officers reportedly tried to signal King to stop by activating their emergency equipment, but King failed to stop his vehicle. Instead, King continued to drive for several more miles, allegedly running a stop sign and running through a red light. Meanwhile, CHP officials notified the LAPD that they were attempting to stop the vehicle. Eventually, an LAPD patrol car assigned to Officers Laurence W. Powell and Timothy Wind, a cruiser assigned to LAPD Officers Theodore J. Briseno and Rolando Solano, and a cruiser from the Los Angeles Unified School District Police (LAUSDP) became involved in the pursuit. King pulled his vehicle curbside, and police from several agencies converged on the scene. According to the Christopher Commission's (1991) investigation of the incident, "11 additional LAPD units (including a helicopter) with 21 officers arrived at the end-of-pursuit scene." The unarmed King initially refused to exit the vehicle, but when he did he was shocked twice with a 50,000-V Taser® by LAPD Sgt. Stacey Koon, savagely hit in the head "baseball-bat style" with nightsticks by Officers Powell and Wind, and repeatedly kicked by Officer Briseno. In all, Rodney King was struck at least 56 times by the LAPD officers. At least 21 and as many as 27 officers stood watching or participated in the beating, including LAPD supervisor Stacey Koon, four uniformed members of the CHP, four LAPD field training officers, and several officers from different law enforcement agencies (Christopher Commission, 1991). Two minutes later, Rodney King was lying crumpled on the ground with 11 skull fractures, a broken cheekbone, a fractured eye socket, a broken ankle, missing teeth, kidney damage, external burns, and permanent brain damage (Kappeler et al., 1998) (Box 8.6).

As Skolnick and Fyfe (1993) observed, "Two cops can go berserk, but 20 cops embody a subculture of policing." The Christopher Commission's (1991) investigation into the LAPD found "a significant number of LAPD officers who repetitively misuse force and persistently ignore the written policies and guidelines of the Department regarding force." The Commission examined records

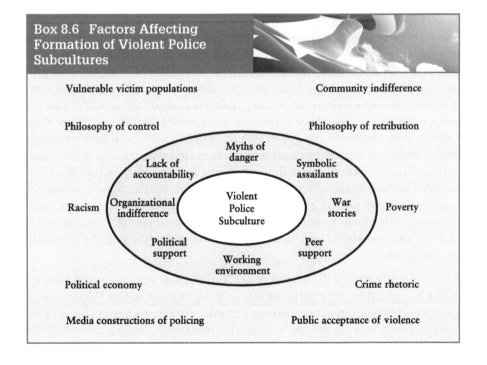

Box 8.6 Factors Affecting Formation of Violent Police Subcultures

from the police patrol officers' mobile digital terminals (MDTs), which police use to communicate with one another, and its review of 182 days of MDT communications uncovered literally "hundreds of improper messages, including scores in which officers talked about beating suspects. … Officers also used the communications system to express their eagerness to be involved in shooting incidents. The transmissions also made clear that some officers enjoy the excitement of a pursuit and view it as an opportunity for violence against a fleeing suspect." The Commission (1991) concluded that:

> The LAPD has an organizational culture that emphasizes crime control over crime prevention and that isolates the police from the communities and the people they serve. With the full support of many, the LAPD insists on aggressive detection of major crimes and a rapid, seven-minute response time to calls for service. Patrol officers are evaluated by statistical measures (for example, the number of calls handled and arrests made) and are rewarded for being "hard-nosed." This style of policing produces results, but it does so at the risk of creating a siege mentality that alienates the officer from the community. Witness after witness testified to unnecessarily aggressive confrontations between LAPD officers and citizens, particularly members of minority communities. From the statements of these citizens, as well as many present and former senior LAPD officers, it is apparent that too many LAPD patrol officers view citizens with resentment and hostility.

The LAPD is not the only police agency that has been plagued with pockets of violent officers. In 1997, one of the most gruesome police brutality cases the nation has experienced came to light in the New York Police Department (NYPD). Abner Louima, an immigrant from Haiti employed as a security guard, went to a Brooklyn nightclub. As patrons left the club at closing time, a fight broke out between two women. Officers from Brooklyn's 70th precinct responded to the disturbance. Louima was arrested by officers Justin Volpe and Thomas Bruder on charges of assault, resisting arrest, disorderly conduct, and obstructing justice. Prosecutors later surmised that Louima was targeted and assaulted because officers thought he was the African-American man who sucker-punched Volpe while police tried to break up the fight. Louima was handcuffed and put in a patrol car driven by Thomas Wiese and Charles Schwarz. When he protested, the police shouted racial epithets, put Louima in a patrol car, and kicked and beat Louima with police radios on the way to the station house.

In the public lobby of the station house, Louima was stripped naked from the waist down and brought in handcuffs to the bathroom where Volpe, wearing gloves borrowed from another officer, shoved a wooden stick into Louima's rectum and then into his mouth, breaking his front teeth. During the assault, the officers taunted him with, "We're going to teach niggers to respect police officers" and "This is Giuliani time, not Dinkins time." After the attack, Volpe was seen carrying the stick and returning the stained gloves to the owner. At 6:00 a.m., an ambulance was called. Although it arrived at 6:25 a.m., it did not leave the station until 7:58 a.m. because paramedics are required to wait for officers to escort them. Louima was taken to Coney Island Hospital, where doctors performed surgery to repair a ripped bladder and punctured lower intestine (Figure 8.4).

Mayor Giuliani visited Louima in the hospital and vowed that justice would be served. He called for 6 months of community forums between city residents and members of the police force. Although two police officers came forward with information about the assault weeks after the investigation, interviews of more than 100 police officers provided little more information, and many speculated that the code of silence was serving as a formidable barrier to the investigation.

In the aftermath of the 2005 London transit system bombings, English police deployed an anti-terror operation. As part of the investigation, police began surveillance of a home in south London. A few days after the bombings, a 27-year-old Brazilian man, Jean Charles de Menezes, emerged from the home and took a bus to the Stockwell Underground station. According to initial police reports, his "clothing and suspicious behavior at the station" led to a confrontation. When confronted by police, he allegedly failed to obey orders and jumped a ticket barrier in the station. The unarmed Menezes was shot and killed by police. Although police initially claimed that he was connected to the transit bombing, it was later learned that there was no connection between

FIGURE 8.4
Abner Louima talks with reporters outside his Miami Lakes, Florida, residence after a federal appeals court threw out the convictions of three of the four white officers sent to prison in the torture of Louima. *Photo courtesy of AP Photo/Richard Patterson.*

the man and the terrorist attacks: "In a statement, Scotland Yard said … that contrary to earlier reports, de Menezes had not run into the Tube station, had not been wearing a padded jacket and that he had not vaulted the ticket barrier" (Anonymous, 2005a). He was apparently shot, seated, and detained, not while scuffling with the police. Following this revelation, police immediately released photographs of the subway carnage and warned the public that these were proper police actions. The "Metropolitan Police Commissioner said he regretted Menezes' death but defended the policy of shooting to kill 'suspected suicide bombers' and warned that more people could be shot" (Anonymous, 2005b). The police had altered their view of crime and created a new and dangerous bridge between representation and experience.

On December 7, 2005, aboard American Airlines Flight 924 in Miami, Florida, a 44-year-old American citizen born in Costa Rica was killed. Rigo Alpizar and his wife were passengers on the flight on their way home to Maitland, Florida. According to a spokesman for the federal air marshals, moments before the shooting Alpizar ran up and down the aisle of the plane yelling, "I have a bomb in my bag." The marshals ordered, "Drop your bag, drop your bag. Come to the ground. I'm a federal law enforcement officer. Police. Drop your bag." When Alpizar failed to comply and appeared to reach into his bag, he was shot and killed.

An investigation following the incident, however, found no witness who publicly confirmed the marshals' account of the shooting, and no bomb was discovered. One witness to the incident said the marshals were too quick to shoot and kill Alpizar. John McAlhany claimed that marshals did not need to use deadly force and that Alpizar never said he had a bomb. "I never heard the word 'bomb' on the plane," McAlhany told a reporter during a phone telephone interview. "I never heard the word 'bomb' until the FBI asked me did you hear the word 'bomb.' That is ridiculous" (Anonymous, 2005c).

McAlhany had been seated in the middle of the plane, and Alpizar was in the back. McAlhany heard Alpizar arguing with his wife, telling her that he had to get off the plane. Alpizar began to run down the aisle; his wife followed informing the other passengers (including the marshals) that he was sick and had a disorder. McAlhany tried to see what happened but only heard five shots. McAlhany was on the phone with his brother when a federal agent put a shotgun to the back of his head and knocked the cell phone from his hand. "They were pointing the guns directly at us instead of pointing them to the ground," he said (Anonymous, 2005c; Morrissey, 2005).

In 2013, the *Illinois Torture Inquiry and Relief Commission* released a report detailing torture by the Chicago Police Department. The Commission fount 17 credible instances were Chicago detectives used torture to elicit confessions from suspects. The detectives known as the "midnight crew" physically assaulted suspects to elicit confessions. The report noted that the detectives often used coercion on mentally handicapped and psychologically vulnerable suspects. In one case, a 15 year old was allegedly punched and kicked, and detectives threatened to throw him out a window during a 16-h interrogation (Meisner, 2013).

Police violence and wrongdoing are the products of a complex grouping of factors that involve the decisions of individual officers, peer support among police, subculture, and organizational socialization, as well as the social and political contexts in which they occur.

These cases of police violence demonstrate that police violence and the emergence of violent police subcultures do not occur in isolation from their social context. Public fear, political rhetoric, and tragic events all shape and contour the acceptability of police violence and even the types of people who are targeted by the police. High levels of public fear can shift social priorities away from police accountability and concerns with police behavior, to wanting the police to do whatever seems necessary to confront these fears.

POLICE STRESS

Stress is a neutral term, but it often carries a negative connotation. Stress can have both beneficial and adverse affects on people. Some people may perform and produce at their best when enough stress is present to encourage or motivate high levels of performance. People experiencing mild forms of stress may have an increased sense of awareness or alertness and may therefore be capable of better performance in certain situations; however, the term is more often associated with its dysfunctional aspects. Some have defined stress in terms of its negative aspects—a personal–environmental fit problem (Lofquist & Davis, 1969). From this model of stress, individuals are seen as being unable to cope with the demands made upon them by their environment. Sometimes, excessive environmental stressors can be debilitating and hinder performance and productivity. Individuals experiencing excessive stress may begin to falter in their occupations and personal lives.

Stress cannot be examined in a vacuum. One way to understand stress is through the demand-control-support model. According to this model, when officers are placed in a stressful environment or situation (demand), it can be mediated through control (officers' ability to deal with the stress and support) formal and informal mechanisms to support officers and assist them in dealing with the stress (Chrisopoulos, Dollard, Winefiled, & Dormann, 2010).

Thus, stress is dynamic varying across officers and situations. Some officers are more adept at dealing with stress than others.

There is a lack of agreement on the extent of police stress and its effects on police officers. In addition, scholars are also divided on the sources of police stress. Some researchers view stress as a personal adjustment problem; that is, certain individuals are not capable of performing under the strains of the occupational demands. Because no two people are alike, stress has differing effects on police officers. From this perspective, it has been suggested that personal needs, values, abilities, and experiences all affect how individuals respond to the stress of their work environment.

A second and very different perspective sees stress as a structural problem that does not reside in any personal maladjustment, but in pathology of the environment, organization, or subculture. Researchers taking this perspective examine factors such as management style, role conflict, and other potential sources of stress. Scholars adopting this structural explanation feel that if people are unable to perform, then it is the environment that is pathological, not the individual. An emerging body of research tends to confirm this position. A study conducted by Hart and Cotton (2003) found that the organizational context of policing, rather than the actual work of the police, influenced officers' intentions to withdraw from the occupation, whether by using sick time or by seeking other jobs. Morale, too, has been shown to be a product of the organizational climate (Griffin, Hart, & Wilson-Everard, 2000). Likewise, Hassell and Brandl's (2009) study of police confirmed that workplace climate has a profound effect on the stress experienced by officers. Nonetheless, it is

Myths of Police Stress

Myth: Policing is inherently more stressful than other occupations.
Reality: There is no conclusive evidence that supports this proposition.
Myth: Working the streets is the most stressful aspect of policing.
Reality: Officers repeatedly report that "organization life" produces more stress than street work.
Myth: Because of stress, police officers experience higher rates of suicide, substance abuse, and divorce than the general population.

Reality: The rates of suicide, substance abuse, and divorce experienced by police are no greater than for populations with similar demographic characteristics.
Myth: The stresses of police work result in a host of health problems for officers, including a shorter life expectancy.
Reality: There is no conclusive research demonstrating that police officers experience health problems at any greater rate than populations with similar lifestyles. Smoking, drinking, poor diet, and a sedentary lifestyle may provide a more adequate explanation for these maladies.

questionable if the police work environment is any more stressful than other work environments. All jobs present levels of stress.

Although research and perspectives on police stress are divided between those who view policing as inherently more stressful than other occupations and those who see policing as no more stressful than other occupations, most would agree that police work can be stressful. Stress has been linked to many problems, including health issues such as cardiovascular disease and depression, which are prevalent in law enforcement (Collins & Gibbs, 2003; Franke, Ramsey, & Shelly, 2002). It has also been linked to maladaptive and antisocial behavior, such as problem drinking, hyper-aggressive behavior, and spousal abuse (Gershon, Barocas, Canton, Xianbin, & Vlahov, 2009; Kohan & O'Connor, 2002).

Sources of Police Stress

Hundreds of studies and articles have been written on the topic of police stress. Most of these articles are not scientific, but rather speculate as to the causes and effects of police stress. David Carter (1994) studied police stress and its sources. He has devised a typology of police stress that consists of seven general sources of police stress. This typology of sources of police stress, or *stressors*, includes (Barker & Carter, 1994:276–277):

1. **Life-threatening stressors**—These are characterized by the embodiment of a constant potential of injury or death. A particularly important aspect of these stressors is the knowledge that violent acts against police officers are intentional rather than accidental behaviors. Because the potential of a life-threatening situation is constant, the stressors are inherently cumulative.
2. **Social isolation stressors**—Included in this category are such factors as isolation and alienation from the community, differential socioeconomic status between the police and their constituency, authoritarianism, cynicism, and cultural distinction, prejudice, and discrimination.
3. **Organizational stressors**—This source of stress is particularly significant but too frequently overlooked (notably at the practical level). These stressors deal with all aspects of organizational life, both formal and informal. Specific stressors include peer pressure, role models, performance measures for evaluation, upward mobility, policies and procedures (or the lack thereof leading to inconsistent and/or unacceptable behavior), job satisfaction, training, morale, inadequate supervision and administrative control, inadequate training, internal organizational jealousy (including "empire building"), management philosophy, the organizational structure, and leadership styles. Thus, simply being a member of an organization and trying to succeed can provide a significant amount of stress for the officer.

4. **Functional stressors**—These are variables specifically related to the performance of assigned policing duties. Included in this category is role conflict, the use of discretion, knowledge of law and legal mandates, and decision-making responsibilities such as the use of force, when to stop and question persons, and how to resolve domestic disputes. If an officer does not have a good understanding of his/her responsibilities and is ill-prepared to handle them, stress will increase.

5. **Personal stressors**—These are stressors that have their primary origin in the officer's off-duty life, such as family problems or financial constraints. Particularly noteworthy in this grouping are marital difficulties, school or social problems of children, family illnesses, and associated personal or family crises. The literature indicates that such stressors clearly influence an officer's on-duty personality, affecting both attitude and behavior.

6. **Physiological stressors**—A change in one's physiology and general health may also affect one's decision-making capabilities, as well as one's tolerance of others' behavior. Fatigue from working off-duty jobs, the physiological impact of shift work (which interrupts the biological clock), changes in physiological responses during critical incidents (e.g., getting an adrenaline rush), and illness or medical conditions are all examples of physiological stressors.

7. **Psychological stressors**—Most of the stressors discussed above could also be classified in this category. For example, fear that is generated when an officer responds to a dangerous call can be a psychological stressor. The fear may be functional if the officer recognizes it as a warning mechanism and becomes more alert as a result. However, if the officer masks that fear and it becomes internalized, it can upset one's psychological balance. Other stress variables in this category include constant exposure to the worst side of humankind and the impact of resolving situations that are of a repulsive nature (e.g., homicides, child abuse, fatal traffic accidents). These situations can have a traumatic effect on oneself, particularly in their cumulative state. Such stressors may also develop into a psychological condition, such as depression or paranoia, which may, in turn, have a significant impact on the abuse of authority.

A survey of police officers conducted by Violanti and Aron (1994) asked police officers to rank the most stressful work activities or situations. Even though police shootings and officers being killed in the line of duty are rare events, officers ranked killing someone or the murder of a fellow law enforcement officer as the most stress-inducing events in their work. This may suggest that the perception of violence and danger rather than the reality of the dangers of police work may be a major source of officer stress.

The disjuncture between the reality of danger in police work and offi- cers' perception of stressors is an ongoing issue for this occupation. More than a decade after Violanti and Aron published their research on police stress, Garcia et al. (2004) revisited the issue and obtained similar results. These researchers split police stressors into three types: occupational, job-related, and external stressors. Once again, they found that, even during a time when crime rates and police killings declined dramatically, police officers still listed injury or death as being the most stressful aspect of their job. The consistency of this finding across studies of police stress, despite changes in the actual level of dangers in police work, suggests that the per- ception of danger by police is more of a cultural artifact than a reality of police work.

Recent research has begun to verify that various situations in the work- place may contribute to stress more than the actual work that officers are called on to perform. Studies indicated that the following factors might contribute more to stress than the dangers and deaths associated with police work:

1. Profanity and sexual jokes in the workplace (Morash, Kawk, & Haarr, 2006).
2. The occupational need to suppress expressions of feelings (Morash et al., 2006).
3. Lack of influence over practices and procedures in the workplace (Morash et al., 2006).
4. Racial and ethnic bias by coworkers (Morash et al., 2006).
5. Poor or destructive coping skills (McCarty, Zhao, & Garland, 2007).
6. Perception of the workplace as unfair (McCarty et al., 2007).
7. Overly rigid rules (McCarty et al., 2007).
8. Strained relationships with coworkers (McCarty et al., 2007).

Occupational stress is also said to affect the families and spouses of police offi- cers. Following is a list of some of the most common family stressors related to living with or being a family member of a police officer (Borum & Philpot, 1993:122–135). This list indicates that many of the stressors experienced by family members are related to the realities of police work, but other issues of concern seem to be related to the perception rather than the realities of police work.

1. Shift work and overtime.
2. Concern over the spouse's cynicism, the need to feel in control in the home, or the inability or unwillingness to express feelings.
3. Fear that the spouse will be hurt or killed in the line of duty.
4. Officers' and others' excessively high expectations of their children.

5. Avoidance, teasing, or harassment of the officer's children by other children because of the parent's job.
6. Presence of a gun in the home.
7. The officer's 24-h role as a law enforcer.
8. Perception that the officer prefers to spend time with coworkers rather than with his or her family.
9. Too much or too little discussion of the job.
10. Family members' perception of the officer as paranoid or excessively vigilant and overprotective of them.
11. Problems in helping the officer cope with work-related problems.
12. "Critical incidents" (injury to the officer or death on the job).

You can read about police chief's view about officers' substance abuse issues by going to: **http://www.policeforum.org/library/subject-to-debate/2012/Debate_Sep-Oct2012_v5web.pdf**

Effects of Police Stress

A number of studies claim that stress has serious negative effects on police personnel. Studies conclude that police officers have higher rates of suicide than the general public and experience job-related deaths at a high rate. Police are said to have high rates of alcoholism and drug abuse. Police officers are also said to have higher rates of mortality resulting from heart disease and diabetes, and some studies have found that police officers run a greater risk of developing colon and liver cancers than members of the general public. Although there has been considerable research into *stress effects* on officers, little research conclusively demonstrates that police officers are plagued by the negative effects of stress to any greater extent than members of many other occupations or the general public. The sections that follow review the research and issues surrounding the negative effects of the stress associated with police work.

Police Suicide

Some police organizations, during specific periods of time (Violanti, 1996a, 1996b), experience higher rates of suicide than the general public. Studies of the NYPD found that it had a higher rate of suicide among its officers than did the general public. Likewise, studies conducted in Washington State and in the Chicago Police Department (Wagner & Brzeczek, 1983), a national study of the United States (Stack & Kelley, 1994), and studies of other countries, found that police officers have higher rates of suicide than the general public (Lester, 1992). Some studies, though, have concluded that police officers have lower rates of suicide than the general public. For example, the study by Dash and Reiser (1978) of the LAPD, as well as a follow-up study of the same department 12 years later, found that LAPD officers had lower rates of suicide than the general public (Josephson & Reiser, 1990). Likewise, Loo's (1986) study of the Royal Canadian Mounted Police found suicide rates lower than those of the general public. Chae (2013) upon investigating police suicide found that organizational stress, critical incident trauma, shift work, relationship problems, and alcohol abuse contributed police suicides.

Comparing police suicide rates with those of the general public, however, may be deceptive because the police differ drastically from the public as a whole. Police departments, for example, are predominantly male and employ people over the age of 21. Police officers have ready access to firearms and most work in urban areas. These factors are highly correlated with suicide.

You can read more about police suicides by going to:**http://www.policeone.com/health-fitness/articles/137133-Police-Officer-Suicide-Frequency-and-officer-profiles/**

Comparisons have also been made between suicide rates among members of the police occupation and rates found in other occupations. Studies show that occupations other than the police also experience higher rates of suicide than the general public. Lester (1983) found that the suicide rate was also high among the self-employed and persons in manufacturing occupations. Labovitz and Hagedorn (1971) found the rate of suicide among male police officers to be lower than that of managers, retail personnel, and the self-employed. Other studies have concluded that members of the medical profession, dentists, and farmers have higher rates of suicide than the general public (Boxer, Burnett, & Swanson, 1995). When studies control for the gender and economic status of the members of a profession, police officers do not appear to have significantly higher rates of suicide compared to many others in the labor force (Stack & Kelley, 1994).

Although the stress of police work may contribute to suicide, a number of other factors may also contribute, including:

1. Abuse of alcohol and drugs.
2. Becoming involved in deviance, corruption, and criminal activity.
3. Ready access to firearms.
4. Depression.
5. Working in a male-dominated organization.
6. Family and economic problems.
7. Alienation and cynicism associated with police culture.
8. Role conflict in the occupation and social situations.
9. Physical and mental health problems.

Alcoholism and Drug Abuse

Police officers are thought to have high rates of alcoholism and drug abuse. For example, in one study conducted in a large urban police department, researchers found that 18.1% of male officers and 15.9% of female officers reported adverse consequences from alcohol use, and 7.8% of the sample met the criteria for lifetime alcohol abuse or dependence (Ballenger et al., 2011). A study by

Kraska and Kappeler (1988) found that approximately 20% of police officers in a single agency abused drugs while on duty. Similarly, in this same study, the researchers found that the rate of on-duty alcohol use among veteran police officers was nearly 20%, with younger officers having an equal percentage of drug abuse. Drug and alcohol abuse may be part of the culture in some police departments. For example, Homish and Leonard (2008) found that drinking social networks such as those found in police departments where "drinking buddies" get together and drink are related to heavy alcohol use. Earlier, Van Raalte (1979) had reported that as many as 67% of the officers he studied admitted to drinking while on duty. Violanti, Marshall, and Howe (1985), as well as Kraska and Kappeler (1988), addressed these conflicting claims and suggested that the study of police deviance is difficult and that there is substantial underreporting of deviance by officers. Violanti et al. (1985) stated that: Alcohol use among police is underestimated. Many officers, fearing departmental discipline, are unwilling to officially report their deviance. Police organizations appear ambivalent toward drinking problems, placing blame on the individual officer and not the police occupational structure (Kroes, 1976). Other departments may "hide" problem drinkers in positions where they will not adversely affect police operations (1976:106) (Box 8.7).

It may, however, be unwise to link police abuse of alcohol and drugs to the stresses associated with police work. Kraska and Kappeler (1988), for example, found that among officers who used controlled substances on duty, every one of them had used controlled substances before becoming a police officer. If police stress were the cause of substance abuse, one would expect at least a few officers without histories of abuse to turn to drugs when faced with the stresses of the job. Police substance abuse seems to be more related to culture and socialization than to the stresses of police work. Obst and Davey (2003:37), for example, found that "joining the police service does have a significant impact on recruits' drinking and socializing behavior. … Drinking with work or police colleagues increased over time in service while drinking with non-work friends and family decreased … recruits joining the police brought a new culture of socializing and drinking together. … Both the frequency of drinking and the quantity of alcohol consumption increased over time in the police service. … These data indicate that the indoctrination into police culture may involve this move toward more frequent and heavier drinking."

Mortality and Health Problems

Police officers are also said to have high rates of mortality resulting from heart disease and diabetes, and other studies have found that police officers run a greater risk of developing colon and liver cancers. Some research indicates that diseases lead to police officers dying at an earlier age as compared to other

Box 8.7 What's Killing America's Cops?

Police are eight times more likely to commit suicide than to be killed in a homicide and are three times more likely to commit suicide than to die in job-related accidents, according to a recent study by researchers at the University of Buffalo–State University of New York, which is said to be one of the few empirical analyses of police officers' risk of suicide, homicide, and accidental death.

The study, which researchers say is also the first to compare police officers' suicide risk to that of other municipal employees, found that police commit suicide at a rate up to 53 percent higher than other city workers, according to the study's lead author, John Violanti, a 23-year veteran of the New York State Police who is now an assistant clinical professor of social and preventive medicine at the university.

Supported by a grant from the National Institute of Mental Health, the study analyzed the deaths of Buffalo police officers and those of other city workers caused by external factors unrelated to disease between 1950 and 1991. The researchers looked at 138 deaths, all of them involving white males, including those of 39 police officers and 99 other municipal workers.

An analysis by a panel of medical examiners who verified the causes of death found that 25 of the police deaths were attributed to suicide, three to homicide, six to accidents, and five were classified as undetermined. In comparison, 13 of the 99 other municipal-worker deaths were labeled suicides, four were the results of homicides, 77 were from accidents, and five were classified as undetermined.

The panel later reclassified the deaths of four police officers and one municipal worker from "undetermined" to suicide, underscoring the belief that police are in a state of denial about the extent of the deadly problem, Violanti told Law Enforcement News.

The study said that police are at higher risk for committing suicide for a variety of reasons, including access to firearms, continuous exposure to human misery, shift work, social strain and marital difficulties, drinking problems, physical illness, impending retirement, and lack of control over their jobs and personal lives.

"There's a very strong denial in policing that this is even a problem," Violanti said. "Suicide accounts for about 1 percent of deaths in the United States, and I think it's a little higher in police work. Because there are so few, police departments think that since they happen once in a while, it's really not a problem. But when you look at the risk factors, do risk-ratios between police and other occupations, and compare them to other causes of death, you see that there is an increased risk. That denial needs to be broken through."

Police officers often erect roadblocks to getting help because they fear being placed on limited duty or being labeled "psychos" by colleagues, Violanti noted. Services offered by departments "are not trusted. They're looked at as not being confidential and cops are afraid to go to them because they're afraid their careers will be ruined. … They won't go, and because they won't go, they don't get help." Most of the victims of police suicides whose deaths have been analyzed in previous studies never sought help, he added.

Violanti said the denial of the problem "runs right through an entire organization," preventing the establishment of awareness and prevention programs. "Middle management is probably a key place to train sergeants, lieutenants, and captains about how to recognize this problem," he said.

A stress-management program needs to be a key part of any effort to prevent police suicides, Violanti added. He noted that the suicide rate among New York City police officers, 12 of whom took their own lives in 1994, fell drastically following the implementation of a suicide-awareness course. "The suicide risk went down after training, and officers were better able to recognize signs of suicide, not only in themselves but in fellow officers."

Source: "What's Killing America's Cops? Mostly Themselves, According to a New Study," Law Enforcement News, November 15, 1996, p. 3.

To read more about the origin of the myth of police mortality rates go to: **http://www.knoxnews.com/news/2011/oct/16/studies-dont-agree-on-law-enforcements-mortality/?print=1**

populations. Brandl and Smith (2012) compared the retired and deceased police officers and other city employees in the City of Detroit and found that police officers died at a significantly younger age. In a similar study, Violanti, Vena, and Petrolia (1998) studied 2693 Buffalo police officers and found that the average age at death was 66 years, significantly lower as compared to the general population. Despite these studies on the extent to which police officers suffer from higher mortality rates because of these ailments, a study of 2376 police officers in Buffalo, New York, found that the overall mortality rate among police officers for a variety of ailments was comparable to the general U.S. population, but police officers showed a significantly higher rate of mortality from certain forms of cancer. Officers were particularly susceptible to cancer of the digestive organs (Violanti, Vena, & Marshall, 1986). As the authors pointed out, these findings may be, in part, effects of stress, but may also be related to an officer's lifestyle and diet. In fact, studies show that police officers lead very unhealthy lifestyles that include smoking, excessive drinking, poor diets, and a lack of exercise (Richmond, Wodak, Kehoe, & Heather, 1998). Other studies call into question the problem of police mortality. Hill and Clawson's (1988) study of the Washington State Police found that, "Contrary to what many people believe, the police do not die at remarkably younger ages than [members of] other occupations."

Reducing Police Stress

Police stress can result in a number of problems for officers and departments, so departments have a vested interest in implementing programs to reduce stress. Essentially, there are two routes for reducing stress. First, is to improve officers' coping mechanisms, and the second is to identify and address modifiable stressors in policing (Gershon et al., 2009). Both tracks should be pursued to decrease the negative effects of stress.

In terms of improving officers' coping mechanisms, research demonstrates that avoidant coping in the presence of high levels of stress is not effective, and it often leads to higher levels of anxiety and burnout (Gershon et al., 2009; He, Zhao, & Archibold, 2002). To this end, Gershon and her colleagues suggest that departments should focus on improving officers cognitive problem-solving skills. This would not only reduce stress, but it would also increase officers' abilities to deal with crime and disorder problems. Other ways to increase officers coping skills include counseling programs, Alcoholics Anonymous programs strictly for police officers and their spouses, or retreats for police families. Police supervisors should constantly monitor their subordinates for poor coping skills and recommend training or programing when such skills are deficient.

Identifying and modifying stressors is another important strategy. Limiting the rotation of shifts, supervisors, and assignments, and providing officers with debriefing sessions could proactively reduce the stress factors in law enforcement. Administrators should strive to improve managers' and supervisors' leadership skills—the need for leaders, not bureaucrats. This should also foster an atmosphere of "fairness." When officers perceive that leaders are fair and concerned about their well-being, they have more job satisfaction and less stress. Reducing stress, whether it is through the improvement of coping mechanisms or modifying stress causing conditions in the department, should be a high managerial priority. Research on the effectiveness of stress intervention programs has been mixed at best (Stevens, Muller, & Kendall, 2006), but departments must try because the negative consequences of stress are too great.

SUMMARY

What we know about police culture and personality is largely dependent on how one views police behavior. Police behavior can be seen from several different perspectives. Although no single perspective gives a clear and complete understanding of the many aspects of police behavior, adopting several alternative points of view allows us to gain a more accurate picture. There is a long history of debate as to whether police officers have unique personalities and cultures that differ from those of members of other occupational groups. It can be said, however, that the role and function of the police set officers apart from other members of society; therefore, the police as an occupational group can be distinguished from other members of society. In making these distinctions, researchers use different models and perspectives of behavior. The general perspectives from which police behavior is viewed include the psychological, sociological, and anthropological perspectives. In addition, several models of behavior—predispositional, socialization, and culturalization—arise when we consider the police and why they behave the way they do.

Research into police behavior has been conducted from a cultural perspective. Each police organization develops a unique and distinct subculture, but many police organizations contain the same elements of culture, including worldview, ethos, themes, and postulates. These elements vary depending on the environment, organization, and social composition of the particular police department, but they provide us with an understanding of the police social character.

In this chapter, police stress was also considered, and it was noted that stress in police work has been examined for more than a decade in terms of whether it exists, its causes, its effects, and how individuals and police departments can cope with its negative effects. It is generally recognized that police stress exists, but there is little, if any, agreement regarding its causes, effects, or extent (Kappeler & Potter, 2005). Some researchers view stress as a personal adjustment problem; others consider stress to be a structural problem that does not reside in any personal maladjustment, but in the pathology of the environment or organization. Although research and perspectives on police stress are divided, most would agree that police work can be stressful. Stress has been linked to many problems, including physiological, psychological, and performance, as well as other health issues. Finally, this chapter considered the approach taken by police administrators to control the negative effects of police stress.

REVIEW QUESTIONS

1. What we know and think about police culture and personality are largely dependent on how one views behavior. How can we gain a greater perspective of the police?
2. What are the major differences between the psychological, sociological, and anthropological perspectives of police behavior?
3. Describe the term subculture and how it applies to the police. How does the law affect police occupational subculture?
4. What is the concept of a cultural worldview and how does it affect the police? How does police isolation reinforce the police worldview?
5. Name and describe David Carter's typology of police stressors. What are the effects of police stress and what are some ways of reducing this stress?

REFERENCES

Adlam, K. R. (1982). The police personality: psychological consequences of becoming a police officer. *Journal of Police Science and Administration, 10*(3), 347–348.

Adorno, T. (1950). *The authoritarian personality.* New York: Harper.

Anonymous. (2005a). *Brazilians push for shooting progress.* CNN. August 24.

Anonymous. (2005b). *Victim's family: Police must pay.* CNN. July 25.

Anonymous. (2005c). *White house backs air marshals' actions: Marshals', witnesses' accounts differ on jet bomb threat claim.* CNN. December 9.

Bahn, C. (1984). Police socialization in the eighties: strains in the forging of an occupational identity. *Journal of Police Science and Administration, 12*(4), 390–394.

Balch, R. (1972). The police personality: facts or fiction? *Journal of Criminal Law, Criminology and Police Science, 63,* 1066–1119.

Baldwin, J. (1962). *Nobody knows my name.* New York: Dell.

Ballenger, J. F., Best, S. R., Metzier, T. J., Wasserman, D. A., Mohr, D. C., Liberman, A., et al. (2011). Patterns and predictors of alcohol use in male and female urban police officers. *The American Journal on Addictions, 20,* 21–29.

Banton, M. (1964). *The police in the community.* London: Tavistock.

Barker, T., & Carter, D. L. (1994). *Police deviance* (3rd ed.). Cincinnati, OH: Anderson Publishing.

Bayley, D. H., & Mendelsohn, H. (1969). *Minorities and the police: Confrontation in america.* New York: The Free Press.

Berg, B. L., Gertz, M. G., & True, E. J. (1984). Police–community relations and alienation. *Police Chief, 51*(11), 20–23.

Bittner, E. (1970). *The functions of police in modern society.* Chevy Chase, MD: National Clearinghouse for Mental Health.

Borum, R., & Philpot, C. (1993). Therapy with law enforcement couples: clinical management of the "high-risk lifestyle". *American Journal of Family Therapy, 21*, 122–135.

Boxer, P. A., Burnett, C., & Swanson, N. (1995). Suicide and occupation: a review of the literature. *Journal of Occupational and Environmental Medicine, 37*(4), 442–452.

Brandl, S. G., & Smith, B. W. (2012). An empirical examination of retired police officers' length of retirement age at death: a research note. *Police Quarterly, 16*, 113–123.

Brandl, S. G., & Stroshine, M. S. (2003). Toward an understanding of the physical hazards of police work. *Police Quarterly, 6*(2), 172–191.

Britz, M. (1997). The police subculture and occupational socialization: exploring individual and demographic characteristics. *American Journal of Criminal Justice, 21*(2), 127–146.

Broderick, J. (1987). *Police in time of change.* Prospect Heights, IL: Waveland Press.

Cain, M. E. (1973). *Society and the policeman's role.* London: Routledge and Kegan Paul.

Carpenter, B. N., & Raza, S. M. (1987). Personality characteristics of police applicants: comparisons across subgroups and with other populations. *Journal of Police Science and Administration, 15*(1), 10–17.

Carter, D. L. (1994). Theoretical dimensions in the abuse of authority by police officers. In T. Barker, & D. L. Carter (Eds.), *Police deviance* (3rd ed.) (pp. 276–277). Cincinnati, OH: Anderson Publishing.

Chae, M. H. (2013). Police suicide: prevalence, risk, and protective factors. *Policing: An International Journal of Police Strategies and Management, 36*, 91–118.

Chappell, A. T., & Lanza-Kaduce, L. (2010). Police academy socialization: understanding the lessons learned in a paramilitary-bureaucratic organization. *Journal of Contemporary Ethnography, 39*, 187–214.

Chrisopoulos, S., Dollard, M. F., Winefiled, A. H., & Dormann, C. (2010). Increasing the probability of finding an interaction in work stress research: a two-wave longitudinal test of the triple-match principle. *Journal of Occupational and Organizational Psychology, 83*, 17–37.

Christopher, W. (1991). *Summary: Report of the independent commission on the Los Angeles police department.* Los Angeles, CA: City of Los Angeles.

Clark, J. P. (1965). Isolation of the police: a comparison of the British and American situations. *Journal of Criminal Law, Criminology and Police Science, 56*, 307–319.

Coates, R. (1972). *The dimensions of police–citizen interaction: a social psychological analysis* (Ph.D. dissertation). College Park: University of Maryland.

Collins, P. A., & Gibbs, A. C. (2003). Stress in police officers: a study of origins, prevalence and severity of stress-related symptoms within a county police force. *Occupational Medicine, 53*, 256–264.

Conti, N. (2009). A Visigoth system: shame, honor, and police socialization. *Journal of Contemporary Ethnography, 38*, 409–432.

Crank, J. P. (1993). Legalistic and order-maintenance behavior among police patrol officers: a survey of eight municipal police agencies. *American Journal of Police, 12*(1), 103–126.

Crank, J. P. (2010). *Understanding police culture.* Cincinnati: Anderson Publishing.

Dash, J., & Reiser, M. (1978). Suicide in urban law enforcement agencies. *Journal of Police Science and Administration, 6*(1), 18–21.

Evans, B. J., Coman, G. J., & Stanley, R. O. (1992). Police personality: type-A behavior and trait anxiety. *Journal of Criminal Justice, 20*(5), 429–441.

Ferdinand, T. H. (1980). Police attitudes and police organization: some interdepartmental and cross-cultural comparisons. *Police Studies, 3*, 46–60.

Franke, W., Ramsey, S. L., & Shelly, M. C. (2002). Relationship between cardiovascular disease morbidity, risk factors, and stressors in a law enforcement cohort. *Journal of Occupational and Environmental Medicine, 44*, 1182–1189.

Garcia, L., Nesbary, D. K., & Gu, J. (2004). Perceptual variations of stressors among police officers during an era of decreasing crime. *Journal of Contemporary Criminal Justice, 20*(1), 33–50.

Genz, T. A., & Lester, D. (1976). Authoritarianism in policemen as a function of experience. *Journal of Police Science and Administration, 4,* 9–13.

Gershon, R. M., Barocas, B., Canton, A. N., Xianbin, L., & Vlahov, D. (2009). Mental, physical, and behavioral outcomes associated with perceived work stress in police officers. *Criminal Justice and Behavior, 36,* 275–289.

Griffin, S., & Bernard, T. (2003). Angry aggression among police officers. *Police Quarterly, 6*(1), 3–21.

Griffin, M., Hart, P., & Wilson-Everard, E. (2000). Using employee opinion surveys to improve organisational health. In L. Murphy, & C. Cooper (Eds.), *Health and productive work: An international perspective* (pp. 15–36). London: Taylor & Francis.

Harris, R. (1973). *The police academy: An insider's view.* New York: John Wiley & Sons.

Hart, P., & Cotton, P. (2003). Conventional wisdom is often misleading: police stress within an organisational health framework. In M. Dollard, A. Winefield, & H. Winefield (Eds.), *Occupational stress in the service professions.* New York: Taylor & Francis.

Hassell, K. D. (2007). Variation in police patrol practices: the precinct as a sub-organization level of analysis. *Policing: An International Journal of Police Strategies and Management, 30,* 257–276.

Hassell, K. D., & Brandl, S. G. (2009). An examination of workplace experiences of police patrol officers: the role of race, sex, and sexual orientation. *Police Quarterly, 12,* 408–430.

He, N., Zhao, J., & Archibold, C. A. (2002). Gender and police stress: the convergent and divergent impact of work environment, work-family conflict, and stress coping mechanisms of female and male police officers. *Policing: An International Journal of Police Strategies and Management, 24,* 687–708.

Herbert, S. (1998). Police subculture reconsidered. *Criminology, 36*(2), 343–369.

Hill, K. Q., & Clawson, M. (1988). The health hazards of "street level" bureaucracy: mortality among police. *Journal of Police Science and Administration, 16*(4), 243–248.

Homish, G. G., & Leonard, K. E. (2008). The social network and alcohol use. *Journal of Studies on Alcohol and Drugs, 69,* 906–914.

Hunt, J., & Manning, P. K. (1994). The social context of police lying. In P. A. Adler, & P. Adler (Eds.), *Constructions of deviance: Social power, context, and interaction* (pp. 153–169). Belmont, CA: Wadsworth.

Josephson, R. L., & Reiser, M. (1990). Officer suicide in the Los Angeles police department: a twelve-year follow-up. *Journal of Police Science and Administration, 17*(3), 227–229.

Kappeler, V. E., & Potter, G. W. (2005). *The mythology of crime and criminal justice* (4th ed.). Prospect Heights, IL: Waveland Press.

Kappeler, V. E., Sluder, R., & Alpert, G. P. (1998). *Forces of deviance: Understanding the dark side of policing* (2nd ed.). Prospect Heights, IL: Waveland Press.

Kirkham, G. L. (1974). A Professor's street lessons. *FBI Law Enforcement Bulletin, 43*(3), 14–22.

Klinger, D. (1997). Negotiating order in patrol work: an ecological theory of police response to deviance. *Criminology, 35,* 277–306.

Kohan, A., & O'Connor, B. P. (2002). Police officer job satisfaction in relation to mood, well-being, and alcohol consumption. *Journal of Psychology, 136,* 307–318.

Kraska, P. B., & Kappeler, V. E. (1988). A theoretical and descriptive study of police on-duty drug use. *American Journal of Police, 8*(1), 1–36.

Kroes, W. H. (1976). *Society's victim, the policeman: An analysis of job stress in policing.* Springfield, IL: Charles C Thomas.

Labovitz, S., & Hagedorn, R. (1971). An analysis of suicide rates among occupational categories. *Sociological Inquiry, 41*, 67–72.

Lambert, A. J., Burroughs, T., & Nguyen, T. (1999). Perceptions of risk and the "buffering hypothesis": the role of just world beliefs and right-wing authoritarianism. *Personality and Social Psychology Bulletin, 25*, 643–656.

Lester, D. (1983). Stress in police officers: an american perspective. *The Police Journal, LVI*(2), 188–190.

Lester, D. (1992). Suicide in police officers: a survey of nations. *Police Studies, 15*(3), 146–147.

Lofquist, L., & Davis, R. (1969). *Adjustment of work*. New York: Appleton-Century-Crofts.

Loo, R. (1986). Suicide among police in a federal force. *Suicide and Life Threatening Behavior, 16*, 379–388.

Lorr, M., & Strack, S. (1994). Personality profiles of police candidates. *Journal of Clinical Psychology, 50*(2), 200–208.

Laguna, L., Linn, A., Ward, K., & Rupslaukyte, R. (2010). An examination of authoritarian personality traits among police officers: the role of experience. *Journal of Police Criminal Psychology, 25*, 99–104.

Manning, P. K. (2006). The police: mandate, strategies and appearances. In V. Kappeler (Ed.), *The police and society: Touchstone readings* (3rd ed.) (pp. 94–122). Prospect Heights, IL: Waveland Press.

Mastrofski, S., & Willis, J. J. (2010). Police continuity and change: into the twenty-first century. In M. Tonry (Ed.), *Crime and justice: A review of research* (pp. 55–144). Chicago: University of Chicago Press.

McCarty, W. P., Zhao, J., & Garland, B. E. (2007). Occupational stress and burnout between male and female police officers: are there any gender differences? *Policing: An International Journal of Police Strategies and Management, 30*, 672–691.

Meisner, J. (2013). Commission finds evidence of police torture in 5 convictions. *Chicago Tribune*.

Morash, M., Kawk, D., & Haarr, R. (2006). Gender differences in the predictors of police stress. *Policing: An International Journal of Police Strategies and Management, 29*, 541–563.

Morrissey, S. (2005). Eyewitness: I never heard the word bomb. *Time*. December 9, 2005.

Muir, W. (1977). *Police: streetcorner politicians*. Chicago, IL: University of Chicago Press.

Niederhoffer, A. (1967). *Behind the shield: The police in urban society*. Garden City, NY: Doubleday.

Obst, P. L., & Davey, J. D. (2003). Does the police academy change your life? A longitudinal study of changes in socialising behaviour of police recruits. *International Journal of Police Science and Management, 5*(1), 31–40.

Redfield, R. (1952). The primitive worldview. *Proceedings of the American Philosophical Society, 96*, 30–36.

Reiss, A. J. (1971). *The police and the public*. New Haven, CT: Yale University Press.

Reiss, A. J., & Bordua, D. J. (1967). Environment and organization: a perspective on the police. In D. J. Bordua (Ed.), *The police: Six sociological essays*. New York: John Wiley & Sons.

Reuss-Ianni, E. (1983). *Two cultures of policing*. New Brunswick, NJ: Transaction Books.

Richmond, R. L., Wodak, A., Kehoe, L., & Heather, N. (1998). How healthy are the police? A survey of life-style factors. *Addiction, 93*(11), 1729–1737.

Rubinstein, G. (2006). Authoritarianism among border police officers, career soldiers, and airport security guards at the israeli border. *The Journal of Social Psychology, 146*(6), 751–761.

Savitz, L. (1971). The dimensions of police loyalty. In H. Hahn (Ed.), *Police in urban society* (pp. 213–225). Beverly Hills, CA: Sage.

Sherman, L. (1974a). *Scandal and reform: Controlling police corruption.* Berkeley: University of California Press.

Sherman, L. (1974b). *Police corruption: A sociological perspective.* Garden City, NY: Doubleday.

Sherman, L. (1980). Perspectives on police violence. *Annals of the American Academy of Political and Social Sciences, 452,* 1–12.

Sherman, L. (1982). Learning police ethics. *Criminal Justice Ethics, 1*(1), 10–19.

Skolnick, J. H. (1966). *Justice without trial: Law enforcement in a democratic society.* New York: John Wiley & Sons.

Skolnick, J. H., & Fyfe, J. J. (1993). *Above the law: Police and the use of excessive force.* New York: The Free Press.

Stack, S., & Kelley, T. (1994). Police suicide: an analysis. *American Journal of Police, 13*(4), 73–90.

Stevens, S., Muller, J., & Kendall, E. (2006). Addressing organisationally induced stress in a police jurisdiction: an Australian case study. *International Journal of Police Science and Management, 8*(3), 198–204.

Stoddard, E. R. (2006). The informal code of police deviancy: a group approach to blue-collar crime. In V. Kappeler (Ed.), *The police and society: Touchstone readings* (3rd ed.) (pp. 201–222). Prospect Heights, IL: Waveland Press.

Swanton, B. (1981). Social isolation of police: structural determinants and remedies. *Police Studies, 3,* 14–21.

Symonds, M. (1970). Emotional hazards of police work. In A. Niederhoffer, & A. Blumberg (Eds.), *Ambivalent force: Perspectives on the police* (pp. 58–74). London: Ginn-Basil.

Van Maanen, J. (2006). Kinsman in repose: occupational perspectives of patrolman. In V. Kappeler (Ed.), *The police and society: Touchstone readings* (3rd ed.). Prospect Heights, IL: Waveland Press.

Van Raalte, R. (1979). Alcohol as a problem among police officers. *Police Chief, 44,* 38–40.

Violanti, J. M. (1996a). Police suicide: an overview. *Police Studies, 19*(2), 77–89.

Violanti, J. M. (1996b). Trends in police suicide. *Psychological Reports, 77,* 688–690.

Violanti, J. M., & Aron, F. (1994). Ranking police stressors. *Psychological Reports, 75*(2), 825–826.

Violanti, J. M., Marshall, J. R., & Howe, B. (1985). Stress, coping, and alcohol use: the police connection. *Journal of Police Science and Administration, 13*(2), 106–109.

Violanti, J. M., Vena, J. E., & Marshall, J. R. (1986). Disease risk and mortality among police officers: new evidence and contributing factors. *Journal of Police Science and Administration, 14*(1), 17–23.

Violanti, J. M., Vena, J. E., & Petrolia, S. (1998). Mortality of a police cohort 1950–1990. *American Journal of Industrial Medicine, 33,* 366–373.

Wagner, M., & Brzeczek, R. J. (1983). Alcoholism and suicide: a fatal connection. *FBI Law Enforcement Bulletin, 52*(8), 8–15.

Westley, W. A. (1953). Violence and the police. *American Journal of Sociology, 59,* 34–41.

Westley, W. A. (1956). Secrecy and the police. *Social Forces, 34*(3), 254–257.

Westley, W. A. (1970). *Violence and the police: A sociological study of law, custom and morality.* Cambridge, MA: MIT Press.

White, S. (1972). A perspective on police professionalization. *Law and Society Review, 7*(1), 61–85.

Wilson, J. Q. (1963). The police and their problems: a theory. *Public Policy, 12,* 189–216.

Wilson, J. Q. (1968). *Varieties of police behavior.* Cambridge, MA: Harvard University Press.

Woody, R. (2006). Family interventions with law enforcement officers. *The American Journal of Family Therapy, 34,* 95–103.

Worden, R. (1989). Situational and attitudinal explanations of police behavior: a theoretical reappraisal and empirical reassessment. *Law and Society Review, 23,* 667–711.

CHAPTER 9

Ethics and Deviance

Who will protect the public when the police violate the law?

—Ramsey Clark

After reading this chapter, you should be able to:

- List and define the various sources of police decision-making.
- Distinguish between police crime, abuse of authority, deviance, and corruption.
- List and define several forms of police deviance based on the desire for economic gain.
- Describe the different forms of police corruption and their different definitions.
- Refute the myth of the "rotten apple."
- Explain the differences between the four definitions of deviance and their theories.
- Discuss the problems of police drug use, sexual deviance, and police sexual violence.
- Distinguish between police quota systems and goldbricking.
- Explain why controlling police misconduct is difficult.

KEY TERMS

- Abuse of authority
- Bribery
- Code of ethics
- Corruption
- Deontological ethics
- Driving while female
- Ethics
- Goldbricking
- Grass-eaters
- Gratuities
- Immanuel Kant
- Jacking-up charges
- Jeremy Bentham
- John Rawls
- John Stuart Mill
- Justice
- Legal abuse

INTRODUCTION

Since before the time of Plato, society has struggled with the issues of ethics and morality. The terms "ethics and morality" are often used interchangeably, with neither having a precise definition. Attempts by scholars to distinguish the two normally result in further confusion as to the precise meaning of each term. In a formal sense, the study of ethics is a specialized branch of philosophy. Unlike

- Meat-eaters
- Morality
- Normative system
- Occupational deviance
- Personal values
- Physical abuse
- Police code of conduct
- Police crime
- Police sexual violence
- Psychological abuse
- Quota systems
- Sexual harassment
- Social norms
- Stacking-up charges
- Utilitarianism
- Values

psychology or sociology, *ethics* is not an attempt to understand the "why" of human behavior but rather an attempt to evaluate behavior in terms of ethical or moral principles. In doing so, one is immediately presented with a number of nearly insurmountable difficulties. How is the term "ethics" to be defined? Should the definition be based on moral concepts and, if so, whose morals are to be considered ethical? Should society be more concerned with the ethics of process or the ethics of result?

The term *morality* can have many meanings. For some, it denotes the capacity of people to make judgments about what is right or good. For others, it describes a person whose behavior is ethical. Still others attach a religious connotation to the term (Ewing, 1953, pp. 11–12). It is perhaps easier, given modern-day confusion about the term, to use the word *values* when discussing police ethics. There are many types of values: social, religious, political, economic, personal, and legal, all of which impact policing and law enforcement. In many cases, these different values seem to be inconsistent or to compete with each other. Determination of what conduct is ethical requires consideration of a wide range of values. In doing so, one must often make a choice between competing values.

Although some behaviors are easily categorized as being right or wrong, new police officers quickly discover a vast gray area. Their responsibilities for order maintenance and provision of services frequently place them in circumstances in which there is no clear distinction between right and wrong or good and evil. Even the law enforcement role, which in theory should present the clearest choices, often requires difficult decisions. The ambiguity of many situations encountered by police officers forces them to make these decisions based on value judgments as to the most desirable course of action. Whether an officer's actions are ethical is determined by evaluating both the choice that is made and the context in which the decision occurs.

As a form of philosophy or method of inquiry, *ethics* can be thought of as a means to evaluate behavior. It is necessary to go one step further, however, and determine the criteria for evaluating the conduct of police officers. How does one define what behavior is good and therefore desirable versus that which is harmful and to be condemned? For some (Moore, 1903), the discussion ends with the conclusion that it is impossible to define terms such as *good, evil, right,* and *wrong*. Others merely adhere to the principle of *utilitarianism*, such that one's actions should ensure the greatest happiness for the greatest number.

Jeremy Bentham and John Stuart Mill first espoused utilitarianism as a form of ethics in the eighteenth century. Utilitarianism, a form of consequentialism, asks that we judge the correctness of an action by its outcome or consequences. If the consequences are good, the action is moral; if the consequences are bad, the action is immoral. Utilitarianism as a framework for ethics raises several issues, such as what is good and who's good should we be concerned with? These views focus not on the behavior but rather its effect on others. In simple terms, adoption of this criterion for determining what is ethical would limit consideration to the ends and not the means by which something is accomplished (Figure 9.1).

British philosopher George Moore (1912) believed that the question of whether an action was right or wrong depends on its consequences. The motives or intentions of the person are not reasonable ways to evaluate behavior; the result of behavior should be the criterion for evaluation. These views focus not on the behavior but rather its effect on others. In simple terms, adoption of this criterion for determining what is ethical would limit consideration to the ends and not the means by which something is accomplished.

FIGURE 9.1 Jeremy Bentham.
Image courtesy of Wikipedia.

Read about police abuses and prejudice by visiting the Website **www.aclu.org/public/gen/14614publ19971201.html**. This site has additional links to related topics.

Deontological ethics does not consider consequences but examines one's duty to act. For example, when police officers observe a violation of law, they have a duty to act. Police officers frequently use this as an excuse when they issue traffic citations that, on their face, have little utility. When an officer writes a motorist a traffic citation for making a prohibited left turn at 2:00 a.m. when no traffic is around, the officer is fulfilling a duty to enforce the law. From a utilitarian standpoint, however, little if any good was served. Here, duty prevailed over good consequences.

Immanuel Kant, an eighteenth century philosopher, expanded the ethics of duty by including the idea of "goodwill." When people act, their actions must be guided by good intent. In the above example, the officer who wrote the traffic citation for the prohibited left turn would be unethical if the ticket was a response to a quota or some prejudice. On the other hand, if the citation were issued because the officer truly believed that it would result in some good, then it would have been an ethical action.

The complexity of choices made by law enforcement personnel mandates an examination of ethics that goes beyond traditional concerns. Decisions in the criminal justice system are often subject to competing interests and values. To judge the ethicality of these decisions, one must first agree on which behaviors are right and wrong. The foundation of values and ethical standards for the criminal justice practitioner comes from many sources. It is with these various sources that we will begin our examination of police ethics. Later in the chapter, we will consider the issues associated with police deviance and misconduct. These behaviors range from the acceptance of gratuities to police sexual violence against citizens (Figure 9.2).

SOURCES OF ETHICS

Police officers must look to a number of sources for guidance in their decision-making. The standard used to evaluate police behavior will often dictate whether an action is considered ethical. Officers must rely on many sources for guidance in making their decisions, including the concept of justice, laws, agency policies, departments' value systems, social norms, and personal values. Defining ethical behavior often depends on the context in which the decision is made and the source from which decision-makers draw perceptions of right and wrong.

Justice

Justice is a concept that is as difficult to define as ethics. For most people, justice implies fairness, and we can readily point to examples in which justice is lacking. Justice is also a relative term, a concept that depends on one's point

FIGURE 9.2 German philosopher Immanuel Kant.
Photo courtesy of Shutterstock.

of view and the circumstances. Philosopher John Rawls (1999) wrote about justice as fairness, developing a theory of justice that consisted of two basic principles. First, people are to be afforded the greatest degree of liberty insofar as it does not compete with the overall liberty of a society. Second, inequalities should be tolerated only to the extent to which they benefit the least well-off members of society. Often, however, our conceptions of justice and fairness are reduced to notions of fairness as embodied in such legal concepts as "due process" that can be interpreted in ways that address only procedural fairness rather than the equitable result of a process or proceeding. When constructed within a framework of competing "rights," legal decisions can lend themselves to creating inequities in the outcomes.

For the police officer, justice may not exist if a suspect is released on a legal technicality. For the defendant, justice exists only if the police are held accountable for their conduct. The justice of a process can conflict with the justice of an outcome. Because our system of justice depends on the premise of impartial application of the law, it is often difficult to separate the two. The law and, perhaps more importantly, its application serve to define the limits of justice in a society. When police engage in unethical acts or deviant occupational practices, it challenges our notions of a free, fair, and just society.

Law

The role of _law_ in a democratic society is best understood in terms of how and why the government was created and structured. The views of those who framed our constitutional form of government were recorded in a series of newspaper articles that have become known as _The Federalist Papers_. Originally intended to persuade the citizens of New York to ratify the Constitution, _The Federalist Papers_ serve as a commentary on the political philosophy of constitutional framers and provide an explanation of their interpretation of the government's role. The sole legitimate purpose of the government was to protect life, liberty, and property. One must ask, however, the protection of whose life, liberty, and property? The greatest dangers to society were factions, or groups of people who would unite for purposes that were in opposition to the rights of others or the interests of the community. Control by _factions_ would result in decisions based purely on majority rule rather than rule of law designed to protect the rights of the minority citizens (Madison, 1787, pp. 56–65) (Box 9.1).

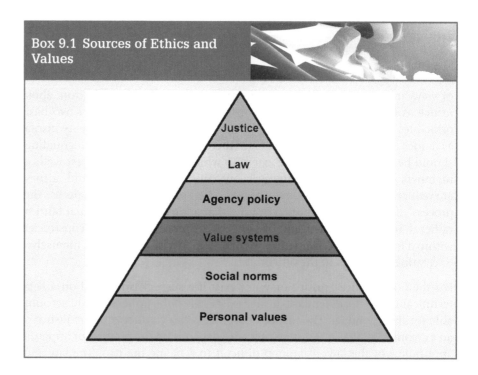

Box 9.1 Sources of Ethics and Values

- Justice
- Law
- Agency policy
- Value systems
- Social norms
- Personal values

In addition to controlling the behavior of individuals, the law also served to control the government. In framing a government that is to be administered by men over men, the great difficulty lies in this: You must first enable the government to control the governed; and in the next place oblige it to control itself. In the words of James Madison (1788, pp. 347–353): "If men were angels, no government would be necessary. If angels were to govern men, neither external nor internal controls on government would be necessary."

Although the law serves as a form of social control over the behavior of and between individuals, it is clear from the writings of the constitutional framers that it was also intended to provide a way for citizens to control the government. Experience had shown that external control of the government by the citizens was not of itself sufficient to prevent abuses. It was also necessary to build in a method of internal controls that would ensure no one group in the government could amass sufficient power to become oppressive.

Thus, it can be said that the law has three roles in our society: (1) to control actions of the government; (2) to control actions of individuals; and (3) to regulate the distribution of rights and property. The purpose of these roles is ultimately to preserve the rights of citizens, to protect them from the government and the majority, and to maintain the status quo of the distribution of rights and property. The extent of control the law should exercise over individuals in doing so has long been a source of debate. The system of internal controls envisioned by the constitutional framers, to a certain extent, relies on the ethics of those in government service and their judgment in the application of law. This is particularly true for the police, whose activities are often conducted outside the public's view (Figure 9.3).

Agency Policy
Police departments operate under a set of policies or guidelines. In addition to specifying the mechanics of performing certain tasks, these regulations set the acceptable limits of an officer's conduct in carrying out sworn duties. They address a host of activities ranging from how evidence is handled and processed to dealing with domestic violence. Violating these policies can result in disciplinary action. Thus, they place limits on officers' behavior in a variety of situations.

Police Department Value Statements
Development of a code of ethics for law enforcement has historically been tied to the movement to professionalize policing. During the 1930s, the International Association of Chiefs of Police (IACP) created a committee to make recommendations on the steps necessary to elevate policing to a profession. One of the five criteria identified as necessary to accomplish this goal was

FIGURE 9.3 Portrait of James Madison by John Vanderlyn, 1816.
Courtesy of www.whitehouse.gov.

the existence of a code of ethics setting forth standards for conduct (Kooken, 1957). It was not until 1957 that the delegates attending the 64th annual conference of the IACP approved the Law Enforcement Code of Ethics. The IACP updated the document in 1989 with a Code of Conduct. Box 9.2 contains the Code of Conduct. It contains statements touching on the exercise of discretion, use of force, legitimate source of authority, cooperation with other police agencies, and the need to develop professional capabilities. The police code of conduct, however, offers little control over police officers and provides only the external trappings of professionalism, because there exists no professional standards committee that reviews and sanctions police officers for violations of their own code. It was only recently that the police profession began to move toward the creation of certifications that could be revoked if officers engage in illegal conduct.

Today, many departments have developed internal value statements. These value statements often closely follow the IACP's Police Code of Conduct; however, by developing these value statements locally or at the department level,

Box 9.2 Police Code of Conduct

Primary Responsibilities of a Police Officer

A police officer acts as an official representative of government who is required and trusted to work within the law. The officer's powers and duties are conferred by statute. The fundamental duties of a police officer include serving the community; safeguarding lives and property; protecting the innocent; keeping the peace; and ensuring the rights of all to liberty, equality, and justice.

Performance of the Duties of a Police Officer

A police officer shall perform all duties impartially, without favor or affection or ill will and without regard to status, sex, race, religion, political belief, or aspiration. All citizens will be treated equally with courtesy, consideration, and dignity.

Officers will never allow personal feelings, animosities, or friendships to influence official conduct. Laws will be enforced appropriately and courteously and, in carrying out their responsibilities, officers will strive to obtain maximum cooperation from the public. They will conduct themselves in appearance and deportment in such a manner as to inspire confidence and respect for the position of public trust they hold.

Discretion

A police officer will responsibly use the discretion vested in the position and exercise it within the law. The principle of reasonableness will guide the officer's determinations, and the officer will consider all surrounding circumstances in determining whether any legal action shall be taken.

Consistent and wise use of discretion, based on professional policing competence, will do much to preserve good relationships and retain the confidence of the public. There can be difficulty in choosing between conflicting courses of action. It is important to remember that a timely word of advice rather than arrest—which may be correct in appropriate circumstances—can be a more effective means of achieving a desired end.

Use of Force

A police officer will never use unnecessary force or violence and will use only such force in the discharge of duty as is reasonable in all circumstances.

Force should be used only with the greatest restraint and only after discussion, negotiation, and persuasion have been found to be inappropriate or ineffective. While the use

of force is occasionally unavoidable, every police officer will refrain from applying the unnecessary infliction of pain or suffering and will never engage in cruel, degrading, or inhuman treatment of any person.

Confidentiality

Whatever a police officer sees, hears, or learns of, which is of a confidential nature, will be kept secret unless the performance of duty or legal provision requires otherwise.

Members of the public have a right to security and privacy, and information obtained about them must not be improperly divulged.

Integrity

A police officer will not engage in acts of corruption or bribery, nor will an officer condone such acts by other police officers.

The public demands that the integrity of police officers be above reproach. Police officers must, therefore, avoid any conduct that might compromise integrity and thus undercut the public confidence in a law enforcement agency. Officers will refuse to accept any gifts, presents, subscriptions, favors, gratuities, or promises that could be interpreted as seeking to cause the officer to refrain from performing official responsibilities honestly and within the law. Police officers must not receive private or special advantage from their official status. Respect from the public cannot be bought; it can only be earned and cultivated.

Cooperation with Other Officers and Agencies

Police officers will cooperate with all legally authorized agencies and their representatives in the pursuit of justice.

An officer or agency may be one among many organizations that may provide law enforcement services to a jurisdiction. It is imperative that a police officer assist colleagues fully and completely with respect and consideration at all times.

Personal/Professional Capabilities

Police officers will be responsible for their own standard of professional performance and will take every reasonable opportunity to enhance and improve their level of knowledge and competence.

Through study and experience, a police officer can acquire the high level of knowledge and competence that is essential for the efficient and effective performance of duty. The acquisition

Continued...

Box 9.2   Police Code of Conduct *Continued*

of knowledge is a never-ending process of personal and professional development that should be pursued constantly.

Private Life

Police officers will behave in a manner that does not bring discredit to their agencies or themselves.

A police officer's character and conduct while off duty must always be exemplary, thus maintaining a position of respect in the community in which he or she lives and serves. The officer's personal behavior must be beyond reproach.

a department can better reflect public sentiment and departmental issues. The department can better codify these values by including them in departmental policies. A value is an "enduring belief that a specific mode of conduct or end-state of existence is personally or socially preferable" (Rokeach, 1973:5). Thus, value statements are permanent ideas delineating how officers should perform their duties. Box 9.3 provides the core value statements for the Los Angeles Police Department.

Box 9.3   Core Value Statements for the Los Angeles Police Department

- Service to Our Communities
- Reverence for the Law
- Commitment to Leadership

- Integrity in All We Say and Do
- Respect for People
- Quality Through Continuous Improvement

Social Norms and Personal Values

Personal values are developed through the process of socialization, as discussed in the previous chapter. In this process, members of a society are taught and internalize which behaviors are considered appropriate. The actual method by which these values are instilled is subject to debate (Sumner, 1966). Individuals are thought to be influenced in their development of values from several sources, including culture, family, school, religion, relationships with others, and occupation. *Social norms*, on the other hand, are the general rules of behavioral expectations that are pervasive in a given group or society. Personal values and social norms can conflict when individuals or groups internalize values that deviate from the existing social norms of the larger society. The influence of the law enforcement profession on a person is often the central point of the discussion surrounding the development of values.

For a number of reasons discussed in Chapters 3 and 8, police officers tend to be a fairly homogeneous group. The process of recruitment selects individuals with a particular set of values. Formal training in the academy serves to solidify these values. The selection and training processes are both designed to weed out those whose values and behaviors do not conform to customary standards. Perhaps the greatest influence on a recruit's value formation is exerted by his or her field-training officer. In addition to teaching new officers the mechanics of law enforcement through example, the field-training officer instills a set of professional values.

The personal values of the officer are developed through two socialization periods: (1) that which occurs before employment; and (2) that which begins with their appointment to the department. For many, this results in the adoption of a new set of values that differ significantly from those of the general public or their personal beliefs. Often these values are instilled into new police officers by their training officers. Sherman (1982) identified a number of inappropriate values that veteran officers teach rookies:

1. **Enforcement decisions**—Decisions about enforcing the law should be governed by the law and who the suspect is.
2. **Disrespect**—Disrespect for police authority should be punished by arrest or the use of force.
3. **Use of force**—Force should be used on those who need it and when it is helpful in solving a crime.
4. **Due process**—Due process only protects criminals and can be bypassed when necessary to solve a crime.
5. **Deception**—Lying and deception are important to police work and should be used when they lead to a conviction or the apprehension of a suspect.
6. **Responding to calls**—You cannot go too fast when chasing a perpetrator or too slow when responding to a service call.
7. **Rewards**—Police work is very dangerous and police officers are paid very little, so it is acceptable for officers to take anything offered by the public.
8. **Loyalty**—An officer's most important duty is to protect their fellow officers.

When values and norms are internalized, the officer is said to be absorbed in the police subculture. This subculture has values and expectations that distinguish it from society as a whole (Kappeler, Sluder, & Alpert, 1998). The officer may find that there is a conflict between socially induced values and those of the profession or his or her personal values. The conflict is often resolved in favor of the set of values that have the strongest reinforcement. Whether this process has a positive or negative effect on police behavior depends on the values instilled and the extent to which these values meet with resistance from the dominant social group.

To learn more about police abuses, visit the Website **https://www.aclu.org/criminal-law-reform/police-practices**

A Conflict of Values

As we have seen, values are obtained from various sources. In many instances, they can conflict, and the police officer must choose between them. The choice of one value over another requires that the officer prioritize them. Few would disagree that the overriding value in law enforcement should be justice and that police officers should follow the law. One can just as easily argue that the law should always take precedence over agency policy that should supersede but should be based on the profession's code of ethics. Only when absent from any other guidance should social norms or personal values form the basis for a decision. In the decisions of the real world, however, the values assume different priorities depending on the individuals and the circumstances involved. What decision do you make, for instance, when the law is unjust or a policy is illegal or unethical?

POLICE CRIME, ABUSE OF AUTHORITY, OCCUPATIONAL DEVIANCE, AND CORRUPTION

The initial focus on police ethics centered on conduct that was illegal: theft, extortion, bribery, perjury, narcotics violations, and the like. In terms of value judgments, the decisions are fairly clear. The activities are illegal; it is unethical for officers sworn to uphold the law to commit crimes for which they would arrest someone else. Police officers who commit crimes are commonly referred to as being corrupt. Although the public and media consider any crime committed by an officer as evidence of corruption, there is considerable disagreement among police experts as to which behavior should be so defined (Hale, 1989; Kappeler et al., 1998). For some, corruption would include *any* wrongful act from accepting a gratuity to committing a homicide. Others may define it very narrowly, excluding a good deal of illegal and unethical behavior. It is instructive to briefly consider some of the terms that have been associated with police wrongdoing. We will consider police crime, abuse of authority, occupational deviance, and corruption.

Police Crime

At the simplest level, according to the Model Penal Code, a crime may be defined as an "act or omission prohibited by law for the protection of the public, the violation of which is prosecuted by the state in its own name and punishable by incarceration" (§1.1014-1). The most serious forms of police deviance—such as police sexual violence or the use of excessive force or illegal drugs—involve acts that are clearly in violation of existing criminal statutes. Yet not all crime committed by persons employed as police officers should be categorized as *police crime* (Sherman, 1974). A police officer who assaults his spouse during an argument is guilty of a crime. The officer who commits a burglary while off-duty has engaged in a crime, as has an officer who purchases illegal drugs or the favors of a prostitute, but none of these acts amount to police crime. In 2007, an allegedly drunken New York Police Department (NYPD) sergeant slashed his ex-girlfriend's tires and smashed her car windows. The 43-year-old veteran officer, Joseph DeMarco, was charged with driving while impaired, criminal mischief, and resisting arrest (Schram, 2007). This officer's actions would not be considered police crimes because they were not directly related to the officer's occupation. The 2007, case of Alameda County sheriff's deputy, Robert Tracy, better illustrates a police crime. Tracy was assigned to guard a crime scene at a hotel. While at the scene, he allegedly took $1000 from the purse of a dead woman. He explained to investigators that he needed money to pay his bills. Tracy was charged with grand theft and embezzlement (Anonymous, 2007a). The factor that probably best distinguishes between criminal acts committed by the police and police crime is the officer's use of their official powers to engage in criminal conduct. That is to say, police crime may be defined as those behaviors where officers use their power and authority as law enforcement officers to facilitate the commission of traditional criminal acts—garden-variety crimes that are committed by both members of the police profession and the public (Kappeler et al., 1998).

Abuse of Authority

Carter (1990) defined police *abuse of authority* as "any action by a police officer without regard to motive, intent, or malice that tends to injure, insult, tread on human dignity, manifest feelings of inferiority, and/or violate an inherent legal right of a member of the police constituency." This sweeping definition covers three general forms of abuse of police authority. First, officers may *physically abuse* others through the use of excessive force. Second, police may *psychologically abuse* citizens through the use of verbal assault, harassment, or ridicule. A third type of abuse is *legal abuse*, where officers violate a citizen's constitutional, federal, or state rights (Carter, 1990). Each of these abuses is made possible by the power and authority of the police but do not necessarily involve personal economic gain. In fact, a great deal of police abuse of authority is a result of attempts to achieve organizational or personal objectives rather than to secure personal economic gain.

This abuse of authority can be expensive. For example, between 2011 and 2013, the City of Minneapolis defended 110 lawsuits for police using excessive force. Plaintiffs received compensation in 59 of the cases. In one case, officers serving a traffic warrant took the suspect to the ground injuring his ribs, grabbed a dreadlock pulling it from his scalp, and fractured his wrist in two places. Also, in 2010, the City paid $3 million in the death of a homeless man who was restrained by officers. The medical examiner ruled the death as a homicide (Furst, 2013).

Occupational Deviance

In 1940, criminologist Edwin Sutherland discussed the criminal activities of upper-class business and professional persons. Although Sutherland referred to his work as a study of white-collar criminals, it represents one of the first efforts to address occupational deviance. In essence, Sutherland observed that many persons employed in business and professional enterprises or who were in political positions routinely engaged in job-related criminal activities during the course of their work. The crimes committed by these professionals, in other words, were made possible because of the very nature of their work.

Police *occupational deviance* also refers to inappropriate work-related activities in which police may participate. More specifically, police occupational deviance may be defined as "the deviant behavior—criminal and noncriminal—committed during the course of normal work activities or committed under the guise of the police officer's authority" (Barker & Carter, 1994). In 2007, "Boston Police Officer Jose 'Flaco' Ortiz allegedly showed up in uniform ... at the workplace of an unidentified man and threatened to kill him and his family if he didn't pay more than $260,000 to drug dealers, according to an FBI affidavit. ... After the man, who was cooperating with law enforcement, agreed to pay the debt 'little by little,' the FBI secretly videotaped meetings ... in which he handed cash to Ortiz while he was in uniform working police details around the city" (Murphy, 2007). It is important to note that the distinguishing factor here is that occupational deviance is made possible because of the power and authority held by the officer. It is not just that the behavior was job-related but that the behavior was substantially facilitated because of the police occupation (Box 9.4).

Corruption

Although many people consider any crime committed by the police as evidence of corruption, there is considerable disagreement among police experts as to which behaviors should be termed corrupt (Hale, 1989). For some, *corruption* would include any wrongful act—from taking a gratuity to committing a homicide. Others may define it very narrowly, excluding a good deal of criminal behavior. McMullan (1961) defined corruption as requiring the misuse of authority for personal gain: "A public official is corrupt if he accepts money or money's worth for doing something that he is under a duty to do anyway, that he is under a duty not to do, or to exercise a legitimate discretion for improper reasons." Similarly, Goldstein (1977) suggested that, for activities to be considered evidence of corruption, they must involve the abuse of a police officer's power or authority for personal gain. Punch (2000) distinguished crimes committed by criminals in uniform from acts of police misconduct that involve violations of departmental administrative rules. The distinction among police crime, occupational deviance, and corruption, according to most scholars, is

Box 9.4 Denver PD Wonders Where the Money Went

With no indication of a break-in at the Denver Police Department's property room, police officials have ordered a criminal investigation into what appears to be an inside job in the theft of $100,000 in seized cash that had been accumulated from 11 separate cases over an 8-year period.

The extent of the theft was discovered in April after interim Chief Gerry Whitman ordered some 70 command officers to conduct an extensive audit of the property room. In March, property bureau clerks failed to locate $30,000 seized in two narcotics cases.

"We have a reasonable suspicion to believe that a crime has occurred, so we're investigating it as a crime," Whitman told The Denver Post.

While police declined to specify which cases the money came from, there were three homicides and eight drug cases involved. One of the homicides, from 1992, remains unsolved. The money, said Assistant District Attorney Chuck Lepley, will not be a "pivotal issue" if the cases are closed. Two of the drug cases, he said, are pending. In the property room investigation, however, prosecutors will have to prove that the money was stolen and who stole it, said Lepley.

No weapons or drugs stored in the property room have turned up missing among the 1 million pieces of evidence and personal property stored there. About 5000 of those items are cash, from $1 and up.

Following the disappearance of the cash, the department is changing its accounting procedures and instituting periodic audits. It also hopes to update its computer system, said Whitman. "We've identified the problem and we're dealing with it," he told The Post.

Whitman has also replaced Captain Miriam Reed as commander of the property room with Captain Ed Connors. Internal affairs investigators are expected to interview as many as 50 employees—both sworn and civilian—who had access to the room.

Source: "Denver PD Wonders Where the Money Went," Law Enforcement News, June 15, 2000, p. 5.

---

that corruption is distinguished by the potential for personal gain and the use of police power and authority to further that gain. Therefore, these activities can be referred to as "corrupt."

Although most actions that are considered corrupt are also crimes, not all offenses committed by an officer constitute corruption. A police officer who drives while intoxicated, abuses a spouse, or uses illegal drugs while on duty is not necessarily corrupt. Crimes committed by police without the misuse of authority are no different from crimes committed by anyone else. There is, however, an important exception to this statement. Police officers are placed in a position of public trust and confidence. When a police officer engages in criminal conduct, it reflects poorly on the entire profession. If enough police wrongdoing occurs, public trust can be lost and police–community relations can become strained.

The distinction between corruption and crime, however, is not always clear. Consider the case of a Pittsburgh police officer who was sentenced to serve 2½–100 years in prison and pay $8322 in restitution for a series of burglaries he had committed (Anonymous, 1988). Bernard Hont, a 9-year veteran, looked for potential targets while he was on routine patrol. He would then commit the burglaries on his off-duty time using a scanner to monitor police radio traffic. Is Hont an example of corruption or merely a burglar who was also a police officer? In either case, the discovery of this type of criminal behavior by the police erodes public confidence in government.

As with any profession, law enforcement will have a certain percentage of members who commit crimes. For these activities to be considered evidence of corruption, they must involve the abuse of a police officer's authority for personal gain (Goldstein, 1977; Kappeler et al., 1998). The types of activities engaged in by police officers that are considered to be corruption include bribery, extortion, narcotics violations, and other criminal offenses.

Bribery

Police officers occasionally are voluntarily offered something of value to influence their performance of an official duty. To constitute _bribery,_ the citizen must initiate the offer to have an officer do or not do something. Examples of bribery may include the motorist who offers an officer $100 to not issue a speeding ticket or a businessperson who pays police to enforce laws that would hinder a competitor. In 2007, a Dallas police officer, Mark Torres, was accused of taking money from a motorist during a traffic stop. He was charged with theft by a public servant, a felony, and was booked into the Dallas County Jail. The officer was placed on administrative leave pending a departmental investigation (Anonymous, 2007g). Two Chicago police detectives were placed on 4 years' probation for accepting bribes from owners of vending machine companies. Eight other officers were acquitted of similar charges. Owners of the vending machine companies paid detectives who reviewed applications for liquor licenses to refer potential customers to them. The owners would then pay officers to overlook falsified financial statements from the license applicants (Gorman, 1989).

Extortion

Extortion is initiated by the officer. Using the threat of arrest or harassment, the officer requires a person who has committed a crime to give them something of value to avoid being arrested. Thirteen NYPD officers were suspended and faced the possibility of criminal charges when it was revealed that they were involved in a scheme to extort money and drugs from narcotics dealers. Because the officers were not members of the narcotics squad, they did not offer protection from arrest. Instead, they promised to omit identifying individual dealers from their intelligence reports. Most discussions of police extortion surround the objective of extracting money from the victim, but this is not always the case. In 2007, Omaha police officer Scott Antoniak was convicted of threatening and raping two prostitutes. According to prosecutors, he threatened to arrest the women if they did not engage in sex with him. Faced with a possible sentence of 50 years, the officer was given only a 5-year term of probation and ordered to write letters of apology to the two prostitutes. Representing the dismissive approach that the justice system often takes to these forms of police crimes, the officer's defense attorney said "Certainly there was a mistake made by this young man. ... Certainly this was a serious mistake. It's not a mistake he can't come back from" (Anonymous, 2007c). Although extortion by the police may seem rare, the Mollen Commission's investigation into the NYPD found widespread corruption, with officers threatening and often using violence to extort money and property from citizens (Mollen, 1994) (Box 9.5).

Narcotics Violations

There were police drug scandals in a number of major cities throughout the 1990s. Los Angeles police officers in the Rampart Division were involved in a bank robbery, theft of cocaine from the police evidence room, and the beatings of arrested drug dealers (Los Angeles Police Department, 2000). In Miami, a group of police officers called the "Miami River Gang" extorted money and stole drugs from drug dealers (Sechrest & Burns, 1992). A report

---

Box 9.5   Shakedown Shakeup: Sting Nails Cops Extorting Immigrants

Chicago Police Superintendent Terry Hilliard has stripped seven officers of their police powers pending an internal investigation into charges that they had lain in wait outside of taverns catering to Polish immigrants and demanded bribes during traffic stops.

The seven, along with as many as five others, were captured on videotape during a 2-year FBI sting operation prompted by a barrage of complaints to the Polish National Alliance.

"In most cases, they have them dead to rights," Fraternal Order of Police president Bill Nolan told The Chicago Sun-Times. "They were under video surveillance while making traffic stops and accosting patrons leaving taverns. They had agents posing as Polish immigrants. They have some on audio and videotape."

The discovery of tracking devices and possibly electronic listening devices in two cruisers may have cut short the department's own probe, said local news sources. Although, in the aftermath of the discovery of the surveillance tools, Nolan had accused the city of casting a wide net in its search for dirty officers, he later said "We are saddened that, once again, the Police Department has to be painted with a brush of corruption because of officers who evidently didn't have the courage or the character to wear the badge we're all proud to wear."

The incidents allegedly took place along the Belmont Avenue commercial strip, a borderline between the Jefferson Park and Grand Central police districts, which caters to Polish immigrants. Nolan said that some of the officers involved had created a "shakedown ring" while assigned to the Grand Central District. They continued taking bribes after being transferred to Jefferson Park, he said.

According to one merchant, police had shaken him down for $70,000. Another claimed to have been robbed of between $18,000 and $20,000. Sources said the officers had apparently waited outside of taverns on Belmont and Milwaukee Avenues, then followed immigrants to their cars, either demanding payment on the street or pulling them over and telling them to "empty their pockets."

Some of those patrons turned out to be FBI agents.

"That's what always happens," Mayor Richard M. Daley told The Sun-Times. "You pick on the less fortunate. You pick on the poor. You pick on the elderly. You pick on, many times, new immigrants."

Source: "Shakedown Shakeup: Sting Nails Cops Extorting Immigrants," Law Enforcement News, October 15, 2000, p. 7.

from the U.S. General Accounting Office described similar scandals in Atlanta, Chicago, Cleveland, Detroit, New Orleans, and Philadelphia. As a result of police corruption, including drug related corruption, the City of New York formed the Mollen Commission. The commission found problematic drug related corruption in the NYPD. The commission pointed out how the cocaine and crack markets contributed to the use of illegal drugs, perjury, burglary, robbery, and police brutality with citizens involved in drug trafficking (Baer & Armao, 1995). These cases demonstrate that drug related police corruption has been widespread and involve shocking behavior. They also show that these problems do not involve individual officers, but become endemic in some departments. Furthermore, the problem remains in a number of departments today.

As an example, Stinson et al. (2012) through an internet search of newspapers identified 188 arrests of police officers across the country for drug related offenses. These officers were from 141 different departments. Cocaine involvement was the most common drug when the type of drug was identified (49%) with marijuana second (39.8%), and a host of other drugs were involved in a much lesser degree. The most common crime committed by officers was drug trafficking (48%) followed by theft/shakedowns (29%) and drug use (27.6%). A variety of other offenses, such as facilitating the drug trade, forged prescriptions, theft from evidence room, sexually motivated drug corruption, and planting evidence, were also identified offenses. This research demonstrates that drug related corruption results in officers becoming involved in a host of criminal activities (Box 9.6).

Box 9.6 Should a Career Go to Pot Over One Dumb Move?

The Illinois State Police went to court in July to try and overturn a ruling by the agency's own independent merit board which called for suspending rather than firing a sergeant who tested positive for marijuana use.

Master Sergeant Mark Atchison, a 42-year-old department pilot from Pawnee, Illinois, told the State Police Merit Board that he had smoked some pot with two family members during a party. "For some stupid reason—I don't know whether it was to relieve their tension or it was total stupidity on my part—I actually took the joint and did a couple of hits," he told the board at his hearing in July 1999.

The board, persuaded by arguments that before the results of a random drug test, Atchison was a good employee with a clean record, voted to suspend him without pay for 6 months. Atchison's attorney argued that his client had never before been seriously disciplined and had tested negative on three previous random drug tests.

The punishment for the February 1999 incident cost Atchison approximately $35,000 of his $66,700-a-year salary. He has been on paid administrative leave from his job as a pilot since last November when he completed the suspension.

State Police officials contend, however, that Atchison should be fired, and the agency is suing in circuit court to have the board's decision either reversed or reconsidered. "It would be very difficult to explain to people in the general public why we would tolerate actions among our own officers that we put people in jail for," Daniel Kent, the agency's deputy director of operations told the merit board.

Source: "Should a Career Go to Pot Over One Dumb Move?" Law Enforcement News, September 15, 2000, p. 7.

THE SCOPE AND FORMS OF POLICE CORRUPTION

Corruption and ethical conflicts are not new problems in law enforcement. In his description of policing in the late nineteenth century, historian Samuel Walker (1980) observed "By 1870 the American police were a long way from fulfilling Robert Peel's idea of police service. The police were hopelessly corrupt, scandalously brutal, and incapable of effectively dealing with crime. Immersed in partisan politics, they also seemed incapable of reforming themselves." To address this problem, a series of commissions were established at the federal, state, and local levels. Some were designed to be permanent, but others were disbanded after completion of their investigation and report (Walker, 1980).

An example of such an effort is the *Knapp Commission's* investigation of the NYPD. The Commission was created in 1970 by the mayor to investigate allegations of corruption. Their report, issued 2 years later, concluded that corruption was widespread in the department. They described those engaging in corrupt or unethical conduct as either grass-eaters or meat-eaters. *Grass-eaters* were those officers who would engage in illegal activities only occasionally or when the circumstances of their work presented an opportunity to do so. The traffic officer might release a speeding motorist or the neighborhood officer might overlook a tavern owner's failure to close on time when offered money or a favor. *Meat-eaters*, on the other hand, were officers who aggressively pursued corrupt activities. They would actively solicit bribes by threatening arrest, cooperating with criminals, or committing crimes themselves (Knapp Commission, 1972).

The Knapp Commission found widespread corruption at various levels in the police department. Sherman (1974) suggested that police departments can be classified according to the amount and type of corruption that exist. The typology he developed portrays corruption as a progressive problem. Departments are classified as being one of three types:

- **Type I. Rotten apples and rotten pockets**—This type of agency is characterized as having individual officers who use their position for personal gain. There is no organized effort among the officers to do so, and they receive no support from the organization for their activities. While this behavior warrants concern, it is not a problem unique to policing. It is possible to find instances in any organization in which individuals have used their position for personal gain.
- **Type II. Pervasive unorganized corruption**—When individual behavior described under Type I is not effectively controlled through investigation and discipline, it develops into pervasive unorganized corruption. Like the "rotten apple" theory, officers are not organized to carry out corrupt activities. The distinction between the two levels is based on the number of officers involved. The first type is said to exist when relatively few of the

officers are committing illegal acts, but the second describes an agency in which a significant number of officers are doing so.

- **Type III. Pervasive organized corruption**—The most problematic type of corruption results when officers begin to act in an organized manner. This type of behavior requires either the active cooperation of police administrators who participate in the illegal acts or their passive assistance by failing to control officer's activities. It was this level of corruption that the Knapp Commission found to exist in the NYPD. Twenty years after the Knapp Commission's findings, the issue of systemic police corruption was revisited by the Mollen Commission. Although Commissioner Kelly denied systemic corruption, the commission uncovered substantial evidence of this form of organized corruption.

The Commission on Police Integrity in Chicago (1997) made the following observations:

> While corruption has been a consistent and pervasive problem in law enforcement, the nature of corrupt activity has changed dramatically over the years. … Low-level passive forms of corruption (i.e., systemic bribery schemes, non-enforcement of the law, collusion) have been replaced by more aggressive forms of corruption. Today's police corruption is most likely to involve drugs, organized crime, and relatively sophisticated but small groups of officers engaged in felonious criminal activities. The cycle of police scandals in New York City provide a clear example of this trend. In the 1970s, New York's Knapp Commission on Police Corruption identified two general forms of corruption—police officers involved in relatively low-level forms of corruption and misconduct, and those officers involved in large-scale corruption. Twenty years later, New York's Mollen Commission revisited the issue and found the face of corruption had changed. Their primary problem was "crew corruption," wherein groups of officers protect and assist each other's criminal activities. The Mollen Commission identified the predominant patterns of corruption in New York City as police officers committing outright theft from street dealers, from radio runs, from warrantless searches, from legitimate raids, from car stops, from drug couriers, and from off-duty robberies. They also discovered cops protecting and assisting narcotics traffickers as well as cops dealing and using illicit drugs themselves. A pattern of perjured police testimony and false crime reports was also identified in New York.

Sherman's typology is an attempt to describe the progressive nature of corruption, its magnitude, and the level of tolerance by police administrators. Different behavior patterns exist even in an agency permeated with corruption.

Policing, like other professions, has its share of individuals who commit crimes. From a public relations standpoint, whether the crime involves corruption or merely common criminality makes little difference. The public will assume a police officer who commits an illegal act is corrupt. Many will also assume that the entire department or profession is also corrupt. Although this assumption may not be accurate, there is evidence that systemic corruption in the police profession is not limited to a few departments or only a few "bad" officers. Consider the Chicago Commission's (1997) observations on corruption in big city police departments across the country:

- **Miami**—Miami has been rocked with a series of drug related corruption cases. In its most notorious case, the "Miami River Cops Scandal," 17 police officers stole cash and millions of dollars in drugs from drug dealers, sold the drugs, and caused at least three deaths. The scandal resulted in the arrest, suspension, or punishment of more than 100 police officers.
- **New Orleans**—For 6 months in 1994, as many as 29 New Orleans police officers protected a cocaine supply warehouse containing 286 pounds of cocaine. The Federal Bureau of Investigation (FBI) indicted 10 officers who had been paid nearly $100,000 by undercover agents. The investigation ended abruptly after one officer successfully orchestrated the execution of a witness.
- **Philadelphia**—Since 1995, 10 police officers from Philadelphia's 39th District had been charged with planting drugs on suspects, shaking down drug dealers for hundreds of thousands of dollars, and breaking into homes to steal drugs and cash.
- **Los Angeles**—In 1994, 27 Los Angeles County sheriff's deputies and one Los Angeles police officer had been convicted of skimming millions of dollars of drug money while they were members of an elite antinarcotics unit. A convicted deputy stated that they stole $60 million seized in drug raids in one 2-year period alone.
- **Detroit**—In 1991, nine officers were charged with conspiracy to abet the distribution of cocaine, attempted money laundering, and other charges. The officers served as escorts for shipments of what they believed to be drug money and cocaine.

Today, there is no shortage of police officers engaged in acts of corruption and abuse of authority. Box 9.7 highlights some current police scandals in many of the same cities mentioned above.

"Rotten Apples" or Systemic Abuse?
Detecting police deviance and corruption is much more difficult than detecting the deviance of ordinary citizens. Police are the primary social institution charged with the detection and control of crime. This greatly reduces the

Box 9.7   Good Cops Gone Bad

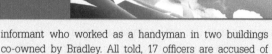

Texas Governor Rick Perry pardons 35 people from the Panhandle town of Tulia who were rounded up in a now-discredited drug sting. Nearly 46 residents, 39 of them black, were arrested during early morning raids on July 23, 1999. The charges were based solely on the word of a Swisher County deputy sheriff, Tom Coleman, who was working for a regional narcotics task force. Coleman now faces perjury charges, and District Attorney Terry McEachern may be sanctioned for possible misconduct by the State Bar of Texas. Two of those arrested, Tonya White and Zuri Bosset, have filed suit in federal court against the 26 counties and four cities involved in the task force.

A federal judge in Pennsylvania orders the unsealing of some 1000 pages of previously confidential internal affairs records containing the names of 13 state troopers who had been disciplined for sexual misconduct. Summaries of the allegations against the officers included sex with teenage girls; the assault and molestation of a suspect while in custody; homosexual rape; and the gang rape of a female who was also injected with an "unknown substance."

While conceding that the witnesses gave her pause, a U.S. District Court magistrate orders three Detroit police officers detained on charges of stealing money and drugs from suspects during illegal searches. The witnesses against officers Troy Bradley, William Melendez, and Matthew Zani include a convicted drug dealer with 10 aliases and an FBI informant who worked as a handyman in two buildings co-owned by Bradley. All told, 17 officers are accused of conspiring to violate the suspects' constitutional rights.

Four former Miami police officers are convicted on conspiracy charges stemming from four shootings in the 1990s that left three men dead and one wounded. Former officers Jorge Castello, 34, Jesus Aguero, 40, and Arturo Beuiristain, 42, are convicted of conspiracy for planting a handgun on a homeless man in a 1997 incident. Oscar Ronda, 41, another former officer, was convicted of obstruction of justice for trying to cover up the crime. The convictions follow by 1 month a report by the Justice Department's Civil Rights Division that stated that the department needs to establish clearer guidelines for the use of force.

Chicago police officers Edgar I. Placencio and Ruben Oliveras, both veteran officers, become the first in the jurisdiction to be charged with failing to report criminal misconduct by fellow officers. The prosecution stems from the investigation of Joseph Miedzianowski, a former officer who was sentenced to life in prison for running a criminal enterprise that transported cocaine from Miami to Chicago. Placencio pleads guilty to a felony civil rights violation and Oliveras to a misdemeanor civil rights charge.

Source: "Good Cops Gone Bad," Law Enforcement News, XXIX(611/612), December 15/31, 2003.

chances that police will focus on themselves as potential deviants or that citizens will perceive the police as engaged in a significant amount of corruption and deviance. Generally, public attitudes toward the police suggest that they are perceived as honest, hardworking, and free from corruption. This public perception creates an intellectual bias and assumption that those charged with controlling crime will not themselves indulge in such behavior.

Manning (1999) provided invaluable insight into the police manipulation of public appearances. He suggested that police are not passive actors in the construction of the police public image. In fact, they cultivate their appearances by "selective systematic presentation of their activities" and by taking "special care to manage or control access to knowledge. … This protects that which they conceal, such as organizational secrets, plans, and the less-than-laudatory features of organizational life." Police, in fact, cultivate the appearance of full and impartial enforcement of the law and are generally unwilling to admit publicly that they have broad discretionary power to interpret the law situationally in their own best interests and to abuse their powers.

One of the most powerful constructions about the police is the administrative and political promotion of the myth of the "rotten apple" (Sherman, 1974). This myth—the corrupt or deviant police officer operating alone and in isolation from the social environment without organizational and peer support—further cultivates the public assumption that police do not engage in significant systematic misconduct. The public perceives the police as a legally controlled institution, bound by the letter of the law, and working only within the confines of legally articulated procedures. This conception of the law is also promoted by members of the legal profession who view law as built on a foundation of precedent that has resulted in a distinct set of doctrines that determines the outcome of cases. This cultivated image of clearly delineated law furthers the general assumption that police will not deviate; their behaviors are thought to be subject to the same review and sanctions as the behaviors of ordinary citizens. As illustrated in countless cases in which police abuse their power, the legal system responds to it very differently than to the criminal behavior of citizens. When an incident of misconduct publicly surfaces, police administrators are quick to point out that the officer involved was a single rotten apple in an otherwise clean barrel—the officer's behavior was an aberration that is not acceptable under existing law nor is it condoned by the police organization. The police thus maintain the public appearance of a profession governed by the rule of law.

> To view a video of LAPD brutality during a May Day event, go to **www.youtube.com/watch?v=4eujQHA8MF0**

The police management of appearances and the rotten apple myth have taken on increasing complexity in recent years. The rise of community policing has been accompanied by a reframing of police imagery. Police have begun reconstituting themselves as scientific problem solvers and community caretakers, transforming their public image from crime fighters to service providers. The police characterize themselves as striving to be accountable to their "clients," "consumers," or "customers" and producing a "quality product" (Kappeler & Kraska, 1998). This new public construction of policing plays down incidents of police deviance (and moves the police further away from legal accountability). Meanwhile, overt police violence appears in the increasing use of police paramilitary units, especially during a time when the public is concerned with terrorism. These events are sanitized for public consumption by emphasizing the services they provide—ridding neighborhoods of drug dealers, protecting us from terrorists, and using a show of force to signal that unacceptable behavior will not be tolerated.

The rotten apple myth is now woven throughout the image of the police as service providers. Incidents of police brutality and corruption are excused as singular aberrations, in contrast to the enormous benefits derived from the community policing movement, such as declining crime rates and winning the war on terrorism. Policing is becoming more aggressive. There is no dearth of police deviance even in community-oriented police departments. Kappeler and Kraska (1998) noted that "police violence is as a whole thus more effectively implemented and public resistance is more proficiently regulated through the mixing of community rhetoric, the circulation of overt violence, and the realignment of the constellation of various social control agencies." The rotten apple explanation for police deviance seems even more palatable in an age in which community policing and waging a war on terror are said to be the dominant orientations of the police institution.

DEVIANT BEHAVIOR

Defining police deviance is a difficult and complex endeavor. The difficulty arises because many of the behaviors considered deviant could also be considered unethical, illegal, or corrupt. There is no clear line between these forms of police wrongdoing and what can be considered deviant. The concept of deviance, however, adds an additional dimension to these forms of misconduct. Deviance can also include behaviors not considered illegal or corrupt. Police officers who sleep on duty, for example, are neither criminal nor corrupt but they can be considered deviant. Compounding the complexity of the idea is the fact that what constitutes deviance is inherently subjective and based on individual as well as group perceptions of behavior. To circumvent the obvious difficulties associated with using subjective conceptions of deviance, theorists have attempted to create uniform but very general definitions of the term. Meier (1989), for example, stated that "deviance refers to differentness," and Matza (1969) suggested "to deviate is to stray, as from a path or standard." Although they serve as a beginning point, these definitions have some problems. Being different, for example, is a matter of degree and depends on context. To be different would include acts from wearing shorts in the winter to committing multiple murders. Because of the vast differences in determining what is deviant by using these simple definitions, we will look at deviance within the context of four sociological paradigms: the statistical paradigm, the absolutist or violation of values paradigm, the reactivist paradigm, and deviance in the context of normative systems.

Statistical Definition of Deviance

The statistical definition of deviance is perhaps the easiest to understand. *Statistical deviance* is any behavior that departs from the average. On the one hand, some behaviors are common and occur with some regularity. These common behaviors would be considered normal. On the other hand, behaviors that are rare or that occur fairly infrequently would be considered deviant. Because the statistical definition requires the use of an average, many persons who may not ordinarily be seen as deviant would be classified as such using this conception. Clinard and Meier (2010) suggested, for example, that if one were to use this definition then those who have never stolen, never smoked marijuana, or never had premarital sex would all be classified as deviant. Thus, behavior that significantly departs from the average even in a "positive" direction is classified as deviant. To illustrate, police who use excessive force to make an exceptional number of arrests would be classified as deviant, as would those who have received an inordinate number of commendations for performance beyond the call of duty. This conception of deviance has some utility for police administrators in that it provides them with a basis to check individual officer behavior against the behaviors of the department as a whole. For example, administrators might want to take a closer look at officers who generate complaints at greater rates than the departmental average (Kappeler et al., 1998).

Absolutist Definition of Deviance

Up until the 1950s, many members of the public and social scientists viewed the concept of deviance as an absolute. Certain behaviors were thought to be *absolutely deviant* or universally and inherently wrong. For the most part, it was implicitly understood that some behaviors were intrinsically deviant. Behaviors typically falling into the category of "deviant" were those involving a violation of criminal law—especially those crimes committed by persons with little social influence or power. The absolutist perspective on deviance is premised on a few important assumptions. First, it is assumed that members of society agree that certain behaviors should be proscribed. Second, it is assumed that people are both acquainted with and understand the rules prohibiting certain acts. In short, the absolutist perspective suggests that there is a consensus in society that some acts are repugnant. To control these behaviors, certain rules have been adopted, endorsed, clearly articulated, and made known to all societal members.

Although the absolutist perspective on deviance continues to be supported by some, it has come under attack by others. The absolutist perspective has been criticized for supposing that there is universal agreement among societal members that certain behaviors should be prohibited. In contrast, some have argued that the values held by Americans are pluralistic rather than absolutist. This criticism points to substantial disagreement in society over which behaviors should be considered deviant. In a similar vein, it has been suggested that those acts considered by absolutists as deviant most often reflect the values and morals of people in power; hence, acts defined as deviant may actually represent a violation of the value positions of only certain segments or classes of society.

The absolutist conception of deviance can also be criticized for its assumption that the vast majority of citizens are aware that certain acts are deviant and that this has been clearly communicated. Statutes, regulations, rules, and social norms proscribe many behaviors; however, not all of these prohibitions are universally known. Even if known, they may not be completely understood because of their complex nature. Finally, in some settings, certain acts are prohibited, while in others they are considered appropriate. Murder, for example, is ordinarily prohibited, but in the case of societies at war, killing becomes an expected and even rewarded behavior. Thus, on several accounts, the absolutist definition of deviance is problematic for the study of police deviance (Kappeler et al., 1998).

Reactivist Definition of Deviance

Often referred to as "labeling," "societal reaction," or "interactionist perspective," the reactivist conception of deviance was developed by Durkheim in the late 1800s but became popular in the 1950s and 1960s. The reactivist perspective represents an important alternative way to conceptualize and to understand deviance. In contrast to the absolutist definition, the *reactivist* paradigm proposes that no act is inherently deviant. Instead, this view of deviance suggests that members of society routinely engage in various rule-breaking behaviors; however, some of those who break rules are labeled deviant while many others are not. Whether an act is labeled deviant depends on the response of others to the particular act. In brief, reactivists propose that the key factor in determining whether an act is deviant is how others react to it. Being labeled deviant is contingent on many factors. These include the status of the person violating the rule, the status of those who feel harmed by the behavior, and the context in which the behavior occurs.

The reactivist conception of deviance is important because it illustrates the relative nature of deviance. That is, what may be classified as deviant in one setting may be considered socially acceptable behavior in another. As an illustration, corrupt police working on a squad together would likely label deviant any newly assigned officer who refused to participate in corrupt activities. It would be unlikely that the same officer would be labeled deviant if assigned to work with a group of officers who were not engaged in corrupt activities. These illustrations are consistent with the reactivist proposition that not all criminal behavior is deviant, and not all deviant behavior is criminal (Kappeler et al., 1998).

Normative Definition of Deviance

Although there are different ways to define or operationalize deviance, generally it is viewed as a violation or divergence from the normative system. The *normative system* definition suggests that deviance is the violation of a norm.

Simply stated, norms may be defined as social expectations or guidelines for conduct. When people violate the norms governing a particular setting, they would be considered deviant. Deviance is relative not only to behavior but also to the social context in which the behavior occurs; therefore, the normative definition of deviance reflects an interactive process among social actors, settings, and norms. In other words, people who are labeled deviant must engage in behavior that is viewed as departing from the bounds of acceptable conduct that governs a particular social group or setting. The process of detecting and labeling a behavior deviant then depends on the behavior, the social context in which the behavior occurs, the formal and informal rules of conduct, and the perception of the behavior as violating existing social norms. Deviance then is based as much on the perception of social control agents and social interpretation as it is on actual behavior: "It is the audience which eventually decides whether or not any given action or actions become a visible case of deviation" (Erikson, 1962).

Norms and values of social and occupational groups differ. As in social settings, what is considered deviant behavior in one occupation may be viewed as perfectly acceptable conduct in another. This makes the study of police deviance an especially difficult task. Police conduct occurs within a unique occupational and normative context. The police occupational group often subscribes to values that depart drastically from those found in many segments of the larger society. This means that behavior unacceptable to the public may not be seen as constituting anything particularly wrong by the police as an occupational group. Because police officers have special powers, authority, and a unique culture, their attitudes, values, and beliefs sometimes conflict with those of private citizens (Box 9.8).

Another complication is that norms and values tend to differ within and between police groups. Members of one police organization may condemn the use of physically aggressive measures to control crime, while another organization may have a history of rewarding its members for aggressive practices. Similarly, different groups within a single police organization may adhere to values and expectations different from other groups or cliques. Police assigned to patrol a neighborhood considered to be violent and crime-ridden might view aggressive practices as necessary police behavior, whereas another group of police assigned to a usually quiet, middle-class neighborhood might be less likely to subscribe to violence as normal police behavior. Given the complexity and diversity of the norms and values that affect the police, the study of deviance necessarily entails an understanding of the differences in norms as they are expressed at the legal, organizational, and subcultural levels. With these distinctions in mind, we will turn to some of the issues surrounding police deviance, such as alcohol and drug abuse, sexual misconduct, police sexual violence, and various work-related forms of deviance.

Box 9.8 Normative System of Police Deviance

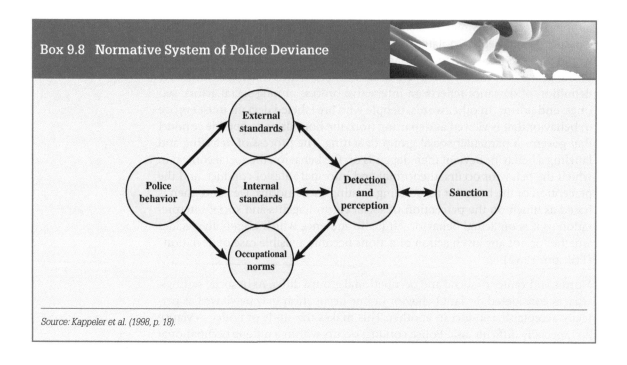

Source: Kappeler et al. (1998, p. 18).

Alcohol and Other Drugs of Abuse

Police drug use has become a major issue in a number of departments with officers using illegal drugs, such as cocaine and marijuana. Also, there are a number of officers who abuse prescription drugs. Stinson et al. (2012) examined news articles from across the country for police drug use and corruption. They found that 27.6% of the cases they found involved officers using illegal drugs. Kraska and Kappeler (1988) interviewed officers in one department and found that 25% of the officers abused illegal drugs. Drug use by police officers is becoming more prevalent. It has a higher acceptance rate within society, and, in some cases, it is acceptable within the police culture. The primary mechanism to combat police drug use is random drug testing. Some departments now randomly test all sworn officers, while other departments test selected groups, such as applicants, officers working in the drug unit, or officers applying for promotion. Given the increased use of drugs by officers, the best policy is to randomly test all officers. A problem with the current state of affairs in police drug testing is that most departments depend on urinalysis. Because drugs like cocaine quickly leave the body they are not always detectable through urinalysis. Hair analysis results in more accurate testing and should be adopted by departments (Mieczkowski & Lersch, 2002).

The Myths of Police Deviance and Corruption

Myth: Policing is free from the deviance and corruption that is found in most other occupations.

Reality: Policing is vulnerable to all the forms of deviance found in other occupations. In fact, policing, in some cases, has higher rates of deviance and criminality than that found in the general public.

Myth: Most police departments never or only rarely experience incidents of deviance or scandal.

Reality: All police organizations experience some form of deviance or scandal at some point in their history.

Myth: Acts of police deviance, misconduct, and corruption are the result of rogue officers and are not widespread often systemic.

Reality: Very few cases of police deviance and misconduct are the results of isolated rogue officers. More often than not deviance is the product of behavioral support systems and is systemic or directly related to the social organization of policing.

Although there is disagreement as to the number of officers who actually abuse drugs, no one would deny that the problem exists and that it has serious consequences. Drug abuse is normally in that category of behavior that is illegal and clearly violative of ethical norms. The potential does exist, however, for officers to abuse medicines prescribed by a physician and which are, in a technical sense, legal to use. This issue is complicated by the fact that 16 states have legalized medical marijuana, and two states, Colorado and Washington, have legalized the drug for recreational use. The ethical question centers on when officers should be relieved of duty in order to prevent harm to themselves, other officers, or the general public. The decision would, on the surface, be simple to make: if the physiological effects of the drug impair performance, then the officer should be relieved of duty.

Studies of alcohol abuse by police officers present conflicting information. Some claim that as many as 25% of police officers have serious problems with alcohol abuse (Kraska & Kappeler, 1988; Kroes, 1976). Lindsay (2008) surveyed 663 officers in Mississippi and found that 18.2% of the respondents at a harmful risk level for alcohol problems. In an earlier study, 2200 police officers in 29 states were surveyed, and 23% of respondents reported some of their peers had drinking problems. The research indicates that a number of officers have alcohol related problems. To a great extent, police officer drinking behavior mirrors the general public. However, it becomes problematic when officers drink on duty. Such behavior has serious consequences for public safety.

A significant problem with police alcohol abuse is officers being apprehended for driving under the influence (DUI). For example, in a 4-month period, four

San Diego police officers were charged with DUI; this problem is endemic across all departments. Departments have implemented a variety of programs to stem the problem. Some provide counseling through wellness centers or police psychologists, others have increased the penalty for the offense, and one department, Salt Lake City, has an arrangement with cab companies to transport off-duty officers when they have had too much to drink. In Texas, police officers can lose their certification if convicted of DUI (PERF, 2012). Given the seriousness of police officer DUI and the negative public attention given to such cases, police departments must ramp up efforts to prevent the problem.

Sexual Harassment

Sexual harassment in the workplace is a significant problem for police agencies. In simple terms, sexual harassment can take one of two forms: (1) requiring an individual to grant sexual favors to obtain, maintain, or improve employment status; or (2) creation of a hostile work environment. The first category of employee harassment occurs when someone in a position to affect another's continued employment, advancement, or working conditions makes unwelcome sexual advances, coupled with the threat of retaliation if refused. This may include actions by supervisors, field training officers, administrators, or other government officials. Such actions are illegal under Title VII of the 1964 Civil Rights Act and may be actionable under 42 U.S.C. Section 1983.

The second type of sexual harassment occurs when suggestive comments, photographs, jokes, obscene gestures, or unwanted physical contact creates a hostile work environment for the victim officer or other police employee. What constitutes a hostile work environment is difficult to define. If the female officers perceive they are working in a hostile environment, then there most certainly exists unethical if not illegal conduct. The ethical problem is determining the point at which behavior resulting from such exposure creates a hostile working environment for other employees. There are two sides to the argument. The first side maintains that officers who find locker-room conversations or photographs offensive are in the wrong profession. This station house behavior is mild compared to what they will encounter on the street. The other side of the argument holds that, just because some people use abusive language, female officers should not have to endure this conduct from their coworkers. Although police cannot control such conduct among the general public, they should not be subjected to it from other officers.

Thus far, we have examined sexual harassment that occurs among officers or employees of the department. There is also the potential for harassment of citizens by officers that may take one of several forms. Officers may engage in bribery or extortion for sexual favors rather than money. Voyeurism is a form of harassment. Officers routinely check parked vehicles and occasionally discover citizens who are engaged in sexual activity. The ability to explain their presence in a given area presents the opportunity for officers to "window-peep." If confronted about their actions, a claim that they were looking for a suspicious subject would satisfy most people. Illegal strip searches of prisoners may also be abused and have been the subject of several court decisions (*Bell v. Wolfish*, 1979; *Mary Beth v. City of Chicago*, 1983). Another problem has been termed *driving while female*, where police officers stop women for traffic violations and demand sexual favors in lieu of a traffic ticket.

Sapp (1994) identified seven categories of police sexually motivated or sexual harassment behaviors:

1. Nonsexual contacts that are sexually motivated;
2. Voyeuristic contacts;
3. Contacts with crime victims;
4. Contacts with offenders;
5. Contacts with underage females;
6. Sexual shakedowns;
7. Citizen initiated sexual contacts.

Police Sexual Violence

Recently, social scientists have begun to examine the various forms of sexual deviance against female citizens. Although sexual harassment has gained media attention in recent years, it is only recently that scholars have paid attention to the sexual violence committed by police officers. *Police sexual violence* (PSV) takes many forms; it is not confined to a single definition or kind of victimization. Instead, PSV involves "those situations in which a citizen experiences a sexually degrading, humiliating, violating, damaging or threatening act committed by a police officer, through the use of force or police authority" (Kraska & Kappeler, 1995). An example of this form of violence and the power differences between citizens and police is illustrated in the case of a complaint against a Houston police officer. In 2007, Officer Thomas Gandy was charged with official oppression following accusations that he forced a woman to undress. According to the complaint, the incident took place at an apartment where the officer was serving a warrant. After serving the warrant, according to the prosecutor, the officer returned to the apartment, searched it, and made a woman remove her clothes. Prosecutors said "The woman told them she was scared and did what the officer told her to do" (Anonymous, 2007d).

In an exploratory study covering a couple of years, Kraska and Kappeler (1995) uncovered 124 documented cases of what they considered to be police sexual violence. Based on their analysis, they developed a continuum of police sexual violence. Box 9.9 shows that continuum and categorizes police sexual violence as unobtrusive, obtrusive, and criminal.

Kraska and Kappeler (1995) concluded that, based on their research, police sexual violence is:

1. Based on operational justifications found in police work;
2. Often institutionally and culturally supported;
3. Evenly dispersed across types of police agencies and officer ranks;
4. Not merely the product of aberrant officers or departments.

Expanding on this research, McGurrin and Kappeler (2002) examined 66 newspapers from around the country and located more than 700 cases of police sexual violence. Their examination of the context of these news articles found that the majority of these incidents involved serious criminal activity, such as rape and sexual assault, not merely locker-room or station house banter. Police sexual activity has been dismissed as merely being "boys will be boys" or as consensual relationships, but many of the cases they examined could be

---

Box 9.9   A Continuum of Police Sexual Violence

Continuum Category	Range of Behaviors	Institutional or Cultural Support	Operational Justification	Range of Legal Sanctions
Unobtrusive behavior	Viewing victims, photographs, and sexually explicit videos; invasions of privacy; secondary victimization	Possible institutional and cultural	Crime control investigation, examine evidence, review evidence for case preparation	Civil lawsuit
Obtrusive behavior	Custodial strip searches, body cavity searches, warrant-based searches, illegal detentions, deception to gain sexual favors, provision of services for sexual favors, sexual harassment	Possible institutional and cultural	Preservation of evidence, ensure security, control contraband, law enforcement, necessary for covert investigations	Civil lawsuit to possibly criminal
Criminal behavior	Sexual harassment, sexual contact, sexual assault, rape	Linked to institutionalized police characteristics	None	Civil lawsuit to criminal

Source: Kraska and Kappeler (1995).

described as predatory behavior by police officers against women. Consider a few recent examples:

- A Dickinson County, Michigan, jury convicted a city police officer, Phillip Bal, of a sex crime. The officer was charged with first-degree criminal sexual conduct and first-degree home invasion stemming from a sexual assault of an Iron Mountain woman at her home. At trial, Bal's attorney argued that the sex was consensual. The officer was also facing additional charges of sex crime stemming from two alleged sexual assaults in bars (Anonymous, 2007e).
- A sheriff's deputy working as a school safety officer was arrested on charges he had sex with a Swain County High School student. Officer Joseph Scott Smith was charged with four felony sex offenses (Anonymous, 2007i).
- An Atlanta, Georgia, police officer was arrested and charged with raping a woman. Officer Lamar Gavin was indicted on charges of rape, burglary, and unlawful eavesdropping. The officer was fired from the department for the alleged off-duty rape (Anonymous, 2007h).
- Multiple criminal sexual misconduct charges were brought against a Detroit police sergeant accused of forcing victims to perform sex acts. Officer Roosevelt J. Tidwell, Jr., according to the Wayne County Prosecutor's Office, not only forced park visitors to perform sex acts but also engaged in sex with a victim. Two couples reported that he allegedly stopped them in Chandler Park and threatened to arrest them unless they performed sex acts while he watched. "Tidwell allegedly stopped citizens for traffic offenses and used them for his own perverse sexual pleasures," Wayne County Prosecutor Kym L. Worthy said in a press release. "We suspect that there may be other victims" (Anonymous, 2007b).

Stacking-Up, Jacking-Up, and Using Cover Charges

Many acts of police deviance are driven by a desire to achieve organizational objectives, such as fighting crime. Overzealous officers can engage in legally abusive conduct not out of a desire for personal gain, as in the case of corruption, but rather from a motivation to apprehend and punish law violators. In many jurisdictions, identical legal violations can be charged as either a misdemeanor or a felony. One example is a charge of possession of a fictitious or altered driver's license versus possession of a forged instrument. Many juveniles obtain false driver's licenses in order to frequent nightclubs and to purchase alcoholic beverages. Police who run across these licenses when making traffic stops will often jack-up the charge against the juvenile, hoping that he or she will "turn" or provide information on where the fake license was purchased. In many jurisdictions, stacking-up and jacking-up charges allow police to accomplish their goal of law enforcement. Police may charge or threaten to charge a citizen with a more serious offense or with several offenses if they fail to cooperate with the real police objective. *Stacking-up* and *jacking-up* charges are often encountered in cases involving drug enforcement activities. Similar to the example regarding a fake driver's license, police will jack-up or stack-up drug charges on a minor violator to obtain information on a major drug distributor.

Police who have violated the rights of a citizen or even committed an outright criminal act may charge the abused citizen in hopes that the number or severity of charges will induce a guilty plea so the incident will never be uncovered or aired in the courtroom. In the Mollen Commission (Mollen, 1994), this practice is referred to as a *cover charge*:

> [O]fficers know that the operation of the criminal justice system itself usually protects them from having to commit testimonial perjury before a grand jury or at trial. The vast majority of charges for narcotics or weapons possession crimes result in pleas without the necessity of grand jury or trial testimony, thus obviating officers' concerns about the risk of detection and possible exposure to criminal charges of perjury.

The distinction between the use of the law to achieve organizational objectives and the use of the law to achieve personal objectives is often blurred.

The court system contributes to the deviance of stacking charges. Often, defense attorneys and prosecutors bargain with offenders concerning criminal charges. Defense attorneys offer prosecutors a guilty plea in exchange for a reduction in charges and a recommendation for a light sentence. Police, well aware of this practice, charge citizens with the most serious crime available, knowing that other criminal justice officials will negotiate the outcome of the case.

For deviant police officers, the law serves not as a control on practice but rather as a device for securing enforcement objectives. The law is often used in a selective fashion because "a wide range of rules can be used to justify any particular disposition an official deems appropriate for his organizational interests" (Ericson, 1981:86). In addition to taking advantage of the discretion and ambiguity afforded by the law, some officers are guilty of outright violation of the law to advance the objectives of the police organization. The Mollen Commission's (Mollen, 1994) investigation into corruption in the NYPD found, for example, that:

> When officers genuinely believe that nothing is wrong with fabricating the basis of an arrest, a search, or other police action and that civil rights are merely an obstacle to aggressive law enforcement, the

Department's top commanders must share the blame. Indeed, we found that for years the Department was content to address allegations of perjury on a case-by-case basis, rather than pursuing the potential for a broader-based investigation. For example, supervisors were rarely, if ever, held accountable for the falsifications of their subordinates. We are not aware of a single instance in which a supervisor or commander has been sanctioned for permitting perjury or falsification on their watch.

Sherman (1974) noted "police failure to observe due process requirements in arresting suspects is an illegal practice, but such practices are usually viewed as supportive of the formal goal of police organizations." Similarly, when the law does not serve to advance the organizational objective of the police, then the police are likely to resort to deviant behavior to secure objectives. Many authors have noted that, while the exclusionary rule was constructed to prevent police abuses of citizens' constitutional rights through the exclusion of evidence obtained illegally by the police, its use has resulted in an increase in police perjury.

Gratuities

The practice of extending gratuities to police officers has been in existence almost as long as the profession itself. Debates over whether it should be permitted are almost as old. *Gratuities* consist of coffee, food, or other items and services given to police officers for a reduced price or free of charge. Many national chains have a corporate policy of providing gratuities to officers. The debate about this practice is usually couched in terms of whether it constitutes an abuse of police authority or is merely an expression of appreciation shown to officers by the community (Box 9.10).

Those opposed to the practice contend that it is an attempt to corrupt the officer in return for future favors. Anechiarico and Jacobs (1996) go so far as labeling gratuities as bribery. Additionally, Prenzler and Mackay (1995) surveyed citizens about the issue and found that police gratuities undermined citizen confidence in the police. Citizens often believe officers should not receive benefits just because of their office, and they see where gratuities can lead to favoritism or corruption. Ruiz and Bono (2004) echo this sentiment noting that the practice is degrading to offices.

Feldberg (1986) believed that this argument was without merit, as officers are capable of distinguishing between gestures of goodwill and attempted bribery. Most officers do not view the acceptance of gratuities as a form of corruption. The public's perception is fairly evenly divided. Depending on how the question is asked, about one-half do not believe the practice creates a problem (Sigler & Dees, 1988).

Box 9.10   Factors Affecting the Sanctioning of Police Deviance

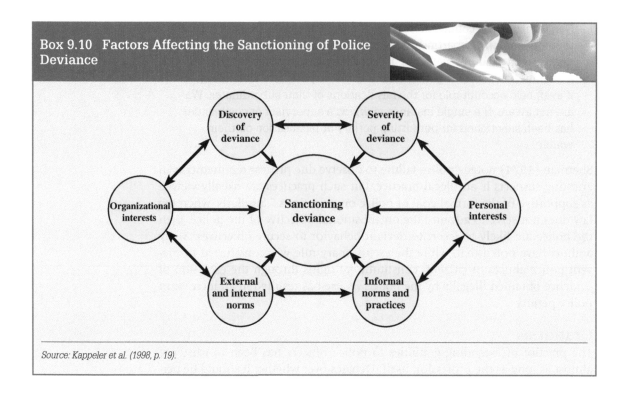

Source: Kappeler et al. (1998, p. 19).

Cohen (1986) provided an excellent discussion of the ethical issues. Gratuities may differ from bribery or extortion in the amount offered and the intent of the officer and citizen; however, the intent and amount are not viable ways to evaluate the behavior. Police services are a valuable resource. If acceptance of gratuities is pervasive in a department, this resource may be allocated on the basis of the availability of "freebies." Those who do not offer gratuities are denied the presence of officers who gravitate to businesses that do offer them. Not all officers accept gratuities; some routinely avoid establishments that offer them. Cohen (1986) also suggested that new officers may be coerced into accepting gratuities rather than risking alienation from other officers. They are forced to engage in behavior that violates their values because of existing social norms. Although not addressed directly by Cohen, once this occurs, they may be more susceptible to other forms of coercion, leading to illegal behavior. Gratuities from merchants are often viewed as "tips" for services performed. This is a normal practice in certain businesses and is not based on expectations of future services (Box 9.11).

How then should we regulate acceptance of gratuities? Is a complete ban necessary, or should officers be allowed to accept minor amounts that are offered as a form of appreciation by the community? Goldstein (1977) identified

> ### Box 9.11   No Free (or Discounted) Lunch for Bradenton Cops
>
> After the firing of an officer for taking food and other items from local merchants, the Bradenton, Florida, Police Department established a policy in September that prohibits sworn personnel from accepting any discounted meals offered by restaurant owners.
>
> The order came from Mayor Wayne Poston, who said he did not want any appearance of impropriety. An internal memo issued by Police Chief Dan Thorpe said "The purpose of this directive is to establish a higher level of integrity and enhance the image of the Bradenton Police Department and its members."
>
> According to Captain Jeffrey J. Lewis, investigators found that Officer Keith Dennis had not so much abused a policy allowing officers to accept small gratuities, such as a fountain drink, but outright stole these items. Records show that Dennis never paid for a cigar, a sandwich, a magazine, and other goods from a 7-Eleven store.
>
> "He would go into the humidor and get a cigar, or take a bottle of Gatorade and tell the clerk, 'I don't have any cash on me now, I'll catch you tomorrow,'" Lewis told Law Enforcement News. "Well, there's a different clerk working the next day, and he would never pay it back."
>
> The department's policy had been that if merchants offered discounted meals with no solicitation on the part of police, then it was all right to accept that generosity. It had been a considered a perk, said Lewis, by officers who make approximately $22,000 a year.
>
> "It was definitely important to officers and it was important to business owners as well, because they liked to have the presence of the uniformed officer in their establishment eating" he said. "It really had worked both ways."
>
> *Source: "No Free (or Discounted) Lunch for Bradenton Cops," Law Enforcement News, October 15, 2000, p. 6.*

problems inherent in either approach. Labeling gratuities as a form of corruption and prohibiting officers from accepting them can be impossible to enforce. Because this form of corruption is not effectively addressed, it may appear that the department is not seriously committed to addressing any form of corruption. Allowing officers to accept gratuities may lower their resistance to other temptations. If the practice is condoned, it is virtually impossible to define the limits of what is acceptable. Is it all right to accept a free lunch but not an expensive dinner? Is a discount on clothing permissible but free admission to a movie theater is not?

Goldbricking versus Quotas

Goldbricking is a term that is used to imply that an officer avoids work or performs only the amount necessary to satisfy department supervisors. In the previous chapter, we discussed the existence of police postulates and defined them as statements of belief held by a culture that reflects its basic orientation. Several of these postulates (Reuss-Ianni, 1983) can be related directly to the problem of goldbricking:

1. Do not give bosses too much activity.
2. Do not do the bosses' work for them.
3. Be aggressive when you have to, but do not be too eager.

4. Do not get involved in anything in another officer's sector.
5. Hold up your end of the work.
6. Do not leave work for the next tour.

With the exception of the last two, these postulates, if adhered to by officers, would result in their performing a minimal amount of work. Only when their inactivity created work for others would they be subject to criticism from fellow officers. These values are in direct conflict with the work ethic that dictates that officers adopt a proactive approach to policing and continually seek out activities to be performed.

Establishing an acceptable level of performance has caused many administrators to be criticized for creating a quota system. *Quota systems* based on the need to produce revenue through the collection of fines or promote activity merely to increase statistics reported to other government officials and the public are clearly unethical. Establishing an acceptable level of activity to ensure that officers are performing their duties is part of the administrator's responsibility. The difficulty arises in distinguishing between quotas and reasonable workload measures.

Perhaps the easiest example to use is traffic enforcement. In theory, police officers enforce traffic laws to prevent accidents. There is, however, a point at which writing additional tickets will have no effect on the accident rate. Officers will typically resist efforts to dictate the level of their activity. Citizens perceive these efforts as establishment of a quota system. Ethical conduct requires the administrator to ensure that a sufficient number of tickets are written to reduce accidents and prevent an officer's goldbricking, while at the same time protecting citizens from unwarranted enforcement actions. The systems, however, can be abused, as in the case of the New York City Police Department. In 2013, it was uncovered that the NYPD administration had established quotas for their now infamous "stop and frisk" program that discriminated against thousands of minorities in that city. If an officer or department adheres solely to quota systems that values enforcement, actions quickly become oppressive to the community.

Goldbricking can take many forms. Calls for service can be ignored or passed on to someone else; suspicious activities or violations can be overlooked; or officers can engage in personal business while on duty, sleep while they are supposed to be working, or engage in any number of other activities. Adherence to the police postulates discussed above can lead to inactivity. Officers generally have a great deal of freedom and mobility, making it possible to engage in personal business while on duty. Today's technology means that officers are no longer restricted to their patrol vehicles. It is possible to pay bills, go shopping, visit with friends, or otherwise goof off while still remaining in contact with the dispatcher and thus avoiding detection (Box 9.12).

Box 9.12   If It Smells Like a Quota and Acts Like a Quota…

Two Mendham Township, New Jersey, police sergeants recently filed suit against local officials, claiming they were unfairly disciplined because they disobeyed an order to write at least one traffic ticket during each shift.

The plaintiffs, Vincent J. Romano and Thomas R. Zenick, both of whom have been Mandham police officers for more than 20 years, contend they were issued written reprimands in June for failing to comply with a directive on issuing traffic tickets in the affluent northern New Jersey community.

"Mendham Township is calling it a performance evaluation, but it smells like a ticket quota and acts like a ticket quota," said attorney Michael Bukosky, who is representing the sergeants.

Law Enforcement News was unable to reach Bukosky for further comment, but the lawyer told The Newark Star-Ledger that the two sergeants were notified on June 10 that they were getting written reprimands for "disobeying a ticket quota." Bukosky further charged that the action was taken without giving his clients a chance to challenge the move in a hearing.

The lawsuit seeks to have the reprimands voided and asks that the directive, which the plaintiffs contend is unconstitutional and violates public policy, be scrapped.

"Both of these officers have been on the force for more than 20 years and have exemplary records," said Bukosky. "Each is well-respected and has no beef with their chief or the township except when it comes to enforcing a policy they strongly oppose."

Mendham Township is "not the type of community where traffic is flying around and there might be reason for a ticket quota," Bukosky continued. "The public shouldn't stand for it. Pity the poor motorists who get stopped on the last day of the month because an officer is short four or five tickets."

Township Attorney Roger Clapp did not return calls from Law Enforcement News for comment. Police Chief Thomas Constanza told Law Enforcement News, "I've been directed by the township attorney to not speak about it."

Source: "If It Smells Like a Quota and Acts Like a Quota…," Law Enforcement News, October 15, 1997, p. 9.

DISCIPLINING THE POLICE

Police officers can be disciplined for a variety of reasons. Discipline generally originates when an officer engages in behavior that is prohibited or fails to take some action—violates a rule or law. Police officers may be disciplined when they violate a statute, city or county ordinance, or a departmental policy. These guidelines provide specific information about how officers should act when performing a specific task. Even though some police departments have voluminous rules and regulations, there are ample gray areas where officers must use their discretion. These gray areas often become contentious when discipline is considered.

When police officers commit crimes or are involved in deviant behavior, it is not always easy to discipline them. A case in Indianapolis illustrates this point. One of the department's officers was charged with driving under the influence, and consequently was suspended. However, it took 3 years for the department to terminate him. Civil service regulations dictate that the merit board cannot hear the case until criminal charges are heard in court (Tuohy,

2013). Such court hearings often take months or even years, as in this case. Indianapolis was, to some extent, fortunate because laws allow officers to be suspended without pay. In many other jurisdictions, when officers are suspected for some offense, they are suspended with pay. Collective bargaining agreements or state statutes in many jurisdictions require that they be paid until officers are found guilty in court or the disciplinary issue is ruled upon. In some cases, officers are paid for several years awaiting the outcome of their case.

Police discipline can be complicated in other ways. Generally, departments bring charges against one or a few officers. However, in 2013, the Cleveland Police Department brought disciplinary charges against 74 officers, including a captain and a lieutenant. The charges stemmed from a high-speed pursuit in 2012 that was completely out of control. At the time of the pursuit, there were 277 officers on duty, with 104 officers becoming involved in the pursuit. As a result of the 23 min chase, officers fired 137 shots killing the two occupants in the vehicle being pursued. Officers reported hearing a gunshot from the vehicle and seeing a gun, but no weapon was found after the pursuit (CNN Staff, 2013). Generally, police disciplinary actions do include such a large number of officers.

The investigation of police disciplinary problems can be conducted by a variety of agencies depending on state statutes, labor contracts, and local government laws. For example, Sauchelli, Schram, and Velez (2013) identify the various agencies that have investigative authority over New York City officers.

- Civilian Complaint Review Board (CCRB): investigates complaints of alleged misconduct with subpoena power.
- Commission to Combat Police Corruption: city agency that monitors and evaluates anticorruption programs and practices.
- NYPD Internal Affairs Bureau (IAB): reviews allegations of police misconduct and can recommend disciplinary action.
- NYPD Quality Assurance Division: monitors compliance with department procedures through audits.
- Investigation Review Section: part of the NYPD Chief of Patrol's Office, investigates complaints not handled by the IAB and CCRB.
- Prosecutors: the city's five district attorneys, two U.S. attorneys and the state attorney general have jurisdiction to conduct criminal investigations into allegations of police wrongdoing.
- Justice Department Civil Rights Division: prosecutes allegations of police misconduct relating to civil-rights violations.
- Supervisors: sergeants, lieutenants, precinct integrity officers, and precinct commanders all review and evaluate the performance of officers.

There is substantial variability in how officers are disciplined. Generally, when officers are charged by the department for an offense or violation, a hearing is conducted by the department or other duly authorized body. Police officers have due process and administrative rights during such hearings. The department will render a verdict based on the information in the case. At that point, officers will accept the verdict or they generally have a right to appeal the verdict and penalty to a higher authority. In some instances, disciplinary cases can weave their way through the appellate court system before there is a final determination.

Oftentimes, officers are opposed to disciplinary procedures. A study by McDevitt et al. (2011) showed that, for the most part, police officers had critical views about the disciplinary process. They questioned officers in seven departments (two small, three medium, and three large departments) and found that 57.6% of the respondents in the smaller departments viewed disciplinary procedures as being fair, while only 21.1% from the larger agencies perceived the process as being fair. This is problematic. When officers perceive some level of unfairness in the department, they are less likely to respect their supervisors. They also are likely to be less committed to the department and its programs and goals. Perceived justice is important in maintaining morale and all departments must make efforts to improve perceptions of procedural justice.

There is some concern that racial biases enter into the disciplinary process where minorities are treated more harshly than white officers. Research has been mixed. Hickman, Lawton, Piquero, and Greene (2001) found no statistical disparity with regard to complaints or findings. However, Lersch and Mieczkowski (2000) found that minorities were overrepresented in citizen complaints in their study. In a recent study in a large Midwestern police department, researchers studied the results of 1706 allegations lodged against officers with the most common allegation conduct unbecoming (35.3%) followed by violation of department procedures (24.7%). They found that minority officers were overrepresented in the number of complaints, and minority officers had higher numbers of complaints that were sustained by the department; however, minorities and whites had about the same percentage or citizen complaints sustained, but minorities had a higher number of departmental complaints sustained. The high number of departmental complaints sustained resulted in minorities having a larger percent sustain rate. When disciplinary action was examined, it was found that minority officers did not receive more severe discipline (Rojek & Decker, 2009). These findings are from one department, and they may vary across departments. They show that all aspects of a disciplinary process should be monitored to ensure that there are no biases in the process.

SUMMARY

This chapter explores the definition and application of ethics and deviance in law enforcement. Ethics is a term that is not easily defined. Traditionally, the study of ethics focused on activities about which there was little disagreement as to their inappropriateness: bribery, extortion, excessive force, perjury, or other illegal behaviors. Contemporary approaches to the topic focus on issues for which there are no obvious or easily agreed upon solutions, such as the use of discretion, appropriate use of force, and other activities that require a value judgment to be made by the officer.

Values are derived from a number of sources: our concept of justice, existing law, agency policy, professional codes of ethics, social norms, and personal beliefs. In many instances, these values conflict, and officers must choose between them. Whether or not others view an action as ethical will depend on which value source they adhere to in making their evaluation. For many of the issues facing law enforcement, there are no clear-cut choices. The inability to predict all of the circumstances that will arise often leaves officers in a vacuum without guidance as to the correct course of action. Equally important is the simple fact that significant numbers of police engage in crime, deviance, and misconduct. Because deviance is based on both group and individual perceptions of what is normal behavior, the concept is difficult to define. Several conceptions of deviance were reviewed, and various forms of deviance and issues associated with the police were considered. Deviance among the police has a long history and remains an important problem facing the police and society even today.

When officers violate prescribed behavioral norms, whether they are laws or departmental policies, officers generally are faced with some form of disciplinary action. The disciplinary procedure results in a determination of guilt or innocence and recommends a punishment that is imposed by the police chief. Officers have due process rights throughout this procedure. Moreover, they have appeal rights should they disagree with the outcome. Outcomes can include anything from a letter of reprimand to termination. Discipline is an important mechanism for instilling the department's ethics and values, and reducing criminal and deviant behavior.

REVIEW QUESTIONS

1. The terms *ethics* and *morality* are often used interchangeably, with neither having a precise definition. Define each and how they are related to each other.
2. Defining ethical behavior often depends on what? What are the main sources of ethics?

3. Describe the difference between police crime and abuse of authority, occupational deviance, and corruption.
4. What is the "rotten apple" myth of corrupt or deviant police behavior and how has it shaped the image of police as service providers?
5. How do the statistical, absolutist, reactivist, and normative definitions of deviance each provide a "lens" or means in which to view police deviance?

REFERENCES

Anechiarico, F., & Jacobs, J. B. (1996). *The pursuit of absolute integrity: How corruption control makes government ineffective.* Chicago: University of Chicago Press.

Anonymous. (1988). Ex-Pittsburgh officer with unusual off-duty "employment" sentenced to 2-1/2–100 years. *Crime Control Digest, 22*(19), 9.

Anonymous. (2007a). *Deputy charged with stealing $1,000 from dead woman's purse.* Mercury News. May 9.

Anonymous. (2007b). *Detroit police officer charged with multiple sex crimes.* Detroit News. April 26.

Anonymous. (2007c). *Former officer gets 5 years probation.* Omaha: KETV. April 24.

Anonymous. (2007d). *HPD officer charged with official oppression.* Houston: KPRC. April 26.

Anonymous. (2007e). *Jury finds ex-Iron Mountain officer guilty of rape.* Associated Press. May 25.

Anonymous. (2007g). *Police arrest Dallas officer accused of taking money during stop.* Dallas: NBC5. June 19.

Anonymous. (2007h). *Police officer charged with rape.* Atlanta: WSB-TV. May 3.

Anonymous. (2007i). *Swain deputy charged with having sex with student.* Ashville: Citizens Times. May 7.

Baer, H., & Armao, J. P. (1995). The Mollen Commission report: an overview. *New York Law School Law Review, 40,* 73–85.

Barker, T., & Carter, D. (1994). *Police deviance* (3rd ed.). Cincinnati, OH: Anderson Publishing Co.

Bell v. Wolfish, 441 U.S. 520 (1979).

Carter, D. L. (1990). Drug-related corruption of police officers: a contemporary typology. *Journal of Criminal Justice, 18*(2), 85–98.

Clinard, M. B., & Meier, R. B. (2010). *Sociology of deviant behavior* (14th ed.). Ft. Worth, TX: Harcourt Brace.

CNN Staff. (2013). *74 Cleveland police officers to face discipline after deadly pursuit.* http://www.cnn.com/2013/08/02/justice/cleveland-police-shooting/index.html. Accessed 15.10.13.

Cohen, H. (1986). Exploiting police authority. *Criminal Justice Ethics, 5*(2), 23–31.

Commission on Police Integrity. (1997). *Report of the commission on police integrity. Office of international criminal justice.* Chicago: University of Illinois.

Ericson, R. V. (1981). Rule for police deviance. In C. D. Sheaing (Ed.), *Organizational police deviance.* Toronto, CA: Butterworth.

Erikson, K. T. (1962). Notes on the sociology of deviance. *Social Problems, 9,* 307–314.

Ewing, A. C. (1953). *Ethics.* London: English University Press.

Feldberg, M. (1986). Gratuities, corruption, and the democratic ethos of policing: the case of the free cup of coffee. In F. Elliston, & M. Feldberg (Eds.), *Moral issues in police* (pp. 267–276). Totowa, NJ: Work Rowman & Allanheld.

Furst, R. (2013). Minneapolis police face lawsuits alleging misconduct. *StarTribune*. http://www.startribune.com/local/minneapolis/219998711.html?page=1&c=y. Accessed 26.08.13.

Goldstein, H. (1977). *Policing a free society*. Cambridge, MA: Ballinger Publishing.

Gorman, J. (March 7, 1989). Two detectives put on probation. *Chicago Tribune*.

Hale, D. C. (1989). Ideology of police misbehavior: analysis and recommendations. *Quarterly Journal of Ideology, 13*(2), 59–85.

Hickman, M. J., Lawton, B. A., Piquero, A. R., & Greene, J. R. (2001). Does race influence police disciplinary process? *Justice Research and Policy, 3*, 97–113.

Kappeler, V. E., & Kraska, P. B. (1998). A textual critique of community policing: police adaption to high modernity. *Policing: An International Journal of Police Strategies and Management, 21*(2), 293–313.

Kappeler, V. E., Sluder, R., & Alpert, G. P. (1998). *Forces of deviance; understanding the dark side of the force* (2nd ed.). Prospect Heights, IL: Waveland Press.

Knapp Commission. (1972). *Knapp commission report on police corruption*. New York: Braziller.

Kooken, D. L. (1957). *Ethics in police service*. Springfield, IL: Charles C Thomas. 15.

Kraska, P. B., & Kappeler, V. E. (1988). Police on-duty drug use: a theoretical and descriptive examination. *American Journal of Police, 7*(1), 1–28.

Kraska, P. B., & Kappeler, V. E. (1995). To serve and pursue: exploring police sexual violence against women. *Justice Quarterly, 12*(1), 85–111.

Kroes, W. H. (1976). *Society's victim, the policeman: An analysis of job stress in policing*. Springfield, IL: Charles C Thomas.

Lersch, K. M., & Mieczkowski, T. (2000). An examination of the convergence and divergence of internal and external allegations of misconduct filed against police officer. *Policing: An International Journal of Police Strategies and Management, 23*, 54–68.

Lindsay, V. (2008). Police officers and their alcohol consumption. *Policy Quarterly, 11*, 74–87.

Los Angeles Police Department. (2000). *Borad of inquiry into the rampart area corruption incident, public report*. Author.

Madison, J. (1787). *The federalist*. Middletown, CT: Wesleyan University Press. The Federalist Papers No. 10. Reprinted in J. E. Cooke (1961).

Madison, J. (1788). *The federalist*. Middletown, CT: Wesleyan University Press. The Federalist Papers No. 51. Reprinted in J. E. Cooke (1961).

Manning, P. K. (1999). The police: mandate, strategies and appearances. In L. K. Gaines, & T. A. Ricks (Eds.), *Managing the police organization*. St. Paul, MN: West Publishing.

Mary Beth G. v. City of Chicago, 723 F.2d 1263 (7th Cir. 1983).

Matza, D. (1969). *Becoming deviant*. Englewood Cliffs, NJ: Prentice-Hall.

McDevitt, J., Posick, C., Zschoche, R., Rosenbaum, D., Buslik, M., & Fridell, L. (2011). Police integrity, responsibility, and discipline. *National Police Research Platform*. http://www.nationalpoliceresearch.org/storage/updated-papers/Police%20Integrity%20Responsibility%20and%20Discipline.pdf. Accessed 15.10.13.

McGurrin, D., & Kappeler, V. E. (2002). Media accounts of police sexual violence: rotten apples or state supported violence? In K. M. Lersch (Ed.), *Policing and misconduct* (pp. 121–142). Upper Saddle River, NJ: Prentice Hall.

McMullan, M. (1961). A theory of corruption. *Sociological Review, 9*(2), 181–201.

Meier, R. F. (1989). Deviance and differentiation. In S. F. Messner, M. D. Krohn, & A. E. Liska (Eds.), *Theoretical integration in the study of deviance and crime: Problems and prospects.* Albany: State University of New York Press.

Mieczkowski, T., & Lersch, K. M. (2002). Drug-testing police officers and police recruits: the outcome of urinalysis and hair analysis compared. *Policing: An International Journal of Police Strategies & Management, 25,* 581–601.

Mollen, M. (1994). *Commission report of the commission to investigate allegations of police corruption and the anti-corruption procedures of the police department.* Commission Report 36. New York: City of New York.

Moore, G. E. (1903). *Principia ethica.* Cambridge, MA: Harvard University Press. 6.

Moore, G. E. (1912). *Ethics.* London: Oxford University Press. 6.

Murphy, S. (May 3, 2007). *Affidavit: Boston police officer extorted money in uniform.* Boston Globe.

Packman, D. (2010). *Officer-involved sexual misconduct starts new years with a surge in cases.* The Cato Institute's National Police Misconduct Reporting Project. http://www.policemisconduct.net/officer-involved-sexual-misconduct-starts-new-years-with-surge-in-cases/. Accessed 04.11.13.

PERF.2012). Police chiefs discuss a tough issue: alcohol and drug abuse by officers. *Subject to Debate, 26,* 2–3.

Punch, M. (2000). Police corruption and its prevention. *European Journal of Criminal Policy and Research, 8,* 301–324.

Rawls, J. (1999). *A theory of justice.* Cambridge, MA: Harvard University Press.

Reuss-Ianni, E. (1983). *Two cultures of policing.* New Brunswick, NJ: Transaction Books.

Rojek, J., & Decker, S. H. (2009). Examining racial disparity in the police discipline process. *Police Quarterly, 12,* 388–407.

Ruiz, J., & Bono, C. (2004). At what priced a "freebie"? the real cost of police gratuities. *Criminal Justice Ethics, 23,* 44–54.

Rokeach, M. (1973). *The Nature of Human Values.* New York: Free Press.

Sapp, A. (1994). Sexual misconduct and sexual harassment by police officers. In T. Barker, & D. L. Carter (Eds.), *Police deviance* (3rd ed.). (pp. 187–199). Cincinnati, OH: Anderson Publishing.

Sauchelli, D., Schram, J., & Velez, N. (2013). NYPD cops say they won't go above and beyond the call of duty over "stop-frisk" lawsuit risks. *New York Post.* http://www.nypost.com/p/news/local/not_busting_our_humps_cops_WazplU7FKqAXtwXh8cCvnO/1. Accessed 28.08.13.

Schram, J. (March 15, 2007). *Cop takes it out on ex's auto.* New York Post.

Sechrest, D. K., & Burns, P. (1992). Police corruption: the Miami case. *Criminal Justice and Behavior, 19,* 294–313.

Sherman, L. (1982). Learning police ethics. *Criminal Justice Ethics, 1*(1), 10–19.

Sherman. (1974). In L. Sherman (Ed.), *Police corruption: A sociological perspective 1974* (pp. 1–39). Garden City, NY: Doubleday.

Sigler, R. T., & Dees, T. M. (1988). Public perception of petty corruption in law enforcement. *Journal of Police Science and Administration, 16*(1), 14–19.

Stinson, P. M., Liederbach, J., Brewer, S. L., Schmalzried, H. D., Mathna, B. E., & Long, K. L. (2012). A study of drug-related police corruption arrests. *Policing: An International Journal of Police Strategies & Management, 36,* 491–511.

Sumner, W. G. (1966). *Folkways.* New York: Dover.

Tuohy, J. (2013). Firing police in Indianapolis takes time: merit board hearings for suspended officers must wait until criminal trials are over. *Indystar.com*. http://www.indystar.com/article/20130822/NEWS02/308210089/Firing-police-Indianapolis-takes-time?gcheck=1. Accessed 24.08.13.

Walker, S. (1980). *Popular justice: A history of American criminal justice*. New York: Oxford University Press.

CHAPTER 10

Civil Liability

The law condemns and punishes only actions within certain definite and narrow limits; it thereby justifies, in a way, all similar actions that lie outside those limits.

—Leo Tolstoy

LEARNING OBJECTIVES

After reading the chapter, you should be able to:

- Explain the difference between a tort and a crime;
- List and define the elements of a state tort action;
- Distinguish between negligence, intentional, and strict liability torts;
- Describe the defenses to state tort actions;
- List and define the elements of a Section 1983 action;
- Describe the most common constitutional violations under Section 1983;
- Describe the defenses to a Section 1983 action;
- List and discuss the steps law enforcement agencies can take to reduce the right of civil liability.

KEY TERMS

- Absolute immunity
- Assault
- Assumption of risk
- Attorney's Fee Act
- Battery
- Breach of duty
- Civil Rights Act of 1871
- Color of state law
- Comparative negligence
- Constitutional violation
- Contributory negligence
- Crime
- Damage or injury

INTRODUCTION

Police officers perform duties that include apprehending criminals, providing citizens with protection, aiding persons in distress, and maintaining the safety of our streets and communities. These are difficult tasks in themselves, but matters are complicated because police officers are often the target of lawsuits. Legal actions against the police arise for many reasons, some of which are inherent in the nature of the police role, the services they provide the public, and their status as government employees (Kappeler, 2006). When police officers fail to perform their assigned duties, perform them in a negligent fashion, or abuse their authority, the possibility of civil liability exists. Civil suits against

- Defendant
- False arrest
- False imprisonment
- Good faith
- Intentional tort
- Legal duty
- Negligence
- Plaintiff
- Probable cause
- Proximate cause
- Qualified immunity
- Strict liability tort
- Tort
- Wrongful death

the police, however, are not always the product of their inability or failure to perform assigned duties. An alarming number of police liability cases are filed against the nation's law enforcement officers claiming misconduct and abuses of authority, ranging from false arrest to allegations of excessive force and brutality. These lawsuits often allege intentional violations of constitutional, civil, and statutory rights.

Certainly, there are police officers that engage in acts of misconduct and knowingly step beyond the scope of their official authority. The beating of motorist Rodney King by Los Angeles police officers following a traffic stop captured the nation's attention. As a result of this beating, attorneys for King filed a civil rights lawsuit against the police asking for a multimillion dollar award in damages. The officers who participated in the King beating were found criminally liable for the assault, and the city of Los Angeles was found civilly liable for the actions of its police officers. King was awarded more than $3.5 million in damages. In October of 2005, in the aftermath of hurricane Katrina, three New Orleans police officers were captured on video beating 64-year-old Robert Davis. One of the officers "grabbed a news producer, leaned him backward over a car, jabbed him in the stomach and unleashed a profanity-laced tirade" (Out, 2006:297). The sexual assault of Abner Louima by New York City police officers, which ended in a $8.8 million settlement (Mauro, 2004), the $70 million price tag the Los Angeles Police Department's (LAPD) Rampart CRASH unit's corruption (Marquez, 2005), and the national concern with the issues of Driving While Black and religious profiling all contributed to a renewed interest in controlling police misconduct. Reminiscent of the Rodney King beating, a television news helicopter captured videotape of three LAPD officers beating an unarmed black man with metal flashlights following a pursuit (LEN, 2004) and the City of New York is settling scores of cases alleging that its Brooklyn booking facility violated citizen's constitutional rights by strip searching people arrested for minor offenses. These settlements come on the heels of a $50 million judgment against the city for the same kind of illegal strip searches. In 2013, the New York Police Department faced a number of legal challenges to its aggressive "stop and frisk" practices. These incidents keep the issue of police misconduct and civil liability in the forefront of public attention. There is growing public concern about the misconduct of police officers in U.S. society and a well-evidenced trend toward suing law enforcement officials for acts of misconduct and abuses of authority. Countless incidents of police wrongdoing are published in the newspapers, shown on television, and eventually addressed by the courts in civil lawsuits.

The filing of a liability suit against a police officer, however, does not always mean the officer has engaged in some obvious or intentional wrongdoing. Some perceive the government as having "deep pockets" and the ability to either pay out-of-court settlements or large punitive damage awards. Therefore, some lawyers and citizens are quick to bring litigation against the government and their most visible agents—the police. This, coupled with a rise in court findings of police liability, has led some to conclude that no other group of governmental employees are more exposed to civil suits and liability than are police officers. Indeed, civil liability is an occupational hazard for many officers and their departments.

THE INCIDENCE OF CIVIL SUITS

The unique vulnerability of the police and a trend toward allowing governmental liability has led to an explosion of lawsuits. Accurate information regarding the actual number and type of lawsuits filed against the police is difficult to obtain. Even so, several trends can be noted from the available information on police liability. First, since the 1960s, there has been a sharp increase in the number of civil suits filed against the nation's police (Kappeler, 2006; Ross & Bodapati, 2006). Second, there has been an increase in civil cases successfully litigated against police officers, police departments, and municipalities (Kappeler, 2006). Finally, although police officers and their departments have a good record in defending themselves from civil lawsuits, there are still a significant number of judgments handed down against the police.

From 1967 to 1971, the number of civil suits filed against the police increased by 124%. In 1976, there were more than 13,400 civil suits filed against law enforcement officers in the United States. This trend continued: between 1967 and 1976, the yearly number of civil suits brought against law enforcement officers increased by more than 500% (AELE, 1974, p. 67). Studies conducted by the International Association of Chiefs of Police (IACP) and other organizations indicate that during a 5-year period, one in 34 police officers was sued. Studies such as these predicted that by 1980 there would be more than 26,000 civil lawsuits filed against the nation's police (AELE, 1980, p. 7). Each year during this decade thousands of civil liability cases were brought before the courts claiming police violations of citizen's rights. Today, it is estimated that there are more than 30,000 civil actions filed against the police each year.

Another way to look at the incidence of police liability litigation is to consider the percentage of officers who have been sued. Two separate studies of Cincinnati, Ohio, police officers found that between 17% and 19% of the officers surveyed had been sued (Hughes, 2001; Novak, Smith, & Frank, 2003). Another study of multiple law enforcement agencies in a single county found that about 27% of the officers had been sued during the course of their careers (Hall, Ventura, Lee, & Lambert, 2003). In all likelihood, these studies underestimate the rate at which police officers are sued by citizens. One can only expect that some of the most liability prone officers and those held liable for the most egregious conduct were either terminated or voluntarily left their departments.

POLICE FEAR OF LITIGATION

One irony of current thinking on civil liability is that while police chiefs have taken a guarded view of the liability situation and generally feel that civil liability has yet to reach a point of crisis (McCoy, 1987), their officers are less confident. This may be due, in part, to the fact that municipal police chiefs are afforded some insulation from personal liability for the actions of their officers. Research shows that some police officers fear civil litigation. A study of 101 police cadets, conducted by Scogin and Brodsky (1991), found that 9% of the officers interviewed felt that their fear of civil litigation had reached a point of being irrational and excessive. Several of the officers interviewed expressed a very simplistic understanding of prevention measures, as well as a fatalistic sentiment regarding potential litigation. This research noted that "Typical [officer] responses were, for example, '... what seems to be the only word in the English language is sue' and 'we can be sued for anything.'" Other officers expressed their risk management precautions in terms of "treating people fairly" and "going by the book." These researchers concluded "the percentage of litigaphobic candidates is considerably higher than the 9% self-identified figure" (Scogin and Brodsky, 1991:44).

A survey of 50 police officers from three different law enforcement agencies in Pennsylvania conducted by Garrison (1995) found that 28% of the officers agreed with the statement that "the idea that a police officer can be sued bothers me" (Garrison, 1995:26). A replication of these studies in Kentucky found that 50% of 220 police cadets in a statewide training academy were worried about civil liability, and 31% thought they worried to excess (Kappeler, 2006). Female police officers showed less anxiety over the potential to be sued even when controlling for age, education, years of experience, and job assignment. In all, lower-ranking police officers seem more concerned with the potential of civil liability than do their chiefs. More recently, a survey of 658 sworn police officers from 21 agencies across the United States found that 15% of the officers ranked civil liability third among the top 10 serious challenges they face on the job (Stevens, 2000). A study of police officers in Cincinnati, Ohio, found that 55% of the responding officers thought civil suits were a "barrier to effective law enforcement" (Hughes, 2001:255).

Lawsuits, Police Perceptions, and Behavior

Such fears are promoted by a lack of understanding of the nature and consequences of police civil liabilities, a general feeling by police officers that they can be "sued and found liable for anything," and that frivolous lawsuits are commonplace. Such misplaced notions are promoted by police officers who feel unjustly threatened by civil litigation. Consider a few of the remarks made by police commanders in very popular police magazines: "Every time a police officer engages in a confrontation with a citizen or performs other official duties, he runs the risk of possible civil litigation… only a small percentage of such suits have any reasonable justification. The remainder are brought by overzealous citizens who perceive some personal harm, however so slight…." (Reynolds, 1988:7). Another police commander remarks: "Any perfectly law-abiding police officer can be sued, perhaps maliciously, by just about anybody at just about any time. That's an unfortunate and unjust side effect of pinning on a badge" (Garner, 1991:34).

Remarks such as these, based on inaccurate information and false perceptions, express unrealistic fears of litigation and can have negative effects. Some have argued that unrealistic fears of civil liability "can seriously erode the necessary confidence and willingness to act. Even worse, law enforcement officers who have an unrealistic or exaggerated fear of personal liability may become overly timid or indecisive and fail to arrest or search to the detriment of the public's interest in effective and aggressive law enforcement" (Schofield, 1990:26–27). Besides the chilling effect fear of liability may have on "aggressive" law enforcement, these views may foster protectionism, police cover-ups, and a division between the police and community. Others have argued that "Civil lawsuits actually allow police departments to ignore abuses committed by officers. Damages paid to victims do not come from the budget of the police department or officers personally. In almost all cases, the city pays any settlement or jury award and the officers' performance evaluations are usually unaffected" (Collins, 1998:2, cited in Out, 2006:301).

Myths of Police Civil Liability

Myth: Police can be sued and found liable for almost any activity.

Reality: The law of police liability is well articulated and police are afforded extensive immunity when carrying out their duties.

Myth: Citizens file a substantial number of frivolous and meritless lawsuits against the police.

Reality: Evidence shows that police face a very limited number of frivolous lawsuits and the courts sanction plaintiffs who file these suits.

Myth: Allowing the police to be sued for their misconduct negatively affects police decision-making and agency operations.

Reality: There is no creditable evidence to suggest that police decision-making or police operations are negatively effected by the threat of civil liability.

Although some have claimed that the fear of being sued and court cases may affect law enforcement practice (Amadi, 2010), research seems to suggest otherwise. Garrison's (1995) survey of police officers found that most police officers did not believe that "a civil suit against a police officer is an impediment to effective law enforcement" (Garrison, 1995:25). In fact, while a slight majority of officers indicated that they thought civil liability had a deterrent effect on police misconduct, the vast majority said that the possibility of being sued "did not affect their thinking in the field" (Garrison, 1995:26). Stevens' (2000) survey of police officers in 21 agencies found that only 11% of the officers reported that concern about civil liabilities promoted alternatives to arrest. Likewise, the Vaughn, Cooper, and del Carmen's (2001) study of Texas chiefs of police found that 61% thought lawsuits had little or no effect on their departmental functions. Additionally, a study of Cincinnati police officers found that 78% of the officers did not think about liability when they stopped a citizen (Kenneth Novak, Brad Smith, & James Frank, 2003).

Some might even argue the social objective of holding police officers liable for their misconduct is to change the way officers go about fulfilling their duties and to give them pause to think about the consequences of their actions. It would seem that the prospect of civil liability has a deterrent effect in the abstract and quiet of the survey environment, but that it does not have a major impact on field practices. One of the most comprehensive studies of the deterrent effect of civil liability lawsuits on the police concludes that "Given the infrequency with which departments seek to gather information from lawsuits, and the barriers when they do try to gather this information," it seems fair to conclude that most law enforcement officials know little about lawsuits alleging misconduct by their officers (Schwart, 2010:1067).

Frivolous Lawsuits

Although there are certainly a small number of frivolous claims brought against the police, examination of published cases decided by the federal district courts indicates that less than one-half of a percent of those cases resulted in a judicial sanction because plaintiffs brought cases that clearly lacked merit (Kappeler & Kappeler, 1992). In 1 year, for example, the issue of sanctions was only brought up twice in police liability cases published by the federal courts. In one case, the court refused to impose sanctions on a plaintiff and in the other case the court refused to impose sanctions against the defendant-sheriff (Singer v. Fulton County Sheriff, 1995). Likewise, of 658 police liability cases decided by the Federal Circuit Courts in 2004, only six cases, or less than 1%, contained a claim of a frivolous lawsuit against the police. One of these six cases was a frivolous lawsuit brought by a police officer against the Boston Police Department (Donahue v. City of Boston, 2004; Kappeler, 2006). One must remember that just as a few clearly frivolous claims are brought against the police, police officers and their legal counsel are as likely to engage in sanctionable misconduct during the litigation of a police liability case (see, Jock v. Tavernier, 2000).

One must also consider the millions of interactions that take place between citizens and the police each day and the number of incidents that result in litigation. With approximately 18,000 state and local law enforcement agencies in the United States employing nearly a million people, the rate of litigation would seem relatively small compared to its potential. In fact, Novak et al. (2003:355) point out,

> ...the police have contact with over 43.6 million people annually. Of these contacts, over half of them (56% or over 24.5 million) are with citizens who are suspects of criminal activity... If we take these figures at face value, we then must conclude that one tenth of 1% of all encounters between police and persons suspected of committing a crime could result in civil litigation.

A study conducted by the IACP concluded that about 40% of the liability cases were brought against the police for officer misconduct—not just technical error or minor rights violations.

There are good reasons for a healthy concern over potential police civil liability, but such concerns are not founded when they are premised on the notion that citizens file an inordinate number of unjustified claims against the police. Legal remedies are available to address the small number of these cases both at the state and federal levels (Davis v. Harrison Township Police Dept, 2013). The feeling that police officers can be sued and held liable for almost anything is similarly unfounded. As noted later in this chapter, the civil litigation process has safeguards to prevent and, if necessary, punish frivolous and unjust claims brought against the police (see Kritzer, Marshall, & Zemans, 1992). Comments such as those cited above only serve to divide the police from citizens and to close minds to an understanding of the complex issues of police civil liability and the need for accountability.

THE COST OF CIVIL LIABILITY

Police civil liability has become a concern of state and municipal government as well as of individual police officers. The cost of a civil suit goes beyond expenses incurred by individual police officers. Such factors as the cost of liability insurance, litigation expenses, out-of-court settlements, and punitive damage awards all make civil liability an extremely expensive proposition for police officers, law enforcement agencies, governments, and, ultimately, taxpayers. A 1998 study by Human Rights Watch noted that taxpayers are often required to pay three times for police misconduct: first, for the officer's salary and training; second, for the defense of the officer who is being sued; and third, for the damage awards handed down by a jury. A survey conducted by the National Institute of Municipal Law Officers found that the 215 municipalities surveyed had more than $4.3 billion U.S. worth of claims in pending liability suits. Some criminal justice scholars reason that if these figures were applied to the existing 39,000 local governments, there could be as much as $780 billion in pending liability litigation against local government (Barrineau, 1994; Bates, Culter, & Clink, 1981). Ross and Bodapati's (2006) study of 151 law enforcement agencies in Michigan found that the average yearly cost of police liability for these agencies was about $13.8 million. The mayor of Los Angeles remarked that the city would "set aside 25 years worth of tobacco settlement money—as much as $300 million—to pay for lawsuits anticipated from the city's latest police corruption scandal" (L.A. Mayor Suggests, 2000; cited in Archbold & Maguire, 2002:224) (Box 10.1).

Facing potential judgments amounting to millions of dollars, municipalities are forced to secure liability insurance to protect them from civil litigation. Insurance policies of this type are extremely expensive. After several lawsuits

Box 10.1 A Few Million Dollar Police Liability Cases

Cleveland, Ohio, A $13.3 million judgment was handed down against two Cleveland police detectives for a wrongful conviction where officers provided false testimony to secure the conviction.

Minneapolis, Minnesota, agreed to pay a nearly $1 million settlement to a man who lost his colon after an alleged beating by police responding to a domestic call at his home. Previously, the City paid a jury award and settlement of more than $1 million to two victims of a bar fight involving an off-duty police officer.

Upper Marlboro, Maryland, Prince George's County was found liable for the death of a Howard University student. An undercover county officer shot the student after following him to a Northern Virginia neighborhood and confused him for a suspect in a gun case. The plaintiffs were awarded $3.7 million in damages.

City of New York, New York, agreed to pay over $7 million to the family of Sean Bell for the New York Police Department's role in his death. Bell was shot and killed by New York City police officers after an altercation while leaving his bachelor party. Officers fired 50 shots at his vehicle but no weapon was found, the officers who approached him were in plain clothes, and never announced themselves.

Palm Beach, Florida, County Sheriff's Office reached a $2 million settlement with Kharmilia Ferguson who

sustained severe brain after her car was struck by a speeding sheriff's deputy's cruiser in a residential neighborhood.

Long Beach, California, must pay former police officers Melissa Clerkin and Lindsey Allison for the sexual harassment they endured in the department. The two officers were forced off the department and a federal jury awarded $3.1 million to the women.

Newark, New Jersey, officials settled a lawsuit stemming out of a police vehicular chase. One of the plaintiffs, Curtis Berry, was paralyzed when he was struck by a stolen sport utility vehicle being pursued by police. The City will settle the case for $3.6 million.

Apple Valley, Minnesota, officials agreed to pay more than $3 million to Gennadiy Balandin, who was paralyzed after being shot by officer Jim Eagle.

Miami, Florida officials agreed to settle a case for $5 million with a community college student who was paralyzed when the car he was riding in was struck by a Miami police patrol car. The officer made a U-turn and ran a red light. A jury awarded the student $15.7 million, but reduced it to $13,674,660 because he wasn't wearing his seat belt.

Source: Compiled by the authors from various newspaper sources.

are filed against a police department, premium rates can skyrocket, or companies may refuse to insure the department at all.

The cost of an average jury award of liability against a municipality is reported to be about $2 million. Although early studies of police civil liability found that individual claims against the police only average about $3000, it is not uncommon for a police liability case to result in a six- or seven-figure award against a city. In 1982, there were more than 250 cases in which juries awarded at least $1 million (National League of Cities, 1985). A study of federal court cases between 1978 and 1995 found that the average award handed down against a police defendant was more than $134,000 (Kappeler, Kappeler, & del Carmen, 1993). A study of federal police liability cases in the state of New York found that the average damage award was about $50,400, but, in some cases, awards exceeded $2 million (Chiabi, 1996). These cases do not represent the growing trend toward out-of-court settlements that cost some cities like New York and Los Angeles millions of dollars each year (del Carmen, 1995; Ross & Bodapati, 2006). Research suggests that more than one-half of all police misconduct cases are settled out of court (Fisher, Kutner, & Wheat, 1989). These enormous awards and settlements have nearly bankrupted some municipalities and townships. Table 10.1 shows the costs of police liability in several cities for select years. As the figures illustrate, the cost of police liability can be

Table 10.1 The Cost of Police Liability in Select Cities

City	Year(s)	Payments	Type of Cases/Notation
Baltimore	2009–2011	10.4 million	All police cases
Chicago	2009–2011	45 million	Brutality and misconduct
Denver	2002–2011	10 million	Settlements in misconduct
Detroit	1986–1997	100 million	All lawsuits
Indianapolis	2012–2013	4.1 million	
Los Angeles	2007–2012	110 million	Excludes traffic
Minneapolis	2006–2012	14 million	
New York	2011	185.6 million	Police abuses
Oakland	2011	7.6 million	All police cases
Philadelphia	2005–2008	9.2 million	(Yearly average)
Portland	2005–2009	3 million	(At least)
San Francisco	1993–1995	1.9 million	Settlements
St. Paul	2006–2012	14 million	Police cases
Washington, DC	1993–1995	4.1 million	False arrest only

Source: Various newspaper reports and Human Rights Watch (1998).

substantial. Likewise, there has been a growing trend for courts to put police agencies under consent decrees, which can be extremely costly. Ross (2012), for example, reports that the consent decree against the LAPD is costing between $30 and $50 million annually.

In an attempt to prevent such large judgments, many cities and their sureties have made it a routine practice to settle many claims of police misconduct out of court for a minor portion of what a jury might award, had the case gone to trial (Kappeler, 2006; Ross & Bodapati, 2006). A study published by the Department of Justice (Bureau of Justice Statistics, 1995) found that three out of four tort cases were settled out of court. Such practices can lead cities to pay large sums of money even in cases in which the police might not be found liable in a civil proceeding. Given the potential for multimillion dollar awards, many municipalities are not willing to gamble on whether juries will find in favor of their police officers or award judgments against them. Some departments have used out-of-court settlements as a risk management technique to reduce the overall cost of police liability (Ross & Bodapati, 2006). These practices can lead to the filing of frivolous civil suits, create morale problems in police organizations, and lead to an unfavorable public perception of police conduct. All in all, police liability is an expensive proposition for individual officers, their departments, government, and taxpayers.

LITIGANTS IN LIABILITY CASES

Unlike a criminal proceeding, liability litigation is tried in civil court. Jurors who are selected from the community in which the alleged wrongdoing occurred generally decide the outcome of these cases. A judge acts as the referee or moderator for the proceeding, instructing the jury on the law of liability, and ruling on the motions of attorneys representing the parties involved. The person who brings a lawsuit against the police is referred to as the "plaintiff." Plaintiffs may include any citizen who has had rights violated and, in rare cases, police officers themselves will bring liability claims against their own department or government. The person, agency, or government that is sued and has allegedly inflicted the damage or injury is referred to as the "defendant." In police liability cases, defendants may include individual officers, supervisors, law enforcement administrators, agencies, and the government entity.

You can watch a video lecture on the stages of a civil lawsuit by going to: **http://www.youtube.com/watch?v=OwxyHAAnpoU**

It is common practice when filing a liability suit for plaintiffs to name as many persons as possible in a civil action. Anyone associated with the injury or damage, such as the officer, department, supervisor, and chief of police, may be named in the lawsuit. This allows plaintiffs to seek out the person or agency with the "deepest pocket." Although an individual police officer may have limited financial resources or "shallow pockets," high-level police administrators and governments have "deeper pockets" and the ability to pay larger damage awards either personally or by raising taxes.

If the officer who inflicted the damage or injury is unknown to the plaintiff, a "John Doe" lawsuit may be filed against the agency or government. In some cases, even though the plaintiff does not know which officer inflicted the injury, a civil action may succeed against police departments and governments.

Considering the enormous costs of police liability, its increasing frequency, and the number of people whose lives are affected by this type of litigation, it is important to understand the framework of federal and state law as it relates to police liability and the delivery of public services. There is no better way for police officers, departments, or police administrators to insulate themselves from civil liability than to have a thorough understanding of the framework of liability law. There are generally two legal avenues for litigating police wrongdoing. First, plaintiffs may file lawsuits in state court claiming that the police negligently or intentionally failed to perform their duties in violation of state law. Second, a civil suit can be brought in federal court in which the plaintiff claims the police violated a constitutional right. These are explored further in the sections that follow.

POLICE CIVIL LIABILITY AND TORT LAW

The term "tort" is derived from the Latin word "tortus," which means twisted or bent. The term was transported into the English language from France following the Norman Conquest of 1066. When translated from the French language, the term simply means "wrong." Originally, crimes and torts were identical and people handled both types of wrongdoing by taking private action against the injurious party. "Gradually the custom of private vengeance was replaced with the concept of criminal law, that is the community as a whole is injured when one of its members is injured" (Barrineau, 1994:1–2). As the law evolved, torts and crimes became distinguishable. Torts are now legal actions between private parties that do not arise from written contracts.

Tort law is best understood when compared to crimes. Crimes are harms punished by the state and spelled out in written legal codes. As such, crimes are viewed as offenses against the state and not just the particular crime victim. It is thought that when a person is victimized by a criminal act, not only are the victim's rights violated, but so are the rights of the community and society as a whole. Crimes are punishable by sanctions, such as community service, fines, probation, incarceration, and sometimes death. In order for a person to be convicted of a crime, a court must find the defendant guilty beyond a reasonable doubt. This requires the state to present a high level of proof that the accused party in fact committed the crime.

A tort, on the other hand, is conduct that interferes with the private interests of individual persons or their property. Persons suffering private interest harms can bring a legal action against the party inflicting damage in a civil rather than a criminal proceeding. Torts are redressed by money awards and are not subject to criminal punishments. People bringing tort actions must show by a preponderance of evidence that the defendant caused the harm by acting in an unreasonable manner contrary to law. This level of proof is lower than that needed to convict a person of a crime.

Although torts are distinguishable from crimes, some torts can also be crimes. Consider the situation in which a police officer intentionally discharges a firearm and kills an innocent bystander. If the officer were tried in criminal court, a finding of manslaughter or murder would be possible, depending on the circumstances surrounding the incident. If the officer were convicted of the crime, this would mean the imposition of a criminal sanction by the state – a fine, probation, or incarceration. The family of the shooting victim may also file a civil lawsuit claiming that the officer's conduct violated the victim's rights. In this civil proceeding, the officer might be found liable for the death of the victim and the family might be awarded money to compensate them for their loss. The officer's conduct would be a violation of criminal law, an offense against the state, and at the same time a tort, in which injury was inflicted on another person.

The type of civil suit brought against a police officer depends on the officer's conduct and existing law. There are three types of torts under state law: (1) strict tort liability; (2) intentional torts; and (3) negligence. Each of these torts requires the plaintiff to demonstrate different elements and meet different levels of proof. In the sections that follow, each of these torts is discussed and its relevance to policing considered.

Strict Tort Liability

Strict tort liability is normally associated with behaviors that are so dangerous or hazardous that a reasonable person who engages in such behavior can be substantially certain the conduct will result in injury or damage. Because behavior of this type is legally unacceptable, persons engaging in these behaviors are held strictly liable for any resulting damage or injury. Under strict tort liability, the police officer's mental state, whether he or she intended to engage in the conduct, is not a consideration. Under strict liability, fault on the part of an officer need not be established. When courts decide strict liability cases, they concern themselves with whether the officer or the agency should bear the burden of financial costs of the damage or injury. Strict tort liability does not usually apply to police officers, even though many of the services they provide and duties they perform obviously involve great danger.

Intentional Torts

Contrasts to strict liability torts are intentional torts. In an intentional tort action, the plaintiff must prove that the defendant's behavior was intentional. That is, the police officer must have "intended" to engage in the conduct that led to the damage or injury. It is important to note that this requirement does not mean the officer "intended" to inflict the injury or damage, only that the officer intended to engage in the conduct that led to the injury. The distinction between strict liability tort and intentional tort is drawn by the foreseeability of danger associated with engaging in a particular behavior and the extent to which the officer's behavior was intentional. Intentional torts are usually behaviors that are substantially certain to bring about injury or damage and the officer knowingly engaged in the behavior.

For example, the police officer that shoots an unarmed fleeing burglar may have intended to discharge the firearm, but may not have intended to kill the suspect. For purposes of proving an intentional tort, it must only be shown that the officer intended to discharge the firearm. For liability purposes, it makes little difference whether the officer actually intended to kill, wound, or scare the suspect. Because the officer intended to discharge the firearm and could be substantially certain that damage or injury would follow, liability would be found, absent of an adequate defense.

There are various forms of intentional tort actions that can be brought against police officers. The type of intentional tort action filed depends on the officer's conduct and existing law. Some intentional torts are based on state statutes that require officers to perform their duties in a certain fashion whereas others prohibit officers from engaging in certain behaviors. Other litigation is based on previously decided judicial decisions that, as a matter of legal policy, make certain types of conduct unacceptable. Some of the most common forms of intentional tort actions filed against police officers are wrongful death, false arrest, false imprisonment, and assault and battery.

Wrongful Death

Wrongful death lawsuits are based on state statutes. The family of the deceased often brings this type of civil lawsuit. Police officers who either take the life of a citizen or fail to prevent the death of a citizen can be held liable for wrongful death under certain circumstances.

Wrongful death claims often arise as a result of police use of deadly force. In most states, the law permits persons to bring a civil action against an officer who either intentionally or negligently kills someone (Hoyt v. Cooks, 2012).

These laws are intended to compensate the family of victims who are wrongfully killed by improper police action. Depending on the officer's behavior and state law, punitive damages can also be awarded against the officer and the police department.

Until recently, many states allowed police officers to use deadly force to apprehend suspected felons attempting to flee the scene of a crime. However, in Tennessee v. Garner (1985) the Supreme Court curtailed the use of deadly force by police officers. The Court held that certain state fleeing-felon laws were unconstitutional. In the Garner decision, the Court said that police officers were only allowed to use deadly force to either prevent the escape of a dangerous felon or to protect themselves or others from serious physical harm. Since that time, it has become easier for the families of shooting victims to succeed in civil actions against police officers who improperly use deadly force to apprehend law violators (Figure 10.1).

In one case alleging wrongful death, the family of a young man sued the police when an officer drove over their son in a city patrol car. A San Antonio

FIGURE 10.1
Seated left to right: Justice Clarence Thomas, Justice Antonin Scalia, Chief Justice John G. Roberts, Justice Anthony M. Kennedy, Justice Ruth Bader Ginsburg. Standing left to right: Justice Sonia Sotomayor, Justice Stephen G. Breyer, Justice Samuel Anthony Alito, Jr., Justice Elena Kagan. *Photograph courtesy of Steve Petteway, Collection of the Supreme Court of the United States.*

police officer was working as a private security officer at a mall. While he was driving through a parking lot, he noticed two men stepping out of a black pickup truck. One of the men first stood on the bumper of the pickup, looked around, and then joined the other man who had entered an unattended, parked, yellow pickup truck. The off-duty officer, suspecting that he was witnessing a theft, followed both vehicles out of the parking lot. After a time, he spotted a San Antonio Police Department car and informed the driver of what he had seen. The second officer began to pursue the two pickups, pulled in between them, and turned on his emergency lights and siren. The yellow pickup left the expressway and drove over the grassy median to the access road; the patrol car followed. The pickup truck slowed down and the driver jumped out and ran. In court, the officer advised that the man appeared to reach for something in his waistband and the officer felt he might be shot. The officer ducked under the dashboard, turned the front wheels to the right and accelerated the patrol car. The plaintiff's son was found under the left front wheel of the patrol car, but no weapon was found. The court stated they did not agree that the flight and alleged movement of the young man's hand to his waistband was proof enough for a judgment favoring the officer on the claim of wrongful death (Guzman v. City of San Antonio, 1989).

Assault and Battery

Assault is behavior that inflicts injury or causes a person to fear the infliction of immediate injury. Assault requires that the officer act in a manner so as to cause an injury or to place a person in fear of harm. It is sufficient for a finding of liability to show that the officer caused an individual to fear for their safety. Damage need not be shown in a civil action other than the distress associated with fear or apprehension of injury. Police officers can be found liable for assault when they engage in conduct that either inflicts injury or causes the fear of injury if they are not acting within the scope of their lawful authority. Consider the situation in which a police officer is interrogating a criminal suspect. During the course of the investigation, the officer moves toward the defendant, grabs him, and threatens to throw the suspect from a second-floor window. This type of behavior could result in liability under an intentional tort claim for assault. Police officers are not afforded immunity for the commission of intentional torts (Houghton v. Forrester, 2010).

> You can learn more about police brutality and civil litigation by reviewing the report "Shielded from Justice: Police Brutality and Accountability in the United States" at: **http://www.hrw.org/reports98/police/index.htm**

Battery, on the other hand, is offensive or harmful contact between two persons. Intentional tort lawsuits can be brought against police officers for battery. This form of conduct does not require that the officer intended to inflict harm or that the officer realized the conduct to be offensive to a person.

It need only be established that the officer acted without the consent of the party and made some form of offensive contact. Consider the situation in which a male police officer performs an illegal search of a woman without her consent and over her protests. If the officer was not legally entitled to conduct the search, and was not acting within the scope of police authority, such a search may constitute a battery, as well as other violations of civil law. An intentional tort claim could therefore be filed against the officer and a court could impose liability. Also, a municipality may be vicariously liable for an assault, by a police officer, under a theory of respondeat superior (Linson v. City of New York, 2012). In extreme circumstances, a serious battery can constitute a constitutional violation. Outrageous police conduct under color of state law is actionable under the due process clause of the Fourteenth Amendment. In police sexual assault cases, where an officer commits a battery, courts have ruled that this conduct violates the constitution as compared to trivial a battery. Rape, however, is a serious battery, and a rape committed under color of state law is actionable under 42 United States Constitution Section 1983 as a deprivation of liberty. In one case, a women was induced by an officer "and his fellow officers to perform oral sex..." by their threat to put her away for 40 years if she refused to cooperate with them. The court held that this behavior constituted a serious battery and violation of the Constitution (Alexander v. DeAngelo, 2003).

False Arrest and Imprisonment
False arrest is the unlawful seizure and detention of a person. It is any unlawful restraint of a person's liberty without their consent. In order to demonstrate false arrest, it is not necessary for the officer to physically restrain the person. It need only be established that a reasonable person under similar circumstances would conclude that they were no longer free to leave, even though no physical contact between the officer and the suspect may have occurred. A police officer who places a person inside a patrol car with a screened cage, several police officers surrounding an individual, or ordering someone to remain at the police station are all examples of conduct that could be seen as behavior intended to detain a person. As such, these behaviors could be interpreted by the courts as making an arrest for purpose of liability. Whether a person has been physically restrained or has stopped or yielded to the show of authority does not determine whether there has been a seizure. Courts consider the totality of the circumstances and whether a reasonable person would have believed he or she was not free to leave. Courts have ruled that a seizure occurs when a police officer:

1. Pursues an individual who has attempted to terminate the contact by departing;
2. Continues to interrogate a person who has clearly expressed a desire not to cooperate;

3. Renews interrogation of a person who has earlier responded fully to police inquiries;
4. Verbally orders a citizen to stop and answer questions;
5. Retains a citizen's identification or other property;
6. Physically restrains a citizen or blocks the citizen's path; or
7. Displays a weapon during the encounter.

Plaintiffs claiming false arrest must show several factors in order to succeed in a civil action against the police. Plaintiffs alleging false arrest must establish that: (1) they were willfully detained; (2) they were unwillfully detained; or (3) they were unlawfully detained. If even one of these three elements is established, then a plaintiff is likely to succeed in a false arrest lawsuit against a police officer.

State courts, however, differ on their interpretation of what constitutes a seizure. The Tennessee Supreme Court, for example, has held that when a police officer activates the blue lights of a patrol car, ordering a defendant to stop, and pursues him for several blocks without probable cause then these actions constitute a seizure (State of Tennessee v. Perry Thomas Randolph, 2002).

Because virtually any detention of a person by the police can constitute an arrest for the purposes of a false arrest lawsuit, police officers are susceptible to this form of lawsuit. Most false arrest claims allege that the arresting officer did not have probable cause to make the arrest and detain the person. One exception to the warrant requirement arises "when a police officer makes an investigatory stop based upon reasonable suspicion, supported articulable facts, that a criminal offense has been or is about to be committed (Terry v. Ohio, 1968).

To affect a warrantless arrest, police officers must have probable cause to believe the suspect has committed or is in the process of committing a crime. If the officer makes an arrest without a warrant, probable cause is always at issue. Whether probable cause to arrest existed at the time of arrest is a determination to be made by the courts. If it is found that the officer did not have probable cause to make the arrest, liability for false arrest may follow.

The best way to prevent liability for false arrest is to secure a warrant before the arrest. In this case, a magistrate determines whether probable cause exists for the arrest. Normally, an arrest made pursuant to a valid warrant provides the officer with a total defense to a claim of false arrest. There are, however, situations in which a warrant does not totally shield an officer from liability. If a police officer provides a magistrate with false information in order to secure an arrest warrant, the officer may be found liable for false arrest. A second potential form of liability is the situation in which a police officer knowingly serves a warrant on someone other than the person named on the warrant.

If the officer cannot show reasonable diligence in securing the identity of the person or the validity of the warrant, liability may be imposed. Usually, however, if an officer is acting in good faith and believes the warrant is valid and for the person arrested, liability is barred.

False imprisonment is similar to false arrest in that it requires an unlawful detention by a police officer. Claims of false imprisonment are distinguishable from false arrest in that an officer may have had probable cause to affect an arrest, but may still be found liable for false imprisonment. An officer who makes a valid arrest may later violate certain rights during a person's detention. Failure to release an arrested person at an appointed time, preventing access to a judge, or preventing a person from posting bail or a bond may result in a lawsuit for false imprisonment. False imprisonment lawsuits have been supported by the courts when police officers: (1) fail to follow proper booking procedures; (2) prevent defendants from being properly arraigned; (3) restrict a defendant's access to court; or (4) improperly file criminal charges against suspects. False imprisonment claims are usually based on the conduct of an officer following an arrest when the officer either unlawfully prolongs detention or violates the rights of a detained person.

NEGLIGENCE

Negligence is inadvertent behavior that results in damage or injury. The distinctions between strict liability and intentional torts leave negligence a residual category. Negligence requires a lesser degree of foreseeability of danger than does an intentional tort. In negligence, the mental state of the police officer is not at issue, because even inadvertent behavior resulting in damage or injury can lead to liability. The standard applied in negligence is whether the officer's act or failure to act created an unreasonable risk to another member of society. Consider the situation in which a police officer is driving a vehicle on an interstate highway. If the officer exceeds the posted speed limit and becomes involved in an accident, the officer could be found liable for negligence in the operation of a motor vehicle.

You can learn more about police negligence and the principles of law discussed here by visiting the Americans for Effective Law Enforcement's home page at: **http://www.aele.org/**

Negligence, however, is more complicated than demonstrating inadvertent behavior and injury or damage. There are four elements needed to establish a case of negligence. Each of these elements must be shown before an officer can be found liable for a claim of negligence. These elements include: (1) a legal duty; (2) a breach of that duty; (3) proximate causation; and (4) actual damage or injury (Box 10.2).

Box 10.2 Playing It Safe: Website Drops Fugitive List

Morris County, New Jersey, officials do not see themselves as having bucked a trend by removing a list of "10 Most Wanted" fugitives from a county website, but rather as being on the cutting edge of responsibility.

The posting was taken down in March by County Prosecutor John Dangler's office after a woman complained that the fugitive list was one of the hits turned up by a search engine given her boyfriend's name. Although the man's name and photograph had previously been removed, the search engine had apparently retained the outdated information.

> "This is a good example of the unintended consequences of putting public records online," Ari Schwartz, a policy analyst for the Center for Democracy & Technology, a Washington, D.C.-based watchdog group, said in an interview with The Newark Star-Ledger. "Anything they put online could be stored forever."

Fearing exposure to civil litigation, Dangler said he had asked for an opinion from the county's lawyer. "We decided to play it safe," he told The Star-Ledger.

But others in law enforcement find cyberspace posting a crime-fighting tool that outweighs any potential for defaming an innocent person.

Unlike Morris County, where the people who make the list are typically those who missed court appearances, the fugitives on the New Jersey State Police site are notoriously wanted criminals. Eight of the 12 Most Wanted are accused of murder, or attempted murder, including Joanne Chesimard, who escaped from prison in 1979 after her conviction for killing a state trooper 6 years earlier.

"I'm not concerned about any of them not being guilty," said a spokesman, Sergeant Al Della Fave. "These people are a danger. People need to know." Although the website list has not helped capture any fugitives in the 3 years it has been posted, Della Fave, nonetheless, called the site a "great tool."…

What concerned the internet administrators at the Morris County prosecutor's office, however, was their inability to stay current with the information spit out by search engines. Said Detective Paul Sagal, the office could not prevent incidents such as the name of someone who has been exonerated from coming up in a search.

Source: Law Enforcement News, April 30, 2001, p. 8.

Legal Duty

Legal duties are behaviors recognized by the courts that require police officers either to take action or to refrain from taking action in particular situations. Police legal duties arise from a number of sources. Laws, customs, judicial decisions, and departmental policy can create duties on the part of police officers.

Criminal law may be a source of police duty. Consider the case in which a state law prohibits drunk driving. A typical state law might read "police officers shall arrest and take into custody any persons operating a motor vehicle under the influence of intoxicants." A court examining this law may conclude that it creates a duty on the part of police officers to arrest drunk drivers. Similarly, a police department policy may require officers who stop suspected drunk drivers to perform field sobriety tests at the scene of traffic stops. If an officer stops a drunk driver, fails to perform a field sobriety test, and fails to make the arrest, and that driver subsequently causes an accident, the officer could be held liable for the injury. The court might conclude that the officer had a duty to perform the field test under departmental policy and a duty to arrest the drunk driver because of state law. Had the officer performed the duties, the injury and damage may not have occurred.

In the past, most plaintiffs were unsuccessful in establishing that the police owed them a legal duty because the courts had ruled that police officers have no duty to protect the general public. This, however, has changed and many courts now recognize that under certain circumstances police may owe a special duty to individual citizens when the actions of the police set a citizen apart from other members of society (Kappeler, 2006). For example, if the police become involved in an investigation and an informant provides the officer with information that leads to the arrest of a fugitive, the police may owe a duty to protect the informant from future harm.

Breach of Duty

The existence of a duty alone is not sufficient to lead to a police officers' liability. A plaintiff in a negligence lawsuit must establish that the officer breached the duty to the citizen. Breaches of duty are determined from factual situations. In the case of the drunk driver, the injured party must show that the officer either acted or failed to act in accordance with the existing duty. Just because police officers have a duty to arrest drunk drivers does not mean that because the police do not arrest every drunk driver, liability is incurred for every injury. The courts are quick to recognize that the police are only liable to specific individuals and not to the general public. Therefore, because a drunk driver injures an individual, if the police had no contact with the driver, the police cannot be held liable for the injury. The same reasoning holds true for crime victims. Just because there has been a rash of burglaries in a community does not mean the police are liable to people whose homes have been invaded. There must exist some special knowledge or circumstance that sets the individual apart from the general public and shows a special relationship between that person and the police. For example, if a home owner called the police and advised them that a person threatened to burglarize their home that evening and the police failed to take any action to prevent the crime, a court might find that such information and the police inaction created a special relationship.

Proximate Cause

Once a plaintiff has demonstrated the existence of a duty and has shown that the officer breached that duty to a specific citizen, one still must prove that the officer's conduct was the proximate cause of the injury or damage. The proximate cause of an injury or damage is determined by asking the question "but for the officer's conduct, would the plaintiff have sustained the injury or damage?" When the answer to this question is yes, then proximate cause is established. If proximate cause is established, the officer can be held liable for the damage or injury.

The proximate cause requirement is designed to limit liability in situations in which damage would have occurred regardless of the officer's behavior. Consider the case when a police officer is involved in a motor vehicle chase. If an officer chases a suspect and the suspect's vehicle strikes an innocent third party, is the officer liable? Generally, if the officer was not acting in a negligent fashion and the officer's conduct cannot be shown to have been the cause of the injury, there would be no liability on the officer's part. The accident may have occurred regardless of the officer's behavior.

Damage or Injury

Providing that a plaintiff has shown the existence of a duty, the breach of that duty, and proximate cause of injury, a negligence suit will still not succeed unless the plaintiff can show actual damage or harm. It must be shown that the damage was such that it substantially interfered with an interest of an individual or their property. General or technical rights violations that do not significantly interfere with the interests of a specific individual or their property do not satisfy the damage element under a negligence tort. Similarly, potential but uncertain future damage or harm is not sufficient to satisfy the damage element of a negligence action. For example, if the police refuse to provide the victim of a crime with police protection, the victim could not succeed in a negligence action until some actual damage or injury has occurred. The potential for future damage alone is not sufficient to satisfy the damage element in a negligence action. There must be actual damage or injury.

Box 10.3 lists some of the major high-risk areas of police negligence. The figure presents typical liabilities of both line officers and their supervisors.

Box 10.3 High-Risk Areas of Law Enforcement Liability	
Liabilities of Officers	**Liabilities of Supervisors**
Negligent operation of police vehicles	Negligent hiring
Negligent failure to arrest drunk drivers	Negligent supervision
Negligent failure to protect crime victims	Failure to direct officer
Failure to respond to calls for assistance	Negligent assignment
Failure to restrain criminal offenders	Negligent entrustment
Failure to investigate	Negligent retention of officers
Negligent service at accident scenes	Failure to discipline

Common Claims of Police Negligence

There are various behaviors in which the police engage that can form the basis of a negligence claim. The following are a few of the most frequent claims of negligence brought against the police. When reviewing this list one must remember that the law of police negligence is highly unique to legal jurisdictions and every form of negligence listed is not always actionable in all jurisdictions (Kappeler, 2006).

Negligent Operation of Emergency Vehicles

Under this claim of negligence, a plaintiff argues that a police officer failed to operate an emergency vehicle with due care for the safety of the public. As a result of the negligent operation and because the officer's actions were unreasonable, the plaintiff sustained injuries. Claims of police negligent operation of emergency vehicles can be brought against the police by innocent third parties who are injured when police officers engage in high-speed pursuit driving. Under such circumstances, if a police officer becomes involved in an accident with an innocent motorist or causes the fleeing suspect to injure an innocent motorist, there is a potential for civil liability. In rare cases, even the fleeing suspect can sue if injured while attempting to elude officers.

Negligent Failure to Protect

This form of negligence may occur if a police officer fails to take adequate actions to protect a person from a known and foreseeable danger. These claims most often arise when police officers fail to protect battered women. There are, however, other circumstances that can create a duty on the part of police officers to protect people from crime. Informants, witnesses, and other people dependent upon the police can be a source of police liability if an officer knows of a potential threat and fails to take reasonable action to prevent victimization. Police officers may owe a duty of protection to the people they have taken into custody. In some cases, police officers may have a legal duty to prevent self-inflicted injury or death. Police officers can create foreseeable zones of risk for which they can be held liable for damages. For example, when officers use firearms, they may create zones of risk that require them to protect all people in that zone. In some cases, the law imposes a duty for the officer to act with reasonable care (Lewis v. City of St. Pete, 2001).

Negligent Failure to Arrest

A claim of negligent failure to arrest or apprehend is similar to a claim of negligent failure to protect. Under this form of negligence, a plaintiff argues that they were injured as a result of a police officer's failure to enforce the law. These claims are usually brought as a result of police failure to arrest suspected criminals. Plaintiffs argue that although there existed probable cause to arrest the suspect and the officer could reasonably foresee that inaction would lead to injury or damage, the officer still failed to take action. One of the most frequent claims of police failure to arrest occurs in situations in which a police officer fails to arrest a drunk driver and that driver later injures an innocent motorist or pedestrian.

Negligent Failure to Render Assistance

In certain circumstances, the police may have a duty to render assistance to sick or injured people. If officers undertake a duty to provide assistance or medical attention and if they do not provide that assistance in a timely and reasonable manner they can be subject to civil liability. This type of claim most often arises as a result of traffic accidents, injuries, or when illnesses strike people in custody.

Negligent Selection, Hiring, and Retention

Police administrators may have a duty to use appropriate and reasonable methods of selecting and hiring police officers. This duty may include the use of proper selection standards and tests as well as conducting adequate background investigations of police applicants. If a police officer is hired in a negligent fashion and that negligence is directly related to a later incident of police misconduct or illegal behavior administrators may be held civilly liable for unreasonable selecting and hiring practices. Likewise, police administrators who knowingly retain or promote employees who have committed illegal acts or patterns of illegal acts can be held liable for negligent retention. This is especially the case if the police-employee's illegal act is clearly related to past acts of misconduct by the same employee.

Negligent Police Supervision and Direction

Negligent supervision and direction involves breaching a duty to provide effective systems for the evaluation, control, and monitoring of police employees' performance. Evidence of a breach of this duty may come in the form of failure to provide written and verbal directives, failure to develop adequate departmental policies and guidelines, or the failure to clearly articulate to employees how duties are to be performed. It may also involve a supervisor's direction to an employee to engage in an illegal activity or the supervisor's approval of an illegal activity (District of Columbia v. Tulin, 2010).

> You can watch a video lecture on police supervisory liability by going to: **http://www.youtube.com/watch?v=exGbI3P-93NA**

Negligent Entrustment and Assignment

Police administrators may have a duty to ensure that officers are properly trained and capable of using equipment or carrying out a given responsibility before they entrust or assign them to that responsibility. A police administrator, for example, who entrusts an officer with a motor vehicle knowing that the officer is incapable of using the vehicle with an ordinary amount of care, could be held liable for negligent entrustment. Likewise, assigning an officer to a duty that the officer is incapable of performing can result in liability if the officer or a citizen is injured while the officer is performing that assignment. An example of negligent assignment would be assigning an officer to conduct a bomb sweep of a building knowing that the officer had no training in the proper execution of that assignment.

Negligent Failure to Discipline and Investigate

Negligent failure to discipline and investigate relates to a police department's failure to provide an effect system of police accountability. This breach of duty could arise by a department's failure to have adequate citizen complaint processes, inadequate internal affairs investigative practices, or failing to effectively and progressively take steps to sanction police misconduct.

DEFENSES TO CLAIMS OF POLICE NEGLIGENCE

There are a number of defenses available to police officers faced with a claim of negligence. Each of these defenses serves to bar or limit the liability of police officers. The most common defenses to negligence include: (1) contributory negligence; (2) comparative negligence; and (3) assumption of risk. In the sections that follow, each of these defenses to negligence is discussed and its various limitations are considered.

Contributory Negligence

One common defense available to police officers faced with a claim of negligence is the defense of contributory negligence. Such a defense holds that if an officer can show that the plaintiff was also negligent in causing the damage or injury, the officer will not be held liable for the damage or injury. This defense is based on the idea that all persons owe a duty to carry out their day-to-day activities in a reasonable manner. It is reasoned that if the plaintiff was engaged in unreasonable behavior that increased the likelihood of damage or injury, the officer should not be held liable. Consider the situation in which a police officer is in pursuit of a speeding suspect. Although the officer might be negligent in the operation of the vehicle, other motorists owe a duty to operate their vehicles in a reasonable manner. If the pursuing officer becomes involved in an accident with a motorist who inadvertently ran a red light, a court might find that the citizen's behavior contributed to the damage. In such a situation, liability would be avoided because of the citizen's own contributory negligence.

Comparative Negligence

Comparative negligence does not totally bar an officer's liability, but rather serves to mitigate the size of the damage award. Consider the same facts mentioned above, in which the officer is in pursuit of a suspect. When the issue comes to court in a jurisdiction using the comparative negligence, the court would attempt to determine the degree of negligence of both the officer and the injured party. If the officer was 30% negligent and the citizen running the red light was 70% negligent, the court would apportion the damage award. If the award were $1000, the officer would be liable for $300. Comparative negligence allows the court to assess fault to both parties and determine the extent to which each party contributed to the accident.

Assumption of Risk

The assumption of risk doctrine is another method by which liability is limited. The general principle behind the doctrine is that one who voluntarily engages in a known and foreseeable dangerous behavior cannot expect to recover damages sustained in conjunction with engaging in the dangerous behavior. For example, a suspect injured while fleeing from the police following an armed robbery cannot expect to successfully sue the police to recover from damages sustained in an automobile chase. In such a situation, the court would hold that the suspect had assumed the risk of injury by choosing to commit the robbery and attempting to flee from the police. Because the suspect assumed the risk of injury, the police will not be liable to the suspect for the damages received (Kappeler & Vaughn, 1989).

POLICE LIABILITY UNDER FEDERAL LAW

The Civil Rights Act of 1871 was enacted by Congress to control the behavior of state officials and to allow persons whose constitutional rights were violated an avenue of legal redress. Following ratification of the Thirteenth and Fourteenth Amendments of the United States Constitution, which abolished slavery and provided due process safeguards, Congress enacted the legislation to assist in controlling the conduct of state officials affiliated primarily with the Ku Klux Klan. The Civil Rights Act of 1871 has since been codified as Title 42 of the United States Code, Section 1983 and legal actions brought under this legislation are commonly referred to as Section 1983 lawsuits. The legislation allows persons whose civil rights are violated by government officials to bring civil suit in federal court to recover damages.

Although the legislation was largely unused before the 1960s, it is now the cornerstone of police federal liability litigation. Between 1871 and 1920, only 21 cases were brought under The Civil Rights Act of 1871 for all types of constitutional violations (Vaughn, 1994). By 1995, the federal district courts alone decided more than 130 claims against the police. The increasing use of the Civil Rights Act may be attributable to an expanded interpretation of the legislation by the Supreme Court and the passage of the Attorney's Fee Act of 1976. The courts have interpreted the Civil Rights Act to allow persons who have had their civil rights violated by the police to bring civil suit against law enforcement officers, police agencies, and governments. Additionally, the Attorney's Fee Act allows counsel representing these parties to collect their fees from judgments against persons or agencies found liable for rights violations. These two factors have led to an explosion in the number of federal cases filed against the police claiming violations of constitutional or federally protected rights.

Title 42 of the United States Code, Section 1983 states that:

> Every person who, under color of any statute, ordinance, regulation, custom, or usage, of any State or Territory, or the District of Columbia, subjects, or causes to be subjected, any citizen of the United States or other persons within the jurisdiction thereof to the deprivation of any rights, privileges, or immunities secured by the Constitution and laws, shall be liable to the party injured in an action at law, suit in equity, or other proper proceeding for redress....

The legislation has two unique elements that must be established for a person to successfully sue a government official for civil rights violations. Persons seeking redress for civil rights violations must show that: (1) the officials were acting under color of state law; and (2) the alleged violation was of a constitutional or federally protected right. If each of these elements is not met, then liability is barred under the provisions of the legislation. As mentioned earlier, a civil suit may still be brought at the state level under a tort action, provided that the elements of a tort can be established.

You can watch a video lecture on Section 1983 lawsuits by going to: **http://www.youtube.com/watch?v=-MrR6kURSI4**

ACTING UNDER COLOR OF STATE LAW

Defendants in a Section 1983 action must be acting under color of state law in order to be held liable for constitutional violations. Acts of private individuals or the acts of law enforcement officers not related to employment are not actionable under the provisions of the legislation. This, however, does not mean that an off-duty police officer performing a police function cannot be held liable for a constitutional violation. Conduct by police officers is deemed as occurring under color of state law when they involve the misuse of power "possessed by virtue of state law and made possible only because the wrongdoer is clothed with the authority of state law." (Honaker v. Smith, 2001:484–85; Wilson v. Price, 2010). A police officer's conduct does not constitute acting under color of state law unless it is "related in some way to the performance of the duties of the state office." (Honaker v. Smith, 2001:485).

Off-duty police officers employed on second jobs can be found to be acting under color of law if they perform police functions. Consider the situation in which an off-duty police officer has accepted employment as a bank security guard. If the bank is robbed and the officer attempts to apprehend the suspect, the officer may be found to be acting under color of law for the purposes of a Section 1983 lawsuit.

Many police actions that lead to the filing of a Section 1983 suit are based on conduct that is outside the scope of an officer's official authority. For example, a police officer that brutalizes a citizen is not acting within the scope of police authority. Courts, however, interpret this type of conduct as being under color of state law even though it is illegal conduct. Often, the distinction between official state action and private action is difficult to make. Generally, however, if officers are carrying out a police function, such as making an arrest or conducting a search, it can be said that they are acting under color of state law for purposes of liability.

In one case, a Chicago police officer was placed on medical leave because of mental unfitness. The department enjoined the officer from carrying a weapon or from exercising his authority as a police officer, and required him to surrender his badge and identification card. Approximately 3 months later, he identified himself as a police officer and shot a subject in the chest, killing him. A subsequent departmental investigation of the shooting eventually found the officer had shot the individual without justification. A civil action under 42 United States Constitution Section 1983 was brought, claiming that the officer was acting under color of state law and that the shooting violated the victim's constitutional rights. The District Court held that the officer was not acting under color of law when he shot the individual because the department had stripped the officer of all police authority 3 months before the shooting. The Court stated that Section 1983 was intended to provide a remedy only to those injured by the abusive exercise of governmental power and because the department had removed the officer's police power, the lawsuit could not succeed (Gibson v. City of Chicago, 1988). If, however, the department had not stripped the officer of his police power, liability may have extended to the department as well as to the individual officer.

You can view a news video on the lawsuits filed against the Chicago Police at: **http://www.youtube.com/watch?v=1aKZN42WgFs**

Courts consider the following factors when making determinations of whether a police officer was acting under the color of law for purposes of liability:

1. Did the police identify themselves as law enforcement officers?
2. Were the officers performing an investigation?
3. Were the official police documents filed?

4. Did the officer attempt an arrest?
5. Did the police invoke powers outside their jurisdiction?
6. Did the officer settle a personal vendetta with police powers?
7. Were weapons or police equipment displayed?
8. Was the officer acting pursuant to state or city law?
9. Does police policy mandate that officers are on-duty 24 h a day (Vaughn & Coomes, 1995)?

VIOLATION OF A CONSTITUTIONAL RIGHT

Conduct that can be redressed under Section 1983 is limited to violations of constitutional or federally protected rights. This means that violations of state laws or city ordinances by a police officer are normally not actionable. For example, a police officer arrests an intoxicated driver and lawfully impounds the motor vehicle. If, under state law, it is unlawful for the officers to conduct an inventory search of the contents of the vehicle, a state law has been violated. However, because inventory searches of motor vehicles are permissible within the provision of the Fourth Amendment of the United States Constitution, the officer's conduct would not be a violation of a constitutional or federally protected right. Although the drunk driver may have grounds for a civil action under state tort law, a Section 1983 lawsuit could not succeed because there was no violation of a constitutional right.

Box 10.4 presents various amendments to the United States Constitution that are related to police liability litigation. Each of these amendments can be a source of police liability if an officer or a department violates its provisions.

Violations of judge-made case law, unlike violations of the Constitution or federal statutes, are not actionable under Section 1983. For example, violations of the exclusionary rule or the rule of Miranda v. Arizona (1966) are redressed by suppression of the illegally obtained evidence or confession, rather than by a civil suit. In one case that illustrates this point, police officers in Lincoln, Nebraska, were responding to a burglary call. The caller stated that an intruder was attempting to gain entry into his apartment through a second-story window. A man, described as a slender white male in his early 20s wearing a white, short-sleeved shirt, fled from the area on foot. One of the officers at the scene used a tracking dog to follow the suspect's scent and was led four blocks from the crime scene to Jackson Warren's parked vehicle. Warren was a slender white male, 19 years of age, who wore a light-colored, short-sleeved shirt. Warren attempted to start his vehicle and leave the scene as the officer arrived. One officer flagged down the suspect's vehicle and ordered him to park the car. Warren was arrested and transported to the Lincoln jail where he was turned over to a detective. The detective had been investigating a number of burglaries and

Box 10.4 Select Amendments to the United States Constitution

Amendment I

Congress shall make no law respecting an establishment of religion, or prohibiting the free exercise thereof; or abridging the freedom of speech, or of the press; or the right of the people peaceably to assemble, and to petition the government for a redress of grievances.

Amendment IV

The right of the people to be secure in their persons, houses, papers, and effects, against unreasonable searches and seizures, shall not be violated, and no Warrants shall issue, but upon probable cause, supported by Oath or affirmation, and particularly describing the place to be searched, and the persons or things to be seized.

Amendment V

No person shall be held to answer for a capital, or otherwise infamous crime, unless on a presentment or indictment of a Grand Jury, except in cases arising in the land or naval forces, or in the Militia, when in actual service in time of War or public danger; nor shall any person be subject for the same offense to be twice put in jeopardy of life or limb; nor shall be compelled in any criminal case to be a witness against himself, nor be deprived of life, liberty, or property, without due process of law; nor shall private property be taken for public use, without just compensation.

Amendment VI

In all criminal prosecutions the accused shall enjoy the right to a speedy and public trial, by an impartial jury of the State and district wherein the crime shall have been committed, which district shall have been previously ascertained by law, and to be informed of the nature and cause of the accusation; to be confronted with the witnesses against him; to have compulsory process for obtaining Witnesses in his favor, and to have the Assistance of Counsel for his defense.

Amendment VIII

Excessive bail shall not be required, nor excessive fines imposed, nor cruel and unusual punishments inflicted.

Amendment XIV

Section 1. All persons born or naturalized in the United States, and subject to jurisdiction thereof, are citizens of the United States and of the State wherein they reside. No State shall make or enforce any law which shall abridge the privileges or immunities of citizens of the United States; nor shall any State deprive any person of life, liberty, or property without due process of law; nor deny to any person within its jurisdiction the equal protection of the laws....

sexual assaults that were similar in nature to the call to which the initial officer had responded. Warren was questioned by the detective as to his whereabouts and background. The detective denied Warren's requests for counsel and failed to advise him of his Miranda rights (Warren v. City of Lincoln, Nebraska, 1989).

Warren brought a civil rights claim under 42 United States Constitution Section 1983 against police officer and the city claiming violations of constitutional rights because the officer did not read him his Miranda warnings before interrogation. The court held that the officers' failure to read Warren the Miranda warnings is not actionable under Section 1983 because the reading of Miranda warnings is a judicially created procedural

You can watch a video lecture on civil liability and constitutional amendments by going to: **http://www.youtube.com/watch?v=41nW_0_Ut3c**

safeguard rather than a right arising out of the Fifth Amendment itself (Warren v. City of Lincoln, Nebraska, 1989).

The following is a list of the more common police behaviors that may indicate a constitutional violation.

1. The use of excessive or deadly force;
2. Illegal search of persons or places;
3. Illegal seizure of items or persons;
4. Invasion of privacy;
5. Failure to protect citizens from crime;
6. Abandoning citizens in dangerous or high-crime areas or situations;
7. False arrests or false imprisonment;
8. Failure to render medical attention; and
9. Unlawful conversion of property.

Municipal Liability for Failure to Train

The allegation of inadequate or improper training of police officers is frequently the basis of a failure to act claim brought under Section 1983. This issue was addressed by the United States Supreme Court in Harris v. City of Canton (1989). In the Harris case, the plaintiff was arrested and brought to the police station in a police wagon. Upon arrival at the station, she was found sitting on the floor of the wagon. When asked if she needed medical attention she responded with an incoherent remark. During the booking process, the plaintiff slumped to the floor. She was later released and taken by an ambulance to a hospital. The plaintiff was diagnosed as suffering from several emotional ailments. The plaintiff brought a Section 1983 suit against the city and its officials, claiming that they violated her constitutional right to due process. Evidence was presented during the trial that showed shift commanders in the police department were authorized to determine, solely at their discretion, whether a detainee required medical care. Testimony was also presented stating that the commanders were not provided with any special training to make such determinations. The district court decided in favor of the plaintiff on the medical claim and the Sixth Circuit Court of Appeals affirmed that decision.

The case was appealed to the United States Supreme Court, which held that failure to train can be the basis of liability under Section 1983 if that failure is based on "deliberate indifference" to the rights of those with whom the police come into contact. The Court stated that "it may happen that in light of the duties assigned to specific officers or employees the need for more or different training is so obvious, and the inadequacy so likely to result in violation of constitutional rights, that the policymakers of the city can reasonably be said to have been deliberately indifferent to the need" (City of Canton v. Harris, 1989:1205; Schneider v. City of Grand Junction Police Dept, 2013). The Court then set forth what may be considered requisites for liability based on "deliberate indifference." These include:

1. The focus must be on the adequacy of the training program in relation to the tasks the particular officer must perform;
2. The fact that a particular officer may be unsatisfactorily trained will not alone result in city liability because the officer's shortcoming may have resulted from factors other than a faulty training program;
3. It is not sufficient to impose liability if it can be proved that an injury or accident could have been avoided if an officer had better or more training; and
4. The identified deficiency in a city's training program must be closely related to the ultimate injury.

Using the Harris case as precedent, the United States First Circuit Court of Appeals decided Bordanaro v. McLeod (1989). In the summer of 1982, an off-duty police officer and a woman were at a motel bar. Shortly after their arrival, an altercation began between the officer and two other patrons. The officer was badly beaten in the fight and ejected from the bar. He then called the police department to report the incident; the entire night-watch of the department was dispatched to the scene. Upon arrival at the bar, the officers found the glass front door locked; they demanded admittance. When the manager hesitated, they shattered the door and threatened to kill the occupants of the lounge. Those involved in the earlier altercation had fled to a room within the motel and the officers pursued them, brandishing "nightsticks, clubs, bats, tire-irons and an ax in addition to their service revolvers" (Bordanaro v. McLeod, 1989:1153). Instead of accepting the manager's offer to open the door with a passkey, officers drilled a hole and sprayed mace into the room while firing shots into the door. After the officers forcibly entered the room, the plaintiffs were beaten unconscious and one died from the injuries.

A civil rights action was brought under Section 1983 against the municipality, the mayor, the police chief, and several individual officers, claiming that the police action constituted numerous constitutional violations. On appeal, the First Circuit Court discussed in detail the issue of municipal liability for police misconduct. The court reviewed the trial evidence and affirmed the jury's finding of municipal liability for failure to train, as well as the imposition of punitive damages against the chief of police and the mayor. Liability was based on the following findings:

1. The department was operating under rules and regulations developed and distributed to the officers in the 1960s;
2. The department's rules and regulations failed to address modern issues in law enforcement;

3. The department failed to provide officers with training beyond that received in the police academy;
4. The city actively discouraged officers from seeking training;
5. There was no supervisory training;
6. The chief of police haphazardly meted out discipline and failed to discipline the officers in the current incident until after they were indicted; and
7. There was no internal investigation of the incident until one year after its occurrence.

The court found liability for failure to train based on the "deliberate indifference standard" as well as liability for the promotion of an "official" policy based on a custom of unconstitutional use of force and unlawful search and seizure. The Bordanaro case applied the standards set forth by the United States Supreme Court in Harris to a specific set of facts and concluded that there was deliberate indifference.

Regardless of who the plaintiffs is, a police officer or a civilian, to establish municipality liability for failure to train police officers in a Section 1983 action, a plaintiff must show five basic elements. A plaintiff must prove that:

1. The training was in fact inadequate;
2. The officer's actions exceeded constitutional limits;
3. The officer's actions arose in a typical situation with which officers must deal;
4. The training demonstrates a deliberate indifference toward persons with whom the police come into contact with; and
5. There is a direct causal link between the constitutional deprivation and the inadequate training (Brown v. Gray, Denver Manager of Public Safety, 2000).

DEFENSES TO SECTION 1983 LAWSUITS

There are a number of defenses that are available to police officers when they are confronted with a claim of liability under Section 1983. Each of these defenses serves to limit, and, in some cases, bar recovery of damages by plaintiffs. The four primary defenses to a Section 1983 action include: (1) absolute immunity; (2) qualified immunity; (3) probable cause; and (4) good faith.

Absolute Immunity

The concept of absolute immunity means that if a civil action is brought against a person protected by this form of immunity, the court will dismiss the lawsuit. This form of immunity is usually reserved for persons involved in the judicial process. Because the role of law enforcement officers in the judicial process is limited, there is only one circumstance for which the court will recognize absolute immunity of police officers. If a police officer is testifying in a criminal trial and commits perjury or provides the court with incorrect information, the officer cannot be sued. The courts reason that it is difficult enough to get people to testify at a criminal trial without the threat of civil liability. Also, courts reason that there exist alternative criminal actions that can be taken against a person who commits perjury. Officers who intentionally provide perjured testimony are immune from civil liability, but may be charged and convicted of a criminal offense.

Qualified Immunity

A lesser form of immunity than absolute is qualified immunity. Qualified immunity extends to police officers who are performing duties of a discretionary nature. Discretionary duties are those tasks performed by police officers who require deliberation or judgment. Qualified immunity for public officials serves important societal purposes and is intended to protect "all but the plainly incompetent or those who knowingly violate the law" (Malley v. Briggs, 1986:341). The qualified immunity of an individual police officer is determined by a two-part analysis (Harlow v. Fitzgerald, 1982; Johnson v. Jones, 1995). The first step in the decision-making process is to determine whether the alleged constitutional violation was a breach of a clearly established constitutional right at the time of the deprivation. The law must have defined the right in a quite specific manner, and that the announcement of the rule establishing the right must have been unambiguous and widespread (Brady v. Dill, 1999; Reichle v. Howards, 2012; see also, Wilson v. Layne, 1999). The determination of whether a right is clearly established can be made by considering the following questions:

1. Is the right defined with reasonable clarity?
2. Has the Supreme Court or a court of appeals affirmed its existence?
3. Would a reasonable police officer understand from existing law that the conduct was illegal (Dickerson v. Monroe County Sheriffs Dept., 2000; Kennedy v. City of Cincinnati, 2010)?

It must be established that law enforcement officers had ample opportunity to know what behaviors were proper before holding them accountable (Anderson v. Creighton, 1987).

If the law was clearly established at the time of the alleged misconduct, the court moves to the second step in the decision-making process: determining whether the officer's conduct was objectively reasonable. It asks the question, would a reasonable law enforcement officer know that their conduct was a violation of a constitutional right? If a court determined that the law was not clearly established or that the officer's conduct was reasonable, the officer is to be afforded immunity from liability (see, Bonner v. Anderson, 1996).

Probable Cause

Police officers who face claims of false arrest or unlawful search are afforded the defense of probable cause. If an officer can show that probable cause existed to either make an arrest or to search a residence, the courts will bar liability. Probable cause means that the officer has a "reasonable good faith belief in the legality of the action taken." The best way to support a claim of probable cause is to secure a warrant either for an arrest or search. By issuing a warrant, a judge makes the determination of whether probable cause exists for the proposed police action. Police action taken in the execution of a warrant is protected by the good faith defense.

Good Faith

When the defense of good faith is used by police officers, the officer, in effect, argues that at the time the act was committed, he could not have reasonably known that the act was unconstitutional or against the law (Harlow v. Fitzgerald, 1982). A good faith defense can be used when an officer executed an arrest warrant believing in good faith that the warrant was valid. Later, if it is determined that the warrant was defective and invalid, the officer can raise the defense of good faith. There are a number of factors the courts will consider as evidence of an officer's good faith actions. These factors include:

1. The officer's actions were based on departmental policy and regulations;
2. The officer was acting pursuant to a valid law that is later invalidated by a court;
3. The officer was acting on the orders of a supervisor and believed the orders to be legal; or
4. The officer was acting on advice of legal counsel and felt the advice was valid (del Carmen, 1987:414).

PREVENTING LIABILITY

Although police officers and their departments have little control over the filing of civil lawsuits against them, they can take measures to reduce the potential for liability. Citizens have a right to file claims against police officers and their departments for alleged rights violations. In order to drastically reduce findings of liability, the police must take an aggressive posture toward risk management (Hopper & Summers, 1989). This means that police departments must identify the areas of high-risk liability and develop programs that target these particular areas. Police can decrease the likelihood of civil suits by:

1. Acting within their official scope of authority;
2. Knowing the law of police liability;
3. Keeping abreast of the changing law of liability;
4. Reading and following departmental rules and regulations;
5. Keeping and maintaining adequate records and documentation on police operations;
6. Seeking the assistance of the county attorney or other counsel on liability matters;
7. Implementing and providing continuing training for police liability (see Worrall, 2001);
8. Selecting officers with higher education and recruiting officers who adhere to and respect the rule of law; and
9. Maintaining good community relations and advising citizens of drastic changes in police policy or operations.

SUMMARY

In this Chapter, police liability was discussed and the difficulty in performing law enforcement duties in a legally hostile environment was noted. Because of the special role and function the police play in society, police officers are particularly vulnerable to civil litigation. There is a general concern among practitioners and scholars alike concerning the growing number of cases filed against the nation's police and the increasing cost of these cases to citizens and cities alike. The cost associated with police civil liability goes well beyond the actual damage awards rendered by courts and can have an effect on the operation of police department and municipal governments. The actual costs of liability judgments against the police were considered, and while the police have had a good record in defending themselves from civil liability, the number of cases the police lose are increasing.

Various reasons that people file lawsuits against the police were reviewed and the roles of the actors in the civil litigation process were briefly discussed. The distinction between crime and torts were made and three different types of torts were considered: (1) strict liability tort; (2) intentional tort; and (3) negligence tort. These state actions make up the vast majority of claims filed against the police in state courts. Federal litigation against the police is also a growing area of concern. Federal liability was considered and the elements of a lawsuit under 42 United States Constitution Section 1983 were presented. Section 1983 actions have become the cornerstone of police civil liability at the federal level. In closing, a number of methods to reduce police liability were enumerated.

REVIEW QUESTIONS

1. The unique vulnerability of police and a trend toward allowing governmental liability have led to an explosion of lawsuits. When does the possibility of civil liability for police officers exist?
2. Do police officers fear being sued and does this affect their behavior?
3. Police civil liability has become a concern of state and municipal government as well as of individual police officers. Why is this?
4. Where does the word tort come from and how is it used in civil liability and the law? What is negligence and what are some defenses available to police officers faced with a claim of negligence?
5. What are the differences between a state tort and a Section 1983 action?
6. Describe the rights afforded to citizens the Bill of Rights and common police behaviors that may indicate a constitutional violation.

REFERENCES

Alexander v. DeAngelo, No. 02-3124 (7th Cir. 2003).

Amadi, E. (2010). The impact of Section 1983 on police operations in the United States. *Journal of Criminal Justice and Law Review*, 2(1–2), 1–10.

Americans for Effective Law Enforcement. (1974). *Survey of police misconduct litigation: 1967–1971.* San Francisco, CA: AELE.

Americans for Effective Law Enforcement. (1980). *Lawsuits against police skyrocket.* San Francisco, CA: AELE.

Anderson v. Creighton, 483 U.S. 635 (1987).

Archbold, C. A., & Maguire, E. R. (2002). Studying civil suits against the police: a serendipitous finding of sample selection bias. *Police Quarterly*, 5(2), 222–249.

Barrineau, H. E. (1994). *Civil liability in criminal justice* (2nd ed.). Cincinnati, OH: Anderson Publishing Co.

Bates, R. D., Culter, R. F., & Clink, M. J. (1981). *Prepared statement on behalf of the national institute of municipal law officers, presented before the subcommittee on the constitution, Senate Committee on the Judiciary, May 6, 1981.* (as cited in Barrineau, 1987).

Bonner v. Anderson, 81 F.3d 472 (4th Cir. 1996).

Bordanaro v. McLeod, 871 F.2d 1151 (1st Cir. 1989); cert. denied, 493 U.S. 820(1989).

Brady v. Dill, No. 98-2293 (1st Cir. 1999).

Brown v. Gray, Denver Manager of Public Safety, Nos. 99-1134, 99-1164 & 99-1232 (10th Cir. 2000).

Bureau of Justice Statistics. (1995). *Three out of four tort cases settled out of court.* Washington, DC: U.S. Department of Justice.

Chiabi, D. K. (1996). Police civil liability: an analysis of section 1983 actions in the Eastern and Southern districts of New York. *American Journal of Criminal Justice*, 21(1), 83–104.

Collins, A. (1998). *Report charges police abuse in U.S. goes unchecked.* New York: Roger Press, Inc. Retrieved August 8, 2006, from www.commondreams.org/pressreleases/July98/070798a.htm.

Davis v. Harrison, Township Police Department, Civil Action No. 2:13-cv-1224. (Dist. W.D. Penn. 2013).

del Carmen, R. V. (1987). *Criminal procedure for law enforcement personnel*. Monterey, CA: Brooks/Cole.

del Carmen, R. V. (1995). *Criminal procedure for law enforcement personnel* (3rd ed.). Monterey, CA: Brooks/Cole.

Dickerson v. Monroe, County Sheriff's Department, 114 F. Supp.2d 187 (W.D. N.Y. 2000).

District of Columbia v. Tulin, No. 08-CV-1116 (DC App. 2010).

Donahue v. City of Boston, 371 F.3d 7 (1st Cir. 2004).

Fisher, W. S., Kutner, S., & Wheat, J. (1989). Civil liability of New Jersey police officers: an overview. *Criminal Justice Quarterly, 10,* 45–78.

Garner, G. (1991). Off-duty: off the hook? *Police, 15*(9), 32–34. 71–73.

Garrison, A. H. (1995). Law enforcement civil liability under federal law and attitudes on civil liability: a survey of university, municipal and state police officers. *Police Studies, 18*(3), 19–37.

Gibson v. City of Chicago, 701 F. Supp. 666 (N.D. Ill. 1988).

Guzman v. City of San Antonio, 766 S.W.2d 858 (Tex. App. 1989).

Hall, D. E., Ventura, L. A., Lee, Y. H., & Lambert, E. (2003). Suing cops and corrections officers: officer attitudes and experiences about civil liability. *Policing: An International Journal of Police Strategies and Management, 26*(4), 529–547.

Harlow v. Fitzgerald, 457 U.S. 800 (1982).

Harris v. City of Canton, 109 S. Ct. 1197 (1989).

Honaker v. Smith, 256 F.3d 477 (7th Cir. 2001).

Houghton v. Forrester, 989 A.2d 223 (MD App. 2010).

Hopper, J. W., & Summers, W. C. (September 1989). Managing the risks and controlling the losses. *Police Chief,* 45–48.

Hoyt v. Cooks, No. 11–10771. (11th Cir. 2012).

Hughes, T. (2001). Police officers and civil liability: "the ties that bind"? *Policing: An International Journal of Police Strategies and Management, 24*(2), 240–262.

Human Rights Watch. (1998). *Shielded from justice: Police brutality and accountability in the United States*. New York, NY: Human Rights Watch.

Jocks v. Tavernier, 97 F.Supp. 2d 303 (E.D.N.Y. 2000).

Johnson v. Jones, 115 S. Ct. 2151 (1995).

Kappeler, V. E. (2006). *Critical issues in police civil liability* (4th ed.). Prospect Heights, IL: Waveland.

Kappeler, S. F., & Kappeler, V. E. (1992). A research note on section 1983 cases against the police: cases before the federal district courts in 1990. *American Journal of Police, 11*(1), 65–73.

Kappeler, V. E., & Vaughn, J. B. (1989). The historical development of negligence theory. *American Journal of Police, 8*(1), 1–36.

Kappeler, V. E., Kappeler, S. F., & del Carmen, R. V. (1993). A content analysis of police civil liability cases: decisions of the federal district courts, 1978–1990. *Journal of Criminal Justice, 21*(4), 325–337.

Kennedy v. Cincinnati, No. 07–00512 (6th Cir. 2010).

Kritzer, H., Marshall, L., & Zemans, F. (1992). Rule 11: moving beyond the cosmic anecdote. *Judicature, 75*(5), 269–272.

L.A. Mayor Suggests Tobacco Money to Pay Off Lawsuits over Corruption (February 17, 2000). The Associated Press State & Local Wire.

Law Enforcement News. (2004). The same only different: reforms, not riots, come quickly on the heels of latest videotaped LAPD beating. *Law Enforcement News, 30*(622), 1.

Lewis v. City of St. Pete, No. 00-12917 (11th Cir. 2001).

Linson v. City of New York, 98 A.D.3d 1002 (App. D. N.Y., 2012).

Malley v. Briggs, 475 U.S. 335 (1986).

Marquez, J. (March 31, 2005). *LA police corruption settlements estimated to reach $70 million*. The Associated Press State & Local Wire.

Mauro, T. (2004). *The Legal Intelligencer, 230*(5), 4. January 8, 2004, Thursday.

McCoy, C. (1987). Police legal liability is 'Not a crisis' 99 chiefs say. *Crime Control Digest, 21*, 1.

Miranda v. Arizona, 384 U.S. 436 (1966).

National League of Cities. (November 25, 1985). *Seeking solutions on liability insurance*. Washington, D.C.: Nation's Cities Weekly. National League of Cities.

Novak, K. J., Smith, B. W., & Frank, J. (2003). Strange bedfellows: civil liability and aggressive policing. *Policing: An International Journal of Police Strategies and Management, 26*(2), 352–368.

Out, N. (2006). The police service and liability insurance: responsible policing. *Policing: International Journal of Police Science and Management, 8*(4), 294–314.

Reichle et al. v. Howards, No. 11–262. Argued March 21, 2012—decided June 4, 2012.

Reynolds, C. D. (1988). Unjust civil litigation. *Police Chief, 7*(12), 8–9.

Ross, D. (2012). *Civil liability in criminal justice* (6th ed.). Cincinnati, OH: Anderson Publishing Co.

Ross, D. L., & Bodapati, M. R. (2006). A risk management analysis of claims, litigation and losses of Michigan law enforcement agencies: 1985–1999. *Policing: International Journal of Police Science and Management, 29*(1), 38–57.

Schneider v. City of Grand Junction Police Dept., 717 F. 3d 760 (10th Cir, 2013).

Schofield, D. L. (1990). Personal liability: the qualified immunity defense. *FBI Law Enforcement Bulletin, 59*(3), 26–32.

Schwartz, J. C. (2010). Myths and mechanics of deterrence: the role of lawsuits in law enforcement decisionmaking. *UCLA Law Review, 57*, 1023–1094.

Scogin, F., & Brodsky, S. L. (1991). Fear of litigation among law enforcement officers. *American Journal of Police, 10*(1), 41–45.

Singer v. Fulton County Sheriff, 63 F.3d 110 (2d Cir. 1995).

Stevens, D. J. (2000). Civil liabilities and arrest decisions. *The Police Journal, 73*, 119–142.

Tennessee v. Garner, 53 U.S.L.W. 4410 (1985).

Tennessee v. Perry Thomas Randolph, No. 99-0493, No. M2000-02293-SC-R11-CD–Filed May 3, 2002.

Terry v. Ohio, 392 U.S. 1, 20–21, 88 S. Ct. 1868, 1879 (1968).

Vaughn, M. S. (1994). Police civil liability for abandonment in high-crime areas and other high-risk situations. *Journal of Criminal Justice, 22*(5), 407–424.

Vaughn, M. S., & Coomes, L. F. (1995). Police civil liability under section 1983: when do police officers act under color of law? *Journal of Criminal Justice, 23*, 395–415.

Vaughn, M. S., Cooper, T. W., & del Carmen, R. V. (2001). Assessing legal liabilities in law enforcement: police chiefs' views. *Crime and Delinquency, 47*(1), 3–27.

Warren v. City of Lincoln, Nebraska, 864 F.2d 1436 (8th Cir. 1989).

Wilson v. Layne, 119 S. Ct. 1692 (1999).

Wilson, et al. v. Price, et al., No. 09-2904 (7th Cir. 2010).

Worrall, J. L. (2001). *Civil lawsuits, citizen complaints, and policing innovations*. New York, NY: LFB Scholarly Publishing.

CHAPTER 11

Police in the Community

"Never doubt that a small group of thoughtful, committed citizens can change the world. Indeed, it is the only thing that ever has."

—Margaret Mead

After reading the chapter, you should be able to:

- Describe the public's perception of the police and discuss how that perception differs across age, race, sex, socioeconomic status, and contacts with the police.
- Discuss and explain how the drug war and a shift toward tough law enforcement have effected the public's perception of the police.
- Describe the general theory of crime prevention and define primary, secondary, and tertiary crime prevention.
- Outline the "broken window" thesis and discuss how is it applied to crime prevention.
- Trace how community policing evolved and describe how Goldstein articulated the basis for community policing.
- Describe the percentage of police departments that have full-time community policing officers and units devoted to community policing.
- List and discuss the challenges to implementing community policing.
- Define police legitimacy and describe how it is best gained.
- Explain procedural justice and how it fosters police legitimacy.

KEY TERMS

- Access control
- Activity support and motivation reinforcement
- Broken windows thesis
- Community policing
- Defensible space
- Environmental design
- Homeland security
- Neighborhood watch
- Philosophical dimension
- Police legitimacy
- Primary crime prevention
- Private security
- Problem-oriented policing

INTRODUCTION

This chapter explores several facets of the relationship between the police and the public. The following section will review the research on how the public views the police and how citizens come to develop their opinions. Also, one of

- Procedural justice
- Programmatic dimension
- Secondary crime prevention
- Strategic dimension
- SARA model
- Surveillance
- Tertiary crime prevention

the major programmatic themes used by the police to influence the community has been crime prevention. Crime prevention programming has been used to positively change police–community relations and public attitudes toward the police, as well as to attempt to reduce the incidence of crime and victimization. The relative effectiveness of a variety of these programs is discussed. Finally, community policing is explored. This philosophy is at the forefront of the police response to community problems today. Basically, it represents an organizational arrangement that attempts to cause the police department to focus on community problems as opposed to focusing on symptoms of problems. Too often, the police only superficially address citizen problems, and community policing causes a more thorough and directed response to problems and issues.

AN OVERVIEW OF PUBLIC PERCEPTIONS OF THE POLICE

Before discussing specific attitudes toward the police, it may be helpful to discuss attitudes within a general cultural context. America is the "melting pot" for the world. Our country traditionally has maintained a liberal immigration policy that has led to the United States being the most multicultural country in the world. As people are raised within their respective cultures, they develop their own culturally defined worldview of how society is and should be ordered. This limited worldview remains fairly stable throughout life. Within this context, a liberal or conservative ideology affects how people perceive the police (Miller, 1973; Packer, 1968; Reed & Gaines, 1982). Also, cultural attributes, such as socioeconomic class and values, affect the nature of people's attitudes toward the police and, to some extent, the type of interactions they have with the police. Finally, the interactions citizens have with the police have profound effects on their attitudes.

For the most part, the general public tends to view the police positively (Benedict, Brown, & Bower, 2000; Kaminski & Jefferis, 1998; Reisig & Giacomazzi, 1998). This is not to say that problems do not exist, and in fact, there are areas within most jurisdictions in which the police are viewed negatively. For the most part, research on citizen perceptions of the police indicates there are four variables (age, contact with the police, neighborhood, and race) that affect citizen perceptions (Brown & Benedict, 2002). However, most researchers would agree that the overall public perception of the police and what they do is positive. This is important because public perceptions of what the police do and how effective they are affect public participation in crime reduction programs and political support for the police, police programs, and crime-related legislation. Also, public support generally is a key consideration when making budgetary and other administrative and operational decisions that affect the police department. There are several benefits to the police and community when good relations exist:

1. Greater cooperation and harmony between the police and all the people of the community;
2. A decrease in the rate of crime and delinquency;
3. Better control of crime and delinquency through more effective enforcement;
4. Establishment of communication lines into the community so that both community and police problems can be worked on and resolved;
5. Improved working relationships with citizens and official groups;
6. More persons interested in police careers, thus enhancing the recruitment and selection of police officers; and
7. Increased governmental support in terms of higher salaries and resources for new programs.

Essentially, the police have a vested interest in maintaining positive relations with all individuals and groups in the community.

When examining attitudes toward the police, it is important to realize that there are numerous groups and subgroups of people within each jurisdiction, and these various groups may have differing perceptions of the police and the effectiveness of the police in dealing with community problems (Brown & Benedict, 2002). In most jurisdictions, there is no such thing as one community; each jurisdiction is composed of numerous communities. These communities of interest are created by geographical boundaries, such as rivers or major highways; by ethnic or racial groups settling together, such as "Little Italy" or "Chinatown," which occur in several larger US cities; or by service landmarks or centers, such as when shopping centers and malls tend to serve areas of a city and draw on a specific clientele. For this reason, public perceptions of the police are examined in general and in terms of the various groups that exist in various communities.

Public Attitudes Toward the Police

As previously noted, most researchers have found that, in general, citizens view the police positively. For example, the Bureau of Justice Statistics and Office of Community-Oriented Policing Services surveyed more than 13,000 people in 13 cities and found that nearly 80% of the respondents were satisfied with the police (Smith, Steadman, Minton, & Townsend, 1999).

Even though citizens support the police generally, this support is not uniform across all groups of people. Perhaps the best way to study and understand citizen support for the police is to study the levels of support across individual and community variables. Decker (1981) and Worrall (1999) note that individual and community variables serve to mold and describe the types and levels of support that exist in a community. Individual variables include factors such as sex, race, and personal experience with the police. On the other hand, community variables include factors such as socioeconomic status, likelihood of victimization, general community attitudes toward the police, and crime rates. These factors are explored in the following sections.

Individual-Level Variables

Most of the studies of police–citizen relations have focused on demographic characteristics of citizens. This research has attempted to determine how different types of people view the police.

Age

The consensus among researchers is that older persons tend to view the police more positively than do younger citizens (Cao, Frank, & Cullen, 1996; Chermak et al., 2001; Reisig & Giacomazzi, 1998). There are several reasons that explain why younger persons do not view the police as positively as their older counterparts. First, younger persons are resistant to and less respectful of authority figures, and police often demand respect from youth (Flexon, Lurigio, & Greenleaf, 2010). Younger persons tend to value their freedom and tend to resent control. When police officers inquire into their activities or stop them for traffic violations, many young people see this as an infringement on their freedom. Second, younger persons tend to have more negative contacts with the police. This is especially true with regard to traffic violations and other minor offenses. Some youths come to believe that the police tend to focus or "pick on" young people because of the increased attention. Third, older people are more vulnerable to crime and victimization, which engenders more positive feelings for the police. Older persons, especially senior citizens, exhibit higher levels of fear and they come to view the police as their allies, regardless of the quality of service provided by the police. When the police provide elderly persons with crime prevention and community relations programs, ratings of the police are extremely high (Zevitz & Rettammel, 1990).

Regardless of reasoning, older persons tend to foster more positive attitudes toward the police than do younger people. Police departments should attempt to alleviate this situation through better training and programs that produce more positive contact with younger people.

Race

Over the years, there has been a substantial amount of research that has examined how minorities view the police. There is a consensus in the research that white citizens tend to view the police more positively than do minority citizens. Weitzer and Tuch (2004) note that whites most often have higher opinions of the police, are more supportive of aggressive crime control measures, and are skeptical of criticisms of the police. African American citizens, on the other hand, consistently rate the police lower (Huang & Vaughn, 1996; Reisig & Parks, 2000; Tuch & Weitzer, 1997; Worrall, 1999). Researchers tend to attribute these lower perceptions to perceived mistreatment. Weitzer and Tuch (1999) found that African American citizens were much more likely to report being mistreated by the police. This research indicates that African American citizens have a tendency to be more critical of the police. Regardless, the police must realize that relations with African American citizens are often strained and departments must develop initiatives to reduce this strain.

Carter (1983, 1985) assessed the attitudes of Hispanics toward the police. His findings coincided with the research on African Americans' attitudes toward the police. Overall, he found that Hispanics: (1) feel less safe concerning crime in comparison to the general population, (2) do not feel that the police are capable of reducing the incidence of crime, (3) feel that they receive less than adequate protection from the police, and (4) generally evaluate the police lower relative to the general population. More specifically, Carter found that Hispanics believed the police did a poor job. Police were believed to have a bad attitude, needed to do a better job of investigating crimes, needed to decrease response times, and in general should reduce the level of discrimination against Hispanics.

However, Cheurprakobkit (2000) found that Hispanics did have a more positive view of the police in comparison to African American citizens, and Spanish-speaking Hispanics were more cooperative and viewed the police more positively than did English-speaking Hispanics. Many Hispanics, though, are fearful of the police and fail to report crimes or seek assistance because of immigration status and fear of deportation (Walker, 1997). Police departments must recognize these problems, especially those evolving around Hispanic victimization, and develop programs to ensure better relations with the Hispanic community.

> You can watch a video interview about the effects of negative encounters with the police by going to: **http://www. youtube.com/watch?v=0lF3ypBmspk**

Again, there appear to be a multitude of explanations for these attitudes. First, minorities have more negative contacts with the police relative to non-minorities (Walker, 1997). Minorities tend to have a higher representation in arrest statistics. Second, minorities tend to be victimized at higher rates relative to non-minorities. Victimization tends to adversely affect one's view of the police, especially when the police fail to apprehend the perpetrator or provide what is perceived as poor service. Finally, as the research suggests, it may be that generally police officers do, in fact, treat minority citizens differently than they treat white citizens. Police officers, especially white officers, typically do not comprehend or understand other cultures, which may cause them to treat minorities differently. The language barrier can be the greatest impediment to developing more positive relations with the Hispanic community.

Sex

Although it is commonly thought that females view police more positively than their male counterparts, the research does not support this hypothesis. There have been several studies that found females view the police more positively (Cao et al., 1996; Reisig & Giacomazzi, 1998), whereas other studies have found the opposite (Correia, Reisig, & Lovrich, 1996). Other studies have found no differences (Chermak et al., 2001; Huang & Vaughn, 1996). On the basis of research, it appears that there is no or little difference.

Socioeconomic Status

It appears that persons from a lower socioeconomic background are less likely to view the police positively (Cao et al., 1996; Huang & Vaughn, 1996). Essentially, minorities in poor urban neighborhoods have some of the lowest approval ratings of the police. The reasons for these perceptions include perceived injustice, lack of concern and attention on the part of the police, and ineffectiveness, especially in comparison to the level of services often provided to more wealthy neighborhoods in the same jurisdiction. Also, these areas have the highest crime rates.

Kusow, Wilson, and Martin (1997) found that African American citizens and whites living in the suburbs viewed the police more positively than did residents of urban areas, and suburban African American citizens viewed the police more positively than did urban whites. Thus, social class seems to play a key role in forming opinions of the police.

Contact with the Police

Positive contacts with the police tend to improve citizens' perceptions of the police, whereas negative contacts lead to more disapproval (Worrall, 1999). However, research indicates that positive contacts have a stronger influence relative to negative contacts (Cheurprakobkit, 2000). When citizens observe the police engaging in what they consider to be "wrongdoing," it has a negative impact on citizen perceptions of the police (Dean, 1980; Cox & White, 1988). Negative contact is sometimes mediated by the context of the contact. Reisig and Chandeik (2001) found that citizens' satisfaction is based on their expectations. If police actions meet their expectations, they are satisfied, but if the police provide an inadequate level of service or exhibit what is perceived as a negative demeanor, citizens become dissatisfied. A study in Chicago, IL, found that citizen perceptions of the police were enhanced when police officers were

FIGURE 11.1
NYPD officer Michael Belogorodsky speaks with a man in Russian in New York. Police departments across the country are stepping up efforts to recruit officers who can speak more than one language, in some cases offering raises or even sending cops abroad as part of immersion programs. *Photo Courtesy of AP Photo/ Seth Wenig.*

polite, helpful, and fair; attentive to citizens' needs and what citizens had to say; and willing to explain the actions that officers were taking. Police officers must use good judgment when interacting with citizens. Even though officers may be making an arrest or issuing a citation, they can do so diplomatically in most cases. This would lead to fewer confrontations and improved relations with the public (Figure 11.1).

Major Incidents
Periodically, there are major police incidents that receive national media attention, which affect public perceptions of the police. Some of these incidents include the Rodney King incident in Los Angeles, CA; the Abner Louima case in New York, NY; and the racist attitudes of Mark Furman in the O. J. Simpson case. Studies indicate that such incidents undermine public trust of the police and cause the public to question the police's integrity (Kaminski & Jefferis, 1998). Moreover, such incidents have a global effect, resulting in a decline in public support across the country. Police administrators must understand that these incidents, even though in faraway cities, can have a rippling effect in their jurisdiction, and they must immediately respond to them by shoring up local support for the police.

The research regarding individual and community differences and their effects on citizen attitudes toward the police is striking. There are numerous differences as a result of these variables. These differences should be considered in police policymaking. Police departments must address these differences of opinion and the causes of any citizen dissatisfaction that may be present. As previously noted, a police department can only be as effective as its relations with its citizens will allow. All police agencies depend on their citizens and should constantly strive to improve relations and develop trust with each and every group and community within their jurisdictions.

CRIME PREVENTION

To learn more about crime prevention, go to Dr. Cecil Greek's crime prevention links at: **http://www.criminology.fsu. edu/cjlinks/killers.html**.

The late 1970s and 1980s brought a significant increase in real and perceived crime as drugs invaded our country. Drugs and crime became potent political issues, with almost all candidates involved in local, state, and federal elections promising to do something about the drug and crime problem. Government and the police responded by shifting to more of a law enforcement orientation. Citizens became more interested in crime than in how their police treated suspects or other population groups. Crime prevention programs and a crime prevention philosophy became a higher priority in police departments.

Another reason for this increased emphasis was that crime prevention programs involved and focused on community leaders and the politically powerful. Crime prevention programs were aimed at the business community, and they sounded good to the middle and upper classes in general who perceived that they were being overly victimized. People were more interested in apprehending and punishing criminals than eradicating social conditions that contributed to increasing crime rates. These people had the political clout to affect governmental policy, and they demanded more attention from government, especially in the area of law enforcement.

The Theory of Crime Prevention

Everyone should realize that the police cannot, nor should they be expected to, be exclusively responsible for combating crime. Police departments do not have the resources or personnel to significantly diminish crime without help from other quarters. In other words, effective crime reduction and elimination programs are not feasible without citizen involvement. Crime is a multidimensional problem that requires multiple responses from a variety of individuals and groups within the community. From this concept, crime prevention was born.

Crime prevention can be divided into three approaches: primary, secondary, and tertiary (Lab, 2010; Brantingham & Faust, 1976). Each type of crime prevention attacks criminality at a different stage of development. Box 11.1 provides an overview of the crime prevention process.

Box 11.1 The Crime Prevention Process

Primary Prevention:
- Environmental design
  - Architectural designs
  - Lighting
  - Access control
  - Property identification
- Neighborhood Watch
  - Surveillance
  - Citizen patrols
- General Deterrence
  - Arrest and conviction
  - Sentencing methods
- Public Education
  - Levels of crime
  - Fear
  - Self-help
- Social Crime Prevention
  - Unemployment
  - Poverty
  - Employment/job training
- Private Security

Secondary Prevention:
- Identification and Prediction
  - Early identification and prediction of problem individuals
- Situational Crime Prevention
  - Problem identification
  - Situation-specific intervention
- Community Policing
- Crime Area Analysis
  - Targeting of high-crime areas
  - Neighborhood dispute resolution
- Substance Abuse
  - Prevention and treatment
- Schools and Crime Prevention
  - Work with potential problem youth

Tertiary Prevention:
- Specific Deterrence
- Incapacitation
- Rehabilitation and Treatment

Source: Lab (2010).

According to Brantingham and Faust (1976), primary crime prevention consists of efforts to identify and manage the conditions within the social and physical environment that provide opportunities for or precipitate crime. *Primary crime prevention*, to a large extent, is rooted in routine activities theory. As depicted in Figure 11.2, routine activities theory notes that crime is a product of a motivated criminal, a suitable target, and a lack of guardianship Box 11.2. Most street crimes are opportunistic, where offenders see a target who is not properly guarded and then commit a crime (Miethe, McCorkle, & Listwan, 2006). For example, a thief may steal something when no one is around or a drug dealer may sell drugs because he or she believes that he or she will not be discovered by the police or reported by a resident or passerby. As identified in Box 11.1, there are numerous program areas that can be used when implementing primary crime prevention. Primary crime prevention programs center around efforts to make criminal activity more difficult, or to enhance apprehension, should an individual decide to commit a criminal act (enhanced guardianship). For example, environmental design programs attempt to make the commission of a criminal act more difficult

FIGURE 11.2
Morgan Atkins of Laramie, WY, paints over some graffiti on a wall downtown as part of a community cleanup day on April 19, 2008. Laramie used the weekend to get a jump on next Tuesday's Earth day.
Photo Courtesy of AP Photo/Laramie Boomerang, Ben Woloszyn.

by hardening or fortifying the target. On the other hand, programs such as neighborhood watches and enhanced police patrols attempt to either deter criminals by an increased presence or increase the probability of apprehension by observing the criminal committing the act. Primary crime prevention represents a first line of defense against crime.

Secondary crime prevention, for the most part, focuses on persons and the community in an effort to identify potential criminals and high-crime areas and to address problems that cause crime. Secondary crime prevention focuses on removing or reducing the criminal's desire to commit crime, whereas primary crime prevention efforts focus on diminishing the criminal's opportunities to commit crime. Examples of secondary crime prevention include police athletic programs and wilderness programs, where youths are provided opportunities for recreation, positive socialization, and character development as alternatives to criminal behavior. For the most part, secondary crime prevention rests with a variety of institutions in our society, including the police, parents, educators, and individuals in the social services who can intervene into the conditions that lead to deviance and crime.

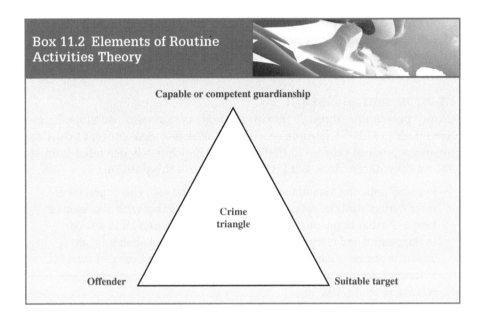

Box 11.2 Elements of Routine Activities Theory

Capable or competent guardianship

Crime triangle

Offender

Suitable target

Finally, *tertiary crime prevention* deals with individuals who have committed criminal acts. Basically, society and the criminal justice system must try to deal with these individuals in such a way that they will not commit additional criminal acts in the future. In some cases, individuals must be incarcerated for long periods of time because they continue to be a threat to society. In other cases, treatment and rehabilitation, coupled with incarceration, might diminish the likelihood of future criminal behavior. Tertiary crime prevention is the objective of corrections, probation, and parole programs.

Although secondary and tertiary crime prevention techniques are important in the crime prevention scheme, we focus on primary crime prevention techniques in this chapter. The police are only nominally involved in secondary and tertiary crime prevention. Other agencies of government and the criminal justice system are more involved in these types of crime prevention programs.

PRIMARY CRIME PREVENTION TECHNIQUES AND PROGRAMS

Primary crime prevention consists of environmental design in an effort to make criminality more difficult; *neighborhood watch* programs attempt to mobilize citizens as a deterrent and to enhance apprehension, deterrence measures by the police, public education, and private security measures that are implemented by the private sector. Primary crime prevention is based on the idea that if it is more difficult to attack a crime target and there is an increase in guardianship, then crime will be reduced. Crime prevention attempts to eliminate opportunity.

Environmental Design

Crime prevention through environmental design was developed from Newman's (1972) "defensible space." The *defensible space* concept posits that creating a physical expression that society is appropriately defended from victimization reduces crime. Lab (2004) summarizes this position:

> For residents, the appearance and design of the area can engender a more caring attitude, draw the residents into contact with one another, lead to further improvements and use of the area, and build a stake in the control and elimination of crime. For potential offenders, an area's appearance can suggest that residents use and care for their surroundings, pay attention to what occurs, and will intervene if an offense is seen (2004:35).

And, indeed, Wilson and Kelling (2005) support this position in their *broken window thesis*. They argue that the physical decline of a neighborhood, to a great extent, invites crime. A neighborhood in physical decline gives the appearance that no one cares about the neighborhood or what happens therein. Once potential criminals sense this situation, they are less inhibited and tend to commit many more serious offenses. Crime and neighborhood decline continue to worsen without positive intervention. Research, however, indicates that there is a trade-off for this intervention: "police intervention itself significantly increased the probability of feeling unsafe."

Accordingly, any fear reduction benefits gained by reducing disorder may be offset by the fact that the policing strategies employed simultaneously increase fear of crime" (Hinkle & Weisburd, 2008, p. 503). Not only must a neighborhood give the appearance that its citizens are concerned with the activities within the confines of the neighborhood, environmental design means that citizens take extraordinary steps to make it appear even more difficult to victimize. These steps include such things as increasing the level and amount of lighting, installing remote cameras, or designing buildings and other structures to maximize observation and access control. In other words, environmental design is concerned with making it more difficult to commit a crime by improving the physical environment or target hardening. Environmental design activities fall into one of three categories: (1) access control, (2) surveillance, or (3) activity support and motivation reinforcement (Lab, 2010).

Access control refers to physical changes that are made to inhibit or control the flow of people into or out of an area. Examples would include an apartment building that has special keys for the residents or employs a guard who only allows residents or approved visitors to enter the building. Another example would be a manufacturer who only allows employees to enter or exit through approved entrances. In both cases, the physical environment is constructed so that persons entering and leaving a premise are controlled and they can be monitored in terms of the possessions they transport with them. In larger terms, neighborhoods can be designed so that streets contain numerous cul-de-sacs, few entrances, and few through streets. Such a design would inhibit strangers from entering the neighborhood and would allow residents to become more familiar with each other and the activities within the neighborhood. Research indicates that residential streets with limited access (dead-end streets and cul-de-sacs) have lowered crime rates (Buck & Hakim, 1993; White, 1990).

The police role in access control centers on advice and advocacy. That is, they should provide advice to individuals involved in the planning of buildings, subdivisions, and other construction projects. They can provide information on how such projects can be constructed to deter crime. Their advocacy role revolves around placing pressure on the jurisdiction's legislative branch to incorporate physical control and access control in zoning and construction ordinances and laws. For example, in addition to advocating the use of proper locks and windows, the police should attempt to ensure that new residential streets and neighborhoods are constructed in such a manner that the possibilities of crime are reduced.

On an individual basis, the police commonly have crime prevention programs that advocate the use of deadbolt locks and more secure windows and patio doors. There is evidence that this type of target hardening works. Bennett and Wright (1984) found that burglars considered the quality of locks and windows when they selected a target. For example, smaller windows were easier to break, and some locks provided an extra deterrent. Along these same lines, Buck and Hakim (1993) found that burglar alarms tended to deter burglars. However, even though some security devices deter criminals, there is some question as to how successful the police can be in getting homeowners to purchase and install these devices. Even if the police are successful in educating the public, the overall effectiveness of the program may falter if citizens subsequently do not take protective measures.

Another form of target hardening the police use is a property identification program. Basically, the police work with individuals or groups to encourage them to permanently mark their property for identification if it is stolen. People are encouraged to engrave their social security numbers or names on their valuables. It is reasoned that engraving social security numbers on property will make it more difficult to resale and easier to trace if it is stolen. Window decals or other insignia should also serve as a deterrent to would-be thieves.

Laycock (1985) found that property identification did have a short-term effect on burglaries when many people became involved in the program. Lurigoi and Davis (1988) found that property identification leads to higher rates of apprehension of burglars and property recovery.

Surveillance refers to physical changes that increase the probability that residents observe offenders. Streets should be adequately illuminated; doorways to buildings should be positioned toward the street so that passers-by can observe activities; and pathways and walkways through parks and other areas should be relatively clear of visual obstructions and hiding spots, such as nearby shrubs and trees. Stealth is a key factor in the decision to commit some crimes, and if the probability for observing law violators is increased, then the probability that a criminal will commit a crime is diminished. The police have two primary roles regarding surveillance: one is advocacy and advice as they attempt to have measures incorporated into construction plans, and the other is routine patrol when they directly observe for wrongdoing Box 11.2.

Box 11.3 Groups that Local Police Departments Regularly Met With to Address Crime-Related Problems

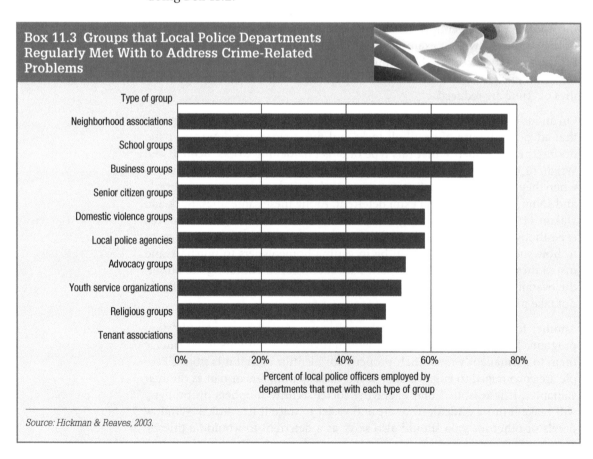

Percent of local police officers employed by departments that met with each type of group

Source: Hickman & Reaves, 2003.

Finally, *activity support* and *motivation reinforcement* refer to building a community atmosphere in which members of the neighborhood or area recognize and know the other members in the neighborhood and look after their welfare. We are too often strangers in our own neighborhoods. We do not take the time to get to know our neighbors, their work habits, and the activities that occur on their premises. Consequently, when criminal activity occurs, we are unable to recognize it. Activity support and motivation reinforcement efforts attempt to develop a more cohesive community, with citizens looking after each other's interests. Police involvement centers on providing information to the public and assisting in organization efforts.

Neighborhood Watches

Neighborhood watches, block watches, or citizen patrols are probably the primary methods used by the police for activity support and motivation reinforcement. That is, once the police initiate or help start these activities, citizens begin to develop more cohesive relations. Garofalo and McLeod (1989) identify two primary expectations for neighborhood watches:

> First, it is meant to reduce crime, both directly, through the "observe and report" function, and indirectly, by being a vehicle for the encouragement of other crime prevention practices. Second, there is a more general hope that NW (neighborhood watches) will kindle a sense of community among residents by giving them a common purpose, and by getting them to talk to each other and watch out for each other (1989:334).

Although surveillance is the primary motive for neighborhood watch programs, they are also involved in numerous other crime prevention activities: operation identification, streetlight improvement, block parenting, household security surveys, and the deployment of other security measures (Lab, 2010). Thus, when a neighborhood group begins a program, it actually has several purposes (Garofalo & McLeod, 1989).

The extent to which neighborhood watches are used in this country is unknown. O'Keefe et al. (1996), in a national survey, found that 31% of respondents reported belonging to a neighborhood crime prevention organization. MacGillis (1983), using the data from an ABC News poll, estimated that approximately 20,000 communities and five million people were involved in such programs. Generally, each program has approximately 10–15 households involved, and new programs are constantly being developed and old ones waning, which makes it difficult to estimate the actual number of programs at any given time.

Neighborhood watches, such as other volunteer organizations, are difficult to develop and maintain. They tend to be organized in middle- and upper-middle-class, well-established neighborhoods. Participants generally are white, own their residences, and have lived in the area for several years. Watches tend to begin as the result of a sensational criminal event and unravel or become disorganized over time. This is because they tend to be somewhat unorganized from the beginning. Meetings are infrequent, and information dissemination among members is sporadic (Garofalo & McLeod, 1989) (Table 11.1).

The effectiveness of neighborhood watch programs is mixed, at best. In most cases, the programs provide a high profile for a brief period of time. They also provide an outlet for police–community relations, and are effective to the extent that they do develop some level of neighborhood cohesiveness that lasts for periods of time. These programs also provide police with contact points for future community intervention. In terms of long-term effectiveness, most of these programs fail to remain active unless some external threat to the neighborhood is present. Even then, it is difficult to maintain interest among the citizen participants for long periods of time.

A variation of the neighborhood watch is community anti-drug programs. Here, citizens band together to fight drugs in their neighborhood. They use a variety of measures: anti-drug rallies, reporting and surveillance programs, citizen patrols, code enforcement where drugs are sold, and drug house abatement (Rosenbaum, Lurigio, & Davis, 1998). Roehl, Wong, Huitt, and Capowich (1995) evaluated several of these programs and found them to be loosely organized. These programs can have several benefits, especially when aligned with the police. They can result in enhanced police patrols and enforcement, better relations with the police, and an increase in arrests in the neighborhood. The police can provide members of these programs with information and ideas on how they can assist in resolving the drug problem in their neighborhood.

Media Program
Police departments began to use public education programs or public relations techniques in the 1960s and 1970s to overcome negative police–community relations. These efforts naturally evolved into crime prevention, where the police used the media and other methods of communication to inform the public about the crime problem, how best to assist the police in their fight against crime, and measures that the citizens could take to neutralize certain crimes and public problems. The police also use the media to control their public image. That is, there is a symbiotic relationship between the police and the media. The media needs the police for easy access to crime news, and the police need the media to help manage how the citizenry view the police and the job they are doing (Kasinsky, 1994).

Media reporting of crime information is the most common type of public education. Crime, especially sensational or unusual crimes, is of significant interest

Table 11.1 Techniques of Situational Prevention

Increase the Effort	Increase the Risks	Reduce the Rewards	Reduce Provocations	Remove Excuses
1. Target harden a. Steering column locks and immobilizers b. Anti-robbery screens c. Tamper-proof packaging	6. Extend guardianship a. Take routine precautions; go out in groups at night, leave signs of occupancy, carry telephone b. "Cocoon" neighborhood watch	11. Conceal targets a. Off-street parking b. Sex-neutral telephone directories c. Unmarked bullion trucks	16. Reduce frustrations and stress a. Efficient queues and polite service b. Expanded seating c. Soothing music/ muted lights	21. Set rule a. Rental agreements b. Harassment codes c. Hotel registration
2. Control access to facilities a. Entry telephones b. Electronic card access c. Baggage screening	7. Assist natural surveillance a. Improved street lighting b. Defensible space design c. Support whistleblowers	12. Remove targets a. Removable car radios b. Women's refuges c. Prepaid cards for pay telephones	17. Avoid disputes a. Separate enclosures for rival soccer fans b. Reduce crowding in pubs c. Fixed cab fares	22. Post instructions a. "No parking" b. "Private property" c. "Extinguish camp fires"
3. Screen exits a. Ticket needed for exit b. Export documents c. Electronic merchandise tags	8. Reduce anonymity a. Taxi driver identifications b. "How's my driving?" decals c. School uniforms	13. Identify property a. Property marking b. Vehicle licensing and parts marking c. Cattle brandings	18. Reduce emotional arousal a. Controls on violent pornography b. Enforce good behavior on soccer field c. Prohibit racial slurs	23. Alert conscience a. Roadside speed display boards b. Signatures for customs declarations c. "Shoplifting is stealing"
4. Deflect offenders a. Street closures b. Separate bathrooms for women c. Disperse pubs	9. Use place managers a. Closed Circuit Television (CCTV) for double-decker buses b. Two clerks for convenience stores c. Reward vigilance	14. Disrupt markets a. Monitor pawn shops b. Controls on classified advertisements c. License street vendors	19. Neutralize peer pressure a. "Idiots drink and drive" b. "It's OK to say no" c. Disperse troublemakers at school	24. Assist compliance a. Easy library checkout b. Public lavatories c. Litter bins

Continued...

Table 11.1 Techniques of Situational Prevention *Continued*

Increase the Effort	Increase the Risks	Reduce the Rewards	Reduce Provocations	Remove Excuses

5. Control tools/ weapons
  a. "Smart" guns
  b. Disabling stolen cell telephones
  c. Restrict spray paint sales to juveniles
	10. Strengthen formal surveillance
	  a. Red light cameras
	  b. Burglar alarms
	  c. Security guards
		15. Deny benefits
		  a. Ink merchandise tags
		  b. Graffiti cleaning
		  c. Speed humps
			20. Discourage imitation
			  a. Rapid repair of vandalism
			  b. V-chips in TVs
			  c. Censor details of modus operandi
				25. Control drugs and alcohol
				  a. Breathalyzers in pubs
				  b. Server intervention
				  c. Alcohol-free events

Source: Center for Problem-Oriented Policing.

to reporters. Graber (1980) found that 22–28% of the news stories in newspapers were devoted to crime. Surette (2006) notes that approximately 25% of television programming is crime related, and Chermak (1994) found that approximately 50% of all crime reporting deals with violence. More important, however, is the fact that the media tends to distort such coverage. Surette (2006) found that journalistic accounts of crime were distorted, emphasizing pathological individuals who commit bizarre acts. Such coverage tends to bias the public and promote fear of victimization that is diametrically opposed to police purposes. The public comes to develop a distorted view of crime. Citizens tend to believe that there are many more rapes, murders, assaults, and violent crimes than actually occur (Kappeler & Potter, 2005). News coverage can create an impression of higher crime rates by reporting on criminal acts in other jurisdictions without clearly specifying where the crime took place. For example, what purposes are served when a Kansas television station reports on a series of homicides in California or Florida? Indeed, even though news journalists do not admit it, television news reporting too often imitates supermarket tabloids.

The best-known crime-prevention media campaign has been "Taking a Bite Out of Crime," which was developed by the Advertising Council. Since 1991, more than $160 million worth of airtime has been donated to the program, with 75% of television stations having aired segments (O'Keefe et al., 1996). O'Keefe and his colleagues found that 80% of the respondents in their national study had reported viewing "Take a Bite Out of Crime" segments. The program had mixed effects in that respondents reported feeling more competent about crime prevention, but, on the other hand, they became more fearful about crime.

The Crime Stoppers program, another media crime prevention technique, consists of a police hot line where citizens report crime-related information on the basis of wanted persons information supplied by the police. There are an estimated 1082 communities using Crime Stoppers programs (Crimestoppers International, 1999). Basically, the program attempts to increase the flow of criminal intelligence information to the police through rewards and depicting or acting out specific criminal events on television.

Crime Stoppers International reports that programming has resulted in more than 700,000 cases being solved, the recovery of more than $1 billion in property, and approximately $3.3 million in narcotics being seized by law enforcement. Rosenbaum, Lurigio, and Lavrakas (1989) found that most of the tips received by the police came from other criminals attempting to eliminate a competitor or even an old score or "fringe players" who hung around or associated with the criminals whom they reported. A problem with Crime Stoppers is that it can overburden law enforcement with worthless calls and tips (Kelley, 1997). Crime Stoppers remains a high-profile program that creates a high level of crime prevention awareness in the community.

There are a variety of media programs available to the police executive. Selection of a particular program should be on the basis of need and how the program fits other crime prevention efforts. Police executives too frequently attempt to use a shotgun approach, where everything available is implemented. Such an approach is unproductive and sometimes can result in destructive or negative effects, such as fear of crime and victimization.

Juvenile Curfews

The preceding sections focus on several primary crime prevention programs. One form of secondary crime prevention that deserves mentioning is juvenile curfews. Although curfews have been in existence for hundreds of years, there has been a renewed interest in them primarily because of the tremendous increase in violent juvenile crime. A survey of America's largest 200 cities showed that 73% had curfew ordinances (Ruefle & Reynolds, 1996). Curfews are somewhat controversial, with proponents believing they reduce crime, whereas opponents say they stigmatize primarily underclass, minority youths. Regardless, there seems to be a high level of support for curfews in many communities (Nelson, 1994).

Special units, such as narcotics, gang, street crimes, or tactical squads, use curfew violations as a method of dealing with other problems. For example, a narcotics unit may stringently enforce curfew violations in areas that have a history of drug dealing. This reduces the number of potential customers and crew members

You can watch a video discussion between a police chief and mayor on the issue of juvenile curfew by going to: **http://www.youtube.com/watch?v=Bqm3XxxRET4**

who are assisting in the drug dealing operation. Gang units may use curfew violations to thwart gang violence or to attempt to prevent younger juveniles from joining gangs. Police units also conduct periodic sweeps of areas such as parks, video arcades, shopping malls, and cruising strips, with a high incidence of juvenile crime to maintain control of the areas.

There are several studies examining the impact of curfews on crime. Cole (2003) found that curfews did not reduce crime in Washington, DC. McDowell, Lofton, and Wiersema (2000) examined the effects of juvenile curfew laws in 57 jurisdictions and found that they did not result in a decrease in crime. Although they are not effective in reducing crime, they remain popular. The police and citizens see these laws as a way to promote parental responsibility and to deal with youth who are potentially engaging in criminal behavior.

There are several reasons why curfews do not work. First, the police tend to use curfew violations moderately. In 2009, the FBI (2010) estimated that 72,203 juveniles were arrested for curfew and loitering violations. This compares to 51,740 juvenile arrests for violent crimes and more than 1.5 million youths arrested for other crimes. Its moderate use is probably attributable to curfew violations being minor offenses that ultimately require a substantial amount of administrative paperwork. Officers probably use it sparingly, and use it primarily as a tool to deal with more serious matters. Officers can place curfew charges against juveniles to deal with a variety of disorder and minor crime problems. For example, it may be much easier, and just as effective, to charge a juvenile with a curfew violation as opposed to possession of drugs or some other minor crime. In many jurisdictions, there is little difference in judicial outcomes, but curfew violations generally result in less administrative hassle for the officer.

Another problem is that curfews generally are not in effect when juvenile crime is highest. Most juvenile crime occurs after school between 8 and 10 p.m., before curfews generally go into effect (Cole, 2003). Males (2000) found that the police tend to target juveniles who are not committing crime or involved in some offense, such as drinking or using drugs. The curfew stops tended to focus on law-abiding juveniles. Hirschel, Dean, and Dumond (2001) found that curfews failed, at least to some extent, because police officers focused on areas that had few crime problems. Obviously, curfews are not a mantra by which to affect juvenile crime problems.

Community Policing

In 1994, Congress passed a Crime Bill that, among other things, funded 100,000 new police officers and allocated approximately $11 billion to law enforcement. In addition to being the most substantial criminal justice funding effort ever to pass Congress, it solidified support for community policing as the primary law enforcement modality for dealing and interacting with the community. Funding to state and local law enforcement agencies was tied to their adoption of community policing. Indeed, governmental leaders, from President Clinton, to mayors and city managers from large and small cities throughout the United States, voiced their support for community policing and demanded their police executives immediately implement it. Many saw community policing as a program that would successfully deal with a wide variety of problems. Community police reached its zenith in 2000 when it was reported that more than 100,300 local police offers were involved in community policing. By 2007, however, that number had declined dramatically to approximately 47,000 officers (BJS, 2010) (Table 11.2).

Community policing evolved from the police–community relations programs of the 1950s and 1960s, team policing strategies of the 1970s, and the increase in citizen fear of crime that began to dominate public policy formulation in the 1980s (Greene, 1987; Walker, 1993). The basis of community policing was first articulated with Goldstein's (1979) article on "problem-oriented policing" and Wilson and Kelling (2005) discussion of community disorder. Basically, Goldstein noted that the police were, more or less, treating symptoms of problems rather than problems themselves, and that the police would never be successful until actual problems were confronted and resolved. He also criticized the police for placing too much emphasis on rapid response to calls for service and doing too little once they arrived at a call. In other words, Goldstein believed that police responses typically lacked substance. Wilson and Kelling, on the other hand, viewed community disorder as the precursor to crime. That is, the "deterioration" of the quality of life in neighborhoods was a slow evolutionary process that begins with minor neglect and disorder problems. If these problems go unchecked over time, they continue to worsen until there is little that residents or government can do to reclaim the neighborhood. Therefore, the best way to attack crime and disorder is to deal with

Table 11.2 Use of Community Policing Officers by Local Police Departments, 1997–2007		
Year	Departments Using the Program, %	Total No. of Officers*
2007	47	47,000
2003	58	55,000
2000	66	103,000
1997	34	16,000

*Rounded to the nearest 1000.
Source: BJS (2010).

minor problems, such as panhandling, unrepaired homes and businesses, and junk cars in yards, before they foster larger ones. Although there is little empirical support for Wilson's position, these two articles spawned a rethinking of US police. Policing began to move from a reactive, law enforcement mode to a proactive, community building mode, whereby the police and the community functioned cooperatively to deal with crime, disorder, and social problems. Moreover, the primary police function shifted from law enforcement to service and order maintenance.

You can view a video interview with a chief of police and the community at: **http://www.youtube.com/watch?v= xFMnp52d_RY**.

Although Goldstein, Wilson, and Kelling laid the foundation for community policing, it was first implemented as community-oriented policing (Kappeler & Gaines, 2008) and problem-oriented policing (Eck & Spelman, 1987; Goldstein, 1990). *Community-oriented policing* evolved through the work at the Police Foundation and the School of Criminal Justice, Michigan State University. The Police Foundation became involved in several programs that attempted to foster better relationships between the police and the community. Michigan State University investigated foot patrols as a method of: (1) fostering better relations with citizens, (2) reducing the fear of crime among citizens, and (3) reducing crime. *Problem-oriented policing* was initially implemented by the Police Executive Research Forum and consisted of efforts to identify crime and disorder problems and develop police and community responses that effectively dealt with both causes and symptoms. From these early efforts, community policing spread throughout the United States (Table 11.3).

There has been a great deal of confusion over what community policing is. To some, it was considered a philosophy or a new way to consider police–community relations, whereas others saw it as a series of interlinked police strategies. Numerous police departments implemented community policing, with each department implementing something different. There has been little, if any, uniformity in the way it has been implemented. Perhaps, Bayley (1988, p. 225) best summarizes the confusion about community policing:

> Despite the benefits claimed for community policing, programmatic implementation of it has been very uneven. Although widely, almost universally, said to be important, it means different things to different people—public relations campaigns, shopfronts and mini-stations, rescaled patrol beats, liaison with ethnic groups, permission for rank-and-file to speak to the press, Neighborhood Watch, foot patrols, patrol-detective teams, and door-to-door visits by police officers. Community policing on the ground often seems less a program than a set of aspirations wrapped in a slogan.

Table 11.3 Full-Time Community Policing Officers and Units in Local Police Departments, by Size of Population Served (2007)	Community Policing Officer			
Population Served	Agencies Using the Program, %	Total No. of Officers	Average No. of Officers	Separate Full-Time Unit, %
All sizes	47	46,919	8	14
1,000,000 or more	100*	2101	153	8S
500,000–999,999	97	4212	133	61
250,000–499,999	98	2315	49	61
100,000–249,999	94	6671	38	61
50,000–99,999	87	6893	18	58
25,000–49,999	69	4347	7	33
10,000–24,999	50	5311	6	17
2500–9999	42	9110	5	7
<2500	39	5959	3	9

Source: BJS (2010).

Although community policing has taken several directions (Rosenbaum, 1994), there does seem to be a common overarching structure to it. There are at least three major dimensions that occur when community policing is implemented: (1) the *philosophical dimension*, (2) the *strategic dimension*, and (3) the *programmatic dimension*. All three dimensions must exist if a department is implementing community policing. It cannot be implemented piecemeal—there must be a commitment to it at all levels of a department. Williams (2003) notes that police administrators must change the police organization to facilitate implementation and long-term acceptance of community policing.

The Philosophical Dimension

Historically, even though there have been sporadic variations in the underpinnings or theme for US law enforcement, it substantively has remained a legal-bureaucratic organization focusing on professional law enforcement. Outputs, such as numbers of arrests, reductions and increases in crime rates, volume of recovered property, numbers of citations issued, and a rapid response to calls, have been more important than the end result of police work. This philosophy translated into a reactive police force that does little to tangibly deal with problems.

Community policing consists of several community-based elements that differentiate it from the traditional professional model. Three of community policing's core ideas are as follows: (1) broad police function, (2) citizen input, and (3) neighborhood variation.

Broad Police Function

Community policing dictates that police departments move from law enforcement or crime fighting as the primary function. The police should have a broader function that also incorporates fear reduction and order maintenance. Indeed, fear reduction and order maintenance become the primary goals for the department supplanting crime reduction. This change in police philosophy emanates from two general directions. First, research examining police operations and crime statistics tends to point out that police have not been effective, nor will they become effective, in combating crime. Crime is a product of social conditions and, therefore, it cannot be controlled through police actions. Crime can be affected only through the control and manipulation of social conditions. The police can, at best, only manage and document most crime. Order maintenance is a legitimate police goal in itself. That is, social control and domestic tranquility contribute to the quality of life. Furthermore, police order-maintenance activities will have an effect on the amount of crime in a community (Mastrofski, 1988).

The focus of order-maintenance policing should be on minor crimes and disorder, which lead to more substantial police problems. Some research indicates that order maintenance can have an impact on minor crime. Katz, Webb, and Schaefer (2001) found that a police strategy focusing on disorder has a positive effect on physical disorder and morals (prostitution problems). Silverman (1999) concluded that crime in New York declined in part because of NYPD's aggressive enforcement of disorder. Braga et al. (1999) examined a Jersey City program that focused on violent places and found the program reduced disorder, calls for service, and crime. When the police use order-maintenance policing, they can improve the quality of life in an area. Yet, there is little proof that order-maintenance policing affects serious violent crime.

Second, fear has a far greater debilitating effect on a community or individuals than do crime rates. The fear of crime results in persons becoming virtual prisoners in their own homes; it inhibits commerce, and it poses a subtle psychological cost to everyone. Research shows that often an individual's level of fear of crime bears no relationship to the actual amount of crime or victimization. However, our traditional approach to fear reduction has been to attack crime:

> The traditional police response to fear has been to attack crime, in the hope that reducing crime overall will ultimately lessen fear. Since traditional policing relies primarily on motor patrol, which is basically reactive, there are obvious structural limitations that make it difficult to provide an effective means of confronting fear of crime separately and directly. Though crime prevention and police/community relations programs have helped broaden the traditional police role in ways that

impinge on fear of crime, these peripheral attempts tended to chip away at problems that demand a bulldozer (Trojanowicz & Bucqueroux, 1990, p. 131).

Police-sponsored fear-reduction programs have the potential to yield positive results in several areas: citizen participation in crime prevention programs, citizen crime reporting, and positive relations with citizens. Several such programs have been implemented and have been shown to be successful in reducing fear of crime. For example, Jim, Mitchell, and Kent (2006) examined a police-business empowerment partnership in a retail shopping center. The collaborative efforts resulted in reduced fear of crime on the part of business owners and shoppers.

Citizen Input

The police have traditionally developed and implemented programs that involved citizens. For the most part, however, these programs bordered on public relations schemes with little consideration given to community or citizen needs. Team policing programs of the 1970s and some of the police–community relations programs of earlier years seriously involved and considered citizens, but for the most part, the police were concerned with educating the public about their own needs rather than listening to the public about citizen needs.

Community policing uses methods that cause the police to work more closely with citizens. To develop a better relationship, police departments have attempted to collect information about citizen attitudes toward crime problems and the effectiveness of the police. For example, the police in Baltimore County (MD), Reno (NV), Atlanta (GA), Newport News (VA), St. Louis (MO), and other cities have requested that citizens complete surveys. Other departments have attempted to collect information by holding town or neighborhood meetings or by regularly meeting with minority and business groups. Gathering information from citizens allows the police to accomplish several tasks. Survey information can be used to evaluate the effectiveness of police programs in terms of fear reduction or attitudes toward the police. They also gauge citizen behavior, such as victimization or crime prevention efforts. Finally, they can also be used to collect data to assist the police in establishing goals and priorities (Peak & Glensor, 2008). Community policing attempts to get citizens involved by encouraging two-way communication between the police and public Box 11.3

Neighborhood Variation

Traditional, professional policing mandated that police officers disavow the existence of police discretion and police every situation and neighborhood the same. That is, the police exerted full or uniform enforcement of the

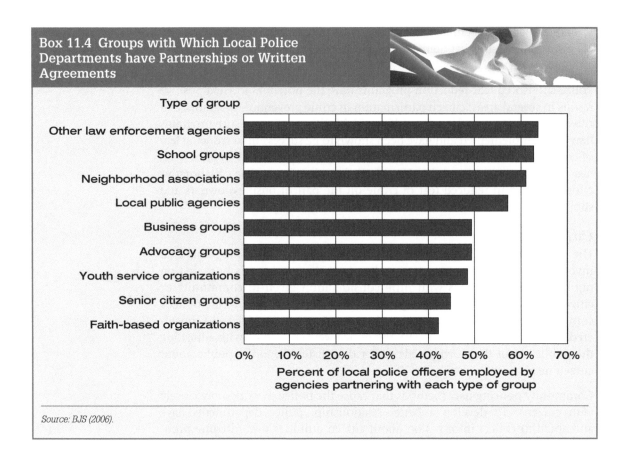

Box 11.4 Groups with Which Local Police Departments have Partnerships or Written Agreements

Type of group

Other law enforcement agencies
School groups
Neighborhood associations
Local public agencies
Business groups
Advocacy groups
Youth service organizations
Senior citizen groups
Faith-based organizations

0%   10%   20%   30%   40%   50%   60%   70%

Percent of local police officers employed by agencies partnering with each type of group

Source: BJS (2006).

law. Community policing, on the other hand, recognizes that a political jurisdiction is composed of several communities or neighborhoods, each with its own set of problems and expectations. Suttles (1972) notes that citizens develop "cognitive maps" where they designate certain places as their neighborhood. Stable neighborhoods have relative homogeneity of activity, people, and values. As ethnic, religious, and other socioeconomic factors define neighborhoods, differential expectations within neighborhoods evolve. Nolan, Conti, and McDevitt (2004) also found that neighborhoods' ability to achieve cohesiveness and stability change and evolve over time. Police departments must diagnose neighborhood problems and apply the most appropriate services. Particular neighborhoods develop expectations not only about what the police should do, but also about what type of behavior by residents and nonresidents is acceptable or unacceptable. Along these lines, Weisburd and Eck (2004) note that the police should develop a set of tools and match the tools or practices to the problems of specific neighborhoods. The application of broad police practices across all neighborhoods does not contribute to crime reduction, lessoning of fear, or better relations with the public.

Community policing dictates that the police follow the "will of the community" when dealing with situations and enforcing the law. For the most part, there is little variation in how the police react to serious crimes or felonies. However, the police must be cognizant of community standards when policing minor infractions of the law and dealing with activities that may be acceptable in one neighborhood, but not another (Kappeler & Gaines, 2008). For example, a citizen working on his or her car while parked on the street would not be acceptable in most upper- and middle-class neighborhoods, but it is a way of life for many people residing in poor neighborhoods. Police officers must rely on community or neighborhood standards when encountering such situations.

Along these lines, the police must recognize that neighborhoods are unique, and each neighborhood has a different mix of crime and disorder problems. The police must understand this mix and respond to specific problems as opposed to relying on global responses. When unique problems are addressed effectively, disorder and fear may be reduced.

The Strategic Dimension

The police must develop strategies to implement the philosophy of community policing. Strategies provide guidelines for the development of specific programs. Some have identified geographical, prevention, and substantive focuses as three parameters that should guide operational planning when implementing community policing.

Geographical Focus

Traditional law enforcement focuses on time and function as opposed to locations or areas within a jurisdiction. In terms of time, police departments revolve around shift work. Patrol officers, detectives, and other officers are assigned to shifts. Police effectiveness is measured by activities across time (i.e., what occurred on a particular shift). In terms of function, police departments are highly specialized, with several different units (patrol, criminal investigation, traffic, and community relations) responsible for their own unique tasks. Officers assigned to one functional area seldom have the time or inclination to work or worry about activities that fall into another functional area. In fact, typically only the chief in small and medium departments and precinct commanders in large departments have full responsibility for a given geographical area. Specialization by time and task inhibits the evaluation, or even articulation, of policing at the citizen or neighborhood level (Table 11.4).

Table 11.4 Community-Oriented Policies for Patrol Officers in Local Police Departments, by Size of Population Served (2007) 			
	Departments with These Features, %		
		Patrol Officer Involvement in Problem-Solving Protects	
Population Served	Geographical Assignments for Patrol Officers	Actively Encouraged	Included in Performance Evaluation
All sizes	31	21	15
1,000,000 or more	92	62	62
500,000–999,999	97	61	39
250,000–499,999	83	61	52
100,000–249,999	89	57	46
50,000–99,999	81	57	39
25,000–49,999	65	33	29
10,000–24,999	52	29	17
2500–9999	26	21	15
<2500	14	11	7

Source: BJS (2010).

For community policing to be successful, there must be some level of geographical permanence. Officers must work a geographical area on a permanent basis so that they become familiar with residents, activities, and social problems. Furthermore, if police officers are permanently assigned to an area, they hopefully will come to identify with the area and take greater care in safeguarding it and working to solve its problems. This "territorial imperative" does not end with police officers. Some note that command staff must also come to identify with and take responsibility for specific geographical areas. Once there is a level of geographical accountability within police departments, officers and units will respond more effectively to citizen and neighborhood needs and demands (Kappeler & Gaines, 2008).

Prevention Focus

First, as previously alluded to, community policing dictates that the police be proactive, rather than reactive, to problems and situations. A central part of proaction is prevention. Prevention is a much more attractive alternative when dealing with crime and disorder compared with enforcement because it reduces the level of victimization in a community. Prevention subsumes several operational possibilities. Prevention refers to ferreting out the problems and conditions that cause crime and disorder. In essence, the police must examine the conditions surrounding crime and disorder "hot spots" in an effort to develop effective measures of eliminating them. Patrol, criminal investigation, and other operational units must become actively involved in prevention.

Second, crime prevention units in police departments must become more active and broaden their range of activities. Historically, crime prevention in a given police agency has centered on a few activities, such as home and business surveys. Crime prevention units must become more active. In addition to their regular target-hardening activities, they should assist operational units by serving as a resource when dealing with specific crime problems or hot spots, and they should work closely with crime analysis and operational units to identify crime and disorder problems and solutions (Weisburd & Eck, 2004).

Finally, a part of a police department's crime prevention responsibility includes attacking the problems and conditions that contribute to, or result in, crime (secondary crime prevention). Police departments must take the lead in implementing programs that attack causes of crime. Here, the police can assume several social welfare roles. Police departments now have programs to assist and refer people in need to appropriate social welfare agencies; they have initiated educational and recreational programs aimed at providing wholesome life skills experiences for underprivileged youth; and, in some cases, police departments have begun to provide direct services to the needy. Crime prevention also means helping people at risk attain a minimum standard of living.

Substantive Focus

Community policing means more than responding to calls or generating activity, such as arrests and citations. As previously mentioned, it means that the police must engage in complex activities that address problems, as well as their accompanying symptoms. It also means that police departments must broaden the range of problems they address, because there are several social problems that result in or are intertwined with crime and disorder. Finally, a substantive focus requires that the police do not act alone. They must actively solicit the support and assistance of other governmental and private agencies in dealing with problems.

Figure 11.3 depicts this process. Generally, an entrenched problem will result in incidents that require a response from the police. Traditionally, the police have responded to these incidents by making an arrest, issuing a citation, or providing information to the citizen. They responded to the incidents, but seldom did anything about the problem generating the incidents. A substantive focus means that the police engage in problem solving to eliminate the problem, which, in turn, will eliminate the incidents or calls for service.

FIGURE 11.3
A neighborhood watch sign in Charleston, SC. *Photo courtesy of Ellen S. Boyne.*

The Programmatic Dimension

The previously described philosophy and strategies must be implemented operationally into specific tactics or programs. For the most part, community policing is implemented operationally through the following: (1) reoriented police operations, (2) problem-solving and situational crime prevention, and (3) community engagement (Box 11.5).

Reoriented Police Operations

The traditional police response to crime and disorder primarily consisted of random, routine patrols. It was believed that random patrols would deter crime through a consistent unpredictable police presence. If patrols were unable to prevent crime, then officers, as a result of their distribution across beats, would be in a good position to observe the criminal activity and apprehend criminals. Finally, if this failed, detectives would be dispatched to investigate the crime and make arrests.

Box 11.5 Problem-Oriented Policing

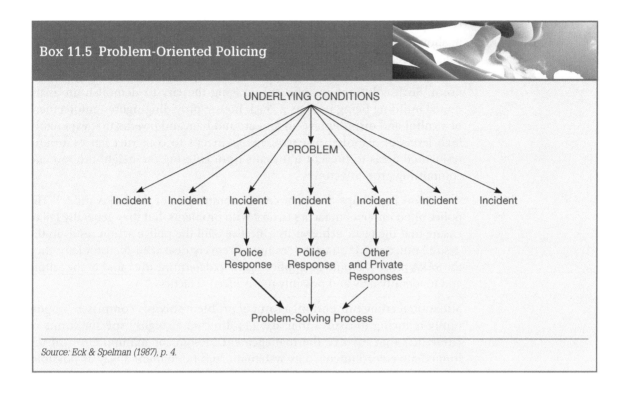

Source: Eck & Spelman (1987), p. 4.

Community policing means going beyond a reactive strategy. It means not waiting to be called, but identifying and targeting problems and implementing solutions. Police operational units must use foot patrols, directed patrols, citizen surveying, and other alternatives to random patrol to target crime and disorder problems. The police must ensure that they have an intensified police presence through many positive and negative citizen contacts. The police must not only focus on serious crime, but they must also attend to minor offenses, disorder, and incivilities. Order maintenance and the provision of service become more important.

Problem Solving and Situational Crime Prevention

Two primary tactics in community policing include problem solving (Eck & Spelman, 1987) and situational crime prevention (Clarke, 1997). Problem solving consists of using the SARA model as shown in Box 11.2. The SARA model consists of the following four-step process: (1) *scanning*, specifically identifying the problem; (2) *analysis*, careful analysis of the problem and its attributes and identification of possible solutions; (3) *response*, implementation of a solution; and (4) *assessment*, an evaluation of police efforts to measure the effectiveness of the solution. Simple questions, such as what is the problem, what is causing the problem, and what can I do to resolve it, should be asked by officers when attempting to solve problems. Effective solutions require comprehensive responses. When effective problem solving occurs, solutions that go beyond traditional police responses become the norm. Such solutions include encouraging the city to demolish an abandoned building being used as a crack house; providing tighter enforcement of alcohol and disorder laws in and around bars and taverns that experience high levels of disorder; or encouraging citizens to construct fences around residential areas to prevent transients from entering the neighborhood and committing property crimes.

Evaluation is perhaps the most critical component of the SARA model. The police often implement tactics to deal with problems, but they generally fail to ensure that the tactic achieves its objective. Did the police action result in the desired outcome? If a tactic does not effectively deal with the problem, then the SARA process should be applied again to determine the cause of the failure and to identify new and possibly more effective tactics.

Situational crime prevention, a form of problem solving, comprises "opportunity-reducing measures that are: (1) directed at highly specific forms of crime, (2) that involve the management, design, or manipulation of the immediate environment in as systematic and permanent a way as possible, and (3) so as to increase the effort and risks of crime and reduce the rewards as perceived by a wide range of offenders" (Clarke, 1997, p. 4). Adherents to situational crime prevention believe that crime is a product of "rational choice," where criminals weigh the likelihood of being discovered with the potential benefits of the act (Cornish & Clarke, 1987). Increases in difficulty in committing the crime or likelihood of apprehension result in reduced levels of crime. Therefore, crime prevention plays a key role in reducing crime (Box 11.6).

Situational crime prevention also relies on routine activities theory. Routine activities theory posits that crime occurs when a motivated criminal converges on a suitable target when there is a lack of guardianship (Felson, 2009). For example, an increase in residential burglary during the 1960s and 1970s has been attributed to decreased guardianship because of increases in empty homes as increasing numbers of single mothers and wives entered the workforce. Also, we find that there are large numbers of crime on routes leading to bars, taverns, adult bookstores, and other entertainment spots. As criminals travel to and from these locations and their homes, they discover homes and businesses with diminished guardianship and, ultimately, commit crimes. An effective method for reducing crime is to increase guardianship. Neighborhood watches, police patrols, and increased citizen activity can increase guardianship, which reduce opportunities for crime.

Box 11.6   SARA Model of Problem Solving

Variable	Activity	Outcome
Scanning	Looking for problems	Concentrations of crime, disorder, drugs, traffic crashes
Analysis	Focusing or defining problem	Understanding the specific problem or situation that causes incidents and calls for service
Response	Devoting resources to problem (personnel and programs)	Crime prevention programs, increased patrols, organizing neighborhoods, closing crack houses, enforcement of substance abuse laws, arrests for panhandling, traffic enforcement
Assessment	Determine if response was successful in dealing with problem; if not, repeat process and develop new, more effective solutions	Did crime, disorder, and drug use subside? were citizens less fearful? was the number of accidents reduced?

Community Engagement

Community policing dictates that the community become involved in protecting itself. People must realize that crime and disorder are not the exclusive domain of the police and government. People have a responsibility to assist the police, especially in their own neighborhoods. Citizens can become involved in a variety of ways. They can form neighborhood watches or citizen patrols, report criminal or suspicious activities, become involved in sports or educational activities for disadvantaged youth, assist non-governmental agencies in providing social services to the disadvantaged, or volunteer services to the police. The police must encourage, motivate, or otherwise induce citizens to become involved. This is best accomplished by planning for and providing opportunities for their involvement. In other words, create a need, and it will be fulfilled with the appropriate amount of effort by the police and the community.

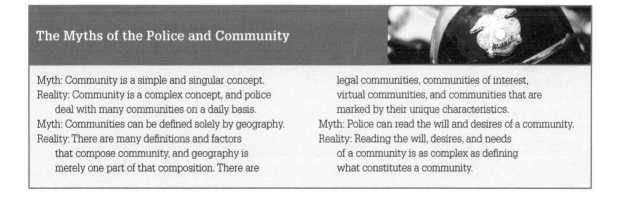

The Myths of the Police and Community

Myth: Community is a simple and singular concept.
Reality: Community is a complex concept, and police deal with many communities on a daily basis.
Myth: Communities can be defined solely by geography.
Reality: There are many definitions and factors that compose community, and geography is merely one part of that composition. There are legal communities, communities of interest, virtual communities, and communities that are marked by their unique characteristics.
Myth: Police can read the will and desires of a community.
Reality: Reading the will, desires, and needs of a community is as complex as defining what constitutes a community.

The police must also become involved in community building and empowerment. In some cases, a neighborhood or community will be so disorganized that it does not have the resources to become involved in helping itself. In these instances, the police must engage the community, identify leaders, and begin building the community. The police must work with religious and civic leaders to increase the level of neighborhood governance, and they must work to improve governance even when a neighborhood has a strong infrastructure. There should be a reduction in crime and disorder concomitant with increases in local governance. In essence, the police must assist in building a neighborhood's ability to ward off crime.

The previous sections provide a theoretical foundation for community policing. Community policing as a model is complex. It is complex because it entails implementation throughout a police department, not just selected units or officers. It is complex because it requires that the police department, at several levels, be in synchronization with the community it serves. Finally, it is complex because it requires police agencies to not only do different things (i.e., meet with the community, allow citizen input into police operations, or emphasize order maintenance over law enforcement), but it also means that police departments perform many of their old tasks differently (Table 11.5).

Table 11.5 Community Policing Activities of Local Police Departments, by Size of Population Served (2007)

Population Served	Department that Did Activity, %			
	Partnered with Citizen Groups to Elicit Feedback	Upgraded Technology to Support Community Polking	Conducted a Citizen Police Academy	Conducted or Sponsored Citizen Surveys
All sizes	38	25	15	15
1,000,000 or more	85	77	85	31
500,000–999,999	100	68	94	65
250,000–499,999	96	57	80	65
100,000–249,999	80	64	83	43
50,000–99,999	83	61	66	47
25,000–49,999	66	43	47	39
10,000–24,999	55	35	27	21
2500–9999	35	23	9	13
<2500	22	15	2	6

Source: BJS (2010).

Experience with community policing abounds. For example, a recent national survey of police departments showed that 68% of police agencies stated they were using community policing (Hickman & Reaves, 2003). Community policing, as previously discussed, encompasses a broad range of activities; therefore, there is no singular model by which to gauge how consistently or successfully community policing has been implemented. Perhaps the most expedient way to understand how it is being implemented is to examine some examples. The following sections examine management issues and operational examples relative to implementing community policing.

Management Issues

The BJS (2010) notes that 14% of police departments have full-time community policing officers and units devoted to community policing. Numerous other departments have adopted community policing more informally and have adopted various elements of community policing. At this point, it appears that community policing has gained considerable acceptance in law enforcement.

However, there are departments that have not fully implemented community policing, and there are others that adhere to traditional policing while applying a few community policing programs. Giacomazzi, Riley, and Merz (2004) have identified several challenges to implementing community policing. First, departments do not always have a vision and mission that emphasize cooperative relationships with the community. They tend to see enforcement and suppression as the primary vehicles for accomplishing their mission. Second, organizational goals are not always consistent with community policing. For example, police departments still rely on crime statistics rather than focusing on fear of crime, community relations, or non-law enforcement services provided to the public. Third, police departments do not always have an organizational structure that is conducive to community policing. Police units should be provided with direction and, in some cases, new police units should be created to ensure that community policing activities occur. Policy changes without actual changes to the department structure prove fruitless or counterproductive. Fourth, the organizational climate must change. That is, managers and supervisors should be trained and directed to pursue community policing activities. Officers should be given assignments that reflect a community policing orientation: working with community groups and neighborhoods. If managers and supervisors are not committed to community policing, then line police officers will not accept it (Peak, Gaines, & Glensor, 2009; Williams, 2003). Finally, the community environment is important. Too many citizens see arrests and crook-catching as the answer to crime problems. The community must understand that crime and disorder will not be eradicated or reduced until those community conditions that cause it are addressed.

Operational Examples

Operationally, community policing encompasses a variety of programs that serve to alleviate problems, make a neighborhood safer, and build a community's capacity to be safer and more orderly. Indeed, police departments have devised and implemented a wide range of community policing programs. For example, several departments have implemented programs aimed at community building and reducing disorder. Houston, TX, implemented its "Positive Interaction Program," which was aimed at identifying citizens who worked with the police in developing community groups and reducing crime and fear in the community. Houston also implemented a "Dispute Resolution Program" in an effort to reduce intra-family and neighborhood violence. Officers were specifically trained in mediation and conflict resolution techniques. Detroit, MI, developed a "Junior Police Cadet Section" that enlisted more than 4000 youths in the city. In addition to emphasizing academic excellence and having its members working on community projects, it also provided cadets an orientation aimed at recruiting them as police officers. The Reno police created "Neighborhood Advisory Groups" that were composed of citizens and met with police officials periodically to discuss community problems and concerns. As can be seen, the police have implemented a variety of programs focusing on the community. Although the police have historically implemented such programs, today they are the norm as police departments implement multiple programs aimed at different segments of the community and different problems. These programs represent a decentralized police–community relations effort.

For more information on police community relations, go to Dr. Tom O'Connor's Website at: **http://www.drtomoconnor. com/1030/1030lect07.htm**

Although police departments are focusing on the "community" when implementing community policing, they have not neglected efforts to directly attack the crime problem. Indeed, crime reduction efforts under the auspices of community policing are more directed in terms of both area and crime problem. The drug problem perhaps has received more attention from community policing than other crime problems. For example, Tampa (FL) police began strictly enforcing trespassing laws and other violations in one of its public housing areas when officers discovered that most of the drug dealers did not reside in the housing project. Tampa police also worked with public housing officials to remove people who did not officially reside in the housing. They had bulletproof, high-wattage lighting installed in the area to thwart drug dealing. San Diego (CA) deployed its "Walking Enforcement Campaign Against Narcotics", which consisted of a mobile squad of officers that moved from one problem area to another using strict, aggressive enforcement to reduce street drug sales. Dallas (TX) implemented its "Community and Law Enforcement Against Narcotics", which was based on a comprehensive governmental attack on drugs. Once an area was identified, police would strictly enforce laws; fire department officials checked for violations of fire codes and ordered unoccupied buildings closed that were unsafe; and the streets department cleared debris, abandoned cars, and discarded furniture that facilitated drug dealing. Essentially, community policing has encouraged police departments to implement new, imaginative programs that are more results oriented than many of the crime reduction strategies.

COMMUNITY POLICING AT THE MICRO-LEVEL: POLICE LEGITIMACY AND PROCEDURAL JUSTICE

The previous sections provided a roadmap for implementing community policing. It is a comprehensive endeavor that realistically affects all aspects of a department when implemented correctly. Most police departments in the United States have implemented some form of community policing, with some being more successful than others. With community policing's problem-solving and community partnership orientation, police departments can develop and implement strategies and tactics that more effectively accomplish agency goals and objectives Box 11.4.

An area that requires more elaboration is the application of community policing at the neighborhood level. In essence, the police must have positive relations with people in the neighborhoods they police. When there are positive relations, citizens are more cooperative, provide more crime information to the police, and tend to violate the law less. There is a substantial body of research that shows minority citizens tend to view the police less positively than their majority counterparts (Reisig & Parks, 2000; Tuch & Weitzer, 1997). Moreover, African Americans report that they are more likely to be mistreated by the police. Some researchers have found that African Americans do not like the police (Brunson, 2007). Hispanics, on the other hand, report more positive views of the police than African Americans (Cheurprakobkit, 2000). Nonetheless, Hispanics often are fearful of the police as a result of immigration issues and show a general distrust of the police. Adding to this problem is that some of the research shows that people in poorer neighborhoods tend to view the police less positively (Cao et al., 1996; Reisig & Giacomazzi, 1998). It is apparent that police–community relations and police practices in minority, poor neighborhoods need improvement. Again, these relations are important in accomplishing police goals.

Producing more positive interactions is only the first step in improving relations. The police should endeavor to build trust, yet merely having positive perceptions of the police does not necessarily engender trust. A contributor to poor perceptions is that the police treat people differently in high-crime, disorderly, disadvantaged neighborhoods (Kane, 2005; Fagan & Davies, 2000; Terrill & Reisig, 2003). It is in these neighborhoods where the police need to have better relations to more effectively combat crime and disorder. Recently, this problem has been analyzed using the police legitimacy and procedural justice paradigms.

Police legitimacy is when people recognize and accept the authority of the police to the point that they willfully obey the law. When people respect and trust the police, they are less likely to violate the law. They have a moral or ethical orientation toward police authority. Research has demonstrated that legitimacy results in people accepting police decisions. This innate acceptance of police authority often is derived from how the public views the police.

Sunshine and Tyler (2003) note that legitimacy when there are credible sanctions for those who break the law (risk); when there is effective control crime (performance); and when services are fairly distributed across people and communities (distributive fairness). In other words, procedural justice is an important underpinning for legitimacy. When these three conditions are not met, people tend to question the police's legitimacy; the police are deemed illegitimate because they are not performing their responsibilities to the level expected and procedural justice is absent. The police tend to do the least effective job meeting these conditions in minority, disadvantaged neighborhoods, resulting in police–community relations problems, but problems can also exist in other neighborhoods.

Citizens' evaluation of police procedural justice occurs in every interaction between the police and the public. If a motorist is stopped by an officer for a traffic violation, the officer's actions and demeanor affect the motorist's perceptions of police procedural justice. These perceptions tend to be global, where the motorist applies those judgments to the police department and policing in general. Moreover, negative perceptions of the police can accumulate in a neighborhood when people feel that police officers treat them unjustly.

Legitimacy should be an important goal for police departments. However, to achieve legitimacy, police departments must make an effort to improve the way officers interact with people (procedural justice). Police officers too often use a professional or even a caustic approach when dealing with citizens, especially in disadvantaged neighborhoods. Officers sometimes have difficultly separating their crime-fighting demeanor from their helping people demeanor. Police legitimacy implies that if police officers can have more positive interactions, there will be an improvement in citizens' acceptance of the law and the police.

SUMMARY

This chapter has focused on the relationship between the police and the community. Several problems and concerns have been addressed. First, citizen perceptions of the police were explored. Research indicates that there are substantial variations in how citizens view the police. The police must be acutely aware of these variations and attempt to build better relations when weak ones exist. Historically, the police have depended on police–community relations and crime prevention programs to solve any problems with the public. However, it appears that such programs are not always effective. The primary reason for their failure was that they too often were used as a vehicle for public relations, and they did not address problems or issues that cause crime and disorder. Police agencies, in essence, cannot use simplistic programs to solve complex problems.

Crime prevention remains an important part of policing. Departments must implement programs that reduce crime. For the most part, departments focus on primary crime prevention tactics. Such programs involve the police working with the community. More important, the police should identify the types of crime and disorder problems in a neighborhood and tailor programs to meet citizens' needs. When crime is reduced, it results in less work for the police, an increase in community relations, and a reduction in fear, all of which are important goals.

By the mid-1990s, policing in America was rapidly moving toward community policing. Many, especially politicians and government leaders, believed that community policing was a panacea that could cure all sorts of problems that historically had plagued US policing. History will probably show that community policing was a failure, primarily because police departments were again searching for simplistic answers. That is, many agencies have rushed to implement parts of community policing, but few have approached it comprehensively. Shortcuts and bits and pieces of community policing will not adequately address the problems confronting law enforcement today. Police departments have to be re-engineered from the top to the bottom, to be successful. All management and operational activities must be systematically examined and synchronized in their efforts to effectively accomplish goals and objectives. By 2000, the use of community policing among local police departments had began to decline.

REVIEW QUESTIONS

1. In general, how do people view the police? How does this differ with age, race, sex, socioeconomic status, contact with the police, and major incidents?

2. Since the late 1970s and 1980s, drugs and crime have become potent political issues, followed by a shift toward tough law enforcement over the protection of civil rights. What has this done to the public's perception of the police?
3. What is the theory of crime prevention and what does primary, secondary, and tertiary crime prevention mean?
4. What is Wilson and Kelling's *broken window thesis* and how is it applied to crime prevention?
5. What did community policing evolve from and in what way did Goldstein articulate the basis for community policing?
6. What percentage of police departments have full-time community policing officers and units devoted to community policing? What are the challenges to implementing community policing?
7. What is police legitimacy and how is it best gained?
8. What is procedural justice and how does it foster police legitimacy?

REFERENCES

Bayley, D. H. (1988). Community policing: a report from the Devil's advocate. In J. Greene, & S. Mastrofski (Eds.), *Community policing: rhetoric or reality?* (pp. 225–238). New York, NY: Praeger.

Benedict, W. R., Brown, B., & Bower, D. J. (2000). Perceptions of the police and fear of crime in a rural setting: utility of a geographically focused survey for police services, planning, and assessment. *Criminal Justice Policy Review, 11*(4), 275–298.

Bennett, T., & Wright, R. (1984). *Burglars on burglary.* Brookfield, VT: Grower.

BJS. (2006). *Local police departments, 2003.* Washington, DC: Bureau of Justice Statistics.

BJS. (2010). *Local police departments, 2007.* Washington, DC: Bureau of Justice Statistics.

Braga, A., Weisburd, D., Warning, E., Green-Mazerolle, L., Spelman, W., & Gajewski, G. (1999). Problem-oriented policing in violent crime places: a randomized controlled experiment. *Criminology, 37,* 541–579.

Brantingham, P. J., & Faust, F. L. (1976). A conceptual model of crime prevention. *Crime & Delinquency, 22,* 284–296.

Brown, B., & Benedict, W. R. (2002). Perceptions of the police. *An International Journal of Police Strategies and Management, 25*(3), 543–580.

Brunson, R. K. (2007). "Police don't like black people:" African-American young men's accumulated police experiences. *Criminology & Public Policy, 6,* 71–101.

Buck, A., & Hakim, S. (1993). Burglar alarms and the choice behavior of burglars: a suburban Phenomenon. *Journal of Criminal Justice, 21,* 497–507.

Cao, L., Frank, J., & Cullen, F. (1996). Race, community confidence and confidence in the police. *American Journal of Police, 15,* 3–22.

Carter, D. (1983). Hispanic interaction with the criminal justice system in Texas: experiences, attitudes, and perceptions. *Journal of Criminal Justice, 11,* 213–227.

Carter, D. (1985). Hispanic perception of police performance: an empirical assessment. *Journal of Criminal Justice, 13,* 487–500.

Chermak, S. (1994). Body count news: how crime is presented in the news media. *Justice Quarterly, 11,* 561–582.

Chermak, S., McGarrell, E. F., & Weiss, A. (2001). Citizens' perceptions of aggressive traffic enforcement strategies. *Justice Quarterly, 18*, 365–391.

Cheurprakobkit, S. (2000). Police-citizen contact and police performance: attitudinal differences between hispanics and non-hispanics. *Journal of Criminal Justice, 28*, 325–336.

Clarke, R. V. (1997). *Situational crime prevention: successful case studies* (2nd ed.). New York, NY: Harrow and Heston.

Cole, D. (2003). The effect of a curfew law on juvenile crime in Washington, D.C. *American Journal of criminal Justice, 27*, 217–232.

Cornish, D. B., & Clarke, R. V. (1987). Understanding crime displacement: an application of rational choice theory. *Criminology, 25*, 933–947.

Correia, M. E., Reisig, M. D., & Lovrich, N. P. (1996). Public perceptions of state police: an analysis of individual-level and contextual variables. *Journal of Criminal Justice, 24*, 17–28.

Cox, T. C., & White, M. F. (1988). Traffic citations and student attitudes toward the police: an examination of selected interaction dynamics. *Journal of Police Science and Administration, 16*, 105–121.

Crimestoppers International. (1999). *CSIte International Statistics.* . http://www.c-s-i.org/stats/html.

Dean, D. (1980). Citizen ratings of the police: the difference contact makes. *Law and Policy Quarterly, 2*, 445–471.

Decker, S. H. (1981). Citizen attitude toward the police: a review of past findings and suggestions for future policy. *Journal of Police Science and Administration, 9*(1), 80–87.

Eck, J., & Spelman, W. (1987). Who ya gonna call? The police as problem-busters. *Crime & Delinquency, 33*(1), 31–52.

Fagan, J., & Davies, G. (2000). Street cops and broken windows: Terry, race, and disorder in New York City. *Fordham Urban Law Journal, 28*, 457–504.

Famega, C. N. (2009). Proactive policing by post and community officers. *Crime & Delinquency, 55*, 78–104.

FBI. (2010). *Crime in the United States, 2009*. Washington, DC: U.S. Department of Justice.

Felson, M. (2009). *Crime and everyday life: insights and implications for society* (4th ed.). Thousand Oaks, CA: Pine Forge Press.

Flexon, J. L., Lurigio, A. J., & Greenleaf, R. G. (2010). Exploring the dimensions of trust in the police among Chicago juveniles. *Journal of Criminal Justice, 37*, 180–189.

Garofalo, J., & McLeod, M. (1989). The structure and operations of neighborhood watch programs in the United States. *Crime & Delinquency, 35*(3), 326–344.

Giacomazzi, A., Riley, S., & Merz, R. (2004). Internal and external challenges to implementing community policing: examining comprehensive assessment reports from multiple sites. *Criminal Justice Studies, 17*, 223–238.

Goldstein, H. (1979). Improving policing: a problem-oriented approach. *Crime & Delinquency, 25*, 236–258.

Goldstein, H. (1990). *Problem-oriented policing*. New York, NY: McGraw-Hill Book Co.

Graber, D. (1980). *Crime news and the public*. New York, NY: Praeger.

Greene, J. R. (1987). Foot patrol and community policing: past practices and future prospects. *American Journal of Police, 6*(1), 1–15.

Hickman, M., & Reaves, B. (2003). *Local police departments*. Washington, DC: U.S. Department of Justice.

Hinkle, J. C., & Weisburd, D. (2008). *The irony of broken windows policing: a micro-place study of the relationship between disorder, focused police crackdowns and fear of crime.* .

Hirschel, D., Dean, C., & Dunond, D. (2001). Juvenile curfews and race: a cautionary note. *Criminal Justice Policy Review, 12*, 197–214.

Huang, W., & Vaughn, M. (1996). Support and confidence: public attitudes toward the police. In T. Flanagan, & D. Longmire (Eds.), *Americans view crime and justice: a national public opinion survey* (pp. 31–45). Thousand Oaks, CA: Sage Publications.

Jim, J., Mitchell, F., & Kent, D. (2006). Community-oriented policing in a retail shopping center. *Policing: An International Journal of Police Strategies and Management, 29*, 146–157.

Kaminski, R. J., & Jefferis, E. S. (1998). The effect of a violent televised arrest on public perceptions of the police: a partial test of Easton's theoretical framework. *Policing: An International Journal of Police Strategies and Management, 21*, 683–706.

Kane, R. J. (2005). Compromised police legitimacy as a predictor of violent crime in structurally disadvantaged communities. *Criminology, 43*, 469–498.

Kappeler, V. E., & Gaines, L. (2008). *Community policing: a contemporary perspective* (4th ed.). Cincinnati, OH: LexisNexis.

Kappeler, V. E., & Potter, G. W. (2005). *The mythology of crime and criminal Justice* (5th ed.). Newark, NJ: LexisNexis Matthew Bender.

Kasinsky, R. G. (1994). Patrolling the fact: media, cops, and crime. In G. Barak (Ed.), *Media, process, and the social construction of crime*. New York, NY: Garland.

Katz, C. M., Webb, V. J., & Schaefer, D. R. (2001). Assessment of the impact of quality-of-life policing on crime and disorder. *Justice Quarterly, 18*, 825–876.

Kelley, J. (January 31, 1997). Police lines often clogged with false, unreliable clues. *USA Today*, 1–2.

Kusow, A., Wilson, L., & Martin, D. (1997). Determinants of citizen satisfaction with the police: the effects of residential location. *Policing: An International Journal of Police Strategies and Management, 20*, 655–664.

Lab, S. P. (2004). *Crime prevention: approaches, practices, and evaluations* (4th ed.). Cincinnati, OH: Anderson Publishing Co.

Lab, S. P. (2010). *Crime prevention: approaches, practices, and evaluations* (7th ed.). Cincinnati, OH: Anderson Publishing Co.

Laycock, G. (1985). *Reducing burglary: A study of chemists' shops, crime prevention unit paper 1*. London: Home Office.

MacGillis, D. (1983). *Crime in America*. Radnor, PA: Chilton Book Co.

Males, M. (2000). Connecticut's juvenile curfew: the circumstances of youths cited and effects on crime. *Criminal Justice Policy Review, 11*, 254–267.

Mastrofski, S. (1988). Community policing as reform: a cautionary tale. In C. Klockars, & S. Mastrofski (Eds.), *Community policing: Rhetoric or reality*. New York, NY: Praeger.

McDowell, D., Lofton, C., & Wiersema, B. (2000). The impact of youth curfew laws on juvenile crime rates. *Crime & Delinquency, 46*, 76–91.

Miethe, T., McCorkle, R., & Listwan, S. (2006). *Crime profiles: the anatomy of dangerous persons, places, and situations*. Los Angeles: Roxbury.

Miller, W. (1973). Ideology and criminal justice policy: some current issues. *Journal of Criminal Law and Criminology, 64*, 141–162.

Nelson, A. (1994). *The Cincinnati curfew ordinance: A preliminary report*. Cincinnati, OH: Human Relations Commission.

Newman, O. (1972). *Defensible space*. New York, NY: Macmillan.

Nolan, J., Conti, N., & McDevitt, J. (2004). Situational policing: neighborhood development and crime control. *Policing & Society: An International Journal of Research and Policy, 14*, 99–117.

Packer, H. (1968). *The limits of the criminal sanction.* Stanford, CA: Stanford University Press.

Peak, K. J., & Glensor, R. W. (2008). *Community policing & problem solving: strategies and practices.* Upper Saddle River, NJ: Prentice-Hall.

O'Keefe, G., Rosenbaum, D. Lavrakas, P., Reid, K. & Botta, R. A. (1996). Taking a bite out of crime: The impact of national prevention campaigns. Thousand Oaks, CA: Sage.

Peak, K., Gaines, L., & Glensor, R. (2009). *Police supervision and management in an era of community policing* (3rd ed.). Upper Saddle River, NJ: Prentice-Hall.

Reed, T., & Gaines, L. K. (1982). Criminal justice models as a function of ideological images: a social learning of alternative of Packer. *International Journal of Comparative and Applied Criminal Justice, 6,* 212–222.

Reisig, M. D., & Chandeik, M. S. (2001). The effects of expectancy disconfirmation on outcome satisfaction in police–citizen encounters. *Policing: An International Journal of Police Strategies and Management, 24,* 87–99.

Reisig, M. D., & Giacomazzi, A. L. (1998). Citizen perceptions of community policing: are attitudes toward police important? *Policing: An International Journal of Police Strategies and Management, 21,* 547–561.

Reisig, M. D., & Parks, R. B. (2000). Experience, quality of life, and neighborhood context: a hierarchical analysis of satisfaction with police. *Justice Quarterly, 17,* 607–630.

Roehl, J. A., Wong, H., Huitt, R., & Capowich, G. E. (1995). *A national assessment of community-based anti-drug initiatives: final report.* Pacific Grove, CA: Institute for Social Analysis.

Rosenbaum, D. P., Lurigio, A. J., & Lavrakas, P. J. (1989). Enhancing citizen participation and solving serious crime: A national evaluation of crime stoppers programs. *Crime & Delinquency, 35*(3), 401–420.

Rosenbaum, D. P. (1994). *The Challenge of community policing.* Thousand Oaks, CA: Sage Publishing.

Rosenbaum, D. P., Lurigio, A. J., & Davis, R. C. (1998). *The prevention of crime: social and situational strategies.* Belmont, CA: Wadsworth.

Ruefle, W., & Reynolds, K. M. (1996). Keep them at home: juvenile curfew ordinances in 200 cities. *American Journal of Police, 15,* 63–84.

Silverman, E. (1999). *NYPD battles crime: innovative strategies in policing.* Boston, MA: Northeastern University Press.

Smith, S. K., Steadman, G. W., Minton, T. D., & Townsend, M. (1999). *Criminal victimization and perceptions of community safety in 12 cities, 1998.* Washington, DC: U.S. Department of Justice.

Surette, R. (2006). *Media, crime, and criminal justice: images and realities* (3rd ed.). Belmont, CA: Wadsworth.

Sunshine, J. and Taylor, T. (2003). The Role of Procedural Justice and Legitimacy in Shaping Public Support for Policing. *Law and Society Review, 37*(3): 513–48.

Suttles, G. D. (1972). *The social construction of communities.* Chicago, IL: University of Chicago Press.

Terrill, W., & Reisig, M. D. (2003). Neighborhood context and police use of force. *Journal of Research in Crime and Delinquency, 40,* 291–321.

Trojanowicz, R., & Bucqueroux, B. (1990). *Community policing: a contemporary perspective.* Cincinnati, OH: Anderson Publishing Co.

Tuch, S. A., & Weitzer, R. (1997). The polls: racial differences in attitudes toward the police. *Public Opinion Quarterly, 61,* 642–664.

Walker, S. (1993). Does Anyone Remember Team Policing? Lessons of the Team Policing Experience for Community Policing. *American Journal of Police, 12,* (1), 33–56.

Walker, S. (1997). Complaints against the police: a focus group study of citizen perceptions, goals, and expectations. *Criminal Justice Review, 22,* 207–226.

Weisburd, D., & Eck, J. (2004). What can police do to reduce, disorder, and fear? *Annals of the American Academy of Political and Social Science, 593*, 42–65.

Weitzer, R., & Tuch, S. (1999). Race, class, and perceptions of discrimination by the police. *Crime & Delinquency, 45*, 494–507.

Weitzer, R., & Tuch, S. (2004). Reforming the police: racial differences in public support for change. *Criminology, 42*, 391–416.

White, G. F. (1990). He police: racial differences in public support. *Justice Quarterly, 7*, 57–68.

Williams, E. J. (2003). Police: racial differences in public support foalizing Innovative change. *Police Practice and Research, 4*(2), 119–129.

Wilson, J. Q., & Kelling, G. (2005). "Broken Windows" and fractured history. In V. Kappeler (Ed.), *The police and society: Touchstone readings* (3rd ed.). Prospect Heights, IL: Waveland Press, Inc.

Worrall, J. L. (1999). Public perceptions of police efficacy and image: the "Fuzziness" of support for the police. *American Journal of Criminal Justice, 24*, 47–66.

Zevitz, R. G., & Rettammel, R. J. (1990). Elderly attitudes about police service. *American Journal of Police, 9*(2), 25–39.

CHAPTER 12

Policing the Drug Problem

It is easier to exclude harmful passions than to rule them, and to deny them admittance than to control them after they have been admitted.

—Seneca

LEARNING OBJECTIVES

After reading the chapter, you should be able to:

- Describe the nature and extent of the drug problem in the United States.
- Discuss the realities of the relationship of drugs and crime.
- Describe the nation's drug strategy and its components.
- Outline the illegal drug delivery system and the groups that participate in this system.
- Describe the drug distribution levels and police enforcement programs designed to target these levels.
- Discuss the role community policing can play in addressing the drug problem.

KEY TERMS

- Buy-busts
- Civil forfeiture
- Civil gang injunctions
- Colombian drug cartels
- Criminal forfeiture
- DARE
- Drug marts
- Drug treatment
- Economic compulsive violence
- Effective education
- Fear arousal
- Fixed-site neighborhood sales
- Forfeiture
- High-level drug kingpins

INTRODUCTION

America's law enforcement community is engaged in an expansive war on drugs. Ever since the mid-1980s, the drug problem has consumed an ever-increasing amount of police administrators and other governmental officials' time and effort as they plan and implement drug reduction strategies. They have sought more effective ways to control the continued and steady increase in drug use and sales. Drug dealers and people in the drug culture control areas within some American cities. The drug related criminality in our major cities makes it even more important for the police to develop effective measures for dealing with the drug problem.

- Informants
- Information dissemination
- Interdiction
- La Cosa Nostra
- Mexican Mafia
- Moral appeals
- Multijurisdict- ional drug task forces
- Mutual societies
- National Drug Control Strategy
- Neighborhood crackdowns
- Outlaw motorcyclegangs
- Periodic markets
- Psychopharma- cological
- Pulling levers strategy
- Raids
- Retail street level
- Reverse stings
- Street sweeping
- Systemic violence
- Third-party policing

This is not our first drug war and, indeed, we can trace the first modern drug war to President Richard M. Nixon when, in September 1969, his administration initiated "Operation Intercept." Since that time, every U.S. president since President Nixon has implemented policies designed to control the drug problem. We have invaded other countries, including Panama, and provided direct military assistance to foreign nations, such as Peru and Colombia. The reduction of revenue from drug sales is a central concern in current conflicts in the Middle East. We have intensified police efforts in our own country to the point that many believe that some of our civil liberties are in jeopardy (see Wisotsky, 1997). We have engaged in national public relations campaigns to foster greater public support for the wars on drugs. Presidents George H.W. Bush and William J. Clinton pushed $11 billion policing programs through Congress with a substantial portion of this funding aimed at more effectively dealing with the nation's drug and crime problems. President George W. Bush and Barak H. Obama have, however, been relatively silent on the drug issue and policing programs generally. Crime problems have taken a backseat to the war on terrorism and homeland security. Irrespective of past efforts, the drug war continues and is being fought on a number of fronts in communities all across our country.

Agencies at the federal, state, and local levels are engaged in the war on drugs. As a direct result of the perceived severity of the problem, many federal law enforcement agencies, regardless of Cabinet affiliation, are engaged in drug enforcement. This includes agencies ranging from the Federal Bureau of Investigation (FBI) to the Investigators with the United States Department of Agriculture. Police departments that previously did not have drug investigative units created them, and in many states, even the smallest cities banded together to form regional drug task forces (Chaiken, Chaiken, & Karchmer, 1990; Schlegel & McGarrell, 1991). In 2009, for example "the DEA State and Local Task Force Program managed 381 state and local task forces… staffed by over 1890 DEA special agents and over 2200 state and local officers" (DEA, 2010, p. 1). Indeed, drug enforcement has significantly altered how police departments are organized and how they operate.

The rhetoric of the drug war is misleading. It would appear, based on drug war pronouncements, that we are aggressively engaging evil chemicals, which destroy our nation's youth. However, our warlike tactics do not target drugs, such as cocaine, heroin, or marijuana; they focus on people. The drama of the drug war affects real people. Sometimes, the police and the criminal justice system are able to rid our streets of truly evil people. In other cases, the police and prosecutors become the predators. As a result of their zeal, they prosecute innocent citizens, and, in other instances, they join the enemy as a result of being corrupted by the immense profits associated with drugs (Miller, 1996). The point is the drug war is being fought in "real" life and the outcome of the war is determined

You can learn more about how the war on drugs has affected on city by going to: http://www.aljazeera.com/programmes/faultlines/2012/08/20128218333383106.html.

not by the police, but by society and our culture. We must not lose sight of justice as we continue to fight this war. We must also keep the drug problem in proper perspective.

THE NATURE AND EXTENT OF THE DRUG PROBLEM

- Undercover operations
- Youth street gangs
- Zero tolerance eviction programs

One of the difficulties in understanding the nature of the drug problem is that there are so many different drugs to consider. Historically, we were concerned with heroin, cocaine, and marijuana. It was believed that these drugs contributed the bulk of the drug problem. Recently, however, a number of other drugs have become problematic. For example, in some parts of the country, methamphetamine has overtaken cocaine as the drug of choice (Herz, 2000). Date-rape drugs such as GHB and Rohypnol, which is 10 times stronger than Valium, are increasingly being used in sex offenses. MDMA or Ecstasy has become popular among many young people, especially at raves and dance clubs. There is an increased concern over the abuse of prescription drugs. Barbiturates such as Amytal, Nembutal, and Seconal, and tranquilizers such as Xanax, Librium, and Valium, are being abused. Recently, the national spotlight focused on the abuse of synthetic narcotics when it was learned that Rush Limbaugh, a conservative pundit and radio commentator, was obtaining and abusing OxyContin. Other synthetic narcotics that are abused include Lortab, Dilaudid, Demerol, Percocet, and Darvon. Different people have a propensity to use different drugs creating a myriad of drug problems and user populations.

For more information about drugs and crime, go to the Bureau of Justice Statistics Drugs and Crime page at: **http://www.bjs.gov/index.cfm?ty=tp&tid=35**.

Perhaps the best way to understand the extent of the drug problem is to review some of the national survey data that gauge America's drug problems. In 2010, *The National Drug Control Strategy* published by the White House provided statistics on drug use in the United States. "Each day in this country, almost 8000 Americans illegally consume a drug for the first time. The risks posed by their drug use, like that of the other 20 million Americans who already use drugs illegally, will radiate to their families and to the communities in which they live" (NDCS, 2010, p. 5). The most commonly used illicit drug was marijuana. It is interesting that 15.2 million people used marijuana, while only 1.9 million used cocaine. In fact, there are more people abusing prescription drugs than all illicit drugs combined except for marijuana. These statistics seem to indicate that prescription drug abuse is a more significant problem than cocaine, ecstasy, methamphetamine, LSD, or heroin.

Another method of examining the scope of the drug problem is by looking at arrest data. The FBI reported in 2009 that there were 1,663,582 drug arrests in the United States. This represents a substantial increase in the past 10 years. Drug offenders constitute more than 50% of the federal prison population and over 20% of state prisoners (BJS, 2010).

It is also insightful to examine drug use by offenders. *The Arrestee Drug Abuse Monitoring Program* (ADAMP) was instituted in 1997, and it collects data on drug use by the jail population. Prisoners from 39 major cities across the country voluntarily provide urine samples. The program has found that nationally, 67% of arrestees had drugs in their system at the time of arrest (ADAMP, 2003). The most common drug found was marijuana, followed by cocaine and opiates. Figure 12.1 shows national data on current drug abuse by type of drug (Box 12.1).

Drugs and Crime

The abuse of illegal drugs may be related to crime and other police problems. The exact nature of this relationship is not clearly understood, and there is considerable debate as to whether drugs cause crime (Kappeler & Potter, 2005) or if the conditions that contribute to criminality also cause drug abuse (Goode, 2011; McBride & McCoy, 2003). It appears that as individuals become more involved in criminality and begin to associate with the criminal subculture, they are introduced to a wider variety of drugs and an increasing number of situations where drugs are abused. The abuse of illicit drugs then becomes part of the culture, and it becomes difficult to separate the drug usage from the criminality.

FIGURE 12.1

U.S. Customs and Border Patrol Agents gather along the International Border Monday, August 16, 2010, near Naco, Arizona. *Photograph Courtesy of AP Photo/Matt York.*

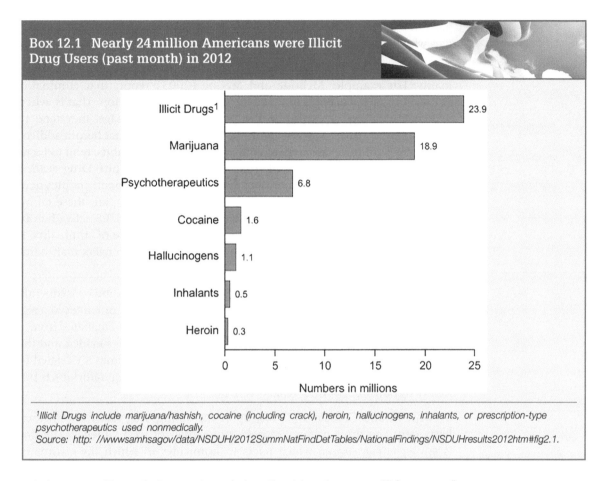

Box 12.1 Nearly 24 million Americans were Illicit Drug Users (past month) in 2012

[1]Illicit Drugs include marijuana/hashish, cocaine (including crack), heroin, hallucinogens, inhalants, or prescription-type psychotherapeutics used nonmedically.
Source: http: //wwwsamhsagov/data/NSDUH/2012SummNatFindDetTables/NationalFindings/NSDUHresults2012htm#fig2.1.

Miethe, McCorkle, and Listwan (2006) describe this culture as a "life as party" culture. People living in this culture become more involved in crime and drug use. Continued drug abuse results in the increased consumption of drugs and, sometimes, the commission of additional criminal acts to obtain drugs.

There is a substantial body of literature that indicates that drug abusers and addicts commonly commit a substantial number of crimes, and perhaps commit thousands of crimes over the lifetime of their addiction. People who begin using drugs at an earlier age tend to commit more crime and use more drugs over a lifetime. They become embedded in the drug culture.

Of course, most, if not all, of these offenders committed crimes prior to their drug use, and even though there may be a strong correlation between drugs and crime, there is little evidence that there is a strong causal relationship (for a discussion of this issue, see McBride & McCoy, 2003). Many addicts may very well have committed these crimes even if they had not used

For alternative views on the drug war, go to: **http://stopthedrugwar.org/home.**

narcotics. Indeed, there are addicts who do not commit crimes as well as criminals who do not abuse drugs.

Researchers have identified distinct patterns relative to drug abuse and criminality. For example, McBride and McCoy (2003) report that criminality among drug abusers tends to fluctuate with levels of addiction. That is, when addicts go through a period of abstinence or reduced usage, they tend to commit fewer crimes. Kowalski and Faupel (1990) found that heroin addicts, although committing a variety of crimes to support their habits, tend to focus on one "main hustle" or type of crime to support their habits. Drug dealing is the main hustle for the majority of drug hustlers, and property crimes tend to constitute the bulk of addict criminality. For the most part, these criminals engage in crimes of opportunity. Less than 2% of the 768 active heroin users in the study said that robbery was their primary mode of criminality. It appears that drug addicts tend to be more like street scavengers than hardened criminals.

Violence has become a central part of the select drug cultures and consequently a significant police problem. Many of our major cities have experienced a significant increase in drug related homicides. This violence emanates from a number of directions: gang wars, rip-offs during drug deals, suicides, and the accidental killings of innocent bystanders. Most of these crimes are related to the illegality of drugs, not their pharmacological effects. Drug trafficking is primarily responsible for drug related violence.

Brownstein and Goldstein (1990), upon examining drug related homicides, have identified three primary causes or categories of such violence. The first is *psychopharmacological*, which refers to homicides in which the victims or perpetrators were abusing drugs, and their diminished mental capacity led to their being victimized or resulted in aggressive behavior and the commission of a violent criminal act. The second is *economic compulsive violence*. Here, drug abusers commit crimes of violence, such as robberies or assaults, in an effort to obtain drugs, money, or something of value that could be used to obtain drugs. The third category of drug related homicides is *systemic violence*. This violence arises from the interaction of participants in the drug culture as they barter drugs, compete for territory, fight with rival gangs, and, in general, settle disputes that erupt while engaged in the buying, selling, and abusing of drugs. Systemic violence is without question the greatest source of drug related violence (Auerhahn & Parker, 2003). Although violence emanates from a variety of directions in the drug culture, which gives rise to numerous police problems, it is drug selling and buying, not use, that is the most significant source for drug related violence.

There appears to be a relationship between the amount and severity of the crime and the type and amount of drugs used. Inciardi and Pottieger (1991) found that crack users with the greatest participation or involvement in the crack business tended to be more involved in crime or drug usage. Similarly, Fagan, Weis, and Cheng (1990) found that serious substance abuse was more prevalent among serious delinquents, but the reverse was not always true. Not all serious drug users had high levels of criminality. The drug crime nexus is tenuous, but it should be remembered that, generally, where drugs are illegal, there will be crime.

To a great extent, we have been preoccupied with the drug problem for the past four or so decades to the point that we have neglected to comprehend the impact of alcohol on crime and violence. Indeed, alcohol may very well make a greater contribution to crime and violence than drugs. The evidence linking alcohol to violence is overwhelming (Auerhahn & Parker, 2003). For example, in his classic study, Wolfgang (1958) found that 60% of the homicides in his study involved alcohol. The same findings occur when rape and other physical assaults are examined. Goode (2011) notes that a high correlation between alcohol and violence occurs in every such study. Karzberg and James (2005) found that of convicted inmates in jails, 48.9% were dependent on or abusing alcohol, and 52% of offenders committing violent offenses were dependent on or abusing alcohol.

THE NATION'S DRUG STRATEGY

It should be remembered that this country has waged several wars on drugs. President Nixon declared war on drugs in 1969 and previously there was a national effort to attack drugs after the Civil War, after World War I, and again in the 1950s when several of our narcotics laws were passed in an effort to deal with the nation's drug problem. One might conjecture that today's drug problem is not new, but that it is only a continuation of the one our country has had for several decades. Regardless, the size and dimensions of the problem today have resulted in a combination of programs to be implemented that, in totality, are designed to deal with all aspects of the problem. The development of our national drug strategy has come from the President, the Congress, and the United States Attorney General. Basically, the components of this strategy are: (1) preventing use through *education* and community action, (2) healing America's drug users by making *treatment* resources more readily available, and (3) disrupting *the drug market* (White House, 2007). Some of the programs associated with these strategies include increased drug testing of students, fight efforts by the states to decriminalize marijuana for medical purposes, encourage faith-based organizations to become involved in prevention and treatment, increase effective treatment opportunities, target drugged driving, increase the use of drug courts, and disrupt domestic and overseas drug markets by increasing the cost of business through enhanced enforcement and asset forfeiture. The plan lays out a hodgepodge of programs rather than a coherent, comprehensive strategy. This three-pronged strategy attempts to attack the problem at all levels and essentially

You can watch a video on the profit motive behind drug enforcement activities by going to: **http://vimeo.com/59416176**.

centers around enforcement, interdiction, prevention, and treatment. Interdiction, prevention, and treatment are discussed in the following sections. Enforcement will receive a more expanded discussion later in this chapter.

Interdiction

The purpose of *interdiction* programs is to deter drug smuggling by seizing or deterring drug shipments entering the United States. The focus of interdiction programs has been on smuggling activities in Colombia and Mexico. The vast majority of this country's illegal cocaine, and some marijuana, come from Colombia, whereas Mexico serves as a major transshipment point for cocaine and marijuana. Additionally, Mexico produces a substantial amount of black tar heroin, marijuana, and methamphetamine. Afghanistan supplies the vast majority of the world's heroin. The wars in Afghanistan and Iraq have resulted in supplying larger amounts of heroin to finance their war efforts in Afghanistan, Pakistan, and Iraq. In 2007, Afghanistan produced approximately 9000 tons of opium, or about 93% of the global production (Associated Press, 2007).

Mexico has emerged as a major drug trafficking problem for the United States. Historically, most of the cocaine and marijuana smuggled into the United States from Central and South America came via sea and air routes. The U.S. government substantially increased patrols and interdiction resulting in larger amounts of drugs being smuggled into the United States over land through Mexico. This has resulted in greater government corruption in Mexico and the formation of large violent organized crime groups. Each year there are hundreds of drug related homicides in Mexico, and the violence is beginning to leach into the United States in border towns in Texas, Arizona, New Mexico, and California. The Drug Enforcement Agency (DEA) reports that Mexican drug trafficking organizations now facilitate the movement of all types of contraband, including drugs, into the United States charging fees to originators. The Mexican drug cartels have become the gatekeepers for drugs coming through Mexico (White House, 2007).

Basically, interdiction has three intended consequences: (1) to increase the amount of personal and financial risk to suppliers, (2) reduce the amount and quality of drugs at the retail levels, and (3) increase the cost of drugs, thereby making them too expensive for some consumers. Interdiction amounts to attempting to seal the country's borders from drug traffickers through air, maritime, and land operations. The agencies principally involved in interdiction are the U.S. Coast Guard, the U.S. Customs and Border Protection (CBP) agency, and the Immigration and Customs Enforcement (ICE) agency. The Coast Guard patrols the coasts around the United States and attempts to intercept boats and ships that attempt to bring drugs into the country. The CBP is responsible for securing the vast land border between the United States and Mexico, an area into which large amounts of drugs are smuggled. The CBP is responsible for inspecting cargo that is exported to the United States, persons arriving or re-entering the country, and packages that are mailed to citizens in the United States. Interdiction of foreign drugs is a monumental task, and one that has had varying levels of success. Finally, the ICE is responsible for removing undocumented immigrants from the United States, especially those who have been convicted of crimes or who are engaged in drug trafficking.

Reuter (1990) and Wood, Tyndall, Spittal, Li, Anis, and Hogg (2003) examined our interdiction policies and concluded that they have little effect upon cocaine trafficking, which has been their primary target. Basically, it is physically impossible to secure vast borders, and as we concentrate on one geographic area, the smugglers will move their operations to another point on the border. Furthermore, as we implement new interdiction techniques, the smugglers alter the methods they use to smuggle their drugs. In the past, smugglers used smaller boats when the Coast Guard increased its efforts in southern Florida to interdict marijuana. When the federal government increased its sea efforts to deal with cocaine smuggling, the smugglers started using overland routes through Mexico. Interdiction is a cat-and-mouse game, with each player attempting to anticipate the other's next move and reacting to it. In the end, losses to traffickers as a result of drug seizures at the borders account for only about 15% of the cost of the drug (White House, 2003) (Box 12.2).

In addition to interdiction programs that attempt to stop drugs from entering the country, a number of police departments have deployed interdiction teams to prevent drugs from coming into their jurisdictions. In many cases, a number of departments will band together to form *multijurisdictional drug task forces*. This allows for the sharing of criminal intelligence, and it allows officers from one jurisdiction to work in other jurisdictions. This sometimes is important, especially if a department is small and most or all of the officers are known or recognizable in the community. Research indicates that these drug task forces are at best moderately effective. McGarrell and Schlegel (1993) found that they increase communications and cooperation between agencies, whereas Pratt, Frank, and Smith (2000) found that task force members felt that the arrangements improved their ability to combat drugs. Finally, Smith, Novak, and Frank (2000) and Mazerolle, Soole, and Rombouts (2007) found that departments involved in drug multijurisdictional task forces were no more likely to achieve their stated productivity (arrests and drug confiscations) as were departments not involved in multijurisdictional task forces. Thus, it appears that multijurisdictional tasks forces may improve cooperation among police departments, but they do not necessarily increase drug arrests. As indicated in Table 12.1, 35% of American police departments are involved in task forces with larger departments participating at a higher rate than smaller departments. Larger

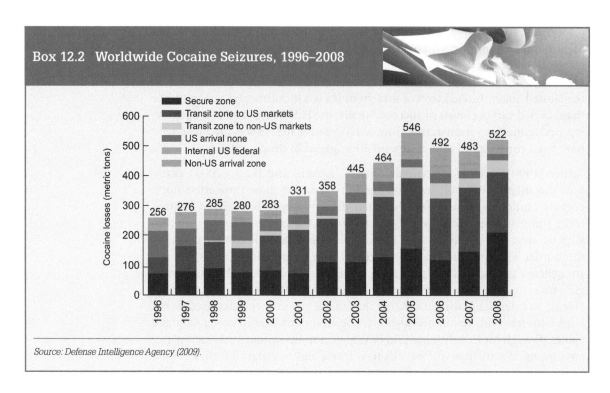

Box 12.2 Worldwide Cocaine Seizures, 1996–2008

Secure zone
Transit zone to US markets
Transit zone to non-US markets
US arrival none
Internal US federal
Non-US arrival zone

Cocaine losses (metric tons)

256, 276, 285, 280, 283, 331, 358, 445, 464, 546, 492, 483, 522

1996, 1997, 1998, 1999, 2000, 2001, 2002, 2003, 2004, 2005, 2006, 2007, 2008

Source: Defense Intelligence Agency (2009).

departments tend to assign more officers to the task forces as compared to smaller agencies. This is the result of larger cities having more difficult drug problems as compared to smaller jurisdictions, and the larger agencies having more personnel for such assignments.

It appears that interdiction effectively has little impact on the amount and market value of drugs (Kappeler & Potter, 2005). Arrests at points of interdiction would yield smugglers and low-level members of drug organizations who could easily be replaced. Finally, Reuter notes that 99% of the price of a drug is profits to the people who distribute it. Therefore, seizures of cocaine and other drugs coming into the United States would have little economic impact within the distribution chain.

Drug Prevention Programs

Research indicates that many youths tend to experiment with drugs. Most of today's prevention programs presuppose that such experimentation is the result of teens' insufficient knowledge of drugs' adverse consequences. Quite the contrary, however, this experimentation generally is the result of complex social relationships, especially with peers, and the social benefits derived from drug experimentation or usage may overshadow the

You can watch a video on the use of K-9 units for drug interdiction by going to: **http://www.youtube.com/ watch?v=SvPXmwBOlsk**.

Table 12.1 Drug Task Force Participation of Local Police Departments by Size of Population Served, 2007				
	Local Police Departments with Officers Assigned to a Multiagency Drug Task Force			
	Officers Assigned Full Time or Part Time		**Officers Assigned Full Time**	
Population Served	**Percent of Departments**	**Number of Officers**	**Percent of Departments**	**Number of Officers**
All sizes	35	13,409	24	8524
1,000,000 or more	100	1625	100	1620
500,000–999,999	94	843	90	747
250,000–499,999	98	367	96	360
100,000–249,999	83	1015	79	916
50,000–99,999	82	1189	77	1064
25,000–49,999	73	1483	62	1111
10,000–24,999	54	2147	41	1089
2500–9999	36	3392	17	1234
Under 2500	14	1348	8	382

Sources: Bureau of Justice Statistics (2010) and Local Police Departments (2007).

social, health, and criminal justice consequences of drug usage behavior. Many even view substance abuse as normal behavior. Drugs are embedded in many youths' culture. Therefore, drug prevention is not a simple matter, and programs based solely on the idea that sufficient knowledge leads to a reduction of drug usage are fatally flawed. Drug prevention strategies basically amount to drug education. There are several varieties of drug education: (1) *information dissemination*, (2) *fear arousal*, (3) *moral appeals*, and (4) *effective education*, that focuses on the personal and social enrichment of students (Botvin, 1990).

A number of years ago, the Bureau of Justice Assistance (1989) implemented a three-pronged drug reduction strategy that has remained as the vehicle for countering America's drug problem. The first strategy, drug use prevention campaigns, includes public service announcements, pamphlets, and other media presentations to assist in educating the public. Second, are those programs that include law enforcement involvement in citizen education. The premier program here has been *Drug Abuse Resistance Education* (DARE), which originated with the Los Angeles Police Department, and it involves educating fourth, fifth, and sixth graders about the perils of drug use. Approximately 80% of schools in the United States use the program.

It should be recognized that the program is expensive. It costs approximately $2000 to train an officer, and nationally the program costs between $1 billion and $1.3 billion each year (Shepard, 2001). This program is recognized as the premier drug education program, even though research indicates that it is ineffective in reducing drug use (General Accounting Office, 2003; Gorman, 2003).

Finally, community involvement programs are designed to involve community groups in the fight against drug abuse. *The National Drug Control Strategy* advocates this method for reducing drugs (White House, 2007), and the federal government has funded numerous community grants to this end. This strategy involves organizing parents, churches, schools, or other groups to raise drug education monies, to help disseminate information, or to conduct programs to establish drug-free communities. Community involvement programs are increasingly more popular as police agencies across the country adopt community policing. However, there is little evidence to suggest that these programs have any effect on drug usage, and some have labeled these programs a failure.

Drug education is an area that ultimately may have the greatest benefit for each dollar spent. Basically, drug education is an attempt to reduce the demand for drugs. If individuals no longer desire drugs, they will not buy them, they will not use them, and street sellers cannot tempt those individuals to abuse drugs. Ultimately, an effective drug control strategy must rest with demand reduction.

We should also consider developing prevention programs around specific drugs as opposed to attacking all drugs. For example, there is little credible evidence to suggest that marijuana presents abusers with health risks. Yet, we continue to attack it just as vehemently as we attack heroin, cocaine, or methamphetamine. This tactic lessens the credibility of our drug education and prevention programs. Perhaps it would be more effective to concentrate on those drugs that cause the greatest behavioral and health problems. In the long run, such a strategy should be much more effective, especially with younger drug abusers.

Drug Treatment

Drug treatment in the United States has been sorely neglected. There has been a great deal of hyperbole about the commitment to drug treatment, but the federal government has devoted relatively few resources to it. The basic reason is that enforcement is more appealing to most politicians and voters, irrespective of the relative effectiveness of either strategy. The American public is adopting increasingly more punitive attitudes toward the control of criminals in general, and many citizens perceive addicts or chronic drug abusers as people who are morally deficient; to spend money on treatment would be an unconscionable waste to society.

Regardless of perceptions, the problem remains, and an untreated drug addict is still someone who will continue to exact a toll on society. Conventional wisdom tells us that the levels of drug related crime, violence, and health problems are directly related to the number of addicts in our society, and the only way to lesson these social problems is to reduce the number of addicts and chronic drug abusers. This line of reasoning mandates that drug treatment be a significant component in any overall drug strategy (Box 12.3).

A variety of treatment programs have been developed in response to the drug problem. Programs have been developed for incarcerated inmates, probationers, and citizens who have not encountered the criminal justice system. Some of these programs depend on therapeutic community or group therapy, whereas others use individual counseling or individual support programs, such as those used to treat alcoholics. Methadone clinics have been established to treat heroin addicts, but methadone has been overly regulated to the point that most of America's heroin addicts are unable to obtain this type of treatment.

One of the more popular modes of drug treatment today is the drug court. Jurisdictions have developed varying standards for drug courts, but essentially give a drug arrestee the choice between incarceration and treatment. Most drug courts consist of three phases. First, the initial phase is where offenders are supervised via frequent meetings and drug testing to get them off drugs. Second, the treatment phase consists of a variety of treatment and education programs. Typical programs include counseling, job training, and General Educational Development or college courses. The treatment stage not only attempts to assist offenders with their drug problems, but also to build their life skills making them less prone to drug use. Finally, the follow-up stage is where offenders have successfully completed drug counseling or treatment, but are continuing their job training programs. As offenders progress from one stage to the next, the level of supervision is reduced, but they continue to be tested from drugs. Typical drug court programs last between 12 and 24 months. Sechrest (2003) found that drug courts are fairly effective in reducing or eliminating offenders' drug use. In fact, White House (2007) reported on one study that found that drug court graduates are rearrested at a rate of 16.4% during the first year of release, whereas drug offenders who did not go to drug court re-offended at a rate of 43.5%. Drug courts can significantly reduce re-offending.

> To learn more about the history of drugs in America and its relationship to organized crime, go to the Schaffer Library of Drug Policy at: **http://www.druglibrary. org/schaffer/govpubs/amhab/amhabc4. htm**.

Finally, it should be noted that we cannot expect drug treatment programs to completely cure addicts. Perhaps we should examine drug treatment in terms

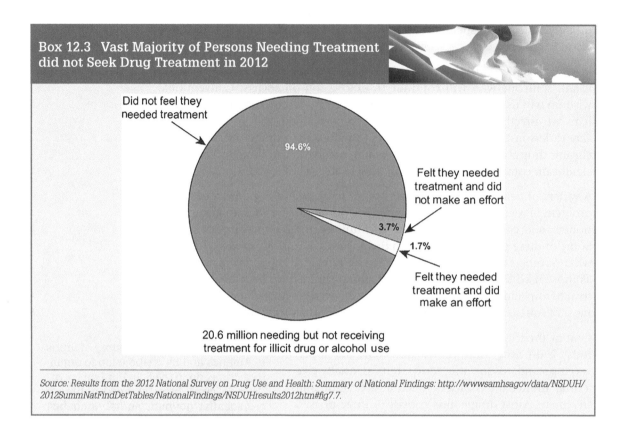

Box 12.3   Vast Majority of Persons Needing Treatment did not Seek Drug Treatment in 2012

Did not feel they needed treatment

94.6%

Felt they needed treatment and did not make an effort

3.7%

1.7%

Felt they needed treatment and did make an effort

20.6 million needing but not receiving treatment for illicit drug or alcohol use

Source: Results from the 2012 National Survey on Drug Use and Health: Summary of National Findings: http://wwwsamhsagov/data/NSDUH/2012SummNatFindDetTables/NationalFindings/NSDUHresults2012htm#fig7.7.

of "remission" and "improvement" as opposed to a total cure (Clear, Clear, & Braga, 2003). Also, treatment often focuses on improving addicts' life skills or ability to cope in society – an absolute necessity if a rehabilitated addict is to remain off drugs. The drug problem is quite intractable and success must be gauged in terms of incremental changes. That is, if a treatment program is able to keep persons off drugs for only a limited time, reduce the amount of drugs consumed, or improve the addict's ability to function within society, then it has been somewhat successful. Such benchmarks may not be acceptable to some, but one must consider alternative costs. Treatment is certainly less expensive than incarceration, and, in the long run, it may be more effective even with minute improvements in addict behavior.

THE ILLEGAL DRUG DELIVERY SYSTEM

There are numerous misconceptions about how drugs are sold or bartered on our streets. The term "drug dealer" often conjures images of Mafia underlings, Colombians, or inner-city gang members. The fact of the matter is, there are a number of individuals and groups whose livelihood depends on drug

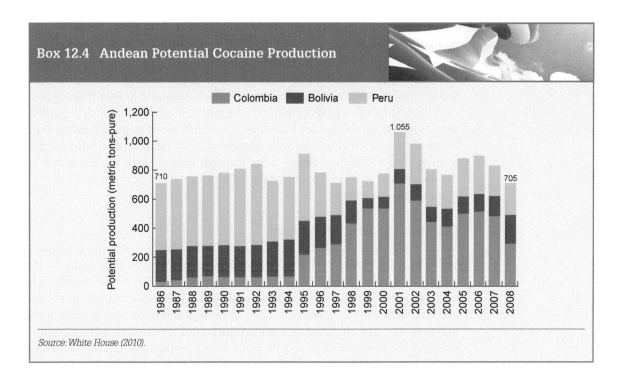

Box 12.4 Andean Potential Cocaine Production

Source: White House (2010).

trafficking. There are a variety of mechanisms and criminal organizations that are involved in the drug enterprise. This section explores the illegal drug delivery system in an effort to provide a better understanding of the enforcement problem facing our police forces.

In addition to the numerous drugs that are manufactured in this country, drugs are imported into the United States from all over the world. Heroin and other opiates come into the United States from Mexico, Afghanistan, Iran, Pakistan, Myanmar, Laos, and Thailand. Cocaine is manufactured from plants grown primarily in Bolivia and Peru and is exported into the United States chiefly by the Colombians. Marijuana was imported from Colombia, Jamaica, Mexico, and Thailand until relatively recently, when the United States developed its own substantial marijuana industry in states such as Hawaii, California, Oregon, and Kentucky (Box 12.4).

Criminal Organizations

A number of criminal organizations that are extensively involved in the drug business exist in this country. Some of these groups have operated for decades, such as the La Cosa Nostra or Mafia, whereas others, such as the Mexican Mafia, are relatively new. The following sections provide a brief description of these organizations and their modes of operation.

Colombian Drug Cartels

Perhaps the best-known drug related criminal organizations are the *Colombian drug cartels*. The Colombian cartels control the world's cocaine production and distribution. Although coca is grown in Peru, Bolivia, and Columbia, it is the Colombians who control its export, which amounts to hundreds of tons each year. The cartels have developed a number of safe havens, such as various islands in the Caribbean and countries in South and Central America, from which to ship their drugs into the United States. Today, most of the cocaine coming into the United States flows through Mexico with the assistance of the Mexican Mafia. The Mexican Mafia distributes most of the cocaine once it enters the United States.

Organized Criminal Groups

Historically, a great deal of drug trafficking in the United States was conducted by the *La Cosa Nostra* or *Mafia*. The Mafia was organized into families in the major cities across the United States. For example, the five families known to operate in New York City were the Gambino, Colombo, Lucchese, Bonanno, and Genovese families (Lyman, 2010). Although the government maintained that these families created a national criminal confederation ruled by a composition of the families, there is little evidence to support this theory. According to Albanese (2010), Albini (1971), and Block (1983), the families were not connected via governance, but the various families would work together on various business or criminal enterprises.

The Mafia was primarily involved in the importation, distribution, and sale of heroin in the country's major cities. The United States witnesses a drug revolution beginning in the 1960s and 1970s in which there was a market for a variety of drugs, including marijuana, LSD, cocaine, prescription drugs, and later methamphetamine. Numerous criminal organizations not associated with the traditional Mafia sprung up to provide drugs for this demand. Many had ties to the Colombian drug cartels and later with the Mexican Mafia. Today, there is a patchwork of criminal drug organizations across the country supplying a variety of drugs. Some are small, while others are quite large. Many of these organizations concentrate on individual drugs, such as marijuana, methamphetamine, cocaine, or ecstasy. These organizations are not organized crime in the traditional sense, but traditional organized crime, the Mafia, plays less a role in drug trafficking today. The Mafia, to a degree, has been supplanted by these newer, independent organizations.

Mexican Mafia

Mexico, like Colombia, has a number of drug cartels operating within its borders and in the United States. These cartels generally are referred to at the *Mexican Mafia*, but they are numerous with each vying for control of drug operations in specific geographic areas and often coming into conflict with one another. The Mexican Mafia started in the 1950s in California prisons where Mexican inmates banded together to protect themselves from other inmate groups. Over time, they evolved into large, complex criminal organizations, and today they exist throughout Mexico and many southern and southwestern states in this country.

The Mexican cartels initially served as "mules" for the Colombians transporting cocaine into the United States. Later, they expanded their operations to not only transporting cocaine, but also going directly to the source, often bypassing the Colombians. The Mexican Mafia also manufactures and distributes large quantities of methamphetamine and heroin in Mexico and the United States. They have deployed elaborate smuggling operations, including building tunnels into the United States from several border towns.

The hallmark of the Mexican Mafia is its violence and corruption. There is no organized crime group operating in the United States that is more prone to using violence, and Mexican Mafia's propensity for violence rivals the Medellin cartel's level of violence in its heyday in the 1970s and 1980s. For example, in 1993, Mexican Mafia henchmen were accused of killing a Roman Catholic Cardinal. Other high-profile murders include a Tijuana police chief, a Mexican federal prosecutor, Tijuana's federal prosecutor, and a Mexican presidential candidate. In 1997, Amado Carillo-Fuentes, who used a fleet of Boeing 727s to transport drugs from Colombia, was killed sparking a war that resulted in at least 60 deaths. Today, the violence and corruption continues to escalate and is leaching across the border into U.S. border cities. Many police and military personnel are connected to the Mexican organized crime groups.

Outlaw Motorcycle Gangs

Outlaw motorcycle gangs have their origin in California where a group of World War II veterans formed the Pissed-Off Bastards of Bloomington shortly after the war. In 1946, about 750 members almost destroyed Hollister, California, after authorities there refused to release one of their members who had been arrested. The havoc was later depicted in the movie The Wild One, which starred Marlon Brando. In the beginning, the motorcycle gangs were seen as mechanisms by which participants could let off steam.

Today, there are motorcycle gangs all across the United States. There are four primary motorcycle gangs with a combined total of 850 chapters and more than 8000 members in the United States. These motorcycle gangs have emerged with their own unique geographic territories. The Hells Angels, although located throughout the western part of the United States, primarily are in California. The Hells Angels currently have between 500 and 600 members with their "Mother Chapter" located in Oakland, California. They are the oldest and probably the wealthiest motorcycle gang. The *Outlaws* were formed in Chicago in 1959 and later absorbed the Canadian *Satan's Choice* gang in 1977. This created the country's largest gang, with approximately 1200–1500 members in 31 chapters. The Outlaws have chapters in Canada and throughout the Midwestern and southern United States. The *Pagans* were established in Prince George's County, Maryland, in 1959. The Pagans have approximately 700–800 members in 44 chapters located between New York and Florida. Finally, the *Bandidos* was formed in Houston in 1966 and currently has approximately 500 members in chapters as far away as Washington State and South Dakota (Lyman, 2010).

Although involved in a number of criminal enterprises, the primary business of the motorcycle gangs is the production, distribution, and sale of methamphetamine. Their members are extremely fraternal, which makes police infiltration very difficult. Entry into a gang usually entails the commission of some criminal act that also assists in keeping police officers out of the ranks and ensures that members do not later become informants. They also depend on violence and the threat of violence as tools to ensure that members remain loyal.

Law enforcement only recently has been able to gain more information about the various gangs' activities because of inter-gang conflicts and wars and from members who feared that their days in the gang were numbered. Still, however, law enforcement has little real intelligence information that can be used to break up the gangs.

Youth Street Gangs

Youth gangs have been a part of our nation's inner cities for decades, but only recently have they become so violent and menacing. Although long involved in criminal activities, it has been only relatively recent that the gangs have become heavily involved in drug trafficking. The violence and drug trafficking activities of youth gangs have become critical problems for law enforcement.

The National Youth Gang Survey reports that there are approximately 27,900 gangs with 774,000 members in the United States (Egley, Howell, & Moore, 2010). The two most infamous youth gangs are the *Crips* and the *Bloods*, which originated in Los Angeles. Each of these gangs is composed of smaller gangs called "sets." Law enforcement officials estimate that there are approximately 190 Crips sets and 65 Bloods sets with a combined membership of approximately 25,000 members. Crips and Bloods now have substantial membership in a number of major cities throughout the country and are ever-spreading eastward. For example, Denver police have documented 700 members in the Denver area. The Bloods were even found in Sioux Falls, South Dakota (population 100,000).

These gangs have their own distinct organization. Although gangs consist of similar elements, they remain very loosely organized:

> The sets are structured along lines of seniority and function. They have caste-like subdivisions within each set, notably (1) original gang members; (2) gangsters, the hard-core members, whose ages range from 16 to 22; (3) baby gangsters, who are between nine and 12; and (4) in some cases, tiny gangsters, who are even younger. Although some age groups go to the late 20s and early 30s, the most violent and active members are those between 14 and 18, many of them "wanna-bes" who want to prove themselves in order to be accepted by other gang members and who are precisely the ones most useful as soldiers in gang activities (Attorney General, 1989, p. 33).

The Crips and Bloods focus on the sale of crack and cocaine. They use a variety of techniques, including heavily fortified "rock houses," spotters who direct customers to waiting salespersons, and sales from motel rooms. Because most urban police departments are concentrating on crack houses, the Crips and Bloods are increasingly using motel rooms, which can be changed frequently in order to thwart law enforcement efforts. The Crips and Bloods are extremely violent and have constant turf wars in most jurisdictions where both gangs reside. This has created another serious law enforcement problem, the killing of innocent bystanders.

Even though the Crips and Bloods receive the greatest attention from the news media and law enforcement, there are a number of other gangs in the United States. The *Vice Lords* and *El-Rukins* are the primary gangs in Chicago and, in combination with the Crips and Bloods, they supply crack to the Minneapolis-St. Paul area. Gangs from Los Angeles and Detroit control approximately 60% of the crack business in Cleveland, Toledo, and Akron. The *Miami Boys* operate out of Florida and have spread their operations into the Atlanta area. There are smaller, local gangs in most large cities throughout the United States (Figure 12.2).

Four caveats relative to youth gangs and drugs must be established. First, government and police officials have sustained considerable efforts to portray gangs as highly organized and structured, but the opposite is more accurate. For the most part, they have an unstable, erratic membership. Youth gangs are loosely defined and organized with a steady succession of leadership and membership. Gang leaders are a constant target for law enforcement and for leaders of other gangs who are intent on exacting revenge. Moreover, leadership can best be described as pluralistic, with a variety of set or group leaders within each gang. Members come and go with members' levels of commitment and association varying over time (Ruble & Turner, 2001).

FIGURE 12.2

A youth whose street name is Inkman is asked by Los Angeles County Sheriff Sgt. Rick Mejia, right, to reveal his Los Angeles gang tattoos in Compton, California, on February 3, 2009. He is wearing a blue baseball cap with the Angels logo. Blue is usually the Crips gang color, while an "A" could mean the Acacia clique. *Photograph Courtesy of AP Photo/Damian Dovarganes.*

Second, the majority of violence associated with youth gangs is not the result of drug wars, but it has more to do with turf and disrespect. Antagonism among gangs is the result of movement and insults by gang members on another gang's turf. When gang members wear their colors, give their own gang signs, or paint their gang graffiti in another gang's area, it invites a violent response from the home gang. To some extent, violence is reduced to ritualistic behavior where members commit violent acts as a part of the gang's creed (Howell & Decker, 2003; Hunt & Liadler, 2004).

Third, the police tend to overuse the gang label. That is, the police tend to label people gang members who are not. Klein (1971, p. 13) defined gangs as: a group who (1) are generally perceived as a distinct aggregation by others in the neighborhood, (2) recognize themselves as a denotable group (almost invariably with a group name), and (3) have been involved in a sufficient number of incidents to call forth a consistent negative response from neighborhood residents and/or law enforcement agencies.

The police tend to label any youth, especially if they are minority, a gang member if they have problems with them. Essentially, the police have been involved in constructing or exaggerating social problems with gang activities. Such social construction is counterproductive because it precludes the police from adopting nongang juvenile programs, and it tends to unjustly label some juveniles as gangsters or troublemakers (Esbensen, Winfree, He, & Taylor, 2004). At a minimum, the above three criteria must be present if a gang actually exists.

Fourth, the potency and ability of youth gangs as purveyors of drugs has been grossly overstated by law enforcement officials and the media (Rengert, 1998). We have created, to a great extent, a panic as a result of our gang pronouncements. Even though youth drug gangs are present in a variety of cities, functionally, they remain little more than street level retailers (Decker, Bynum, & Weisel, 2004). Dunston (1990, p. 7) best summarizes the situation:

> … drugs are controlled by organized crime groups. Young, weak, undermanned, and poorly organized street gangs cannot compete with the older more powerful and violent groups. The fragmented street gangs do not have the network or the power to distribute or control drugs on a large scale. What we see are drug organizations employing youths in various aspects of their drug business…. The primary difference between a drug organization and a youth gang is that in a drug organization all members are employees while youth gang membership only requires affiliation. We do not see our youth gangs become drug organizations.

Clearly, Dunston makes an important point. Although youth gangs are often portrayed and perceived as being rather ferocious, they generally remain small-time players relative to other drug trafficking organizations.

Along these same lines, much has been said about gangs' abilities to spread from city to city. In fact, it appears that the gangs, particularly the Bloods and Crips, have developed and implemented a clear strategy by which to take over drug markets in other cities. This spread, however, appears to be little more than happenstance (Maxson, 1998). Starbuck, Howell, and Lindquist (2004) point out that youth gang members are not worldly nor do they possess substantial life skills. The spread of gangs has generally occurred when members, along with family or close friends, move to another city and discover an opportunity to sell drugs as opposed to a predetermined bureaucratic plan. Youth gang members clearly do not have the skills to effectively move from one locale to another. Generally, the police are facing localized gangs who have established business relations with gangs from other cities.

Youth gangs remain a police problem. However, it must be noted that the problem is not as critical as commonly thought or portrayed. The best strategies for dealing with youth gangs and drugs are localized efforts to thwart dealing, target gang leaders for arrest, and interdict drugs as they come into the jurisdiction. Constant pressure is the best way of dealing with youth gangs (see Sanders, 1994).

DRUG ENFORCEMENT TECHNIQUES AND PROGRAMS

The nation's drug problem has placed extreme pressures on law enforcement. Parents are afraid that their children will become addicted; drug related crimes have increased significantly; and violence involving individuals in the drug world, as well as innocent bystanders, has increased dramatically. It seems that each time the police devise a new strategy to counter some facet of the drug problem, the drug smugglers and dealers react with changes in their business practices and operations to thwart the police. Fighting the drug war is analogous to a chess game, with each side reacting to the other's previous moves and continuously contemplating the other's impending moves. Policing drugs is extremely complicated, with the police, at best, attempting to control the problem rather than having any hope of eliminating it.

Given the current situation and the fact that the problem cannot be eliminated, the police must establish priorities to guide planning and decision-making. Priorities for specific police agencies will vary because the problems confronting each community are different. However, Moore and Kleiman (2003, p. 248) have identified six goals that are useful in ordering police operations:

1. Reduce the gang violence associated with drug trafficking and prevent the emergence of powerful organized criminal groups;
2. Control the street crimes committed by drug users;
3. Improve the health and economic and social well-being of drug users;
4. Restore the quality of life in urban communities by ending street-level drug dealing;
5. Help to prevent children from experimenting with drugs;
6. Protect the integrity of criminal justice institutions.

The police have developed a number of law enforcement strategies over the years that, whether used independently or in combination, have resulted in varying levels of success. The police have altered their approaches to the drug war and have adopted more aggressive tactics. The following sections will describe, evaluate, and provide examples of how these various strategies have been implemented.

Attacking High-Level Distributors

Attacking the *high-level drug kingpins,* or "Mr. Big," is a much-discussed topic in political and law enforcement circles. Many believe that if the high-level distributors were arrested or their activities disrupted, it would unsettle large drug distribution and sales networks at the street level. Drugs would become more difficult to obtain, users would have to pay higher prices for their drugs, and overall, drug consumption would decrease. It is assumed that only the kingpins have the elaborate smuggling and transshipment operations to deliver drugs to our cities and towns. Also, there is a great deal of public demand for law enforcement officials to focus on these people. It seems reasonable to the public that the police should focus on those who are getting rich at the expense of our wasted youth. When police only arrest street peddlers, public confidence is eroded and charges of corruption or incompetence usually are forthcoming.

For the most part, law enforcement at the drug distributor level has been left to the federal agencies, such as the FBI and DEA, which have the resources, technical skills, and the investigative expertise to operate the expensive, time-consuming investigations required to go after the kingpins. Kleiman and Smith (1990, pp. 82–83) summarize how federal law enforcement approaches the problem:

> … long term, high level undercover operations; developing informants, often by making cases against low-level dealers which can then be bargained away in return for their help against their suppliers ("working up the chain"); searching through police files, financial records, telephone logs, and the like to demonstrate connections; and, most powerful but most expensive, electronic surveillance (wiretaps and, less frequently, bugs).

Regardless of the method used, investigating the higher-level distributors and smugglers is extremely expensive, requiring large numbers of personnel and equipment over extended periods of time. Local and state agencies often do not have the resources for such long-term investigations and must depend on federal assistance.

Perhaps the best known and probably one of the most effective investigative techniques for dealing with high-level drug operatives has been the *Racketeer Influenced and Corrupt Organizations Statute* (RICO). The RICO statute was passed as a part of the *Organized Crime Control Act of 1970*. The statute makes it a crime to conspire with others to commit specific serious crimes: murder, kidnapping, gambling, arson, robbery, bribery, extortion, or trafficking in narcotics or dangerous drugs. All the prosecution must show in these cases is that the defendant participated in at least two such crimes in a 10-year period. The prosecution need not show that the defendant knew the other participants, only that he or she participated in a criminal organization. Because dealing drugs consists of an organization and the seller must obtain the drugs from another source, or the smuggler must move the drugs to shippers and sellers, RICO cases are fairly simple to establish when drugs are involved. The RICO statute has significant penalties, up to 20 years imprisonment on each count.

Another enforcement technique increasingly being used at all levels, but particularly at the Mr. Big level, is asset *forfeiture*. For example, in 2006, the U.S.

Department of Justice Asset Forfeiture Program controlled $1.33 billion in assets as a result of asset forfeiture. As shown in Table 12.2, local police departments in the United States received more than $320 million in 1999 as a result of asset forfeiture. Money generated through the asset forfeiture programs oftentimes is used by police agencies to support additional drug investigative and enforcement operations. In some cases, police departments have come to rely on asset forfeiture funds as a part of their budget, which results in pressure on departments to continually acquire funds through this channel.

There are two types of forfeiture; criminal and civil (see Worrall, 2003). States have differing versions of forfeiture statutes, so there is little uniformity among them. The types of property that often are seized include:

1. Contraband, such as controlled substances that are illegal to possess.
2. Derivative contraband, which includes conveyances used to transport contraband, such as aircraft, vessels, and vehicles.
3. Direct proceeds, such as cash.
4. Derivative proceeds, such as real estate or stock. Vehicles and cash are the most frequently seized assets; however, units of government are becoming more active in seizing real property, such as homes, farms, or businesses when used in the drug business because of their high dollar return to the unit of government (Stellwagon, 1985, p. 5).

Table 12.2 Drug Asset Forfeiture Receipts of Local Police Departments by Size of Population Served, 2006

| Population Served | Percent of Departments with Receipts | Value of Money, Goods, and Property Received | | |
		Total	Per Department[1]	Per Sworn Officer[1]
All sizes	33	$307,542,062	$73,200	$1033
1,000,000 or more	62	$23,742,200	$2,802,100	$644
500,000–999,999	74	$25,906,900	$1,063,500	$703
250,000–499,999	89	$36,392,300	$838,100	$1218
100,000–249,999	89	$50,931,700	$298,500	$1028
50,000–99,999	82	$61,684,200	$175,000	$1385
25,000–49,999	68	$37,804,500	$64,300	$967
10,000–24,999	57	$40,211,500	$38,800	$1135
2500–9999	33	$15,537,400	$11,300	$743
Under 2500	12	$15,331,200	$25,300	$3388

Note: Table based on asset forfeiture receipts during calendar 2006. The value of goods and property is based on estimates provided by reporting agencies. Computation of per officer averages includes both full-time and part-time employees, with a weight of 0.5 assigned to part-time employees.
[1]Excludes departments without receipts.
Sources: Bureau of Justice Statistics (2010) and Local Police Departments (2007).

Criminal forfeiture is applicable only after a successful criminal prosecution. If the government can show that the defendant used the property in the commission of a crime or obtained the property by using the profits from the crime, the government can initiate criminal forfeiture proceedings. *Civil forfeiture*, on the other hand, does not require a criminal conviction. In fact, civil forfeiture can be initiated without a criminal prosecution. Civil forfeiture is brought against the property itself. If the property was used in the commission of a crime or was obtained through illegal profits, it can be seized civilly.

Police use of civil forfeiture has led to a number of problems. First and foremost, the police have, on occasion, initiated civil forfeiture against individuals who were not involved in the drug business or other criminal enterprises. For example, Indiana police attempted to seize a house because a previous owner (two owners removed) had bought it with drug money. The current owner had no knowledge of the history nor was he involved in any criminal activity. The police have seized large sums of money from citizens and forced them to prove that the money was not derived as a result of illegal activities, something that can be done as a result of civil forfeiture. In these instances, the rule of law has circumvented our basic idea of justice.

A second problem is that police agencies have developed drug strategies with the specific intention of increasing asset forfeiture activity. Small sheriff and police departments now have drug units patrolling interstate highways with a goal of forfeiture. They have a stated goal of interdicting drugs, but many of them have a real goal of increasing asset forfeiture. Police routinely stop anyone remotely fitting a drug profile, which means that minorities are increasingly being unjustly hassled by the police. Forfeiture has also resulted in increased police corruption in which police officers keep assets that are seized or, in some cases, keep money and drugs without arresting offenders (Miller & Selva, 1997). Asset forfeiture has turned policing into a high stakes business where the goal of drug control has sometimes been lost.

Going after the high-level distributors, although appealing to our basic instincts, may have little effect on the drug market itself. That is, the drug operation controlled by Mr. Big may not be disrupted. Mr. Big most certainly will have lieutenants who might easily take Mr. Big's place once he is convicted and no longer able to control his operations. Second, there are always other organizations ready and willing to fill any market void (e.g., as occurred when several of the Colombian drug cartels were dismantled). That is, there are always new marketing organizations starting and older ones are ever-attempting to expand. Even if Mr. Big and his organization were eliminated, the void may only be momentary. Finally, enforcement techniques may only be successful on the less well-organized or amateurish organizations. The drug business, after all, is predicated on the survival of the fittest. Enforcement may help to strengthen the better-organized cartels or organizations and enable them to control increasingly larger portions of the market making them more dangerous. Thus, it is not entirely clear how effective high-level enforcement efforts are in reducing drug availability.

Drug Enforcement at the Retail Level

Drug enforcement at the various retail levels is a primary responsibility of local and state police organizations. Typically, the tactics used include *undercover operations*, the use of *informants*, and *buy-bust sweeps* in which officers attempt to purchase drugs from dealers and then arrest them. These operations sometimes result in a series of cases whereby arrests are made up the distribution line in an attempt to arrest the higher-level dealers and suppliers. Primary responsibility for drug enforcement generally is vested with a special drug unit. Table 12.3 shows the distribution of drug units by size of department. A higher percentage of larger departments have these units and assign larger numbers of officers to them.

Enforcement at the *retail* or *street level* serves a number of purposes. First and foremost, it is aimed at making drug transactions riskier and more inconvenient,

Table 12.3 Special Units for Drug Enforcement in Local Police Departments by Size of Population Served

	Full-Time Unit for Drug Enforcement		
	Number of Full-Time Officers		
Population Served	Percent (%) of Agencies	Total	Average[1]
All sizes	18	12,212	6
1,000,000 or more	88	337	233
500,000–999,999	97	1199	32
250,000–499,999	93	964	25
100,000–249,999	83	1791	12
50,000–99,999	66	1545	6
25,000–49,999	43	1025	3
10,000–24,999	26	1040	2
2500–9999	14	833	2
Under 2500	6	440	1

[1]*Excludes agencies not having a unit with full-time officers.*
Sources: BJS (2006) and Hickman and Reeves (2006).

which, in turn, leads to reduced drug consumption. Left unchecked, drug dealing would become increasingly indiscreet, which would result in additional usage and increases in associated criminal activity. Street enforcement programs in this regard are aimed at inconveniencing the user as well as the dealer. Second, street level drug enforcement leads to safer neighborhoods. Drug dealing, associated criminality, and other problems naturally cluster in specific geographic areas within jurisdictions. This concentration of the drug problem causes residents to have extremely high levels of fear, victimization, and isolation. Police street level drug enforcement programs are aimed at alleviating these problems at least temporarily. Finally, street level enforcement produces the arrest statistics and public visibility that police departments and units of government produce to pacify the public and prove that action is being taken (Reinarman & Levine, 1989).

In the past, police street drug operations have been expansive, sporadic, and nondirected. Arrests were made wherever officers could make the arrests. Drug enforcement essentially was a part of extensive street enforcement programs where officers had little tolerance when drugs were encountered as the result of traffic stops, drunk arrests, or other street stops. Enforcement amounted to the random selection and arrest of offenders, which basically had little impact on the problem because of the sheer volume of offenders that always remained in the community. The goal of these operations was to produce large numbers of arrests that were used for political leverage. If the numbers were high, the police department was deemed effective.

As the drug problem became more pronounced, police departments began to focus their efforts. They developed strategies and tactics that were designed to attack specific problems or hot spots, or at least to have more of an impact on the areas or populations with the greatest problems. Before discussing specific strategies, it should be noted that there are different types of drug markets, and the police should tailor their enforcement efforts based on the nature of the drug market being addressed. Rengert (2003) has identified four types of drug marketplaces. First, there are *mutual societies*, which entail a group of friends or acquaintances selling to each other. Mutual societies are most commonly found at teen hangouts or parties. A significant amount of Ecstasy and other club drugs are distributed by mutual societies. Second, *periodic markets* are distribution points where sales are made at limited times. Examples include rock concerts, areas near schools where dealers sell drugs to students before and after class, or around movie theaters during evening hours. Third, *fixed-site neighborhood sales* are locations where a trafficker constantly sells drugs. Examples include liquor stores or bars, crack houses, and street corners. Finally, *drug marts* are locations that are out of control where large numbers of dealers hawk their drugs and are usually located in entertainment districts, high crime areas, or public spaces.

Traditional Enforcement

Responsibility for drug enforcement traditionally was housed in a specialized drug unit. Detectives assigned to the unit identify drug dealers and problem areas and then attempt to make cases. Tactics primarily included buy-bust and reverse sting operations. *Buy-busts* occur when undercover officers attempt to buy drugs from dealers and then arrest the dealer. *Reverse stings* are when undercover officers pose as drug dealers and arrest customers who attempt to purchase drugs from them. Buy-busts remove dealers, while reverse stings remove customers. Both tactics can be used to alleviate problems in specific areas. Mazerolle et al. (2007) found that these enforcement tactics had little impact on drug and crime problems, but they may be useful when coupled with other enforcement strategies.

Another traditional tactic is *raids*. Here, the police raid locations, such as crack houses and residences, and commercial establishments, such as hotels and clubs where drugs are sold. These fixed-site operations often are responsible for large numbers of drug sales. Cohen, Gorr, and Singh (2003) found that raids had short-term effects on drugs and crime in an area. It appears that for raids to be effective over the long term, they must be followed by tactics that focus on drug trafficking in the immediate area.

Another traditional tactic commonly used is to offer lenient sentences to drug dealers who cooperate with the police by assisting in the arrest of other drug dealers. Usually for this to occur, the arrested dealer must facilitate the arrest of several other dealers or dealers at higher levels in the drug trafficking organization.

Gang Strategies

As discussed above, perhaps the most frightening and troublesome part of the nation's drug problem has been the emergence of drug gangs. Many of these gangs operate openly and in complete defiance of law enforcement. There is an abundance of violence and criminality associated with the various drug gangs and their activities. Also, as discussed in Chapter 10, fear of crime is almost as debilitating as actual victimization, and the appearance of drug gangs has substantially increased citizens' level of fear.

Given the problems posed by youth gangs, many departments have established gang units. Huff and McBride (1990) noted that gang units engaged in four different functions: (1) intelligence, (2) enforcement and supervision, (3) investigation, and (4) prevention. The emphasis placed on these functions varies from department to department. Webb and Katz (2003) examined several gang units and found them to be loosely organized, responding primarily to specific incidents as opposed to adhering to an over-arching strategy. Gang unit officers tended to be more reactive than proactive. Even though they gathered intelligence, it seldom resulted in a cohesive plan. The gang units also tended to isolate themselves from the rest of the department, which restricted the sharing of information. Community policing dictates that gang units work with other police units and focus on significant gang problems as opposed to garnering arrests or bean counting. Decker and Curry (2003) note that gang suppression must be linked with gang prevention if it is to be successful. Results from any suppression program will be short-lived unless there is a prevention program to help sustain the decrease in gang and drug activities.

You can view a video about gangs and the LAPD at: **http://www.youtube.com/watch?v=Vp8VmyhlUek**.

Another innovative program to deal with gang violence and drug trafficking was Boston's *Operation Nightlight*. A predecessor program to Nightlight was *Operation Ceasefire*. Ceasefire was an effort by the Boston police to reduce gang violence by reducing the number of guns in gang members' possession. The police focused on people selling guns to gang members and established a strong deterrence to gang violence by quickly making arrests. When Ceasefire started, 60% of Boston's homicides were attributable to gangs.

Ceasefire evolved into Nightlight when the Boston police forged a working relationship with the probation department. Police probation teams patrolled the city responding to gang related crime and violence. The teams used a *pulling levers strategy* where they used police and probation sanctions to deal with violent gang members. Many of the gang members who were causing problems were on probation. When they came to the attention of the Nightlight teams, probation sanctions were used to intensify supervision: longer probation time, increased home visits by officers, changes in supervision terms, and special prosecution. McDevitt, Braga, Nurge, and Buerger (2003) found that Nightlight had a significant impact on violence. Subsequently, Nightlight has been adopted by a number of jurisdictions across the country.

Another innovative gang strategy is *civil gang injunctions* (CGIs), which has been used in a number of jurisdictions in California (Maxson, Hennigan, & Sloane, 2003). CGIs are usually precipitated by an outbreak of gang violence. Once a problem occurs, the police work with prosecutors to obtain a civil injunction preventing gang members from associating with one another. In some cases, association is prohibited anywhere in the jurisdiction, whereas in other cases it may limit association in certain areas of the jurisdiction (e.g., where gang violence or drug trafficking has been occurring). Maxson, Hennigan, and Sloane (2005) found that CGIs were popular with citizens because it gave the appearance of combating gang problems. CGIs also tend to reduce citizens' fear of crime. However, there is scant evidence that they are effective in combating gang problems.

Citywide Street Sweeps

Citywide drug sweeps have been one of the most common reactions to increases in drug problems. *Street sweeps* amount to an increase in visible police activity in the target areas. Here, the police attempt to apply the greatest amount of pressure possible to all avenues of the street drug market. Suppression through arrests or the threat of arrest is the goal of such programs. The police attempt to disrupt open drug sales by forcing sellers to move indoors or making them frequently move to other locations so that buyers have difficulty finding their dealers. Tactics commonly used by the police include an increased presence through patrols, buy-busts, observing and arresting dealers and buyers during transactions, and arresting or "hassling" users or customers when they enter an area known for street drug dealing.

Street sweeping and repression tactics are being used increasingly by departments. Like other programs, there is some question as to the utility of street sweeping programs. Critics charge that only the small-quantity street dealers are arrested as a result of street sweeping while the distributors are left untouched. Thus, the programs commonly have little impact on the high-level distributors, and the distributors remain in a position to recruit more street dealers. They also charge that the programs merely displace the problem from one area to another. When things get "too hot" in one area, the dealers set up shop somewhere else, or the dealers will start using another method to sell their drugs, such as eliminating the use of crack houses and starting to deal out of hotel rooms. Moreover, police departments do not have the resources to maintain street sweeping for long periods of time. In some cases, the drug dealers lay low until the intensified enforcement ends. Critics argue that the anticipated disruption in the drug operations as a result of police operations often only amounts to a minor inconvenience to dealers and buyers (Kleiman & Smith, 1990). Finally, critics warn that some of the tactics deployed by the police often violate suspects' and innocent bystanders' civil rights, which later may lead to negative repercussions.

To read more about community antidrug efforts, go to the National Criminal Justice Reference Service at: **http://ncjrs.org/txtfiles/anti.txt**.

However, Sherman (1990) argues that such tactics may have residual effects. Street sweeping disrupts and confuses the drug marketplace, even if it is only for a short period of time. Sherman found that dealers and potential buyers avoid swept areas for extended periods of time after a street sweeping or crackdown. It may be that total recovery from a street sweeping may take at least several months. Therefore, a series of crackdowns in an area may indeed be effective. That is, the police should plan a series of sweeps using various tactics in an area. Collectively, the street sweeps might have a sustained effect on drug sales.

Neighborhood Crackdowns

Neighborhood crackdowns are similar to street sweeps, except that the police usually identify hot spots as areas that deserve concentrated long-term attention. Neighborhood crackdowns are necessary when drugs suddenly begin to enter a neighborhood in large quantities, or when, after several years of marginal drug sales, the dealing escalates and becomes open, the level of criminality and victimization increases substantially, or when the residents become so fearful of the conditions in the neighborhood that they are afraid to leave their homes. These conditions generally prompt the police to institute a crackdown.

Smith (2001) examined a neighborhood crackdown in Richmond, Virginia, where large numbers of officers were assigned to a 50-block area for 1 month. Police officers were joined by code enforcement officers and maintenance workers to clean up the area. Strict enforcement was coupled with efforts to clean up the neighborhood. The increased enforcement resulted in a significant decline in the amount of crime in the target area. Moreover, crime was not displaced to other areas, and crime fell in some areas immediately surrounding the target area. Unfortunately, 6 months after the program, crime rates approximated pre-crackdown rates, indicating, as Sherman (1990) suggested, that a series of random crackdowns might be more effective than individual crackdowns.

In a similar study, Popkin and her associates (1995) examined the impact of street sweeps in two Chicago public housing areas. Authorities first swept the buildings and attempted to eliminate as much crime as possible. The second phase of the program consisted of security and tenant patrols. These patrols attempted to provide better guardianship and management over public areas to reduce crime and drug trafficking opportunities. A third component consisted of drug prevention and treatment services. Some of the programs initiated were Narcotics Anonymous groups, "Just Say No" clubs, tutoring programs, and Boy and Girl Scout programs. Residents reported positive gains in a number of areas, including perceived violence in and around the facilities, a perception of reduced drugs, and a more positive perception of social and security programs at the facilities. Unfortunately, the study did not report the program's impact on actual criminal and drug trafficking activities.

However, Weisburd and Green (1995) examined a similar program in Jersey City where neighborhood crackdowns were coupled with police surveillance. A total of 56 high-crime and drug trafficking hot spots were identified through crime analysis mapping. Each hot spot was assigned to a team who was charged with attacking the problem. Typically, the teams would conduct a series of mini-crackdowns to reduce the problem. To ensure that the problem remained under control, patrol officers were instructed to enhance patrol time and enforcement. Detectives were assigned to monitor the area and determine if additional enforcement actions were needed. Weisburd and Green report that the program resulted in a reduction in drug trafficking, and the enforcement actions did not seem to displace the problem to other areas of the city. This study demonstrates that for drug enforcement to be effective, police departments must apply several strategies in tandem over a period of time.

Public Housing and Drugs

Historically, public housing has experienced some of the most severe drug and crime problems (Fleisher, 1995). The problems have been so difficult that in some instances the police have referred to housing projects as "jungles" (McInerney, 1988). However, Mazerolle and Terrill (1997) caution that we should not condemn public housing too quickly. They found that, although public housing had high levels of crime and drugs, the problems often are concentrated in a small number of public housing dwellings or units. In the past, the police only provided nominal service to residents. The advent of problem-solving and community policing provided the police an impetus to retake these areas and instill law and order.

The police have tried a wide range of tactics in public housing, and, indeed, public housing has served as the proving grounds for many new police programs. The street sweeping tactics discussed above were often implemented in public housing, and they usually are a prelude to other more long-term programs. Other tactics were also used. Most notably, many jurisdictions implemented *zero-tolerance eviction programs* (Webster & Connors, 1992). Although different cities used a variety of approaches, essentially, when a resident of public housing was arrested for any drug charge, the resident and his or her family were evicted and barred from public housing. Not only could they not live there, in some jurisdictions, they were not allowed to visit other residents once evicted. Critics of eviction noted that the program perhaps punished innocent persons who were not involved in drugs. Proponents noted that eviction of only the wrongdoer was ineffective because he or she ultimately would sneak back, and the eviction would become meaningless. They also noted that such a strict policy forced family members to assume some measure of responsibility for other family members.

A number of departments have instituted no trespassing programs. Essentially, the public housing areas were "posted," and when the police encounter a stranger or suspicious person who is not a resident, they can initiate trespass charges. In some cases, they warn the trespassers and place charges after subsequent violations. Public housing has always been a magnet for drug trafficking and other types of crime, and trespass laws provide the police a tool with which to deal with nonresident criminals who generally constitute a large part of the problem. Enforcement of trespass laws not only enables the police to remove undesirables from the area, they also provide a deterrent.

Most police departments, as a result of community policing, have taken measures to "clean up" public housing. Historically, public housing has deteriorated into ill-kept areas wrought with crime and disorder. Police departments have made efforts to physically clean up public housing as well as clean up the crime. In terms of physical clean ups, the police have begun to more strictly enforce trash ordinances. They have forced the removal of abandoned and junk vehicles, and generally began to cause more building codes to be enforced. Such actions are rooted in Wilson and Kelling (1982) "Broken Windows" philosophy. If neighborhoods are clean and well kept, it projects an image that its residents are willing to take actions against criminality and acts of disorder.

In terms of cleaning up crime in public housing, the police have become more judicious in their enforcement actions. Historically, the police would ignore numerous minor violations, especially in poorer neighborhoods. Violations ranging from panhandling to public drunkenness to drug trafficking were ignored. The police disregarded many violations that they otherwise would enforce in more affluent neighborhoods. Today, many police departments are enforcing these violations.

Third-Party Policing

Another tactic in dealing with the drug problem is third-party policing. *Third-party policing* is where the police attack a drug or crime problem by attempting to engage third parties who have a vested interest in the crime or people involved in criminal activity. According to Buerger and Mazerolle (1998), it is the systematic integration of civil remedies into law enforcement that enables the police to better control the actions of potential lawbreakers, victims, and respective guardians. Most of these activities are civil in nature, but the police, where possible, use criminal remedies as well. For example, if a business or dwelling were being used to sell drugs, the police would ask city officials to perform inspections and demand that the owners get the property into compliance. If the property does not come into compliance, then the city will institute forfeiture and condemnation proceedings against the owner. Because, in many cases, the owner is different from the occupants, the owner is forced to apply pressure on his or her tenants, evict them, or face the possibility of losing the property. This aspect of third-party policing is similar to tactics that have been used in public housing.

Green (1996) studied third-party policing in Oakland and found that, when used in combination with other enforcement tactics, it substantially increased the police's ability to police hot spots or trouble areas. In Oakland, the police would identify a location as a target based on the amount of drug activity, crime, and disorder associated with the address. The police would then collect information and request various city inspections. The police, as a result of the program, made an average of slightly more than six contacts with a targeted property before the problem was abated. In about 50% of the cases, the tenant was evicted. "No Trespassing" signs were often posted on abandoned or empty property and trespassing laws were used to remove squatters and other tres- passers, particularly drug dealers and abusers.

Coldren and Higgins (2003) studied a similar program in Chicago where the police identified high crime and disorder areas and subsequently used nui- sance abatement through building inspections to counter the problems. They found that bureaucratic entanglements often resulted in the inspections being delayed or not occurring at all. In the case of Chicago, partnering with code enforcement was not always effective. Chicago demonstrates the difficulty in forming partnerships with other governmental agencies.

Third-party policing is an example of how the police use coercion to force prop- erty owners into becoming more responsible. Today, a number of departments are holding landlord academies where they attempt to educate landlords on their property responsibilities and the potential results of not controlling their tenants. It is a tool that can be used to attack a wide variety of crime and dis- order problems. It seems that the most effective police response to a problem oftentimes is a multifaceted response in which the target is attacked from a number of different directions.

COMMUNITY POLICING AND DRUGS

The preceding sections detailed various alternatives, strategies, and programs that have been used by the police to combat the drug problem. They have achieved varying degrees of success; in some instances they have been able to affect the drug business and related problems, while in other cases, they only marginally deterred drugs or had no impact whatsoever. Needless to say, the drug problem is very frustrating to police officials from the perspective that there is no correct or uniformly effective response to the problem. It is obvious that most drug problems are extremely complex requiring a complex police response.

We have spent and continue to spend billions of dollars on the war against drugs, and, at best, we have only marginally affected the drug problem. We must therefore devise a realistic and workable strategy for law enforcement. Many believe that community policing, which was detailed in Chapter 11, is the answer to this perplexing problem. President Clinton made community policing one of his top priorities, and the vast majority of U.S. Department of Justice grants to states and local police are tied to community policing. Essentially, officials must continually evaluate the drug, crime, and disorder problems and react to those problem areas that cause the greatest harm. Such prioritization allows the police to address the most pressing problems and perhaps provide citizens the greatest levels of relief. Community policing has been de-emphasized, at least at the federal level, as a result of the threat of domestic terrorism. It remains to be seen if this change in policy will filter down and affect how departments address the drug problem.

Regardless, community policing represents a comprehensive philosophy that has a number of associated strategies and tactics. It includes enforcement, community involvement, prevention, and community enhancement. The police attack problems while simultaneously improving the community's ability to withstand problems and keep them from occurring. Traditionally, the police have deployed simplistic responses to complex problems. Community policing dictates that typical police responses be abandoned for more complex, long-term responses (Kappeler & Gaines, 2008). A primary strategy used in community policing is problem solving, which is of particular importance in dealing with drug problems (Figure 12.3).

FIGURE 12.3
Bensalem, PA, community police officer Theresa Nelson has a chat with 8-year-old Victoria McDaniel, near McDaniel's residence. *Photograph courtesy of AP Photo/Tim Shaffer.*

Problem solving means that departments and officers must examine problems in their totality and develop solutions that address the problems. Problems need not be limited to law enforcement concerns and may include social and economic needs. Weisel (1990, p. 77) provides an excellent description of problem solving at the officer level:

> This problem-oriented approach to policing is one mechanism dealing with drug-related problems. For example, an officer who faces the problem of a drug hot spot in a particular location must identify what conditions contribute to that problem. If truant youths are the culprits, and poor lighting and a litter-strewn environment constitute the background for the activity, and nearby abandoned dwellings provide a cache for drugs, then all of those contributing factors are part of the problem. A problem-solving officer, for example, would not disregard the lighting issue, claiming it was not a police problem. If a condition contributes, directly or indirectly, to a drug problem, as might poor lighting at a drug spot, then it is clearly a condition for which the police should take the lead to develop a solution.

Community policing requires that police departments expand their roles, rely on nontraditional policing methods, and cooperate with other governmental and social agencies. In the past, police officers would not intervene in situations or conditions unless they were of a law enforcement nature. Problem-solving officers must recognize that there are numerous conditions and situations within a neighborhood that contribute to crime and these conditions must be dealt with in order to reduce the amount of associated criminality. Expansion of the police role is central to police effectiveness. Second, officers must be innovative, sometimes using nonenforcement techniques to solve problems. For example, eviction of drug dealers from public housing, the removal of abandoned automobiles, demolishing abandoned buildings, constructing fences around neighborhoods, or providing additional lighting are just a few of the non-law enforcement tools that can be used to accomplish police goals. Third, police officers must cooperate with social workers, sanitation workers, building inspectors, and private citizens to ensure that the best solutions are provided. The police cannot, nor should they be expected to, solve all of society's ills on their own. Finally, police managers must deploy a management system that is conducive to officers using innovative nontraditional methods to deal with problems. Such a management structure should focus downward, rather than upward (Weisel, 1990) (Box 12.5).

A prime example of how community policing can be implemented was discussed above where the Chicago Police Department implemented a drug eradication program in two of its public housing areas. In that example, the police

Box 12.5   Chicago Desk Jockeys Hit the Streets

Every day for the next few months, 200 Chicago police officers – many of whom now sit behind desks – will sit in squad cars in the middle of the city's open-air drug markets as part of a new strategy for waging war on narcotics and gangs.

As many as 1000 additional officers will be dispatched to the streets each week, with officers taking their turns 1 week out of every 5 at Chicago's 100 top hot spots.

> "Half of our homicides every year are somehow related to drugs and gangs," Michael Bayliss, a spokesman for the department, said in an interview with Law Enforcement News. "So to the extent that we could disrupt that activity, we hope to reduce violence. One way... is enhancing our visibility right in the midst of open-air drug markets, which seem to be the areas where violence takes place."

According to police data, 74% of all murders took place outdoors during the first 9 months of last year.

Target areas will be chosen by evaluating street intelligence, monitoring calls for service related to narcotics sales, and by using the department's computer analysis system called CLEAR, short for Citizen Law Enforcement Analysis and Reporting.

The program holds entries on more than 4 million arrestees dating back 12 years. Each entry has more than 30 data points, including name, address, age, nicknames, and tattoo descriptions.

"We're trying to squeeze as much out of our resources as possible," said Bayliss. "This is just another creative way we're taking a look at."

The tactic is one of a number of initiatives implemented by Superintendent Phil Cline since she took the top post in October. Cline said he would put into action two proven strategies used in the past by the agency: building street corner conspiracy cases, and increasing Operation Double Play missions.

Homicides were down 7% through Decker & Curry, 2003 compared to the same period the year before – 587 as compared to 629. The department recorded 646 killings overall in 2002. In fact, the city is on target for having its lowest number of homicides since 1967. There have also been 700 fewer shootings last year.

In a street corner conspiracy investigation, police develop a case against narcotics operations by identifying everyone in the organization, from lookouts to sellers, all the way up to the leadership ranks. Since 1998, more than 50 cases of this type have been built against 1700 defendants by the department. Ninety-seven percent of the defendants were convicted.

Under Operation Double Play, narcotics teams arrest drug dealers, and tactical officers posing as dealers take over the location. Since August, 2966 customers have been arrested this way and 1178 cars seized. Seven of every 10 arrestees are from the suburbs or outside the community.

"Overwhelmingly, the people who buy drugs in these communities do not live in them, but they contribute to the violence that takes place so they must be held accountable." Cline said in a statement.

Source: Law Enforcement News (2004).

---

combined enforcement with education, prevention, and treatment in an effort to attack a specific problem (Popkin, Olson, Lurigio, Gwiasda, & Carter, 1995). Prior to community policing, the police would have only been interested in sweeping the drug infested areas, and once the sweeps were completed, they would move on to some other problem.

Perhaps one of the most ambitious community police programs was *Weed and Seed*, a program implemented in 19 cities ranging from a population of 35,000–2.8 million. The programs consisted of three phases: (1) weeding,

(2) community policing, and (3) seeding (Lyman, 2010). Weeding consisted of police efforts to remove drug dealers and violent offenders from the community. The local U.S. Attorney supervised this phase of the program, and it consisted of aggressive police operations and vigorous prosecutions. Once criminals were weeded from an area, the police implemented community policing to help keep the area free of criminals. Tactics included: foot patrols, neighborhood watches, and various community relations programs aimed at enhancing police–citizen relations. Finally, seeding refers to efforts to revitalize, enhance, and empower neighborhoods. The focus of seeding was to help residents learn to identify and resist potential problems while restoring neighborhoods. Roehl (1995) evaluated the Weed and Seed Programs, and, unfortunately, found that, for the most part, they failed to achieve their lofty goals. The primary problem was that a majority of the efforts and resources went into weeding (80%) with little consideration for community policing and seeding (see Kappeler & Gaines, 2008). Likewise, Costanza, Helms, Ratansi, Kilburn and Harmon's (2010) study of a weed and seed program in New Britain, Connecticut, found the program altered the geography and place of crime and increased arrest rates without really reducing crime rates. They also observed that "The relative absence of substantial seeding and the preponderance of weeding activities may need to be reconsidered from a much more critical framework, especially in light of the recent economic turbulence confronting local jurisdictions throughout the country" (p. 66).

Community policing represents a unique philosophy and strategy to approach the drug problem. Of great importance is the fact that it recognizes that police must use innovative techniques that go beyond enforcement. The police, in essence, must work as educators, social workers, and city inspectors as they tackle drug and crime problems. Moreover, they must encourage neighborhood and citizen support and involvement. Community policing recognizes that problems are complex and can only be solved through comprehensive wide-ranging responses.

SUMMARY

The drug problem consumes vast amounts of police, government, and citizen resources. Drugs are responsible for large amounts of crime, social problems, disease, and community destruction. Heretofore, we have, at best, been only marginally effective in the fight against drugs, and many argue that we have failed miserably (Trebach, 1990). Efforts to stem the tide of drugs have been severely criticized. For example, Krisberg (1996) characterizes our current crime control efforts as a "make believe war," whereas Herman (1993) characterizes many components of the war on drugs as merely "hot air." These critics advance the idea that many of the drug war efforts are largely to satisfy public reactions as opposed to solve an intractable problem. Still others attack the drug war because of its adverse impact on citizens' civil rights (Halsted, 1992; Skolnick, 1990). As failed attempts at control, many are calling for an outright legalization of drugs, while others call for increased treatment and prevention and some measure of decriminalization (Faupel, Horowitz, & Weaver, 2009; Goode, 2011). This policy debate basically keeps the police in the middle and creates a basis for continued criticism and the police attempt to follow unclear, debatable social policies.

Regardless, drugs and drug laws have created a criminal element in our society that has untold proportions. A variety of criminal organizations ranging from eastern Kentucky marijuana cultivators to the Mexican Mafia have evolved to reap the profits from drugs. Add to this the numerous individual entrepreneurs, some of whom are prone to violence, who enter into the business for the quick profits. Law enforcement, indeed, is faced with a rogues' gallery of adversaries that makes for a difficult task.

Drugs are a primary focal point for police planning and operations. In addition to traditional police practices, the police have developed a number of innovative and creative strategies in an attempt to ameliorate the problem. The situation has caused the police to search for other, more effective means of dealing with the problem. This has resulted in police practices that differ drastically from those of earlier years. Also, the police are beginning to realize that they will not be able to solve the problem, and, at best, it is hoped that it can be controlled to some extent. Harm reduction and problem management are increasingly becoming the goal of police efforts, and if this goal can be achieved, a police department has been able to make great strides.

REVIEW QUESTIONS

1. To where can we trace the modern drug war? According to the FBI, how many drug arrests are made in the United States annually?
2. Where does our national drug strategy come from and what are the basic components of this strategy? What is meant by the term interdiction?
3. What are some of the drug prevention programs and strategies?
4. In addition to the numerous drugs that are manufactured in this country, drugs are imported into the United States from all over the world. From what countries do we import most of our heroin and other opiates?
5. What countries grow and manufacture cocaine?
6. From what countries was marijuana usually imported and which states lead the marijuana industry within the United States?

REFERENCES

ADAMP (2003). *Arrestee Drug Abuse Monitoring II in the United States*. Ann Arbor, MI: Inter-university Consortium for Political and Social Research.

Albanese, J. (2010). *Organized crime in our times* (6th ed.). Newark, NJ: LexisNexis Matthew Bender.

Albini, J. (1971). *The American Mafia: Genesis of a legend*. New York, NY: Appleton-Century-Crofts.

Associated Press. (August 28, 2007). Record Afghan opium crop expected. *Los Angeles Times*, A5.

Attorney General of the United States. (1989). *Drug trafficking: A report to the President of the United States*. Washington, DC: U.S. Government Printing Office.

Auerhahn, K., & Parker, R. N. (2003). Drugs, alcohol, and homicide. In L. Gaines, & P. Kraska (Eds.), *Drugs, crime & justice* (pp. 120–134). Prospect Heights, IL: Waveland.

BJS. (2006). *Local Police Departments, 2003*. Washington, DC: Bureau of Justice Statistics.

BJS. (2010). *Prisoners in 2009*. Washington, DC: Bureau of Justice Statistics.

Block, A. (1983). *East side-west side: Organizing crime in New York, 1930–1950*. New Brunswick, NJ: Transaction.

Botvin, G. (1990). Substance abuse prevention: theory, practice, and effectiveness. In M. Tonry, & J. Wilson (Eds.), *Drugs and crime* (pp. 461–520). Chicago, IL: University of Chicago Press.

Brownstein, H., & Goldstein, P. (1990). A typology of drug-related homicides. In R. Weisheit (Ed.), *Drugs, crime and the criminal justice system* (pp. 171–192). Cincinnati, OH: Anderson Publishing Co.

Buerger, M. E., & Mazerolle, L. G. (1998). Third-party policing: a theoretical analysis of an emerging trend. *Justice Quarterly*, *15*(2), 301–327.

Bureau of Justice Administration. (1989). *FY 1988 report on drug control*. Washington, DC: BJA.

Chaiken, J., Chaiken, M., & Karchmer, C. (1990). *Multijurisdictional drug law enforcement strategies: Reducing supply and demand*. Washington, DC: National Institute of Justice.

Clear, T., Clear, V., & Braga, A. (2003). Correctional alternatives for drug offenders. In F. Esbensen, S. Tibbetts, & L. Gaines (Eds.), *American youth gangs at the millennium* (pp. 332–351). Prospect Heights, IL: Waveland.

Cohen, J., Gorr, W., & Singh, P. (2003). Estimating intervention effects in various settings. Do police raids reduce illegal drug dealing at nuisance bars? *Criminology*, *41*, 257–292.

Coldren, J. R., & Higgins, D. F. (2003). Evaluating nuisance abatement at gang and drug houses in Chicago. In S. Decker (Ed.), *Policing gangs and youth violence* (pp. 131–162). Belmont, CA: Wadsworth.

Costanza, S. E., Helms, R., Ratansi, S., Kilburn, J. C., Jr, & Harmon, J. E. (2010). Boom to bust or bust to boom? Following the effects of weed and seed zoning in New Britain, Connecticut, from 1995–2000. *Police Quarterly*, *13*, 49–72.

DEA. (2010). *State & local task forces*. http://www.justice.gov/dea/programs/taskforces.htm.

Decker, S. H., & Curry, G. D. (2003). Suppression-based approaches to gangs and youth violence. In S. Decker (Ed.), *Policing gangs and youth violence* (pp. 17–50). Belmont, CA: Wadsworth.

Decker, S. H., Bynum, T., & Weisel, D. (2004). A tale of two cities: gangs as organized crime groups. In F. Esbensen, S. Tibbetts, & L. Gaines (Eds.), *American youth gangs at the millennium* (pp. 247–274). Prospect Heights, IL: Waveland.

Defense Intelligence Agency. (2009). *Interagency assessment of cocaine movement*. Washington, DC: Office of National Drug Control Policy.

Dunston, L. (1990). *"Reaffirming prevention." Report on the task force on juvenile gangs*. Albany, NY: New York State Division for Youth.

Egley, A., Howell, J. C., & Moore, J. (2010). *Highlights of the 2008 national youth gang survey*. Washington, DC: Office of Justice Programs.

Esbensen, F., Winfree, T., He, N., & Taylor, T. (2004). Youth gangs and definitional issues: when is a gang a gang, and why does it matter? In F. Esbensen, S. Tibbetts, & L. Gaines (Eds.), *American youth gangs at the millennium* (pp. 52–76). Prospect Heights, IL: Waveland.

Fagan, J., Weis, E., & Cheng, Y. (1990). Delinquency and substance use among inner-city students. *Journal of Drug Issues, 20*(3), 351–402.

Faupel, C. E., Horowitz, A. M., & Weaver, G. S. (2009). *The sociology of american drug use* (2nd ed.). New York, NY: McGraw-Hill.

Fleisher, M. (1995). *Beggars & thieves: Lives of urban street criminals*. Madison, WI: The University of Wisconsin Press.

General Accounting Office. (2003). *Youth illicit drug use prevention: DARE long-term evaluations and federal efforts to identify effective programs*. Washington, DC: GAO.

Goode, E. (2011). *Drugs in american society* (8th ed.). New York, NY: McGraw-Hill Book Co.

Gorman, D. M. (2003). The failure of drug education. In L. Gaines, & P. Kraska (Eds.), *Drugs, crime, and justice* (pp. 310–317). Prospect Heights, IL: Waveland.

Green, L. (1996). *Policing places with drug problems*. Thousand Oaks, CA: Sage.

Halsted, J. (1992). The anti-drug policies of the 1980s: have they increased the likelihood for both wrongful convictions and sentencing disparities? *Criminal Justice Policy Review, 6*(3), 207–228.

Herman, E. (1993). Drug 'wars': appearance and reality. *Social Justice, 18*(4), 76–83.

Herz, D. (2000). *"Drugs in the heartland: Methamphetamine use in rural Nebraska." Research in brief* (April). Washington, DC: National Institute of Justice.

Hickman, M. J., & Reeves, B. A. (2006). *Local Police Departments, 2003*. Washington, DC: U.S. Department of Justice, Bureau of Justice Statistics.

Howell, J. C., & Decker, S. H. (2003). The youth gangs, drugs, and violence connection. In L. Gaines, & P. Kraska (Eds.), *Drugs, crime, & justice* (pp. 150–174). Prospect Heights, IL: Waveland.

Huff, R., & McBride, W. D. (1990). Gangs and the police. In R. Huff (Ed.), *Gangs in america* (pp. 142–174). Los Angeles, CA: Roxbury.

Hunt, G., & Liadler, K. (2004). Alcohol and violence in the lives of gang members. In F. Esbensen, S. Tibbetts, & L. Gaines (Eds.), *American youth gangs at the millennium* (pp. 229–238). Prospect Heights, IL: Waveland.

Inciardi, J., & Pottieger, A. (1991). Kids, crack, and crime. *Journal of Drug Issues, 21*(2), 257–270.

Kappeler, V., & Gaines, L. (2008). *Community policing: A contemporary perspective* (5th ed.). Newark, NJ: LexisNexis Matthew Bender.

Kappeler, V. E., & Potter, G. W. (2005). *The mythology of crime and criminal justice* (4th ed.). Prospect Heights, IL: Waveland Press.

Karzberg, J., & James, D. (2005). *Substance dependence, abuse and treatment of jail inmates, 2002*. Special Report. Washington, DC: Bureau of Justice Statistics.

Kleiman, M., & Smith, K. (1990). State and local drug enforcement: in search of a strategy. In M. Tonry, & J. Wilson (Eds.), *Drugs and crime* (pp. 69–108). Chicago, IL: University of Chicago Press.

Klein, M. (1971). *Street gangs and street workers*. Englewood Cliffs, NJ: Prentice-Hall.

Kowalski, G., & Faupel, C. (1990). Heroin use, crime, and the 'main hustle.' *Deviant Behavior, 11*(1), 1–16.

Krisberg, B. (1996). Distorted by fear: the make believe war on crime. *Social Justice, 21*(3), 38–49.

Law Enforcement News. (2004). Chicago desk jockeys hit the streets "Increased police presence to target open-air drug markets." Vol. XXX, No. 614, p. 5.

Local Police Departments. (2007). Washington DC: BJS.

Lyman, M. (2010). *Drugs in society: Causes, concepts, and control* (6th ed.). Cincinnati, OH: Anderson Publishing Co.

Maxson, C. (1998). *Gang members on the move*. Bulletin. Washington, DC: Office of Juvenile Justice and Delinquency Prevention.

Maxson, C., Hennigan, K., & Sloane, D. C. (2003). For the sake of the neighborhood?: civil gang injunctions as a gang intervention tool in southern California. In S. Decker (Ed.), *Policing gangs and youth violence* (pp. 239–266). Belmont, CA: Wadsworth.

Maxson, C., Hennigan, K., & Sloane, D. (2005). It's getting crazy out there: can a civil gang injunction change a community? *Criminology & Public Policy, 4*(2), 577–606.

Mazerolle, L. G., & Terrill, W. (1997). Problem-oriented policing in public housing: identifying the distribution of problem places. *Policing: An International Journal of Police Strategies and Management, 20*(2), 235–255.

Mazerolle, L., Soole, D., & Rombouts, S. (2007). Drug law enforcement: a review of the evaluation literature. *Police Quarterly, 10*(2), 115–153.

McBride, D., & McCoy, C. (2003). The drug-crime relationship: an analytical framework. In L. Gaines, & P. Kraska (Eds.), *Drugs, crime, and justice: Contemporary issues* (2nd ed.) (pp. 100–119). Prospect Heights, IL: Waveland Press.

McDevitt, J., Braga, A. A., Nurge, D., & Buerger, M. (2003). Boston's youth violence prevention program: a comprehensive community-wide approach. In S. Decker (Ed.), *Policing gangs and youth violence* (pp. 53–76). Belmont, CA: Wadsworth.

McGarrell, E. F., & Schlegel, K. (1993). The implementation of federally funded multijurisdictional drug task forces: organizational structure and interagency relationships. *Journal of Criminal Justice, 21*, 231–244.

McInerney, M. J. (1988). Moonlighting at the green: a cop's eye view of life in Chicago's most notorious housing project. *Chicago Tribune*, 14. 10 July, section 10.

Miethe, T., McCorkle, R., & Listwan, S. (2006). *Crime profiles: The anatomy of dangerous persons, places, and situations.* (Los Angeles: Roxbury).

Miller, R. L. (1996). *Warriors & their prey: From police power to police state*. Westport, CT: Greenwood Press.

Miller, J., & Selva, L. (1997). Drug enforcement's double-edged sword: an assessment of asset forfeiture programs. In L. Gaines, & P. Kraska (Eds.), *Drugs, crime, and justice: Contemporary issues* (pp. 275–296). Prospect Heights, IL: Waveland Press.

Moore, M., & Kleiman, M. (2003). The police and drugs. In L. Gaines, & P. Kraska (Eds.), *Drugs, crime & justice* (pp. 248–267). Prospect Heights, IL: Waveland.

NDCS (2010). *The National Drug Control Strategy.* Washington, DC: Office of the Executive, President of the United States.

Popkin, S., Olson, L., Lurigio, A., Gwiasda, V., & Carter, R. (1995). Sweeping out drugs and crime: residents' views of the Chicago housing authority's public housing drug elimination program. *Crime & Delinquency, 41*(1), 73–99.

Pratt, T., Frank, J., & Smith, B. (2000). Conflict and consensus in multijurisdictional drug task forces: an organizational analysis of personnel attitudes. *Police Practice and Research, 1*(4), 509–525.

Reinarman, C., & Levine, H. (1989). The crack attack: politics and media in America's latest drug scare. In J. Best (Ed.), *Images of issues: Typifying contemporary social problems* (pp. 115–137). New York, NY: Aldine de Gruyter.

Rengert, G. F. (1998). *The geography of illegal drugs*. Boulder, CO: Westview.

Rengert, G. F. (2003). The distribution of illegal drugs at the retail level: the street dealers. In L. Gaines, & P. Kraska (Eds.), *Drugs, crime, & justice* (pp. 175–193). Prospect Heights, IL: Waveland.

Reuter, P. (1990). Can the borders be sealed? In R. Weisheit (Ed.), *Drugs, crime, and the criminal justice system* (pp. 13–26). Cincinnati, OH: Anderson Publishing Co.

Roehl, J. (1995). *"National process evaluation of the weed and seed initiative." Draft report*. Washington, DC: National Institute of Justice.

Ruble, N. M., & Turner, W. (2001). A systematic analysis of the dynamics and organization of urban street gangs. *American Journal of Family Therapy, 28*(2), 117–135.

Sanders, W. B. (1994). *Gangbangs and drive-bys: Grounded culture and juvenile gang violence*. New York, NY: Aldine de Gruyter.

Schlegel, K., & McGarrell, E. (1991). An examination of arrest practices in regions served by multi-jurisdictional drug task forces. *Crime & Delinquency, 37*(3), 408–426.

Sechrest, D. (2003). Drug courts: what is their future? In L. Gaines, & P. Kraska (Eds.), *Drugs, crime, & justice* (pp. 318–331). Prospect Heights, IL: Waveland.

Shepard, E. (2001). *The economic costs of DARE* (Research Paper #22). Syracuse, NY: Le Moyne College, Institute of Industrial Relations.

Sherman, L. (1990). *"Police crackdowns." NIJ reports, March/April*. Washington, DC: National Institute of Justice.

Skolnick, J. (1990). A critical look at the national drug control strategy. *Yale Law & Policy Review, 8*(1), 75–116.

Smith, M. R. (2001). Police-led crackdowns and cleanups: an evaluation of a crime control initiative in Richmond, Virginia. *Crime & Delinquency, 47*(1), 60–83.

Smith, B. W., Novak, K., & Frank, J. (2000). Multijurisdictional drug task forces: an analysis of impacts. *Journal of Criminal Justice, 28*(6), 543–556.

Starbuck, D., Howell, J., & Lindquist, D. (2004). Hybrid and other modern gangs. In F. Esbensen, S. Tibbetts, & L. Gaines (Eds.), *American youth gangs at the millennium* (pp. 200–215). Prospect Heights, IL: Waveland.

Stellwagon, L. (1985). *Use of forfeiture sanctions in drug cases*. Washington, DC: National Institute of Justice.

Trebach, A. (1990). A bundle of peaceful compromises. *Journal of Drug Issues, 20*(4), 515–531.

Webb, V. J., & Katz, C. M. (2003). Policing gangs in an era of community policing. In S. Decker (Ed.), *Policing gangs and youth violence* (pp. 17–50). Belmont, CA: Wadsworth.

Webster, B., & Connors, E. (1992). *"The police, drugs, and public housing." research in brief* (June). Washington, DC: National Institute of Justice.

Weisburd, D., & Green, L. (1995). Policing drug hot spots: the Jersey city drug market analysis experiment. *Justice Quarterly, 12*(4), 711–735.

Weisel, D. (1990). Playing the home field: a problem-oriented approach to drug control. *American Journal of Police, 9*(1), 75–96.

White House. (2003). *National drug control strategy*. Washington, DC: U.S. Government Printing Office.

White House. (2007). *National drug control strategy*. Washington, DC: U.S. Government Printing Office.

White House. (2010). *National drug control strategy*. Washington, DC: U.S. Government Printing Office.

Wilson, J. Q., & Kelling, G. (1982). Broken windows: police and neighborhood safety. *Atlantic Monthly, 249*, 29–38.

Wisotsky, S. (1997). Not thinking like a lawyer: the case of drugs in the courts. In L. Gaines, & P. Kraska (Eds.), *Drugs, crime, and justice: Contemporary issues* (pp. 321–356). Prospect Heights, IL: Waveland Press.

Wolfgang, M. (1958). *Patterns in criminal homicide*. Philadelphia, PA: University of Pennsylvania Press.

Wood, E., Tyndall, M., Spittal, P., Li, K., Anis, A., & Hogg, R. (2003). Impact of supply-side policies for control of illicit drugs in the face of the AIDS and overdose epidemics: investigation of a massive heroin seizure. *Canadian Medial Association Journal, 168*(2), 165–169.

Worrall, J. (2003). Civil asset forfeiture: past, present, and future. In L. Gaines, & P. Kraska (Eds.), *Drugs, crime & justice* (pp. 268–287). Prospect Heights, IL: Waveland.

CHAPTER 13

Terrorism and Homeland Security

Nothing is easier than to denounce the evildoer; nothing is more difficult than to understand him.

—Fyodor Dostoevsky

LEARNING OBJECTIVES

After reading the chapter, you should be able to:

- Define the term terrorism and discuss the complexities surround the definition of terrorism.
- Discuss some of the major crimes that are part of the definition of terrorism.
- Characterize the geographic distribution of terrorist acts and the frequency of these events in North America.
- Define WMD and delineate between the three major types of weapons.
- Describe the various types of extremist groups and their motivations.
- Describe and list the roles and responsibilities of the Department of Homeland Security.
- Discuss the role local police agencies play in threat assessment and providing homeland security.
- Describe the initiatives the New York Policy Department (NYPD) have undertaken to address homeland security.

KEY TERMS

- Al Qaeda
- Arizona Patriots
- Biological weapons
- Bioterrorism
- Chemical weapons
- Critical infrastructure
- Dirty bombs
- Extremists
- Fighting Jewish Organization
- Fusion centers
- Hamas
- Hezbollah
- Homeland security
- Intelligence-led policing
- Islamic Jihad

INTRODUCTION

On September 11, 2001, the terrorist group al Qaeda conducted coordinated attacks on the United States using commercial airliners as weapons. The terrorists crashed two airliners into the World Trade Center in New York and another into the Pentagon in Northern Virginia. A third airliner was destined for the White House, but passengers attempted to subdue the terrorists

- Jewish Defense League
- Kach
- Ku Klux Klan
- National Infrastructure Protection Plan
- Nuclear weapons
- Oklahoma Constitutional Militia
- Patriots Council
- Public education programs
- Response-protection decisions
- Target assessment
- Terrorism
- Threat assessment
- Threat identification
- Weaponized
- WMD

who crashed the jet in a field in Pennsylvania. The attack resulted in almost 3000 casualties. The 911 attacks in 2001 were not the first attacks by al Qaeda against the United States. In 2000, al Qaeda linked terrorists attacked the USS Cole in Aden Harbor, Yemen. The attack resulted in 17 deaths, and in 1998, al Qaeda operatives detonated car bombs at the U.S. embassies in Dar es Salaam, Tanzania, and Nairobi, Kenya. The attacks killed 223 people including 12 Americans.

The 911 attacks resulted in a major shift in American foreign policy, military operations, and national security. Foreign policy quickly was altered to include the development of relations with countries to ferret out terrorists and destroy them. The American military focus on large symmetric wars began to develop asymmetric modes of intervention. Congress passed legislation creating the Department of Homeland Security. The 911 attacks resulted in a seismic shift in how the American government operated.

Local police agencies were not immune from this shift. Although many terrorist groups are global, attacks occur in a local jurisdiction. When a terrorist attack occurs on American soil, the police and other first responders are the first to be on the scene to mediate the effects of the attack. Moreover, because terrorist attacks are local, the police, through intelligence gathering, have an important role in preventing attacks. Terrorist attacks are rare, but when they occur they can have a significant impact on communities. For example, on April 15, 2013, Dzhokar and Tamerlan Tsarnaev detonated two bombs made with pressure cookers at the Boston marathon. The bombs killed three people and injured an estimated 264 others. The bombings were a grim reminder that the threat of terrorism is ever-present and terrorist acts affect local communities.

This chapter examines terrorism and homeland security. Terrorism is examined to provide perspective to homeland security. More importantly, as discussed later in this chapter, Homeland Security is a complex governmental activity that spans governments at the federal, state, and local levels.

TERRORISM

The term terrorism is not easily understood or defined. It is a political term with many different connotations. One might view a particular group as terrorists, whereas another may see the group as a group that is fighting for freedom and justice. For example, Israelis see Hamas and Hezbollah as terrorists, whereas Palestinians see these groups as freedom fighters. Perspective plays an important role in defining terrorism. It is difficult to define terrorism. The following section examines the geographic dispersion of terrorist attacks.

Geographic Dispersion of Terrorist Attacks

Today, terrorist groups throughout the world are waging war on countries, institutions, political ideologies, and political or ethnic groups. Recently, we have witnessed major terrorist events in the United States, India, Spain, Great Britain, Russia, Japan, Kenya, Tanzania, Turkey, Saudi Arabia, and Indonesia, to name just some of the affected countries. The National Consortium for the Study of Terrorism and Responses to Terrorism (2013) reports that, in 2012, there were 6771 terrorist attacks worldwide. Moreover, these events seem more deadly, sophisticated, and better planned as compared to those in the past. We are witnessing attacks on high-profile targets, and the attacks are carried out using weapons that inflict substantial death, injury, and damage. The fear of terrorism comes, in part, from the aggregation of incidents, media attention, and presenting terrorism as affecting the entire world. As Table 13.1 shows, however, terrorist attacks are not evenly distributed across countries. The table shows the 10 countries with the largest numbers of terrorist attacks in 2012.

North America (the United States and Canada) has experienced the fewest incidents of terrorism. For example, the average number of terrorist attacks in the United States between 2002 and 2010 was 16 per year—a much smaller number as compared to other countries (START, 2011). Terrorist attacks are not equally distributed across the United States. Table 13.2 shows that terrorist attacks are concentrated in just a few states. Thus, some states and areas are

Table 13.1 Ten Countries with the Largest Number of Terrorist Attacks in 2012

Country	Total Attacks	Total Killed	Total Wounded	Average Number Killed per Attack	Average Number Wounded per Attack
Pakistan	1404	1848	3643	1.32	2.59
Iraq	1271	2436	6641	1.92	5.23
Afghanistan	1023	2632	3715	2.57	3.63
India	557	231	559	0.41	1.00
Nigeria	546	1386	1019	2.54	1.87
Thailand	222	174	897	0.78	4.04
Yemen	203	365	427	1.80	2.10
Somalia	185	323	397	1.75	2.15
Philippines	141	109	270	0.77	1.91
Syria	133	657	1787	4.94	13.44

Source: National Consortium for the Study of Terrorism and Responses to Terrorism (2013).

Table 13.2 Terrorist Activities at the State Level	1991–2000	2002–2010
California	15% of U.S. attacks	24% of U.S. attacks
New York	7%	6%
Florida	6%	5%
Oregon	6%	1%
Washington State	4%	6%
Illinois	4%	3%
New Mexico	3%	4%
Texas	3%	3%
Ohio	3%	1%
Michigan	2%	6%

Source: START (2011).

more threatened as compared to others (e.g., almost one-quarter of all attacks in the United States have occurred in California).

It is also important to note that the number of terrorist attacks in the United States has been declining. As noted above, after the 911 attacks, the yearly average of attacks has been 16, whereas, prior to the 911 attacks, the annual average was 41.3. Box 13.1 provides a graph depicting the number of annual attacks.

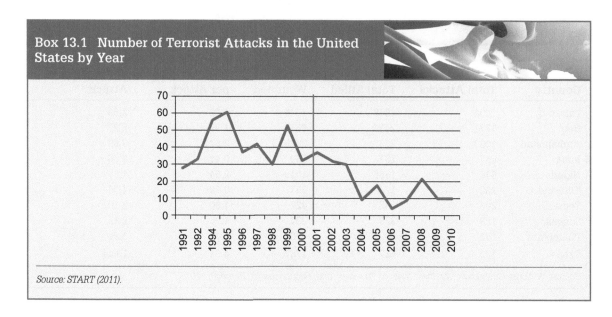

Box 13.1   Number of Terrorist Attacks in the United States by Year

Source: START (2011).

Acts of terrorism differ, with some attacks requiring months of planning and coordination and the expenditure of hundreds of thousands of dollars. For example, the 9/11 Commission estimated that the terrorist attacks in Northern Virginia and New York cost between $400,000 and $500,000. Other high-profile attacks, like the London transit bombing, are funded with a few thousand dollars gained from credit card fraud and by passing bad checks. There is no evidence that the Boston Marathon bombers received any funding, but constructed their bombs using a few hundred dollars.

Defining Terrorism and Its Variations

It is difficult to define terrorism because there are so many attacks, and these attacks have a variety of intertwined motivations, including economic, political, social, and religious. Moreover, the multiple groups committing terrorist acts have different and sometimes multiple motivations. As such, a variety of definitions have evolved, but each definition has an inherent political perspective and is designed to define differently those who use violence to maintain versus those who seek to use violence to secure political power.

Under U.S. Federal Criminal Code, Chapter 113B of Part I of Title 18, terrorism is defined as:

> activities that involve violent ... or life-threatening acts ... that are a violation of the criminal laws of the United States or of any State and ... appear to be intended (i) to intimidate or coerce a civilian population; (ii) to influence the policy of a government by intimidation or coercion; or (iii) to affect the conduct of a government by mass destruction, assassination, or kidnapping; and ... occur primarily within the territorial jurisdiction of the United States ... [or] ... occur primarily outside the territorial jurisdiction of the United States.

Although the United Nations (UN) has never adopted a formal definition of terrorism, primarily because it would have to include acts of state terrorism, one UN panel (2007) described it as an act: intended to cause death or serious bodily harm to civilians or noncombatants with the purpose of intimidating a population or compelling a government or an international organization to do or abstain from doing any act.

Laqueur (1987) suggested that terrorism is the illegitimate use of force to achieve a political objective by targeting innocent people. The Federal Bureau of Investigation (FBI) has defined it as "the unlawful use of force or violence against persons or property to intimidate or coerce a government, the civilian population, or any segment thereof, in furtherance of political or social objectives." These definitions, of course, favor those who have the power to define what constitutes "illegitimate" and "lawful" violence or force. Thus, to a great degree, terrorists are those without political or social power who attack the powerful, usually the government and its representatives or corporations, to wrestle power from political elites. Because they are not powerful enough to attack the government itself in conventional terms, they attack civilians and critical infrastructure to create fear, chaos, and economic instability. To the civilian injured in a terrorist attack, it makes little difference if a state's covert military personnel, political activists, or religious zealots have detonated the bomb.

Another way to examine terrorism is as a term by itself associated with crime. Terrorism is always in conjunction with the violation of a criminal statute, homicide, arson, kidnapping, use of a weapon, etc. In order to better understand terrorist events, the crimes associated with the event must be articulated. In some cases, it may be more prudent and informative to analyze these crimes to gain insights into terrorism and terrorist events (Table 13.3).

Terrorism represents the lowest level of conflict that can be waged, primarily because the combatants often represent a group without state power and they are without the resources to fight on a larger conventional scale. If terrorists are successful, they will create an atmosphere whereby others become interested in their cause. They will also cause economic and social hardships that result in the government taking punitive, drastic courses of action that often are aimed at innocent civilians. Because terrorists can blend in with the population, it is difficult to differentiate terrorists from civilians. When the government responds

Table 13.3 International and Domestic Terrorist Incidents by Tactic, 1998–2007

Tactic	Incidents	Injuries	Fatalities
Armed attack	6682	7765	11,826
Arson	850	179	295
Assassination	1719	1122	2484
Barricade/hostage	55	1412	604
Bombing	14,290	75,137	22,710
Hijacking	31	5	26
Kidnapping	1529	143	1353
Other	149	427	118
Unconventional attack	56	3019	3047
Unknown	448	309	600
Total	25,809	89,518	43,063

Source: Data from Memorial Institute for the Prevention of Terror (MIPT) Terrorism Knowledge Base. www.mipt.org/.

to terrorist acts with repression or by retracting civil liberties, the terrorists often are able to gain more support and recruit more people to join their fight. This can escalate into guerilla warfare when the opposition gains the personnel and resources to directly fight the government. If the government continues to repress the citizenry and the opposition continues to gain support, the guerilla war can evolve into civil war and, with sufficient support, the emergence of a new state. Unfortunately, history shows that nations are often born of acts their victims would call terrorism. Although terrorism without the political support of a population cannot result in the overthrow of a government, it can lead to actions and conditions that ultimately accomplish this objective. It is, however, a risky and deadly tactic that most political groups denounce.

To learn more about terrorism and terrorist incidents, visit The National Counterterrorism Center's Website at **www.nctc.gov/**

Terrorism has its roots in economic inequality and repression, political power, and religion. In numerous countries, the governments are run by and for the political and economic elite and repress large segments of the population. These elites amass large amounts of wealth, whereas the majority of people are poor, living in substandard conditions, and often lacking food, shelter, and other basic essentials. Ultimately, small groups rise up and begin terrorist campaigns against the ruling classes. Sometimes they use terrorist or small guerilla operations. Many countries are hotbeds for these types of problems. Political power often involves one political party attempting to wrestle power from a ruling political party. They often have militias and money to fund the conflict. Frequently, this funding comes from nations that have a direct political interest in supporting the groups and weakening or overturning an existing regime.

In other situations, nations fund and support other states in their exercise of political repression against their own minority populations fueling conflict. When nation-states provide the economic and military resources necessary to repress citizens, they may become the targets of terrorist activities.

Religion plays a key role in a substantial amount of terrorism. White (2008) identified three causes around which religious violence centers. First, some religious groups feel they must purify the world in the name of their god. For example, some Muslims believe that all Christians and Jews should be killed. Likewise, some Christians have bombed abortion clinics, killing innocent healthcare workers. Other Christian groups have killed minorities and attacked governments. Second, some groups believe they are the chosen ones, and they must destroy all other people in the name of righteousness to defend themselves or the lands they have taken from others. In this sense, religion is not a cause of terrorism; it is used as one motivation for terrorism. Finally, people may become so consumed in a particular cause that they resort to violence to advance their beliefs.

WEAPONS OF MASS DESTRUCTION

Weapons of mass destruction (WMD) can be defined as any weapon that when used can result in mass casualties. Generally, we think of WMDs as being biological, chemical, or radiological in nature. However, large amounts of conventional explosives are also considered WMDs. Terrorists have never successfully used a WMD against the United States, and most terrorists around the world use conventional or homemade weapons. The National Counterterrorism Center (2009) reported that most attacks "were perpetrated by terrorists applying conventional fighting methods such as armed attacks, bombings, and kidnappings." Box 13.2 shows the primary methods of attack used by terrorist groups in the United States. Notice that the most common modes of attack are traditional weapons; they commonly have been used throughout history. Also, WMDs, such as chemical and biological weapons, are very uncommon. When they have been used, they have been on a very small scale.

WMDs, however, are of great concern to political leaders, the media, and the public (Henry & King, 2004). Exploding a small nuclear device in Chicago, New York, or Los Angeles would inflict substantial destruction and would have long-term residual effects. Such an incident would overload first responders and hospitals and would substantially affect the economy. In essence, in addition

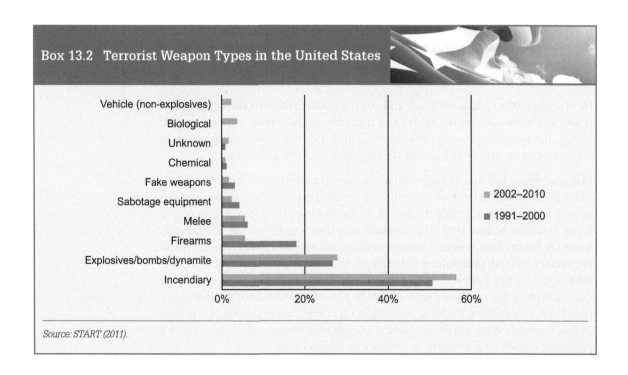

Box 13.2   Terrorist Weapon Types in the United States

Source: START (2011).

to the initial loss of life and property, a WMD attack could cripple the economy of a city or nation, resulting in numerous problems that could last for years or decades. To some extent, the primary purpose of using WMDs is not the initial deaths and injuries. Destroying a primary communications center might result in initial deaths and injuries and loss of property, but the loss of communication would have a dramatic impact on a society. WMDs include a wide range of weapons potentially more dangerous than conventional weapons.

WMDs differ from conventional weapons because they target a wide, rather than a specific, area. WMDs have the potential to spread destruction across a wide area, affecting hundreds or thousands of people. Moreover, they have long residual effects; for example, considerable effort, time, and expense would be required to clean up an area attacked by a biological, chemical, or nuclear device. These long-term effects would result in significant health problems, public fear, and disruption to the economy.

Nuclear Weapons

Of all the WMDs, nuclear weapons raise the greatest concern. Even a small nuclear device detonated in a large city could result in catastrophic destruction and casualties. Moreover, the presence of nuclear materials (i.e., radiation) would result in long-term problems for a country.

Terrorists can acquire nuclear weapons in two ways. First, they could steal or purchase one, or, second, they could acquire the materials and construct one themselves. Of these two possibilities, the Union of Concerned Scientists (www.ucsusa.org/) has suggested that the greater likelihood is that terrorists would attempt to acquire the materials and construct a device themselves. If terrorists are able to acquire all the necessary components, it is not difficult to construct a nuclear weapon. Only a small amount of fissile material (highly enriched uranium or plutonium) is required to build a bomb. A crude weapon could be constructed from about 12 kg of highly enriched uranium or 4 kg of plutonium. Several Middle Eastern countries currently have the knowledge and capability to build these weapons, and some of these countries are sympathetic to extremist causes. Indeed, scientists in Pakistan have shared technical information with other countries in the Middle East.

Another problem is that the materials necessary for building these weapons are stored inadequately, especially in Russia and countries that broke away from the former Soviet Union. In many cases, the materials are stored with substandard security, and large quantities of materials are unaccounted for. Even the United States cannot account for all of its fissile materials. Additionally, the production of tactical battlefield nuclear weapons by the United States makes these devices smaller and easier to transport. A tactical nuclear weapon can easily fit into a piece of luggage.

In terms of nuclear weapons, three different threat scenarios exist, and each has a different level of probability: (1) a dirty bomb, (2) attacks on nuclear power plants, and (3) diversion of fissile material or weapons. Dirty bombs use conventional explosive materials but are wrapped in or contain some type of radioactive material. The radioactive material is dispersed as the result of a conventional explosion, resulting in contamination. A dirty bomb does not necessarily have to contain highly enriched uranium or plutonium; it could contain radioactive waste products that are produced at commercial power plants. Radioactive waste generally has fewer security precautions as compared to highly enriched uranium or plutonium. Additionally, Iraq is littered with hundreds of thousands of radioactive depleted uranium ammunition rounds used by the U.S. military in the Gulf War.

There have been several plots and a single attempt to use dirty bombs. In 1996, Islamic rebels from Chechnya planted a dirty bomb in a park in Moscow. Although not detonated, it contained dynamite and cesium-137, a byproduct of nuclear fission. In 2002, Jose Padilla, a Brooklyn-born convert to Islam, also known as Abdullah Al Muhajir, was arrested by federal authorities for plotting to construct and detonate a dirty bomb in the United States. He was held in military detention for almost 4 years without the benefit of counsel until the Justice Department faced a Supreme Court showdown over his detention and transferred him to the criminal justice system for trial in federal court. In 2007, Padilla was convicted not of plotting to use a dirty bomb as was initially claimed but of conspiring to kill people and support terrorism—all overseas. Prosecutors failed to present any evidence of the dirty bomb allegation to the jury.

The effectiveness of dirty bombs as WMDs, however, is questionable. Because a dirty bomb has never been detonated in public, it is difficult to predict the impact. Research generally shows that these devices are not very efficient as WMDs for two reasons. First, to inflict massive damage, these devices would have to be very large in terms of both the amount of radiation they would have to release and the amount of conventional explosives necessary to disperse the radiation. This makes dirty bombs impracticable for their destructive features. Second, research predicts that these devices would neither sicken nor kill a substantial number of people as compared to other WMDs. The use of one of these devices, however, would instill great panic and potentially disrupt the economy. Although the media has focused public attention on these devices, there are far more destructive devices and techniques that should be of concern.

Crashing a large aircraft or dropping large amounts of explosives on a nuclear power plant could have disastrous effects as compared to dirty bombs. Such an explosion could cause a reactor's core to melt down (such as occurred in 2011 at the Japanese Fukushima Power Plant and at the Chernobyl Nuclear Power Plant, located in the former Soviet Union) or cause spent fuel waste to be spread across a large geographic area. The effects could be devastating, and the cleanup could take decades. Russia is still dealing with the aftermath of the Chernobyl disaster, which occurred in 1986. The extent and magnitude of the cleanup in Japan is unknown at this time but could take decades.

Finally, diversion of nuclear material remains a threat. Numerous sites throughout the world contain the materials needed to make a bomb, and, in many instances, the security is suspect. Moreover, some countries are sympathetic to terrorist causes or need hard currency, and they may be tempted to provide terrorists with a bomb or bomb-making materials. Examples include states from the old Soviet Union, North Korea, and Pakistan. The actual threat of a nuclear attack by terrorists, however, must be put into perspective. FBI Director Robert (2007) remarked that "Although a nuclear terrorist attack is the least likely to occur due to the required technical expertise and challenges associated with acquiring weapons-usable material, the intent of terrorists to obtain this material is a continuing concern."

Biological Weapons

Although given far less attention by the media, biological weapons represent a more realistic threat to the United States and the rest of the world. A number of contagions could pose an enormous health threat to large numbers of people. Diseases, such as smallpox and anthrax, have the potential to infect large numbers of people over a wide geographic area. Containment and prevention are perhaps the greatest issues. There is a great deal of speculation that terrorist groups possess or are attempting to possess biological weapons. There was substantial publicity and public fear in 2001 when someone sent anthrax via the mail to several locations in the United States, causing five deaths and infecting at least 17 people. Although the case remains unsolved, some believe that right-wing domestic extremists in the United States carried out the attacks. Evidence shows that the bacterial strain used in the attacks was derived from the Ames strain first studied at the U.S. Army Medical Research Institute of Infectious Diseases in Fort Detrick, Maryland, and later transferred to research laboratories across the country.

There is some confusion over what exactly constitutes bioterrorism. Here, bioterrorism means the use of microorganisms to inflict harm on a civilian population. The target for a biological attack may not be people; toxins have been used to destroy crops and livestock. This exemplifies how biological warfare can have multiple targets and devastating effects on living conditions and local economies. The U.S. Centers for Disease Control and Prevention (2007:1) has defined a bioterrorist attack as:

> … the deliberate release of viruses, bacteria, or other germs (agents) used to cause illness or death in people, animals, or plants. These agents are typically found in nature, but it is possible that they could be changed to increase their ability to cause disease, make them resistant to current medicines, or to increase their ability to be spread into the environment. Biological agents can be spread through the air, through water, or in food. Terrorists may use biological agents because they can be extremely difficult to detect and do not cause illness for several hours to several days. Some bioterrorism agents, like the smallpox virus, can be spread from person to person and some, like anthrax, cannot.

Ackerman and Moran (2006) identified three types of biological agents suitable for bioterrorism:

1. Bacterial organisms such as those that cause anthrax, plague, and tularemia.
2. Viruses, including those that cause smallpox and Ebola.
3. Toxins, including botulinum toxin (derived from a bacterium), ricin (derived from the castor bean plant), and saxitoxin (derived from marine animals); toxins are not alive and cannot multiply like bacteria or viruses, and therefore have the same attributes associated with chemical weapons.

Biological agents are not biological weapons. Mere possession of an agent does not make it a weapon. The agent must be weaponized; that is, a would-be terrorist must develop or possess a mechanism that can disperse or disseminate the agent. There is an incubation period associated with most biological agents, a time period (1–2 weeks) before onset of the disease within the host or victim. This allows perpetrators to distance themselves from the scene before law enforcement officials become aware of the act. It also provides a time for medical experts to begin responding to the problem. Both contagious and noncontagious biological weapons exist; for example, anthrax is not contagious like smallpox. We know very little about the effectiveness of biological weapons in terms of casualties. Most of the information we have is from military uses and experiments. Perhaps the greatest problem with many biological agents is their effect on the population. An outbreak of smallpox or other virus could result in a great deal of disorder, because they are highly contagious and transmitted rather easily. A significant concern is that the virus is still stored in Russian and American laboratories.

As for the possibility of a terrorist group using these weapons against the United States, FBI Director Mueller (2007) testified before Congress that "Few if any terrorist groups are likely to have the capability to produce complex biological or chemical agents needed for a mass casualty attack, but their capability will improve as they pursue enhancing their scientific knowledge base by recruiting scientists as some groups are doing."

Chemical Weapons

As displayed in Box 13.3, the Center for Disease Control and Prevention (CDC) has compiled a listing of the various chemical compounds that may be used in some type of chemical attack. Chemical warfare was a primary weapon used in World War I and in the Iraq–Iran War. In 2013, it was claimed that Syria used chemical weapons against rebels who were attempting to overthrow the Assad government. One million casualties occurred in World War I as a result of combatants using chemical weapons, and Iraq used chemical weapons against Iran almost daily in their conflict. The largest manufacturers of chemical weapons are located in the United States, Germany, Britain, and France. Chemical weapons are not new nor are they produced in any meaningful quantity by terrorists. Ironically, countries continue to develop new and more deadly compounds that pose a risk to themselves should they be used by terrorists.

The various types of chemical weapons have different levels of toxicity and lethality. Insecticides, for example, have a low level of toxicity but are readily available. Moreover, although evidence suggests that insecticides have been used, the results have been limited to nonexistent. On the other hand, weapons grade chemicals are potentially dangerous. Chemical weapons, such as mustard gas, Sarin, and VX, are extremely lethal. As with biological weapons, the effectiveness of a chemical threat is based largely on the delivery system. To have a significant impact, hundreds of thousands of pounds of the chemical would have to be effectively released, and many experts believe that chemical

Box 13.3 CDC Categories of Chemical Weapons of Mass Destruction

- Biotoxins
- Blister agents/vesicants
- Blood agents
- Caustics (acids)
- Choking/lung/pulmonary agents
- Incapacitating agents
- Long-acting anticoagulants
- Metals
- Nerve agents
- Organic solvents
- Riot control agents/tear gas
- Toxic alcohols
- Vomiting agents

weapons cannot produce the same level of casualties as nuclear or biological weapons. Although governments have used chemical weapons for decades, one of the very first terrorist uses of chemical agents against a civilian population did not occur until 1995. Aum Shinrikyo, an apocalyptic cult group, released Sarin into a Tokyo subway. The incident killed at least 12 people and injured more than 5000 people. In essence, an effective attack would only be capable of causing hundreds to a few thousand casualties. A primary difference between chemical agents and biological agents is that the chemical agents have an immediate effect, which cripples any potential response and delays issuing a warning to civilian populations.

Because the vast majority of all WMDs and their necessary delivery systems are produced, distributed, sold, stored, and used by nation states, a logical and rational first step in combating terrorism would be to either eliminate or restrict the distribution and sale of or to adequately store and secure the materials before they become weapons of extremist groups.

The Myths about Terrorism

Myth: The number of terrorist incidents in the United States is increasing dramatically.

Reality: Actually the number of acts that can be classified as "acts of terrorism" has been dramatically decreasing in the United States for decades.

Myth: Radicalized Muslins commit the vast majority of terrorist acts in the United States.

Reality: Right-wing extremist groups, often motivated by racism and religious intolerance, have carried out the vast majority of terrorist acts committed in the United States.

Myth: Terrorists armed with WMDs pose the greatest and most realistic threat to the American public.

Reality: The vast majority of terrorist acts committed in the United States have been carried out using conventional weapons. The use of a WMD is an event even worldwide.

EXTREMIST GROUPS

There are literally hundreds of extremist groups around the world. These groups can work in isolation, they can be connected to a main group or cause, they can be sponsored by states, or they can be state-sanctioned groups. As with the concept of terrorism, it is difficult to define exactly what constitutes an extremist group. We might initially think of extremists as those groups that constitute a terrorist organization, have a violent political orientation, or possess a militant orientation to an issue. We must also keep in mind that extremists come from almost all countries, races, religions, and ethnic groups. White Christian extremist groups living in the United States include the Christian Identity Movement, Christian Defense League, and the Covenant, the Sword,

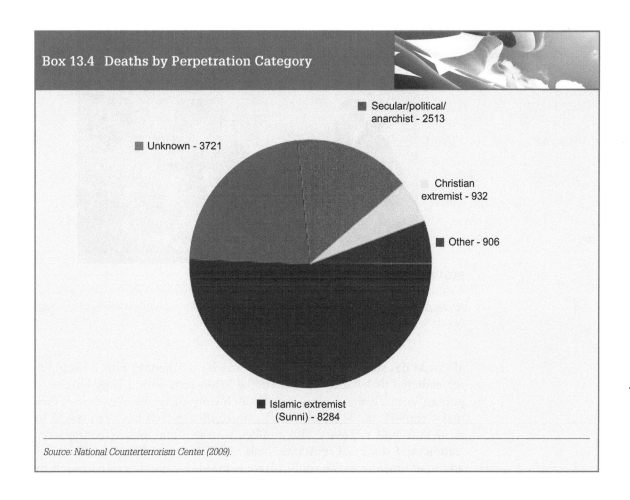

Box 13.4 Deaths by Perpetration Category

- Secular/political/anarchist - 2513
- Unknown - 3721
- Christian extremist - 932
- Other - 906
- Islamic extremist (Sunni) - 8284

Source: National Counterterrorism Center (2009).

and the Arm of the Lord. Jewish extremists living in Israel include Gush Emunim, the Jewish Fighting Organization, and the Kach Party. Box 13.4 categorizes the religious or political ideology and the number of deaths caused by extremist groups in a single year. In the sections that follow, we briefly consider a few of the many extremist groups to illustrate the point.

Extremist Groups and the Middle East

It was only in the aftermath of 9/11 that the American media and politicians turned their focus on Arab Muslim extremists. Despite this current unprecedented attention, relatively few Muslim groups have expressed a desire to do domestic harm to the United States (National Intelligence Council, 2007). LaFree, Yang, and Crenshaw (2009) examined international terrorism groups from 1970 to 2004 and identified 53 groups that were anti-American, of which 31 were radicalized groups from the Middle East. Of these groups, only

FIGURE 13.1

President Barack Obama participates in national security briefing aboard Air Force One before landing in Afghanistan, May 1, 2012. *Photograph courtesy of www.whitehouse.gov; official White House photograph by Pete Souza.*

al Qaeda has successfully launched an attack on American soil. It should be remembered that hatred for the United States rests with a large number of political conflicts that have spanned both history and geography. One of these major conflicts is the Israeli–Palestinian conflict, which has been waged for more than half a century. This conflict, with its bombings, wars, fractionalization, and sustained resistance, fuels unrest in the Middle East. The scope and long timeline of the conflict have embroiled a number of parties in the conflict. This is not to say that other conflicts or interests have not produced anger toward the United States. There are groups throughout the rest of the world who have also directed their anger toward the United States because of its policies, but the numerous groups in the Middle East seem to be the most outraged (Figure 13.1).

Hamas

Hamas (Islamic Resistance Movement) is one of the larger extremist groups operating in the Middle East. It is housed in Palestine and is at the center of the Israeli–Palestinian conflict. In 2006, Hamas won a controlling number of seats in the Palestinian Parliament; since then, after thwarted attempts at reunification of Hamas and the Palestinian Authority, as well as much violence, Hamas has maintained control of the Gaza Strip. Both groups are fighting for ultimate control of Palestine. Many of the members of Hamas are well educated, possessing advanced degrees in science and engineering. The group is made up of two wings: a political wing, which provides social services for the Palestinian people, such as hospitals, schools, and libraries, and a militant wing (Izz ad-Din al-Qassam Brigades), which carries out acts of resistance to the Israeli occupation. Many of Hamas' activities are thought to be funded by Saudi Arabia, Kuwait, and Iran. Hamas enjoys great support among Palestinians because of corruption and ineffectiveness in previous Palestinian governments and because it is seen as a movement that defends Palestinians from Israeli occupation. Its militant wing carries out attacks against Israel, including suicide bombings, and often targets civilians. In 2006, the militant wing called on Muslims around the world to attack American targets. The political wing, however, has denounced this statement and claims to be interested only in operations against Israeli occupation. The militant wing is organized into cells, some having only a few members. To some extent, leaders may be unable to control the decision-making and actions of some of the cells. Although Hamas has never carried out a suicide attack outside of Israel, the Gaza Strip, or the West Bank, U.S. officials are concerned because they claim to have covert cells in America.

Hezbollah

Hezbollah (Party of God) is a predominantly Shiite organization that is strongest in Lebanon. Hezbollah was first formed during the Lebanese Civil War with the principle goal of eradicating Western colonialism and establishing an Islamic government in Lebanon. Some accuse Hezbollah of carrying out the 1983 Beirut barracks bombing, which killed more than 300 American and French troops; however, the group has denied this claim. The United States and Great Britain regard Hezbollah as a terrorist group, but most in the Arab world view it as a legitimate resistance force. Like Hamas, Hezbollah enjoys a great deal of popular support among the Lebanese people and has won numerous seats in the Parliament. Hezbollah enjoys public support because of its position in the conflicts and because it provides a great deal of social services to the people. Hezbollah gained regional and international recognition when it battled Israel in the Lebanese Civil War (1982–1990) and again during the Israeli invasion of Lebanon in 2006. The organization has ties to Syria and Iran, with Iran providing most of the financial and material support for its operations.

To learn more about counterterrorism efforts, visit the Website of The U.S. Department of State, Office of the Coordinator for Counterterrorism, at **www.state.gov/s/ct/**

Al Qaeda

Special attention should be given to al Qaeda because this group is responsible for the 911 attacks, the attacks on U.S. Embassies in Africa in 2000, and the 1998 attack on the USS Cole in Yemen waters. It truly is an international terrorist organization with activities in several countries including Iraq, Afghanistan, Pakistan, Yemen, Somali, and Mali. Al Qaeda (the base) is perhaps the most publicized and feared terrorist group in the world. This Sunni Muslim group was led by Osama bin Laden and might be better thought of as a network of groups rather than a single formal organization. The group's origin can be traced to Dr Abdullah Azzam, who was a leader in the anti-Soviet jihad after the Soviet invasion of Afghanistan. Bin Laden became involved in the resistance to Soviet occupation, recruiting, funding, and organizing the Afghan Mujahideen, which was supported covertly by the United States.

Al Qaeda espouses an ideology of "defensive jihad," which responds to what it sees as attacks against Muslims, the occupation of Muslim lands, and the operation of repressive governments, such as Saudi Arabia, Egypt, Algeria, and Afghanistan. The group and its network seek to expel Western forces from "holy territories," such as the Gulf, Afghanistan, and Iraq. The group also wants to install Muslim theocratic governments and has launched jihad against anyone or any government that is seen as interfering with this objective.

Al Qaeda claims to have cells throughout the world, operating in as many as 65 countries with membership in the tens of thousands. It also claimed responsibility for the 9/11 World Trade Center attack. These claims, however, cannot be substantiated because the very nature of al Qaeda's networked structure makes it difficult to accurately estimate its size or global reach or to even determine if its members are directly responsible for particular attacks. Further complicating the matter is evidence that the 9/11 operation was financed by nation-states and conducted by hijackers from Saudi Arabia, United Arab Emirates, Lebanon, and Egypt. A 2007 National Intelligence Council (2007:6) report stated that "Although we have discovered only a handful of individuals in the United States with ties to al-Qa'ida senior leadership since 9/11, we judge that al-Qa'ida will intensify its efforts to put operatives here."

Al Qaeda has provided material support and training for a number of other terrorist and insurgent groups. Al Qaeda has trained or supported resistance and insurgent campaigns in Afghanistan, Tajikistan, Bosnia-Herzegovina, Kashmir, Mindanao, Chechnya, Lebanon, Nagorno-Karabakh, Algeria, and Egypt. Al Qaeda provides training in camps and sends fighters to support Muslim struggles in other counties. Al Qaeda is part of the fight against American troops in Afghanistan. Some believe that Osama bin Laden and his group have attempted to procure WMDs. Al Qaeda is often alleged to be the organizer of potential attacks by other terrorist groups against the United States.

Since the 2001 9/11 attacks, the United States has exerted enormous resources and resolve in combating al Qaeda. Intelligence services have made efforts to collect information about the group and its activities including fostering more cooperative relations with other countries' intelligence services. The Central Intelligence Agency and the Department of Defense have launched hundreds of drone attacks on al Qaeda and the Taliban in Afghanistan, Pakistan, and

Northern Africa. As a result of intelligence gathering and drone attacks, the senior leadership of al Qaeda, including bin Laden, is said to have been largely decimated.

Extremist Groups in the United States

We must also consider the existence of homegrown extremist groups willing to resort to violence or terrorism. The prime example is the bombing of the Alfred P. Murrah Federal Building at Oklahoma City. On April 19, 1995, Timothy McVeigh and Terry Nichols detonated about 5000 pounds of explosives, killing 168 people. The bombers belonged to a right-wing group that was opposed to the government, and their actions were motivated by the government's botched intervention in Waco, Texas, and Ruby Ridge, Idaho. McVeigh said he developed a hatred of the government while serving in the U.S. Army. The novel *The Turner Diaries*, a right-wing hate book popular with some racist groups, also influenced him. *The Turner Diaries* was written by William Luther Pierce, a former leader of the National Alliance, a white separatist group that advocated the extermination of all Jews and people of color to create a "White world." Terry Nichols was tried in 1997 and found guilty of conspiring to build a "weapon of mass destruction" and on several counts of manslaughter. McVeigh was found guilty on several counts of murder, sentenced to death, and executed in 2001.

Hundreds of right-wing extremist groups in the United States have members who might plot similar incidents. FBI Director Mueller (2007) cautioned that "While much of the national attention is focused on the substantial threat posed by international terrorists to the homeland, we must also contend with an ongoing threat posed by domestic terrorists. … Despite the fragmentation of white supremacist groups resulting from the deaths or the arrests of prominent leaders, violence from this element remains an ongoing threat to government targets, Jewish individuals and establishments, and non-white ethnic groups."

There is a range of extremist groups in the United States possessing a variety of fanatic ideas, the two most common types are general hate groups and patriot groups, although their ideologies sometimes overlap and it is difficult to distinguish where a particular group fits. Generally, hate groups are comprised of radicalized members who propagandize and sometimes commit crimes against other religious or ethnic groups. They often view non-whites as inferior and desire to have an exclusive white society. They include groups such as the Ku Klux Klan (KKK), neo-confederate groups, Christian identity, and racist skinheads. The number of hate groups in the United States is in the thousands, with the KKK being the most common (Potok, 2013). Patriot groups are opposed to our government or fear that the government is going to take away their freedoms. They are opposed to the new world order and constantly engage in conspiracy theorizing about the government and government officials. Some of these groups believe that America has lost sight of its Christian principles and strive to move the country to a more conservative path. Patriot groups include the John Birch society, sovereign citizen movement, militias, and patriot groups. The number of patriot groups grew substantially with the election of President Obama and is estimated to be approximately 1360, up from 149 in 2008 (Potok, 2013). Table 13.4 provides a listing of the 10 states with the largest number of extremist groups.

There are a number of hate crimes and terrorist acts committed by these groups and individuals each year. Some are minor in nature, whereas others shock the national conscious. A fairly recent example is the mass killing at a Sikh Temple in Wisconsin. Michael Page who had connections with the neo-Nazi movement killed six Sikhs and wounded six other people including a police officer. Page thought he was killing Muslims (Elias, 2012). Other examples of hate crimes by extremists include:

- In June 2013, two members of the KKK were arrested in New York for plotting to construct a radiation weapon targeting Muslims or government officials.
- In August 2012, seven people associated with the sovereign citizens movement ambushed and killed two Louisiana deputies.
- In April 2012, two Minnesota men were indicted on weapons and drug charges. Prosecutors alleged that they planned to attack the Mexican consulate in St. Paul with a truckload of gasoline and oil that would be set on fire.

Table 13.4 Ten States with the Largest Number of Extremist Groups	
State	**Number of Groups**
California	82
Texas	62
Florida	59
Georgia	53
New York	38
Mississippi	36
Ohio	36
Pennsylvania	35
Alabama	30
Virginia	30
Source: Potok (2013).	

- In November 2011, four members of a North Georgia militia were arrested for plotting to bomb federal buildings, attack cities with ricin, and murder police officers.
- In October 2011, a white supremacist and his girlfriend went on a killing spree in Washington, Oregon, and California. When stopped by the police, they stated they were on the way to Sacramento to kill more Jews (Southern Poverty Law Center, 2013).

These cases demonstrate the scope of the violence carried out by American extremists.

Simone, Freilich, and Chermak (2008) surveyed the nation's state police organizations, and their research found that right-wing extremist groups are located in almost every state and that they were present in more states than Islamic Jihadists (see Box 13.5). Additionally, in 2009 and 2010, both the Department of Homeland Security and the Southern Poverty Law Center warned of the rise of right-wing extremist groups in the United States (Lake, 2009; Southern Poverty Law Center, 2010). The Southern Poverty Law Center (2010) reported a 244% increase in active Patriot groups in 2009, many of which are armed militias who view the federal government as the enemy.

Simone and his colleagues also asked the state police agencies whether the various groups pose a national or state threat. Box 13.6 summarizes their responses. Note that the most significant concern was from Islamic jihadists, but they responded that other right-wing and environmental groups pose a significant threat.

The Boston Marathon bomber renewed our collective interest in homegrown terrorism. There has been a long line of such terrorists: Adam Gadhan, aka

Box 13.5 State Police Organizations' Perceptions of Extremist Groups Operating in Their States (Percent Responses)

- Neo-Nazi (92%)
- Militia/Patriots (89%)
- Racist skinheads (89%)
- Freemen/sovereign citizens (87%)
- Extreme animal rights groups (76%)
- Extreme environmental groups (73%)
- Ku Klux Klan (KKK) (73%)
- Christian identity (70%)
- Extreme anti-tax groups (67%)
- Extreme anti-immigration groups (65%)

- Islamic Jihadi groups (62%)
- Extreme anti-abortion groups (62%)
- Extreme black nationalist groups (54%)
- Odinists (35%)
- Left-wing revolutionary groups (32%)
- Idiosyncratic sectarians (32%)
- Other extremist groups (11%)
- Doomsday cults (8%)

Source: Simone et al. (2008).

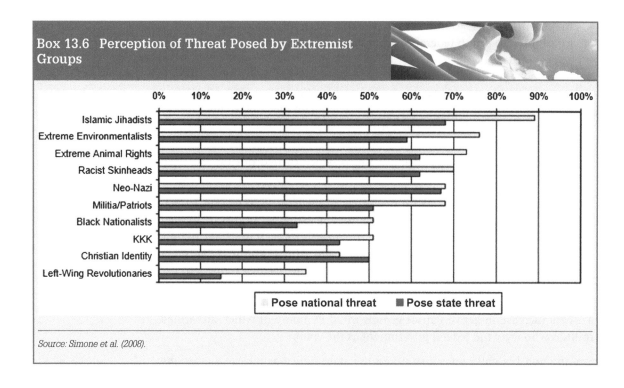

Box 13.6 Perception of Threat Posed by Extremist Groups

Source: Simone et al. (2008).

Azzam the American, who became a prominent spokesman for al Qaeda. Gadhan was born in Orange County, California; John Walker Lindh, better known as the American Taliban; Nidal Malik Hasan, the Fort Hood shooter; and Richard Reed, the shoe bomber.

A review of homegrown terrorist attacks in the United States shows interesting results. Most of these attacks, plots, and conspiracies tend to show that they are conducted by incompetent plotters. For example, the Times Square bomber, Faisal Shahzad left a car bomb in New York City's Times Square in 2010. The bombs consisted of gasoline and propane tanks with fireworks as a detonator. The plot was quickly discovered, and there was only a low probability that the bomb would have detonated. There have been numerous other attacks and plots with the same level of incompetence. Brooks (2011) advises there are several reasons for these terrorists' lack of skills. First, the United States has an array of security measures that makes such attacks very difficult. Second, many of the aspiring terrorists do not have the tradecraft to be successful terrorists; they have little or no training. Finally, the security environment prevents people from attaining the necessary skills. This is not to say committed terrorists will not be successful. However, completing an act of terrorism requires a substantial amount of skill and knowledge. We have been able to tamp down opportunities to obtain the needed information. Regardless, radicalized Americans remain a threat to local communities.

The Arizona Patriots

The Arizona Patriots are a group of white supremacists that believe in Posse Comitatus and Christian Identity ideology. In the 1980s, they began planning attacks against the U.S. government and Jewish centers. At one point, the group sent a threatening letter to state officials in Arizona demanding their resignation. As a result of undercover operations, several of its members were arrested and convicted of plotting to bomb the Simon Wiesenthal Center, an FBI and Internal Revenue Service office, and the Jewish Defense League (JDL). The group also intended to carry out robberies to finance its cause. These plans included the use of homemade bombs, chemical gases, and a plot to destroy the Hoover Dam "as a distraction." Like Timothy McVeigh, these plots were inspired by *The Turner Diaries*, racism, and Christian Identity ideology. Some believe that the group is rebuilding itself following the imprisonment of some of its members.

Patriot Council

The Patriot Council is an antigovernment right-wing group founded by U.S. Air Force Colonel Frank Nelson. The group draws from radical right Christian Identity ideology and focuses on issues of taxation and governmental power and rejects the legitimacy of government authority. No documented cases of terrorism have been directly linked to the group, but members of the group have considered bombings and the assassination of federal officials. One plot included plans to use ricin, a biological toxin, against government officials and insulations. Members of the group went so far as to secure the castor beans necessary to make the toxin and actually extracted ricin from the beans. As a result, members of the groups were arrested and were among the first to be charged under the Biological Weapons Anti-Terrorism Act. As with most terrorist groups, it is difficult to know whether the plot was merely the result of a few rogue members or sanctioned by the group.

Oklahoma Constitutional Militia

The Oklahoma Constitutional Militia, also known as the Universal Church of God, is a small, right-wing, anti-Semitic group. Willie Ray Lampley formed its militant arm in the 1990s. This group networked with other racist Christian Identity groups that advocated American white supremacy. Lampley saw himself as a prophet whose duty was to follow God's edicts to kill "sinful" people, such as homosexuals, abortion clinic doctors, and civil rights proponents. In the 1990s, members of the group were arrested and convicted for planning to bomb gay and lesbian bars, several abortion clinics, and the offices of the Southern Poverty Law Center and the Anti-Defamation League.

Ku Klux Klan

The KKK is one of the oldest and most well-known terrorist groups in America. The organization rose out of reconstruction in 1866, was founded by veterans of the Confederate Army, and continues to preach hatred against minorities, Jews, homosexuals, Catholics, immigrants, and Communists. The group's ideology is based on a fusing of white supremacy, Christian Identity, and belief in a worldwide Jewish conspiracy. The group was so powerful and intertwined with the state in the 1860s that Congress passed legislation (the Ku Klux Klan Act) to attempt to control the group's activities and control its influence over the justice system.

The group reemerged in the early 1900s and, at the height of its power, claimed somewhere between 4 and 5 million members of numerous local chapters across the country. The group carried out literally hundreds of lynchings and acts of terror and intimidation, from burning crosses to beating minorities. During the 1950s and 1960s, the group murdered women and children by bombing churches. One of the most infamous attacks conducted by the KKK was the bombing of the 16th Street Baptist Church in Birmingham, Alabama. The attack took place on Sunday, September 15, 1963, and was designed to instill fear in members of the civil rights movement. KKK members Bobby Frank Cherry and Robert Edward Chambliss detonated a bomb as 26 children were assembling for prayer service. The explosion killed four young teenage girls and injured more than 20 children (Table 13.5).

Although the KKK is most often depicted as being composed of men from the South that exclusively target people of color for violence, this was often not

Table 13.5 U.S. Locations with Growing KKK Chapters and Membership			
South	**Midwest**	**Great Plains**	**Mid-Atlantic**
Alabama	Indiana	Iowa	Maryland
Arkansas	Kentucky	Nebraska	New Jersey
Florida	Michigan		Pennsylvania
Georgia	Ohio		West Virginia
Louisiana			
Mississippi			
South Carolina			
Tennessee			
Texas			
KKK, Ku Klux Klan. Source: ADL (2007).			

the case. The KKK has been active in New England, Canada, the South, and the Midwest, and it has targeted many groups because of race, religion, and political affiliation. The KKK targeted both Communists and Socialists and even killed uniformed Africana soldiers returning home from World War I.

Some might argue that the group is no longer in existence, but several variants of the KKK have emerged at the national level in American society, such as the Imperial Klans of America, American Knights of the Ku Klux Klan, and Knights of the White Kamelia. In 2006, the Anti-Defamation League reported that "The Ku Klux Klan, which just a few years ago seemed static or even moribund ... has experienced a surprising and troubling resurgence due to the successful exploitation of hot-button issues including immigration, gay marriage and urban crime." Today, this extremist group is estimated to have at least 150 chapters and as many as 8000 members across the nation.

Extremist Groups and Israel
The Jewish Defense League
In 1968, the JDL was founded in New York City. The group was founded by Rabbi Meir Kahane, who later moved to Israel and formed the Kach party. The organization began as a group of vigilantes whose purpose was to protect orthodox Jews. Going far beyond merely protecting New York's Jewish population, the group began to conduct an extensive campaign of terror. Initially, the group targeted governments that it thought were anti-Semitic but rapidly expanded their attacks to include bombings and assassinations. The JDL was responsible for the assassination of Alex Odeh, Director of the Arab-American Anti-Discrimination Committee. The group targeted both Soviet and Palestinian institutions. For decades, the group was one of the most violent and active terrorist organizations operating in the United States. In 2001, two JDL members were arrested for planning to kill a Lebanese-American Congressman and blow up a mosque in California. The JDL and its offshoots have a presence in Eastern Europe, Canada, Australia, South Africa, Russia, France, and Britain. In 2005, a dispute over leadership split the groups into factions—JDL, B'nai Elim, and the Jewish Task Force. As late as 2007, JDL members were active in political protests, and, in one case, were accused of assaulting a controversial Canadian extremist at a demonstration (Mahoney, 2007). Ironically, the group is not designated by the U.S. State Department as a terrorist group nor is it on its watch list.

Kach
Kach ("Thus") is a political offshoot of the JDL. Kach is an extreme nationalist group that operates in Israel, the West Bank, and the Gaza Strip. The group follows what is called "Kahanism" (named after its founder) ideology, which espouses extreme right-wing Religious Zionist ideals. These ideals include a belief that Israel should be a theocratic government and that it should reserve

citizenship exclusively for Jewish people. To achieve these goals, proponents of the ideology would deport all gentiles or reduce their status to resident aliens without political rights.

Rabbi Kahane, the JDL founder, established the group in Israel during the 1970s. The group advocated the annexing of all Palestinian lands and the violent removal of all Arabs from these lands. Before his assignation, Kahane openly advocated the use of terror against both the Israeli government and Arab peoples. In 1984, Kahane was elected to the Israeli Knesset. His movement was opposed to any peace settlement with Palestine. Following the Oslo peace accords, one member of his group killed 29 Muslim worshippers and injured another 125 in a mosque in the southern West Bank city of Hebron. In large part because of the attack, Israel was forced to outlaw the group.

In 2005, the group threatened Israel officials who supported "disengagement" from Gaza. Just before Prime Minister Ariel Sharon initiated his plans for disengagement, Eden Natan-Zada, a Kach sympathizer and deserter from the Israeli army, carried out an attack against a bus of Arabs in Shfaram, Israel. Today, the group has splintered into many factions, but former affiliates are still active in both violence and running for political office.

Fighting Jewish Organization

The Fighting Jewish Organization (EYAL) was a nationalist group that can be traced to conflicts over British-mandated Palestine and the birth of the State of Israel. The British Mandate was a form of governance in the Middle East between 1920 and 1948. It involved the control of Jordan, Israel, the West Bank, and the Gaza Strip. EYAL members can trace their roots to two right-wing terrorist organizations that carried out terrorist attacks in British Mandated Palestine—the Irgun and the Stern Gang. The group also is an extension of the Kach movement and its ideology. The group is also noteworthy because it shows the historical complexity and controversial nature of terrorism in Israel. As part of the Oslo Peace Accords, Israeli Prime Minister Yitzhak Rabin agreed to turn over the West Bank to the Palestinians. An extremist, Yigal Amir, with ties to EYAL's founder, Avishai Raviv, assassinated Rabin. It was later learned that Raviv was a member of the Israel Secret Police (Shin Bet) investigating right-wing radical groups. Some have speculated that Shin Bet founded EYAL; the group was disbanded after Raviv's exposure. Members of the groups have been absorbed into groups associated with the Kach movement.

HOMELAND SECURITY

Although homeland security encompasses all levels of government, it is primarily a federal responsibility with its primary objective of defending the country and responding to terrorist attacks and other disasters. The Department of

Homeland Security (DHS) is the Cabinet-level department with this responsibility. Former President George W. Bush organized the DHS by combining a number of agencies from other Cabinet-level departments. The department currently has approximately 180,000 employees and is the largest Cabinet-level department in the federal government. As discussed in Chapter 1, the DHS consists of a number of agencies including Customs and Immigration Enforcement, Transportation Security Agency, Customs and Border Protection, Secret Service, Coast Guard, and a number of other agencies. It was formed to better coordinate the numerous agencies and can play a role in mitigating the effects of a terrorist attack on the United States. Additionally, it has a number of corollary responsibilities. Through the Federal Emergency Management Agency (FEMA) and other agencies within the department, the DHS responds to natural and synthetic disasters, including potential terrorist attacks. The DHS plays a significant role in preventing terrorism and minimizing any potential devastation. Additionally, traditional and organized crime is associated with terrorist organizations, especially in the areas of procuring financial resources and money laundering. These agencies are involved in thwarting and investigating these activities and crimes, especially as they relate to terrorist organizations (Figure 13.2).

In order to better understand homeland security, it must be remembered that state and local governments are involved in the process. To a large extent,

FIGURE 13.2
Homeland Security Secretary Jeh Johnson at MetLife Stadium in East Rutherford, NJ, to tour security operations for Super Bowl XLVIII. On January 29, 2014. *Photograph courtesy of the Department of Homeland Security.*

prevention and mitigation have become responsibilities of state and local offi-cials even though several federal agencies, such as FEMA, are involved in these activities. When there is a terrorist attack or some other incident, local and state governments are the first to respond. In such instances, the federal gov-ernment uses a layered response. A layered response essentially means that fed-eral resources will only be used when local and state governments are unable to mitigate the situation (Gaines & Kappeler, 2012).

The federal government responds to the emergency only after it is determined that the local and state governments are unable to deal with the emergency. This protocol was legislated by the Stafford Act. The Stafford Act requires that when there is a disaster, state authorities request assistance from FEMA by con-tacting the state director. The state manager then communicates the request to the head of FEMA and presents the request to the President of the United States. If the President declares an emergency, federal assistance is provided.

Most efforts to assist state and local units of government, including the police, have hinged on block grants to the states with little coordinated direction. Block grants allow the federal government to give the appearance of action, but it does not have to assume any responsibility, should the monies be spent in areas that are not productive. This has resulted in a patchwork of action. The federal government, however, has failed to fully fund a number of the required initiatives, placing greater strain on state and local governments. O'Hanlon (2003) observed that funding had been inadequate for those cities most likely to be targets. Hobijn (2002) estimated that, in 2002, homeland security had cost the states approximately $4 billion, and the U.S. Conference of Mayors estimated the costs at $2.1 billion for larger cities. The security initiative has resulted in a number of unfunded liabilities for state and local governments. In the meantime, it is estimated that the federal government has spent $690 billion on homeland security between 2002 and 2011 (Mueller & Stewart, 2011).

What is Included in Homeland Security

A primary role for the DHS is to protect the nation's critical infrastructure and assets. An example of critical infrastructure would be our rail system, water-ways, or banks. If these infrastructure assets were destroyed, it would result in the loss of lives or have a devastating effect on the economy. Assets include icons and monuments that, if destroyed, would do significant psychological harm to the country (e.g., the Washington Monument, the Lincoln Memorial, or the Golden Gate Bridge). The DHS has identified three categories of critical infrastructure and assets.

According to the DHS (2006), there are three primary categories of critical infrastructure and assets. First, human assets refer to the large numbers of peo-ple who congregate as a result of living conditions, working conditions, or social events (Gaines & Kappeler, 2012). This could refer to sporting events, shopping malls, parades, etc. It includes any situation where a large number of people could be targeted in a single or multiple attacks. The Boston Marathon is a prime example. Second, is physical infrastructure. Physical infrastructure includes transportation, manufacturing facilities, government buildings, and so on. Attacks on physical infrastructure would have a negative effect on the local or national economy. Finally, there is cyber infrastructure. Cyber infrastructure consists of the hardware and software networks that conduct the nation's telecommunications business. Everyone uses the internet every day whether to buy goods, conduct banking, or work. Virtually everything is, to some extent, dependent on our cyber infrastructure. There would be disastrous effects if Wall Street, the banking system, or the energy grid were hacked.

The Office of the President (2003) has identified a list of the key physical assets that should be addressed in homeland security:

- Information technology;
- Telecommunications;
- Chemicals;
- Transportation;
- Emergency services;
- Postal and shipping services;
- Agriculture and food;
- Public health and health care;
- Drinking water and water treatment;
- Energy;
- Banking and finance;
- National monuments and icons;
- Defense industrial complex;
- Key industry/technology sites;
- Large gatherings of people.

The National Infrastructure Protection Plan

In 2006, the DHS published the National Infrastructure Protection Plan. This document is a guideline for organizing security in the United States. The plan is designed to provide coordination among the numerous federal, state, and local agencies in protecting the nation's critical infrastructure and key resources. Essentially, the plan enumerates a process consisting of six steps that are central to protecting physical, cyber, and human assets:

1. Establish security goals or performance targets that constitute a protective posture.
2. Identify assets, systems, networks, and functions within and outside the United States that require a level of protection.

3. Assess risks in terms of a direct or indirect attack on particular assets and the probability that a target will be attacked.
4. Establish priorities in terms of risk and levels of current protection and mitigation systems.
5. Implement protective programs for those high-priority assets, especially those that currently have low levels of protection.
6. Measure effectiveness in terms of progress toward hardening assets and preventing attacks.

Woodbury (2005:2) developed a simpler prevention model, especially as it applies to critical infrastructure. He identified four subprocesses:

1. **Threat identification**—Identify those groups and individuals who would commit terrorist attacks and monitor those groups to determine immediate and long-term intentions.
2. **Threat assessment**—Once potential adversaries and intentions or plans are identified, determine their capabilities to conduct an attack. In other words, do they have the financing, logistical support, and personnel?
3. **Target assessment**—Identify possible and plausible targets. What critical infrastructure and population concentrations are likely targets, what degree of protection currently exists, and what actions should be taken to harden targets? What resources are currently available to prevent and mitigate a possible attack?
4. **Response-protection decisions**—Develop a process to make decisions about risk management.

These four subprocesses comprise a national prevention system; as such, each of the four subsystems must be addressed for adequate prevention to exist. The first two subsystems center around intelligence gathering and dissemination, while the latter two subsystems focus on identifying possible targets, protecting targets, and planning responses should a target be attacked. These processes are hierarchically interdependent in that failure in one area negates success in other areas; for example, failure to adequately assess targets means that response-protection systems likely will fail or be inadequate.

The prevention of terrorist attacks is a complicated matter. First, attacks can involve domestic citizens or groups of persons who reside within a country or those based in another country; for example, foreign as well as domestic right-wing terrorists have attacked targets in the United States, which complicates the identification and investigation of groups and incidents. Making matters worse, covert governmental operations are known to use terrorist-type attacks against civilian populations to advance political agendas. Second, attacks are secretive, making discovery difficult or impossible. In some cases, it is difficult to determine who or what group was responsible for an attack or if it was carried out by a government. Secrecy also complicates preventive efforts. Third, any country has a host of potential targets. Targets range from population centers or gatherings to institutions, such as government buildings, financial institutions, communications centers, and transportation arteries. Finally, attacks can come in many forms. WMDs are a primary concern, but conventional weapons (bombs or explosives) are most often used and result in substantial destruction. For these reasons, prevention presents multiple challenges.

Threat Identification

In terms of threat identification, prior to the wars in Iraq and Afghanistan, the greatest and most significant threat to the United States was al Qaeda, which was responsible for the 9/11 attacks on New York and Northern Virginia. The invasion of Iraq resulted in the United States becoming a focal point for a great deal of anger on the part of numerous terrorist groups; for example, Sheik Ahmad Bahr, the leader of Hamas, speaking at a mosque in Sudan, called for all Americans to be killed (Anonymous, 2007). Threat identification requires that these groups be identified and monitored to identify specific and credible threats; however, it is a difficult task to identify all possible groups or cells with the intent to commit a terrorist act. Nonetheless, our intelligence and law enforcement agencies must endeavor to do so. Although al Qaeda remains the foremost adversary in the public's mind, it is important to keep in mind that it has inspired others through its rhetoric and deeds. These groups do not have the capabilities of al Qaeda and other older, more well-established terrorist groups, but they might be seen as opportunistic terrorists whereby they, a potential target, and the means intersect. These groups are dangerous from the perspective that they are isolated and generally intent on committing a single significant terrorist act. This modus operandi makes it difficult for authorities to discern their existence and strategies.

Threat Assessment

When identifying possible attackers, policymakers must also consider the types of potential attacks. Generally, WMDs have driven a substantial number of policy decisions. Policies have been promulgated that address all types of WMDs, but clearly some of these weapons are more threatening than others. The possibility of terrorists using particular WMDs is greater as compared to others. As an example, even though some bacteria are deadly, many cannot be passed on among citizens like viruses can; thus, viruses are more likely to be used as a terrorist weapon. Certain viruses, such as smallpox, are difficult to obtain but pose enormous dangers. There is limited access to viruses as a result of enhanced guardianship, and if a virus is obtained then it must be transported long distances through areas observed by a number of governments. This is not to say that such WMDs will not be used, but there are other weapons that can produce similar results and are more easily obtained. There are considerations regarding the potential use of various weapons that should be included in any prevention policy.

Another factor to consider when gauging threat assessment is the ability of a group to acquire specific WMDs and other weapons. Although many states possess a variety of WMDs, they are not inclined to provide them to terrorist organizations for fear that the weapons would be traced to the originating country, and the victim country would retaliate (Ackerman & Snyder, 2002). Moreover, a state being associated with the use of WMDs would raise numerous diplomatic and strategic issues. To some extent, states have a vested interest in keeping WMDs out of the hands of terrorists. This is not to say that states will not supply these weapons, but the use of conventional weapons is far more probable.

Target Assessment

In terms of target assessment, the first step is to identify potential targets, but, realistically, any country has literally thousands of targets. The two general categories of targets are critical infrastructure and population groupings. Critical infrastructure includes transportation, telecommunications, financial institutions, governmental buildings, medical care facilities, and petrochemical facilities. Population groupings include permanent and temporary assemblies of large numbers of people. Permanent populations include high-density populations located in cities and shopping areas where people congregate on a constant basis. Temporary population groupings include sporting and other cultural and entertainment events that draw large numbers of citizens. These population groupings are also vulnerable to attack.

The DHS is working to establish a national critical infrastructure database to guide prevention efforts. Moteff (2006) reported that the DHS established preliminary target criteria, such as refineries with a capacity of 225,000 barrels of oil per day, commercial centers with a potential loss of $10 billion, or events or activities that involve more than 35,000 people. These types of targets should receive the highest priority. Even though the criteria are somewhat restrictive, they still include hundreds of potential targets, and they may omit numerous targets that could be appealing to terrorists or that might result in substantial political consternation. Target assessment has been quite problematic, and prevention must begin with the identification of possible targets, which is of great importance at the local level. It is the cornerstone for strategic planning.

Because any terrorist attack or disaster occurs in a local community, the first responders include the police, fire services, and other emergency responders. For this reason, police departments must identify the potential targets and other vulnerabilities that exist in their jurisdictions. Once these targets are identified, the police, in conjunction with other emergency personnel, should develop response plans for each potential target. Response-protection decisions cannot be made without first identifying potential targets and accessing the effects of an attack on them or their destruction as a result of a disaster.

In addition to attempting to build a database, the DHS has developed a formula for prioritizing potential targets. The formula $[R = f(C \times V \times T)]$ where risk (R) is equal to the function of consequences of attack (C), the vulnerability of the target (V), and the threat or risk of a terrorist attack (T). The formula assumes that adequate information exists for each of the three variables. Consequences and vulnerability can be calculated, but often the threat is an unknown because planners do not have information about terrorists' intentions. Thus, security planners often must rely on consequences and vulnerability when prioritizing critical infrastructure protection.

Response-Protection Decisions

When potential attackers, their capabilities, and possible targets and vulnerabilities have been identified, decisions must be made concerning infrastructure protection. The national, state, and local governments must identify likely targets and develop protection and response plans. For the most part, these actions occur at the local level with state and federal support. On its face, this process appears to be rational and straightforward, but the process is so expansive and political, even for the smallest jurisdiction, it likely will not occur in a comprehensive, useable manner. The DHS has attempted to construct a national critical infrastructure database, but its efforts have fallen short of expectations. It is a rational process in an irrational world.

A factor complicating the protection of critical infrastructure is that the vast majority of these assets are privately owned. Although the government regulates many types of critical infrastructures, it only has tangential authority to mandate protective measures or changes. The various affected industries are not likely to volunteer changes, especially when they are costly and adversely affect corporation profits. Industry likely will lobby Congress to pay for any changes that contribute to infrastructure protection. Indeed, Gilmore (2003) noted that the presence of federal funding is a predictor of prevention status. In essence, the government may not be able to enact the requisite changes for enhanced infrastructure protection and therefore reduce vulnerability for specific targets.

HOMELAND SECURITY AND LOCAL POLICING

National security has major implications for state and local governments and their police. Should a terrorist attack or major disaster occur, state and local police are among the first responders. They must control the situation and mitigate the damage as much as possible. Moreover, the federal government has approached homeland security from a top-down perspective. The federal government, to a large extent, has moved into the areas of airline security and is mounting efforts in border security, although border security has little to do with reducing the threat to potential local targets. For the most part, the federal government has concentrated on identifying and arresting terrorists or threat identification. There is substantial consternation over the role of local police agencies in protecting assets; however, we must "think globally and act locally." Essentially, attacks on a local asset can come from almost anywhere in the world, but local authorities will assume a large amount of the responsibility to prevent an attack and mitigate it if one does in fact occur.

Homeland security is just one of many responsibilities for local police agencies. Police departments must respond to crime and calls for service. As a consequence of staffing, many only have the resources to properly attend to core responsibilities. Some jurisdictions have significant gang or drug problems that usurp large amounts of resources. Thus, the homeland security function must compete with these other responsibilities. Ortiz, Hendricks, and Sugie (2007) examined police departments' implementation of homeland security and found that it has been prioritized in varying degrees. For the most part, departments have conducted business as usual irrespective of homeland security. Agencies in large cities, such as New York, Chicago, Washington, and Los Angeles, have developed homeland security units within their departments. They do so as a result of our larger cities being terrorists' primary targets. Many cities, however, have not incorporated homeland security strategies to the extent that is necessary. As noted in Table 13.6, only 9% of agencies have officers assigned to an antiterrorism task force. These task forces are on the front line of combating terrorist threats.

Local agencies must develop strategies and policies to deal with security. As noted, it is the local agencies that will, at least initially, be responsible for protection and response. Some departments have created homeland security units to deal with the issue. The Washington, D.C. Police Department created a unit because Washington is a potential target. The functions carried out by this unit include:

- Provide 24-h emergency operations center capabilities;
- Serve as the central communications point during regional emergencies;
- Develop plans and procedures to ensure emergency response and recovery capabilities for all emergencies and disasters;
- Conduct an assessment of resources and capabilities for emergencies;
- Coordinate emergency resources for emergencies and disaster incidents;
- Provide training and conduct exercises for all emergency first responders, city employees, and the public;
- Coordinate all major special events and street closings;
- Provide public awareness and outreach programs (Washington, D.C. Police Department, 2013).

Table 13.6 Antiterrorism Task Force Participation of Local Police Departments by Size of Population Served, 2007				
	Local Police Departments with Officers Assigned to a Multi-Agency Antiterrorism Task Force			
		Officers Assigned Full Time or Part Time		**Officers Assigned Full Time**
Population Served	**Percent of Departments**	**Number of Officers**	**Percent of Agencies**	**Number of Officers**
All sizes	9	2693	4	1141
1,000,000 or more	100	365	100	364
500,000–999,999	90	121	84	105
250,000–499,999	80	105	80	101
100,000–249,999	54	196	43	146
50,000–99,999	29	200	16	97
25,000–49,999	16	262	7	65
10,000–24,999	10	663	3	145
2500–9999	5	347	2	87
Under 2500	4	433	1	31

Source: Reaves (2010).

Currently, it appears that the states and local units of government are engaged in four security activities: (1) threat assessment via intelligence gathering, (2) critical infrastructure identification, (3) partnerships between law enforcement and critical infrastructure security personnel, and (4) public education.

Intelligence-Led Policing and Threat Assessment

The Homeland Security Council (2007) defined intelligence-led policing (ILP) as "an approach to law enforcement using data collection and intelligence analysis to set specific priorities for all manner of crimes, including those associated with terrorism. ILP is a collaborative approach based on improved intelligence operations and community-oriented policing and problem solving, which the field of law enforcement has considered beneficial for many years." Threat assessment at the local level implies that local police departments must become involved in identifying potential terrorists and suspect activities, although there is some debate as to whether terror intelligence gathering should be a federal function or involve state and local agencies (Thacher, 2005).

Most major police departments have some form of intelligence gathering capabilities or a crime analysis unit. Intelligence analysis differs from crime analysis, which often focuses on investigations or the deployment of police personnel or resources. "Intelligence is a formal process of taking information and turning it into knowledge while ensuring that the information is collected, stored, and disseminated appropriately." (Peterson, 2005:11). According to Peterson (2005:7), ILP requires the following steps:

1. **Planning**—Identifying the outcomes an agency wants to achieve from its collection efforts – setting priorities.
2. **Collecting**—Collecting and processing large amounts of information using a variety of collection modalities and collecting information about all types of crime, criminal behavior, and terrorist activities.
3. **Analysis**—Converting information into intelligence, a process of deriving meaning from data – interpreting the intelligence information so that it is usable by police units.
4. **Dissemination**—Getting intelligence to those who have the need and the right to use it in whatever form is deemed most appropriate.
5. **Reevaluation**—Examining intelligence products to determine their effectiveness; to ensure the department collecting and providing intelligence information that is useful in achieving priorities.

Of course, one of the major difficulties in collecting terrorist intelligence at the local level is that, unlike other organized crime groups, little is known about who might be a terrorist and their potential activities. For the most part, there is an absence of baseline data or information to guide intelligence and investigative activities. It is likely that both the police and public will evidence bias in the assumptions they make about terrorists and their activities, defaulting to popular media constructions that focus almost exclusively on international groups from the Middle East. It is too late to gather information about possible terrorists once they have been identified as terrorists. Nonetheless, departments are encouraged to begin gathering information on "persons of interest." Source of intelligence information is generally collected from (Peterson, 2005:6):

1. Physical surveillance (either in person or by videotape);
2. Electronic surveillance (trap and trace or wiretap);
3. Confidential informants;
4. Undercover operators;
5. Newspaper and internet reports;
6. Public records (e.g., deeds, property tax records).

ILP is compatible and complementary with community policing and homeland security. As summarized by Chappell and Gibson (2009:328), "Intelligence-led policing is a philosophy of policing that builds on prior policing strategies and research, such as problem solving and community policing. It promotes the gathering and analysis of information and intelligence to solve

Table 13.7 Full-Time Intelligence Personnel in Local Police Departments with Primary Duties Related to Terrorist Activities by Size of Population Served, 2007

| Population Served | Percent of Departments with Full-Time Intelligence Personnel | | | | | |
| | Sworn | | | Non-Sworn | | |
	Percent (%) of Departments Using	Average Number	Total Number	Percent (%) of Departments Using	Average Number	Total Number
All sizes	11	3	3994	1	2	238
1,000,000 or more	92	69	882	46	12	73
500,000–999,999	94	13	392	26	4	31
250,000–499,999	76	3	127	28	2	28
100,000–249,999	59	2	207	13	2	42
50,000–99,999	29	2	201	3	2	20
25,000–49,999	17	1	201	2	1	21
10,000–24,999	11	2	394	1	1	16
2500–9999	8	3	831	—[1]	1	8
Under 2500	8	2	759	0	0	0

[1]Less than 0.5%.
Source: Reaves (2010).

all types of crime, including terrorism. Homeland security policing, on the other hand, is a strategy of policing that focuses specifically on the prevention and response to terrorism." Community policing, to be effectively implemented, requires that police departments forge working relationships with citizens and communities (Kappeler & Gaines, 2011). This allows the police to better identify problems and react to them. Such relationships are conducive to the police collecting information about potential terrorists and suspect activities. In other words, the public becomes the "eyes and ears" for the police departments, assisting them in gathering information for intelligence purposes (Table 13.7).

Fusion Centers

In some of the major metropolitan areas, the FBI has partnered with state and local officials to form terrorism early warning groups, or fusion centers (Sullivan, 2006). The fusion center provides overarching coordination of all response and counterterrorism elements within a community. Essentially, information is fed into the fusion center from all agencies within a geographic area. The information is then analyzed. Once analyzed, threat or activity intelligence is generated and supplied to affected constituents. The teams include medical personnel and fire department personnel, as well as law enforcement personnel. The medical personnel can provide the fusion center with information about suspicious diseases or illnesses (early warning systems for biological attacks) and the firefighter personnel can provide information about suspicious fires or chemical releases. This team model allows all possible information to be analyzed in a central facility. The fusion center also allows for more comprehensive planning and a better coordinated response should an event occur.

Fusion centers have several important benefits. First, the fusion centers have resulted in a number of departments to increase their efforts in the homeland security domain (Ortiz et al., 2007). Second, they assist in developing cooperative and coordinated efforts by local agencies. Fusion centers generally cover metropolitan areas resulting in representatives from a number of jurisdictions participating in them. This results in a more comprehensive or regional approach to homeland security. Third, fusion centers provide a template or map to guide police departments in collecting intelligence and other information. This guidance allows departments to better identify the types of information that are needed. Finally, fusion centers provide an interface with the federal intelligence community through the FBI coordinators. This results in more information-sharing in all directions.

An important component of fusion centers and ILP is the Suspicious Activity Reports (SARs). SARs are reports detailing suspicious activities or persons and are generated by a variety of agencies. They are the primary documents that are fed into the intelligence process. When entered into a database, they represent a comprehensive view of potential crime and terrorist activities in a jurisdiction (Box 13.7).

Critical Infrastructure Identification

At some point, local police departments will take inventory of the critical infrastructure or potential targets within their jurisdictions. Communities will need to identify assets and develop response plans, especially given the numerous potential targets that may exist and because attacks on different types of targets present dissimilar challenges to the police and other first responders. Thus, it is important for local police departments to create their own catalog or database of all possible targets in the jurisdiction, especially those that would result in significant damage if attacked.

The identification of these critical infrastructure assets serves two primary purposes. First, the database allows the department to develop response plans comprehensively; that is, a police department should have a response plan in place for all of these locations. Second, it results in focusing attention

Box 13.7   Fusion Process Overview

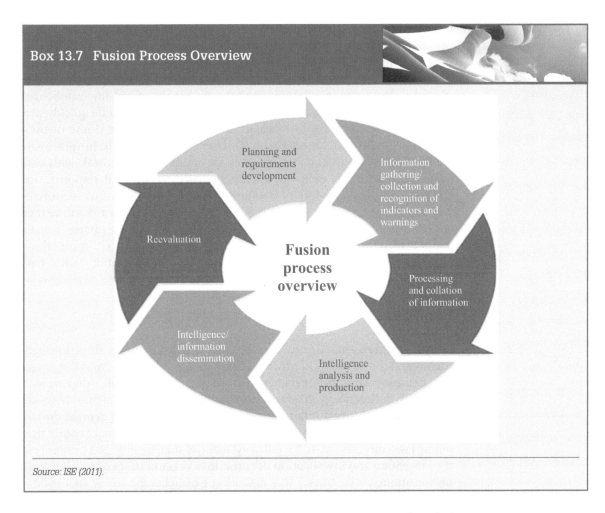

Fusion process overview

Planning and requirements development

Information gathering/ collection and recognition of indicators and warnings

Reevaluation

Processing and collation of information

Intelligence/ information dissemination

Intelligence analysis and production

Source: ISE (2011).

on areas that are of interest to potential attackers. Once assets are identified, the police department should focus intelligence operations near and around these locations. It is likely that attackers will conduct reconnaissance on a potential target. Due vigilance may result in the suspects being identified before the act.

Police departments currently have critical incident response plans for natural disasters, airplane crashes, and major crimes, such as hostage situations, etc. These plans include information about command and control, tactical responses, and use of other support agencies, such as disaster, medical, fire, and chemical and radiological personnel. These plans are flexible because they can be used to deploy resources for a host of problems anywhere within a jurisdiction. Police agencies use these plans sparingly, as there are only a few instances that call for their application. Donahue and Tuohy (2006) suggested that these plans often fail for a variety of reasons, including unco-ordinated leadership among the various responding agencies; failed communications, including inoperability of communications systems and a lack of desire for agencies to communicate with each other; weak planning, whereby plans are developed in a vacuum without the benefit of real-life experiences; and resource constraints, as most emergencies of any magnitude quickly strip a jurisdiction's resources to maintain a maximum response. Some of these problems can be overcome through tabletop exercises or drills; however, generally when these drills occur critiques are conducted piecemeal, with each agency examining its own response as opposed to the total response, and the critiques generally focus on what went right as opposed to identifying and documenting failures and problems. Police agencies must examine their critical incident response plans and ensure that they are comprehensive and applicable to threats. Pelfrey (2005) advised that planning is the most critical aspect of prevention. Many departments are well equipped but do not have adequate plans in place.

Enforcement and Critical Infrastructure Security Personnel

Private security is mentioned here because it is a significant force in safety. Each year, more is spent on private security than public police, and the private sector employs larger numbers of personnel than do public police departments (Morabito & Greenberg, 2005). Policing and private security are not necessarily mutually exclusive domains; for example, Green (1981:25) defined the role of private security as "those individuals, organizations, and services other than public law enforcement and regulatory agencies that are engaged primarily in the prevention and investigation of crime, loss, or harm to specific individuals, organizations, or facilities." This definition highlights the substantial overlap between private security and the police. Private security continues to grow, and its role in public safety is enhanced as the result of the homeland security orientation.

Private security personnel are assigned to guard much of the critical infra-structure in this country. Historically, there has been little cooperation or communication between the police and private security personnel even though they, to some extent, have parallel responsibilities; however, the need to secure critical infrastructure has changed this perspective. Now, police departments are encouraged to develop formal working relation-ships with private security firms. Such relations would: (1) improve joint response to critical incidents, (2) coordinate infrastructure protection, (3) improve communications and data interoperability, (4) bolster information and intelligence sharing, (5) prevent and investigate high-tech crime, and (6) devise responses to workplace violence (Ohlhausen Research, Inc., 2004).

It is logical for the police to develop and formalize these relationships. The police and private security personnel have common goals, and, to a great extent, private security personnel are more informed about problems, critical points, and vulnerabilities. Many of these facilities have controlled access and activities; therefore, security personnel are more likely to observe people and actions that are out of the ordinary or suspicious and, independently or in cooperation with the police, investigate them. At a minimum, the police should be aware of those facilities that are target hardened through private security and have procedures that include private security personnel when responding to those installations.

Partnerships with the police are critical. Some of the activities that must occur include:

1. Cooperative training on the development and implementation of potential suspect profiles;
2. Mapping potential targets in a jurisdiction to include security assets;
3. Development and coordination of critical incident plans outlining responses to attacks and disasters;
4. Better communication between law enforcement and the private security industry.

Although everyone in law enforcement is well aware of domestic terrorism, few departments have initiated comprehensive planning and programing. Threats of terrorism likely will remain for the next several decades, and the police must enhance their capabilities to respond to them. Private security will play a key role in this new priority.

Public Education

On May 9, 2007, the FBI arrested six suspects who had planned to attack and kill soldiers at Fort Dix in New Jersey. An alert clerk who was asked to copy a videocassette onto a DVD supplied the initial investigative lead. The cassette contained footage of the suspects training for their attack. The alert store clerk notified the police, which resulted in an extended FBI investigation and subsequent arrests. In May 2010, New York police prevented a terrorist attack in Times Square because of an alert street vendor who noticed smoke coming from a parked car. The vehicle had been filled with propane tanks, gasoline, explosive devices, and a timing device. Because of the vender's observation and quick reporting to the police, the vehicle was prevented from exploding and causing serious injury (Grynbaum, Rashbaum, & Baker, 2010). These incidents exemplify how law enforcement can obtain valuable intelligence information from the public.

There have been efforts to develop public education programs to achieve results similar to those in New Jersey. These programs encourage citizens to observe for and report suspicious persons and activities. These programs are similar to some of the drug and crime citizen reporting systems used in the United States. Here, police media campaigns urge citizens to call the police and report criminal or drug activities. Lyon (2002) advised that the police should develop programs in communities in close proximity to possible problems. One of the problems with these types of programs is that, in some cases, police departments receive many more citizen calls or tips than can be processed. When the police fail to respond to the calls, it results in lowered citizen evaluations of police performance and a reluctance to call the police in the future. Additionally, only relatively few calls lead to an investigation. The reporting of suspicious persons or possible terrorists will be even more problematic, as citizens most likely will report racially or different persons who are not involved in any suspicious activities. Nonetheless, public education is an essential component in identifying suspicious persons and activities.

NEW YORK CITY AND HOMELAND SECURITY

The 9/11 attacks that occurred in New York City raised its awareness. City and police officials are acutely aware that their city remains a potential target for terrorists, and there are numerous potential targets including Wall Street; city, state, and federal buildings; sporting events; television and Broadway audiences; a mass transit system that carries more than 6.5 million passengers daily; and petrochemical facilities. Consequently, New York City has made a number of changes to prevent future attacks and to better enable the city to respond should an attack occur. It is illustrative to examine some of the actions the city has taken; especially considering that it likely has instituted more safeguards as compared to other cities.

First and perhaps foremost, the NYPD has reorganized to include several security elements within the department. The department has more than 37,000 police officers, with approximately 1000 assigned to "terrorist" duties. One of the tactics used by these officers is the "surge." Essentially, each day about 200 officers are sent to a specific location, usually a potential target. They surge in the area as a show of force. Officers observe for and investigate suspicious persons and activities. Along these same lines, the department has increased the number of bomb-sniffing canines and routinely deploys them throughout the city. These specially trained canines serve as a deterrent, in addition to possibly locating explosive materials (Gaines & Kappeler, 2011).

The city is proactively using counterterrorism tactics in the mass transit system. Each week, NYPD officers conduct more than 300 explosive screening deployments in which officers physically check bags, briefcases, and other containers or conduct an external swab of these containers for explosives. NYPD transit bureau supervisors are provided with radiation sensors, and random radiological screening occurs on facilities. These sensors are also mounted on aircraft to search for radiological emissions. Various mass transit facilities are inspected daily to ensure that all alarms and access control systems are operational. Canine units are often used in mass transit to detect explosives (Falkenrath, 2007). Essentially, the department has substantially increased its efforts to deter attacks and to detect potential attackers.

The NYPD is actively involved in gathering intelligence about terrorist operations. The department created a Counterterrorism Bureau, whose analysts and detectives examine terrorist organizations, potential terrorists, and bomb-making technology. The department has dispatched officers to a number of foreign countries to work with counterterrorism personnel. When the Madrid bombing occurred, an NYPD officer in Israel was immediately dispatched to Madrid, where he collected intelligence information and forwarded it back to the New York Counterterrorism Bureau. The modus operandi information collected overseas may be helpful in detecting and preventing attacks in New York City. The NYPD Counterterrorism Bureau cooperates with federal agencies but is not dependent on them (Figure 13.3).

New York also deployed an array of security hardware for the Lower Manhattan Security Initiative, which resembles London's Ring of Steel. Essentially, New York City has installed security cameras throughout its boroughs. Eventually, about 3000 cameras will be installed, with approximately 2000 of them owned by private businesses (Gaines & Kappeler, 2011). The London Metropolitan Police Department used similar cameras to identify suspects after the subway

FIGURE 13.3
Customs and Border Protection's (CBP) Office of Air and Marine helicopter patrols the air space around New York City. *Photograph courtesy of the Department of Homeland Security.*

bombings in 2005. New York City is also considering movable roadblocks that can be activated remotely should a problem occur. In the future, the NYPD may install facial recognition programing to enhance the identification of suspected terrorists or criminals. The city is also installing radiation detection devices around its port of entry to screen cargo for radioactive materials.

New York is ahead of other major cities in the United States and has essentially gotten in front of the DHS. City officials see New York as a plausible target and are attempting to prevent attacks. This move has resulted in a different NYPD. Counterterrorism is now one of its primary objectives. It is likely that other major cities will follow New York's lead. For example, Pelfrey (2007) surveyed departments in South Carolina and found that many departments of all sizes had begun implementing homeland security programing.

SUMMARY

As a result of the 9/11 attacks on New York and Northern Virginia, homeland security has become a primary national initiative. The DHS was created in the aftermath of the attacks by combining a number of federal agencies that are involved in providing homeland security related activities. The DHS is one of the largest federal agencies with over 180,000 employees. Its responsibilities range from border security to cyber security. At the same time, these agencies still have a number of responsibilities that existed prior to adding homeland security duties.

Homeland security revolves around the protection of critical assets, including infrastructure, human, and cyber assets. As such, the DHS has developed a plan and priorities for securing these assets. These assets exist in every community, with some jurisdictions having more assets than others. This results in states and local communities having an important homeland security role. Police departments have a number of important homeland security responsibilities. First, they must identify the critical infrastructure in their jurisdiction and prepare response plans should one be attacked. Second, they must increase their capacity to collect intelligence about possible terrorist attacks and other suspicious activities. This means that they should incorporate ILP and work with fusion centers. These efforts result in much more knowledge about potential terrorism. Police departments must also develop homeland security related public education programs. These programs are designed to encourage people to report suspicious persons and activities. They increase the eyes and ears on the street. Citizens often observe these activities before they come to the attention of the police.

Homeland security is a critical police function. Because terrorist attacks are so rare, many police departments have become complacent. Police administrators

Box 13.8 A U.S. First, NYPD Gains Global Reach through Interpol Database

The New York City Police Department (NYPD) will be the first law enforcement agency in the nation to have direct access to Interpol's I-24/7 network, a high-tech tool for fighting crime and terrorism that contains the international crime-fighting organization's databases.

With access to the encrypted network, officers can instantly obtain fingerprints, photographs, and other details about persons they have detained. These may include whether the suspect has a stolen passport, or is wanted for criminal activity anywhere in the world, said Interpol's General Secretary, Ronald K. Noble.

"One issue that's very important for police officers around the world is when they stop someone on the street, for them to know whether that person is known to police anywhere in the world, to know the characteristics of that criminal record that the person might have, and to know whether the person is being actively searched." he said at Interpol's Terrorism Awareness Conference hosted in November by the NYPD.

The I-24/7 uses Internet technology to link Interpol's 181 member nations to its databases. Eighty members are already connected, and the remaining ones should be linked by June. All police departments in the United States will eventually be in the system, said Noble.

"What has become obvious in the war on terror is that the major cities of the world have emerged as the true front lines." said Police Commissioner Raymond W. Kelly. "They

are both the likeliest source of criminal finances and support for terrorist groups as well as the likeliest targets."

Establishing and maintaining relationships around the world are vital since September 11, said Noble. In 2000, Interpol identified 219 suspected terrorists; in 2003, that figure soared to 1489.

It is not any specific threat, but the growing presence of terror-related organizations abroad that has the NYPD particularly concerned, said David Cohen, the department's deputy commissioner for intelligence.

"What are they doing about it? How do you define it? How do they understand it?" he asked. "What are the methods of operation? So we can bring that back to the NYPD and better position ourselves to prevent anything from happening here." One policy change that Interpol has instituted recently is that red notices, a wanted list for people who belong to terrorist groups, can now be issued for group members who have not committed a terrorist act. Prior to the change, a person needed to be charged with a crime before a red notice could be issued.

"This is a new and important policy change that will help police around the world keep citizens safer by helping police apprehend and extradite terrorists before they commit terrorist acts." Noble said.

Source: A U.S. First, NYPD Gains Global Reach through Interpol Database (2004).

should take action to ensure that this does not happen. A terrorist attack in a community can have long-term devastating effects on the community (Box 13.8).

The newly identified targets by police and the expanded geographic focus are based on the identification of the groups and regions thought to be most threatening to the United States. As seen in New York City, this approach has resulted in a shift in organizational priorities and reorganization. It means that these new responsibilities must be integrated into departments. It is problematic in that, for the most part, police departments are expected to pursue traditional goals and objectives. In the end, police departments are becoming more complex as the number of public and government expectations increase.

REVIEW QUESTIONS

1. What factors influence our definitions of terrorism?
2. What motivates groups to engage in terrorism?
3. How does the U.S. Federal Criminal Code define terrorism? How is defining terrorism a problematic endeavor?
4. What is meant by WMD, name some examples, and how can they have an impact on society?
5. Where do extremist groups come from? Describe Hamas, Hezbollah, Islamic Jihad, and al Qaeda. What are some extremist groups within the United States?
6. What is the primary responsibility of The Department of Homeland Security? How does the DHS affect national and local policing?

REFERENCES

Ackerman, G., & Moran, K. (2006). *Bioterrorism and threat assessment. Weapons of mass destruction*, Stockholm, Sweden. http://www.wmdcommission.org/files/No22.pdf.

Ackerman, G., & Snyder, L. (2002). Would they if they could? *Bulletin of the Atomic Scientists, 58*(3), 40–47.

ADL. (2007). *The ku klux klan rebounds with new focus on immigration*. Washington, D.C.: Anti-Defamation. http://www.adl.org/PresRele/Extremism_72/4973_72.htm.

Anonymous. (May 1, 2007). *Top Hamas Official: "Kill All Americans"*. Jerusalem Post. http://www.jpost.com/MiddleEast/Article.aspx?id=59873.

Brooks, R. (2011). *Stupid terrorists? Why homegrown terrorists are often incapable of deadly attacks in the United States*. http://kb.osu.edu/dspace/handle/1811/49726.

Carter, D. (2004). *Law enforcement intelligence: A guide for state, local, and tribal law enforcement agencies*. Washington, D.C.: Office of Community Oriented Policing Services.

CDC. (2007). *Emergency preparedness and response. Bioterrorism overview*. http://www.bt.cdc.gov/bioterrorism/overview.asp.

Chappell, A. T., & Gibson, S. A. (2009). Community policing and homeland security policing: friend or foe? *Criminal Justice Policy Review, 20*, 326–343.

DHS. (2006). *National infrastructure protection plan*. Washington, D.C.: Department of Homeland Security.

Donahue, A., & Tuohy, R. (2006). Lessons we don't learn: a study of the lessons of disasters, why we repeat them, and how we can learn from them. *Homeland Security Affairs, 2*(2), 1–28.

Elias, M. (2012). Massacre in Wisconsin. *Intelligence Report, 148*, 29–36.

Falkenrath, R. (March 6, 2007). *Prepared statement of testimony before the committee on homeland security*. U.S. House of Representatives.

Gaines, L. K., & Kappeler, V. E. (2011). *Homeland security and terrorism*. Upper Saddle River, NJ: Pearson/Prentice Hall.

Gilmore, J. (2003). *Forging America's new normalcy: Securing our homeland, protecting our liberty*. 5th Report of the Advisory Panel to Assess Domestic Response Capabilities for Terrorism Involving Weapons of Mass Destruction ("Gilmore Commission"). Arlington, VA: Rand.

Green, G. (1981). *Introduction to security*. Stoneham, MA: Butterworth.

Grynbaum, M. M., Rashbaum, W. K., & Baker, A. (May 2, 2010). *Police seek man taped near Times Sq. bomb scene*. The New York Times.

Henry, V., & King, D. (2004). Improving emergency preparedness and public-safety responses to terrorism and weapons of mass destruction. *Brief Treatment and Crisis Intervention, 4*(1), 11–35.

Hobijn, B. (2002). What will homeland security cost? *Economic Policy Review, 8*(2), 21–33.

Homeland Security Council. (2007). *National strategy for homeland security*. Washington, D.C.: U.S. Department of Homeland Security.

ISE. (2011). *National network of state and major urban area fusion centers*. Washington, D.C.: Information Sharing Environment. http://www.ise.gov/Pages/NFCP.aspx.

Kappeler, V. E., & Gaines, L. (2011). *Community policing: A contemporary perspective* (6th ed.). Newark, NJ: LexisNexis Matthew Bender.

Kappeler, V. E., and Gaines, L. K. (2011). *Community Policing: A Contemporary Perspective*. (6th ed.). Waltham, MA: Anderson Publishing.

LaFree, G., Yang, S., & Crenshaw, M. (2009). Trajectories of terrorism: attack patterns of foreign groups that have targeted the United States. *Criminology & Public Policy, 8*, 445–474.

Lake, E. (April 14, 2009). *Federal agency warns of radicals on right*. The Washington Times.

Laqueur, W. (1987). *The age of terrorism*. Boston: Little, Brown.

Lyon, W. (2002). Partnerships, information, and public safety. *Policing, 25*, 530–543.

Mahoney, J. (April 20, 2007). *Activists confront controversial educator: Demonstrators charged as scuffle erupts over ex-teacher tied to white supremacists*. The Globe and Mail.

Morabito, A., & Greenberg, S. (2005). *Engaging the private sector to promote homeland security: Law enforcement-private security partnerships*. Washington, D.C.: U.S. Department of Justice, Bureau of Justice Statistics.

Moteff, J. (2006). *Critical infrastructure: The national asset database*. Congressional Research Service Report. Washington, D.C.: Congressional Research Service.

Mueller, J., & Stewart, M. (2011). *Terror, security, and money: Balancing the risks, benefits, and costs of homeland security*. New York: Oxford University Press.

National Consortium for the Study of Terrorism and Responses to Terrorism. (2013). *Annex of statistical information: Country reports on terrorism 2012*. College Park: University of Maryland.

National Counterterrorism Center. (2009). *2008 Report on Terrorism. Office of the Director of National Intelligence*. Washington, D.C.: National Counterterrorism Center.

National Intelligence Council. (2007). *National intelligence estimate: "The terrorist threat to the U.S. Homeland"*. Washington, D.C.: Office of the Director of National Intelligence, National Counterterrorism Center.

O'Hanlon, M. (2003). *Protecting the American Homeland: One year on*. Washington, D.C.: Brookings Institution.

Office of the President. (2003). *The national strategy for the physical protection of critical infrastructure and key assets*. Washington, D.C.: Author.

Ohlhausen Research, Inc. (2004). *Private security/public policing: Vital issues and policy recommendations*. Alexandria, VA: International Association of Chiefs of Police.

Ortiz, C., Hendricks, N., & Sugie, N. (2007). Policing terrorism: the response of local police agencies to homeland security concerns. *Criminal Justice Studies, 20*, 91–109.

Pelfrey, W. V. (2005). The cycle of preparedness: establishing a framework to prepare for terrorist threats. *Journal of Homeland Security and Emergency Management, 2*(1), 1–21.

Pelfrey, W. V., Jr (2007). Local law enforcement terrorism prevention efforts: a state level case study. *Journal of Criminal Justice, 35*, 313–321.

Peterson, M. (2005). *Intelligence-led policing: The new intelligence architecture.* Washington, D.C.: U.S. Department of Justice, Office of Justice Programs.

Potok, M. (Spring 2013). The year in hate and extremism. *Intelligence Report,* 40–68.

Reaves, B. A. (2010). *Local police departments, 2007.* Washington, D.C.: U.S. Department of Justice, Bureau of Justice Statistics.

Robert, S. M., III (January 11, 2007). *Statement before the Senate Select Committee on intelligence.* (Washington, D.C.).

Simone, J., Freilich, J. D., & Chermak, S. M. (2008). *Surveying state police agencies about domestic terrorism and far-right extremists, research brief.* College Park, MD: National Consortium for the Study of Terrorism and Responses to Terrorism.

Southern Poverty Law Center. (2010). Active "Patriot" groups in the United States in 2009. *Intelligence Report, 14* (Spring (137)).

Southern Poverty Law Center. (2013). *Terror from the right: Plots, conspiracies and racist rampages since Oklahoma City.* http://www.splcenter.org/get-informed/publications/terror-from-the-right. Accessed 11.12.13.

START. (2011). *Background report – 9/11, ten years later.* College Park: University of Maryland. http://www.state.gov/documents/organization/210288.pdf. Accessed 25.11.13.

Sullivan, J. (2006). Terrorism early warning groups: regional intelligence to combat terrorism. In R. Howard, J. Forest, & J. Moore (Eds.), *Homeland security and terrorism* (pp. 235–245). New York: McGraw-Hill.

Thacher, D. (2005). The local role in Homeland security. *Law & Society Review, 39,* 635–676.

United Nations Panel. (2007). *United Nations Reform.* New York: U.N. Web Services Section, Department of Public Information.

A U.S. First, NYPD Gains Global Reach through Interpol Database. *Law Enforcement News, XXX*(616), (2004), 3.

Washington, D.C. Police Department. (2013). *Homeland security protecting DC.* http://mpdc.dc.gov/node/19192.

White, J. (2008). *Terrorism and homeland security* (6th ed.). Belmont, CA: Wadsworth.

Woodbury, G. (2005). Measuring prevention. *Homelss Security Affairs, 1*(1), 1–9.

Glossary

Absolute deviance behaviors that were thought to be universally and inherently wrong; especially behaviors involving violations of the criminal law when they are committed by persons with little social influence or power.

Absolute immunity a legal doctrine that holds that if a civil action is brought against a person protected by this form of immunity, the court will dismiss the lawsuit. This form of immunity is usually reserved for persons involved in the judicial process.

Abuse of authority any action taken by a police officer without regard of motive, intent, or malice that tends to injure, insult, tread on human dignity, manifest feelings of inferiority, and/or violate an inherent legal right of a citizen.

Access control the process of making physical changes to an environment to inhibit or control the flow of people into an area.

ADA Americans with Disability Act that protects persons with disabilities from discrimination in the work place. This requires that if a police agency rejects a disabled person for employment, it must show that the disabled person cannot adequately perform a job.

Administration the management of governmental affairs that includes control of the organization and structure of an agency.

Administrative discretion the decision-making power granted to administrators that creates a vehicle through which uniform policies and procedures are developed.

Administrative reform initiated by police administration, which is an important source of change. This type of change was brought about to provide quality law enforcement services to the public and to offset the control and domination exerted by politicians.

Affirmative action an organized effort or plan to improve the employment opportunities of members of minority groups and women because of past discrimination.

Agency policy the formal policies and standard operating procedures of an organization. It specifies the mechanics of performing certain tasks; these regulations set the acceptable limits of an officer's conduct in carrying out sworn duties.

Allocation of personnel refers to making decisions about how many officers should be assigned to the various units in the police department.

Anthropological perspective holds that officers are influenced and shaped by their culture. Beliefs and values are transmitted from one generation of officers to the next in a learning process by which a cultural group teaches what behaviors are acceptable and unacceptable.

Appointment based on qualifications the principle that holds only qualified persons should be selected for police service and that the organization has an inherent obligation to train its employees.

Arrest apprehending or detaining a person to bring them forth to answer an alleged or suspected crime. Generally an act constitutes an arrest if a reasonable person would assume that they were no longer free to leave and their movement has been restricted in some meaningful way.

Assault a criminal offense that involves behavior that inflicts injury or causes a person to fear the infliction of immediate injury; for example, by striking at someone or even holding up the fist in a threatening or insulting manner. When the injury is actually inflicted, it is a battery.

Assessment center an assessment center consists of several tests, some of which are job simulations where candidates act out real situations from the job. In addition, an assessment center can contain paper and pencil tests and oral interviews.

Assumption of risk a legal doctrine that holds one who voluntarily engages in a known and foreseeable dangerous behavior cannot expect to recover damages sustained in conjunction with engaging in the dangerous behavior.

613

Attorney's Fee Act a law that allows counsel representing the parties that have been violated to collect their fees from the judgments against persons or agencies found liable for rights violations.

Authoritarian personality is characterized by conservative, aggressive, cynical, and rigid behavior. People having these characteristics are said to have a limited view of the world and see issues in terms of black and white.

Authoritarianism a form of government in which one person or a small number of people control state power; law, police, military, and other public and semipublic institutions such as school and church.

Automated traffic control involves devices, located in unmarked vehicles along the roadway, that were developed to monitor traffic, and detect speeding violations, photograph the vehicle, and produce a traffic citation.

Autonomy a cultural ethos that is evident in the police subculture's use of and concern about discretionary law enforcement.

Background or character investigation consists of a process whereby officers contact applicants' references and ascertain information about their work record, ability to get along with neighbors and others in the workplace, lifestyle, and criminal history.

Basic training is training designed to provide officers with a rudimentary level of competency before entering into police work. It provides officers with basic skills.

Battery is the unlawful touching of a person of another. It must be either willfully committed or done without due care.

Beat boundary geographic area an officer is in charge of patrolling.

Behavioral model views drug usage as a learned behavior in which abuse is the result of peer pressure and other social contacts.

Bill of Rights the first 10 amendments of the United States Constitution are known as the Bill of Rights and afford American citizens certain rights and protections in matters of freedom of speech, religion, and due process, etc.

Bioterrorism means the use of microorganisms to inflict harm on a civilian population. This definition includes terrorist groups and other groups such as organized crime or hate groups.

Bow Street Runners Henry Fielding's group of six householders who agreed to serve as paid, regular constables. This small plain-clothed force, first known as Mr Fielding's people or the "thief takers" was successful in breaking up number of criminal gangs. Later, in 1750, they were called the Bow Street Runners. That group's

responsibility was to patrol the streets to investigate and, when necessary, arrest criminals.

Bravery a cultural ethos that encourages the display of courage related to the perceived and actual dangers of law enforcement.

Breach of duty is the violation of an obligation, engagement or duty; the breach of a duty, is the refusal or neglect to execute an office or public trust, according to law. A police officer who fails to make an arrest when it is required by law has breached a duty.

Bribery is something offered voluntarily of value to influence performance of an official duty. Establishing bribery requires the state to prove that a person gave, offered or promised something of value to and that the person acted with the intent to influence an official act.

Brutality when officers willfully and wrongfully use force that exceeds the boundaries of their authority.

Bureaucracy is a form of social organization in which order, rationality, and hierarchy are the most important elements. Bureaucracy is a way of organizing social life to control the behavior of large groups of people. Bureaucracy is marked by the formal and uniform application of rules and driven by "rational" goals.

Buy Busts sweeps in which officers attempt to buy drugs from dealers and then arrest them.

CALEA The Commission on Accreditation for Law Enforcement Agencies is the body that oversees the national accreditation of police agencies.

Call outs calls for police to respond immediately to a situation at hand. The term is often used in reference to police tactical or SWAT teams.

Career development to a great extent, career development efforts have been limited by civil serviced, labor contracts, and other personnel restrictions that limit how employees are hired, transferred, and promoted within governmental agencies. Career development in law enforcement essentially has taken two directions: expansion of the number or levels of rank within the department or expansion of the number of specialized positions such as investigator, crime prevention specialist, or planner in the department.

Case law is written law created by judges when deciding disputes. Case law is also known as common law.

Child pornography is the exploitation and abuse of minors by depiction of them in sexual situations.

Civil gang injunctions are usually precipitated by an outbreak of gang violence. Once a problem occurs, the police work with prosecutors to obtain a civil injunction preventing gang members from associating with one another.

Civil law regulates social relations arising from private, commercial, or contractual relations. Family law, the law of contracts, and business law are all considered forms of civil law. Certain codes for operating businesses, housing restrictions, and safety regulations are often embodied in the civil law.

Civil Rights Act of 1871 enacted by Congress to control the behavior of state officials and to allow persons whose constitutional rights were violated an avenue of legal redress. The Act was later codified as 42 U.S.C. Section 1983 and is the basis for federal liability of governmental employees.

Civilian review boards a group of citizens that attempt to maintain effective discipline of the police, provide satisfactory resolution of citizen complaints against officers, maintain citizen confidence in the police, and influence police administrators by providing feedback and review of police practices.

Classical organizational theory was developed by Max Weber, which delineated six principles that are used in police departments today.

Code of ethics a document that serves to guide and restrict behavior of members of a professional group.

Collective bargaining this is where employees organize in a union or other organization to present their demands and grievances to management.

Color of law is a threshold legal question for determining civil liability of a governmental official. It is the determination of actions were undertaken by virtue of state law and made possible only because the officer is clothed with authority of state; pretense of law and includes actions of officers who undertake to perform their official duties, but also include acts done beyond their lawful authority.

Community is a collection of individuals living in a particular area who have shared interests.

Community officer uses discretion liberally and has a primary objective of helping people.

Community policing a style and form of policing predicated on the belief that the community must become involved in protecting itself. People must realize that crime and disorder are not the exclusive domain of the police and government. People have a responsibility to assist the police, especially in their own neighborhoods.

Community-oriented policing evolved from work done at MSU in which fear of crime was found to be more problematic that crime itself. Researchers advocated that police departments should form partnerships with citizens and citizen groups to address crime and fear issues.

Comparative negligence a civil law doctrine that allows a plaintiff to recover some portion of the damages caused by another's negligence even if the original person was also negligent and responsible for causing the injury. The degree of negligence of both the officer and the injured party.

COMPSTAT was first developed by the New York City Police department and is an acronym for computer statistics in some locations, while other jurisdictions refer to it as compare statistics.

Conduct energy device (CED) is a hand-held weapon shaped like a handgun that delivers an instantly, incapacitating 50,000-V shock to its target.

Constables in the American colonies constables were among the first law enforcement officers. Constables were charged with surveying land, checking weights and measures serving warrants and meting out punishment. Constables were often assigned to oversee night watches many of which later developed into police departments.

Constitutional government constitutional government describes the social arrangements between a government and its citizens.

Constitutional violation conduct that can be redressed under Section 1983 is limited to violations of constitutional or federally protected rights. This means that violations of state laws or city ordinances by a police officer are normally not actionable.

Contingency management there is no one best way to manage and that managerial decisions should be based on the particulars of the problem under consideration.

Contributory negligence a concept in civil law that prevents a party from recovering for damages if they contributed in any way to the injury. For example, if an officer can show that the plaintiff was also negligent in causing the damage or injury, the officer will not be held liable for the damage or injury.

Convenience norms one of the four primary roles over which the police have responsibility. This role includes investigating traffic accidents, issuing traffic citations and parking tickets, directing traffic, and suggesting engineering changes to facilitate traffic flow.

Corruption the misuse of official authority for personal gain.

County police law enforcement organizations that report to a county commission or other form of county government and are independent of the sheriff.

Court control responsible for determining the constitutionality of a law, they also have the authority to govern procedural aspects of the law and to limit the manner in which it is enforced by the police.

Crime harm punished by the state and spelled out in written legal codes. A crime is an offense against a public law that is defined and punished by statutes and by the common law.

Crime analysis the examination and mapping of crime and calls for service to discover patterns. Once patterns have been discovered police have better information about criminal activities and how to respond to them.

Crime control model crime control model that places a high priority on moving cases through the system.

Crime fighters are zealots who see their role as enforcing the law, and view other police activities as being outside "real" police work. They typically are associated with legalistically styled police departments.

Criminal investigation the processes, techniques, and methods that focus on solving crimes reported to or discovered by police.

Criminal justice system criminal justice system is composed of three primary and discernible components: police, courts, and corrections.

Critical infrastructure includes transportation, telecommunications, financial institutions, governmental buildings, medical care facilities, and petrochemical facilities.

Culturalization model a model that assumes that culture determines both personality and behavior.

Culture differences between large social groups. These include varying beliefs, laws, morals, customs, and other characteristics.

Damage or injury substantial interference with an interest of an individual or his or her property.

Drug Abuse Resistance Education (DARE) involves educating fourth, fifth, and sixth graders about the perils of drug use.

Day watches watches to supplement the activities of the night watches. However, the day watch generally was separate, both in terms of activities and management, from the night watches.

Deadly force any level of force that is likely to lead to serious physical injury or death. Deadly force can only be used in instances where the officer believes there is a threat of immediate and "great bodily harm" to the officer or to another person.

Decentralization the dispersion or distribution of political or police functions and powers; the delegation of power from a central authority to regional and local authorities. In the case of American policing this means that police forces are controlled at the federal, state and local levels rather than being centralized at the national level.

Defendant in a criminal case, the person accused of the crime. In a civil case, the person, agency, or government that is sued and has allegedly inflicted the damage or injury.

Deinstitutionalization this occurred in the 1960 and 1970s when thousands of mentally ill patients were released from state hospitals, and laws restricting involuntary commitment of mentally ill people were enacted.

Demeanor the attitudes and manners exhibited by citizens when encountering the police. Citizens and offenders who fail to show deference to the police by cooperating are more likely to be treated fairly. When citizens are antagonistic toward officers, their complaints are not taken seriously and the officer is more likely to initiate formal actions.

Democracy The concept of democracy includes belief in such fundamental principles as respect for the rule of law, individualism, civil rights, human dignity, constitutionalism, social justice, and majority rule.

Deontological ethics a consideration not of the consequences of an act, but an examination of one's duty to act.

Deviant behavior occurs when an officer violates the norms or rules of conduct expected of a member of the police profession. Deviance may take the form of legal or illegal behavior that is committed either on or off duty.

Differential police response responding to citizen calls by means other than dispatching an officer.

Directed patrol consists of a variety of strategies: saturation patrol, stakeouts, surveillance of suspects, and decoys. Its implementation recognizes that crime and other police hazards are not equally distributed across and time and that recognizable patterns can often be identified.

Discretion the effective limits on a public official's power leave him or her free to make a choice among a number of possible courses of action.

Discrimination results when an officer acts on the basis of their prejudices, and this overt act results in negative consequences for the person who was the object of the prejudice.

Disenfranchised populations include the mentally ill, public inebriates, and the homeless, although most of the people in these categories are homeless and society tends to deal with them as homeless.

Disparate impact employment techniques and practices could not discriminate against classes or groups of people that fell under the protection of the civil rights act.

Disparate treatment prohibited treatment of workers that discriminate against persons falling into certain classifications. Employers cannot discriminate against individuals because of their race, color, sex, national origin, or religion.

DNA deoxyribonucleic acid, allows police officers and scientists to identify a person based on the scientific examination of blood, semen, or even a single cell of tissue.

Domestic violence an incident that results in physical harm or threats of harm by one household member against another. This includes partners, spouses, former spouses, parents and children, or others who live or have lived together.

Downtime this refers to any time that an officer is not committed to some call or police activity.

Draconian a termed used to describe cruel and aggressive punishments or law enforcement practice. Derived from 621 BCE Athenian ruler Draco who revised the legal system and sought to do so with a vengeance of bloodshed.

Driving While Black (DWB) is the police use of race to determine which drivers to stop for minor traffic violations and the use race to determine which motorists to search for contraband.

Drug abuse is the excessive use of a drug (as alcohol, narcotics, or cocaine) without medical justification to the extent that its use adversely affects the user.

Drug cartels criminal organizations that are extensively involved in the drug business.

Drug marts locations where large numbers of dealers hawk their drugs and are usually located in entertainment districts, high crime areas, or public spaces.

D-runs directed patrol runs. One strategy that police agencies utilize to augment or replace routine patrol.

Due process is the ideal that laws and legal proceedings should be fundamentally fair. The due process clause of the Constitution guarantees that the government cannot take away a person's basic rights to "life, liberty or property, without due process of law" or fundamental fairness.

Due process model due process model that places a greater emphasis on protecting citizens' rights.

Early warning systems are designed to identify officers who as a result of their performance may exhibit behavioral problems in using force and dealing with citizens. The benefits of such a system are that it potentially could reduce the number of civil suits against the department, reduce the incidence of excessive force and abuse, and ultimately foster better police community relations.

Economic compulsive violence drug abusers commit crimes of violence, such as robberies or assaults, in an effort to obtain drugs, money, or something of value that could be used to obtain drugs.

Economic status discretion socioeconomic status has been shown to affect the manner in which police respond to requests for service and the probability of being arrested.

Educational standards the requirement of higher education in police selection. Proponents argue that college educated officers are more effective problem solvers and possess a better understanding of people and their problems, and therefore increase the quality of police services in the community. Educational opponents argue that education has little effect on police officers, and can in some cases, cause problems in police departments.

Enacted roles the actual activities and tasks carried out by the police that may or may not be in accord with legal authority or public desire.

Enforcement discretion how officers enforce the law, provide services, and otherwise maintain order.

Enforcers are officers who emphasize law enforcement at the expense of due process and individual rights. Enforcers believe that the "ends always justify the means".

Environmental design citizens will take extraordinary steps to make it appear difficult to victimize.

Equal Employment Act a law passed in an effort to clarify misunderstandings and legal issues that had developed as a result of decisions rendered by the Supreme Court. It prohibited the use of statistical or other adjustments that would give minorities an advantage over majority candidates in the selection process. It also reaffirmed disparate impact as a method of determining whether discrimination existed.

Ethos subcultural sentiments, beliefs, customs, and practices. Ethos often includes the ideas valued most by a subculture or an occupational group.

Excessive force is where an officer applies too much force in a specific situation. It is unreasonable or unnecessary use of force.

Excessive use of force is where officers legally apply force in too many incidents.

External controls are imposed on the department by other agencies or individuals outside the agency. This control can be achieved through civilian review boards, legislative oversight, or through the court system.

Extortion using the threat of arrest or harassment, the officer requires a person who has committed a crime to give them something of value to avoid being arrested.

Extremists are those groups that constitute a terrorist organization, have a violent political orientation, or posses a militant orientation to an issue.

Factions a concern of the constitutional framers with a group of like-minded and politically oriented individuals whose control would result in decisions based purely on majority rule rather than rule of the law designed to protect rights of the minority citizens.

False arrest person, agency, or government that is sued and has allegedly inflicted the damage or injury.

False imprisonment is an intentional detention of the person not authorized by law. It is any illegal imprisonment, without any process whatever, under color of law without regard to whether a person has committed any crime.

Federalism federalism is a form of political organization that distributes authority and power among levels of government.

Federalist papers a series of position papers penned by our constitutional framers recorded in this series of newspaper articles. These serve as a commentary on the political philosophy of the founding fathers and provide an explanation of their interpretation of the government's role.

Federalization is the shift of municipal police agencies to take on greater federal responsibilities and an internationalization of federal agencies.

Field Training Officer program (FTO) field officer training programs are designed to supplement basic training and have as their primary objectives: (1) to reinforce learning that occurred in basic training, (2) to ensure that officers are able to apply that which was learned in basic training, and (3) to provide more detailed information about specific aspects of the job.

Fixed-site neighborhood sales locations where a drug trafficker constantly sales drugs.

Fleeing Felon Doctrine a legal doctrine that allowed police officers to use deadly force against any escaping felon, and required that police weigh the dangerousness of shooting a suspect with the probability of immediate or future harm caused by the suspect.

Follow-up investigation the process of formally observing or studying by close examination and systematic inquiry the evidence of a crime for the purposes of criminal prosecution.

Foot patrol a form of preventative patrol where officer walk an assigned beat.

Force continuum outlines the level of force that officers can use when subduing a suspect. It is based on the principle that officers should use only that force necessary to effect the arrest or subdue a suspect.

Forfeiture is being divested or deprived of the ownership of something as a penalty for the commission of a crime or the alleged commission of a crime. Under certain circumstance one need not be convicted of a crime to forfeit property.

Frankpledge system medieval policing style practiced in England prior to the industrial revolution. Each male above the age of 12 was required to form a group with nine neighbors into a "tithing". Ten tithings were grouped into a "hundred". Hundreds were supervised by a hundredman. The frankpledge system handled all criminal and civil matters for the tithing and the hundred.

Gambling often considered a form of vice, includes a wide variety of activities, all of which include the element of chance. Bets or wagers are risked by a player who hopes to win by beating the odds.

Gender ideology is a system of beliefs that attempts to justify differential treatment.

George Moore a philosopher who believed that the question of whether an action was right or wrong depends on its consequences. The motives or intentions of actors are not reasonable ways to evaluate behavior.

Globalization an increasing worldwide integration of social, cultural, and economic systems especially, markets for goods, services, labor, and capital.

Goals the desired ends of our actions but do not necessarily follow our actions.

Goldbricking term that is used to imply that an officer avoids work or performs only the amount necessary to satisfy department supervisors.

Good faith is acting honestly and without deception; to act in a fair and equitable manner. Police officers are afforded some immunity from civil liability if they can demonstrate that at the time the act was committed, one could not have reasonably known that the act was unconstitutional or against the law.

Government a political institution of the state that uses organization, bureaucracy, and formality to regulate social interactions and is most often recognized among societies that emerge as nation-states.

Gratuities consist of coffee, food, or other items and services given to police officers for a reduced price or free of charge.

Greek city-states following the Dark Age the Greek world reemerged between about 800 and 500 BCE. Greece experienced a major population growth in its centers. During this time the Greeks developed a well-defined division of labor and a clearly delineated political structure. Eventually, there were more than 150 city-states, as they were known, in Greece—each of which had its own laws and judicial system.

Hammurabi King of Babylon around 1750 BC who developed a system of coded laws.

Hate crimes crimes that manifest evidence of prejudice based on certain group characteristics.

Hawthorne studies an attempt to determine how to improve worker productivity. The Hawthorne studies resulted in the discovery of worker morale and its impact on productivity.

Hedonistic approach to what is good would be the amount of pleasure one receives from his or her actions.

Hierarchy of needs a multidimensional approach to motivation.

Hobbes, Thomas British philosopher who used the principles of materialist physics to defend ethical egoism and a social contract theory of the state.

Homeless a social-economic condition whereby people have no fixed permanent residence. A significant part of the population that has been disenfranchised from the rest of society and presents a special challenge for the police.

Hot spots geographic locations that have a disproportionate amount of crime; chronic repeat call locations.

Human relations theory improving the internal workings of the police department by allowing larger numbers of officers from throughout the department to become involved in matters which previously were the exclusive domain of top management.

Human trafficking is the recruitment, harboring, transportation, provision, or obtaining of a person for labor or services, through the use of force, fraud, or coercion for the purpose of subjection to involuntary servitude, peonage, debt bondage, or slavery.

Immanuel Kant a philosopher who expounded on the ethics of duty by including the idea of good will. When people act, their actions must be guided by good intent.

In-service training attempts to keep veteran officers abreast of new or innovative procedures and techniques in law enforcement, and it is designed to provide specialized expertise to officers.

Institutional barriers the formal and informal barriers police departments erect to dissuade minorities from seeking employment or continuing employment if they are hired.

Intentional tort behaviors that are substantially certain to bring about injury or damage and the officer knowingly engaged in the behavior.

Interdiction deter drug smuggling by seizing drug shipments entering the United States.

Internal controls policies, practices, and directives that are enacted within a law enforcement agency designed to limit police practice. Police departments must actively establish policies and other guidelines to control officers' behavior. Policies and procedures not only control what officers can do; they also provide guidance when officers are confronted with situations where they need assistance.

Investigative commission a panel, board, or group usually appointed by politicians to investigate police corruption and police practices.

Investigative function is directed at solving crimes reported to the police, apprehending criminals, and recovering stolen property.

Iron fist and velvet glove is a phrase used to describe the police provision of social service only to mask its use of force and aggressive law enforcement practices.

Isolation an emotional and physical condition that makes it difficult for members of one social group to have relationships and interact with members of another group.

Jeremy Bentham a philosopher who espoused utilitarianism, which means that actions should ensure the greatest happiness for the greatest number of people.

John Stuart Mill a philosopher who espoused utilitarianism with Jeremy Bentham which means that actions should ensure the greatest happiness for the greatest number.

Jurisdiction is the political or geographic location in which a police officer may use the authority to enforce the law.

Kansas City Patrol study the most frequently cited and perhaps most in-depth study of the effectiveness of routine preventive patrol.

La Cosa Nostra was formed in 1930s after several Italian immigrant gangs or families consolidated their power. Today, the LCN consists of families operating in approximately 25 cities with more than 2000 members and several times that many associates.

Labor riots around 1835, a series of riots swept through the country. The riots and their devastating effects demonstrated the ineffectiveness of the day and night watch systems in cities. These riots are what caused the watchmen to become a police organization and labor unions to form.

Latent investigations are instituted once a crime it is turned over to the detective unit. This is also referred to as a follow-up investigation.

Lateral expansion expansion of the number of specialized positions such as investigator, crime prevention specialist, or planner in the department.

Law enforcement role one of the four primary roles over which the police have responsibility. This role includes investigating criminal activities, arresting perpetrators of crime, investigating crimes in progress, serving warrants, and interrogating suspects.

Legal duty behaviors recognized by the courts that require police officers either to take action or to refrain from taking action in particular situations.

Legalistic style legalistic-style police department is one in which authority is highly centralized or bureaucratic and requires officers to enforce one set of uniform standards on the public.

Legalistic-abusive officer refers to officers who typically come from legalistically oriented departments. These officers see themselves as the protectors of the "right" moral standards.

Leges Henrici in 1116, Henry I, son of King William, issued the Leges Henrici, which established offenses against the crown. The Leges Henrici also established judicial districts and separated crimes into felonies and misdemeanors.

Legislative control branch of government that can affect the exercise of discretion in three ways: (1) enactment of laws, (2) allocation of funds, and (3) legislative oversight.

Less than lethal force any level of force not likely to lead to serious physical injury or death. Often associated with equipment like water cannons, rubber bullets, Tasers, and chemical sprays.

Lipit-Ishtar code this code of law, which was unearthed in the 1940s predates Hammurabi's code by at least 300 years.

Locke, John British philosopher who outlined the central tenets of empiricism in philosophy and in political theory argued that civil authorities rule only with the consent of those who are governed. Developed one perspective of the social contract.

London Metropolitan Police first modern English police department created in London in 1829.

Magna Carta this document, signed by King John in 1215, guaranteed basic civil and political rights.

Management refers to the processes that occur within the structure of an organization.

MBO represents the application of systems theory from the top down within an organization. That is, police executives establish goals for the police department, and then successive units and unit managers within the department establish lower-level goals and objectives.

Media image media ages of police work are that policing is all about crime fighting, excitement, and danger.

Medical standards applicants must be physically capable of performing the many tasks and responsibilities that are required of police officers. Consequently, applicants are given a complete medical examination to ensure that they are healthy and can meet the demands of their job.

Mental illness is any disease or disorder of the mind that causes behavior or emotional problems that impairs a person's ability to function in society.

Mesopotamia thought to be the first civilization which begun about 3500 BCE located between the Tigris and Euphrates rivers.

Mexican Mafia a number of drug cartels operating in Mexico within its borders and in the United States. These cartels are vying for control of drug operations in specific geographical areas and often coming into conflict with one another.

Militarizing law enforcement the blurring of the lines that separate the military and domestic police forces. This trend is made evident with the adoption of military tactics by police agencies.

Models of criminal justice the due process model emphasizes due process and individual rights. The crime control model, on the other hand, focuses on the rights and protection of society as a whole and gives the police larger measures of discretionary power to maximally protect society.

Modus operandi files files that describe how known suspects commit specific crimes.

Moral model attributes drug usage to people who are bad or evil. This model dictates that punishment and moral education are the best preventive and treatment measures.

Multijurisdictional drug task forces a number of police departments have deployed interdiction teams to prevent drugs from coming into their jurisdictions. In many cases, a number of departments have band together to form these groups.

Mutual societies this entails a group of friends or acquaintances selling to each other, which are commonly found at teen hangouts or parties.

Necessary force because force cannot be separated from the job of police work it must be used with restraint to accomplish lawful objectives, this force is referred to as necessary force.

Negligence inadvertent behavior that results in damage or injury. It is demonstrated by showing the lack of reasonable care; actions which a reasonably prudent person would not do, or the failure to do something which a reasonably prudent person would do, under the circumstances.

Neighborhood crackdowns similar to street sweeps, except that the police usually identify an area that they feel deserves concentrated, long-term attention.

Neighborhood watch programs that attempt to mobilize citizens as a deterrent to crime and to enhance apprehension, deterrence measures by the police, public education, and private security measures that are implemented by the private sector.

Net-widening the ideas that police officers possessing less-than-lethal weapons may be more inclined to use these weapons in cases where they would not have been legally justified in using traditional weapons. As technologies improve police may be more likely to apply force to a greater number of people in less serious cases or in cases where citizens simply defy police authority.

Night watches early form of policing where constables walked around at night and every now and then stopping and listening. The constables assigned to night watches often were lazy, drank on the job, and cared little about the citizens.

Norm enforcement police function associated with standardized expectations of social positions. These expectations can be very specific or diffuse and are often associated with social institutions.

Norman conquest William, the Duke of Normandy, invaded and conquered England. The Normans brought with them a sense of collective security as opposed to individual rights and commenced to centralize governmental activities and operations.

Normative system a model that suggests deviance is the violation of a set of established norms; defined by social expectations or guidelines for conduct.

Occupational deviance refers to inappropriate work related activities in which police may participate. This is the deviant behavior—criminal and noncriminal—committed during the course of normal work activities or committed under the guise of police officers' authority.

Offender variables in discretion attributes of the offender that influence officers to take action. They include considerations of gender, age, race, socioeconomic status, and demeanor.

Oleoresin Capsicum (OC) is a spray or pepper spray weapon used by the police to subdue suspects. Pepper spray contains derivatives from the cayenne pepper, and when a suspect's face is exposed to it, it results in the eyes burning and swelling shut, nasal passages drain, bronchial passages constrict, and breathing becomes more difficult.

Omnipresence an appearance that the police are everywhere.

Open systems view organizations as total systems within an environment, and realize that the environment affects the police organization and vice versa or out of an area.

Optimists are officers who have a high regard for due process but have little regard for social order. To them, people are more important than crime. Optimists are committed to their jobs and tend to emphasize community service.

Oral interview board evaluates the remaining candidates and determine which ones should be hired by the department. The oral interview board usually ranks the remaining candidates, and selections are made consecutively from this list, or in other cases, candidates are evaluated on a pass–fail basis.

Order maintenance role one of the four primary roles over which the police have responsibility. This role includes forcing a panhandler or drunkard to vacate an area, investigating suspicious persons or vehicles, investigating domestic disturbances, breaking up bar fights, quelling a riot or disorder, and intervening in noisy parties or gatherings.

Organization is a collective that is brought together to accomplish a mission. They are distinguished by formal rules, division of labor, authority relationships, and limited or controlled membership.

Organizational authority derived from their positions within the organization, rather than from their personality, their standing in the community, or from some other source.

Organizational documentation is the process of ensuring that all or most communications are in writing; serves to inform others about what has previously occurred within the department and to hold people accountable.

Outlaw motorcycle gangs have their origin in California where a group of WWII veterans formed a group that rode motorcycles. They evolved to form gangs across the United States and became extensively involved in drug trafficking.

Paramilitary unit officers equipped with an array of militaristic equipment and technology. They often refer to themselves in military jargon as the "heavy weapons unit" implying that what distinguishes them from regular police is power, culture, weapons, and assignments.

Participative management refers to developing formalized organizational arrangements whereby officers at lower levels of the organization can have input into departmental matters, especially those that directly affect them.

Patrol is the practice of covering a district or beat by police to make observations for the purposes of documentation and/or the detection or prevention of crime; it may be accomplished by a number of methods including using vehicle, watercrafts, horses, aircrafts, or on foot.

Patrol function the primary unit responsible for answering calls, providing police services, and preventing crime.

Peel, Robert Sir English politician; British prime minister 1834–1835, 1841–1846; established permanent police force; source of word "bobby".

Peelian reform in 1829, Peel introduced a bill in Parliament, An Act for Improving the Police In and Near the Metropolis, or the Metropolitan Police Act. The Act provided for a single police authority that would be responsible for an area that covered approximately a 7-mile radius from the heart of the city.

Periodic markets distribution points where drug sales are made at limited times.

Personal barriers refer to minorities lack of interest in law enforcement as a career choice.

Personal values normative beliefs developed through two socialization periods: (1) that which occurs before employment as an officer, and (2) that which begins with appointment to the department. For many, this involves the adoption of a new set of values that differ significantly from those of the general public or personal interests.

Physical agility physical fitness has long been recognized as a requirement to become a police officer. The issue has been, however, what level of physical fitness is required to be able to adequately perform police activities.

Plaintiff is the person who initiates a civil lawsuit a by filing a complaint.

Police code of conduct value statements on the exercise of discretion, use of force, legitimate source of authority, cooperation with other police agencies, and the need to develop professional capabilities.

Police crime illegal behavior in which the officer uses official power of his/her job to engage in the conduct.

Police force a group of trained officers charged by a government with maintenance of public peace and order, enforcement of laws, and prevention and detection of crime. Police forces are authorized by law to use force to achieve their objectives.

Police functions police functions are the tasks and activities associated with neither a role of police nor their mission, and that the best way to improve relations with the public is to educate them about the police.

Police roles police roles refer to a basic or standardized social position that carries with it certain expectations.

Police sexual violence those situations in which a citizen experiences a sexually degrading, humiliating, violating, damaging, or threatening act committed by police officer, through the use of force or authority.

Police state is a phrase used to describe a society that totally manages all aspects of social life by the use of state force and power.

Police types consists of three types: (1) legalistic-abusive officers, (2) task officers, and (3) community service officers.

Political entrenchment a phase of American history in which politicians saw the police as a mechanism for solidifying their power by controlling political adversaries and assisting friends and allies. The police department was not only responsible for enforcing the city's laws but, in many respects, it was the primary social service agency of the time.

Pornography is the depiction of lewd, obscene, or erotic sexual behavior without any artistic merit or value.

POSDCORB planning, organizing, staffing, directing, coordinating, reporting, and budgeting. These seven functions, broadly speaking, comprise police administration, and outline how police administrators structure and manage their police departments.

Postulates statements of belief held by a culture that reflect its basic orientations.

Praetorian Guard created by Augustus Caesar, their functions were to protect him from assassination. The Praetorian Guard consisted of nine cohorts, each with 1000 men.

Predisposition model behavior is predetermined by a static, preexisting personality that is shared by people entering the law enforcement profession.

Preferred role those tasks and activities that the public would have police do.

Prejudice is a judgment or opinion developed without the benefit of knowledge or facts.

Preliminary investigation an initial inquiry into a reported crime. The process remains the same regardless of whether the investigation is to be conducted by a patrol officer or a detective.

Prescribed role those tasks and activities that are required of police by law.

Primary crime prevention efforts to identify and manage the conditions within the social and physical environment said to cause crime.

Private security individuals, organizations, and services other than public law enforcement who work to protect property and assets.

Privatization instances in which private security personnel are given full or limited police powers.

Probable cause is a reasonable belief that a person has committed or is about to commit a crime. Probable cause merely requires that the facts available to the officer warrants a "man of reasonable caution" to conclude that crime has been committed by a person. Probable cause is necessary to a make a legal arrest.

Problem-oriented policing this style of policing addresses symptoms of crime rather than crime itself to help reduce the potential for crime to be committed in the first place. There has been little, if any, uniformity in the way it has been implemented.

Problem solvers are police officers that tend to be more sympathetic to people's needs, viewing people as clients, not adversaries. They are community oriented and view the law as one of many instruments that can be used to solve a specific problem.

Problem-solving groups was organized to focus on a specific problem or a set of problems.

Procedural guidelines a system of written rules that include policies (which describe the department's position relative to some problem or area of concern), procedures (which describe how officers are to perform some function such as documenting the storage of physical evidence), and rules or general orders (which explicitly describe what an officer can or cannot do, such as the type of weapons the department will allow an officer to carry while on duty).

Procedural law procedural law refers to laws that prescribe how police officers apply substantive laws.

Professional officers consider a complete range of solutions and mediate the "rule of law" and citizen needs when they select solutions.

Professionalism as reform efforts gained momentum and politics played a less obvious and less intrusive role in policing, law enforcement in this country began to be viewed as a profession. The professional phase of law enforcement began in 1920s. The professional phase of policing can be analyzed and best understood using three general perspectives: the law enforcement role, the bureaucratic role, and science and technology.

Professionalization process by which norms and values are internalized as workers begin to learn their new occupation.

Programmatic dimension operationalization into specific tactics or programs.

Prostitution is the practice of engaging in sexual behavior in exchange for money.

Proximate cause once the plaintiff has demonstrated the existence of a duty and has shown that an officer breached that duty to a specific citizen, this still must be proven. This is done by asking the question, "but for the officer's conduct, would the plaintiff have sustained the injury or damage?" When the answer to this question is yes, then proximate cause is established.

Psychological perspective a view that personality is fixed and does not change significantly by occupational choice or personal experience.

Psychological screening these tests attempt to identify individuals who have personality "problems". Such personality problems include emotional instability, excessive dependency, paranoid tendencies, sexual identity problems, schizophrenia, depression, and neurotic or psychotic tendencies.

Psychopharmacological refers to homicides in which the victims or perpetrators were abusing drugs, and their diminished mental capacity led to their being victimized or resulted in aggressive behavior and the commission of a violent criminal act.

Psychopharmacological effect crimes in which victims or perpetrators were abusing drugs, and their diminished mental capacity led to them being victimized or resulted in aggressive behavior and the commission of a violent criminal act.

Pulling levers strategy where police and probation sanctions are used together to deal with violent gang members.

Qualified immunity a defense that protects "government officials…from liability for civil damages insofar as their conduct does not violate clearly established statutory or constitutional rights of which a reasonable person would have known". *Harlow v. Fitzgerald*, 457 U.S. 800, 818 (1982). "Therefore, regardless of whether the constitutional violation occurred, the officer should prevail if the right asserted by the plaintiff was not clearly established or the officer could have reasonably believed that his particular conduct was lawful". *Romero v. Kitsap County*, 931 F.2d 624, 627 (9th Cir. 1991).

Quality circle is a group of volunteer employees from the same unit or work area who meet on a regular basis to discuss and study problems confronting their area within the department.

Quota systems the need to produce revenue through the collection of fines or promote activity merely to increase statistics reported to other government officials and the public.

Racial profiling occurs when police target someone for investigation, detention, or arrest on the basis of race, color, national origin, or ethnicity.

Reactivist deviance proposes that no act is inherently deviant. Instead, view of deviance suggests that members of society routinely engage in various rule-breaking behaviors. However, some of those who break rules are labeled deviant while many others are not.

Realists are those officers who have little concern for social order or due process. They take a "to hell with it" attitude and typically withdraw from as many of their responsibilities as possible.

Reasonable force is the least amount of force necessary for a police officer to effect an arrest or enforce a lawful order.

Reciprocators are those officers who are sympathetic toward citizens and have difficulty applying coercive force. These officers want to help people, but they are hesitant to use force.

Recruitment is defined as the development of a pool of sufficiently qualified applicants from which to select officers.

Reform Era a long, slow evolutionary process punctuated with numerous gains and losses. For the most part, police reform activities, can be discussed in terms of investigative commissions, reform initiated by police administrators, and political reform.

Residency requirements a departmental requirement that limits recruiting within the local jurisdiction or state.

Reverse discrimination being denied admittance or not being hired because openings are being reserved for minorities.

Reverse stings where undercover police officers pose as drug dealers and arrest customers who attempt to purchase drugs from them.

Riots and strikes around 1835 a series of riots swept through the country. The riots and their devastating effects demonstrated the ineffectiveness of the day and night watch systems of the cities. Strikes also played a role in the development of modern day police organizations. The objective of police forces were to protect the "scabs", to protect coal company property and factories, and to generally to assist in breaking the strikes through arrests and physical violence.

Roman Empire state initially ruled by Augustus Caesar who was the first Roman ruler to implement a police force, the Praetorian Guards, which was to protect him from assassination. Later he formed a group of vigils to fight fires.

ROP programs repeat offender projects, designed to effect the arrest of large numbers of offenders who commit disproportionately large numbers of offenses.

Rousseau, Jean-Jacques Swiss political philosopher who held that the citizens of the state form a collective body ruled by the general will, resulting in a freedom and equality.

Routine preventive patrol provided by officers in marked police vehicles dispersed throughout an agency's jurisdiction. Officers are assigned to patrol specific areas, often termed beats or districts. The geographic boundaries of patrol areas are generally based on some form of workload analysis. Agencies attempt to balance the officer's workload by dividing the city into areas that would have equal amounts of activity.

Rule appliers are bureaucrats who operate "by the book". They remain detached from their jobs and the citizens they serve.

SARA Model consists of a four-step process, which involves (1) scanning, (2) analysis, (3) response, and (4) assessment. This is method of effective problem solving which can be used by police officers.

Saturated patrol attempts to deter crime or problems in a specific area by deploying large numbers of officers. Strategies are employed that concentrate officers in a given area to create a total police presence.

Screening in applicants a process whereby procedures are employed that identify the "best-qualified" applicants, and selections are made from this more restricted pool.

Secondary crime prevention focuses on persons and the community in an effort to identify potential.

Secrecy The quality or condition of being secret and often is the result of a fear of loss of autonomy and authority as external groups try to limit police discretion and decision-making ability.

Selection once an applicant pool has been established, police administrators attempt to select applicants who possess the qualities necessary to perform police duties at a high level. We use the word "attempt" here since selection is not a scientific proposition. It is a process composed of objective and subjective judgment.

Self-medication model defines addiction as a symptom of some mental defect.

Separation of powers each branch of government operates independently acting as a source of checks and balances on governmental power and authority.

Service role one of the four primary roles over which the police have responsibility. The term given to define the majority of police work as opposed to the preconceived notion many officers have prior to joining the force in which they see their priority being law enforcement.

Service style service-style agencies are usually found in homogeneous middle- and upper-class communities that generally surround metropolitan areas.

Sexual harassment this can take one of two forms: (1) requiring an individual to grant sexual favors to obtain, maintain, or improve employment status, or (2) creation of a hostile work environment.

Shire-reeves later known as sheriffs, were appointed to collect taxes, seize property, and squash political dissent.

Situational variables in discretion the context in which officers perform police activities. They could include the presence of others, whether officers were summoned by someone else or the visibility of their actions.

Slave patrols slave patrols helped to maintain the economic order and to assist the wealthy landowners recover and punish their slaves who essentially were considered their property.

Social contract members of society are assumed to have entered an agreement to create the state and a government to acquire security and order for the entire society.

Social control Social control is the collective practices by which a group attempts to ensure that individuals conform to the norms and values of the group.

Social differentiation as villages grew in population and resources, civilizations began to develop social differentiation, usually beginning with slavery, and a surplus of material resources based on trade, production, warfare, and the exploitation of labor.

Socialization model behavior is based on group socialization and professionalization. Officers learn how to behave and what to think from their shared experiences as police officers.

Social norms the types of behaviors that are considered appropriate by society.

Society the totality of networks and patterns of social interaction occurring between members of a bounded social group including those interactions within organizations and institutions.

Sociological perspective police officers learn their social personality from training and through exposure to the unique demands of police work.

Solidarity an effect of the socialization process that breeds a unity of interests or sympathies among the police group.

Specialization provides a number of benefits to the department including simplified training, placement of responsibilities, administrative control of operations and activities, development of expertise for handling complex police problems, and in some cases officers are provided career enrichment.

Split force patrol the patrol force was split into two separate patrol groups: the patrol call-answering group and the criminal interception group.

State a political creation that has the recognized authority to use and maintain a monopoly on the use force within a clearly defined jurisdiction.

State police state police agencies were created for a number of reasons: (1) to assist local police, which frequently did not have adequate training or resources; (2) to investigate criminal activities that transcended jurisdictional boundaries; (3) to provide law enforcement in rural and other areas that did not have local or county police agencies; and (4) to break strikes and labor movements.

Statistical deviance is any behavior that departs from the average or mathematical mean.

Strategic dimension provide guidelines for the development of specific programs.

Street sweeps a law enforcement of deploying officer in a specific area to create safer neighborhoods and alleviate fear of residents living in high-crime areas where drug use and sales are high.

Stress a condition where people are said to have an inability to cope with a situation or environment. This is a neutral term, but it often carries a negative connotations. Stress can have both beneficial and adverse affects on people.

Stress effects adverse physiological and psychological effects by officers; but there is little evidence to prove that officers feel more stress than others of different occupations.

Stressors sources of stress related to the police occupation.

Strict liability behaviors that are so dangerous or hazardous that a reasonable person who engages in such behavior can be substantially certain the conduct will result in injury or damage.

Subculture a group that while sharing many of the values and beliefs of the larger, more dominant culture, also have separate and distinct values.

Subculture of violence some police organizations have emphasized bravery and danger elements of policing to such an extent that they have created an environment conducive to citizen victimization.

Substantive law substantive law refers to criminal statutes that define which behaviors are acceptable and which behaviors are unacceptable in our society.

Suicide by cop is a victim-precipitated homicide where the victim takes action that causes the police to use deadly force.

Surveillance physical changes that increase the probability that the offenders are observed by residents.

Suspect-oriented techniques are where agencies direct officers to concentrate on known suspects or classes of individuals.

Symbolic assailant is further refined in appearance by taking on the characteristics of marginal segments of society as police frequently come into contact with the most powerless members of society.

System variables in discretion the idiosyncrasies of the criminal justice system that may influence officers to exercise their discretion. They include such factors as the officer's perception of the law, peer group relationships, community attitudes and the system's capacity to process events.

Systemic violence violence that arises from the interaction of participants in the drug culture as they barter drugs, compete for territory, fight with rival gangs, and in general settle disputes that erupt while engaged in the buying, selling, and abusing drugs.

Systems theory postulates that organizations were a part of their environment, and therefore they should closely monitor and react to changes in the environment. Systems theory dictated that administrators view their organizations as systems.

Taser® is a hand-held weapon shaped like a handgun that delivers an instantly, incapacitating 50,000-V shock to its target.

Task officers are street-level bureaucrats who follow the department's rules and regulations without exception.

Tennessee v. Garner a Supreme Court case that dictated the circumstances in which police officers could use deadly force to make an arrest. The court ruled that an officer could not use deadly force to prevent escape unless the suspect posed a significant threat of death or other serious injury to the officer or others.

Terrorism the threat or intentional use of violence that is directed at civilians for the purpose of achieving a political objective.

Tertiary crime prevention deals with individuals who have committed criminal acts. Society and the criminal justice system must try to deal with these individuals in such a way that they will not commit criminal acts in the future.

Themes related to the belief systems or "dynamic affirmations" maintained by its members. Themes are more specific and viable indicators of a culture than worldviews or ethos, as they help to shape the quality and structure of the group's social interactions.

Theory X and Theory Y Theory X is management oriented with a general emphasis on control. Theory Y is people oriented with an emphasis on management and employee cooperation when approaching work.

Third party policing where the police attack a drug or crime problem by attempting to engage third parties who have a vested interest in the crime or people involved in criminal activity.

Title VII legislative action taken in this country to prohibit discrimination in employment. The act defined discrimination as the act of drawing distinctions from which to make selection and other personnel decisions based on considerations of race, color, sex, national origin, or religion.

Tort is a negligent or intentional civil wrong not arising out of a contract or statute. A tort is an act that injures someone in some way, and for which the injured person may sue the wrongdoer for damages.

Tough cops see their jobs as keeping criminals under control. They typically use very repressive methods and are more concerned with the outcomes of their actions rather than the actions themselves.

TQM attempts to change an organization's culture to encompass workers, cooperative teamwork, feedback, and customers as important considerations in organizational enterprise.

Traffic function is the responsibility for reducing the frequency and severity of automobile accidents and facilitating the orderly flow of traffic.

Unnecessary force any level of unauthorized force that does not contribute to achieving a lawful objective by the police or force used by well-intentioned officers who are unable to handle a situation and resort to violence too quickly or needlessly.

Use of force deadly or nondeadly force to control the behavior of individuals in order to protect life and property.

Use of force continuum a model that outlines the level of force that officers can use when subduing a suspect. It is based on the principle that officers should use only that force necessary to effect the arrest or subdue a suspect.

User-financed police services refer to police departments that charge citizens fees for certain services.

Utilitarianism actions should ensure the greatest happiness for the greatest number.

Vertical expansion expansion of the number or levels of rank within the department.

Vertical staff meetings vertical staff meetings included representatives from all levels of the department. Such an arrangement allowed for input from every level within the department.

Vice comes one of the first acts by King William was to separate law enforcement and the judiciary by creating judges who traveled about the realm to hear cases.

Vice crimes refers to criminal activity that is against the public order or public morality. Vice includes activities such as prostitution, gambling, pornography, the illegal sale of alcoholic beverages, and the trafficking in drugs and narcotics.

Vigils formed by Augustus Caesar to guard and fight fires during the Roman Empire.

Vision standards departmental requirement for minimal vision standards that states what level of vision would be necessary to adequately perform duties.

Vizier the chief official of Egyptian government who had responsibility over agriculture, labor, the treasury as well as justice.

Warrant an official legal order authorizing a specific act, such as an arrest or the search of a person or home. A written order directing the arrest of a party. A search warrant orders that a specific location be searched for items that may be used in court as evidence.

Watchman style refers to policing that emphasizes order maintenance and crime control, and generally can be found in larger industrialized cities such as New York or Albany.

Workload analysis determines the frequency of each activity performed by the unit and the average amount of time spent for each occurrence.

Worldview the manner in which a culture sees the world and its own role and relationship to the world.

Wrongful death officers who either take the life of a citizen or fail to prevent the death of a citizen in a manner that renders them subject to civil liability for their actions.

Youth street gangs highly violent gangs of young persons that have become involved in drug trafficking, crime, and violence.

Author Index

Note: Page numbers followed by t indicate tables; b, boxes.

Subject Index

Note: Page numbers followed by f indicate figures; t, tables; b, boxes.

Lightning Source UK Ltd.
Milton Keynes UK
UKOW07f1230301215

265546UK00003B/26/P